Play Therapy in Action

Play Therapy in Action:
A Casebook for Practitioners

edited by

Terry Kottman, Ph.D.

and

Charles Schaefer, Ph.D.

A JASON ARONSON BOOK

ROWMAN & LITTLEFIELD PUBLISHERS, INC.
Lanham • Boulder • New York • Toronto • Oxford

The poem "Elephant in the Room," by Terry Kettering, is reprinted by permission of Bereavement Publishing Company, Inc., 8133 Telegraph Drive, Colorado Springs, Colorado 80920.

A JASON ARONSON BOOK

ROWMAN & LITTLEFIELD PUBLISHERS, INC.

Published in the United States of America
by Rowman & Littlefield Publishers, Inc.
A wholly owned subsidary of The Rowman & Littlefield Publishing Group, Inc.
4501 Forbes Boulevard, Suite 200, Lanham, Maryland 20706
www.rowmanlittlefield.com

PO Box 317
Oxford
OX2 9RU, UK

Copyright © 1993 by Terry Kottman and Charles Schaefer
First Rowman & Littlefield edition 2004

British Library Cataloguing in Publication Information Available

Library of Congress Cataloging-in-Publication Data

Play therapy in action : a casebook for practitioners / edited by Terry Kottman and Charles Schaefer.
    p. cm.
  Includes bibliographical references and index.
  ISBN 1-56821-058-2 (hardcover)
  1. Play therapy—Case studies. I. Kottman, Terry. II. Schaefer, Charles E.
  [DNLM: 1. Mental Disorders—in infancy & childhood—case studies. 2. Play therapy—in infancy & childhood—case studies. WS 350.2 P7224 1994]
RJ505.P6P54 1994
618.92'891653—dc20
DNLM/DLC
For Library of Congress   93-15666

Printed in the United States of America

⊖™ The paper used in this publication meets the minimum requirements of American National Standard for Information Sciences—Permanence of Paper for Printed Library Materials, ANSI/NISO Z39.48-1992.

To our spouses, Anne & Rick,
who help us remember to play

CONTENTS

Acknowledgments   ix

Contributors   xi

Preface   xv

1   Introduction   1
Terry Kottman, Ph.D.

2   Audrey, the Bois d'Arc and Me: A Time of Becoming   5
Lessie Perry, Ph.D.

3   Family Theraplay for the Family Tyrant   45
Ann Jernberg, Ph.D., and Emily Jernberg, M.A.

4   Gentleman Jim and His Private War:
Imagery Interaction Play Therapy   97
Joop Hellendoorn, Ph.D., and Marie-Joze De Vroom, M.A.

5   The King of Rock and Roll: An Application
of Adlerian Play Therapy   133
Terry Kottman, Ph.D.

6   To Show and Not Tell: Cognitive-Behavioral Play Therapy   169
Susan M. Knell, Ph.D.

7   "Born on My Bum": Jungian Play Therapy   209
John Allan, Ph.D., and Susan Levin, Ph.D.

8   Child, Protector, Confidant: Structured Group
Ecosystemic Play Therapy   245
Kevin O'Connor, Ph.D.

9   From Meek to Bold: A Case Study of Gestalt Play Therapy   281
Violet Oaklander, Ph.D.

10   Where in the World is . . . My Father?
A Time-Limited Play Therapy   301
Richard Sloves, Psy.D., and Karen Belinger Peterlin, C.S.W.

11   Internal and External Wars: Psychodynamic Play Therapy   347
     Donna M. Cangelosi, Psy.D.

12   Ann: Dynamic Play Therapy with Ritual Abuse   371
     Steve Harvey, Ph.D., A.D.T.R., R.D.T., R.P.T.

13   Oh, But a Heart, Courage, and a Brain:
     An Integrative Approach to Play Therapy   417
     Jan Faust, Ph.D.

14   As the Child Plays, So Grows the Family Tree:
     Family Play Therapy   457
     Ruth A. Anderson, Ph.D.

15   "Please Hurt Me Again": Posttraumatic Play Therapy
     with an Abused Child   485
     Jamshid A. Marvasti, M.D.

16   It's All in the Game: Game Play Therapy   527
     Steven Reid, Ph.D.

17   Two by Two: A Filial Therapy Case Study   561
     Louise F. Guerney, Ph.D., and Ann D. Welsh, M.S.

18   I Brought My Own Toys Today! Play Therapy
     with Adults   589
     Diane Frey, Ph.D.

     Index   607

ACKNOWLEDGMENTS

We want to express our appreciation to the authors of each of the chapters for the hard work they put into writing and the love they put into working with children of all ages.

We also want to thank Marlene Shea for her dedication and effort, her diligence and organization. Without her there would be no words on the pages.

CONTRIBUTORS

John Allan, Ph.D., is professor of child counseling in the Department of Counseling Psychology at the University of British Columbia, Vancouver, Canada. He is on the board of the Association of Play Therapy, vice-president of C. G. Jung Institute Pacific Northwest and author of *Inscapes of the Child's World: Jungian Counseling in Schools and Clinics*.

Ruth A. Anderson, Ph.D., is a counselor educator in the Department of Family Sciences at Texas Woman's University in Denton, Texas. Her doctorate is in marriage and family therapy. One of her interests and areas of research is children in the context of the family. She is a former elementary and high school teacher.

Donna Cangelosi, Ph.D., is senior clinical provider/psychologist at the Division of Psychological Services, Fairleigh Dickinson University, Hackensack, New Jersey. She has recently coedited *Play Therapy Techniques* with Dr. Charles E. Schaefer and is currently writing children's books that address issues related to parental divorce and separation anxiety. Dr. Cangelosi is a member of the American Psychological Association and the Association for Play Therapy.

Jan Faust, Ph.D., is an assistant professor in the Center for Psychological Studies at Nova University. She developed and directs the Pediatric Psychology Program within Nova University Community Mental Health Center. Through this program, Dr. Faust conducts treatment outcome research designed to investigate the effectiveness of psychodynamic family systems and behavioral therapies with abused and traumatized children. She resides in Ft. Lauderdale, Florida with her husband Louis and daughter Nina.

Diane Frey, Ph.D., is professor of counseling at Wright State University, Dayton, Ohio. She has authored or coauthored five books and numerous articles and chapters on the topics of play therapy, self-esteem, and the gifted. Dr. Frey is on the executive board of the National Council for Self-Esteem, the board of the Association for Play Therapy, and the editorial board of the *International Journal for Play Therapy*. She has served on the editorial boards of the *Journal of*

Counseling Psychology and the *Elementary School Guidance and Counseling Journal.* Dr. Frey is an internationally known speaker.

Louise Guerney, Ph.D., is a Registered Play Therapist-Supervisor of the Association for Play Therapy (APT) and a member of APT's Board of Directors. She is a professor of human development and counseling psychology at the Pennsylvania State University, University Park, Pennsylvania, and director of the Filial Therapy Program of the Individual and Family Consultation Center in the College of Health and Human Development.

Steve Harvey, Ph.D., A.D.T.R., R.D.T., R.P.T., is a licensed psychologist working with children and families. He consults with school districts, courts, and social service systems in addition to being adjunct faculty of Narpoa Institute. Dr. Harvey teaches internationally and has a practice in Colorado Springs where he resides.

Joop Hellendoorn, Ph.D., is an associate professor in the Department of Special Education at the University of Leiden (the Netherlands). She serves as the director of a graduate course and of a research program in child psychotherapy. She has published six books and numerous papers on play and play therapy, and is a member of the editorial board of two Dutch professional journals. Dr. Hellendoorn is approved as a Registered Play Therapist-Supervisor by the APT.

Ann Jernberg, Ph.D., is founder and director of the Theraplay Institute in Chicago. She has written numerous chapters and articles on attachment and play and has lectured in the United States and abroad. Her book *Theraplay* has been translated into German and Japanese. Ann and Emily Jernberg are mother and daughter.

Emily Jernberg, M.A., is finishing her Ph.D. in clinical psychology at the University of Michigan after having been awarded a Powers Fellowship for the study of attachment and loss. She has been a research assistant to Marvin Zonas, Ph.D., in Chicago and to Jerome Kagan, Ph.D., T. Berry Brazelton, M.D., Edward Tronick, Ph.D., and Denny Wolf, Ph.D., in Boston.

Susan M. Knell, Ph.D., is a licensed clinical psychologist and currently the director of the Diagnostic Assessment Center of the Child Guidance Center of Greater Cleveland, Ohio. Dr. Knell holds appointments at Cleveland State University and Case Western Reserve

University. She developed the cognitive-behavioral approach to play therapy, and is the author of *Cognitive-Behavioral Play Therapy* and numerous articles in the area of child clinical psychology.

Terry Kottman, Ph.D., L.P.C., N.C.C., is an assistant professor of counselor education at the University of Northern Iowa. Dr. Kottman has worked extensively with children and their families in the process of developing Adlerian play therapy and has written numerous articles on the subject. She has given workshops throughout the country. She is a Registered Play Therapist-Supervisor and she is the president of the Education Section of the North American Society of Adlerian Psychology.

Susan Levin, Ph.D., is a Registered Play Therapist and Play Therapy Supervisor who has worked for over 14 years in the fields of child counseling and special education. She received a fellowship grant from the Social Sciences and Humanities Research Council of Canada (SSHRC) for her doctoral research. She is currently a SSHRC Post-Doctoral Fellow researching the intentional communication of autistic children at the Hadassah-Luizo Canada Research Institute in Jerusalem, Israel.

Jamshid A. Marvasti, M.D., is a child psychiatrist and the director of the Sexual Trauma Center in Manchester, Connecticut. He is on the faculty of the St. Joseph College Institute for Child Abuse Intervention in West Hartford, Connecticut. Dr. Marvasti maintains a private practice specializing in the psychotherapy of trauma victims/ survivors and is an attending physician in the Department of Psychiatry at Manchester Memorial Hospital. He has presented numerous papers and has written articles and book chapters on the topic of child sexual abuse.

Violet Oaklander, Ph.D., is a certified Gestalt therapist with a private practice in Santa Barbara, California. Her book, *Windows to Our Children*, has been translated into seven languages. Dr. Oaklander has given seminars and workshops around the world on her unique approach, which combines Gestalt therapy theory, philosophy, and practice with a variety of creative, expressive, and projective techniques.

Kevin O'Connor, Ph.D., R.P.T.-S., is professor and director of the Ecosystemic Clinical Child Psychology Program at the California

School of Professional Psychology–Fresno. His primary research interest is in the area of adult–child interactions and he focuses on the treatment of young children in his private practice. He is the executive director of the Association for Play Therapy and the editor of that organization's quarterly newsletter. He coedited the *Handbook of Play Therapy* and authored *The Play Therapy Primer*.

Lessie Perry, Ph.D., R.P.T.-S., is a licensed counselor in private practice in Denton, Texas. She uses play therapy exclusively in the treatment of abused and traumatized children. Dr. Perry is a Registered Play Therapist-Supervisor and serves on the board of the Association for Play Therapy. She coauthored "Diagnostic Assessment of Children's Play Therapy Behavior" in *Play Diagnosis and Assessment*.

Karen Belinger Peterlin, C.S.W., is chief of service, Manhattan Children's Psychiatric Center, New York, New York.

Steven Reid, Ph.D., is director of the Pediatric AIDS Early Intervention Program, Herbert G. Birch Children's Center, Brooklyn, New York. He served as vice-president of the Association for Play Therapy from 1985 to 1987. Dr. Reid coedited the book, *Game Play: Therapeutic Use of Childhood Games*.

Richard Sloves, Psy.D., is director of short-term therapy, child and adolescent psychiatry, Kings County Hospital Center, Brooklyn, and clinical assistant professor of psychiatry, Health Science Center of Brooklyn, the State University of New York.

Marie-Joze de Vroom, M.A., is a Ph.D. student at the University of Leiden (the Netherlands), working on a controlled study on the effects of time-limited imagery interaction play therapy.

Ann D. Welsh, M.Ed., is a Ph.D. candidate at Penn State University. She is interested in using play therapy with families who have children with special needs, combining her background in early childhood special education with family counseling. She teaches psychology and early childhood education at Harrisburg Area Community College.

PREFACE

The upsurge of interest in play theory and practice over the past decade has been dramatic. Each year an ever-growing number of publications and presentations in this field appear. The current interest in play therapy with children has its roots in the seminal works of such pioneers as Hermine Hug-Hellmuth, Melanie Klein, Margaret Lowenfeld, David Levy, and Virginia Axline.

In recent years, we have witnessed the application of the healing powers of play by therapists from other theoretical orientations, including Adlerians, cognitive-behaviorists, family therapists, and Gestalt therapists.

The purpose of this book is to bring together in a single volume concrete applications of play therapy by seasoned clinicians from various theoretical perspectives. There is no attempt to present any one theoretical or technical point of view. On the contrary, our goal is to reflect the broad spectrum of approaches that now exist in the field. We believe that the major psychopathologies in children present the therapist with different problems and therefore require different approaches.

Another guiding belief underlying this volume is that descriptive studies that carefully detail psychotherapy process are among the most useful and practical resources for both students and practicing therapists. The richly detailed case study by Virginia Axline, which is contained in her book *Dibs: In Search of Self*, is an example of the extraordinary power of a clinical case presentation. Her book has influenced a number of readers to pursue careers as play therapists.

One cannot overemphasize how important it is to study childhood psychopathology and psychotherapy in terms of the particular case, rather than the average child. This is important if one is to gain greater insight into the clinical complexities of behavior change for a particular child with a particular behavior problem.

This casebook offers step-by-step treatment guidelines for a number of childhood difficulties, including internalizing, externalizing, and post-traumatic disorders. It should be of interest to both students and more advanced practitioners in a variety of mental health disciplines, including social work; psychiatry; clinical, counseling, and school psychology; expressive arts therapy; child-life therapy; and psychiatric nursing.

Terry Kottman
Charles Schaefer

1

Introduction

Terry Kottman, PH.D.

Play Therapy in Action: A Casebook for Practitioners is a book of case studies, representing 17 different approaches to play therapy. This text serves to illustrate the wide range of applications that can successfully employ play therapy practices. However, this sampling is not all inclusive. There are many other therapeutic approaches using play than those presented here.

Over the past several years, as I trained and supervised students and mental health professionals in the area of play therapy, I have wanted to share with them my sense of the rich variety of ways to use play therapy with clients. The material presented in this book is meant as a supplement for professional training and supervision. These case studies can provide an introduction to the practical application of theory and techniques. The information contained in this text is not designed to provide a complete program of training as a play therapist. Dr. Schaefer and I hope that the reader can use this book to begin to identify directions for further study in play therapy. There are many ways to conceptualize children and many ways to intervene with them. The approach that is best for each individual professional will be the one in which the therapist can feel confident and comfortable, the one that incorporates the therapist's views about people and lets the therapist express all of the aspects of his or her personality.

Dr. Schaefer and I wanted each of the case studies to capture the essence of the theory the chapter illustrates, the spirit of the child in the case, and the process of that particular approach to play therapy, and we believe that they have done exactly that. The authors wrote the case studies informally and in the first person, as though they were discussing the case with a professional colleague. To protect the confidentiality of the clients and their families, the authors have preserved the essential features of the process in their case studies, but have changed significant identifying information.

We asked each of the authors to follow a set format in the writing of the chapter so that all of the case studies contained the same kinds of information. In the Introduction to Theory section, the authors provide background information about this theory/approach. They cover important theoretical constructs and terms, a short history of the theory, and its application to play therapy. The authors also discuss techniques, strategies, and processes particular to their chosen method of working with clients.

In the section entitled Presenting Problem and Background Data, the authors describe the child, the presenting problem and background data/ on the child, and the child's family. This part of each case study explains any relevant family, medical, and educational history. In this section the authors provide answers to the following questions:

1. Why was the client referred to them?
2. What was their professional position when they saw the client?
3. Why did the family decide to seek help at this particular time?
4. What was the implicit contract—was there a difference between the way the authors saw the presenting problem and the way the family described it?

The Theoretical Conceptualization section of each chapter contains the authors' conceptualizations of their clients, and analysis of the presenting problems and psychological issues according to specific theories. In this section, the authors describe their therapeutic goals and specific play therapy strategies.

In the Process of Play Therapy section, the authors include descriptions of the growth of their relationship with the child and the interventions and techniques they used. They describe each phase of therapy: What happened? What were the themes and issues that arose for the child? The authors also discuss the role of the therapist, techniques for limit setting, and criteria for termination decisions. If they also worked with parents, they detail these interactions.

In some of the chapters the authors have included actual selected transcripts of representative interactions between them and their clients. Several of the play therapists have also provided a running commentary that explains their reactions, thoughts, and feelings explicating the connection between what they say and do in the play room and the theory they are illustrating.

For all of the chapters, the Results and Follow-up sections contain descriptions of the results of the play therapy relationship and provide any available follow-up data on the outcome of the case. The authors detail what happened with their clients and the families as a result of the play therapy intervention.

We wanted the authors to use the Discussion Section as a forum to air their thoughts and feelings about this particular case and about the form of play therapy they used with the particular client. To help them in this process, we asked them to consider the following questions:

1. How did this particular type of play therapy lend itself to working with this child? What worked and what did not? Why?
2. Did anything about the process of this case or its outcome surprise them?
3. What are their predictions about the future of this child and this family?
4. What did they learn about themselves in this process? What did they learn about their theory?
5. What did they learn about children?
6. What did they learn about play therapy?
7. Looking back on the case, what other strategies might have been effective with this child?
8. What would they change about their interaction with this child if they had the chance?

2

Audrey, the Bois d'Arc and Me: A Time of Becoming

Lessie Perry, PH.D

There is a piece of a bois d'arc stump living by the corner of my 25-year-old house. Though I was able to build around eight trees on the lot, I chose to cut down three others—one being the corner bois d'arc. At frequent intervals over the past 25 years, I have snipped, pruned, sawed, covered with rock salt, withheld water, and employed other means of tree extermination, but with no success. Every spring and from time to time during the long Texas growing season, new, green-leafed sprouts emerge from the shored-off piece of stump. Though stunted and misshapen, the bois d'arc continues to grow and become the tree it was meant to be.

This case study is about a little girl who reminds me of that bois d'arc. The concept of living things being always in the process of becoming not only holds for the bois d'arcs, but for human beings as well—an especially significant factor in the field of psychotherapy. For human beings, the process of becoming is embodied in the concept of self-actualization, a lifelong journey—a journey toward health, adequacy, and self-realization. Person-centered play therapy provides "good growing ground" (Axline 1947, p. 10) for children's journeys of self-actualization, of becoming.

INTRODUCTION TO PERSON-CENTERED THEORY

History

Person-centered play therapy emerged from the counseling theory. This theory has moved through several labels—initially it was "non-

5

directive," later it was "client-centered," and it is now "person-centered." The writings of the theory's originator, Carl Rogers (1942, 1951) best represent the person-centered approach to counseling. Two of Rogers's associates, Virginia Axline (1947) and Elaine Dorfman (1951) pioneered and designed person-centered play therapy for children. Other contributors to person-centered play therapy include Ray Bixler (1949), Haim Ginott (1959, 1961), Louise Guerney (1983), Garry Landreth (1982, 1991), Dell Lebo (1955), and Clarke Moustakas (1959).

In 1940, Rogers presented a paper to the Minnesota chapter of Psi Chi, a national psychology fraternity, on his thoughts about counseling and psychology. The furor aroused by this presentation led him to believe he had an original contribution to make to the field of psychotherapy. At this meeting, Rogers presented the following concepts:

1. Individuals have an innate drive toward growth, health, and adjustment. People are always behaving in ways that they perceive will facilitate their self-actualization.
2. The feeling aspect of an event is more important than the intellectual or cognitive aspect.
3. The immediate therapeutic situation is more valuable to the therapy process than the individual's past history.
4. Therapeutic relationship is a growth experience. When the client perceives the therapist as being genuine and sincere, warmly accepting and valuing the client as a separate individual, and having the sensitive ability to see the client's world and self as the client sees them, then the client will move in the direction of maturity and self-integration.

Rogers first examined and measured the phenomenon of client change in successful and unsuccessful therapy cases. He then developed a theory of therapy to explain what had happened in those cases. Through observation of the therapy process, he formed a conceptualization of individual personality development and behavior. As he wrote his initial theory, he consistently reminded the reader that theory was only a way of thinking about people and change. Theory, like the person, is fluid and constantly changing as new understandings emerge. What remained for him, as stubborn facts, were the phenomena of personality and behavior change in therapy—these he endeavored to explain with his theory.

Personality Development and Behavior

I will present the theory in the form of propositions or tenets similarly set forth by Rogers (1951). In writing about the theory of personality development and behavior and the process of person-centered therapy, I have used the word *child* to denote the client. The words *person* and *adult* in place of child would be equally appropriate. I used female pronouns for convenience and because the client in this case study is female; however, the theory applies equally to both genders.

Each child lives in a continually changing world of experience of which she is the center. Rogers (1942, 1951) called this private world the experiential field. The field includes all that the organism experiences, whether or not the organism consciously perceives the experience. We do not consciously perceive many of our sensory and visceral sensations, but may become conscious of them if we perceive the sensations to be connected to the satisfaction of a need. Probably only a small portion of this private world is consciously known. There are many sensations that I experience or impulses I feel that I permit into consciousness only under certain conditions. An important aspect of this proposition is that the child herself is the only one who can know this private world in any complete or genuine way.

The child reacts to the experiential field as the field is perceived; this perceptual field is "reality" to the child. The child does not react to some absolute reality (whatever philosophers might decide that is), but to her perception of reality. Semanticists have noted that words and symbols bear to the world of reality the same relationship as a map to the territory that it represents. A similar relationship exists between perception and reality. "We live by a perceptual 'map' which is never reality itself" (Rogers 1951, p. 485). The child is always checking her perceptions against one another or adding to them so that the perceptions become more reliable guides to "reality." When perception changes, the reaction of the child changes.

The child responds as an organized whole to the experiential field. One of the characteristics of the child's behavior is the tendency toward total, organized, goal-directed responses. When one avenue of meeting her perceived need is blocked, the child will develop another avenue. If the child perceives she is not loved following the arrival of her baby sister, she might physically attack her sister. When someone blocks this behavior, the child could become whiny and cling to her mother, unwilling to go to school. When her mother reprimands her for this behavior, she might begin wetting her bed at night. The child is at all times a total organized system in which a change of any part (in this case, the birth of her sister) produces changes in other parts (in this instance, the whiny, clingy behavior and her reluctance to attend school).

The child has one basic need—to actualize, maintain, and enhance herself. Though the child is born with many needs that are physiological, psychological, emotional, intellectual, and social in nature, all needs are aspects of the one fundamental need to self-actualize. In responding to the need to self-actualize, the tendency is for the child to move in the direction of greater independence, autonomy, self-regulation, self-government, self-responsibility, and socialization. The move toward growth and self-actualization is not a smooth one; the child must travel through struggle and pain toward growth and enhancement. Unless the child perceives her power to freely choose her behavioral responses to her experiences, she may mistakenly choose regressive behavior for self-enhancing behavior.

Behavior is the goal-directed attempt of the child to satisfy her needs as experienced in the field she perceives. The child's needs occur as physiological tensions that, when perceived, form the basis of behavior designed to reduce that tension and to enhance the child's existence. She perceives these needs both consciously and subconsciously, and behavior is an expression of the child's reaction to the field. Past events do not cause behavior. Present needs and tensions are the only ones that the child endeavors to satisfy or reduce. Of course past experiences modify the meaning of present experiences, but there is no behavior except to react to a current need.

Emotions accompany and usually facilitate the child's goal-directed behavior. The unpleasant and/or excited feelings (e.g., anger, anxiety, fear, and frustration) tend to accompany the seeking effort of the child. The calm and/or satisfied emotions (e.g., happiness, delight, joy, and love) tend to accompany the experience of a need being met. The intensity of the emotional reaction varies according to the perceived relationship of the behavior to the self-actualization of the child.

In later propositions, the development of the self will involve some modification of the proposition that behavior always enhances the child. Meeting the needs of the self sometimes is in opposition to meeting the needs of the child, and the emotional intensity becomes governed more by the child's self-concept than by the child's visceral experiences.

Behavior is best understood from the internal frame of reference of the child herself. To understand the child and explain her behavior, the therapist attempts to see the child's world of experience as nearly as possible through the child's eyes. Knowledge of the child's frame of reference depends upon communication. In play therapy, we do not limit the child to verbal communication, but provide play as the medium for her to project her view of herself and her world. Toys are her words; play is her communication. The more all of her experiences are available to her consciousness, the more she can choose to communicate a more complete picture of her experiential field. The safer and less defensive the child feels and the freer she feels to express any and all thoughts, the more adequate will be her communication of her field. The increasing communication brings more of her experience into her area of awareness, and thus she is free to present a more accurate and total picture of her world.

Gradually a part of the perceptual field becomes the self. The child begins to differentiate the *me, I,* and *myself* from her environment. In person-centered theory, the self is not synonymous with the child. Person-centered therapists use the self in a restricted sense as the awareness of being. As an infant, the child becomes aware of a feeling of control over parts of her world of experience, and those parts become organized in a self structure. As a result of interaction with the world, and especially as a result of others' evaluations of her, the child forms her concept of self. Because as infants we are dependent on others to meet our needs, we primarily learn who and what we are from our perceptions of how others value us.

Maladjustment

The values attached to experiences and the values that are a part of the child's self-structure/self-concept are values sometimes not experienced directly. They may be taken over, introjected from the significant others in her life, and distortedly perceived as having been experienced directly. From her experiences, the child forms a learned sense of self that she bases on her perception of the regard she has received from others.

Individuals seek those experiences that they see as enhancing and place a negative value on those experiences seen as threatening. Infants have no trouble with the value of their experiences. They like to be comfortable; they dislike being hungry. Soon the infant's own valuing system comes into conflict with the evaluation held by others. Because of the need to be loved by significant others, such as parents and caretakers, children may choose the conditions of worth expressed by parents, rather than their own valuing system. Parental conditions of worth appear in statements like "Big boys don't cry" and "You can't be thirsty, you drank a big glass of Kool-Aid just a while ago." Children begin to accept the values of others instead of their own internal valuing system. Self-alienation begins.

As experiences occur, they are either (a) perceived and organized into a relationship to the self; (b) ignored, though sensed as a sensation, because the experiences have no significance to the self; or (c) denied or distorted because the experiences are threatening to the self (Rogers 1951). When the individual separates the internal valuing process, which she based on her own perceptions, from the experience and replaces it with parental attitudes and values, she forms her self based on distorted sensory perception. Self-alienation increases.

Because of the denied or distorted sensory perceptions, the individual begins to consider behavior that has no organismic value enhancing to the self. Conversely, the individual considers behavior that has organismic value as opposing the maintenance of self. Whenever a person distorts or denies her awareness of experience, she is in a "state of incongruence between the self and experience" (Rogers 1959, p. 226). She begins to exclude certain perceptions, not because they are derogatory, but because if she acknowledges them, it would be contradictory to her self-concept. She begins to repress organismic experiences, not give them symbolization, or only give them distorted symbolization to prohibit the intrusion of perceptions inconsistent with concepts of self. "Psychological maladjustment exists when the organism denies to awareness significant sensory and visceral experiences, which consequently are not symbolized and organized into the gestalt of the self-structure" (Rogers 1951, p. 510). When the difference between experiencing and self become so great, tension arises, anxiety increases, and the individual begins to employ defense mechanisms to reduce tension and lower anxiety. Maladjustment follows.

Adjustment

Psychological adjustment or freedom from inner tension exists when the child's concept of self is at least roughly congruent with all of her experiences. When she can accurately admit to awareness all of her sensory and visceral experiences and organize those experiences into one system that is internally consistent and that is, or is related to, the structure of self, the child experiences integration—adjustment. Conscious acceptance of impulses and perceptions greatly increases the possibility of conscious control. The concept of all experiences being available to consciousness is synonymous with the child's sense of autonomy and self-government. The important fact is that all experiences are *available*, not necessarily present in consciousness. No longer must the child deny experiences that she perceives as being contradictory to her concept of self. The child has come to accept deeply the fact that "I am what I am." She can lose her self-consciousness and be spontaneous as she accepts all that she is.

In the presence of a complete absence of any threat to her self-structure, the child can perceive and examine experiences that are inconsistent with her self-concept and then revise her concept of self to assimilate and include such experiences. In person-centered therapy, by means of the relationship and the therapist's handling of the relationship, the child is gradually assured that the therapist accepts her as she is. The therapist accepts each new aspect of the child that she reveals. It is then that she can gradually bring into conscious form the experiences she has denied. Once those experiences are conscious, the concept of self is expanded so that she can include all experiences as part of a consistent, integrated self.

When the child perceives and accepts all her experiences, she becomes more understanding of others and accepts others as separate individuals. The child who denies some experiences must continually defend against those experiences. Therefore, she views all experiences defensively as potential threats. In interpersonal relationships, she perceives words or behaviors of others as threatening even when they are not so intended. The child attacks others because they represent the feared experience. She has no real understanding of the other as a separate person because she perceives the other mostly in terms of a threat or nonthreat to the self. But when all experiences are available to consciousness and are integrated, then there is no need to defend, no need to attack. The child perceives others for what they really are: separate individuals behaving in terms of their own meaning, based on their own perceptual maps.

"Good Growing Ground" Therapy

The play therapy setting, Axline's (1947) "good growing ground," must provide the appropriate climate for children to experience themselves fully and to experience their own potential for growth. The person-centered play therapist's objective is to create a relationship in which children feel secure and safe enough to experience all of their emotionalized attitudes that in the past have seemed too threatening to admit to awareness (Moustakas 1959). The factors of the therapeutic relationship that produce good growing ground for play therapy include the role of the therapist, playroom limits, and the playroom toys. The therapeutic relationship enables the child to experience and respond to her need for self-actualization.

Therapist's Role

Axline (1947) based the therapist's role on the following eight principles. As a person-centered play therapist, I. . .

1. Develop a warm, friendly relationship so that I form good rapport with children.
2. Accept children exactly as they are.
3. Maintain an accepting environment where children feel free to express all of their emotions.
4. Recognize and acknowledge the children's feelings in a manner that helps the children gain insight into their behavior.
5. Demonstrate a deep respect for the children's ability to solve their problems. The responsibility for choices and change is the child's.
6. Make no attempts to direct children's play or conversation. Children lead; I follow.
7. Do not hurry the therapeutic process.
8. Establish only the limits necessary to meet safety, legal, and ethical standards.

As the therapist, I define my role in the relationship through words and actions. My statements in the playroom structure the relationship. The following are some examples:

> In here you can play with all the toys in *most* of the ways that you choose. You can decide. The window is not for breaking. I'm not for hurting. We have five (one) more minutes before our time is up for today. I can tell you would like to leave the playroom, but our time is not up yet. This is our special time. I will not be telling your parents what you say or do in here unless I think you will get hurt or will hurt someone else. Then I will tell you "that is something we need to talk to Mom (Dad) about." I am not going to tell you what other children do or say in the playroom, just like I am not going to tell them what you do or say. Of course, you may tell anyone what you or I do or say in here if you wish.

All of these statements are not given in the initial session. Rather, I use them as the need arises.

My actions also delineate my role. I remain in "my chair" in the same location in the room. The playroom is the children's world, and they may explore, create, or roam around, unencumbered by me. I am not their playmate, director, evaluator, teacher, or instructor; I am their therapist, and my job is to communicate that I am here, I understand, I care (Landreth 1991). I maintain a relaxed, yet involved, stance. I observe their play at all times: I lean forward and as Garry Landreth says, I "listen with my eyes." My speech cadence matches the child's. I accept all feelings. I am nonjudgmental. I am consistent and predictable. I never do for the child what the child can do for herself.

Playroom Limits

The freedom of the therapeutic relationship is anchored in limits. Some have said that without limits there can be no therapy. Limits offer freedom within a boundary of a safe and secure environment. I go a step further and agree with Bixler (1949): limits are therapy. Limits define the boundaries of the relationship, tie the therapy to reality, remind children of their responsibility to self and the world, offer security and permit freedom, and make the therapy experience a living reality (Moustakas 1959). Ginott's (1959) rationale for limits included the following: (a) redirecting aggression into symbolic outlets, thus providing the child with catharsis; (b) insuring the physical safety of the child and the therapist; (c) strengthening the child's ego controls; (d) enabling the therapist to remain accepting, empathic, and caring; and (e) maintaining legal, ethical, and social standards, as well as budgetary considerations.

In the playroom, the focus is on the process of setting the limit within the therapeutic relationship rather than the limit itself. The child's desire to break a limit is the therapeutic encounter; therefore, the procedure of limit setting is crucial. Landreth (1991) outlined the process in limit setting using the acronym ACT:

A—I acknowledge the child's feelings, wishes, wants, and behavior;
C—I communicate the limit broken by the behavior;
T—I target acceptable behavioral alternatives.

Using ACT I would say to a child client when she walks toward the wall with a hammer raised to strike,

A—"I see you would like to hit the wall,
C—but the wall is not for hitting with the hammer.
T—The tree stump is for hitting or you could hit the wall with the orange foam bat."

I accept and respect all feelings, wishes, desires, fantasies, thoughts, and dreams, and I allow the child to express them in words and symbolic play.

In person-centered play therapy, limits are kept to a minimum, presented only when needed, and are "predictable and consistent as a brick wall" (Guerney 1983, p. 39). Limits in my playroom include (a) a predetermined time-limited play session; (b) toys remain in the playroom; (c) children may not hurt themselves, me, or other children; (d) children may not damage expensive toys, such as a bop bag and doll house, or the room itself; and (e) children may not exceed the usual social standards, for example, undress (except shoes, socks, and sweaters), urinate, defecate, masturbate, or touch me in a sexual manner. I have added an additional limit that most person-centered play therapists do not include: all works of art remain in the playroom and I keep them in the child's folder until we terminate therapy. Just as children's psychological concerns are represented in their play, so also are their difficulties projected in their art work. The issue of confidentiality and the children's right to privacy must be respected. Just as I would not disclose the content of an adult's therapy session, neither do I disclose a child's play, verbalization, or art work.

Playroom Toys

Toys are children's words, and play is children's communication. Therefore, the selection of toys is another dimension of the good growing ground. I keep toys in view, in good repair, in the same location, and ready for children's use. As therapists do not require adults to "clean up their language," neither do person-centered therapists require children to clean up their toys at the end of a session. Playroom toys help children express all feelings, but particularly those feelings that are the most difficult and threatening to the self to admit, such as dependence, anger, fear, hate, and aggression (Guerney 1983).

The playroom contains both structured and unstructured items. Unstructured toys, such as sand, water, paper, paint, and clay, offer children the opportunity to express and release strong feelings. They can deform, spread, tear, bury, spill, shape, or destroy with such items (Moustakas 1959). Structured toys, such as guns, knives, swords, darts, bop bag, and hammer and nails, offer opportunities to express hostility and aggression in a socially acceptable manner. Puppets, family doll figures, masks, clothes, and hats encourage the expression of thoughts and feelings through the use of drama. Children use cars, trucks, boats, paper, and pencils for playing games and to express emotions and attitudes through nonhuman toys. Animal figures, such as the snake, spider, dinosaur, lion, and tiger, help represent children's real and imaginary fears.

Play items should be simple, easy for children to manipulate, durable, and designed for rough handling. I avoid mechanical toys because they do not provide children a creative outlet for self-expression. Landreth

(1991) has provided a detailed list of toys recommended for a person-centered playroom.

BACKGROUND DATA
AND PRESENTING PROBLEM

The focus of person-centered therapy is on the person in the here-and-now therapeutic encounter. I do not use any standardized questionnaire to secure a family history, nor any tests or diagnostic measures for evaluating the child. I do seek to understand the parents, the client, and the family dynamics. Whenever possible, I have an intake session with the parent or parents without the presence of the child. The parents have experienced great distress themselves by the time they decide to contact me, and they need time to express their concerns fully. It is difficult for children to sit still and listen over an extended period of time. In the first session with the child, however, I ask the parents to briefly restate their feelings and concerns. In this manner, I demonstrate that there are no secret communications between me and the parents. I show respect for my client, the child.

Audrey was a 6-year-old second grader. Audrey's mother, Mrs. A., was in her late twenties and had been diagnosed with terminal cancer. During a three-month stay in a hospital 350 miles from home, doctors removed Mrs. A.'s right arm and part of her right shoulder. Mr. and Mrs. A. had separated following Mrs. A.'s return home from the hospital. Mr. A. now lived with another woman and her children. The woman had taken care of Mr. and Mrs. A.'s children during Mrs. A.'s hospitalization. Three weeks prior to the initial session, Mrs. A. had been confined for two weeks in a local hospital for severe depression and suicidal tendencies. Hospital personnel had released Mrs. A. and she was in psychotherapy with another therapist. The school counselor had referred Audrey and her 9-year-old brother Harold for therapy. Audrey was an average student, but she cried "all the time," did not want to leave her mother and go to school, and had threatened "I'll shoot myself and go to heaven with Mommy." Audrey's brother was a straight-A student and refused to talk about his mother's illness.

Mrs. A. expressed a need "for space" and for "my children to mind me." Audrey slept with her mother or her brother due to sparseness of furniture and space and as a result of a history of both children often sleeping in their parents' bedroom. According to Mrs. A., Audrey was her favorite child and Audrey had always identified with her mother. As a result of chemotherapy, Mrs. A. had lost her hair and wore a wig. Her hair was beginning to grow back, and Audrey liked to rub Mrs. A.'s reappearing soft hair. Audrey said she hated her father and cried when she and her brother visited their father every Tuesday evening and every other weekend. Audrey's brother was the maternal grandmother's favorite grandchild, and he spent as much time at her home as he could. Audrey had no favorite adult family member, but she was fond of a 12-year-old cousin.

THEORETICAL CONCEPTUALIZATION

Because every child has the same basic need, the need to self-actualize, my approach to each child is the same—to provide a therapeutic relationship in which the child can fully experience all parts of self and her life experiences. Landreth (1991) pointed out, "When we focus on the problem we lose sight of the child" (p. 78). That does not mean that I have the same perception of every child. On the contrary, my job must be to see the child and the child's world as this unique individual perceives self and life.

Audrey's family was in crisis. The needs of each family member were of such a profound nature that they required individual treatment for every family member. Audrey, Harold, and Mrs. A. faced the loss of the family structure as it had been, the physical disability of Mrs. A., Mrs. A.'s possible death, the financial poverty that often accompanies separation and divorce, and the loss of trust and hope in the future—the destruction of their world. Life, as each had known it, had disappeared.

Perceiving so many life-threatening experiences can be overwhelming. Feelings of uncertainty, confusion, helplessness, hopelessness, despair, impotency, anger, frustration, fear, and rage engulfed Audrey, Mrs. A., and Harold.

Due to the high-risk factor involved in the crisis, I recommended twice a week therapy sessions for Audrey and instructed the mother to see that all guns were secured in a locked place. I referred Audrey's brother to another play therapist. Mrs. A. was presently receiving individual therapy. I recommended the family encourage Audrey's relationship with her cousin. All family members were struggling with their own emotions in response to Mrs. A.'s battle with cancer and to the dissolution of Mr. and Mrs. A.'s marriage. Audrey's cousin appeared to be the person who could understand the family dynamics and with whom Audrey would be willing to share her thoughts and feelings.

Audrey's cousin could give Audrey some of the emotional support she needed.

Audrey was living as the center of a changing world of experience filled with threatening factors—she felt abandoned when her mother was hospitalized twice; she felt powerless and angry over the separation and impending divorce of her parents; she was worried about having less money due to the parental separation; she was sad and apprehensive about the move from the family's home into a small apartment; she missed the ability of Mrs. A. to physically care for her as a result of the amputation of Mrs. A.'s arm; she was afraid to lose her mother so she denied the possibility of Mrs. A.'s death; she felt anxious as she experienced the concern of the family for Mrs. A.'s health. Audrey was not symbolizing or was symbolizing in a distorted fashion these sensory and visceral experiences and therefore could not organize those experiences into the gestalt of her self-structure. In other words, Audrey was in a state of incongruence between her experiences and her self-concept.

Audrey had halted her move to differentiate the "me," "I," "myself" from the environment. The process begins around the age of 3 and is usually accomplished by the age of 6. However, Audrey's identification with her mother had become fixated. Audrey was afraid to let go of her identification with her mother because of the illness and possible death of her mother. Some of the values Audrey attached to her experiences were introjected from the significant others in her life. As Mrs. A. denied the terminal nature of her cancer, so did Audrey. Mrs. A.'s rage and feelings of abandonment connected to Mr. A.'s move out of the house were values also introjected into Audrey's experiences. Audrey's self was being formed on distorted sensory perceptions. Audrey was basing her perceptions on parental attitudes and values rather than her own internal valuing system.

As a result of Audrey's perceptual map being based on the values of others, Audrey's basic need to self-actualize, which usually moves the child toward greater independence, autonomy and self-responsibility, became distorted. Audrey did not perceive her power to freely choose her behavioral responses to her life experiences so she mistakenly chose regressive behavior (e.g., sitting on her mother's lap, separation anxiety, crying, refusal to sleep alone). Her predominant feelings (anger, anxiety, fear, and frustration) are the feelings that accompany the seeking efforts of the individual as she attempts to get her needs met. Audrey's emotional reaction was intensive because she perceived her behavior as a means to actualize her self.

Audrey's task and my goal for treatment was for Audrey to fully experience herself and her world in the midst of what appeared to be devastating events—a monumental task for a 6-year-old girl. As Audrey perceived me as being sincere and genuine, accepting and valuing her as a person of worth, having the ability to see her world and her as she herself saw them, then she would move in the direction of growth, maturity, and self-integration. She would be able to fully feel all of her feelings. Literally she would be back in touch with herself. Audrey then would be able to symbolize her experiences and live in a state of congruence between self and experience.

PROCESS OF PLAY THERAPY

Family Time

At the beginning of each session, I have a family group time when all members of the family may be present. I prefer to talk about the child and the family with my child-client present. In this way, children will know that I respect their right to privacy and confidentiality. In Audrey's case, because of Ms. A.'s deteriorating physical condition, we only held the family time during the first three months of therapy.

During the initial session, Audrey and her brother Harold fussed with each other, constantly interrupted their mother, and refused to be orderly or cooperative. Audrey was always in physical contact with her mother (sitting on her lap, leaning on her arm, touching her hair). Audrey denied she thought about killing herself. She separated from her mother and entered the playroom with no hesitation or tears. At the end of the session, however, when we could not find her mother's car, immediately Audrey appeared anxious and tears came into her eyes.

Excerpts from Play Sessions

The following are excerpts from the sessions. I use "A" to denote when Audrey talked and "L" when I spoke. An explanation or clarification of my interventions are on the right side of the page. An excerpt from the first session follows.

Dialogue	Commentary
L: In here, Audrey, you can play with all the toys in most of the ways that you like.	I begin every first session with these words. The child leads the therapy. I follow. I say "most of the ways" implying that there are limits.

A: [pointing to the Slinky®]
What's this?

L: Hmm?

I joined in Audrey's exploration and questioning. I did not name toys. I wanted to see the world through her eyes. Children choose to use the same toy in many different ways. A child once said of the Slinky®, "Oh, I know. It's a motorized giraffe!"

A: [Audrey moves around the room examining the content of the room. She picks up the baby bottle.] What do you do with this?

Audrey was in the exploratory stage of therapy. She was not only exploring the physical contents of the room, but she was also exploring the boundaries of our relationship. She was asking, "What is your role? What is my role?"

L: You can decide.

My message was, "You are in charge."

A: [She continues her exploration. Touching the tips of the paint brushes, she asks wistfully:] Can I paint?

L: Sounds like you would like to. You can decide.

My response said, "I hear and understand your desire. I do not give permission . . . Permission comes from within you." My job was to wait upon Audrey. She led. I accepted her uncertainty. Uncertainty was part of her life and who she was at the moment.

Painting was to become one of Audrey's primary avenues of self-exploration, self-revelation, and self-actualization. Audrey was a prolific painter and declared as she painted at the beginning of the eleventh session, "I do this (paint) every time." Near the end of the first session,

Audrey returned to the easel and painted a " 'Mixed-Up Picture' like Harold's" (Figure 2–1).

Harold had evidently painted a similar picture during his therapy session. The painting seemed to represent Audrey's inner emotional life: a life filled with "mixed-up" feelings rooted in her "mixed-up" life— her mother's surgery, hospitalization, and illness; parents' separation, move to another house, and father's move to another family.

Audrey painted a picture (Figure 2–2) during the third session that could be her perception of my role in her life.

Audrey placed me in the middle. Audrey was "seated" on the right side of me, though she had no visible support such as a chair, and her mother was on the left. The painting seemed to symbolize my entrance into their relationship. As Audrey painted, I thought but did not say that perhaps I would be able to help Audrey with the separation from her mother that must occur.

Dialogue	*Commentary*
A: This is you. I am here and Mommy is over here.	Audrey spent much time on hair. Hair was important in Audrey's world: Mrs. A.'s loss of hair as a result of chemotherapy; the regrowth of her soft hair that Audrey liked to rub; and Mrs. A.'s inability to comb and care for Audrey's hair because of the removal of her arm.
L: So I'm in the middle, between you and your mom. . . . I noticed you were very careful about the hair.	I did not speak directly to the issue of separation or loss of hair, rather I spoke to the image or play Audrey held forth as the symbol for her experiences.
A: Mommy used to braid my hair, but she can't anymore.	Audrey chose to respond to the hair rather than me in the middle of things.
L: I guess you feel sad cause Mama can't do your hair. [Audrey nods.]	I asked no questions; rather I put a feeling word on her experience.

Figure 2-1. "Mixed Up Picture"

Figure 2–2. Ms. A., Me, and Audrey (her view of the relationship)

In silence, Audrey produced the painting in Figure 2–3 during the fourth session.

Dialogue	Commentary
L: Oh, I wonder whose house that is.	Audrey did not respond. I had not stayed with Audrey in her need for silence. My need to know got in the way. My job was *not to know*, but *to be* with Audrey on her journey.

Audrey placed the house left of the center of the page, suggesting a wish to return to the past. Silently I wondered if the heavy line down the house was Audrey's portrayal of her divided home. The divorce of Audrey's parents had become final that week. Harold had moved to his father's house because the quality of his school work had declined and Mrs. A. was having difficulty disciplining him. When she had completed the picture, Audrey titled it "My Home." The therapeutic value of this painting, however, does not rest with my understanding of what Audrey was painting. The therapeutic value was the freedom Audrey had to play out of her experience.

Audrey tested the boundaries of the child–therapist relationship during the fifth session.

Figure 2-3. "My House" (a house divided)

Dialogue	Commentary

A: Want to know a secret about Harold?

L: Sounds like you want to tell me.

I acknowledged her wish.

A: Yeah. [Then she tells me the "secret."] But don't tell Mommy!

L: You want to be sure I don't tell Mom the secret. I don't tell Mom what you do or say in

I explained the boundaries of this relationship and the issue of confidentiality.

here unless I think you might
get hurt. Then I would tell
you, "We will need to talk to
Mom about that." Of course
you can tell Mom anything
you choose about what happens in here. . . .

A: [Audrey makes "sand pies"
and washes the dishes at the
sink.] Come help me.

L: You wish I would help you   I never do for children what chil-
wash all those dishes, but my   dren can do for themselves. To
place is here (in the chair).   me, my act of helping wash the
                                       dishes would have said that I was
                                       able and she was not. Once again,
                                       I defined our relationship.

A: Come help me! You made this
mess!

L: [Nodding my head] Ah, you   I acknowledged and accepted her
are angry because you say I   anger and frustration. I thought of
made the mess and should   other "messes" in Audrey's life—
clean it up. [I remain in my   divorce and dying—and how she
chair. She bangs the dishes   might angrily wish that I and the
around and finally turns to   other adults would "clean it up."
other play activity.]

Audrey continued to explore the boundaries of the relationship
during this session by asking if she could nail, shoot the gun, put water
in the baby bottle, dump the animals out of the basket, and wear
the monster mask. My responses included: "You can decide," "Sounds
like you want to," "You are not real sure," and a number of noncom-
mittal "hmmms." These responses affirm that she sets the direction of
therapy and that I, the therapist, will follow her lead. I believed that
Audrey would take her therapy in the way that met her need to
self-actualize.

Eventually Audrey broke a known limit: she poured a cup of sand on
the floor.

Dialogue	Commentary
L: I know you like to pour sand, but sand is not for pouring on the floor. You can pour it in the sandbox or the pan, not the floor.	I set limits: A—I acknowledged the desire. C—I communicated the limits. T—I targeted acceptable alternatives.
[Audrey sweeps up some of the sand and spills no more during that session, though she does spill sand during other sessions.]	I do not require children to clean up their play, as I do not require adults to "clean up" their verbal communication.

At the sixth appointment, Audrey and Mrs. A. came in smiling and laughing. The cancer had gone into remission.

Dialogue	Commentary
A: Jesus made a miracle!	
L: You are very happy that Mom is better!	I empathized with Audrey's joy.

During that session Audrey painted a picture (Figure 2-4) that she titled "Dance Studio." She was taking dance lessons.

Dialogue	Commentary
A: In the middle of the dark blue sky flowers are born!	
L: [Matching her exuberance] Oh, new flowers!	I spoke to the image. No interpretation was necessary. The doctor's report had given birth to new life and hope in Audrey. The healing power in play therapy is the freedom of expressing all that you experience.

During the seventh through the thirteen sessions, Audrey introduced fantasy stories into her therapy. The stories did not appear profound—

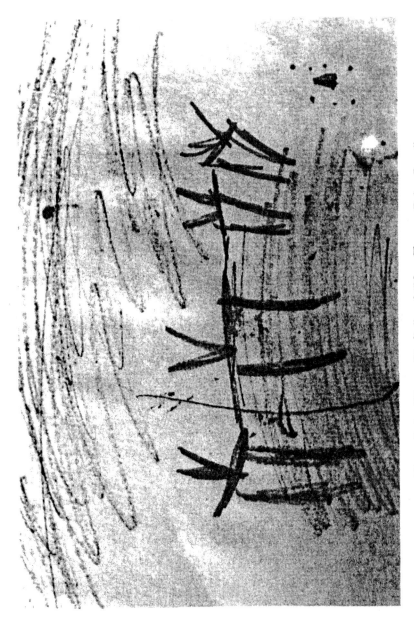

Figure 2–4. "Dance Studio" and "New Flowers Being Born"

television artists giving instructions on how to paint . . . children going on a hayride . . . television artist painting a tornado. The therapeutic value of this play lies less in the content of the material and more in Audrey experiencing my valuing and prizing of her and her play as she felt free to be whoever she was at the moment.

Audrey's world changed dramatically prior to the fourteenth session. Mrs. A.'s cancer began growing again. Audrey finger painted a black picture (Figure 2-5) with strong physical physical movements using her fingernails to scratch out the white areas. She did not talk. She expressed her despair, hopelessness, and rage nonverbally.

Dialogue	Commentary
L: [Sporadically, I verbally observe:] You covered all of that . . . Umm, you squished it with your fist . . . Oh, I see you scratched it hard with your fingernail.	I spoke to the image, no further. My words conveyed the message that I am here, I understand, I care.

Over the next four weeks tornados became a primary theme in Audrey's paintings. Tornados disappeared after the thirtieth session. It seemed to me that perhaps Audrey believed that everything was out of control, whirling around, moving very fast, and she felt scared as she would if she were in the grips of a tornado. Audrey painted a "gray tornado" and a "tornado that hit the house." As Audrey painted "Tornado in the Playroom" during the eighteenth session (Figure 2-6), we talked.

Dialogue	Commentary
A: I think about Mama dying. I don't want to but I do . . . but she doesn't (die).	
L: So even though you don't want to think about Mom's dying, you do. And you are puzzled because Mom doesn't die. It is all so strange.	I didn't try to explain; I accepted Audrey as she was at the moment.

Figure 2-5.   Untitled (perhaps a silent impression of cancer)

Figure 2-6. "Tornado in the Playroom" (a picture of life's storms)

Audrey took the therapy where she needed it to go—into the midst of her tornado. I empathized with Audrey's wish not to think about her mother's dying and at the same time with her puzzlement and confusion that her mother had not died. I offered no rationalizations, explanations, or solutions. I believed Audrey could handle the dying of her mother if she fully sensed and expressed what she experienced.

Mrs. A.'s physical condition had worsened. She was no longer able to maintain a separate living setting for herself and Audrey. Following the eighteenth session Mrs. A. and Audrey moved in with Mrs. A.'s parents. Hospice workers, nurses, psychologist, and friends provided in-home care for Mrs. A. Audrey and Mrs. A. now had their own bedrooms. Mrs. A.'s mother began transporting Audrey to therapy. Audrey appeared more calm and less anxious.

Now another fantasy theme emerged—wicked witches and Cinderella. During the eighteenth through twenty-second sessions, Audrey was the "Wicked Witch of the North" and filled the witch's hat with sand and stomped on it. She also played the part of Cinderella in the story of the poor stepsister who had to work and work while the stepmother and stepsisters had a good time at the party. Audrey never completed the Cinderella story with the fairy godmother, the ball, or the prince. Audrey's perception seemed to be that her life was hard, while the lives of others were easy. Perhaps in Audrey's eyes her real stepmother and stepsisters she visited on weekends were laughing and having a party while all that Audrey experienced was pain and hard times. My interventions were restatements of the content of the story, so she knew I accepted and valued her story. I did not try to get her to make the story have a happy ending. I spoke to the story characters' feelings.

Dialogue	*Commentary*
L: I bet Cinderella is mad at having to work and work and be dirty while others get to play . . . Maybe she feels lonely there all by herself like that.	I identified feelings that Audrey seemed to be experiencing and projecting on the story characters. I do not believe interpretation is necessary or helpful. I stayed within the context of the story.

Mrs. A.'s condition continued to deteriorate. A couple and their two children moved into Mrs. A.'s parents' home to assist with the care of Mrs. A. People were constantly in and out of the house providing support services for Mrs. A. and her family. During the twentieth session Audrey painted Figure 2-7.

Figure 2-7 "Disaster"

Dialogue	*Commentary*
L: I wonder what you're painting.	I didn't wait. I let my desire to know get in the way.
A: [I cannot hear exactly what she says. She says either "It's Mom" or "It's for Mom."]	By mumbling Audrey could be saying that I didn't need to know.
L: I'm sorry I didn't hear you.	I still did not get Audrey's "real" message.
A: I'll tell you when I'm finished.	Audrey reminded me of who was in charge of the therapy.

Audrey continued to paint until she finished. I remained quiet. My job was to join Audrey in her journey.

Dialogue	*Commentary*
A: The name (of the picture) is "Disaster." That's what happened to Mommy—a disaster.	
L: Hmm. I see.	Nodding my head affirmatively, I conveyed that I understood and accepted Audrey's evaluation of what happened to her and to her mother.

Audrey then went to the dollhouse and threw dollhouse figures in every room. I have four family sets of four or five family members, plus four extra infant figures, so there were twenty-three doll figures in the five-room house. They were "sleeping." There were people sleeping everywhere—on the table, floor, even the bathtub. Audrey took the zebra and the elephant and had them "look in" through the window "at the sleeping people." Audrey stuck the elephant's head through the window and made a loud trumpeting noise over the little girl doll sleeping in the bed. Audrey threw the girl doll across the room.

Dialogue	Commentary
A: The little girl jumped out of the house.	
L: She was scared of the loud noise.	I intended my intervention to say I understand and to attach a feeling to the story.

Audrey became so anxious that she abruptly left the scene of the story. She played "a song for you" (the therapist) on the xylophone and then with other toys. This was a form of play disruption. Play disruption is a behavior suggesting emotional discomfort and is an indicator of maladjustment (Perry and Landreth 1991). Erikson (1963) defined play disruption as the "sudden and complete diffuse inability to play" (p. 223). He believed that play disruption occurs when the subject matter of the play suddenly becomes too painful for the child. Children switch from the microsphere, or the play world in which they are immersed, to the world shared with others, the macrosphere. The anxiety that surrounds this switch leads to the cessation of the child's play and is the key factor in distinguishing play disruption. In the playroom, the therapist can recognize play disruption when the child is intensively involved in play and abruptly stops at a point that appears to be especially threatening for the child. Facial expressions suggestive of fear or despair, stiffening of the body, staring into space, sudden concern with realistic aspects of the environment, sudden interest in unrelated objects, and requests to leave the room are behaviors that might indicate play disruption.

Either I went too far ahead of Audrey and verbalized a feeling she was not ready to acknowledge or the content of the story was too threatening to Audrey's self-concept to fully symbolize this experience or a combination of these two circumstances. Later in this session Audrey returned to the dollhouse and her story. The people in the house "were so mad at the elephant and the zebra that they [the people] killed them."

Audrey's elephant story was a dramatic symbolization of what she was experiencing. There were people everywhere in her house. Her mother's cancerous condition was further complicated with emphysema. Mrs. A. could only say two or three words and then she had to gasp for breath and coughed uncontrollably. Mrs. A. feared dying from suffocation. I thought perhaps that Audrey thought her mother sounded like a trumpeting elephant. Watching the people taking care of her mother, Audrey might have perceived their help as killing her

mother elephant. The following week Audrey told me that she was
going to live with her father. The little girl indeed jumped out of the
house, but this time Audrey was able to verbalize her ambivalent
feelings. "I'll be sad (to leave) 'cause I'll miss her, but I don't want to see
Mommy hurting," she said.

Beginning in the twenty-second and continuing through the thirty-
first session, Audrey directed therapy toward a new theme: suffocation,
death, and burial. Audrey made a strong, invincible female doll a central
figure in her stories. She named the powerful female doll "Nardia."
Sometimes Nardia was a little girl like Audrey; sometimes she was a
mother figure. Frequently I had trouble clearly understanding which age
character Nardia represented. I believe the confusion lay not only in me,
but also within Audrey as she experienced the conflict between her
identification with her mother and her own sense of identity. Through
her story enactments, however, Audrey gradually became a separate
entity from her mother.

Over the next nine sessions, Audrey presented a series of repetitive
stories that she acted out with the dolls in the sandbox. Nardia was
"covered with sand," "suffocated," "died," and "buried." Audrey
placed "grave markers" (funnels) in the sand over the buried Nardia.
Audrey rescued Nardia, shook the sand off, and pretended she gave
Nardia a shower, but did not wash Nardia's hair. In one story, Audrey
had Nardia dig and burrow herself under the sand.

Dialogue	*Commentary*
A: [As Audrey buries the doll] She covers herself, suffocated, and died.	
L: I see.	My message was I'm here and I understand. I believed in Audrey's ability to handle death as she had handled the other parts of her life.
A: They think she's in heaven. She floats away above every-one. [She gently waves the doll over her head.] She gets out, goes home, and takes a shower, but doesn't wash her hair.	

L: Oh, so she suffocates and dies . . . floats around over everyone, then gets out and washes off except (for) her hair.

I continued being with Audrey even when the play was "irrational" and a form of denial. I believed she was where she needed to be.

During the twenty-sixth session, Audrey and I shared a profound experience. A hospital bed had replaced Mrs. A.'s bed at her parents' home. This bed could be elevated and adjusted to provide Mrs. A. more comfort. The family had rearranged Mrs. A.'s room so she could look out over the flower garden. Audrey told the following story using Nardia and two adult female dolls to act out the story in the sandbox.

Dialogue   *Commentary*

A: Here's the sister and the mother. They are all buried. [She piles dirt on the dolls. She lays the sand bucket sideways and puts Nardia in it.]

A: Nardia is in a special beautiful room. She wouldn't let anyone in unless the rug and the room are clean.

L: I see.   I'm here. I understand.

Audrey laid back in the sandbox, resting her head on the rim. She made "a hospital bed" by pulling and mounding sand between her spread legs. Audrey said, "It's wonderful! I can lean back!" Audrey placed Nardia on the "bed" between her legs. She was deep in her fantasy. Audrey appeared quiet, contented, peaceful, and satisfied. I was deeply moved and joined with her in the silent treasuring of the moment. I thought, *I am witnessing a birthing.* Perhaps the story was Audrey's own birth memory; perhaps it was the birth of her new self apart from her mother; perhaps the girl, Audrey, was the mother of the woman. I do not know. I did not need to know the meaning for it to be a transformation experience for Audrey. I do know that the experience for me and Audrey was profound. After awhile, Audrey continued the story.

Dialogue	*Commentary*
A: They found her, but her eyes were closed. She was dead. The two sisters carried the mother to the hospital. She was upset about her child being dead. I have to go to the bathroom.	
L: Well, our time is up for today. We can stop by the bathroom on our way to the car.	In the hall Audrey said she didn't have to go to the bathroom. Audrey had become so threatened by her play that she brought about play disruption so she could get some distance from the painful experience.

At the next session, Audrey painted a heart and added the words, "I love my mommy." Mrs. A. died the next day. At the funeral, Audrey cried and she sang. Audrey was able to express the full range of emotions she was experiencing—her sorrow at the loss of her mother and her joy surrounding the love of her mother. At the session following her mother's death, Audrey shared what her experience was like.

Dialogue	*Commentary*
A: My mommy died.	
L: You miss your mom.	

Audrey drew the picture in Figure 2-8. I thought Audrey was drawing a picture of her own sadness and tears. I was only half right. The painting was of her sadness, but not her tears.

Dialogue	*Commentary*
A: It's my mommy. She's in heaven. She is saying,"I miss Audrey."	Audrey was not ready to experience her loss, but played out grief from her mother's viewpoint.

Figure 2–8. "Mommy in Heaven Says, 'I Miss Audrey' "

I believe this symbolization was helpful for Audrey. She could hold in her mind's eye this picture of her mother thinking of her and missing her. It has been said that as long as someone remembers you then you still live. Audrey symbolized such an image for herself. In heaven, her mother would always remember and miss her. Later, Audrey returned to the picture and added the smaller figure on the lower section.

Dialogue	*Commentary*
A: Here's Audrey down here. It's a mess!	Audrey found the strength to add her own feeling of despair about her life.

Beginning with the twenty-eighth session I noticed gradual changes in Audrey's play. She continued her burial and Cinderella stories, but she no longer produced the tornado paintings. Perhaps Audrey's storms were over. Cinderella continued to work and be dirty, but now Cinderella was "clean" sometimes. Repetitive play was still present in the burial stories, but Audrey played less frantically and with fewer repetitions of the burial theme during any one session. She used the army helmet as "the coffin" and more often Nardia remained buried and did not "get out and go home and take a shower." The play was more final.

Dialogue	*Commentary*
A: They (Nardia and the two adult female dolls) are in dirt heaven.	
L: Ahh, in dirt heaven.	
A: They are lonely.	
L: They are lonely in heaven.	Audrey was projecting her loneliness onto the dolls. She was not ready to own this feeling. I waited.

From the thirtieth session on, Audrey's play began to include more positive themes and affects: a "secret recipe" that won a prize and a strong "captain on the job." Audrey's paintings also reflected feelings of adequacy and a sense of her self as a worthy individual and a more positive view of her life. "Designs by Audrey" was the title of a pleasant, calm, and gentle painting of muted pastel shades of blue, yellow, and green flowing together in an integrated expression of self (Figure 2–9).

Audrey continued therapy for six weeks following Mr. A.'s death. Audrey's father called and canceled two successive appointments, saying that other activities interfered, and then without any notice the family moved out of town. I worried that Audrey would have difficulty at the abrupt manner of termination. I was angry and sad that Audrey and I had not gotten to say goodbye to each other. But then I realized that maybe Audrey had. Our final therapy session was held in the spring of the year, but her picture was "Christmas Tree Decorations" (Figure 2–10).

As Audrey painted, I puzzled silently over the subject matter Audrey

Figure 2-9. "Designs by Audrey" (in pastel blue, green, and yellow)

Figure 2-10. "Christmas Tree Decorations" (perhaps a celebration of the healing power of play)

had chosen to use. How and where did Christmas fit in here? Perhaps there was a miracle after all—not in the curing of Mrs. A.'s cancer, but in Audrey's use of the power of play to heal herself and continue her journey of self-actualization.

RESULTS AND FOLLOW-UP

I had no direct contact with Audrey for three years, though occasionally I would hear positive reports about Audrey's life from a member of Mrs. A.'s family. Mr. A. and the woman who had cared for Audrey and Harold during Mrs. A.'s hospitalization married. Audrey and Harold were living with their father, stepmother, and stepsisters in another town. Audrey and Harold enjoyed regular visits with Mrs. A.'s mother and father. When I did talk with Mr. A. three years later, he said Audrey's therapy had been very beneficial for her and had helped her through a difficult period. He was proud to report that Audrey was a happy, active child. She was a straight-A student, played softball on a winning team, and wrote poetry. According to her father, "She is a live wire and a delight to be around."

DISCUSSION

Person-centered play therapy worked. In the face of seemingly over-whelming circumstances, Audrey used play to fully experience all aspects of her life and to assimilate those aspects into an integrated system of self. She adequately maintained, enhanced, and actualized her self in the midst of her disintegrating world. Within the warm, accepting, safe, respectful person-centered relationship and with no suggestion or direction from me, Audrey addressed the threatening issues in her life through stories and paintings. She presented her divided home, her joy when Mrs. A.'s cancer went into remission, the image of the deadly cancer, the whirling events of her storm-tossed life, her life as a stepchild and stepsister, the dying and burial of her mother, the eternal presence of her mother, and the strength and belief in herself that she came to know and prize.

The nonthreatening nature of person-centered therapy was particu-larly appropriate for this threatened child. In therapy, she could choose how, when, and to what degree she would handle her concerns. The "techniques" of person-centered therapy that are embodied entirely in the child–therapist relationship were also beneficial, since Audrey needed someone to accompany her on her walk through this frightening time of her life.

For myself, the therapy experience forced me to address my own unresolved issues connected to death and dying. Death is a fact that I had chosen to address only when I was forced to by my own physical illness. I have never explored the process of dying at least with any acknowledged feelings. The nothingness I face as I contemplate death or nonliving has seemed overpowering, so I filled my thoughts with fantasy that I could master, rather than reality that I could not. Not so for Audrey: she filled her therapy life with fantasy that brought her reality under her control. She led and I followed her working through the process of dying, being buried, living in heaven, and remembering the ones living on earth. Having accompanied Audrey on her experience of dying and death, I am more open to experiencing my own mortality. The beauty and peace that I witnessed in Audrey's therapy life assures me that death, like life, is a part of a never-ending process and I have nothing to fear and no need to escape.

I dealt with another personal issue: my image of myself as a person who must make others happy. I could not take away Audrey's pain and sorrow. On the contrary, my job was to facilitate her fully experiencing her distress. Audrey reminded me that all persons, even a 6-year-old child, can grow and become if they do not deny or distort what they experience, regardless of the awesome nature of the experience. Like the bois d'arc, Audrey refused to stop growing. She *became* and I believe she will continue to become who she is meant to be.

I have enumerated, outlined, and elaborated person-centered theory and therapy — how children struggle to self-actualize, how they live by a perceptual map of their own making, how they have an individualized organismic valuing system, how they deny and distort experiences when the experiences do not support their self-concept, how they become alienated from their self, how they once again fully symbolize all their experiences in a person-centered play therapy relationship. A "good growing ground" play therapy setting activates the reparative processes that reside within the child and allows the child to heal herself.

REFERENCES

Axline, V. (1947). *Play Therapy: The Inner Dynamics of Childhood*. Boston: Houghton Mifflin.
Bixler, R. H. (1949). Limits are therapy. *Journal of Consulting Psychology* 13:1–11.
Dorfman, E. (1951). Play therapy. In *Client-centered Therapy*, ed. C. R. Rogers, pp. 235–277. Boston: Houghton Mifflin.

Erikson, E. H. (1963) *Childhood and Society*. 2nd ed. New York: W. W. Norton.

Ginott, H. (1959). The theory and practice of "therapeutic intervention" in child treatment. *Journal of Consulting Psychology* 23:160–166.

———— (1961). *Group Psychotherapy With Children: The Theory and Practice of Play Therapy*. New York: McGraw Hill.

Guerney, L. F. (1983). Client-centered (nondirective) play therapy. In *Handbook of Play Therapy*, ed. C. E. Schaefer and K. J. O'Connor, pp. 21–64. New York: Wiley.

Landreth, G. L., ed. (1982). *Play Therapy: Dynamics of the Process of Counseling With Children*. Springfield, IL: Charles C Thomas.

———— (1991). *Play Therapy: The Art of the Relationship*. Muncie, IN: Accelerated Development.

Lebo, D. (1955). The development of play as a form of therapy: from Rousseau to Rogers. *American Journal of Psychiatry* 112:418–422.

Moustakas, C. (1959). *Psychotherapy With Children: The Living Relationship*. New York: Harper & Row.

Perry, L., and Landreth, G. (1991). Diagnostic assessment of children's play therapy behavior. In *Play Diagnosis and Assessment*, ed. C. E. Schaefer, K. Gitlin, and A. Sandgrund, pp. 643–662. New York: Wiley.

Rogers, C. R. (1942). *Counseling and Psychotherapy*. Boston: Houghton Mifflin.

———— (1951). *Client-Centered Therapy: Its Current Practice, Implications, and Theory*. Boston: Houghton Mifflin.

———— (1959). A theory of therapy, personality, and interpersonal relationships as developed in the client-centered framework. In *Psychology: a Study of a Science. Study I. Conceptual and Systematic. Vol. 3: Formulations of the Person and Social context*, ed. S. Koch, pp. 184–256. New York: McGraw Hill.

3

Family Theraplay for the Family Tyrant

Ann Jernberg, PH.D., and Emily Jernberg, M.A.

INTRODUCTION TO THERAPLAY

Although we like to think that every child is able to collect his or her share of good parenting, there are, unfortunately, too many children denied these experiences from early on. Among children so deprived are some who are adopted, others who do not meet their parents' needs, yet others who are compelled to meet their parents' needs ("superbabies"), and children who bring into the equation their own unique, but perhaps frustrating, temperaments. In conceptualizing exactly what these disadvantaged children have missed, we look, for contrast, at the typical, happy nursery scene: a parent and an infant in interaction with one another. We find typical, happy parent–infant interactions to be characterized by at least five distinct dimensions: structuring, challenging, intruding/exciting, nurturing, and playfulness. We may, for example, see the parent in this happy scenario chattering or singing to, snuggling with, making delighted faces at the baby, or marching two fingers up the baby's tummy, playing "I'm coming to get you." Babies tend to react to such interactions with pleasure, with heightened self-esteem, and with a view of the world as a caring, admiring, pleasurable, and invested place in which other people regard them as unique, special, handsome, and wonderful.

Deprived of these joyful, engaging physical experiences, children often come to see themselves as ordinary and drab if not burdensome, and the world as a place that is unloving, discounting, rejecting, painful, and not to be trusted. Some children may manifest their feelings of

45

worthlessness and despair by becoming aggressive or withdrawn, others by becoming psychosomatic, suicidal, drug-abusing, or depressed. Lively, positive, physical, personal, and engaged, "Theraplay" strives to give these children the experiences they never had and it strives to do so within a context that is trustworthy, limit-setting, nurturing, playful, and exciting.

We (Jernberg 1979, Jernberg et al. 1987) first developed Theraplay in the 1960s as a means of supplying short-term, but intensive therapy to thousands of disturbed/disadvantaged children enrolled in the several hundred Head Start programs in Chicago. Thus we first formulated Theraplay to serve a large number of Head Start children having myriad emotional, social, and learning problems. As the Theraplay component grew in exposure, obvious effectiveness, and resultant popularity, we began to receive urgent demands from non–Head Start populations for treatment using this method. Thus it was that over the past thirty years we have gone on to mold and expand Theraplay to fit a variety of other populations (including ones from the private sector) and other problem areas (including foster adoptive and stepfamilies) as well as to utilize other resources (e.g., parents to participate as co-therapists) (Jernberg 1989, 1991). We found the nonverbal, noninterpretive, nonenhancing characteristics of Theraplay particularly helpful for a variety of children including those who are non-engaged (e.g., autistic), too verbal, ideational, and intellectualizing (e.g., obsessive compulsives), or too distractible to keep their minds on the content being presented (e.g., attention deficit disorders). Furthermore, we observed that verbal expression only seems to exaggerate the problems of "superbabies" (i.e., children who perform musically, theatrically, academically far beyond their emotional developmental level).

Gradually we came to understand that many children fitting these behavioral characteristics had failed to make a proper early attachment to their parents. We found that the reasons for this could be a function of the parent, a function of the child, or a function of a poor match between the two (Jernberg 1979, 1989, 1993). Often the parents intended "the best" for their children, but for one or another of the above reasons were unable to deliver it. Thus, for example, a parent with a basically healthy child might be depressed, preoccupied, physically ill, in an unhappy marriage, or caught in a maze of reality frustrations. By the same token, some parents may attempt to provide a caring, optimistic environment, but be blocked in carrying out their good intentions by a child who withdraws, is aloof, is overactive or runs away. Yet other parent–child dyads may present a pairing of a temperamentally soft-spoken, dreamy parent, for example, with a rambunctious, noisy child.

Or, equally mismatched, an energetic, active, ambitious parent may find him- or herself with a lethargic baby.

Of crucial importance for our new treatment was the notion that we needed a therapy that could bond poorly bonded parent and child at the most primitive (preverbal) level. We have found Theraplay, which so closely replicates parent–infant bonding, to be particularly useful for the populations of children described above. Thus we use Theraplay as the therapy of choice when dealing with many of the aforementioned children. Jernberg (1993) has made a case for the importance of playfulness for attachment-enhancing. The component of play in the context of other, more traditional, therapeutic qualities (e.g., empathy) is essential. In contrast to the focus on "work" or pathology, conveyed through some other methods of therapy with children, however, Theraplay conveys optimism, joy, and health. In contrast to the traditional utilization of verbally reported dreams, memories, and fantasies, Theraplay uses direct, physical, personal, active engagement. In contrast to the kinds of therapy in which it is the child who determines a session's scenario, in Theraplay it is the therapist who is in charge.

Theraplay sessions take place on one or two gym mats in a room containing minimal "props." Large pillows are scattered throughout and an enclosed closet contains lotion, baby powder, baby bottles, pretzels, M&M's, raisins, water pistols, and plastic garbage bags (for adolescent water pistol fights), Band-Aids, straws, beans, crepe paper strips (for adolescent neckties), newspapers (for crumpling "basketballs" and for kicking and punching through), dress-up hats, necklaces, and shaving cream. Doughnuts, popsicles, milk or juice cartons, and watermelon chunks (for seed spitting contests) are supplied as needed. There are either one or two therapists in the room with the child and one therapist (the interpreting therapist) with the parent(s). Needless to say, in even the simplest of cases (e.g., one Theraplay therapist with the child and one interpreting therapist sitting with the parent), there must be constant communication between therapists. These conferences take place during the detailed planning phase that precedes each session and during the reviewing phase that follows.

Prior to the first session, the therapist invites parents in for an intake interview. This interview generally follows a traditional format. The therapist formulates hypotheses on a continuous basis throughout the interview with each hypotheses leading to yet another effort to refute or verify. Additionally, the therapist elicits certain relevant historical data with the intention to answer the questions, "What kind of a world was this child born into?" "What kind of a world greeted each of his or her parents?" "How did this marriage come about?" "What is the marriage like today?" "What about sibs?" (both parental sibs and the child's). At the end of the 45-minute interview, the therapist tells the parents that one parent will be returning a week or so later with the child for the first Marschak Interaction Method (MIM), followed one week after that by an MIM session with the other parent and child. (In one-parent families there is only one MIM.)

The MIM (originally named the Controlled Interaction Schedule) (Marschak 1960) consists of a series of seven or eight structured tasks performed by parent and child sitting side by side at a table (or with child lying down and parent propped up with pillows if the child is an infant). Specific tasks are selected from a larger repertoire of tasks according to information gleaned in the intake interview. Depending upon hypotheses formulated at the intake, regarding, for example, parental style, child's degree of resistance, and so on, tasks may include "Teach child something new," "Feed each other M&M's," "Tell child about when he or she was a baby," "Dress each other up in hats."

A week or ten days later, both parents are invited to attend a feedback session. This is our opportunity to begin to instill the Theraplay philosophy. Often we use the feedback session to begin to model empathy and to focus on the positives. Thus, we may communicate to a parent how difficult it must be to have a child who responds so minimally to all the lovely things the parent does. At the close of the feedback session, the therapist informs the parents that they will next be coming in for the first of eight weekly half hour Theraplay sessions. The therapist tells them that there will be no expectations of them, particularly in the first four sessions. They will be sitting observing the session with an interpreting therapist who will be explaining to them all that is going on in their child's session, discussing with them what happened during the week preceding, and alerting them to what they can expect in the days to follow (e.g., "It looks as though he is just about to enter what we call 'the negative phase.' It will be important that you prepare his teachers and others for a possible oppositional period.")

The second four sessions begin as did the first four, with one significant variation. During the last fifteen minutes of these final four sessions, the parents join their child and his or her therapist in the Theraplay space.

The goal of Theraplay is to enhance children's view of themselves and to increase their joy in the world. This could not be made to happen as quickly without the intensely personal, physical, and eye-contacting nature of the relationship between child and therapist. To the extent this is possible, all Theraplay activities are carried out in a joyous, playful, and lighthearted spirit, while conveying empathy and extraordinary interest in every feature, every gesture, and every mood of the child. Through activities modeled on the healthy, attachment-enhancing behaviors between parent and infant, the primary goal of Theraplay is to enhance the attachment between parent and child. It is this attachment that will make possible the child's view of him- or herself as unique and wonderful and allow him or her to see his or her world as pleasurable and trustworthy.

PRESENTING DATA AND BACKGROUND

Marie, age 9, was referred for panic attacks and recent weight loss by her mother, a frightened, and never successfully treated panic-attack victim herself. Mrs. Brewster (Marie's mother) sought treatment with Theraplay because she had seen someone in her community benefit from this form of therapy.

Due to the urgency of the situation and the logistics of long-distance travel, Ann Jernberg (A. J.) deviated from the usual face-to-face Theraplay intake format and conducted the intake interview with Mrs. Brewster over the telephone. A. J.'s initial inclination was to refer Marie for hospitalization, but Marie's mother pleaded for at least a trial at Theraplay treatment. In discussing hospitalization with Marie's pediatrician, he commented that the situation was "not yet dire enough" to warrant psychiatric hospitalization. When challenged about this position, he explained that until Marie's picture became yet more life-threatening there would be no money to pay for hospitalization.

When Marie first came to the Theraplay Institute she had been experiencing panic attacks every day for the previous nine weeks. "It's been getting worse," Mrs. Brewster explained. The attacks began when Marie had the flu, but, despite her physical recovery from that illness, Marie had refused ever since to go out to public places. She also had dramatically curtailed her caloric intake and complained of gastrointestinal (GI) disorders such as nausea and vomiting (or, more frequently, feeling sick and throwing up.) At the time of referral Marie weighed 63 pounds—a loss of 17 pounds in the preceding two weeks according to both her mother and the pediatrician.

Her panic attacks began each morning and prevented her from eating breakfast, often lunch, and sometimes dinner. Marie was getting worse; now she was refusing to leave the house altogether. Among Mrs. Brewster's many questions during this first telephone session was the following: "How do I get her to go to school? This morning she lay on the floor; she wouldn't move." Once Mrs. Brewster had managed to get Marie into the school building for the day, she reported, the problems did not abate. Marie frequently called home from the school pay phone complaining of various physical ailments and demanding that she be taken home immediately. As acute as the panic attacks and the GI disorders seemed, however, there was a more chronic, underlying problem that had apparently been festering for the previous year or so. Marie, it appeared, had changed in many ways that were only high-lighted by the dramatic problems of the last few weeks. "Last year Marie was fun-loving. This year she thinks she's becoming unpopular. 'I don't have any friends,' she says." Mrs. Brewster added that "for the last year and a half, Marie's been worried." Over the last year or so, others had also noticed a subtle shift in her character. Mrs. Brewster noted that "the teacher and the school nurse called me in" concerned about how withdrawn and subdued the once jovial and outgoing Marie had become. During the same period Marie had grown proficient in using the severe temper tantrums to terrorize her mother. In order to avoid her "blowing up," her mother was now at the point of acquiescing to Marie's every demand.

Asked about her relationship with Marie, Mrs. Brewster reported, "Me and Marie have always locked horns as far back as I can remember. She's not a happy kid. She's always given me a hard time. As mother and daughter, it hasn't been very good over the years. She's *always* needed an extreme amount of attention." Asked if Marie was a wanted child, Mrs. Brewster noted, "No, she wasn't. She wasn't planned." In contrast, the second pregnancy (which resulted in twin girls) was intentional. Mrs. Brewster reported that while she was pregnant with the twins she never told Marie, then age 5, about her pregnancy. To this day (four years later) she hadn't talked with Marie about it on the grounds that "she's too young" and that "*my* mother never talked to me about these things."

In contrast to her own stressful relationship with Marie, Mrs. Brewster reported that Marie's relationship with her father was positive. "Her relationship with her father has always been pretty good. He's an easy-going guy, the Play Guy. I'm the Disciplinarian. She gets very angry with me."

Interview With Marie

The setting for the initial interview with Marie was unusual, to say the least. Since my (A. J.) partner, Phyllis Booth (who would later function as one of Marie's theraplay therapists), was occupying the downtown office, I was working at home that day. My apartment is a one-bedroom apartment and the furthest Marie would allow her parents to stray from her was into one of the two rooms, the living room, This left the bedroom for Marie and me to talk. One further complication was that my dog—with Marie's prodding—opted not to stay with the parents in the living room, preferring, instead, to sit on Marie's lap for the duration of the conversation. Therefore, this was an interview not with Marie alone, but with Marie tightly clutching a Toto-like terrier.

Although Marie was 9 years old, there was no childlike bounce, no spontaneity, no bubbly-like quality about her. Instead she looked more like a 20-year-old actress in a television drama. Every move, every utterance seemed to serve the purpose of concealing who she really was. She appeared to be in a constant state of appraising what the adult wanted from her, and smiled or frowned or looked concerned accordingly. Although she wore no makeup, her widened eyes seemed to have been painted with mascara. All of this evoked in me a series of bewildering feelings, as though I were relating to a cardboard poster, not to a human being. Marie's only moments of genuine affect broke through at those times when she bordered on going into a panic attack. At those times she might say abruptly, but with sincerity, "I'm leaving," "I'm feeling sick," or "I'm going to throw up."

Marie told me that her problem was a fear of throwing up at school. "People tell me it's in my head." She acknowledged that this might, indeed, be true since the throwing up did not happen all the time. Her worst fear was that she would throw up in front of Linda, a girl in her class whose friendship she was always seeking. "Then Linda wouldn't like me," she explained. She told of watching a kindergarten child throw up in the cafeteria last year. She noticed at that time how "all the kids moved away from him." She was convinced that she could not afford to be more unpopular than she already was. She gave me a list of friends from her past to prove how unpopular she was: Helen, who used to play with Marie "all the time," now turned her back on Marie. Mary was a good friend last year; now Mary was not open or at ease with Marie, and Marie felt uncomfortable around Mary.

In answer to my question about siblings, she said she had twin sisters, age 5. Asked to describe her positive and negative feelings about them, she answered that she had never expressed any negative feelings. In fact, she could not even begin to think that she *could* have any negative feelings. Asked what she remembered of her mother's pregnancy with her younger sibs, she insisted that she remembered nothing. (Mrs. Brewster reported that during her absence while giving birth to the twins, Marie's aunt had stated that Marie had "acted like a crazy person.") I then inquired of Marie as to whether anybody had ever spoken to her about sex. Marie answered that no one ever had. She said that she did not know anything about it. This disclosure was immediately followed by: "I'm getting sick. I'm going to throw up." In testing for the intensity and pervasiveness of this reaction, I changed the subject away from sex and Marie abruptly recovered. When the subject of sex came up a second time, her reactions were similar. We then talked about her two favorite activities: food and painting. What she liked about food, she said, was spaghetti—because of her *grandmother's* spaghetti sauce. She also liked to paint. She was currently painting a bird and a horse. She would have liked to ride and to teach her bird to talk, but she had no access to horses, and "the bird's too old and when he dies, they aren't going to get me another one."

THEORETICAL CONCEPTUALIZATION

While the family presented the problem in purely symptomatic terms, the Theraplay team (Phyllis Booth, Sandra Lindaman, and I) viewed it as multidynamic, that is, as a problem having its origins in Marie's earliest failure to attach to a mother who, by her own account, was largely rejecting of the baby Marie. Add to this original deficit, the subsequent birth of adorable and greatly loved twins and we could understand why Marie's self took a nose dive. Now the "false self" Marie felt required to wear (with regard to experiencing or expressing her negative feelings or her sexual curiosity) and the mask she was presenting to us became wholly understandable.

With regard to the difference between the way we saw the presenting problem and the way *the family* described it, they and we might as well have been speaking two different languages. The family (including the extended family) perceived that they were beset by a demon. Our formulation, in contrast, was that we were dealing with a very small frightened, needy, but tyrannical child.

For this particular case, we chose to use an unusual amalgam of approaches. Only some of these would be Theraplay in the strictest sense. Our basic goal was to bond Marie to an overidentified yet rejecting, frightened, and guilty mother. The means by which we planned to treat Marie included nurturing this young girl who had been described by some observers as "a child of 4 going on 24." Our intention in so nurturing her was to bring her through a corrective infancy, so that she could become the natural, expressive infant she had never felt able to be.

Specifically, the two therapists (Phyllis and Sandra) had multiple goals. The first goal was to encourage Marie's regression. At the very least, we would encourage her to act the way she would have liked to have acted when her sisters were born. At the most, we hoped to encourage her to regress all the way back to the stage where baby Marie initially had to lock horns with a rejecting mother. The second goal was to encourage Marie to freely express her current and, heretofore repressed, angry feelings. And, related to this, the third goal was to replace Marie, the actress, with Marie, the normal-acting 9-year-old little girl.

Clearly, these goals were intertwined. Yet it was important for each treatment session to plan to focus on different goals at different times. Among these goals was that of extinguishing the actress, Marie. We realized that this goal might encompass one or more entire sessions and require a somewhat different (not strictly Theraplay) format in addition to Theraplay *nurturing* activities (e.g., feeding, lotioning, fanning, and stroking). Theraplay nurturing in these sessions had to take priority over *challenging*, for example, or *structuring*. We planned to meet our second objective, the expression of anger through physical means such as kicking and punching holes in newspapers, pushing the therapist with large pillows and throwing crumpled newspaper at the therapist in a mock "snowball fight." Although not strictly Theraplay, we intended to extinguish Marie's phony, "on stage" behavior by confronting it directly. That is, we planned to help her differentiate "real" from "on stage" behaviors, sometimes by encouraging Marie to deliberately act "on stage" while at other times by commenting joyfully whenever we encountered the "real" Marie. At other times, by modeling for her what the difference looked like, we hoped to help her learn the difference.

Although always tailor-made to the unique problems and special history of each specific child, *nurturing* and *structuring* activities along with *intrusion* (e.g., surprising, stimulating, catching off-guard) are typical of the treatment of most children referred for Theraplay. What would be unusual in Marie's case was the effort we would have to make to extinguish phony and "on stage" behaviors. (As it turned out, even though Marie would frequently go through the motions of cuddling, sucking, and laughing, initially there was a quality that smacked of her remaining a distant observer rather than becoming an active participant.)

Our purpose was to help Marie and her mother get along better—so that their relationship did not consist of constantly "locking horns"—and to change eating and food as a battlefield into eating and food as a pleasurable or at least neutral area in their relationship. We wanted to institute boundaries and to help them accept the social and emotional roles appropriate to mother and child. In addition, we wanted to give them both a greater capacity to experience affect. We wanted this to include an enjoyment of life itself and the experiencing of pleasure just from being with one another. This could only happen, however, if Marie gave up her effort to be a grown-up caregiver (including her adult posture of distance and control), in favor of becoming the child she should be, one who thrives on intimacy, warmth, and spontaneity. In her relationship with her mother, in other words, we wanted to move Marie from taking charge of and nurturing her mother to be trusting that she could depend on her mother as a safe and caring object.

At the same time we wanted to move Mrs. Brewster toward being this safe object, who could confidently convey to Marie that she welcomed Marie as a whole person, a legitimate child. We hoped Mrs. Brewster could begin to appreciate that Marie had feelings of the kind that most children have toward their parents and that Marie's anger, dependency, and wish for closeness were all appropriate.

Since Theraplay is scheduled for only half an hour once a week and continues for only a limited number of sessions, it is the parents who ultimately become the full-time Theraplay therapists. Therefore, it becomes as important to train the parents as it is to treat the child. Her own mother having been distant and also suffering from panic attacks, we knew that we would have to provide Marie's mother a model of a mother. We would provide the maternal model, not only through the behavior of the Theraplay therapist on the mat with Marie, but also by having her experience direct nurturing and empathic responsiveness from the interpreting therapist (IT). The IT sits coaching the parents behind the scenes, listening carefully, and in some cases, like Marie's, redirecting aspects of the marital relationship. In this case, Mr. Brewster was helped to provide Mrs. Brewster with enough support and nurturing so that she, in turn, could stop rejecting their daughter. We aimed to change Mr. Brewster's alienated, sometimes smug, and often too playful behavior into that of an empathic support for his very needy, unhappy, frustrated wife. Finally, we felt that we needed to provide both parents—but particularly the mother—with an ongoing font of wisdom about human development, human sexuality, and human relations. This included not only giving guidance on how to educate her daughter about sex (including providing age-appropriate books on sex education that Mrs. Brewster could share with Marie), but also giving both parents hints about how best to relate to relatives and neighbors given their newfound insight into Marie's inhibitions and in light of their new appreciation of the sibling rivalry of Marie toward her sisters. Again, because of the geographic realities, this work had to be done primarily by telephone, generally once or twice a week.

As is typical of family Theraplay sessions, the two parents sat with the interpreting therapist (A. J.) out of view of Marie. Marie concurrently played with her two therapists (Phyllis Booth and Sandra Lindaman). Each session lasted for half an hour.

Behind the one-way mirror A. J. discussed with Mr. and Mrs. Brewster their experiences with Marie the preceding week, answered their questions, supported them in their failures and frustrations, and helped them to support each other as they coped with the dismay or anger one or the other or both of them might be feeling toward Marie.

The Marschak Interaction Method (MIM): A Method to Evaluate Parent–Child Interactions and Organize Treatment

The Marschak Interaction Method (MIM) (Jernberg 1991, Marschak 1960, 1980) is a tool for assessing the relationship between two people. Only one adult at a time performs the MIM with the child. Tasks are printed on different-colored index cards—one color for each dimension. Dimensions elicited by means of the MIM include attachment-enhancing, stress-reducing, guiding purposeful behavior, alerting to the environment, and playfulness. The clinician schedules a parental feedback session a week or ten days following the final MIM administration. The MIM serves not only to begin the imparting of knowledge, awareness, and relationship style for the parents, but also serves to direct the Theraplay therapist in the tailor-made planning of the Theraplay, itself, so that it is specifically suited to each particular child. Thus, for example, the therapist of a child whose parents proceed pedantically on the task "teach child something he or she doesn't know" will proceed very differently from the therapist of a child whose parents either lightly and playfully or chaotically taught him or her something.

The MIMs with Marie and her mother before Theraplay showed many problems in their relationship. In the first MIM it was hard to tell who was the mother and who was the child. In that MIM we saw a mother who had the capacity to say good things, but who was also tentative, awkward, and disengaged. She behaved as if she was afraid of Marie. She turned to Marie for guidance and Marie fulfilled the role of peer and guide, directing Mrs. Brewster with a cold, low affect in a disengaged manner.

THE PROCESS OF THERAPLAY

Theraplay therapists move naturally and energetically. There is a wide variation in the activities, from quiet and soothing to vigorous and active. Often, both a skilled and a trainee therapist work with the child or a skilled therapist works alone. However, because of the urgency of Marie's situation, we used two fully trained therapists. During the Theraplay session, it is the therapist, not the child, who is in charge. In a team situation one therapist is in charge of both the child and the other therapist. Detailed planning and choreography are essential, particularly when there are two therapists.

The Theraplay Sessions

Theraplay Session 1

Therapists: Phyllis Booth (therapist 1) and Sandra Lindaman (therapist 2)

We establish from the start that the therapist (therapist 1 if there are two) is in charge; the child is the center of attention, but will not dictate the agenda. Based on her performance on the MIM, we could be reasonably certain that Marie had been a loner. Marie received minimal indulgence at home (i.e., she "toughs it out"). Marie did not see herself as beautiful or worthy. In this and the following Theraplay sessions, we tried to instill in Marie feelings of adequacy and worthiness.

[Therapists wheel Marie into room on chair—laughing.]

PB: She did it! She did it!

SL: Let's see if we can twirl her around.

[MARIE has a slight smile, fairly flat affect; frequent long glances at camera.]

PB: Oops, did that hurt? Let's do it again.

SL: And I'll help you.

PB: Oh, that was fun! Now come on over here, Marie. And, Sandra, you sit right here. I think that's just right, that's perfect. [Marie is tucked securely under Phyllis's arm, facing Sandra and Phyllis.] Sandra, have you seen this pretty girl?

SL: No.

PB: I want to check to see if your nose is warm or cold, Marie. Sandra, what do you think?

SL: I bet it's cold.

PB: Okay, let's check.

[MARIE crosses arms; slight smile; rigid body.]

PB: Let Sandra check.

[The therapists do not allow Marie to remain uninvolved.]

SL: It's very warm.

PB: Let's check your hands. Oh, you have warm hands!

SL: And the warmest nose! I need to check again—yep, that's a warm nose you have, Marie.

[MARIE looks away, toward camera.]

PB: [Takes Marie's hands.] Now Marie, you have to decide—what about my nose or Sandra's, which is warmer?

MARIE: Yours is cold, yours is warm. [Smiles briefly as she touches each nose.]

PB: Now let's see. I have to compare yours and Sandra's. You're right, Sandra's got a cold nose.

In the following exchange, Phyllis saw a hand-drawn pink heart on Marie's arm. Instead of the expected scolding, the adults gave Marie praise. Also, instead of stoically ignoring a scratch on her skin, the Theraplay therapists lavished attention on this "wound," trivial though it might have been. But the wound was not viewed in a morose or scared context; rather it was cheerfully, nonthreateningly, lovingly "confronted."

PB: [Looking at Marie's arm] Oh Sandra, look!

SL: Wow!

PB: Marie has a special heart, and look. . . .

MARIE: I just rubbed my arm with a marker. [Quiet voice, intense look at arm.]

SL: You had a pink marker?

PB: And you know what else, Sandra? I think that little scratch spot there is just asking for some attention. [Pulls Band-Aids out of pocket.] Uh huh, here we are, a special Band-Aid. Right there, Sandra.

SL: [Puts Band-Aid on Marie's arm.] There you go.

[MARIE raises eyebrows dramatically, surveys Band-Aid on arm, eyes on camera.]

PB: That's right. [Gets lotion.] You know, I want to check something out. Do you think the lotion would turn pink from the marker?

SL: No.

PB: Ooh. Well, no, it didn't. [Sees another mark.] Oops, look at you, there's another one!

SL: She wasn't going to tell us about that one.

[MARIE smiles.]

PB: A secret heart. Wait, that one is so lovely, that deserves its own lotion.

MARIE: I did it by accident.

PB: You do good planning things and good accidents. All right. [Puts lotion into own hands.] I think this ought to be warm, let's check. Sandra, you need to get some. [Puts some lotion into own hands, then into Sandra's.] Oops, I see something special here.

MARIE: I should have cleaned my nails.

PB: No, you shouldn't, then we wouldn't have known you have those wonderful colors.

SL: [Rubs Marie's arms, applying lotion.] Did you do that or did somebody else do that?

MARIE: I did it.

[SL looks up with surprised, delighted expression.]

PB: What did you find?

SL: Between these fingers, more green.

PB: [Laughs.] Can you imagine that?

The therapists wanted to teach Marie that she was beautiful and special. The therapists mirrored Marie's behavior and were intruding and playful. They managed to get Marie to engage in eye contact without her realizing it was happening. Although Marie initially avoided the intrusion, the therapists persisted. She finally allowed herself to enjoy the admiration as she began hesitantly to admit the therapists into her private world.

PB: Now, I think we could use a little bit of lotion on Marie's rosy cheeks. You know your cheeks are lovely and rosy. [Puts lotion in own hands.] I'm going to warm it up. You have . . . [Touches Marie's face with fingers and turns face toward her.] Let me look at you. You have very special eyes.

[MARIE averts gaze; looks at cameras, somewhat sullen, very little interaction on Marie's part.]

PB: Oops—I have to go looking for those eyes . . . there they are. You know, you're fast about that. Watch it Sandra because she can make her eyes go so fast, you can hardly catch up with them.

[SL "chases" Marie's eyes with her own.]

[MARIE smiles.]

PB: Marie, make it so that Sandra can't catch your eyes—way up, that's it. [Laughs.] Did you catch them?

[All three laugh.]

SL: No, I couldn't.

PB: Now, let's see if you and Sandra can just keep your eyes focused right on each other. I'll count and we'll see how long you can keep going . . . 1 . . . 2 . . . 3 . . .

MARIE: [Laughs and closes eyes.] I blinked. I couldn't help it!

[Unable to make or to continue eye contact.]

PB: Blinks are okay. I bet you can do it to five. 1 . . . 2 . . . 3 . . . 4 . . . 5 . . . 6 . . 7 . . . 8 . . . 9 . . . 10. Yeah! Marie, you sure are neat!

[MARIE smiles, rubs lotion off arm.]

The following interaction not only further enhanced Marie's self-esteem and feelings of empowerment and strength, but also encouraged her to actively express some of her repressed angry feelings. In this safe, controlled setting she could act on these feelings without endangering anybody. She could take her anger out on the therapist who may well have symbolized her mother. Hence Marie learned that it was "okay" to be angry and to express emotion.

PB: Now, I think you brought along some muscles. Let's see if you did. Let's check. Do you have a muscle here? Oh, yeah! Okay, pull tight against my hand; pull hard. Oh, that's it.

SL: Oh, she's strong!

PB: Let me fix a couple of pillows; I don't want you to get hurt. And I'll be right behind you. Sandra, you kneel. Marie, you stand up. Good, that'll work well. What's the signal, Sandra? How about sticking your tongue out?

SL: When I stick my tongue out, then that's when you push.

[They wanted to get Marie to focus on Sandra's face.]

[MARIE pushes Sandra over.]

[All laugh.]

PB: Neat! I bet you could do that again.

SL: I think she has a lot more pushing still left in that arm.

PB: What's the signal this time?

SL: The signal this time is when I wiggle my nose . . . You have to watch me really closely.

[MARIE vigorously pushes Sandra away.]

PB: Okay!

SL: All right!

PB: Marie, this time you give the signal. You tell Sandra what it's going to be.

MARIE: Umm, I don't know.

PB: It could be eye-blinking, nose wiggles, ear wiggles . . . Are you good at ear wiggles? [Phyllis puts her arm around Marie.]

MARIE: I could try. [Wrinkles face/ears and pushes against Sandra.]

SL: Boy, she *is* strong!

PB: Yeah, you *are*, my gosh!

Here the therapists placed some sparkles on Marie to serve as a token of the session she could take home with her as transitional objects.

PB: Where is that lotion? Because you made hearts on your arm, we can make a heart on your cheek, here, and I'm going to make it with a little lotion. Sandra, you put the lotion on. Let's try it here first, on her arm first. We need to know how the sparkles'll work. [Blows excess sparkles off lotion on arm.]

[MARIE very carefully blows arm with Phyllis.]

PB: It doesn't quite make a heart, but it does make a nice circle. Great! You know, when you go home to bed tonight, you're going to have a few sparkles left, even when we clean it off. Okay, Sandra, what colors do you want? Blue?

SL: Gold.

[MARIE tilts head to side to help keep sparkles on cheek.]

PB: Hey, you're helping real well here and that's important.

SL: Ooh, you're right!

PB: All set. Oh, I like that.

SL: It's going to stay.

[MARIE smiles, looks in mirror held by Sandra at sparkles on cheek, brushes excess sparkles off shirt.]

PB: Good! Wonderful! Oh, that's neat!

[MARIE glances at camera.]

PB: Okay, let's put it on Sandra's cheek. Marie, put some right here.

MARIE: [Cautiously puts lotion and sparkles on Sandra's cheek.] That's not very good.

PB: That's great!

[MARIE smiles, eagerly rubs lotion off hands.]

The following scene illustrates further how the therapists nurtured and admired Marie. Note how the therapists did not allow Marie to tyrannize the interchange; how they acknowledged and responded to Marie's facial grimace, yet continued to follow their Theraplay agenda: making Marie feel special.

PB: Oh, look, a dimple, right on the bottom of your chin! Right in your lovely chin, a nice red dimple. Okay. You gave me an idea. You made a wonderful face. Do that again. Neat-O.

[MARIE makes face to camera.]

PB: Now, let's get some hats.

[SL picks out hats from box.]

PB: Oh, a yellow one.

SL: [Places hat on Marie.] Oh, I like that.

PB: Oh, lovely!

[MARIE raises eyebrows dramatically, looks coyly into mirror, then camera.]

SL: Marie, you look so nice!

PB: You know what I think we need? Sandra, did you notice that Marie has such wonderful eyebrows?

SL: Yes.

PB: Raise them up like that again. Oh, wonderful. You can do all kinds of things with those eyebrows.

Following is another example of the therapists encouraging Marie to demonstrate anger/aggression. Note, in the basketball scene, how Marie got to throw paper wads at the maternal authority figure, but did so within a safe context.

PB: Grab those little papers, and I have some big paper of mine. What's your best punching arm? Is it your left or right arm?

MARIE: [Shrugs.] I don't know.

PB: Well, we'll find out. Ready?

SL: Now, when I say "go," you're going to punch right through these, Marie. Ready, set, go!

PB: Wow!

SL: Marie, take the one on the right. When I say "go," you're going to punch the paper. Ready, set, "go!" Wow, there's no question about that arm!

PB: It's a little tougher to do two, and colored paper is even harder.

MARIE: With this one now. [Holds up other arm.]

PB: No, let's try this one again. [Holds Marie's original arm up.] This is a hard job. Ready set, go!

MARIE: Ow, that hurt.

PB: Oh, better fix it. [Holding Marie's arm.]

SL: Uh, huh. We take care of every hurt.

[MARIE pulls arm away and shakes head.]

PB: Oh yes. Sandra, get a little lotion.

[SL rubs lotion on Marie's hand while Phyllis holds arm.]

PB: Marie, you punched so hard! Now let's see, I think . . . let's try the left hand. Ready, set, go.

[MARIE bounces forward on sofa, and eagerly thrusts fists through newspaper.]

SL: Wow! You are really good at that. Let's try two.

[MARIE punches, does not go through.]

PB: Oh, that was a hard one. Let's try it again. Ready, set, go!

[MARIE punches through successfully, smiles broadly, glances at camera.]

PB: Yeah! Ready, get the champion puncher. It's harder when it's small and folded like this. Do you think you can do two?

MARIE: Fold it in half.

PB: Listen to this smart girl. Good idea! That's going to be tough, though. This may take two arms and a foot. You watch out Sandra because this is going to be . . . she's going to really get this one.

[MARIE punches paper halfway through.] [All laugh.]

SL: I've never seen anyone do it halfway.

PB: Turn it around and see if we can break through the other side.

MARIE: Oh, I can't.

PB: Go ahead.

[MARIE: punches through successfully; giggles gleefully.]

PB: Yeah! You get to make a bunch of balls. First of all, Sandra make a basket for us; see if she can get it in your basket. Ready, set, go. All right. Back way up to the wall. Ready, set, go. [Whispers to Marie] Let's throw a whole bunch at Sandra.

[Throw free-for-all, during which Marie laughs wholeheartedly, jumps up and down in seat, and throws with increasing vigor.]

PB: Sandra, put a hat on your head. [Whispers to Marie] Do you think we can knock off her hat? I don't know if we can do it or not. Ready, set, go!

[MARIE throws crumpled paper at Sandra's hat.]

PB: Good shot, Marie!

SL: I'm going to close my eyes. Keep going. Almost! You guys are good!

PB: Let's go close. Yeah, we did it! [Hugs a stiffened Marie.]

Again, despite Marie's efforts to fend them off, the therapists made Marie feel cared for and nurtured. In the interplay with the pretzels, the therapists playfully distracted Marie, thus changing the focus from the worrisome, serious aspect of food and eating.

PB: You know, let's cool Marie off.

[Both therapists fan Marie.]

MARIE: You don't have to do that.

PB: I don't *have* to do that, but I *like* to do that because I like to cool you off.

[SL feeds Marie grapes, gently pushing her hand away when Marie tries to feed herself.]

MARIE: I'm not very hungry.

PB: Okay. Want to feed one to Sandra? [Puts pretzels on Marie's fingers.] [Sings] Bells on her fingers, rings on her toes. I think, uh-oh. Let's see, Sandra. Marie, can you take a bite off of one of these places without breaking them off?

[MARIE bites pretzel.]

PB: Great. Okay, Sandra, Marie—let's see who can take bites without having the pretzel break and come off Marie's fingers. [All three take turns biting the pretzel on Marie's fingers.]

PB: [Takes bite.] Hmm, good.

MARIE: I have a loose tooth.

PB: Oh, let's see. It's almost ready to come out, but it will be a little while yet. Okay, Sandra, it's a challenge. [Takes bite of Marie's pretzel, and other half of pretzel falls to ground.]

SL: That's what happens when you bite it off.

[All laugh.]

PB: You know what, I bet we could do one more.

[MARIE takes little bite.]

PB: Hey, you made it real neat. You know, I think I've had enough. Do you want another bite?

[MARIE shakes head no.]

PB: No, Okay, But you know, there's some nice water I've got; those were pretty salty. Why do they make pretzels so salty? You know what, take another drink and let me see if I can hear you swallow. I heard it. Did you hear it?

SL: I heard it.

MARIE: I didn't hear it.

PB: One more drink or is that enough?

[MARIE drinks.]

PB: Did you hear it?

SL: I heard it.

PB: Good.

A finale had the therapists nurturing Marie, who was allowed (encouraged) to regress and accept her "specialness," even though she knew that she was "big."

PB: I think what we need to do—we'll leave the sparkles and take the pink lotion off. [Sprays soap foam on own finger, applies to lotion on Marie's chin.] It's coming. Oh boy, very good. You know, I forgot to check your chin before. You have a soft chin, it's just right. Did you know, this is soap foam called "Baby Juice"? Doesn't it smell good? And it makes your skin so soft. Now, I think this girl could sit right up on my lap. [Pulls Marie onto her lap.]

MARIE: Oops.

PB: Oops, there you are. Okay, that's it. Okay, Sandra, you know that we have that song that would be just right.

[Therapists sing together]

Twinkle, twinkle little star,
What a pretty girl you are.
Nice long hair and rosy cheeks,
Bright brown eyes from which you peek,
And a special smile on each cheek.

PB: You have such a lovely, sparkly smile and such gorgeous eyes!

[MARIE starts to slip from therapist's lap.]

PB: We've got you, You're Okay. You're Okay. [Sings] Twinkle, twinkle little star, What a special girl you are. Sandra, could you get a hold of her, cause she's a big, she's a big girl.

SL: [Picks Marie up.] Let's see if you could catch her.

1 . . . 2 . . . 3 . . . Do you think there's a Mommy or Daddy who could catch her?

[Mr. and Mrs. Brewster approach.]

SL: Oh, she just fits, look at that. See you Friday.

The second session consolidated the lessons learned in session 1. Since the techniques and goals were so similar to those in the previous scene, in the interests of space and time we will skip ahead to session 3.

Theraplay Session 3

Therapist: Phyllis Booth

Marie was still "on stage." This was an important session in getting Marie to be "real." Getting Marie to be "real" proved to be the greatest challenge to the Theraplay method. It required unusual techniques, such as enlisting Marie as a "colleague," in that the therapist helped Marie to observe herself when she was "unreal." Because we thought two therapists might hinder Marie's development (allowing her to flee from one to the other, thus retaining her "unreal" agenda), these sessions used only one therapist: Phyllis Booth. Thus Marie had less of an "audience" for her acting.

Marie learned to enjoy eating in a fun, safe environment. She learned to communicate her wishes directly regarding satiety or desire for more nourishment. Eye contact was selected as the means to get Marie communicating. The therapist needed to persevere to keep Marie from avoiding her (the therapist's) gaze.

[PB feeds Marie with cup.]

[MARIE sits on sofa, with legs together, arms crossed, under Phyllis's outstretched arm; turns head away from proffered cup.]

PB: Turn toward me a minute. Okay, what you need to tell me is when the water is up to your mouth because I can't see it. So blink once with your eyes if the water is up to your mouth and blink twice if you want me to stop. Can you do that? It's going to be tricky.

MARIE: [Blinks once, again looks away.] Umm, wait.

[Waves hand.] I thought it was . . .

PB: Well, that was one. I got to you, but I didn't get the signal to stop. You look at me, so I can see you blink. Did it work? Do it again, looking right at me.

[MARIE blinks and this time continues to face therapist; smiles.]

PB: Did it work? Ooh, we've got a good system. Okay, I'm going to try one more drink. Let's see if we can. Got it? Did it go right inside your tummy?

Again, Marie's physical problems were attended to in a nonthreatening, nonjudgmental, supportive way.

PB: Now, I need to check . . . you know, you were right, it's still there. And look how well that scrape has healed up! And you know what?

MARIE: It got worse.

PB: I think it got picked off a little bit; got bumped off or something. [Gets lotion.] Yeah, it's a little bit rough. Now that's interesting, this one's getting better, but are you saying this one just stays like this most of the time?

MARIE: Yeah, it's a broken blood vessel.

PB: I see, uh-huh. [Applies lotion.] Now this one, I bet next time you come I won't be able to see it. Now this one, I'm going to put lotion around it, all around. Do you have something special that your mom puts on? Something like that to make it heal?

MARIE: Well, I put lotion on it.

PB: Oh, Okay. Do you have these more in the wintertime when it's so dry?

MARIE: Yeah, sometimes. [Slight laugh.]

Here was the first of many efforts on the therapist's part to engage Marie in a search for who was the "real" Marie. Of even more concern, Marie, herself, seemed to have difficulty discerning when she was acting and when she was genuine. The following is the therapist's building rapport with Marie through showing her a nonthreatening clapping game.

PB: Can you feel the tingling in your hands?

MARIE: Yeah.

PB: [Looks directly into Marie's face.] Hey, where did you go? I notice that sometimes when I'm talking to you, you go a long way away and then when I call you back, it's not the real Marie that comes back. Can you tell the difference between the real Marie and a . . . Can you tell the difference between the real Marie and the one with a tense smile?

MARIE: Hmm, Hmm. [Looks flustered, giggles tensely, and looks at camera.]

PB: Here, I want you here, sit over here. I want you to think about making a bunch of faces that are not the real Marie and then one of these faces needs to be the real Marie.

[MARIE makes face.]

PB: Hmm, there's one that's not the real Marie.

[MARIE makes another face.]

PB: And that's, that's not the real Marie.

[MARIE makes another face.]

PB: Let's see, that's not the real Marie. I'm making it hard for you because I'm watching everything. When you have a face you want me to tell you about you lift up that hand.

[MARIE makes face, tentatively raises hand.]

PB: That one's the real Marie.

MARIE: Hmm, I don't know. [Makes self-conscious face with raised eyebrows, scrunched lips, tilted head.]

PB: Now that's a pretend one. I can't tell about that one. It started out as if it was going to be the . . .

MARIE: I don't know! I can't! [Whining, hitting sofa, but still smiling.]

PB: Now that's not a real one, that's a pretend.

[MARIE sighs.]

PB: That looks like the real Marie. Is it? Is it?

MARIE: Sorta, sometimes.

PB: Sometimes you don't even know when it's real—we'll have to work on that.

[MARIE nods, high-pitched, tight laugh.]

PB: Now, let's see, do me two more.

[MARIE makes dramatic, seductive faces.]

PB: Those didn't feel like the real Marie. That felt like it started out not to be Marie.

MARIE: I don't know, I can't tell.

PB: Oh golly, we'll have to work on that. I'll tell you, let's do it different this time. You make a face. This won't be real because you're not feeling it now. You make a face that's supposed to be either mad, happy, sad, or grumpy.

MARIE: Wait a second, I have to think. [Taps teeth with fingernails.]

PB: You have to think about that, that's right. I want to be right over here so I can see.

MARIE: Happy, mad, sad, or . . .?

PB: Grumpy. Is that a mad face?

[MARIE nods head.]

PB: Was I right? Good. That was a good one. Can you do a sad face?

MARIE: Yup. Oh, how am I going to do that one?

PB: That one is hard, isn't it?

[MARIE makes face.]

PB: Grumpy? It's hard to tell grumpy from sad, isn't it?

[MARIE nods.]

PB: I'm going to do one. [Makes face.]

MARIE: Mad?

PB: Yeah, good for you. [Makes face.]

MARIE: Sad? [Looks pleased at having guessed correctly.]

PB: Yeah.

[MARIE smiles again.]

In the following, the therapist provided a sense of continuity through the increasingly safe theme of Marie's hurt toe.

PB: While I'm down here I need to check that special toe.

[MARIE has a self-conscious smile, glances at camera.]

PB: You know what I think? That look you just gave me wasn't a real one, but it was sorta saying, "Be careful."

MARIE: [Smiles, pulls pants up.] These pants are very, very tight.

PB: [Looking at toe.] Uh-huh, I think it's moved up a little tiny ways. Now, Band-Aid. Ta-dum!

[MARIE giggles.]

PB: Here it comes.

[MARIE has a fake, tense smile.]

PB: [Looking directly into Marie's face.] Now what was that?

MARIE: I don't know! [Protesting and looking away from Phyllis.]

[In response to Phyllis's suggestion that they make a bib to keep popsicles from spilling on her, Marie makes a grossly exaggerated smile.]

PB: That was one of those not real ones.

[MARIE laughs.]

PB: Make another not real one. You know what? I like the way your eyes and your eyebrows and your nose look and your mouth looks and the way your face looks when there isn't a smile. Cause that's the real Marie.

MARIE: [Shakes head, flips hair back, smiles tensely.] Couldn't swallow.

PB: Oop. Oh my goodness. All you have to do with popsicles is wait and it will swallow right down. [Sings.] "I like Marie, yes, I do; I like you, I like you very much."

[MARIE points to mouth.]

PB: I should have noticed. That's my job to notice. You were not ready for the next bite. I could tell that. Now, let's see if I can tell. I think you're ready for the next bite and I'll know for sure if you'll open your mouth when I bring this up.

[MARIE opens mouth; rests hand on Phyllis' leg; looks directly at Phyllis.]

PB: Yes, pretty good. The interesting thing about this, those little bits of strawberry in there sometimes you take a bite and there's a strawberry hanging on the edge. [Takes a bit.] You know what I discovered. I can melt it in my mouth. Can you do that? Like sucking the juice out of it. We're going to check and see if you want more.

[MARIE opens mouth.]

PB: Yeah, a little more. I'm going to take a suck, too. Can you hear it? No, you couldn't hear it very well. But you heard a little. Let's see if I can hear yours. Hmm, I can hear little crunches and sucks.

MARIE: I'm not hungry anymore.

PB: Well, do you know, all you have to do, you don't have to tell me that. When I put it toward your mouth, you just close your mouth, that's our signal. I just wonder if Marie needs anymore of this.

[MARIE closes mouth.]

PB: Uh, she's not hungry anymore.

[MARIE smiles, looks comfortable snuggled against Phyllis.]

PB: Look at all she ate. I'm glad she liked that. [Gets mirror.] Let me check your tongue. Did it get pink? I think it's a little pinker than it was before.

Here Phyllis was trying to get Marie to be as limp and relaxed as a "rag doll." Note the nurturing, structuring, challenging aspects of Theraplay in this scene. Note the difficulty Marie had relaxing and letting Phyllis take total charge.

[MARIE giggles.]

PB: Let's see. I'll do the holding. You just let your muscles go. Oh, I don't think you're letting go. It's coming, good. Let's see if your tummy is soft and floppy. Let it go. Oh, is that hard to do, is that ever hard to do. Push hard against my hand, make it tight, tight, tight. Oh good, good, let it go. That's neat. Let's see if your cheeks get soft and floppy. Good. Let's see if your chin gets soft and floppy. Good. Oh, that's tight, tighten it up. Now soft and floppy. [Touches Marie's forehead.]

MARIE: I can't do my forehead. [Genuine smile, moves head into Phyllis' hand; by now there are fewer and fewer glances in the direction of the camera.]

PB: No, I don't know how to make my forehead soft and floppy. Now, let's check to see if you are all soft and floppy. Now, I'm going to tell you one part to wiggle and see if you can manage to wiggle that part only. I see it—that is remarkable! The control; that's neat. All right. The toe with the Band-Aid on it. You know what? This is the time of year for those pricklies that stick out. So I'm going to put a Band-Aid on it. Because they get kind of sticking out sometimes. Is that hurting?

[MARIE shakes head no.]

PB: Where did you go? You were off a long way over there, weren't you? And do you know what happened? I was looking here and when I looked up, Marie was gone and there, you're back again.

[PB begins to put on Marie's shoes.]

MARIE: I can put them on.

Marie turned topic away from her genuineness back to Band-Aids. Marie also attempted to thwart Phyllis' nurturing.

PB: I know you can put them on, but I don't get much chance to put them on so I'm going to put them on you. I'm going to put this on the other foot today so this part of your leg will get the support.

[MARIE pulls up her pant leg.]

PB: [Stops Marie.] Oh, I get to do that. You just try to take care of everything, don't you? [Looks at Marie's expression.] Yeah, it's real hard to stay real. Can you stay real and stay with me?

MARIE: Oh, I can't, I can't.

PB: It feels funny, doesn't it. We'll have to keep working on that. Let's see. You know, it's really neat to have shoes with flowers on them. Some people like their shoes real snug and some like them loose. I'm going to check and see. My hunch is medium for you. I'll tie it just like this. I think that's Okay. Wow, I get to double knot it. Now this is the tricky toe.

MARIE: It doesn't hurt when you put it on.

PB: Is it getting better?

MARIE: Yeah, it was really bad.

PB: It must've really hurt when you first got it. How did it happen?

MARIE: I was walking in my room. I wanted to see, I took a bath and when I was going to my room, I went like this with my toe and I bent it back.

PB: Ooh. Did that hurt?

MARIE: I just started crying.

PB: I might have cried too. And you ran to your mom. Did she take care of it?

MARIE: She put a Band-Aid on it. That's what the black part is underneath, some blood left over.

PB: Do you think so?

MARIE: I think so.

PB: Okay. I'll check and see if this is just right. I'm going to do something different this time. A new trick. Let's see, if I stand up and you stand up. We'll roll this (paper with painted foot prints on it) up and you can take it home and you can decide with your mom and dad where you want to hang it up someplace.

For the sake of brevity, sessions 4 and 5, which reinforced those tactics illustrated in the previous sessions, have been omitted from this protocol. Note the emphasis on producing expression of anger as regression. As with all Theraplay sessions, the five Theraplay characteristics—structurting, challenging, intruding, playfulness, and nurturing—were essential to the therapy.

Theraplay Session 6

Therapists: Phyllis Booth, Sandra Lindaman

Note below when Phyllis and Sandra did the following: paid attention to physical ailments in a nonthreatening manner, convinced Marie that she was special in her own right, dissuaded Marie from acting "unreal," maintained eye contact, provided challenges that Marie could master, increased Marie's tolerance for complexity, and permitted Marie to regress. As with previous sessions, the Theraplay therapists accomplished these tasks within a fun, structured, safe environment, and ensured continuity from one session to the next.

[PB and SL carry in Marie.]

PB: Put her down gently.

SL: Okay.

PB: Let me look at you.

[MARIE starts to untie shoe.]

PB: Nope, we'll wait on that. We'll decide whether we take it off or keep it on. I haven't seen you, it's been three weeks, hasn't it Sandra? Sandra, can you see yourself in her eyes? Can you see yourself?

SL: Uh-huh.

PB: Now, I don't know how cold outside it is. The way I can tell is if I touch your nose. You've got a warm nose. Not hot. But it's certainly not icy cold out. Okay. Let's check a few things here. Look at that, look at how these (sores on arm) have healed up so beautifully.

SL: Ooh, yeah! Oop, a little bit still there.

[MARIE looks intensely at Phyllis and Sandra as they lotion her arms.]

PB: But the scab is wonderful. It's a good scab. And look at those eyebrows! [Unties Marie's shoes.] Goodness. This foot is stuck. I can do it. You know what? I think another pillow would make Marie more comfortable.

SL: Okay. And look at her hair! [Pins Marie's hair with clip.]

PB: I want to do something. I want to make a special face for Sandra and she has to guess. Wait a minute. You and I have to have a special . . . [Whispers in Marie's ear, makes face.]

SL: Sadness?

PB: Yeah. Okay, Sandra, can you make a face? Now Marie and I have to guess. What do you think, Marie?

MARIE: Mad.

[SL nods yes.]

PB: Uh-huh. [Whispers to Marie.] Wipe it off, we'll try again.

MARIE: I don't know. [But makes face.]

PB: You're doing it.

SL: I'm not a good guesser. Is it an angry face?

PB: Yeah, we tricked you. Okay. Now, let's check out those shoes. Now, I think the dark spot will be halfway up. Wow!

SL: Ahh!

PB: It looks like a mountain in there. It is way up!

SL: It is very up and there's a new nail underneath it.

PB: Oh, and wonderful, delicious toes.

[SL blows Marie's feet.]

PB: All right. [Gets finger-paints to paint feet.]

SL: Okay. The special toes, right?

MARIE: Ooh! It's cold!

SL: Oh my gosh, oh my gosh!

PB: Warm it up. Do you know what? There's a bruise here. [Kisses it.] How did you get that bruise?

MARIE: I don't know.

PB: Now, Sandra, do you think we can get her to stand up?

SL: Yeah. Bend your knees a little bit, there, Marie.

PB: That's perfect, that's perfect.

SL: Okay.

PB: Up we go.

SL: Ooh!

PB: Great! Look at that nice high arch under there.

SL: And it goes over like that, especially here.

PB: Now that's interesting. We got a better print of the toes on that foot than the other one. Oh, goozily, goozily. This is wonderfully goozily.

SL: You look a little uncomfortable. Why don't you scoot back? [Pushes Marie gently.]

PB: There, that's better.

SL: You know, Phyllis, her hair is longer than last time.

PB: Oh yeah, and the bangs in front are longer, too.

MARIE: When I put my hair up it looks like this. [Appears comfortable, pleased with the attention, and genuinely engaged in the interaction.]

PB: So you have a little fringe up in the front, and then a few little, lovely curls here. [Fans with pillow.] Yes, yes. Now, we have to do Follow the Leader going across the room in funny ways.

SL: Okay. I've got a great one. [Does it.]

PB: Oh, what's it called?

MARIE: [Volunteers.] Crab walk.

PB: Oh, it's got a name and everything. Marie, you do one.

MARIE: Frontwards it's called spider walk. [Executes walk in opposite direction.]

PB: Oh, here she comes.

SL: Here she comes, here she comes!

PB: Now I'll do one. [Does funny walk.] Okay Marie, you go across the room in a special way. You make up one. Not too hard for us.

[MARIE does seal walk, laughing and having a good time.]

PB: Oh, neat-o!

SL: Okay, you have to watch me and see if I get that one right, Marie. [Imitates Marie.]

MARIE: Yup!

PB: Okay, Okay, see if I can do it. [Awkward imitation.] Oh my golly, it's not quite right is it? Okay, now, I've got one. [Does new walk.]

SL: Okay, Marie, see if you can do that one.

[MARIE does Phyllis' walk.]

PS and SL: Great

SL: Okay, okay, I got one.

PB: You've got another one? Okay. Let's see if you can do it.

SL: [Grabs Marie and Phyllis and all three walk entwined.] Okay! Yeah, we did it!

PB: Okay, let's see if we can all sit down together. What I want to have is a special greeting. So I'll do one thing and you'll add something to it and Sandra will add something else to it. So my first greeting is "Hello, Marie" and then you have to say "Hello, Sandra" like this.

MARIE: [Looks directly at Sandra.] Hello, Sandra.

PB: Right and then add something to it.

MARIE: Hello, Sandra. How ya doing?

SL: All right, now I'm going to do what Marie did and add something to it. Hello, Marie, how are you doing? [Rubs Phyllis' nose.]

PB: Hello, Marie. How are you doing? [Rubs Marie's nose, then rubs Marie's shoulder with her own.] Now Marie, you need to add something to it.

MARIE: I don't know. [But touches Sandra's toes with her own after Phyllis whispers something to her.]

SL: Okay, let's see if I get this right . . . And now I have to add something.

PB: Okay. All right. One more, one more you have to add.

MARIE: I don't know .. . . Oh! This! [Holds Sandra's hands and swings arms.]

PB: That's a great idea.

SL: Should we just practice that once? Then we'll all three remember. [All three go over routine again; Mr. and Mrs. Brewster enter Theraplay scene.]

PB: Now come on Mom and Dad. Come over here.

DAD: Shoes off?

PS: You'll be more comfortable. Look at Marie's toe; there's a special mountain there and it's rising up. Let's do our made-up greeting. We'll start with you, Mom. We'll prompt you, but you probably won't need any extra help. [Marie greets Mrs. Brewster with series of greetings from earlier scene.] Mom, now you need to add to that.

[MOM tickles Marie's ear.]

PB: Okay! Marie, do you think you could try and do it with Dad?

DAD: Do we have enough room here?

PB: Yeah, here, we'll pull her back. Neat idea, neat! [Marie tickles Dad's ear.]

SL: You know what? We were so busy greeting and Dad said something about Marie's new tooth . . .

PB: Oh yes, oh yes!

MOM: She lost her tooth. Yeah, Dad had to pull it.

MARIE: He went like this and I didn't even feel it. I tasted blood and I felt it but I didn't know it was out, but I tasted blood and I said, "Wait a second, what is this?"

DAD: It was on her lap.

PB: Wow! And how is the tooth fairy at your house? Did she remember to come?

MARIE: [Enthusiastically and genuinely.] Okay, well my grandma gave me a dollar and my grandpa gave me a dollar and then the tooth fairy gave me two dollars. [Smiles and looks at Dad.]

PB: Well, this is a good house for teeth. And on top of that you have a brand new tooth already poking its nice head in there.

MARIE: Well, it was still loose when the new one was coming in.

PB: Now, Mom, would you tell Marie how you and Dad met? [This was an effort to pair Mom and Dad without Marie intervening.]

MOM: [Looking past Marie at Dad.] Uh, I think she's heard some of this story. We used to sit next to each other in bookkeeping class and I was best friends with his old girlfriend, Laurie, and I had a date for the prom and at the last minute the guy called me and told me he couldn't make it so my friend said, "Why don't you call Jeff?" So I called up your dad and he says, "Oh, I'd love to." So in a few hours before the prom, he shows up in a Corvette he had borrowed from a friend, in a tuxedo that wasn't quite right, didn't fit. He only had two days' notice. He had a corsage and yellow roses and he came to the door and I thought he was the sweetest guy for making all that effort to be there with a tuxedo for me on such a short notice.

PB: You know, I think he must have been a very handsome young man. [Puts arm around Mrs. Brewster.]

MOM: And I thought he was just the best guy for doing something like that.

DAD: Then what?

MOM: Then we got married two or three years later and thought about having a little Marie, just like you.

[MARIE smiles and hides face briefly.]

PB: Isn't that neat? What do you remember, Dad? What color was her dress?

MARIE: Hah! [Gleefully, giggles.]

MOM: A good test!

DAD: Her dress was blue.

MOM: No, Laurie's dress was blue.

[MARIE opens mouth, smilingly wags scolding finger at Dad, then reaches to pat his knee reassuringly.]

PB: What color *was* your dress?

MOM: Cream-colored.

SL: Then those roses were just right.

PB: I can just see you two and I think you must have been a very nice couple at the prom.

MOM: Yeah, but your dad still doesn't like to dance. So Marie and I dance together.

PB: Okay. Now we want Dad . . . maybe, Dad, you should come over here because you two need to try hats on Marie. In fact, Marie's going to sit on my lap over here. Let's see if we can make this really cozy and nice. Okay. Very good. There she is and Dad, before you get too comfortable, let Sandra get that out of the way. I want you to try, oh, about five different hats and your job is to decide which one you think Marie likes best and which you think looks best on her.

MOM: That black one, I think. There's a wig she might enjoy. She was looking at it the other day.

MARIE: I was going to put it on Mommy, but . . .

MOM: Another one, I was thinking there was another one. How about this, is this it?

PB: There are two of them. Well, you can try both of them.

MOM: Curly or straight?

MARIE: I don't care.

PB: Well, Mom, you just have to decide and then you look and see, yeah.

MOM: [Puts wig on Marie.] Yeah, what a mod hairstyle. I like Marie in this. Gives her a little lift. [Gestures to Marie's hair.]

DAD: Marie would like this one I think.

PB: You think she might? Okay, let's try it on and see how it fits.

DAD: It looks sorta like an Easter hat.

PB: Does, doesn't it?

MOM: I think that looks pretty nice—springy.

PB: I think we have Dad too far away. Why don't we move these hats over here so Dad can come a little bit closer.

MOM: You got one. I like this one.

DAD: That's nice.

PB: Look up at your mom. What do you think?

[MARIE smiles and looks at both parents.]

MOM: Yeah.

DAD: Yellow? Is yellow your favorite color, Marie?

[MARIE shakes head no.]

DAD: No? Blue?

MARIE: Blue.

MOM: I think I like the green one.

MARIE: I like the blue one.

MOM: What do you think, Marie? How about this one? [Puts wig on her own head.] Looks like I still have a perm, huh?

MARIE: It's a bit darker.

PB: The color has changed a little. Okay. You know what? Move this out of the way and, Mom, I want you to stand over here, on your knees, facing Marie. And, Marie, you stand up facing Mom. That's right. Mom, here's your pillow. Marie, you have this pillow. Dad, you're the referee.

DAD: Okay.

PB: And these two ladies are going to have a pillow-pushing contest and I'm going to be behind Marie and, Dad, you have to say "We have Marie, the challenger." You know, you just . . . And the rules are when you say "Go," they have to push really hard against each other behind their pillows. And I'm going to be back here in case Mom pushes Marie over and Sandra's behind Mom in case Marie pushes Mom over. Dad, you get to decide when it's time to stop. And certainly stop if anyone gets hurt or anything.

DAD: In corner one, Marie, the champion, and in corner two, Mom, the challenger. 1 . . 2 . . Go!

[MARIE pushes with great effort.]

PB and SL: Come on, you can do it!

DAD: Come on, Marie . . . Stop.

[MARIE smiles.]

PB: Dad, I think you need to cool them off and Mom needs to be cooled off, too. She's been working hard. All right. Now, let's have a second round. Now was that last round a draw?

DAD: I think Marie gained some ground, she got a couple inches. Okay, again: Ready, set, GO! [Again, pillow-pushing contest between Mom and Marie.] Stop. You're going to break poor Mommy's back.

MARIE: Oh, no! [Burying head in her pillow.]

PB: No, it's okay, nobody will get hurt.

[MARIE looks up from pillow.]

PB: Oh, no. Sandra will take care of Mom. It's okay. If you need anymore help from Sandra, let her know, Mom, cause this is a strong girl!

[MARIE jumps up and down, waving fist and displaying muscles.]

PB: Okay, the third round is the charm.

DAD: Ready, set, Go!

[MARIE pushes with great vigor, but Mom holds her own and pushes Marie back.]

DAD: Whoa!

PB: Did anyone get hurt? No? Okay. We'll always stop before anyone gets hurt. Okay. I think we'd better have you sit down right here and we'll have Mom sit down beside you and, Dad, you come over here. I think we need a little more fanning. Here's the fan right here. Now, where's that water? Mom, would you give her water; she may be thirsty. Great. Now, very good Dad.

[MARIE sits with legs crossed, starts to help Mom give her drink.]

PB: [Gets Fruit by the Foot.] Do you know what this is?

MARIE: [Vigorously nods head yes, smiles.] Fruit by the Foot!

PB: Oh great! Okay Dad, the first thing we should measure is her nose.

[DAD puts hat on Marie.]

PB: [Takes hat off Marie.] Then we'll tear off a little piece the length of her nose and she can eat it.

[MOM strokes Marie's nose, they exchange glances, and smile at each other.]

DAD: One bite, Marie. You like that. Mmm.

[MOM strokes Marie's hair, forehead.]

PB: Mom, measure from her elbow to her fingertips.

DAD: She has such long fingers.

PB: Okay, Mom, you put one end in your mouth and one end in Marie's mouth. Dad, you come over here and see how they're doing.

[MARIE smiles, devours ribbon of fruit until she reaches Mom's mouth.]

DAD: Oh, they're racing to see who can eat it the fastest. Marie's very fast! Oh, she's got it!

PB: The noses are in the way. Okay, Dad I want you to measure from the knee down to the heel.

DAD: [Measures with Fruit by the Foot.] It's pretty long. That's about it.

PB: Okay, take off the paper. Mom, you tell them when to start this. Ready, set, GO.

[MARIE grabs one end, puts it in her mouth, and races up the ribbon toward the end of Dad's mouth.]

MOM: Oh, Marie, look at you!

PB: Now, Sandra, here's a piece left over. I think it might go right around her wrist.

SL: An interesting ring, kind of hanging down.

PB: Now Marie can wear that ring home and she can decide when she wants to eat it. Now, I think there must be shoes around here.

MOM: I got a sock.

PB: Mom, you hide it on you.

[MARIE puts ring up to mouth.]

PB: [Laughs.] You can hardly bear to wait. Well, wait till we get these socks on.

[MARIE finds sock in Mom's shirt, smiles, looks at Mom's face.]

PB: Now Dad has hidden one on himself, Marie.

[MARIE finds sock in Dad's shirt, smiles, looks at Dad's face.]

PB: Good, Mom's going to take one, Dad the other. Marie gets to say when they should go.

[MARIE smiles.]

PB: Dad, you'll have to come around, you can't do it clear on the other side like that.

MARIE: [Giggles.] Daddy won!

PB: All right. Sandra, you and I get to do this. So, we want you people, all three of you lovely people to go home and have some fun and remember us. You can decide when you want to do it. See if you can make that greeting even longer. You know, how we've been doing that. So, when Dad comes home from work tomorrow, see if you can add something to it. And when you come home from school and say "Hi, Mom," see if you can remember it. And Sandra and I will try to remember it. And we hope to hear from you and see how things are going. [Gives Marie footprint picture.]

MOM: We will.

Working With The Parents

Just as Marie's therapists set limits during sessions, I worked with Mrs. Brewster to teach her, also, to take charge with Marie. Mrs. Brewster learned to use the word "nevertheless" to stay in charge. As Mrs. Brewster followed that suggestion, calls from a miserable Marie at school requesting to be taken home were met with "Nevertheless, I want you to stay at school. I do not want to hear how rotten you are feeling." In the past, Marie's pitiful details of her physical ailments had invariably led to Marie's coercing her mother to bring her home from school. On one particular day Marie called twice, asking Mrs. B. to take her home.

When Mrs. B. each time firmly refused, Marie called asking to stay after school. Mrs. B. may have won that victory, but she still felt as though she were at the mercy of Marie's guiles. Marie had her own way of trying to be in control. As Mrs. B. grimly described it. "Marie knows how to get to me with panic attacks." To maintain control, Mrs. B. adopted various techniques from the Theraplay sessions. As Marie's therapists used structuring for Marie during sessions, I encouraged Mrs. B., also, to provide structure for Marie at home. For example, she reported that one day she asked Marie how her homework was going and Marie complained she could not possibly write an essay about her trip to Florida. I suggested that Mrs. B. provide structure by telling Marie to make a list of twelve things about Florida. Marie finished the essay later that night and set off for school the next day without difficulties.

As expected, Mrs. B. needed close supervision around the issue of sex education. I gave her two sex education books and advised her to read them herself. A check-in telephone talk revealed that she had, indeed, read them, but had done so virtually in the dark, in a corner of her house in deep secrecy and with little understanding. This led to a discussion of what she had gleaned from her material, what were the distortions, and why it was that she needed to distort. At the end of that phone talk, I advised her to discuss the material with Marie. In a subsequent phone talk, she confessed, "Well, I gave her the books. It was one of the hardest things I'd ever done. I entered the room. She was busy watching TV. I dropped them on her bed table, saying, 'Here, read these,' and ran out of the room." After several Theraplay sessions, Mrs. B. became more comfortable taking charge when she talked to Marie about sex, although there were times when she went overboard in applying the Theraplay technique. She once said proudly, "I had to sit on Marie with the sex book. I sat on her for 15 minutes while I explained things and asked her questions. Sometimes she answered; for example she told me about her older friend's discussion of periods. Afterward, I could say to her, 'I know that book made you uncomfortable.' " We had not had in mind that she would force Marie to talk about sex, and we worked with her to use a more reasonable approach. We were, however, pleased with the willingness of Mrs. B. to acknowledge Marie's discomfort, while still persevering in her own agenda.

In other phone talks, I helped Marie's mother to understand Marie's feelings of rivalry and anger toward the twins who were so cute and lively that the relatives and neighbors came in droves to fawn over them, never giving Marie a second glance. Asked to explore what might be Marie's feelings about these rivals, Mrs. B. replied, "Why she loves them of course. Everybody does." Asked if she had any younger siblings herself, she said, "Yes, I have a younger sister."

AJ: And did you always feel loving and kindhearted toward her?

MOM: Well, yes I did.

AJ: Always?

MOM: I think so.

AJ: Can you think of one older sister who does not always love her little sister or brother?

MOM: Well, yes, I think that my sister's little girl sometimes has it in for her brother.

AJ: Oh, how come?

MOM: Well, that little boy gets an awful lot of attention.

AJ: More than his sister?

MOM: Yes, I should say so.

AJ: What kind of attention does he get?

MOM: Well, you know everybody makes a fuss over him all the time.

AJ: Like for example?

MOM: Well, people are always coming over bringing him presents, taking him out to McDonald's or Candyland.

AJ: Now, let's get back to Marie. Through her eyes, what do her sisters get that she doesn't get?

MOM: Well (with obvious appreciation of the similarity) people are always coming over and bringing them toys from Toys-R-Us and taking them out to Dairy Queen.

AJ: So, deep down, secretly, how do you think she feels about that?

MOM: Well, only deep down and secretly, because I sure would never let her breathe a word of this, I think she might resent them.

AJ: Now, how about you and your little sister. Do you ever think deep down and secretly you might have resented her?

MOM: I might have.

AJ: Suppose you had said that out loud?

MOM: Why, they would have washed my mouth out with soap.

AJ: Could you ever say to anybody that you resented her or were mad at her?

MOM: No, never.

AJ: Is Marie free to say that about anybody?

MOM: No, never.

AJ: So, what do both of you do when you feel angry?

MOM: We smile and keep busy.

AJ: And have panic attacks and act phony? And neither one of you ever lets anybody know who you really are.

MOM: I guess that's right.

AJ: So, is that how you want the two of you to live the rest of your lives?

MOM: No. It isn't.

AJ: So, you can see now what the job is that you and I will have to do to get Marie well.

Another series of telephone calls concerned sojourns to the grocery store in which Marie publicly displayed increasing regression. The usual trips with Marie and Mrs. B. had focused on the shopping list while the sisters played freely in the aisles. In place of accompanying Marie and her mother on these shopping trips, the twins began staying at grandmother's house. Gradually Marie's mother began lifting Marie into the shopping cart and wheeling her up and down the aisles. Finally, Mrs. Brewster provided her lollipops to suck or ice cream bars to lick on during these grocery cart rides. At times when Mrs. B. wanted to infantilize and be close to the twins, she admitted her annoyance with Marie's newly expressed baby-like behavior. Marie often demanded her attention, frequently crying like a little baby. But Mrs. B. found she also could be pleasantly surprised when she accepted Marie's regressions. She said once, "Marie began to act like a baby. I gently put her in the shopping cart and wheeled her like a baby and it stopped." At other times, too, she enjoyed treating Marie like an infant. She reported tenderly that for a "few minutes each day we go into her room, I hug her, I tell her how beautiful she is, and I run my fingers through her hair."

During the final Theraplay session, Mrs. proudly told how she had acted when Marie "blew her stack." Marie was "really getting into being with her friends" and, in the process, "not doing her homework." Following our advice to maintain control and to structure, Mother had forbidden Marie to visit her friends on weeknights before her homework was done. Marie had had a temper tantrum. Instead of being over-whelmed, guilty, and helpless, Mrs. B. calmly told Marie what she had rehearsed with me during the prior session: "I can understand how you must feel, but I want you to know I love you." Mrs. B. stuck to her edicts, the tantrum subsided, Marie eventually finished the homework and Mrs. B. "felt okay" about the whole affair. The contract was for our usual initial MIM administration followed by eight Theraplay session. However, because of Mr. B.'s work schedule, the long travel time, Mrs. B.'s inability to drive, and the parents' satisfaction with Marie's progress, Marie's parents suggested after session 6 that they consider the remaining two sessions "money in the bank" (saved-up sessions upon which they could draw as necessary.) Thus it was that session 6, not session 8, became the terminating session.

RESULTS AND FOLLOW-UP

Perhaps the most dramatic evidence that we had achieved the Theraplay goals came when we compared the mother–daughter pre- and postTheraplay MIMs. Although, for purposes of careful selection of the MIM tasks, the intake and the MIM are typically scheduled a week apart, we felt that the urgency of Marie's situation did not even allow of one week delay. Therefore we decided to administer the MIM immediately. Administered intermittently throughout the treatment, the MIM can also be useful for gauging progress toward Theraplay goals and for identifying areas that still need work. Marie and her mother were administered the MIM twice—once before and once after Theraplay. The MIMs demonstrated the change in the overall quality of their relationship as a function of Theraplay—from awkward, uncomfortable, confusing, indirect, and tentative to straightforward, relaxed, intimate, playful, and engaged. A comparative analysis of several tasks, before and after Theraplay, illustrated these changes.

Task 1: Pigs

Adult and child make the squeaky pigs play together.

MIM Session I: PreTheraplay

MOM: [Reads instructions on card.] Adult and child make the squeaky pigs play together.

[MARIE giggles.]

MOM: Here's two little piggies. Hi little piggy. [Marie and Mrs. B. each squeaks her pig at the other's pig.] Lots of noise, huh? Umm, boy, this is kind of strange, huh? What's the nursery rhyme of the little pigs? The wolf with the pigs?

MARIE: No, it's three little pigs. [Appears very uncomfortable.]

MOM: Oh, gosh, we're missing the third little pig. Where is he? I never . . .

MARIE: Let's go on. [Very nervous.]

MOM: You want to go on to the next one?

MARIE: Yes, please.

Marie's mother was tentative and awkward; she gave the impression of fumbling incompetence and a distance from the material. She did not know the nursery story that she tried to tell. She was incorrect about the most basic fact of it—that there were three pigs. She asked for the third pig but she never finished her explanation. Marie was the teacher—correcting Mrs. B. and politely telling her when to move along to the next task. Mrs. B. made an enormous effort to make conversation, but she tried to engage Marie in an intellectual, forced discussion. Marie, for her part, was cold, controlling, and polite, although she was also clearly uncomfortable. While Mrs. B. tried to appease, Marie was aloof.

MIM Session II: PostTheraplay

MOM: [Reads card.] Remember this one? The pigs again.

MARIE: Oh.

MOM: Oh, there's the piggy. Hi, little piggy, how are you? [Comfortably approaching Marie's pig with her pig.]

[MARIE—genuine, pleased laugh.]

MOM: Cat got your tongue today? Hmm?

MARIE: I guess so.

MOM: You guess so? You want to keep playing this one?

[MARIE—shakes head down.]

This session was much more focused. Instead of reaching for other topics, Mrs. B. was present in the here and now. She playfully interpreted Marie's speechlessness. Mrs. B. was interested in exploring the pig ("How are you?") and in exploring Marie ("Cat got your tongue?"). She was clearly a parent in MIM session II, while in MIM session I she looked to Marie for guidance. Furthermore, although both

MIM sessions I and II lasted the same amount of time, in MIM session I Mrs. B. seemed to be motivated to stop before Marie gave trouble, while in MIM session II she seemed to be quite comfortable about continuing.

Task 2: Teaching

Adult teaches child something she doesn't know.

MIM Session I: PreTheraplay

[MOM reads card and looks at Marie for guidance.]

MARIE: Uh, fractions . . . I don't remember very well.

MOM: Well we need paper for that, don't we. [Gets paper from therapist.] Do you want to know how to convert a fraction, Marie?

MARIE: Okay, whatever "convert" means.

MOM: Okay, well I think you were doing this the other day, kinda. See, ½ is equal to how many sixths?

MARIE: Well? Well how do you do it?

MOM: Okay How many 2's do you have? How much do you have to multiply 2 for it to become 6?

MARIE: Three.

MOM: So you'll do the same to the top number. Multiply the top number by 3 also.

MARIE: It would be 6. I see, it's just like ½ the bottom number?

MOM: Well, when you're going from small numbers to bigger numbers, you're going to multiply. If you're going from bigger numbers to smaller numbers you have to divide. Okay. So let's say you have 8/12 . . . how many fourths do you have?

MARIE: Oh, smaller to bigger is dividing, right?

MOM: Right, you're going bigger to smaller, so 4 into 12 is 3. Well, that wasn't as good to give you, Marie, because you had to divide that by 3. Can't divide 8 by 3, can you? 3 into 8??? Let's give another example. How about 3/9, into how many thirds?

MARIE: Mmm . . .

MOM: Okay, you're going from a bigger number to smaller numbers. So what do you have to do?

MARIE: Divide.

MOM: Right.

MARIE: 3 divided by 9 is 2 . . . no, 3.

MOM: Right.

MARIE: 3 divided by 3 is 1.

MOM: Right. Okay, do you think that's enough of this?

MARIE: Sure.

MOM: Or do you want to keep doing this?

MARIE: Sure, we'll go onto the next one.

MOM: Okay.

Unlike the previous task in which Marie clearly voiced her displeasure in aloof tones, in this task Marie participated fully. Furthermore, Mrs. B. truly taught, perhaps leading us to think Mrs. B. would be in charge, but we saw that Marie still played the parental role. She initiated the topic without Mrs. B. asking and she made efforts to engage her mother. Her overcompliance came through in the way she went along with her mother's suggestions.

MIM Session II: PostTheraplay

[MARIE mumbles something inaudible to mother.]

MOM: I'm supposed to teach you something, you're not supposed to teach me. How about fractions? Do you know fractions already?

MARIE: I know some things.

MOM: How 'bout . . . um . . . how . . . 'bout . . . um. Do you know how to make chocolate frosting?

MARIE: Didn't you teach that to me already?

MOM: Do you know it? [Lots of eye contact.]

MARIE: No. [Shakes head, looking directly at mother.]

MOM: First you take butter and soften it . . . then you beat it and beat it and beat it until it's real creamy. Then you add the powdered sugar and then the chocolate and you keep beating it and beating it and licking the spoon to make sure it's yummy.

MARIE: I know, it tastes good then. [Nods, laughs.]

MOM: Okay, go on to the next one.

Mrs. B. again made an effort to introduce the same dry intellectual topic of fractions, but here she caught herself and replaced it with a fun, experimental topic about a playful situation in which she could symbolically feed and nurture Marie. She also took charge from the beginning. Although Marie tried to regain control—"Didn't you teach me that already?"—Mrs. B. both acknowledged that she heard Marie and stayed in control, calmly asking, "Do you know it?" Then she continued with her explanation. As the videotape of the session showed, whereas in MIM session I, Mrs. B. looked only at the piece of paper, in MIM session II, she looked at Marie.

Task 3: Band-Aid

Adult asks child, "Where on you should I put this Band-Aid?"

Session I: PreTheraplay

MOM: Wanna read this one?

MARIE: [Reads card.] Where are you going to put it? [Shows her finger.]

MOM: Well, we know your toe's been hurting you.

MARIE: Wanna put it there?

MOM: Band-Aid's 'sposed to be in envelope 3. [Searches for envelope.] Where is envelope 3?

MARIE: Would you like to put it on my toe? No?

MOM: Where do you want me to put it, honey? On your toe or on your finger? Is your finger sore from chewing on it?

MARIE: Yeah.

MOM: Settling down a bit?

MARIE: Yeah.

MOM: See, this isn't so bad. [Whispers.]

MARIE: Ooo, a Batman Band-Aid. Nice!

MOM: Jane and Jill (Marie's twin sisters) would like this.

MARIE: Yeah.

MOM: Maybe not.

This task showed evidence of how Marie and Mrs. B. "locked-horns" and demonstrated the subtle, but meaningful confusion in their communications. Marie and Mrs. B. contradicted directions. Marie initiated and coached and structured for her mother. Not only did she begin the task and asked Mrs. B. where Mrs. B. wanted to put the Band-Aid, but she indicated at the same time where her mother should put it. Mrs. B. seemed not to want to touch Marie and Marie had to help her. Rather than acknowledging Marie's request, however, Mrs. B. countered with a suggestion of her own (toe as against Marie's choice of her finger). Again, Marie sounded like the parent reflecting her mother's wish and then firmly setting the limits on her own body. ("No," when her mother wanted to put the Band-Aid on her legitimately "hurting" toe.) When Mrs. B. began to place the Band-Aid on, Marie responded positively to her mother ("Ooh"), but Mrs. B. pulled away from Marie and referred to Marie's twin sisters. Although the communication was subtle, Marie's invitations to be nurtured were met with disregard and distance. Marie probably wondered how she could win.

MIM Session II: PostTheraplay

MOM: [Reads card and initiates.] Okay. Where should I put this Band-Aid on you, Marie?

[MARIE pulls back sleeve and shows elbow.]

MOM: Yeah, the place where you were picking it before. Trying to get you to stop picking at it.

MARIE: It still bothers me.

MOM: I know, you're doing much better. [Puts Band-Aid on daughter's elbow.] Too tight?

[MARIE shakes head; direct eye contact.]

MOM: Feel better?

MARIE: Hm-mmm. [Nods approval, smiles.]

MOM: Next one.

This session was more energetic, lively, and natural than was MIM session I. Both Mrs. B. and Marie built on one theme (Marie's sore elbow), instead of shifting the focus of attention as in MIM session I. Here Mrs. B. was truly engaged with Marie. (This interaction is much like scaffolding, the process that occurs between a mother and her baby when the baby is learning language. In scaffolding, the mother adds to her child's comments, giving the baby the message that the mother is engaged and encouraging language learning to occur.)

Task 4: Lotion

Adult and child each take one bottle of lotion and apply lotion to each other.

MIM Session I: PreTheraplay

[MARIE reads card mother has given her, holds hand out for mother to lotion.]

[MOM laughs, but doesn't lotion Marie.]

MARIE: This is so hysterical. [Laughs nervously, squeezes lotion out on mother's hands.]

MOM: You want to do me first?

MARIE: [Squeezes lotion into her own hand.] Too much, sorry.

MOM: That's okay.

MARIE: You've got blue all over your hands.

MOM: Yeah, it's from that ink.

[MARIE applies with tips of her fingers.]

MOM: Put the extra up here. Now it's your turn?

MARIE: I can't put this up any further. [Pushes Mother's sweater up her arm.]

MOM: Yeah, there's not too many areas to do this.

MARIE: Yeah.

MOM: Your hands are cold?

MARIE: Yeah.

MOM: Sorry.

MARIE: Now I'm really cold.

MOM: [Shakes head and reaches for Marie's other hand to lotion.] Now your hands'll be so smooth. [Then rubs lotion on Marie's cheeks.] Cheeks are a little red.

MARIE: Ow! [Submits to mother's putting lotion on cheeks, but makes dramatic grimace.] I *have* to put that stuff on. [She uses lotion for sensitive skin.]

MOM: It's on my dresser if you want it.

Both Mrs. B. and Marie seemed uncomfortable in this task that required mutual nurturing and both seemed to want to be nurtured first. (Marie: "You do mine." Mrs. B. "You want to put it on me first?") Marie assumed the caretaker role first; while putting lotion on her mother, she apologized and she reflected her mother's "blue"-ness. When Mrs. B. put lotion on Marie, they both became uncomfortable. Mrs. B. seemed to expect that Marie might find it unpleasant to be nurtured. Then she suggested that Marie needed the lotion (because of Marie's red cheeks), rather than that she was putting lotion on Marie because they could both enjoy the process. Marie, for her part, conveyed to her mother that Mrs. B. was indeed hurting her and making her cold.

MIM Session II: PostTheraplay

MOM: Oh, this is good. We didn't have to do this last time. [Drops object on floor.]

[MARIE picks up dropped object.]

MOM: Thanks, Marie. [Rolls up own sleeves.]

[MARIE smiles, rolls up own sleeves.]

MOM: Ready? [Each squeezes out lotion on the other's hand at the same time, and they gently rub lotion on each other simultaneously, arms, and hands intertwined and moving.] Ooo, it's cold! Soft, cold and soft. [Dabs on Marie's nose; each applies lotion to the other's cheeks.] Pretty good, isn't it?

This session was comfortable; Marie and Mrs. B. were close and tender. The videotape showed that Marie gave her arm to her mother and anticipated her mother's applying lotion. They enjoyed the reciprocal contact and did not even need to talk. This was truly a mutual interaction—comfortable, soothing, and without friction. This engagement was like a mother with her baby. Queried at the end of the session about each other's favorite tasks, Marie said that Mrs. B.'s favorite task was the lotion. Mother confirmed this.

Task 5: Feeding

Adult and child feed each other raisins.

MIM Session I: PreTheraplay

MARIE: Oh, gosh. This is so strange. Oh, raisins. Oh, man.

MOM: What are we going to eat?

MOM: I know you haven't been very hungry lately. Will you eat some, a couple?

MARIE: One.

MOM: Just one? Oh, we're supposed to feed each other, right? Okay, here's one. [Feeds child.] I'm hungry.

MARIE: Eat 'em all, then. [Laughs.]

MOM: You're supposed to feed me.

MARIE: Open wide.

MOM: Thank you. You want another one? [As she holds one up to Marie.]

MARIE: [Shakes head no.] I don't like raisins. [Reaches in box for raisins.]

MOM: Since when don't you like raisins?

MARIE: [Shrugs.] I like raisins, but . . .

MOM: Just not today. One more? You've already had two raisins.

[MARIE takes offered raisin.]

Perhaps in no other task could we more easily see the confusion and struggle that centered around feeding and the process of nurturing. As in the previous task, Mrs. B. both suggested that Marie would find being fed by her distasteful ("I know you haven't been very hungry lately. Will you eat some, a couple?") and expressed an eagerness for Marie to nurture her ("I'm hungry. You're supposed to feed me."). Marie limited her mother's nurturance of her ("One raisin. I don't like raisins."). Marie's confusion in struggling with and complying with her mother ("I don't like raisins . . . I like raisins, but . . .") was clear. Mrs. B.'s participation in this struggle was also clear ("You had two raisins.").

MIM Session II: PostTheraplay.

[MOM offers open box of raisins to daughter.]

[MARIE takes raisin and puts in mother's mouth, thus beginning an interchange of taking turns feeding each other raisins.]

MOM: I think that's it. [Box is empty.]

[MARIE nods.]

Mrs. B. and Marie comfortably fed each other. Marie fed her mother first, but the interaction was mutual. Mrs. B. initiated the task by confidently opening the raisin box and unambiguously offering it to Marie. They performed this task in a simple and natural way.

Following our termination, calls from the parents became fewer and fewer. They seemed increasingly satisfied with having mastered a new technique and feeling comfort with a strategy that was obviously working. Mrs. B.'s own self-confidence grew by leaps and bounds. "I'm no longer threatened when I see her express her anger. Rather, I celebrate how far she's come." Marie's success was apparent in several areas. Mrs. B. reported that Marie was gaining weight and said that rather than begging to be taken home, Marie asked to stay after school. Toward the end of treatment, Mrs. B. observed that Marie wanted to sleep over at a friend's house. "She went and I noticed no nervousness. She has more energy and actually jumped up and down. She told me when she came back, 'You know, I really felt bad when I got there, but then I had a good time.' "

Mrs. B. reflected on the changes in her relationship with Marie: "I can see a tremendous change in her and it's much more relaxed between us. I really enjoy her now. I feel less guilty." Difficult areas remained for Marie and her mother. Mrs. B. reported that Marie still threw tantrums when she was asked to unload the dishwasher, her only chore. At times Marie sobbed "for no reason." However, Mrs. B. now asks Marie "Why?" and Marie seems to feel better in response. We feel confident that as Mrs. B. increasingly accepts the "real" Marie, Marie will feel more understood and less alone. Although Marie and Mrs. B. may continue to "lock horns" for some time, this occasional conflict seems less threatening to both of them so they are more able to work together to overcome their difficulties. In her final phone call, Mrs. B. asked whether we would be willing to begin Theraplay with her cousin and child "because she's seeing the changes in Marie and me and wants them for her own family."

DISCUSSION

In all honesty, given the severity of the presenting problems, the three therapists involved in this case were nothing short of surprised at the outcome. It is the nature of Theraplay to be intense, personal, and engaged, and it is probably this combination that worked so well. Theraplay allowed us to improvise and modify our usual format to include the sessions designed to "make her 'real,' " for example. Also, whereas we might ordinarily have felt confident that Marie's spontaneity in time would have emerged on its own, we could not allow ourselves that kind of time in this case. A major contributor to the strategy we used was the urgency of trying to intervene in a potential life-and-death crisis such as we seldom encounter in day-to-day child therapy. It was this crisis that mobilized each one of us far beyond what we ordinarily might have expected of ourselves, in a sense leaving no stone unturned, no potential solution unexplored. Had it been possible, we certainly would have wanted to extend the treatment time; unfortunately, as those of us who work with children are too often made aware, it is the reality of the adult world and not the child's that ultimately determines the treatment confines. Our predictions about the future of Marie and her parents are generally positive. There will be difficulties, of course, as there are with any developing child, but we are quite sure that when these occur we will hear from the family.

In the process of dealing with this complex, uniquely troubled child, we kept an open mind as we devised new strategies. We learned about ourselves, as did the parents about themselves, that certain risks (e.g., focusing on the "real" Marie) paid off better than a more rigid model might have. Thus we learned that through being the health-enhancing agents we were, we all could grow. We learned again about children, as these parents learned of children, that they are not as brittle as they appear; that if we provide them the opportunities, children will not only welcome them, but make good use of their own instinct for resilience and survival.

ACKNOWLEDGMENT

Many thanks to Susan Lindaman, M.A., for her insightful comments on session 6.

REFERENCES

Jernberg, A. (1979). *Theraplay: A structured New Approach for Problem Children and Their Families*. San Francisco: Jossey-Bass.
_____ (1989). Training parents of failure-to-attach children. In *Handbook of Parent Training*, ed. C. Schaefer and J. Briesmeister, pp. 392–413. New York: Wiley.
_____ (1991). Assessing parent–child interactions with the Marschak Interaction Method. In *Play Diagnosis and Assessment*, ed. C. Schaefer, C. Gitlin, and K. A. Sandgrun, pp. 493–515. New York: Wiley.
_____ (1993). Attachment formation. In *The Therapeutic Powers of Play*, ed. C. Schaefer. New York: Jason Aronson.

Jernberg, A., Booth, P., Koller, T., and Allert, A. (1987). *Manual for the Administration and the Clinical Interpretation of the Marschak Interaction Method (MIM), Pre-school and School Age*. Chicago: The Theraplay Institute.

Marschak, M. (1960). A method for evaluating child–parent interaction under controlled conditions. *Journal of Genetic Psychology* 97:3–22.

_____ (1980). *Parent–Child Interaction and Youth Rebellion*. New York: Gardner.

4

Gentleman Jim and His Private War: Imagery Interaction Play Therapy

Joop Hellendoorn, PH.D., and Marie-Joze De Vroom, M.A.

INTRODUCTION TO THE THEORY OF IMAGERY INTERACTION PLAY THERAPY

The method of child psychotherapy called imagery interaction play therapy originated in the Netherlands in the 1950s. This method was developed specially for children rather than derived from therapy for adults. Its roots lie in European phenomenological psychology, which emphasizes the personal perception of events in daily life and the meaning that an individual gives to them (Mook 1989). The meaning a person attaches to his or her experiences determines the way he or she approaches the world; for example whether this person is open, confident, careful, distrustful, offensive, and so forth.

All child therapy methods make use of imaginative play (Van der Kooij and Hellendoorn 1985). Imagery interaction play therapy, however, differs from other methods in that it highlights the therapeutic qualities of play itself. This is in contrast to both client-centered and psychoanalytic play therapy. In client-centered therapy, the focus is more on the personal relationship between the child and the therapist. In psychoanalytic therapy, the emphasis is on translating the play content in such a way that the child gains conscious insight into his or her own experiencing.

There are two reasons why we think it important for children to be able to express their experiences through imaginative play instead of through words (Langeveld 1955, 1964). First, verbal ability and self-reflection are not as well developed in children as they are in adults.

And then, even adults have difficulty putting their personal and emotional experiences into words. Second, open discussion of their problems could bring children into a loyalty conflict with their parents. On the one hand, children's problems are often related to their parents, while on the other hand, children are highly dependent on their parents and are attached to them in many ways.

Through the medium of imaginative play, the child has the opportunity to communicate in a more covert way, revealing what also remains concealed (Vermeer 1973). The therapist tries to share the play world of the child by joining in the play the child initiates. When communicating in the play world, the child finds it easier and safer to express feelings of anxiety, anger, and other negative emotions. The play world also makes it possible for the child to experiment with new ideas and alternative solutions without actually hurting or damaging anyone. The therapist helps children to develop their own play themes and to work these through, and the therapist guides them in more constructive directions. The working hypothesis is that by influencing the expression of an experience, the experiencing itself is altered, leading to new ways of giving meaning to events in daily life.

Imagery Interaction Play Therapy Techniques

In imagery interaction play therapy, the therapist plays together with the child in the play world the child creates. This joining in can take place in a number of ways. First, the therapist's attitude should convey interest and involvement; for example, the therapist might sit at the same level as the child or explore the play materials together with the child. Second, the therapist could become a more active co-player; for example, the therapist could engage in bringing furniture to the doll's house, or help assemble an army, or construct a canal in the sandbox. And, finally, the therapist should join in verbally. The specific techniques that we discuss below all aim at strengthening, deepening, and influencing the child's experiencing as expressed in imaginative play.

Verbalizing or Phrasing

The first technique is *verbalizing* or *phrasing* what the child is playing out at a given moment, thus giving more specific meaning to what the child does.

Eight-year-old Tom makes a dog climb a mountain, but then suddenly the dog tumbles down. The therapist might accompany this verbally: "The dog climbs a mountain, . . . higher and higher, . . . but when he is nearly at the top . . . he falls down again."

Because an effective verbalization or phrasing should capture the essence of the events as well as of the emotions and thoughts the child shows in play, it is important to pay attention to tone of voice, tempo, and vocabulary. These verbalizations have a number of different purposes:

1. Structuring: The therapist helps the play become more unified by combining separate play fragments into a coherent whole. Structuring it also often helps children become more explicit themselves about their meaning.

   Rita selects different toys and puts them in the sandbox. Her actions seem still tentative, without much specific meaning. The therapist might verbalize these actions as they take place: "There comes a horse . . . and there a tree. And on the other side a fence . . . and behind that crocodile . . . and a tiger . . . and a lion. It looks like all the wild animals have to be on that side of the fence."

2. Strengthening of meaning: The aim of these verbalizations is to help clarify the child's meaning and position.

   Tom repeats his play of the dog climbing the mountain a couple of times, but every time the dog falls down. The therapist can then strengthen the meaning by saying: "Again and again that dog tries to reach the top of the mountain, but every time he fails to reach it."

3. Anticipating future events: These verbalizations bring about continuity in a play story.

   Seven-year-old Brian lines up two big troop formations opposite each another. Therapist: "That looks like it could become a fight."

4. Articulating the feelings and thoughts of the play figures: In this way, the therapist implicitly validates the child's feelings and thoughts.

   Janice (5 years old) plays a little girl who is at home alone and hears the footsteps of burglars outside the house. Therapist: "I bet that girl feels really frightened."

5. Phrasing of therapeutic messages or interpretative play interventions: The therapeutic message resembles an interpretation in the psychodynamic sense, except that in imagery interaction the phrasing remains consistent with the play format. Such a message is always related to the therapy goals. Two examples:

> Seven-year-old Johnny, who terrorizes his family with his unpredictable temper tantrums, lets a little red car drive around so furiously that all the other toys are crushed or flung aside. The therapist takes the part of some bystanders (small plastic toys) who are also threatened and says: "Let's take ourselves off, quick! As long as he is so furious we cannot stay here together with that car. When he leaves off racing, later on, maybe we can come back." Then the therapist takes another little car and races with Johnny. In this way, Johnny gets room to indulge in his wild racing. But at the same time, the therapist conveys the message that such wildness can be disturbing for others and, as a result, you may feel lonely.

> Seven-year-old Helen is always at loggerheads with her mother. In her play, a puppet mother beats up a boy. The therapist identifies with the child, but at the same time conveys the message that there must be some reason behind this: "Ow, that hurts . . . ow! . . Something must have happened there. Perhaps that boy did something he shouldn't have . . . or there is something else why his mom is so mad . . . perhaps she is tired . . . or something else again."

The interpretive intervention can also be put in the form of a question, inviting the child to give his or her own interpretation, which may also strengthen the therapist–child interaction.

> In the case of Tom and his dog, the therapist could say: "I wonder, . . . how could it be that all his attempts fail?"

Stimulating

The second technique of imagery interaction play therapy is *stimulating*, which is related to verbalizing. Stimulating means encouraging the child to engage in more focused and more intensive play. When it is difficult for a child to start to play, the therapist may offer suggestions about possible play materials or may encourage the child to manipulate the different toys. To further stimulate play, the therapist may suggest incorporating new play materials, play space, or play content.

> Jenny is playing with the doll's house. She furnishes the house, puts some puppets in it, puts them to bed, and then says: "That is finished." The

therapist says, using a lowered and somewhat mysterious voice: "Hmmmm, they are all in bed now. . . . It is dark in the house . . . and very quiet . . ."

Stimulation may also be necessary when a child encounters barriers that are difficult to overcome. By joining the play, the therapist makes it clear that the child's action is not forbidden, but permitted by at least one adult. If this is not enough to help the child cross the barrier, the therapist must be careful to space further suggestions so that the child does not feel pressured.

A type of stimulation we often use in imagery interaction play therapy is "sensopathic play." This kind of play is characterized by tactile or other sensory involvement with more or less formless material, such as sand, water, or clay. The child touches, senses, tastes, or smells the material present and undergoes its substance and its properties rather than actively changing it. Sensopathic play is a basic form of play, already found in very young children. This seemingly regressive play often helps children to relax and, consequently, to deepen and intensify the play experience. To some children, however, the regressive form- lessness of sensopathic play can be threatening. They may need more structured interventions.

Setting Limits

Just as it is important to stimulate play now and then, it is also sometimes necessary to *set limits*. For example, when a child uses so many play materials that he or she loses all track of the situation, the therapist will need to set a limit. Such limit setting is often necessary with young children, who are easily distracted by everything they see around them. Sometimes, a therapist has to slow down a child, when he or she crosses a limit or is about to do so. The therapist first tries to integrate limit setting into play.

"Mmm, the water is getting so high, it is almost flooding. Shall we say this is enough?"

If this produces no effect, the therapist will probably need to leave the play world and clearly tell the child what is permitted and what is not, while at the same time accepting the fact that the child may want to do something that is not allowed.

In addition to limits that are valid for all children (such as: time, no taking home of play materials, no willful destruction of play materials, no hurting of others or oneself), sometimes individual children need specific limits. These specific limits must be directly related to the therapy goals. For example, when a goal for a particular child is to stimulate him or her to take on a more active position, it might be appropriate to set a limit to the playing of magical solutions to all problems coming up during play.

Counterplay

The last imagery interaction play technique is *counterplay*. The therapist takes on a role in which he or she can personalize other aspects of the play world than those the child does, while conveying therapeutic messages at the same time.

> Eight-year-old Monica is in therapy for problems that are related to the overstressed ideal-child image of both herself and her parents, which forces her always to be nice. She takes the role of mother of a baby doll whom she spanks good and hard: "She is bad, bad, bad . . ." The therapist takes the role of a friend of mother's, coming to tea: "How mad you are at that girl of yours. She really must have done something awful. I know how it is, mine is the same, sometimes they are just horrible. But that is just how children are: sometimes they are good, and sometimes not."

It will be clear that, to intervene in this way, the therapist needs to have much insight into the meaning of the role for that child. For this, the play therapist relies on what is known about the history of the child, on the results of previous assessment, and on the formulated therapy goals (for more case illustrations, see Hellendoorn 1988).

From our own research (Harinck and Hellendoorn 1987), one result is worth special mention here: Of all possible child behaviors, imaginative play is the one in which the therapist seems best able to influence the child. Moreover, imaginative play behavior of the therapist appears to strongly facilitate imaginative play of the child. Thus, it seems really worthwhile to give therapeutic interventions this imaginative format.

Parental Counseling

The treatment of a child can never stand on its own, for a child is part of a family. Having a child with problems can be very difficult for parents. Moreover, often the parents need to develop different attitudes toward their child. This is why the counseling of parents is an essential part of imagery interaction play therapy. Usually, we prefer the counselor and the therapist to be one and the same person. Working with the child and the parents simultaneously has many practical benefits. Because everything is in the same hands, there can be no difference of opinion about method and priorities. Also, it helps to prevent one-sided identification. Although rivalry between therapist and parents may be more likely to arise, the therapist can deal with this issue more directly. Another important advantage is that the therapist gets to know the child well and is able, as a result of direct experience with the child, to empathize with the parents. After all, the child's difficult behavior will probably be evident in therapy, too! In this way it is often easier to actively involve the parents in the whole process. Nevertheless, situations may occur in which the relationship between parents and child is so tense that one could justifiably speak of two "parties." In such cases, it is advisable that different therapists treat the parents and the child.

Indications for Imagery Interaction Play Therapy

An important feature of imagery interaction play therapy is that it gives children the opportunity to express their problems covertly, through play. For children whose problems are related to their parents, open discussion of their problems could bring them into a loyalty conflict. For these children, the method is especially suitable. Imagery interaction also works well with children with covert symptoms, such as somatic complaints. The method is also appropriate for children who cannot overcome a traumatic event or have difficulty coping with a handicap. People who have experienced traumatic events generally relive these events through images. Imagery interaction play therapy helps them make these images more concrete and work them through. Play therapists can also use this method with children who are rather chaotic, but in such cases it is important that the therapist provide a sufficient amount of structure.

Furthermore, for therapy to be successful, it is necessary that parents be prepared to examine and change their own behavior and attitude toward their child (with the help of the counselor). The child should be between 4 and 10 years, the age at which children like to engage in imaginative play. For older children, other imaginative techniques than play (e.g., drawing, clay work, storytelling) may be more appropriate.

Therapy Goals, Strategy, and Evaluation

To determine whether therapy is indicated, the therapist must conduct a thorough assessment of both the child's and the family's problems. It must be clear why the child needs therapy. The play therapist needs to formulate therapy goals, directed toward both the child and the parents. Usually, we distinguish ultimate goals and intermediate goals. Ultimate goals reflect what the therapist wants to accomplish with this therapy, such as ability to express emotions in an understandable way, better ability to cope with new problems, tantrums reduced to at most once a fortnight. These also form the criteria for termination of therapy. Intermediate goals are steps on the way toward the ultimate goals. They are often related to in-therapy behavior, such as establishing a working relationship between therapist and child, attaining personally meaningful imaginative play, confronting personal problems in play, clarifying a specific problem. Next, the proposed way of attaining these goals must be set forth in a strategy plan. Finally, it is very important that the therapist evaluate every session. The treatment plan (consisting of therapy goals and strategies) provides a basis for these short-term as well as for longer-term evaluations. Harinck and Loeven (1985) found that therapists who paid much attention to the formulation of goals and strategy plan, and who made regular written evaluations of their sessions, were more successful.

PRESENTING PROBLEM AND BACKGROUND DATA

Jimmy was 7 years and 6 months old, when he was referred for assessment to the "ambulatorium" at our university. The ambulatorium is an outpatient clinic of the Departments of Special Education and Developmental Psychology for parents and children with behavioral and child-rearing problems. Its main purpose is to provide a practice base for students and faculty members of both departments. Schools, doctors, and other experts refer clients for services.

In Jimmy's case, his mother (Ellen) and his teacher agreed that something had to be done, because Jimmy tended to withdraw into his own small world where they could no longer reach him. On the other hand, he could be extremely difficult. Especially in company, he did not listen, rebelled against almost anything, and constantly claimed Ellen's attention. Whenever she was on the telephone, Jimmy always needed to know exactly who she was speaking to and about what. On the slightest provocation from outside, his reactions were extremely vehement. In school, too, if he did not daydream, he interfered constantly with other children. This was not only a nuisance for them and the teacher, but it also prevented him from getting his own work done. Accordingly, his grades were low. He had almost no friends. During the previous four years he often wet his bed, and recently he had complained about severe pains in his right leg. The direct cause of referral, though, was his mother's finding some notes in his desk about not wanting to live any more, which naturally alarmed her very much.

The family consisted of Ellen with her two children, Jimmy and his 13-year-old sister Mandy. Four years before, the father (Brian) left the family. Ellen had noticed that something had been bothering him, but his announcement that he was leaving them came as a complete surprise to her. Even after four years she was still unable to understand what had happened. This was not made easier by Brian's living near them and often dropping in for dinner or just to see the children. As Ellen said herself: "In this way, the children and I constantly had to say goodbye again." At the same time it kept their hope for a reunion alive. During the months right before Jimmy entered therapy, however, the rift had suddenly deepened because of Brian starting an affair with Ellen's best friend. Very emotionally, Ellen now wanted a divorce and a regular visiting schedule for the children.

Four years previously, after Brian's departure, the family's income diminished considerably, even though Ellen increased her own working time (as a receptionist in a small office) from 16 to 24 hours a week. Consequently, they had to move to a much smaller apartment, with attendant change of school for both children. Ellen felt very much alone and depressed. For a time, she tried to find help in a therapy group, but she felt her problems were too different from those of the other participants to be understood. Moreover, she had trouble finding a baby-sitter during therapy hours and the children were often very rebellious when she came home after a session. So she quit therapy after a few months. Instead, she applied herself to giving the children a good home. But more and more, she felt herself incapable of this. Her daughter Mandy, just becoming adolescent, was rebelling violently, often telling Ellen she wanted to live with Brian and quarrelling constantly with Jimmy. As Ellen said, "The atmosphere in the house is just hopeless, impossible, it seems as if we can never do anything nice together and can only shout at one another."

Ellen thought that Jimmy was perhaps the most affected by the family's breakup, because "he was so much his father's boy, they were practically inseparable." Apart from his visits to Brian (now every second weekend), about which he never told anything, he did not see anybody socially. Ellen reported, "Often he comes home from school and immediately goes to his room, still with his coat on, and sits there until dinnertime." He almost always played alone with his technical Lego and his cars or read comics. By then, Ellen felt powerless toward him, and guilty at the same time: "He is often so surly, there are so many things he does not want, whatever I try. It just seems I cannot do anything well. And now these death wishes . . . That is really the last straw."

To complete the intake procedure, we had an interview with Brian, Jimmy's father, a well-educated man who traveled abroad frequently for his firm. At first he denied there was any problem. Later, he conceded there might be something wrong, but he tended to ascribe this to his ex-wife, who he believed never understood feelings and who cared only about outward appearances and about money. When the children were with him, he had no discipline trouble. However, if Ellen insisted on professional help, he would not refuse his permission, provided he would be kept up to date.

THEORETICAL CONCEPTUALIZATION

Assessment started with a family observation of Ellen, Mandy, and Jimmy in the playroom. We asked them to build a village together in the large sand tray. We told them they could do this in any way they chose. All three family members then spontaneously chose their own corner of the sand tray and started their own part of the village. Jimmy claimed the largest part. Ellen tried to divide the available space fairly, but was overruled by both children. Jimmy started to put up two armies, Ellen created a homely scene with table, chairs, and tea service. Mandy was the only one who really built something like a village, but soon had trouble defending this against Jimmy's advancing armies. For safety, she decided to build a wall around her villa park. Ellen stated: "This is not a nice village. Everybody wants something else. Please do not attack my part." Since Jimmy kept on advancing, Ellen tried to contain him: "It will soon be night, then the armies have to draw back . . . Please Jimmy, you take all our space, you disturb us all . . . Now please, keep outside my fences." Jimmy, however, just continued to strengthen his armies, even though the counselor announced time was up. Jimmy refused to stop and cried "I am not ready yet." Ellen and Mandy started to clean out the sand tray, and Jimmy became really angry. Furiously, he swept away all toy figures, and refused categorically to help stacking them away when Ellen asked him to.

This session made clear that the family members were quite unused to working together in any way. There was no discussion about how to tackle the exercise. Each person started on his or her own and did whatever he or she wanted. Jimmy claimed much attention and got it without listening to anybody else. Ellen tried to create the image of a happy and harmonious family, but failed. Mandy succeeded best in keeping her own part safe, although her face clearly reflected her disagreement with what happened between Ellen and Jimmy. She had not wanted to come with the family in the first place and said very little during the whole session. She also was quite resolute in refusing to come again if we should wish so.

Further assessment (by intelligence, achievement, and projective tests) revealed that Jimmy was a very intelligent and sensitive, but underachieving boy. He perceived his world as most uncertain and unsafe. Everywhere he saw dangers lurking, with practically no real help available for him from the adults in his life. He felt quite alone, left by both parents, by Brian literally, by Ellen emotionally. His feelings toward Brian were ambivalent: very much dependent on him on the one hand, but furious on the other because Brian was just not there. Ellen's attention, which he got, he experienced as overprotective and restrictive. His sister "tried to boss him around." In relations with peers, he "felt sick." Often in bed or while playing, his leg pained him. A deep feeling of depression became noticeable as the assessment day progressed. "So now there is nothing any more," he said.

However, there were also some positive points. In the first place, his attitude toward work and his concentration during achievement testing were unexpectedly good. He also responded well to the different projective and play techniques and showed strong imaginative ability. There, he was able to express his rage and feelings of loneliness and to counter them with aggressive play acts, although he evaded and withdrew from gentler and more sensitive emotions. In a brief interview, he could also tell us something of what bothered him: that he saw Daddy so little, that Daddy did not play with him as often as he would like, but that he was great for rough-and-tumble. He craved having Brian back in the family and was unrealistically hopeful that somehow this might still happen. He also expressed interest in coming back to play in our playroom.

Jimmy was clearly in need of intensive help. His attitude toward life and his daily living environment was full of rage, distress, depression, and other negative meaning, so much so that there was almost no room left for his attributes to help him function. There seemed to be two ways left for him to cope with life: (a) by withdrawing in his lonely fantasy world in which he could partially admit his grief and in which he could be powerful; and (b) by pretending that there was no distress or grief in himself, but that everybody else was against him and nobody gave him the attention he needed. That second way of coping made him a disturbing and interfering boy both at school and at home.

However, it was also clear that Jimmy was not the only problem in the family. Between all family members, there was a definite lack of cohesion. They showed themselves unable to relate in a positive way and shared an inability to mourn the separation. Ellen's feelings of powerlessness and guilt aggravated this situation. These family problems formed strong indications for some form of family therapy. However, these had to be weighed against Mandy's refusal to participate and against the (by this time) acute distress Jimmy was experiencing. Therefore, we decided instead to offer a treatment plan consisting of individual play therapy for Jimmy, accompanied by intensive counseling for Ellen. During the interviews with Ellen, an indirect eye could be kept on Mandy and the problems she might develop (apart from her heavy adolescent rebellion) in working through her part of the separation from her father.

When we discussed this treatment offer with Ellen, she reacted positively and with relief. But she said she could not decide this on her own. She wanted Brian included in making this decision. Was this a genuine and fair wish to share responsibility with him over the children and not to leave him out or was it a more or less conscious effort to rein him in again as part of the family? Perhaps a bit of both. On the positive side, we considered that she had never in any way grudged or hindered her children's visits to their father. Therefore, we decided to grant Ellen's wish.

Discussing our offer with Brian also gave us an opportunity to invite him for counseling interviews. Although, again, he judged there was no real problem with Jimmy, he agreed to take part even though he still tended to put the blame on his former wife. We also talked about his son's problem with accepting that he had really left for good. Brian then admitted that this was partly his fault. After leaving the family he had felt so guilty that he could not resist often visiting them, thereby keeping everyone's hopes alive. However, since by now it was clear to him that there was no way for him to go back, he wanted the divorce too. He was now ready to talk to the children about it, which he had never done before! When asked whether he would have a joint interview with

Jimmy at our institute about the irreversibility of the separation, after some hesitation, he agreed. We made an appointment with him for some weeks after the start of therapy.

Now that all concerned had agreed to therapy, what would be the best therapy method for Jimmy? In his play and projective tales, Jimmy had shown a well-developed imaginative ability, which afforded him good opportunities for expression. Since it was much more difficult for him to openly talk about his problems and because of the loyalty he showed toward both his father and his mother, play seemed a better medium for him than talking. Playing, the interaction with an adult was less strained than in a vis-à-vis situation. Therefore, we chose imagery interaction play therapy as our intervention strategy. There were no contraindications. All conditions necessary were met: (a) Jimmy's problems were primarily personal conflicts; (b) he liked play and the playful interaction with an adult and seemed motivated to use this medium; (c) his integrative powers seemed satisfactory; (d) his perspective was clear, since he would live with his mother and sister; and (e) his parents both agreed to the help offered and both showed the motivation to start a process of change.

Jimmy was then referred to the first author [J. H.] as therapist, working in the same institute.

I [J. H.] formulated the following intermediate goals for the play therapy:

1. establish a working relationship between Jimmy and myself;
2. further clarify his relationship with the other family members, including Brian; and
3. get acquainted with the way he expressed his life themes in play, and help him to fully develop these themes and to confront his problems in play.

My ultimate goals were:

4. work through his separation problem toward his father;
5. help him find better (less destructive) ways of coping with adversity; and
6. normalize his interactions with his mother, father, sister, and peers.

Concurrently with their child's therapy, we always invite the parents for regular counseling interviews. As said in the Introduction, we prefer to keep child therapy and parent counseling in one hand, if that seems at all possible. I find it infinitely easier to talk with the parents if I know the child and his or her sometimes impossible behavior first-hand, because then we have some immediate common ground. However, when there is fundamental conflict between child and parent, I sometimes feel a need to guard both parties' privacy in such a way that it is better to work with a separate parent counselor. In this case, there seemed enough positive factors in the mother–son relationship for the one-therapist model. The decision about who should work with Brian was a bit more tricky. To counsel both the mother and the father in a divorce case has the advantage, again, of keeping all threads together. But the parents often make this impossible because they try to encapsulate the counselor or try to play off the counselor against their ex-partner. It certainly needs a lot of experience to recognize the danger signs. With 25 years of experience, I felt competent to deal with this. Moreover, in the ambulatorium there are regular staff meetings about the therapy clients, where we work to spot possible pitfalls and where we have the opportunity to mobilize a colleague counselor any time.

For Ellen, the counseling goals were:

1. helping her to express and work through her own feelings and to make her own decisions about her life and her family;
2. giving her more insight in Jimmy's development and personal problems; and
3. helping her find better ways to cope with daily parent–child interaction, with Jimmy as well as with Mandy.

For Brian, the goals were:

1. helping him to actualize his parental role in a positive way, separate from but not opposite to Ellen; and
2. increasing his insight into Jimmy's problems and finding ways to cope with them.

THE PROCESS OF PLAY THERAPY

I scheduled Jimmy for a once-a-week therapy, and I saw him in play therapy for 77 sessions, spaced over 2½ years. Ellen came also once a week during the first half year, but later that frequency lessened. Brian came about once a month.

Start Phase: The First Six Sessions

In the imagery interaction play therapy process, there are usually three main phases: the start phase, the working-through phase (which lasts longest), and the termination phase. In the start phase, the play therapist and the child get acquainted, establish a working relationship, and explore the possibilities for the child in the playroom. Exploration takes a large part. Gradually, specific toys may become more attractive for a child, which is usually a sign that specific meanings come more to the fore and may be included in play themes of growing personal importance.

Jimmy's first sessions were characterized by an all-pervading restlessness. His play themes were brief and he was easily distracted and tended to avoid serious play by talking about minor happenings at home or at school. As a play therapist, I must constantly decide whether a topic of discussion is of personal importance or whether it serves to ward off real involvement in a different activity. If at all possible, I try to confine "social talking" to the start and the end of a session, so as not to impede the serious play work. Usually, if a child starts talking about other topics than play itself, I give a brief reaction and then make a remark about "the cars that are still driving" or "the animals that are waiting" or whatever is going on in play. Naturally, in the later stages of therapy talking may become more important and thus take up more time.

As I do with all children during the first session, I talked with Jimmy about the reasons for his coming to therapy:

JH: Sometimes children don't feel well; they may have a lot of troubles or they may be sad, or quarrel a lot . . .

J: I quarrel a lot with Mandy.

JH: Exactly.

J: But that is not my fault. She is always nagging at me and she bosses me and I don't want that.

JH: Well, perhaps it does not even matter so much whose fault it is, but it does not feel good to quarrel so much.

J: No.

JH: And then perhaps at school . . .

J: Today went very well at school.

JH: Today went well, that's fine, but there are other days when you cannot work or you cannot concentrate . . .

J: Mmmm . . .

JH: And there are not many children you play with . . .

J: No, they never ask me . . . But anyway, when they ask me I feel sick in my stomach, so I do not like to go with them.

JH: No . . . so there are a lot of things that are not well or not nice, or that perhaps you would like to have otherwise. Well, that is why you have come here. Most children come here because there are a lot of bad or sad or disagreeable things they have to cope with. And you know what we do here?

J: Mmm?

JH: Play. We play a lot. You and I are going to play together, sometimes about nice things, but also often about sad or nasty things.

J: At home I go play when I want to forget something.

JH: Yes, and you may have found that that helps sometimes.

J: Yeah.

JH: Now, here it is a bit different, because here we play together. And here we can also play things that you cannot forget. And you'll see, when we do that together, that helps too. So that is why Mom and Dad and I thought that this might be something for you.

J: Mmm. Well, I liked it when I was here before.

JH: Well, that is okay then. So for the next year or so, you are coming every week on _____ (day) at _____ (time). And we will play together.

J: Okay.

JH: And one other thing. Children are better in playing, but grown-ups are usually better in talking. That is why you come to play, and Mom comes to talk with me. And did you hear that your Dad also sometimes comes to talk?

J: About me?

JH: Sometimes about you, when there are things they find difficult. You know, you sometimes have troubles, but they also find it often difficult to know just how to do things with you. [J. laughs.] You know what I mean? [Small nod.] But most of all the grown-ups talk about themselves. Just as you may also sometimes want to talk about Mom or Dad or Mandy or someone else, but mostly you just play for yourself. Okay?

J: Yeah . . . where are those armies again?

Jimmy's main themes during these first sessions were (a) not being able to escape, (b) threatening monsters, and (c) defense against an unknown enemy. He played the first theme several times in different versions. The most striking example was in the third session, when he first built a sand mountain, dug a tunnel in it, and then barricaded the tunnel with fences and traffic signs: no way in, no way out, no through-way. He then called the tunnel a "haunted house." After looking at it for a few moments, he selected a single little black toy man and put it on top of the mountain: "That is the first man on earth." He then quickly destroyed the whole scene and started something else.

He played the second main theme (feeling threatened) with crocodiles and dinosaurs, who attacked everything in their orbit. Jimmy played this with almost fanatic pleasure. I sustained this theme and his need of power.

J: They bite real hard.

JH: They bite real hard, so all those animals they catch feel a lot of pain . . .?

J: Sure, if they are not dead, which most of them are. And they deserve it.

JH: They deserve it. . . . How come?

J: Because they had been bad, bad, bad . . . [He slaps a dinosaur hard on a toy bull.]

JH: That dino is just mad at that bull. And he lets him feel it.

Jimmy also played the third theme (defense against an unknown enemy) in many different ways. The armies that he already had used during the assessment returned and would remain central throughout the whole of this therapy. Jimmy needed strong armies almost every time and he spent a lot of time finding their right order and structure. Sometimes there were two armies who fought till all participants were dead. Sometimes there was only one army put into the sand, directed toward the outside. I commented:

JH: That looks like there is something outside, like they want to defend themselves against an enemy.

J: No no, there is no enemy, they just defend their cars.

JH: There is no enemy, but still . . . they do not feel safe.

Next, Jimmy closed all entrances to his sand castle to the soldiers and their cars. An airplane flew over it, but saw nothing and crashed in the sand. Abruptly, he stopped play, cleared away the toys he had used and tidied up the room, as if to pretend that it had never happened.

In these first six sessions, we worked well towards the three intermediate goals. Our working relationship (goal 1) was growing. Together we were developing some essential play themes, in which he was actively involved and started to confront his problems (goal 3). There was still a lot to be done toward clarifying his relation to the other family members (goal 2). However, I could also tackle this point from the side of his parents, in their counseling sessions.

First Interviews with Ellen

During this first phase, I worked on a once-a-week basis with Ellen, Jimmy's mother. She needed much time for herself, because of her bitterness about everything that had happened to her. "There I am, a divorcee with two children, working like mad to give them everything, and see what happens. . . . Everything just falls apart." On the one hand, she knew very well she often made mistakes in her handling of the children. On the other hand, she very easily felt criticized and even attacked. Therefore, I started to compliment her on the good job she had done in bringing up two children under difficult conditions, one of whom (Mandy) was doing fine in school.

When I told her about the restlessness that marked Jimmy's play behavior during the first sessions, she at once said: "Oh, he has that from me. I am restless myself. It just seems I cannot sit still. There always is so much to be done." Since she also seemed to regret that she had so little time together with her children, I asked her for the next week to think about when throughout the day she might be able to create more time and what she would like to do with it. The next session, she told me she had decided to take a half hour after dinner to read with Jimmy. "That might also keep him away from the TV."

One of Ellen's big problems was that she tried so hard, but succeeded so little, in giving her children a good life. One example: "When they come back on Sunday night, I always cook something special, but they just do not appreciate it." When I asked for more details about what happened on those Sunday nights, Ellen discovered that the children, coming back from their father, were always rather grumpy. Therefore, this really was not a good opportunity to profit by her efforts. She then decided to give the children just a nice, but easy snack on those Sunday nights and to choose another night for her special dinners. This worked much better, especially when she let the children choose their favorite dishes.

All this, trivial though it may seem, meant that Ellen began trying to place herself more in the children's position so as to better understand them. She then proceeded to complain about Jimmy's sudden rages. I helped her little by little to begin to accept that these tantrums were not really *her* problem, but *his*. If he was angry, *he* was angry. And if his anger was directed against her or against Mandy, this did not necessarily mean that they had really done something. It might just be that they were the only people present, whereas his anger was against the whole world. Slowly, she started to take his moods less personally.

After the first six weeks, Jimmy and Ellen both stated that they would like to continue. Although there certainly was not much change yet, they felt a bit more relaxed knowing that there was a place outside now where they could talk, complain, play, or have tantrums as much as they liked, instead of doing that against each other.

JOINT INTERVIEW OF BRIAN AND JIMMY

As it seemed that by now Jimmy and I were well under way toward the intermediate goals (establishing a relationship, getting acquainted with his main themes, confronting these themes in play), this was a good time to have the joint interview with Brian and Jimmy. I also felt this might give me more insight in the nature of their relationship.

So that week Jimmy came with his father instead of with his mother and he seemed rather excited about it. He was very eager for me to meet his dad and told me proudly how much Brian traveled and how much he knew about foreign countries. I started the interview with an explanation about its purpose: to talk openly about what had happened and about the divorce, even though this might be difficult for them both.

J: There is no need to talk, I know all about the divorce.

JH: Well, that is what sometimes you may like to think. But there are also times when you are worrying a lot about Mom and Dad, and why they split up.

B: And besides, I have never really told you about it myself, and I would like to do so now.

Jimmy's face fell, as his father started to tell him, guided a little bit by me. Brian tried to really find words that Jimmy might be able to understand and, as we had discussed before, refrained from taking the blame for the divorce or from putting it on anyone else. When Brian finally said that by now he was convinced that he would never come back to live in the family and that he also wanted a legal divorce, Jimmy started to cry. I supported him by saying that even though he had known this all the time, it was still very difficult to hear it and talk about it. Then I suggested he might want to sit with Brian, and at once he crept on Brian's lap, and had a long cry.

I left them alone at that point for some 15 minutes. When I came back, Brian and Jimmy seemed very close. Therefore, it was a good opportunity to make clear, that throughout his life his dad would be there, even though he was living somewhere else in the same city. Jimmy could often go and see him. Ellen had agreed that whenever he wanted to go or call Brian, that was fine with her. In any case, there was every other long weekend (from Friday afternoon until Sunday night) that he would spend with his dad, just as he had done for the last year. I suggested that it might be a good idea for them to sometimes talk about being together and apart at the same time. I ended the interview by giving them Richard Gardner's *Boys and Girls Book about Divorce* to read together.

As there was still some time left, I suggested Jimmy might like to go to the playroom for a little while. He at once said he wanted to show his dad where he usually played. During the 10 minutes that were left, in the presence of Brian, Jimmy played briefly, but intensely, with a toy gun and the toy soldiers, shooting down one after the other. This play, as can be imagined, was the topic of my next interview with Brian. He had never seen his son in that fierce mood and said that he now understood that Jimmy was really troubled.

In all, this joint interview served different purposes. The father–son relationship was strengthened and deepened and it gave Brian some insight in Jimmy's problems.

Working Through Phase: (Sessions 7–38)

This phase took about ten months and thirty-two sessions. By now, Jimmy had grown more relaxed in the playroom. For a time, he played quite a lot with sand and water (making "horrible mud"), like a much younger child. This heralded his entry into the real working phase of therapy. This entry was also marked (as is quite usual in child psychotherapy) by more specific interest in me as a person and in the playroom situation. The Feast of S. Nicholas (a popular family festival in the Netherlands) gave him an opportunity to ask me with whom I spent that evening and whether I had children of my own. When in session 15 he found several small toys in the sandbox (which should not have been there) he asked: "Was there a child here before me with you?" In this phase, these questions show that the child somehow wants a special relationship with me, but is worried whether that is possible. As I always do, I took these opportunities to tell Jimmy that of course I have a family outside the institute (just as he has) and that there are other children coming, but that during this particular hour I am there for him only, that during this hour this is our room and nobody else's.

At the start of the working through phase, the mountain motif returned, but in a somewhat different form. First, Jimmy made a large and very high mountain. He chose a mother kangaroo and gave her a baby in her pocket, "So you can see she is the mother." He put both of them on top of the mountain. Then there came a lot of other small animals who tried to climb the mountain, but did not succeed. Again and again they tried, but to no avail. Even the dinosaurs could not help them. Since this was the first time he introduced a "mother motif" in his play, I decided to keep my verbalizations simple and cautious. For instance, while verbalizing the difficult plight of all the animals, "The piglets try to get up the mountain, to mother kangaroo up there, but no . . . And then the ducks . . . And that little horse . . . But he doesn't succeed either . . ." I refrained from verbalizing the animal's or the mother's feelings. In this way I hoped to support his theme, to help him give more structure to his play, without pressuring him.

Next, Jimmy started to dig a large hole in the mountain, deeper and deeper, "down to the bottom," as he said. All this was played with great intensity, in which I supported him by emphasizing the physical effort of digging so hard. In this way I strengthened the sensopathic element in his play. This play session conveyed to me an image of two sides in Jimmy: his inability to reach his mother and his searching for a solid base. The session ended with Jimmy firing a toy gun at the dinosaurs.

During the next session, he repeated this theme. This time, however, the piece of mountain on which mother and baby kangaroo were placed became really precarious, and with apparent pleasure he then let the mountain fall down. I commented: "Nobody could reach that kangaroo and now see what happened to her. She was so high, she has fallen deep." This interpretive verbalization implied that falling was her own fault for being so unattainable. My verbalization was clearly inspired by Jimmy's grin when the mother kangaroo came down with the mountain. This conveyed that he enjoyed the (make believe) power he experienced in his play over mother; if he could not reach her, he would make her fall down and reach him.

For his part, Jimmy was delighted with the words "high-and-deep" I used and started to make a word song: "Climbing high—falling deep, climbing deep—falling high [hahaha], climbing—falling—high—deep—low. Have you ever climbed low and fallen high? How would you do that?"

This, by the way, was an example of his sense of humor, which I had noticed before. He loved making little jokes, especially word jokes, and he also liked me to make them up for him. In a therapeutic relationship, it always helps to find small points of "togetherness" such as this. With Jimmy, it helped us over many difficult moments. Jimmy used it for that purpose too. After a very intense play (like the above) he would often break the tension with some small joke or game that made us both laugh.

In the next sessions, the mountain became more threatening. No longer was it just an unattainable summit, it could also suddenly fall apart. And another new detail came up: it could spit fire when it wanted. This made the mountain even more of a self-image than it had been before. During these plays we talked about fire-spitting mountains and how dangerous these could be, especially for the people living around. An example:

J: See how high he can spit? [He lets a fountain of sand erupt.]

JH: Wow, that is a really forceful mountain. Can he do it again, I wonder?

J: Of course he can! [He shows me.]

JH: He can do it again and again, just as he likes. Isn't that some mountain!

[J repeats the eruptions.]

JH: But what about those animals down there?

J: Bad luck to them . . . because . . . they will all be flooded, all dead.

JH: But they don't know that yet. They stand there and perhaps they do not know what will happen to them.

J: Of course they don't know. This is a real volcano, can't you see? And now . . . something is going to happen . . . [He keeps us in suspense, while he stirs his finger in the crater of the volcano.]

JH: It must be very scary for them to stand there, not knowing when something terrible will happen.

J: No, it all happens very sudden, you know. [Suddenly, Jimmy lets the volcano erupt. The animals are completely covered with sand.] There, you see, there, all dead, under the lava.

JH: They are all under the lava, they couldn't prepare themselves, it just happened. It must be difficult for animals and people to live near such a volcano and never feel safe, never know when something will happen.

In this and similar conversations we covertly talked about Jimmy's own tantrums and rages and how these affected the people around him. However, as is characteristic of imagery interaction play therapy, I took care not to interpret this directly to Jimmy. It is our experience that many children stop expressing themselves so freely, once they have to acknowledge that these feelings or actions are, in fact, their own. So long as this remains tacitly understood, imaginative expression and the therapeutic work done through play stays fluent.

Gradually, the mountain theme changed again. From session 15 on, while constructing the mountain at the start of the play hour, more aesthetic aspects crept in. It became a most beautiful mountain, a volcano made by an artist, a masterpiece. It also was not allowed to erupt so suddenly any longer and the fire now could be extinguished with sand. At the same time, it seemed that some of Jimmy's rage inside began to abate and to find more acceptable paths. He still could become very angry, but now this was usually traceable to a real cause.

Starting at session 19, while Jimmy still kept most of his play in the sand tray, the mountain theme changed again. It now became a sand fort, with many corridors, open and secret, in it. Every session he took a lot of time building up this fort and placing toy soldiers on all sides. Usually, after finishing the building, all of the soldiers shot at one another indiscriminately and ended up dead. I commented that it must be difficult for those soldiers, because they never knew who would shoot them. Sadly, Jimmy told me: "They fight for peace." I answered: "It must be a very difficult peace to attain, if they have to fight so hard for it." Jimmy agreed with this statement.

This new fight again escalated, until in session 23 even the dinosaurs got involved again and destroyed everything in the sand tray. When he ended this play hour by fiercely shooting around with the toy pistol, it seemed he had reached rock bottom. Nobody and nothing remained standing. These are difficult moments for any therapist. However, I was sure this play was not just destructive, but meaningful as a fighting process.

Therefore, I tried to play with him throughout the destruction process. Jimmy did not allow me to do so. But he seemed to like it when I stayed near him and made some subdued fighting noises. His whole world seemed to be just destruction and I wanted to share this as much as I could. Still, one other positive note remained: for the first time he asked me to help him (placing the caps in the pistol). As his play partner, I naturally did so.

What could this play fight mean in terms of Jimmy's experience? On the one hand, it could be related to the fights between the family members or to his conflict with Brian. On the other hand, it could also refer to his own inner conflicts. Because of the intensity of his expression, I tended toward the last possibility, that in this play he expressed his own conflicting feelings about himself and (secondary) toward all family members. I did not bring this up during the session, since, again, it is one of the tenets of imagery interaction play therapy that life themes can be played out and do not need to be talked about. However, interpreting the play themes for myself is important because it helps me prepare my interventions.

The fight theme remained central for seven more long sessions, with lasting intensity. Jimmy did not give me much chance to intervene. At first, as stated above, he could only just stand my presence in this play. Gradually, I tried to verbalize a bit more, which he accepted. However, as soon as I tried to take an active part, he said: "No, you just sit there and look." Again and again, all participants in a fight were killed and then destroyed. Once or twice, I suggested that perhaps, if they should start working together, some soldiers or animals might have a better chance to keep alive and attain a real peace. But although Jimmy admitted that "this might be a good idea," it did not happen; "they keep on acting like crazy." Evidently, although he could now rationally admit that there could be alternative ways of feeling and interacting, he was not ready yet emotionally to try these out.

In session 30, however, the first change became visible. After the usual fight, with everyone dead and destroyed by the dinosaurs, Jimmy announced, "The workmen came to make a new mountain." That new mountain was at first to remain "empty and quiet." At the same time, the indiscriminate shooting became more of a fight between two parties. This was the first sign that a new, alternative (play) world might be in the offing.

This positive change may have come a bit too fast for Jimmy. In session 31, the no-through-way tunnel motif from the starting sessions returned. Again, he built a mountain tunnel with many traffic signs around it and with all entrances closed. I remarked on this recurrence of the mountain: "It's a long time since there was such a mountain here where nobody could go in or out or through." Jimmy acknowledged this with a brief "Mmm." He just went on with his mountain but accepted that I helped him smoothing its surface.

In session 32, he rebuilt the fighting fort. But from that session on, two or even four soldiers remained alive after the fight and started to build a new world. The conflict, whatever it was, was not quite over yet, but something constructive could start now from the ashes, even though in this new world there were as yet no people. In this period, too, he began to accept that I join in more actively in his play. He even, once or twice, asked me to take the part of one of the parties in the conflict.

Whenever I play a part myself (either by choice or by the child's order), I always ask the child for directions: "How am I to play this?" This is especially important in a fight, where I might easily become an adversary to the child. Following Jimmy's directions, my party always lost. Each time, I showed regret at the loss by my party who still were so weak, but I also loudly proclaimed my admiration for the other (Jimmy's) side for their strength and braveness.

In session 36, another constructive change occurred: the mountain now became a place for people to live. With care, Jimmy built a small house and dug a well for the family that would come to live there. He let me help him do this and together we speculated about what kind of people they would be. Here, too, it was difficult to know what exactly this family and this house meant to him. Did it mean that Jimmy could live better with himself? Or did it refer to living with his family? Perhaps a bit of both, although my own guess, again, would be that Jimmy's feelings about himself were central. However, in such cases where the interpretation is not quite clear, I find the play format particularly helpful. Whatever may be their more specific meaning, I can keep talking about the (play) house and the (play) family, I can join in and can verbalize whatever I see happen. In this way I remain quite near my child client, even though I do not understand exactly what he or she means.

But Jimmy's new world was not quite sure yet. Once he said, "It looks like being destructed by a flood." In my intervention, I tried to incorporate the different interpretations of "the family" and "the house" just discussed: "Oh dear, they had just settled a bit, and now perhaps a flood is coming. Well, they certainly hope that will not happen. They have worked so hard, they really need a bit of peace and quiet now." Jimmy grinned and left it at that. During the next sessions, this small new world gradually expanded, remaining relatively peaceful. There were some threats from outside, but these "came to nothing."

Interviews with Ellen During the Working-Through Phase

During these months, I gradually reduced the interviews with Ellen, at first still weekly, to once in two weeks. A lot of things happened. Most importantly, the family was allocated a row house with a small garden in a newly built neighborhood. It was a great relief to move there from the small apartment they had occupied for the previous years. At the same time, it meant a lot of extra work for Ellen, which underlined that now she had to make decisions and order things on her own. At first, she felt this as a heavy responsibility, the more so since it was really difficult for her to make ends meet. But gradually, helped a bit by me, she also began to enjoy the fact that nobody could question or even countermand her decisions, something she had been rather used to since she had lived with her parents until her marriage. She also found that one of her brothers and some friends were quite ready to assist her with the actual moving. The children, too, looked forward to the move and to having a room of their own, which they were allowed to organize as they wanted, even if on a very limited budget.

You may wonder whether this move, which took place around session 18, was not a topic in my sessions with Jimmy. It was, but only a minor one. Almost every session, we spent a few minutes talking about daily occurrences, but although of course I was interested in what happened to the rest of the family at that time, this was not central to the therapeutic work Jimmy did in his play. His "new world" only started to appear months after the move and (although of course material surroundings influence a child) had quite a different meaning. The move as a "new start" was much more central to my work with Ellen, coupled as it was with her day-to-day handling of household and mothering tasks. It certainly helped her to feel more competent about herself in many other ways. By talking with me about these everyday occurrences (how to organize everything, the color of the curtains, and the placement of the stove), she gained more confidence in her relationship with me, so that her initial problem in feeling criticized diminished. She now became much better able to discuss her dealings with her son and daughter. In this phase of therapy, Ellen reported mainly problems with Mandy, who was very careless about her own room and her clothes and other belongings. Ellen said, "I want her to see for herself when something needs cleaning." Here, too, it became necessary for her to place herself in the other's position. No two people are the same, and what the one sees as slovenliness is no problem for the other. Moreover, things that are important to a mother may be of no interest to her children. I suggested to Ellen that she could not reasonably expect the children to remember to do things that were of no importance to them. She would need to make it her rule to regularly remind them. If she did not, this would only spoil the atmosphere without doing any good. On the other hand, if she wanted some help, she needed to find out what things *were* important to the children or what *they* liked to do. These tasks would be much easier accomplished by themselves.

A recurrent theme in our discussions during these months was

Ellen's problem in accepting negative feelings toward her and in herself. "I need everything and everyone to be nice. Why can we not just be positive instead of being angry?" Even though she hardly allowed this to herself, she felt often very angry with her children, with her ex-husband, and sometimes with others. This gave me an opportunity to relate her ideas about motherhood and about family life to her own upbringing. At first, characteristically, she told me that they were "an ideally happy family, with never an angry word." As I was used to with her by now, while further discussing different aspects of her home life, small cracks began to appear in that ideal image. She did not often visit her parents though they were both alive and lived not far away, because "they disapprove of what I do, of my working so much and being divorced and so on." It appeared there had been a lot of anger in her family, but never openly, always contained under a nice and smiling front.

Ellen even realized, after some time, that this might also have troubled her marriage; that she had been unable to admit the negative feelings that had gradually marred that relationship. The more she reflected on her marriage, the more she saw that her former husband's departure had not really been so sudden. "But that makes me all the more reluctant to start again. You can cause so much pain and I really am afraid of feeling that pain again. Just now, when I see someone who is interested in me, I am just plain rude. I do not want it."

In the course of this year of therapy, Ellen grew toward more awareness of herself as a worthwhile person, much better equipped to understand her children as persons separate from herself. She also reported a change in the atmosphere at home: less constrained, more relaxed, with more positive moments. At the same time, the negative sides were more clearly recognized, but these became livable.

As to Jimmy's referral problems, after a brief increase during the first months, these had noticeably decreased. Ellen reported that tantrums now occurred only occasionally, particularly in new or special situations, for example, on a holiday and during a firework display. Jimmy was less restless now, just as Ellen herself had found more moments for relaxation. Jimmy also adapted more to the family routines. There had been no repetition of the death wishes, and he was much easier for Ellen to talk with, less withdrawn in his own ideas. Since this change was reflected in Jimmy's play sessions, we decided to think about termination of treatment. Because of the intensity of the original problems, I suggested a gradual ending, with a decrease in session frequency over about four months, to begin in the new school year that would start in a month.

During this same period, I had infrequent contacts with Brian,

Jimmy's father, because he was often traveling and was only home on weekends. His relationship with Jimmy, which became more personal in character after the joint interview, developed without great problems. They had read the Gardner book together and found a lot of common points in it.

Jimmy's teacher showed herself very much interested, both in Jimmy as a person and in his therapy. She appreciated many things about him (e.g., his sense of humor) that made it easier for her to accept his sometimes still difficult behavior. She noticed he had trouble concentrating in the classroom, where children were mostly working on their own assignments and where, therefore, it was usually not very quiet. He liked to be more on his own, in the "silence room," and she allowed him to go there often. She also thought he was gradually making better progress in his work.

Premature Termination Phase: Sessions 39–47

Although at that point in time all conditions for a successful termination seemed fulfilled, this was not to be. When I first broached the subject of decreasing frequency with Jimmy himself, toward the end of the summer holidays, he reacted vehemently: "I do not want to come less often. That is not fair." I tried to find out what he felt was the unfairness, but he was unable to put that into words. Therefore, I concluded this might be an attempt to control the situation like he had done before he came to me and I decided to go through with my decision. In his first session under the new regime, he reverted to the old theme of killing everyone in sight. "They are all dead. Nobody stays alive, they have all lost and nobody has won."

In the next sessions, Jimmy was very much preoccupied by the Second World War and by Hitler. His new group at school was a combined one, half of the students being older children whose history lessons were about World War II. He listened to what they were doing while he was supposed to work on his own tasks. What he told me was rather confused, especially about there being no certainty about Hitler's suicide, so he might come back any moment. I then suggested we play the war. He wanted to play Hitler while he gave me the role of the conquered people. Gradually his play became confused as he changed roles and wanted to murder Hitler. Still, his main object was "freeing more countries," which to me meant that the positive side still prevailed.

In session 43, the war came again. First, Jimmy built a house. It had to be built high on a mountain, "because there will be floods." And then rather a funny detail, that reminded me of his mother: "We will give them some flowers on the table, that is nicer, even if it becomes war." Contrary to what I had become used to, he did not accept my help in any way; he had to do everything by himself. And then a fierce shooting began, mowing away everything in that small world he had built for himself. I could only verbalize this in a supportive way. I also verbalized that "even though the house was high on the mountain, it was not safe from the war."

Rather unexpectedly, after about four weeks in the new school year, I had an emergency call from his new teacher, Mark. Ellen had told him that treatment was almost at an end, whereas he, himself, thought that Jimmy was doing very badly. He was not concentrating at all and his grades were very low. Moreover, Mark, a young teacher highly thought of by Ellen, told me he feared there was much amiss in the family. He suggested Ellen might have an alcohol problem. He urgently asked me to come and see him. It did not seem right to exclude Ellen from this contact, so I suggested we organize a joint conference.

Before that date, I had one more appointment with Ellen. I told her about Mark's alarm and suddenly she began to cry. Everything had gone so well and she had been so grateful, but since the summer it seemed that everything was "falling apart." Mandy was becoming an "impossible adolescent," who had declared she did not want to live with her mother any more, but wanted to move over to her father's. Jimmy was back to his tantrums and she, herself, was "just nowhere."

There was one important point, however, that she had not told me about yet. Since some weeks, there was a new man in her life, Edwin. She had not mentioned this before, because it was still so very uncertain. They both were divorced and they wanted to be very careful and certainly not live together yet. That was the one ray of light in her life just now.

This change in the family's situation seemed to explain quite a lot with regard to the actual crisis. It reactivated, as it were, the problems they had known before. Their relationship with ex-husband and father had become problematic again because of the intrusion of this new friend and father figure, however much in the background. My decision to work toward termination meant one more separation to deal with, which had been just too much.

In one of the next sessions, Jimmy asked me whether I had met and talked to Edwin. I told him, no, because he was just Ellen's friend. Then he asked whether I had seen his dad lately, and I said, yes I had, because he was Jimmy's dad and would remain so. This seemed to calm him down a bit, which gave me an opportunity to verbalize and reflect his confused feelings about his father just now. This may seem to digress from the tenets of imagery interaction play therapy. However, this point was so clear from Jimmy's questions, that I did not feel any problem in bringing it out in the open.

He then chose to play with the dollhouse. This was a new choice for him and he had to be reassured first that it was quite in order for a boy to play with it. Then he said, "In that house, there lives an enemy." He threw small blocks as "hand grenades" toward the house. I verbalized how hard he tried to overcome the threatening enemy. But he repeatedly stated that the enemy was still not dead, that he (Jimmy) was unable to kill him. Clearly, in this play he expressed his anger at this new person in their lives. At the end of this session, he wanted to play a board game, another thing he had never done before. I wondered if this was an effort to reaffirm his relationship with me.

By now, it seemed that the termination decision had been premature or was at least outdated by all the new developments. But how to reverse that decision without losing out on what had been gained during the previous period? Honesty seemed, as usual, the best policy. I invited Ellen, Mandy, and Jimmy for a "family session." Even though Mandy did not come, it became a special hour. We talked about the last year and about the things that had changed for the better. We also talked about the new changes that seemed to make everything more difficult just now. Therefore, I suggested that it seemed a good idea to resume the once-weekly frequency of therapy, with Ellen coming every two weeks. I also told Jimmy that I now understood better why he had said "It is not fair." He nodded very seriously: "Yes, I told you so."

Next, mother and son talked about Edwin. Nudged on a bit by a previous discussion with me, Ellen made it clear to Jimmy that Edwin would not become his new dad; he already had a fine father, who would remain so always. This cleared the way for a more domestic discussion about the many chores in the house, which Jimmy tended to avoid as much as he could. However, he showed himself ready to help a bit more. Asked what chore appealed to him most, he decided he would do the vacuuming twice a week, plus clean up his own room once a week. This was solemnly written down as an agreement by which they both were to stand.

I wished to end this session on a somewhat lighter tone. The Christmas holiday was just starting and I would not see Jimmy and Ellen for some weeks. I also was curious about the quality of their relationship, which I felt had changed for the better during the previous year. Did they know each other better by now? To test this, I asked them whether they could name something the other especially liked. Fortunately, they could. They discussed these points cheerfully and went home in a positive mood.

A New Working-Through Phase: Sessions 48–69

After this joint session, therapy intensified again. However, I introduced one important change: during each session we talked for a little while about school and schoolwork, so that I could keep an eye on how he was progressing there. We also regularly evaluated his household tasks.

In the first sessions after resuming the once-weekly frequency, the full intensity of the previous play came back. The troops he first put down with great care were then slaughtered and nobody stayed alive. But there was also a new and interesting development. More and more, he directed aggressive play acts against himself. Calling himself Gentleman Jim (after a cowboy film he had seen), he used the one-way screen mirror to aim and shoot at his own image. I was not allowed to take part directly in this play, but I could sit beside him and look at his mirror image and talk to him in his role of Gentleman Jim. What he did was still clearly a form of imaginative play. He was not just shooting at himself, but at the image, at the role he played and in which many of his own characteristics were present. Therefore, it was evident that he was actually fighting himself, or, rather, those aspects of himself that bothered him. We talked quite a lot about Gentleman Jim and how he felt about standing there, looking so powerful and still being vulnerable. During session 53, he "really" shot Gentleman Jim, fell down on the floor, and let me bind his wounds. He seemed to enjoy this physical care, but immediately afterward bounced up again and repeated the whole process.

This theme came back in five more sessions. One of these sessions started very peacefully. Jimmy built a castle in which all the people had their own place. He then returned to the role of Gentleman Jim who walked around with his hands (on his pistols) in his pockets. Jimmy cried: "There, take cover, they're shooting!" For a moment he played two roles at the same time: the attacker and Gentleman Jim, himself. In the last role he fell down, shouted "I surrender, I surrender," rolled over, and then fired his pistol. I commented:

JH: Now he is not such a gentleman, more like a bad guy.

J: No no, he is a good guy.

JH: I don't think so. When you surrender and then shoot anyway, you are not a good guy.

J: There really are no laws when you are almost dead.

JH: Well, anyway, everybody had better be very careful and not just trust what someone says.

This brief fragment shows how much ground Jimmy had lost. Moreover, these fighting sessions were interspersed with sessions in which he did not play imaginatively at all. Instead, he chose Gardner's *Talking, Feeling, and Doing Game,* in which the emphasis was on his interaction with me. To me, this meant that although he still worked hard at himself, he was also feeling some resistance to this process.

Perhaps this was caused by his problems in school, which did not abate. Indeed, his teacher, Mark, became more and more negative about Jimmy and again suggested a special school. Since Jimmy's self-image with regard to his schoolwork was very low and since he never completed his tasks, we tried out a behavioral program during a few weeks. Mark would write down with him, every morning, what tasks he should do during that day and what would be the best order. For every task completed, he would get a compliment and a bonus point. For every five bonus points, he would receive 15 minutes free time, to do what he liked. Even though the program was developed in cooperation with both Jimmy and Mark, it was not successful. Later, Mark called me and said it was really against his and the school's philosophy to give so much guidance. In this school, children were supposed to work independently. He felt that a program such as this would increase Jimmy's dependence and would not lead to more autonomous behavior. In the meantime, he appeared to become increasingly irritated by Jimmy's lack of interest in the schoolwork and by his concentration problem. Moreover, Jimmy developed some bizarre behaviors (such as praying before going to gym class or bouncing up like a clown in the middle of a lesson), which gave ever more fuel to Mark's low opinion.

Just before Easter, the relationship between Jimmy and Mark reached an all-time low when Jimmy took some money from Mark's desk and was punished for this in front of the whole class. Jimmy then refused to go to school again. Ellen, though shocked by the theft of money and having punished Jimmy herself for it, was also indignant about the way Mark had handled the situation. Since she found both Mark and the headmaster of the school against her when she protested, she asked me to help her find another school for Jimmy. Although we usually try to mediate and find a joint way out of the problems, I myself despaired by now of a better cooperation. Since in the next school year his group would stay on with Mark, I decided that a school change, although always an upheaval, might be preferable.

Fortunately, we were able to find another school, with a much more structured regime and no combined groups, where the principal and the teachers were willing to take the risk. This, by the way, was a school with a strong mainstreaming philosophy, providing a lot of individual guidance. Jimmy cried when he heard about the school change, afraid as he was to lose the few friends he had. However, Ellen and I discussed with him that the regime of his present school really was not suited to him, that they expected an attitude and concentration to work that he could not attain.

Eventually, Jimmy resigned himself to the change. And although this was not easy for him, it still brought relief. In the next sessions (from session 63 on), I saw a gradual return to more differentiated and less self-directed imaginative play. More variety in his play themes and in the use of toys became apparent. The wars he waged were now more balanced, as they had been at the end of the first working-through phase.

In one rather special session, he chose to paint, quite a new activity for Jimmy. At first it was difficult to find out exactly what he put on the paper. It was a strange figure: "a devil." Since he seemed to identify strongly with the devil on his paper, for once I left the strict play format I adhered to in his sessions and interpreted this directly to him: "This seems like the devil you sometimes feel in yourself." Jimmy did not deny this, but did not otherwise react. Therefore, I felt it was more profitable to return to the imaginative level and talk about the devil he had drawn, what that devil felt or would do. To this, he did respond: "That devil sometimes wanted to kill everyone. But then again, sometimes he felt sorry for those people."

Ellen, strengthened by her decision to put Jimmy in the new school, slowly felt her competence return. This also made her more capable to deal with Mandy's adolescent rebelliousness. Her new relationship with Edwin also had a positive influence on her self-experience. Fortunately, after the first shock, both children started to appreciate Edwin more realistically and to give him a (limited) place in their lives. Together we thought it a good idea to continue with the present frequency of sessions until after Jimmy should feel settled in the new school, before starting a new termination phase. Moreover, I felt that this time Jimmy himself should be an active partner in making that decision.

When I told him about this, he answered, "That's good." Then he asked me about another child he had met in the waiting room for the last few weeks: "Such a small boy, does he also come to play? What is wrong with him?" Of course, this question was in fact an indirect way of asking about himself: why had he come here? I decided that by now he had grown enough to tackle this question more directly and we discussed the reasons for his first coming here (by now almost two years ago). He then said: "Yes, I am not so angry any more, just sometimes at Mandy. But she is difficult, you know. But not at Mom, I help her much more. And only a little at Dad, when he goes away by himself." I supported him in this and said: "Last year when I said we would end your playing here, you were angry at me too. And you know, I think you were right. It really was too early. I should have listened better to you. So this time I said to myself: *I* think Jimmy is much better and we need perhaps not go on for very much longer. But there are new things coming to Jimmy, which may be difficult. So *he* must tell me when the time is there, first to go to once every two weeks, and then when we can say goodbye." Jimmy listened attentively and said: "I think it will not be very long." I asked him to let me know.

Second Termination Phase: Sessions 70–77

Even though the second working-through phase was difficult, we attacked some essential problems. Jimmy's separation problem, reactivated by my decision to terminate, had become much clearer (goal 4). By now, he was better able to cope with new problems by himself and to take responsibility for his actions (goal 5). During the first weeks in the new school he also made a good adjustment. At home, the problems had already decreased (goal 6). Thus, a more positive termination now became possible. Indeed, after about four sessions in the new school year (in session 70), Jimmy himself announced that now was the time to reduce frequency and we decided to go on once every two weeks until the Christmas holiday.

Fortunately, in this last phase, nothing dramatic happened. More and more, we talked about other things besides play. Jimmy told me about his new school, where he settled down well and had already found a friend. His new teacher (an experienced and sympathetic woman) was positive too. Her empathic attitude can best be illustrated by what she told me about Jimmy's Monday mornings: "I can always see when he has been to his father during the weekend. On those Mondays, he is a bit grumpy and does not work well. So I leave him a bit, and do not ask too much of him, but give him an assignment he likes to do. And then, in the afternoon, he usually is all there again."

RESULTS AND FOLLOW-UP

In most of my therapies, particularly when they are terminated on positive grounds, the last session is a bit more festive. We may have a drink together and I usually let the child choose anything special he or she would like to do. Jimmy wanted to walk with me through town. And so we did. Coming back, he gave me a small green plant he had bought for me and admonished me to take good care of it. Of course I promised to take very good care of it. He then took a cheerful leave and went home with his mother, with whom I had had my last interview the week before. Since then, we have exchanged Christmas cards, and at the end of the school year I had a brief telephone conversation with Ellen who told me they were still doing well.

DISCUSSION

I have not concealed my own thoughts and feelings about this therapy throughout the previous description. It will have become clear that Jimmy was not an easy client, but that the rapport between him, his mother, and me helped a lot in quickly establishing a relationship and also helped us through the difficult second year. However, I would like to briefly reflect on why this therapy almost failed. One important point was my inattentiveness to Jimmy's reaction when I first broached the subject of termination. Afterward, I felt I should have listened better to him. Didn't I know him well enough to recognize that what he said was no pretext just to keep me there without any real cause? Probably, as adults, even though experienced in working with children, we still tend to think our own judgment of better quality than that of a child. Perhaps in general we should act more upon what the child clients themselves say.

The second problem was Jimmy's relationship to his male teacher. I am almost sure I have missed something vital in what went on between them, which might explain the deterioration of both their relationship and Jimmy's schoolwork. Afterward, I reflected that possibly Jimmy had more problems in relating to men than to women. Admittedly, he had many conflicts with his mother, but still their relationship had a firm base. To me, he related well, as he also did to his first and his last teacher, all women. Maybe I should have foreseen this problem: that he found it almost impossible to admit another man (than his father) in his life. Particularly so at that specific time, when Ellen's boyfriend had just entered the scene (which, of course, I did not know about until later). In that case, I might have noticed the teacher's growing irritability and Jimmy's ways of throwing coals on that fire much earlier in the process. Had I been more alert, maybe something could have been done to prevent the change of school. However that may be, the new school seemed well geared to take care of a somewhat difficult child like Jimmy. In our last contact, Ellen reported that his grades were fine and that he looked forward to having a male teacher in the next school year.

The third point I should have paid more attention to was what it meant to Jimmy, with his specific separation problem, to separate from his therapist. Of course, I am always alert that suggesting a possible end to therapy may activate or reactivate many problems, and particularly so in the case of children with separation as their referral problem. Still, I rather casually assumed that Jimmy would react about the same as other children. Maybe one of the messages of this case is: However long your experience, never think you have seen all sorts of problems. Each child will still be different.

REFERENCES

Harinck, F. J. H., and Hellendoorn, J. (1987). *Therapeutisch Spel: Process En Interactie (Therapeutic Play: Process and Interaction)*. Lisse, Netherlands: Swets & Zeitlinger.
Harinck, F. J. H., and Loeven, L. (1985). Therapeut-ervaringen met beeldcommunicatieve speltherapie (Therapist experiences with imagery interaction play therapy). In *Therapie, Kind en Spel (Therapy, Child and Play)*. ed. J. Hellendoorn, pp. 239-273. Deventer, Netherlands: Van Loghum Slaterus.
Hellendoorn, J. (1988). Imaginative play technique in psychotherapy with children. In *Innovative Interventions in Child and Adolescent Therapy*, ed. C. E. Schaefer, pp. 43-67. New York: Wiley.
Langeveld, M. J. (1955). Bevrijding door beeldcommunicatie (Freedom through imagery interaction). *Nederlands Tijdschrift voor de Psychologie* 10:433-455.
_____ (1964). De mens en de beelden (Man and his images). *Nederlands Tijdschrift voor de Psychologie* 19:89-110.
Mook, B. (1989). Play and play therapy. *Journal of Learning about Learning* 1:5-20.
Van der Kooij, R., and Hellendoorn, J. (1985). *Play, Play Therapy, Play Research*. Berwyn, PA: Swets North America.
Vermeer, E. A. A. (1973). Projectieve methoden bij pedagogische advies-en hulpverlening (Projective methods in child counseling and therapy). In *Pedagogiek in ontwikkeling (Developing Pedagogy)*, ed. T. Bolleman, pp. 149-170. Tilburg, Netherlands: Zwijsen.

5

The King of Rock and Roll: An Application of Adlerian Play Therapy

Terry Kottman, PH.D.

The wailing from the waiting room turned out to be a 7- or 8-year-old boy, standing on a chair, playing "air guitar," and crooning a song. As the song wound down, he jumped off of the chair, walked up to me, and said, "Hi, I'm Rex, the King of Rock and Roll, and I'm not going to answer any bullshit questions that bitch is going to ask me!!!"

In Adlerian play therapy, the concepts and strategies of Individual Psychology combine with the basic approach of play therapy to create a unique procedure for helping children who are experiencing interpersonal and intrapsychic difficulties (Kottman 1987, Kottman and Warlick 1989, 1990). To help children better understand their thoughts, feelings, and behaviors, Adlerian play therapists serve as equal partners in the play therapy process. By conceptualizing children in terms of Adlerian personality theory, play therapists can creatively choose strategies designed to help individual clients catch themselves at self-defeating behaviors; become more cognizant of their own control over ideas, emotions, attitudes, and actions; and develop confidence in their ability to make wise decisions and cope successfully with life's problems (Ansbacher 1983, Kottman 1987, Kottman and Warlick, 1989, 1990, Manaster and Corsini 1982, Sweeney 1981).

INTRODUCTION TO ADLERIAN THEORY

Individual Psychology (also know as Adlerian psychology) grew from the ideas developed by Alfred Adler in the early decades of the

133

twentieth century. Adler's theory of human personality and development was proactive and positive. He believed that people are creative,
unique, and self-determining. According to Adlerian theory, people are
born with a predisposition toward making connections with other
people, moving toward a sense of belongingness in the community of
human beings. He called this concept "social interest" (Ansbacher and
Ansbacher 1956). Because infants and children are relatively weak and
powerless, they feel an inherent lack, a sense of inferiority. Adler
believed that people spend their lives trying to overcome these feelings
of inadequacy and inferiority (Dinkmeyer et al. 1987).

As a child develops, he or she observes and makes subjective
interpretations of other people's actions and reactions. The child decides
upon ways to belong and to gain significance in relationships with other
people. Based on these perceptions about how he or she gains significance with others, the child begins to formulate a kind of private logic
upon which to base a life-style (Adler 1930, Ansbacher and Ansbacher
1956). Life-style is the "unity in each individual—in his thinking, feeling,
acting, in his so-called conscious and unconscious, in every expression
of his personality" (Ansbacher and Ansbacher 1956, p. 175). A person's
life-style is his or her characteristic way of operating in the social field,
based on the collection of subjective convictions about self, others, and
the world (Griffith and Powers 1984). Because children are excellent
observers, but frequently make faulty interpretations, sometimes the
beliefs underlying their developing life-styles are "mistaken" (Dreikurs
and Soltz 1964).

Maladjustment grows from mistaken concepts about self, others, and
the world. A maladjusted person uses "private logic" and acts "as if"
these mistaken convictions were true. Feelings of inferiority can also
contribute to psychological and/or behavioral difficulties. Adlerians
define maladjustment as discouragement or a lack of courage in dealing
with life's problems (Ansbacher and Ansbacher 1956).

There are four basic goals in Adlerian therapy: (a) build an egalitarian
relationship with the client; (b) develop an understanding of the client's
private logic, life-style, and goals; (c) assist the client to gain insight into
his or her life-style, mistaken beliefs, faulty goals, and self-defeating
behavior; and (d) help the client develop the courage to consider
alternative methods of coping with difficult situations and begin to learn
new skills for interacting with others (Dinkmeyer and Dinkmeyer 1983).
The attainment of each of these goals constitutes a phase in the process
of Adlerian therapy. In Adlerian play therapy, the play therapist uses
the play therapy process to work toward the four basic goals.

Adlerians make several assumptions about human behavior and

human personality. Each of the following sections describes one of the basic tenets of Individual Psychology and its application and importance in Adlerian play therapy.

All Human Behavior is Purposive

Adlerians believe that all human behavior is directed toward goals, that people are constantly striving toward some purpose (Dinkmeyer and Dinkmeyer 1983). To understand and change human behavior, the Adlerian counselor must determine what clients are trying to accomplish with their behavior, either in the real world or in their minds (Thompson and Rudolph 1988). To an Adlerian, the cause of the behavior is irrelevant—it cannot be changed. What can change are people's purposes. However, if clients' behaviors are "working" for them, if they are attaining their goals, then behavior will not change. It is the counselor's job to help clients recognize their purposes and reexamine whether they wish to continue to pursue them. The counselor may also want to work with other people in clients' environments, in order to reduce the likelihood that inappropriate behavior or attitudes continue to move them toward their ultimate purposes.

Children who are having difficulty in coping with life's problems are usually striving toward one of four goals: attention, power, revenge, or inadequacy/withdrawal (Dreikurs and Soltz 1964, Lowe 1971). Although they can switch from one goal to another, most children have one predominant purpose that is the focus of their efforts. In some cases, children will switch goals depending on the setting and the other people in the environment. In play therapy, Adlerians use observation of play, conversations with children, their parents, and their teachers, and their own personal reactions to determine children's goals.

The majority of the children I have worked with in play therapy, including Rex, the King of Rock and Roll, have been striving toward the goal of power. Children who seek power believe that the only way they can feel safe and belong is through being in control—of themselves and/or of others (Dreikurs and Soltz 1964). Their behavior can include arguing, fighting, bullying, refusing to do chores or school work, passive-aggression, disobedience, stubbornness, deliberate forgetfulness, or any other form of power struggle. When other people encounter these children, they feel angry and challenged. Upon being corrected or redirected, power-seeking children will increase their bid for control by escalating their negative behaviors.

In my experience, there are typically three kinds of situations that contribute to children being motivated by power. There are children who have too much control, children who have too little control, and children who live in situations in which it appears that no one has any control. I try to understand these circumstances in working with children in Adlerian play therapy. While my ultimate goal with all three categories of power-motivated children is the equal sharing of power in the relationship, my initial approach will vary. The balance of power factor will also have an impact on the parenting suggestions I make to parents in our consultations.

Human Beings Want to Belong and Their Behavior Must be Examined in its Social Context

All people seek to belong, to be a part of a group (Dinkmeyer and Dinkmeyer 1983). In order to belong, they seek out ways of gaining significance within their social context. If they cannot determine methods of gaining significance in constructive, useful ways, they will employ techniques for belonging in destructive, useless ways. The first group that children want to belong to is their families. They look around the family—at the family atmosphere, the family constellation, the family values—and analyze what they can do to stand out and be important. Then they try out the resultant behaviors and attitudes for a time, observe the reaction of the family system, and reevaluate. If the behaviors and attitudes gain them some level of significance, be it positive or negative, they may decide that this is their ticket to belonging. During this process, they are also deciding on many of the basic convictions about self, others, and the world that constitute their life-styles.

Because of this social-embeddedness, it is important that Adlerian play therapists always consider children's behavior in the context of their social milieus. To gain a complete understanding of their clients, they must observe children in their interactions in all social contexts or provide children with the means for "playing out" those social contexts during their sessions.

Another aspect of the systemic nature of Adlerian play therapy is the inclusion of parents and other family members in the play therapy process. If possible, the Adlerian play therapy will try to incorporate family sessions and parent consultations as an integral part of play therapy. In these sessions, the play therapist uses family members as sources of information and perceptions about the client, engages family

ge process designed to support any changes
therapy, and teaches new skills to family
pist may teach communication strategies,
ethods, and other skills that can help family
s of interacting and building cooperative

ngs Can Learn Social Interest

health and potential for growth and positive
l of social interest (Ansbacher and Ansbacher
sense of connectedness with other human
the individual to the members of his or her
to all the people and creatures of the world
nd Ansbacher 1956). A person with adequate
st character traits such as identification and
ng behaviors such as cooperation and contri-
27). "Social interest is not inborn but it is an
has to be consciously developed" (Adler 1929,
p. 31). Children begin to learn social interest from their parents and
other family members, who must then teach them to make connections
to siblings, peers, teachers, and others (Manaster and Corsini 1982).

In play therapy, the Adlerian counselor uses social interest in three
different ways: (a) as a therapy goal with children, (b) as a way of
measuring children's progress, and (c) as a element in parent skills
training (Kottman, in press). Many of the children who are referred to
play therapy have relatively low levels of social interest. They have not
learned a sense of connectedness with people, and consequently they
do not manifest sufficient ability to identify, empathize, or cooperate
with others. One goal in play therapy is to help children learn to value
other people. The play therapist begins this process by building a
personal relationship with clients. Later in the process, the play therapist expands this social interest by introducing siblings or other children
to share the play therapy process.

In deciding whether a client has made significant improvement, one
of the elements an Adlerian play therapist examines is social interest. At
the beginning of play therapy, the play is frequently characterized by
egocentric, insular themes, with the child showing little interest in
making an emotional connection with the play therapist or anyone else.
As the child grows and changes, the play therapist looks for signs that
the child is learning to value interpersonal relationships and is developing an enhanced desire to cooperate with others.

Because the play therapist is not meant to serve as a surrogate parent, it is important to shift the primary burden of teaching social interest to the child's parent(s). In parent consultation sessions, the Adlerian play therapist helps the child's parent(s) learn how to foster the parent–child attachment. The parent(s) also must learn to encourage the child to cooperate and identify with others, including siblings, relatives, peers, teachers, and neighbors.

Human Personality has a Unity and Human Beings Must Be Viewed Holistically

"The doctrine of the unity of the personality gave Individual Psychology its name. This name, which is so often misunderstood, is derived from the Latin word *individuum*, which literally means 'undivided,' 'indivisible'" (Dreikurs 1953, p. 56). Adlerians believe that every person's personality has an underlying coherence, an order that is equal to more than the sum of the parts (Griffith and Powers 1984). Every facet of the personality fits together into a unique whole, all having equal significance. According to this holistic view, each person is an organic unit in which thoughts, feelings, and actions are all self-consistent behaviors (Griffith and Powers 1984) that are equally important and occur simultaneously.

Because Adlerians view personality as indivisible, they consider all aspects of the human being as equally important and worthy of investigation in the therapeutic process. The play therapist looks for both assets and liabilities in every facet of the child's personality. The intellectual, physical, emotional, spiritual, and interpersonal components of each child contribute to the total picture of the child. The play therapist tries to include and invoke all of these elements of each child in the play therapy process.

In Adlerian play therapy, the holistic view of children's personalities also insures that the play therapist gives equal weight to thoughts, feelings, and actions. In both assessment and intervention, the play therapist considers all three of these components of behavior.

Stages of Adlerian Play Therapy

There are four overlapping stages in Adlerian play therapy: (a) building the relationship with the child, (b) investigating the child's life-style, (c) helping the child gain insight into life-style, and (d) reorientation/

reeducation. During the first stage of Adlerian play therapy, the primary goal of the process is building an egalitarian relationship with the client. During the first session, I try to set the parameters for the equal nature of the relationship by explaining all of the logistical information about the play therapy process, just as I explain to an adult about the therapy process. I ask the child what his or her parent has said about the reason for coming to play therapy. Many times parents, feeling overwhelmed by the problems they are experiencing, may convey negative connotations about coming to play therapy. Since children tend to incorporate negative messages such as these into their life-styles, I want to have an opportunity to reframe the presenting problem in a way that is more hopeful and acknowledges their uniqueness and creativity and my joy in having the privilege of working with them (Kottman, in press).

In building the relationship, I also use tracking, reflection of feelings, restatement of content, tentative hypotheses, encouraging, and questioning strategies. I use a four-step limit-setting procedure that engages the child in decision-making so that he or she will have input into the limits set and the consequences for choosing to violate the limits. I actively interact with the child, using role playing and playing to engage the child and to build rapport (Kottman, in press, Kottman and Warlick 1989).

During the relationship phase of play therapy, the Adlerian play therapy uses the parent consultation time to begin building a partnership with the parent(s). It is important for the parent to feel heard and understood. While it may not be appropriate for the play therapist to agree with the parenting strategies the parent(s) have used up to this point, it is important to validate feelings and to look for positive aspects of the parent–child relationship.

The second stage of Adlerian play therapy involves gathering information so that the play therapist can get a clear picture of how the child's private logic and basic convictions combine to form his or her life-style. To gain understanding of these aspects of the child's world view and behavior patterns, the play therapist explores the goals of behavior, family atmosphere, and family constellation (Kottman in press, Kottman and Warlick 1989). The Adlerian play therapist may also solicit the child's early recollections to help in the life style investigation (Kottman and Johnson in press).

To identify the child's primary goal of behavior, Adlerian play therapists examine children's behavior, the reactions and feelings of other people who encounter those children, and children's responses to correction. They watch the child's actions in the playroom and in the waiting room. Sometimes, they even visit the child's school and observe his or her actions in the classroom and on the play ground. Other sources of information about the child's goals of behavior are parents, siblings, teachers, and peers. Play therapists must also monitor their own reactions to the child in the course of their interactions. These personal feelings will be their most important barometer in forming hypotheses about the child's goal of behavior.

Family atmosphere is another important element in conceptualizing the child. The atmosphere in the family depends on the parents' attitudes toward discipline, their parenting strategies, their relationship with each other, and their own life-styles and basic convictions (Dewey 1971). Family atmosphere affects the child's self-concept, beliefs about others, behavior patterns, and ways of gaining significance. There are several ways to investigate family atmosphere in play therapy: (a) observe the child playing with the doll house, the puppets, and the kitchen utensils; (b) observe the interaction in the waiting room and in the play room among family members; (c) ask the child or the parent(s) questions about discipline patterns and other factors (Dinkmeyer 1977); (d) ask the child to draw family portraits and describe the interaction among family members (Knoff and Prout 1985, Kottman in press).

As each child is born into a family, he or she claims a psychological position in the family constellation (Pepper 1979). Each birth-order position has certain characteristic assets and liabilities. The Adlerian play therapist investigates the child's psychological position in order to help find ways to capitalize on the child's assets and help overcome his or her liabilities. Methods for exploring the family constellation include asking the parent(s) or child questions about the actual birth order and about psychological traits of each child and using child-drawn family pictures and questioning strategies to explore personality characteristics (Knoff and Prout 1985, Kottman, in press).

The Adlerian play therapist can also explore the child's recollections. Adler believed that each person selectively remembers events that represent his or her world view (Ansbacher and Ansbacher 1956). Although not all children can give the kind of detailed information necessary to form a complete picture based on early recollections, a series of these early memories can sometimes help the play therapist understand basic convictions, private logic, and life-style. The play therapist can either ask the child to "tell me something that happened when you were little," or to draw pictures of early recollections (Borden 1982, Nelson 1986). As the play therapist gradually gathers six to ten early recollections, patterns and themes emerge that will help in the understanding of the child's life-style (Kottman, in press).

During parent consultation in the second phase, the Adlerian play therapist gathers information from the parent(s). This information will include the parental perspective on goals of behavior, family atmosphere, and family constellation. The play therapist also explores the family of origin of the parent(s) and what they learned about parenting and about themselves, others, and the world in growing up. This information helps the play therapist formulate ways to teach parenting skills to the parent(s) and to determine how the personal issues of the parent(s) are interfering with the interactional processes in the family.

Based on the information gathered in the second phase of the play therapy, the play therapist begins to formulate working hypotheses about the child's private logic, basic convictions, and life-style. In the third phase of the play therapy, the Adlerian play therapist begins to share these hypotheses in order to help the child gain insight into his or her underlying patterns in thought, feelings, and action. In the process of helping the child grow in self-understanding, the play therapist uses tentative hypotheses or guesses, metaphors, art work, bibliotherapy, humor, "spitting in the soup," pointing out parallels between what happens in the playroom and what happens in the child's other relationships, and other techniques. In this phase of the therapy, the Adlerian play therapist is "technically eclectic," choosing intervention strategies based on the individual child and his or her parent(s).

In the third phase of Adlerian play therapy, the play therapist uses parent consultations to (a) help parent(s) gain an understanding of the child's private logic, basic convictions, and life-style; (b) help the parent(s) gain an understanding of how their own private logic, basic convictions, and life-style may have an impact on their parenting effectiveness; and (c) teach parenting skills. During this process, the play therapist supports the parent(s) in trying new ways of perceiving and interacting with the child and encourages changes in attitudes and behaviors.

The fourth phase of Adlerian play therapy is the reorientation/ reeducation phase. During this time, the play therapist helps the child gain the skills needed to effect any changes the child has decided to make in beliefs, attitudes, feelings, and actions. The play therapist's role during this phase is to use the play process to help the child learn and practice alternative behaviors. This may involve helping the child engage in problem solving, teaching, role playing, storytelling, and other counseling strategies.

The parent consultation component of the fourth phase involves helping the parent(s) consistently carry out changes in their approach to themselves and the parenting process. The parent(s) usually need support in establishing democratic discipline procedures and encouragement in maintaining the personal and interpersonal growth they have achieved. Toward the end of the play therapy, I usually have the parent(s) and child spend time in the playroom together, working on improving their relationship and communication skills.

Historical Context of Adlerian Play Therapy

Although Adler, Dreikurs, Dinkmeyer, and others worked with children from an Adlerian framework, they did not use play therapy techniques. Yura and Galassi (1974) and Nystul (1980) wrote articles suggesting play therapy techniques could be appropriate interventions for Adlerians. However, neither of these manuscripts gave detailed information about how to specifically go about using an Adlerian orientation in a play therapy setting with a child.

When I was a doctoral student I began reading every article I could find on play therapy and on strategies for applying Adlerian techniques with children, determined to formulate a method for combining the two. I took what I was learning into my play therapy sessions with children and Adlerian play therapy began to evolve. With help from my colleagues, students, and clients, I have refined the method over the years (Kottman and Johnson in press, Kottman and Stiles 1990, Kottman and Warlick 1989, 1990).

PRESENTING PROBLEM AND BACKGROUND DATA

When I first met Rex, the King of Rock and Roll, I was the director of a community outreach mental health clinic located on a university campus in the southwest region of the United States. The clinic provided counseling services for children from the community and their families. We also did educational and psychological assessments for children and served as a practicum and internship site for graduate students.

One morning, I was sitting in my office doing paperwork when I heard a long squealing wail in the waiting room of the clinic. I walked over to the door of my office and peered into the waiting room. There, standing on one of the chairs, was a small, 7- or 8-year-old boy with shoulder length black hair and a "tail" that went down to the middle of his back, playing "air guitar" and crooning the words to a song I did not recognize. Looking straight at me, he continued to "play" and sing for another 2 or 3 minutes. As the song seemed to wind down, he jumped off the chair, walked over to the door of my office, and said, "Hey, lady, I'm Rex, the King of Rock and Roll and I'm not going to answer any bullshit questions that bitch is going to ask me!!!" He was pointing to one of the doctoral interns who was walking down the hall, having interviewed his aunt as part of the psychological testing provided by the clinic. Not knowing what was going on, I simply reflected his feelings and acknowledged that we could not force him to do anything that he did not want to do. He smiled triumphantly and strutted down the hall with the doctoral student.

During our weekly staffing, I discovered that Lila Court, Rex's aunt, had brought him for testing because, although he appeared to be extremely intelligent, he was failing second grade. He refused to do most of the work, telling his teacher in no uncertain terms that it was not worth his trouble. He spent most of his time in school drawing pictures of guitars, amplifiers, and other musical equipment, refusing to participate in academic, social, and physical activities in his classroom. He also refused to participate in music or art experiences, saying that they were "for babies and dweebs, not for cool dudes, like me." Rex was alternately verbally abusive and kind and helpful to his teacher and the other children. His teacher's report to the testing team noted that she had not been able to discern any type of pattern in this erratic behavior.

Lila reported that she had noticed a similar mixture of behaviors and attitudes at home with her. She said, "It's kind of like that little girl in that poem. When he's good, he's very, very good and when he's bad, he's HORRID." Rex sometimes helped his aunt around the house without being asked, but when she requested help, he almost always refused and became verbally abusive toward her. When he did not get his way, he had "terrible temper tantrums, screaming and cussing at me." Lila was disturbed by this type of behavior, but she was even more upset by the possibility that Rex might not be promoted to third grade.

In gathering family information, the doctoral intern had found that Rex was an only child and that he lived with his aunt in a lower middle class neighborhood. Lila was 34 years old and had never been married. Lila's only sibling, Danny, was Rex's father, and he had legal custody of Rex. According to Lila's account, Danny was the lead singer of a modestly successful rock group. Jeannie, Rex's mother, had been a "roadie" with Danny's band. Jeannie had gotten pregnant during a brief relationship with Danny, but Danny had refused to marry her. When Rex was several months old, Jeannie had arrived at Lila's house and announced that Lila would "make a much better mother than she would and so she could raise the kid." Neither Danny nor Lila had seen Jeannie or heard anything from her since.

The morning Jeannie dropped Rex off at her house, Lila called Danny and asked him what he wanted her to do with the baby. Danny had informed Lila that she would need to take care of Rex so that Danny could pursue his musical career. He promised to provide financial support. Lila reported that she "didn't really know what to do, but Rex was a really cute baby and I knew that Danny couldn't take care of him. Even if he could have, he probably wouldn't have. I didn't want Rex to grow up with nobody to love him or take care of him, so I took on the responsibility of raising him."

The money from Danny was extremely erratic. Some months he would send a great deal of money and then other months he would send nothing at all. At the time of the assessment, Lila was working for a record store, selling records to supplement the money she received from Danny.

Danny reportedly came into town five or six times a year. Lila stated that Danny frequently "did drugs, even in front of the kid. He wants to take Rex out clubbing with him, too. Lately he says that he even wants Rex to come on the road with him." Lila reported that she dreaded the times when Danny visited them. Danny "breezes in and spends a lot of money on Rex and Rex thinks he's wonderful. When he leaves, Rex is just so sad and angry. He gets really wild and won't listen to me or do anything I want. After a few weeks, things calm down and just when things start going good for us, Danny shows up again." When she complained to Danny about this pattern and about his lack of reliable support, Danny told her that if she "didn't do what he wanted and let him take Rex whenever he wanted to that he would take Rex away from me." She also mentioned that Danny had said this several times in front of Rex and, while Rex looked frightened whenever Danny told her this, Rex used similar threats to get her to let him do whatever he wanted.

During the informal interviews, Rex had, indeed, followed through with his threat and refused to answer questions that he thought were too "personal." He had done remarkably well on the educational portion of the battery. The intelligence assessment results showed that Rex had an IQ in the superior range. The academic testing yielded achievement in all academic areas at significantly above grade level. The personality instruments showed a child with below average self-esteem and elevated tendencies toward delinquent and conduct-disorder type behavior. Rex had also refused to draw any pictures for subjective instruments, such as the House-Tree-Person and the Kinetic Family Drawing, saying, "This is way too babyish for me to do. Cool dudes just don't do that sort of thing. Anyway, I don't have to do anything that I don't want to."

In our synthesis of the assessment information, the clinic personnel could not find any data to indicate that Rex had any type of learning problems or academic deficiency keeping him from performing in school. We decided the factors that were contributing to his poor academic performance and his discipline problems were psychological in nature and recommended that Rex come in for Adlerian play therapy with me to work on his interpersonal skills, his self-esteem, and his self control. We also suggested that his aunt participate in "parent" consultation and perhaps attend a parenting class. We wondered about suggesting family therapy with Lila, Rex, and Danny, but we decided to wait and see what developed with our other strategies. We were skeptical, based on the information that Lila had supplied, about whether Danny would attend family therapy anyway.

THEORETICAL CONCEPTUALIZATION

I usually conceptualize children and their problems based on the information I gather in the first several sessions with them and in my consultations with their parents to start forming hypotheses about their goals of behavior, their mistaken beliefs, their life styles, and their assets. Because of the assessment results, I had more data about Rex than I normally have about the children with whom I work. I began formulating my theoretical conceptualization and my goals for the play therapy and parent consultations even before we started to build our relationship.

It seemed to me that the goal of most of Rex's behavior was power. He used his actions and his attitudes to show others that they could not control him and to keep himself safe. During our first session, he told me that his mother had "disappeared. She didn't really love me that much and she isn't coming back to get me—ever. I will always either live with Aunt Lila or my dad. I can't decide which one I want to live with. Sometimes my dad wants me to live with him and sometimes he doesn't. I think my Aunt Lila always wants me to live with her, but sometimes she gets real mad at me, so maybe she doesn't." Judging from both Lila's and Rex's descriptions of their family arrangement, I was guessing that Rex fit into the third category of children whose goal is power. He was in a situation in which neither he or his aunt felt powerful or in control. Their lives seemed to be chaotic and out-of-control. Rex appeared to lack a sense of security and safety. He did not seem sure from day to day where he was living, who was "in charge," who loved him, or who his "parents" were. Based on these feelings of insecurity, Rex had decided to impose his own will on the world and on other people with whom he had contact. If no one else was going to take responsibility for making sure that he was safe and secure, he was going to have to be very powerful in order to protect himself and insure that he got the material and emotional support that he needed.

Rex was the only child in a family in which the atmosphere was chaotic and conflictual. As such, he was exposed to the adults' struggle for control and power. Lila's uncertainty about her legal and emotional status in Rex's life seemed to undermine her ability to establish consistent patterns of discipline. Her fear that Danny would take Rex away weakened her emotional commitment in her relationship with Rex. She always kept a part of herself emotionally detached from Rex because she was afraid that Danny would take him away and "break my heart." Because there were no siblings or other responsible adults in his life, Rex got no relief or support in dealing with this emotional turmoil, which resulted in his extreme discouragement.

Based on his subjective assessment of the family and his place in it, Rex seemed to be interpreting reality in light of the following mistaken beliefs:

1. I must be in control of all situations in order to make sure I am safe and secure and to make sure I get what I need and want.
2. I cannot trust adults or other children to make sure that I am safe or help me find ways to belong.
3. The best way to stay in control is to tell others what they must do and to keep other people off-balance by having tantrums if I do not get what I want.
4. My mother left me because she did not love me. I can't count on people to love me or stay with me.
5. I do not need other people to like me. It is much more important to be sure that they do what I want.
6. My aunt is not very powerful and she cannot protect me or herself from my father.
7. My father is very powerful. He gets what he wants by threatening other people and always keeping them off-balance.
8. No one can help keep my aunt and me safe from the world. I am all alone.

According to Adlerian theory, Rex did not have to be aware of these ideas for them to influence his feelings and actions. Most of the time, these mistaken beliefs were probably out of Rex's awareness. However, he continued to base his life-style on these convictions and, using private logic, he chose to "act as if" these beliefs were an accurate representation of the world. Based on these mistaken beliefs, Rex seemed to have developed the following life-style:

I am . . .

powerless unless I can control others. Sometimes the best way to control others is for me to act "out of control."
in danger from others unless I learn to control them.
not able to trust people to stay with me or to love me.

Others are . . .

not to be trusted.
out to try to get what they want, at my expense.
trying to make me do things that I don't want to do.
uncaring. They don't love me enough to stay with me and take care of me.

The world is . . .

a scary place in which I cannot count on anyone or anything.
a dangerous place in which I must take care of myself.
a confusing place where I am not sure how to get love and nurturing.

Therefore, I must . . .

act in a way that minimizes my risk of getting hurt and not getting what I need and want.
use my temper and other behaviors to get what I want and need.
show other people that they cannot tell me what to do.
remember never to trust anyone, especially adults.
try to be like my father because he is the most powerful person I know.

My goals with Rex were to help him (a) feel secure with me by providing consistency and a sense of routine in the playroom, (b) feel powerful and in control by initially allowing him to make almost all of the decisions in the playroom, (c) learn to share power and learn to trust that I would help him get the material and emotional support he needed, (d) realize that he was not all alone and that he could get support from others, and (e) understand that his father was not all-powerful and that he did not have to act like him if he did not choose to do so. I wanted him to realize that he did not have to use negative behavior all the time in order to feel safe and to give himself a feeling of control. My goals with Lila were to (a) help her learn ways of recognizing the times when Rex was trying to take control and to point out what his goals were when he was doing this, (b) help her gain a sense of being more powerful and able to establish a set routine that the family followed consistently, (c) help her explore how she wanted to define her relationship with Danny and the relationship between Rex and Danny, and (d) help her learn how to assert herself in order to establish the boundaries and structure in her relationship with Danny and in the relationship between Rex and Danny.

THE PROCESS OF PLAY THERAPY

Building the Relationships with the Parent and the Child

When possible, I meet with one or both the parents of each child I see in play therapy before I meet with the child. I use this initial session with the parent(s) to (a) begin to build a partnership in which we will work together to help the child, (b) begin to build a relationship with them in which I can give them support for making changes in regard to their parenting skills and on personal issues that are preventing them from being the best parent(s) they can be, (c) explain the nature of Adlerian play therapy and the process that I will be employing with them and with the child, and (d) begin to gather information about the family and the way the child gains significance in the family.

Since Lila was essentially serving as Rex's sole parent, I decided to treat her as such. I met with her for an entire session of parent consultation before I met with Rex in a play therapy session. Having heard most of the information I knew about the family second-hand, it was important that I use this time to formulate my own impression of Lila and the family situation first-hand. I also wanted to start building rapport with Lila. Like many of the parents I work with, when I first met Lila she was terrified that I was going to tell her that she was not doing a good job as a parent. Since she was not sure that she had the right to that role, she was even more insecure than most of the parents with whom I work.

In that initial session, she was extremely timid and embarrassed as she told me how she had always "let Danny do whatever he wanted, ever since he was born." She fidgeted and stammered as she nervously related the story of her family of origin. She was 10 years old when Danny was born and their parents were "old and tired. They really let me raise him and I guess I didn't do a very good job because he sure is spoiled and irresponsible." She seemed to feel guilty about how Danny had turned out and was afraid that Rex would grow up the same way. It was obvious as she talked about her relationship with Danny and Rex that she felt responsible for both of them, but had very little sense of power in her relationship with either of them. She got very agitated as she talked about how "Danny just comes to get Rex and thinks he can do whatever he wants to just because he's his real parent."

When I asked her how she could stop this from happening, she burst into tears and told me that there was nothing she could do about it. After I reflected her feelings of fear and helplessness, I probed a bit further about these threats. When I asked her to repeat Danny's actual wording, the best she could remember was that he had said, "He's my son and I can do what I want." Lila seemed to be completely intimidated by Danny's threats and her perceptions of what would take place if Danny decided he wanted Rex to live with him. At the same time, Lila was determined to protect Rex from "the kind of wild life Danny leads."

I used an Adlerian form of confrontation called "spitting in the soup" to suggest that she had more power than she thought she did. Considering that she had been Rex's sole emotional and primary financial support, I believed she might have more legal rights than she had considered. I also gently suggested that she might be letting her fear and sense of powerlessness exaggerate the direness of Danny's threats— she was thinking that he was going to do all these terrible things with Rex, when what Danny had actually threatened was to take Rex to live with him. While this was definitely frightening, she might be giving him even more power by forgetting that it was unlikely that Danny would actually take on the responsibility for the full-time care of a child.

During the course of this consultation, we had touched upon many of the themes that would be present in the nine months that I worked with Rex and Lila. We had talked about Lila's feelings of personal powerlessness, her difficulty in providing structured parenting, the way her private logic sometimes led to her assuming the worst in any situation she did not like, and her feelings of inadequacy as a parent. These were themes that greatly influenced her relationship with Rex and the formation of his own life-style.

Because I felt that Lila would need a great deal of support in order to gain enough personal power to be able to begin to change their circumstances, I arranged to see her once a week for a 50-minute parent consultation. My customary practice is to see each child for 30 minutes of a session and then see the parent(s) for 20 minutes. I varied this with Rex and Lila because I believed that both of them would need maximum support and understanding to make the kind of changes that were necessary.

Based on the data about Rex's family constellations, family atmosphere, and goals, I could also begin to use some of the strategies from the second and third phases of the Adlerian play therapy process. However, I had to be very cautious with this, because if I had rushed this process too much, before we had truly established our relationship, I could have easily prevented the relationship from forming. Few, if any, clients are ready to gain insight into their life-styles before they have a solid attachment to the counselor.

Since I believed that Rex's goal of power was based on his chaotic, out-of-control family situation, my treatment plan required me to begin the relationship by establishing that he could initially control things in the playroom. I knew that in order for him to feel safe in the play therapy sessions, he would have to believe that he was the boss. I also wanted to show him that he could gain power in appropriate ways without having to be a tyrant. As he learned to trust me and feel secure in the playroom and in our relationship, I would gradually move to share the power in the playroom so that he could experience a situation in which he could be safe and secure but not have to be in charge.

The first time Rex came to the clinic, he did not stop in the waiting room. He came directly into my office and announced, "I know you. I already talked to you before on the day that lady asked me all those questions. My Aunt Lila says you're going to play with me and teach me not to be like my dad. You can't make me not be like my dad, you know!" I reflected his feelings, made a tentative hypothesis about the underlying message in this statement, and reframed our relationship by saying, "I can tell you are feeling kind of afraid that I will try to get you to be different. I am happy to be with you just the way you are. It sounds to me like your dad is really important to you and you want to let me know that I can't keep you from being like him." Rex looked at me rather suspiciously and nodded pensively. Then he looked angry and asked, "How do you know that?" I replied, "I'm not sure how I know that. It was a guess. I work with a lot of kids and sometimes they tell me things like that. Let's walk down to our playroom and maybe we can figure it out together." With these responses, I let him know that I would not try to force him to do anything that he did not want to do and that we would be equal partners in the play therapy process.

Rex was very bright, articulate, and suspicious, so it was fun and exciting doing play therapy with him. His mind worked so quickly, shifting from one thought to another easily, it was sometimes hard to keep up with him. During that first session, we walked into the playroom and he was very excited at all of the toys there. He went around the room, touching things and asking me to tell him what they were. I replied, "In here, you can decide that" or "I bet you can figure that out for yourself." He got very angry with me, shouting, "Just tell me what they are. You know and you can tell me." I reflected his feelings of frustration and suspicion with my refusal to try to influence him and made some interpretations about how he was testing to see if I was going to try to be the boss. Several times I also pointed out that he had already told me that I could not boss him around, but he was not sure that he could trust that. He ignored the first of these interpretations, but the second time I made this type of interpretation, he replied "I know you're just pretending that you don't want to tell me what to do. All grown-ups I know want to tell me what to do and they yell at me when I don't do it. If I don't do what you want, you probably won't let me come here anymore."

During the first eight sessions, while we were building our relationship, this theme came up repeatedly. During the first two sessions, Rex continually repeated his skeptical remarks, doubting my willingness to let him have power over decisions and most of his behavior. In the second session, when I stated a limit on his shooting the dart gun at the mirror in the room by saying, "It's against the playroom rules to shoot at the mirror," he looked very angry. I continued with the rest of the limit, reflecting his purpose and engaging him in generating alternate behaviors, by saying, "I can tell that you want to see what I will do if you shoot at the mirror. I bet you can think of something in the room besides the mirror or me that would be all right for you to shoot." When I said this his face cleared and he smiled at me. After several seconds had passed though, he frowned and shouted, "I don't know what is okay! You try to make me decide everything! Don't you know I'm just a kid!?" I reflected his feelings of confusion and insecurity by saying, "You're afraid that you will make a choice that is not okay and I might get angry." I also tried to encourage him by adding, "In here, I will tell you what is against the playroom rules, but I won't get angry if you make choices different than the ones I might make. In here, there are lots of things you can decide and some things that I will decide." When I said this, he nodded and aimed the dart gun at the wall, looked at me, and smiled. I acknowledged that he had "figured out something that was okay to shoot," and reflected his feelings of pride and accomplishment.

As time passed, Rex continued to test my willingness to let him have control over many aspects of the relationship. During the first six sessions, every time I returned the responsibility for making a decision about something to him, he screamed at me and accused me of tricking him or of asking too much of him because he was "only a kid." The few times when I made a decision without consulting him or answered an informational question with a factual answer, he also got furious at me for "telling him what to do." I could tell that it was hard for him to trust that I would be consistent in my desire for us to be equal partners in our relationship. Rex's reaction to my giving him control seemed to vary from smugness to anger, from delight to terror. In addition to his wanting to control things, Rex also wanted a strong adult in his life to take care of him and keep him safe. This need for security, nurturing, and protection was in conflict with his belief that he could not trust anyone to take care of him. As he began to trust me and feel safe in the playroom, his reactions to my returning responsibility to him seemed to mellow. He no longer made doubtful remarks or yelled at me that he could not make important decisions because he was "only a kid." In the seventh session, he asked me what he should paint in a picture and before I could respond, he said, "I know. I know. I can decide that for myself." He turned and smiled at me and said, "I think I will paint my house and my aunt and me. I *can* decide stuff in here."

During those first eight weeks, there were three other important play themes that Rex used in every session: violence and aggression, nurturing, and singing. He spent about 20 minutes in each session punching, kicking, and otherwise trying to maim the stand-up punching bag. Sometimes he said that it was his teacher, sometimes it was his aunt, sometimes it was his father, sometimes it was me, and sometimes it was an unnamed "bad guy." I did not limit this behavior because I felt that Rex needed an appropriate symbolic way to act out his aggression and anger. I did point out how determined he was to make sure that the punching bag not get a chance to defeat him. I used this play to reflect his feelings of anger and frustration and to make guesses about his goal of power. He frequently would be so physically involved in his attacks on the punching bag that he would break out in a sweat. I pointed out how tired he got from being angry and trying to show the punching bag who was boss.

He spent 5 to 10 minutes in each session asking me to make "food" for him in the kitchen area. He wanted me to go through all the motions of fixing his favorite foods, putting them on a plate, and serving them to him. This was one of the areas that he used to test my adherence to our power-sharing. He frequently wanted me to guess what his favorite food was that week and feed it to him. It was my sense that this was some type of test to see if I would be willing to read his mind in order to be able to nurture him. Since I believed that it was essential that Rex learn to ask for what he needed from others with words instead of the negative behaviors he had been using to communicate, I would only "feed" him when he would tell me what he wanted me to fix him. I used the "whisper technique" to give him control of the interaction. Every time he told me to feed him "something," I would whisper, "What do you want me to feed you?" At first he got very angry at me, yelling, "You decide! You're supposed to take care of me." When he would do this, I would say, "I really want to take care of you, but you have to let me know what you need." When he told me what he wanted, I used encouragement to point out that he had the ability to ask for what he wanted and the ability to make decisions and communicate those decisions to others. When he refused to tell me what he wanted, I reflected his fear and reluctance, "Sometimes it's kind of scary for you to tell people what you want. I bet you're kind of afraid if you tell them that they might not give it to you." During the first eight to ten sessions, most of the time he would initially refuse to tell me what he wanted me to fix him. After a few minutes of my avoiding getting into a power struggle with him and simply reflecting his feelings and his purpose, he would assert his control by saying, "Okay, I'll tell you what to fix and I want it NOW."

During these beginning sessions, Rex would intermittently burst into song. I had difficulty understanding the words to many of the songs and when I asked about them, he seemed both irritated and smug, telling me that they were "rock songs" and that I was "probably too old to know about them." During the third session, in one of these interludes, Rex strutted around the room, singing, and rhythmically moving his hips and pelvis. After several minutes of this, he stopped, grinned at me, and said, "I told you, I am the King of Rock and Roll." While sometimes Rex seemed to simply sing because he enjoyed it, other times he would strut and wiggle and then visually check out my response. Sometimes it seemed to me that he was trying to shock me and other times it seemed as though he was trying to impress me with this behavior. I made guesses about both of these possibilities. While I occasionally got a recognition reflex when I made comments about him "wondering what I thought about it when he acted like his dad," at other times he just ignored me or got angry and accused me of telling him that he should not be like his father. After the first five or six sessions, I noticed a pattern in his singing. When he was singing songs composed by other people—usually rock songs in the repertoire of Danny's band or songs he had heard on the radio—the purpose of his singing was enjoyment or shock value. When he was singing songs he composed on the spot, he was usually reacting to something I had said or done. Sometimes these songs were a form of recognition reflex—a response to my guesses or comments—and sometimes they were a way of communicating with me—telling me things that he could or would not say directly.

Rex had not mentioned his mother since the first session when I had asked about her. In session 8, this changed and he introduced the subject of his mother. He used a self-composed song to communicate during this interchange.

Dialogue	*Commentary*
R: [Hitting and punching the punching bag.] This is my mother. She was a bad mother.	
TK: You're pretty angry at your mother	I was surprised and I simply reflected feelings.
R: [Turning and looking at me angrily.] Nobody can say anything bad about my mother. Not my dad, not my aunt, not you. If anybody says anything bad about her, I will kick their butt.	Rex seemed to perceive my reflection of his anger as threatening to his mother and he responded by threatening me.
TK: Sounds like you want to protect your mother from anybody saying bad things about her.	I was making a guess about his purpose. I might have also made a tentative hypothesis about his feeling guilty about being angry at his mother, but this did not occur to me at the time.
R: Right, I will kick their butt like this. [Demonstrating on the punching bag.]	

TK: You want to show me that I better not say anything bad about your mom? You love her and you are going to protect her and keep her safe. I bet you wish that somebody would protect you like that.

Again, I asked a question about his purpose and a guess about his need to feel safe and protected.

R: I don't need anybody to keep me safe. I can keep myself safe. I am Mr. Tough Man. [Begins to sing a song about "Mr. Tough Man."]

I was not really expecting him to agree with my guess, but it was interesting to me that he began to sing a self-composed song.

Exploring the Child's Life-Style

I began tentatively exploring the components of his personality early in our relationship. Even in our first meeting, the primary goal of Rex's behavior was evident. From the beginning of our acquaintance, Rex established that he was not going to let anyone else control him. In the assessment staffing, I began to see the patterns of his family atmosphere and family constellation emerge. During the first eight sessions of play therapy, I continued to investigate Rex's goals of behavior and the effects of the family atmosphere and the family constellation on the formation of his personality. I watched his behavior, especially in the kitchen area, since he totally ignored the dollhouse. His play with the nurturing themes seemed to indicate that, while Lila was providing warmth and love, he needed more consistent, steady support from her. Sometimes he was careful and controlled in his use of the kitchen utensils and sometimes he was violent, throwing them around and yelling. This play seemed to reinforce the idea that I was forming based on Rex's and Lila's answers to my questions about discipline and the relationship between the two important adults in Rex's life: Danny and Lila. Lila's insecurity in the parenting arena and her worry that Danny would take Rex away from her combined with the mixed messages Rex received from Danny and Lila about the value of routine and structure to create a chaotic, inconsistent family atmosphere.

Based on my observation of Rex's behavior in the playroom with me and in the waiting room with Lila, I began to use my knowledge about typical only children to formulate a list of potential strengths and problem areas for Rex. I asked Rex several questions, such as "Of all your friends, which one is the most like you? How is he like you? Of all your friends, which one is the most different from you? What are the things that you like about yourself?" to help me get a better picture of how Rex gained his significance at home and with his friends.

Rex's behavior and attitudes had many typical characteristics of an only child (Pepper 1971). On the positive side, he got along well with many adults. He had an advanced vocabulary and could converse about many subjects in a manner unlike that of most 7-year-olds. He was very intelligent and he used his intelligence to charm others. Rex was very creative, using his musical talent and imagination to compose amusing lyrics and beautiful melodies. He was extremely self-entertaining, endlessly devising ways to keep himself occupied. He also liked to be the center of attention. When he achieved that aim in constructive ways, such as singing and being charming, this was a positive attribute. However, more often than not, he chose to be the center of attention in destructive ways, such as having temper tantrums and generally demanding that others pay attention to him. Also on the liability side, Rex frequently seemed only interested in himself and what he wanted. His social interest was relatively low and he did not spend a great deal of time or energy trying to understand others. He believed that the best way to get things that he wanted was to force others to do things for him, rather than relying on his own resources. He frequently got what he wanted by "playing" his father against his aunt. Whenever Rex did not get what he wanted, he believed that he was being picked on or treated unfairly. Knowing the characteristic interactional patterns of only children helped me to look for Rex's assets and liabilities.

In sessions 9 through 12, I shifted my focus slightly. Although I continued to work on our relationship, I wanted to make sure that I understood Rex's private logic, basic convictions, and life-style. Consequently, in session 9 I asked him to do a Kinetic Family Drawing (Knoff and Prout, 1985), in which I requested that he draw each member of his family, "doing something." Although he had refused to do a similar drawing during the assessment, Rex quickly agreed to draw his family. He made sure that I knew that he was in charge, though, by telling me that he would draw the picture with crayons instead of with the pencil I offered.

He started the portrait by drawing his father in the middle of the page, very large in black crayon. In the picture, he drew his father with big, fierce looking eyebrows, smiling and holding a guitar. On the right side of the paper, Rex drew a picture of himself—also in black, looking exactly like his father, except much smaller. There was a large gap between the picture of his father and the picture of himself. Very close to the picture of himself, in between him and his father, he drew a picture of his aunt, even smaller than the picture he had drawn of himself. She was holding her hand out to him and smiling at him. I asked him to describe each of the people in the picture and to tell me what they were doing. He began by describing his father, saying that he was big, he got his way a lot, he fought with Lila a lot, and that he was playing his guitar and singing a new song. He described himself by saying that he was big, "just like my dad and I'm strong, too." He said that in the picture he was "making a song up, just like I do for you sometimes." In describing his Aunt Lila, Rex said, "She's nice and she tries to get me to do what I'm supposed to do, but I don't always do it." When I asked him what she was doing in the picture, he replied, "She's trying to hold my hand, but I'm busy and I don't want to hold hands with her." When I asked him if he was done with the drawing, Rex said, "No. I have one more person that I have to draw." He turned the paper to the back side and drew a dot in the middle of the page. When I asked him about this, he replied, "That's my mother. Don't you remember anything? I told you that she disappeared." He seemed very agitated and annoyed. When I reflected this by saying, "You seem like you're kind of mad at somebody," he abruptly stood up and said, "I don't like drawing pictures for you and I'm not going to do it anymore."

When I use drawings to help me understand the relationships between children and how they view themselves, others, and the world, I base most of my interpretations on common sense. Overall, there seemed to be a lack of family cohesion in the drawing. This made sense to me, given what I already knew about the family atmosphere. It was interesting to me that there did not seem to be a great deal of conflict between Danny and Lila in the drawing. Based on the relative size of the figures, Rex did not believe that Lila had enough power to be any kind of a threat to Danny's control of the family. My interpretation of the drawing suggested that Rex viewed his father as a powerful, somewhat scary person, who was more interested in his musical career than in his son. The placement of the people in the drawing seemed to indicate that Rex felt closer to his aunt than to his father, but wished that he could be more like his father. Lila's reaching out to Rex seemed consistent with what I had observed in their relationship—she really wanted to be a nurturing caretaker for him. However, the fact that Rex was "too busy" to touch her seemed to illustrate the uncertainty both Rex and Lila felt about their ability to trust each other and their relationship. I was not sure what to make of Rex's inclusion of his mother as part of the drawing. She seemed to linger in his mind as a person who should be in his life and provide love and stability. The anger he directed toward me every time that he brought her up seemed displaced, covering his hurt and a sense of abandonment.

In session 10, I tried to use the drawing to ask Rex some questions about the relationship between the various family members, but he refused to even look at the picture. Instead, he spent the first part of the session punching and kicking the punching bag and the second part of the session burying soldiers in the sand. He repeated this pattern in sessions 11 and 12, spending the last 5 minutes of both of these sessions asking me to cook food and serve him, telling me exactly what he wanted even before I used the whisper technique to ask.

Based on his reaction to my questions about his drawings, I decided not to ask Rex to give me early recollections. I had a pretty clear understanding of his life-style already, and I wanted to avoid any potential power struggle with him. Although I usually use cleaning up the playroom as a time to practice cooperation and partnership, I chose to delete this strategy with Rex because I believed that it would hinder rather than help our growing relationship.

In my parent consultations with Lila, I was exploring her perceptions of Rex and how he gained significance. I was also exploring Lila's views about herself, others, and the world. I realized that Lila was a typical oldest child in many ways: overresponsible and trying to "save the world." At the same time, her lack of confidence in herself and her abilities undermined her sense of control and power. In her relationship with Danny, she had always catered to his desires and whims. It was very difficult for her to imagine changing the dynamics of their relationship. One of the ways I encouraged her to own her power in the relationship was to suggest that she consult a lawyer about her legal rights in regard to Rex. She was extremely reluctant to do this, having never challenged Danny's position before. I did not get into a power struggle with her about this, but told her that when she was ready she would talk to a lawyer about the situation.

By the end of session 12, I had formulated the theoretical conceptualization of Rex presented earlier in the chapter. I had been using tentative hypotheses to share some of my ideas about Rex's private logic, basic convictions, and life-style since the second or third session, but now I was ready to move into the third phase of Adlerian play therapy.

Helping the Child Gain Insight

The bulk of the work I did with Rex in the third phase of our play therapy relationship was making interpretations in the form of tentative hypotheses and using his play metaphors to convey my thoughts about his self-concept and his attitudes toward others and the world. Rex's

THE KING OF ROCK AND ROLL   **159**

metaphors revolved around control and nurturing in his relationships with Lila, Danny, and me. For example, Rex came into session 13 and asked me if I still had his drawing. I told him that I did, and he said that he wanted to tell me a story about it. He told me a story about a storm that came up to the house where he and his Aunt Lila were living and blew them away and "nobody ever saw us again." Over the next five sessions, Rex repeated this story, with variations ranging from the storm blowing him and Lila to "a real neat place and then home again" to the storm blowing "everybody, me and Aunt Lila and even my dad and my mom, and nobody ever came back." I reflected the various feelings that Rex expressed verbally and nonverbally in this story and made some interpretations about how scary it was that a storm could change everybody's lives and take people away. Whenever I made a guess that it was hard to not be able to decide where you were going and what you were going to do, he frowned and nodded in agreement or started singing a song he had composed with a refrain of "Right again little lady."

In session 15, Rex introduced a new game. He wanted me to play bowling with him, but he wanted me to always miss and never knock down any pins so that he could win every time. In session 15 to 18, I agreed to play by these rules. In session 19, I began to phase in the idea that in our play partnership we could share the power and Rex could still be safe. I told him that I was going to change the rules and that I could knock down any pins I hit. He was angry at first and told me that he would not play if we did not play by his rules. After I had reflected his anger and his need to control by winning, he said, "Okay, you can win sometimes too. We'll play by the new rules this time and next time we'll see." I replied that we could either take turns playing by his rules one time and my rules the next or we could just see who would win by who knocked down the most pins—I assured him that he could choose one of these two ways of playing.

In sessions 20 and 21, we alternated bowling with "his" rules and "my" rules. When he realized that he would win most of the time anyway, he decided that we could play "my" rules all of the time, saying, "That's more fair and I can usually win anyway." This became a ritual for us. At the beginning of each session for the rest of the time I saw Rex, we played three games of bowling. By session 25, he was arranging his own shots so that I won at least one of those times—usually due more to his skill at manipulating his own score than due to my skill at bowling. I reflected his desire to take care of me. This behavior was an indicator to me that Rex was learning social interest. He wanted to make sure that I did not feel inadequate or out of control.

I continued to make interpretations about how Rex felt a need for control and how he gained significance in the family. I also made guesses about his relationship with his father ("You would kind of like to be big and strong like him, but you also wish he would be nicer to you and to Aunt Lila.").

In session 24, Rex let me know in a metaphoric way that he did not like some of my interpretations.

Dialogue	*Commentary*
R: [Hitting punching bag.] I'm going to show him. He keeps bugging me and he won't leave me alone.	I realized that the "mean guy" was probably a representation of me.
TK: You're really mad at that "mean guy." You want him to just leave you alone.	I used Rex's metaphor to reflect his frustration and anger at me. I did not want to interpret his metaphor. Rather, I used it to communicate with him, just as he was using it to communicate with me.
R: [Punching the bag.] He can't make me do anything I don't want to do. I wish he would just quit talking to me. I don't like what she . . . I mean . . . he says.	Rex seemed to be trying to tell me that he was unhappy with some of the interpretations that I had been making about his family and the relationships in his family. My sense of this was confirmed by his slip when he changed the gender of the "mean guy" to female.
TK: You sound kind of like you have something you want to say to the "mean guy." Pretend he can hear and talk. What would you like to tell him?	One of my goals with Rex was to encourage him to ask directly for what he wanted and needed. However, I knew that he was not yet ready to ask me directly to stop making guesses. I was hoping this question would give him an avenue for asking for what he wanted a little more directly.
R: Just leave me alone! That's what I'd say.	

TK: Can you say that to the
    "mean guy?"

R: No. I don't want to. That was   I had probably moved too quickly
    your idea. Not mine.   by pushing this. Rex let me know
                                      that he was not yet ready to even
                                      move a little closer to asking for
                                      what he needed and he certainly
                                      was not going to do it just because
                                      I had asked him to.

During this phase of the therapy, I used encouragement to point out Rex's assets and to emphasize the changes I was seeing in his attitudes and his relationships. When he demonstrated his creativity and knowledge, I made comments such as "You sure do know how to sing." "You look really proud of yourself for making up a new song." "You like to show me that you learned some new things in school." I acknowledged behavior changes with comments like, "When you first started coming to the play room, you said that you couldn't shoot the dart gun and now you try shooting the animals down with it." and "You want me to know that you could have knocked all the bowling pins down, but you decided that I should win this game." By session 30, Rex was pointing these things out to me, making comments like, "I know how to make up lots of neat songs," and "I know how to do lots of things for myself. You don't need to help me do that anymore." He was starting to own his assets and was willing to share control and responsibility with me.

At the same time, I was teaching Lila Adlerian parenting strategies (Dinkmeyer and McKay 1989). She was learning to actively listen to Rex and to reflect his feelings. She was also learning about the goals of behavior and how to respond to Rex when he tried to control situations by using temper tantrums. I was teaching her to give Rex choices so that he could have age-appropriate power and how to set up logical consequences when Rex did not abide by the family rules that they had set up. While she was not always successful in consistently carrying out these parenting strategies, Lila had seen a "remarkable" improvement in Rex's attitude at home. She had set up a routine for them to follow at home and they were "getting along pretty good." Rex was still having some difficulty with his behavior and attitude at school, but his grades had improved enough that he passed second grade and was doing reasonably well in the beginning of third grade.

Although I had not mentioned contacting a lawyer for several months, Lila announced that she had talked with a lawyer in session 30. She had previously made an appointment and canceled it when she found out how much the lawyer charged per hour. However, after Danny threatened to take Rex and "never let me see him again, I realized how much I love Rex and don't want to let him go." The lawyer had told Lila that she did not have any legal rights, but that she could probably adopt Rex if Danny would agree to give up his parental rights. She found this discouraging, but said that she was going to try to convince Danny that Rex would be "too much trouble for him to take care of on the road." She believed that this strategy had a chance of success because Danny's band had just cut a second record and the recording company wanted them to tour in Europe and Japan for a year.

By session 32, Rex seemed to have developed a great deal of insight into his basic convictions and private logic. He had begun to shift his destructive striving for control into more constructive avenues. Although he still frequently wanted to be in control of situations, he was willing to share control with others and he usually used socially appropriate methods of gaining power instead of temper tantrums. He still needed to learn social skills for making friends with children instead of constantly demanding adult attention. While Rex still wanted to be like his father, he realized that his father was "not always a nice guy. He kinda pushes people around and they don't like it." He had decided that he wanted to live with his Aunt Lila and "just visit Dad sometimes." He had not mentioned his mother since session 25, when he said rather wistfully, "I hope my Aunt Lila doesn't ever disappear like my mom did." I was not sure that he had resolved this issue, but he did not respond—either verbally or nonverbally—when I brought up conversation about his mother or tried to introduce metaphoric play scenarios that included a mother.

Reorientation/Reeducation

My primary job during the reorientation/reeducation phase was to help Rex operationalize his altered outlook. I used this time to help him learn socially appropriate ways of feeling powerful and in control. Many times, I simply pointed out how I felt when he "bossed me around," made a guess that maybe sometimes other people also felt that way, and led him into brainstorming other ways of getting what he wanted. His creativity blossomed during these times, and he generated many new ways to get what he wanted without resorting to coercive methods. Sometimes I made suggestions for behaviors that he could try with his Aunt Lila, with other students in school, and with his teacher. Before he tried these new behaviors outside the playroom, we practiced them with each other in the session. After we had practiced several times, he would come back to our sessions and report how the suggestions had worked.

In session 33, I asked Rex if he would be willing to stay in the playroom for his aunt's parent consultations and help me teach her some techniques. He agreed to this as long as he could still have his own time "by myself with just you and me." We began to work on their communication patterns, especially on negotiation skills. Lila was still letting Rex control many of their interactions and not insisting on his following the structures they had set up around his going to bed. I wanted to help them practice sharing power and making democratic decisions in which Rex had a reasonable amount of power, but felt safe and protected by Lila's strength. The following interaction occurred in session 34:

	Dialogue	*Commentary*
TK:	Okay. I want both of you to tell me what happens when it's time for Rex to go to bed.	I wanted them to interact cooperatively to relate the conflict objectively.
LC:	Well, I set the timer like we agreed and then Rex wants to change it to make it a longer time.	
R:	I don't like to go to bed that early. I want to go to bed later.	
TK:	Did you agree to that time?	I wanted to make sure that Rex felt like he had some power in the decision-making process.
R:	Yeah. But I changed my mind. It's too early. It's not even dark yet then. I want a different time.	
LC:	Actually, it is still pretty light at 8:00.	
TK:	Rex, can you talk to your Aunt Lila and tell her what you would like to do?	Instead of using me as a switchboard, I wanted to encourage them to talk to each other.

R: I'm going to make this puppet talk. [Puppet says to Lila:] I want to go to bed later. I don't like going to bed when it's still light.

This was fine. Children are sometimes more comfortable using toys to communicate.

TK: Lila, can you tell Rex's puppet what you would be willing to do about this bedtime?

Since Rex had decided to communicate through the puppet, I wanted Lila to use that venue.

LC: I would be willing to change your bedtime to 8:15. That's a little later.

They began the negotiation process in earnest.

R: Is it dark then?

LC: [Turning to me:] It's not really dark then, is it? I'm not sure how much later I want him going to bed. He gets so grumpy if he doesn't get a good night sleep.

TK: Talk to Rex's puppet about that. I know that you guys can work this out by yourselves.

I wanted them to talk directly to one another without using me for an intermediary.

LC: [To the puppet:] Let's see. I don't want Rex to be a grump. Do you?

R: No, but I want him to get to stay up a little later.

LC: How about 8:20 and then I will read you guys a bedtime story until 8:30.

R: We can try. Let's see how light it is then.

This negotiation process was typical of the types of intervention strategies that I used with Rex and Lila during the fourth phase of therapy. Before we were done, I wanted to bring in another child and have Rex practice his newly acquired skills in the safety of the playroom, but this never happened. We planned for Rex to bring several friends from his class, but the logistics never worked out. Lila had started to work on convincing Danny to let her adopt Rex and she felt much stronger about setting boundaries on Danny's interactions with Rex. In session 38, Rex, Lila, and I all agreed that they were ready to start "rocking" without me. We had phased their sessions to every other week at the beginning of the reorientation/reeducation phase and I believed that they now had the insight and the skills to continue on their own. We had one more session to bring a sense of closure to the relationship. As we had done many times in play, Rex and I fed each other, this time with real food. I brought some of the foods that we had pretended to feed to one another in many of our nurturing sessions and we shared them with Lila. At the end of the session, Rex told me that he had made up a song for me and he sang me a lullaby with a rock and roll beat, ending with the words, "And I will always remember you, lady."

RESULTS AND FOLLOW-UP

I happened to be in the record store where Lila worked a year after we had terminated our sessions. She looked happy to see me and wanted to let me know that "things are going great for us." She reported that Rex had done extremely well in the third grade and had been placed in a talented and gifted program for the fourth grade. She had found a choir program for him and he was talking about starting a rock group of his own. Although his behavior was "far from perfect," it was much improved. He still got into an occasional power struggle with her and with his teacher, but overall things were calmer and more peaceful. Danny had decided that "having a kid was nice, but too much trouble." He had consented to giving up his parental rights and Lila was in the process of legally adopting Rex. She reported that Danny "actually seemed relieved and spent more time with me and Rex than he did before all this." Now that she was officially going to be responsible for Rex, Danny had given up getting into power struggles with her over Rex and simply enjoyed his interaction with them.

DISCUSSION

Rex was a relatively typical example of a child whose goal is power. He believed that he needed to gain control of others and of situations in order to provide himself with emotional stability and safety. In many ways, given his family situation, he was right. Adlerian play therapy works well with children who are motivated by power. It provides a framework for understanding these children and for helping them change their feelings, thoughts, and actions. Adlerian play therapy also gives the therapist a method of helping the parents and the other members of the child's social context to make changes so that the child's behavior stops "working." As Lila made changes to her own private logic and learned parenting skills, she began to shift the balance of power in the family so that she could provide a safe and secure relationship in which both she and Rex could grow.

As I pondered the process of play therapy with Rex, my only major regret is that we did not get any kind of closure on his abandonment by his mother. In Adlerian play therapy, sometimes the client leads while the therapist follows and sometimes the therapist leads while the client follows. I chose to follow Rex's lead in the issue of his mother. He did not want to address his mother's desertion, either directly or with recognizable metaphors, and in respecting his wishes I may have left an important issue unresolved. As I write this, however, I remember that issues are seldom actually "resolved," even in adulthood. When we address an issue in therapy, we usually get better at dealing with it, but important issues do not simply go away. Rex will have another chance, another time, when he is ready, to work on his thoughts and feelings about his "disappearing" mother.

I learned many things about communicating and about love from Rex. Rex had a unique and creative way of using his play and his songs to let me know about his needs, thoughts, and feelings. Rex taught me to "listen" with my ears and with my heart for messages that were not always obvious or simple, but were, nevertheless, very real.

REFERENCES

Adler, A. (1927). *Understanding Human Nature*. New York: Premier.
_____ (1929). *Problems of Neurosis*. London: Kegan Paul.
_____ (1930). *The Education of Children*. South Bend, IN: Gateways Editions.
Ansbacher, H. (1983). Individual Psychology. In *Personality Theories, Research, and Assessment*, ed. R. J. Corsini, and A. Marsella, pp. 69–123. Itasca, IL: F. E. Peacock.

Ansbacher, H., and Ansbacher, R., eds. (1956). *The Individual Psychology of Alfred Adler: A Systematic Presentation in Selections from His Writings*. New York: Basic Books.

Borden, B. (1982). Early recollections as a diagnostic technique with primary age children. *Individual Psychology* 38:207–212.

Dewey, E. (1971). Family atmosphere. In *Techniques for Behavior Change*, ed. A. Nikelly, pp. 41–48. Springfield, IL: Charles C Thomas.

Dinkmeyer, D. (1977). Concise counseling assessment: the children's life style guide. *Elementary School Guidance and Counseling* 12:117–124.

Dinkmeyer, D., and Dinkmeyer, D. (1983). Adlerian approaches. In *Counseling and Psychotherapy with Children and Adolescents: Theory and Practice for School and Clinic Settings*, ed. H. Prout and D. Brown, pp. 289–327. Tampa, FL: Mariner.

Dinkmeyer, D., Dinkmeyer, D., and Sperry, L. (1987). *Adlerian Counseling and Psychotherapy*. 2nd ed. Columbus, OH: Merrill.

Dinkmeyer, D., and McKay, G. (1989). *Systematic Training for Effective Parenting: The Parent's Handbook*, 3rd ed. Circle Pines, MN: American Guidance Service.

Dreikurs, R. (1953). *Fundamentals of Adlerian Psychology*. Chicago: Alfred Adler Institute.

Dreikurs, R., and Soltz, V. (1964). *Children: The Challenge*. New York: Hawthorn/Dutton.

Griffith, J., and Powers, R. (1984). *An Adlerian Lexicon*. Chicago: The Americas Institute of Adlerian Studies.

Knoff, H., and Prout, H. (1985). *Kinetic Drawing System for Family and School: A handbook*. Los Angeles: Western Psychological Services.

Kottman, T. (1987). An ethnographic study of an adlerian play therapy training program. Unpublished doctoral dissertation, University of North Texas, Denton, TX.

_____ (in press). Adlerian play therapy. In *Handbook of Play Therapy*, vol. 2, ed. K. O'Connor, and C. Schaefer. New York: Wiley.

Kottman, T., and Johnson, V. (in press). Adlerian play therapy: a tool for school counselors. *Elementary School Guidance and Counseling*.

Kottman, T., and Stiles, K. (1990). The mutual storytelling technique: an Adlerian application in child therapy. *Journal of Individual Psychology* 46:148–156.

Kottman, T., and Warlick, J. (1989). Adlerian play therapy: practical considerations. *Journal of Individual Psychology*. 45:433–446.

_____ (1990). Adlerian play therapy. *Journal of Humanistic Education and Development* 28:125–132.

Lowe, R. (1971). Goal recognition. In *Techniques for Behavior Change*. ed. A. Nikelly, pp. 65–75. Springfield, IL: Charles C Thomas.

Manaster, G., and Corsini, R. (1982). *Individual Psychology*. Itasca, IL: F. E. Peacock.

Nelson, A. (1986). The use of early recollection drawings in children's group therapy. *Individual Psychology* 42:288–291.

Nystul, M. (1980). Nystulian play therapy: applications of Adlerian psychology. *Elementary School Guidance and Counseling* 15:22–30.

Pepper, F. (1971). Birth order. In *Techniques for Behavior Change*, ed. A. Nikelly, pp. 49–60.

_____ (1979). The characteristics of the family constellation. *Individual Psychology* 16:11–16. Springfield, IL: Charles C Thomas.

Sweeney, T. (1981). *Adlerian Counseling: Proven Concepts and Strategies*. Muncie, IN: Accelerated Development.

Thompson, C., and Rudolph, L. (1988). *Counseling Children*. 2nd ed. Pacific Grove, CA: Brooks/Cole.

Yura, M., and Galassi, M. (1974). Adlerian usage of children's play. *Journal of Individual Psychology* 30:194–201.

6

To Show and Not Tell: Cognitive-Behavioral Play Therapy

Susan M. Knell, PH.D.

INTRODUCTION TO
COGNITIVE-BEHAVIORAL THEORY

Psychotherapy with preschool-age children presents some unique challenges. Treatment planning can be difficult, given the wide range of individual differences in development and the transient nature of many common problems during the preschool period. Since young children are not as cognitively sophisticated as older children or adults, the play therapist must present materials and information in a way that will be both understandable and potentially of benefit to the child. Cognitive-behavioral play therapy (CBPT) (Knell 1993, Knell and Moore 1990) is one type of treatment that offers promise in working with preschoolers.

Cognitive-behavioral play therapy is based on behavioral and cognitive theories of emotional development and psychopathology and the interventions derived from these theories. Historically, behavior therapies for children developed in part as an effort to help children and parents translate knowledge gained in therapy to the natural environment. Behavioral approaches to child management are often taught directly to parents or significant adults (e.g., teachers). However, behavior therapies can also be implemented directly with a child. In either case, the therapist attempts to discover factors that reinforce and maintain the child's problematic behaviors so that these behaviors can

Note: This case is discussed in a different form in Dr. Knell's book *Cognitive-Behavioral Play Therapy*.

169

be altered. Social learning theory considers an additional component with its emphasis on observational learning and more cognitive aspects of behavior.

Although the introduction of social learning theories began the process, psychological professionals have been slow to accept the role of cognitive factors in behavior therapy. With the introduction of self-control strategies to modify behavior, there has been more emphasis on internal factors, such as thought processes and their impact on behavior and pathology. Some behaviorists have challenged the movement toward incorporating cognitive factors into therapy, while others argue that cognitive theories bridge the gap between behavior change and thought.

Cognitive therapy is a structured, focused approach that helps an individual make changes in thinking and perceptions, and ultimately, behavior. Although cognitive therapies were designed for adults, there have been recent adaptations for children and adolescents. Unfortunately, adaptations of cognitive interventions for use with children have not been subjected to the same empirical study as have adult interventions. Additionally, the need for more emphasis on normal development and developmental psychopathology has been a problem in much of the child therapy literature to date (Masten and Braswell 1991).

Cognitive-behavioral play therapy provides a theoretical framework for working with children based on cognitive-behavioral principles. It is a potentially powerful arena for children to learn to change their own behavior and become active participants in treatment. CBPT incorporates cognitive and behavioral interventions within a play therapy paradigm. The cognitive-behavioral play therapist uses play activities, as well as verbal and nonverbal communication. CBPT emphasizes children's participation in treatment and provides a framework for their involvement by addressing issues of control, mastery, and responsibility for their own behavior change. By incorporating the cognitive components, children may become active participants in change. For example, by helping children identify and modify potentially maladaptive beliefs, they may experience a sense of personal understanding and empowerment. Integrating cognitive and behavioral interventions may offer effects of the combined properties of all approaches.

The principles of cognitive therapy for adults (Beck and Emery 1985) can be applied with some modifications to children. Thus, CBPT is based on the cognitive model of emotional disorders. It is brief, time limited, structured, directive, and problem oriented. It depends on a sound therapeutic relationship, in which one role of the therapist is educational. CBPT is a collaborative process, although the nature of collaboration between child and therapist is different than that of a therapist with an adult. Both the inductive method and Socratic method are important, but play a different role in CBPT with children than in work with adults.

The potential efficacy of CBPT may be related to six specific properties. First, CBPT involves the child in treatment through play. Because the therapist deals with the child's issues directly, rather than through a parent or significant adult, he or she can address issues of resistance and noncompliance. Second, in CBPT, the play therapist focuses on the child's thoughts, feelings, fantasies, and environment. It is possible to deal with a combination of situation-specific factors (e.g., soiling), as well as the child's feelings about the problem (e.g., anger, sadness). Third, CBPT teaches the child adaptive strategies for coping with difficult situations. For example, the play therapist can teach a child to replace maladaptive thoughts with positive self-statements. Fourth, CBPT is structured, directive, and goal oriented. The therapist works with the child and family to set goals and helps the child work toward these goals. Fifth, CBPT incorporates empirically demonstrated techniques. Modeling, one empirically supported technique, is a frequent tool in CBPT. Modeling is the basis of much of CBPT because of the need to demonstrate specifically, concretely, and nonverbally for young children. Finally, CBPT allows for an empirical examination of therapy so that the clinician can assess treatment effectiveness.

Although CBPT is unique, it is similar to other play therapies in its reliance on a positive therapeutic relationship, based on rapport and trust; the use of play activities as a means of communicating between therapist and child; and the message that therapy is a safe place. It differs from other play therapies regarding philosophy about the establishment of goals, selection of play materials and activities, use of therapy to educate, and the use of praise and interpretations. Thus, CBPT is an active intervention in which the therapist and child work together in establishing goals and choosing play materials and activities. In contrast to other play therapies, the cognitive-behavioral play therapist may be part "educator," in that he or she teaches new skills to the child. Finally, the cognitive-behavioral play therapist uses praise and interpretations to help the child acquire new skills and behaviors and gain understanding.

There is a wide range of intervention strategies that the therapist can use in CBPT. The play therapist typically intervenes through one of several methods: modeling, role-playing, and behavioral contingencies (Braswell and Kendall 1988).

The first, *modeling*, is part of most cognitive-behavioral interventions with children. Although modeling is important in work with children of all ages, it is particularly critical in very young children who do not understand more verbally oriented treatments. Extensive research shows that modeling is an effective way to acquire, strengthen, and weaken behaviors (Bandura 1977). When used in therapy, modeling exposes the child to someone or something (often a stuffed animal or other toy) that demonstrates the behavior to be learned. It can be particularly useful when the child can relate positively to the model. The play therapist can also use modeling in a variety of other forms, such as films, books, and dolls. Because of the nature of the young child's limited cognitive and verbal abilities, modeling is an important component of CBPT.

The play therapist can use modeling in CBPT to demonstrate adaptive coping methods to the child. The model may verbalize problem-solving skills as a particular behavior is demonstrated. In this way, the model can talk in a manner compatible with positive problem solving. Talking out loud provides a number of cues for the child (e.g., auditory, visual), as well as a concrete example. Thus, the play therapist can present the more verbal components of CBPT, through modeling, in a way that the child is most likely to understand.

A second method of delivery, *role-playing*, allows the child to practice skills with the therapist and receive ongoing feedback regarding progress. Role-playing between child and therapist is usually more effective with school-age, rather than preschool-age children. However, for younger children, it is possible to deliver role-playing through modeling. In this way, the models role-play situations, and the child observes and learns from watching them. For example, a shy child may observe as a puppet who is reluctant to be with others "practices" interacting with other puppets. The child listens and watches the puppet, as well as the feedback the puppet receives from the therapist.

Behavioral contingencies, the third method of delivery, are often a significant component of CBPT. With young children, this typically involves reinforcing or rewarding the child for acquiring new skills. For example, the therapist may label the child's behavior and praise the child for attempts to develop new skills. The therapist may also teach and encourage the child to use positive coping self-statements. The therapist can use specific behavioral contingencies in the session and also can encourage and assist the parents in setting up contingencies in the home and other environments.

The play therapist has a wide array of behavioral and cognitive techniques available in CBPT to be delivered through one of the three methods just described. Common behavioral techniques include forms of contingency management, a general term describing techniques that modify a behavior by controlling its consequences. These include positive reinforcement, shaping, stimulus fading, extinction, and differential reinforcement of other behavior (DRO). Common cognitive techniques include cognitive change strategies such as identifying and changing beliefs. Each of these techniques is briefly described, but will be highlighted later in the clinical case discussion.

Positive reinforcement involves social reinforcers, such as praise, or material reinforcers, such as stickers. Therapists often use positive reinforcement in combination with other procedures and may be direct (e.g., praise for playing appropriately) or more subtle (e.g., encouraging the child to explore certain topics rather than others). If a particular problem is the focus of treatment, the therapist may use praise as the child exhibits mastery over the problem.

In some instances a child is missing certain skills necessary to behave in a particular way. The therapist can reinforce the child through *shaping* successive approximations to a desired response. The therapist gives positive reinforcement for a behavior that is not the desired response, but is close to it. As the child comes closer and closer to the desired response, the therapist rewards each approximation and eventually the child reaches the desired behavior.

If a child has some of the requisite skills for a behavior, but only exhibits the behavior in certain circumstances or with certain people, the therapist can use *stimulus fading*. In such situations, the therapist may become a discriminative stimulus for behaving. Thus, the child might learn to use some of these positive skills in a setting with the therapist and then transfer the skills to other settings.

The therapist can extinguish behaviors by withholding reinforcement. *Extinction* itself does not teach new behaviors, so therapists frequently use extinction in conjunction with a reinforcement program. In this way, a therapist can reinforce a child for learning a new behavior, at the same time that he or she is using extinction to extinguish another behavior.

This is often done through *differential reinforcement of other behavior* (DRO), where the therapist reinforces behaviors that are different from, or incompatible with, the maladaptive behavior. The main idea is that the unacceptable behavior cannot occur if a competing, more desirable behavior is taking place (e.g., reinforcing a child for appropriately playing with a toy, while extinguishing the child's efforts to break toys).

While the behavioral methods used in CBPT usually involve an alteration in activity, cognitive methods deal with changes in cognition. This is an important distinction, because cognitive theories suggest that changes in affect *and* behavior occur as a result of changes in thinking. In cognitive therapy with children, the therapist helps the child to identify, modify, and/or build cognitions.

Cognitive change strategies aim to help the individual change faulty cognitions. One way this is done is through hypothesis testing, in which the therapist helps the client to learn to treat thoughts, beliefs, assumptions, and expectations, as hypotheses to be tested scientifically. The therapist helps the client identify problem areas and design "experiments" to test these thoughts. This examination typically involves a three-pronged approach in which the therapist and client look at the evidence, explore the alternatives, and examine the consequences. Thus, together the therapist and the client identify, "counter," and change maladaptive beliefs.

Cognitive-behavioral therapy (CBT) utilizes a combination of these approaches to help the individual change. Some authors have questioned the applicability and appropriateness of using CBT with preschool-age children (e.g., Campbell 1990), citing developmental issues that might preclude the young child from understanding and benefiting from such interventions. Further, the use of "collaborative empiricism," considered a critical component of CBT (Beck et al. 1979), is difficult for very young children.

At first glance, one might assume that preschoolers and young school-age children lack the cognitive skills to engage in cognitive interventions that most therapists currently use with older children and adults. While children have the capacity to misinterpret and distort reality, their inferences may be consistent with *their* perceptions of reality, although they are not necessarily accurate. Their cognitive abilities are also more limited than those of the adolescent and adult; therefore, the hypothesis-testing inherent in this approach is problematic. Finally, children may have difficulty exploring situations, providing alternative explanations, and understanding consequences.

There is, however, ample data to suggest that preschoolers' ability to understand complex problems may be enhanced by specific techniques, such as providing concrete examples and using less open-ended questions (Bierman 1983). By capitalizing on the child's strengths, rather than weaknesses, CBPT incorporates play and deemphasizes complex cognitive and verbal interventions. Play allows the child to reenact problem situations and potentially gain mastery over events and circumstances. The therapist can assist in this mastery by providing the "experiments" in the play situations and by assisting the child in looking at the evidence, exploring the alternatives, and examining the consequences. For example, the therapist can structure some of the play with the child to reflect alternative scenarios, as the child then experiences different reactions and consequences for the same situation. The therapist can also help the child to develop adaptive coping self-statements (e.g., Meichenbaum 1985). Often in the form of self-affirmation, self-statements for very young children can be simple and contain a component of self reward (e.g., the message: "I am doing a good job"). The cognitive-behavioral play therapist should create and maintain a collaborative therapy environment with the child.

One aspect of the cognitive-behavioral approach is in encouraging and facilitating the child's language to describe experiences and emotions. Despite dramatic growth in general vocabulary during the preschool and early school-age years, the child's descriptive vocabulary for words depicting emotions is still limited. Many youngsters do not have even the most rudimentary words to express their feelings (e.g., happy, mad, sad). The therapist helps the child develop a "feeling" word vocabulary, learn to match behavior and feelings, and express certain maladaptive behaviors in more adaptive, language-based ways.

We turn now to consideration of the assessment and treatment through CBPT of a young child. In the following case presentation, the methods and techniques described are highlighted in the implementation of a treatment plan.

PRESENTING PROBLEM AND BACKGROUND DATA

Chrissy L. was a 6-year, 2-month-old Caucasian girl referred by her pediatrician. She presented with an approximately three-year history of elective mutism and spoke only with her parents and several other children. She refused to speak to all other adults except two individuals whom she had known for over one year: the mother of one of her friends and a college student in the neighborhood.

Chrissy had a speech dysfluency, diagnosed when she was 3 years old. Her parents, Mr. and Mrs. L., reported that shortly after her third birthday, a preschool teacher had pressured her to stop stuttering. At about the same time, her peers teased her excessively when she spoke. She subsequently stopped talking in most settings. She had been enrolled in two separate speech and language programs, but had refused to speak in either of them. In the first program (when she was 4 years, 11 months), Chrissy took turns and initially appeared interested, but quickly became bored and fidgety. A second attempt at speech/language intervention occurred shortly before Chrissy's sixth birthday when her parents placed her in speech therapy with another child with an expressive language disorder. Again, Chrissy participated nonverbally, but did not talk.

When Chrissy turned 5, although she was eligible, Mr. and Mrs. L. did not send her to kindergarten in the hopes that the extra time before school entry would give her time to mature and ultimately talk. The next year, although she was still not talking, Chrissy entered kindergarten. She appeared to be comfortable at school, told her parents how much she enjoyed it, and seemed quite excited about school activities. However, she only spoke to other children when it appeared that no adults were watching. As soon as a teacher, principal, or other adult came into view, she stopped speaking. She was an active participant at school, for example taking toys in to "Show and Tell," but would only "show" and not "tell." She enjoyed showing her parents what she learned at school, and often repeated for her parents what she was learning (e.g., alphabet, numbers). However, because Chrissy would not speak in the classroom, the teacher had no way of knowing what, if anything, Chrissy was learning. After several months in kindergarten, Chrissy began to mouth words when her classmates were reciting or singing, but would not speak. She would not move her mouth when it appeared that an adult was watching. School personnel were very concerned about Chrissy and were considering placing her in a special classroom for severely behavior disordered children.

Chrissy was a clever and nonverbally communicative child. Frequently she could communicate her wishes and needs without speaking and much of the time people were able to guess what she wanted. Her efforts to communicate nonverbally were often quite creative. For example, in mid-December after her sixth birthday, Chrissy asked her parents to help her prepare a "wish list" for Christmas. She dictated the items to her parents and insisted that they write down her name, address, and telephone number at the top. Several days later, the family took Chrissy to a shopping mall so that she could see Santa Claus. Mr. and Mrs. L. observed with anticipation, wondering if and how Chrissy would communicate with him. Was Santa considered an "adult?" Would Chrissy talk to him, or would she remain silent? When she reached the front of the line, Chrissy took out the list from her pocket and handed it to Santa Claus. Because she insisted on having her name, address, and telephone number on the top of the list, it appeared that Chrissy felt that she did not need to talk with Santa because he had all the "vital" information. Her parents had not realized that Chrissy had the list with her, nor that she had anticipated her visit with Santa when she asked them to help with her Christmas list.

Apparently many adults had attempted to get Chrissy to talk. This included friends, relatives, and professionals with whom the family came in contact. It was Mr. and Mrs. L.'s impression that Chrissy was aware of this. She seemed sensitive to attempts to "trick" her into talking and her response was always to be uncooperative with these efforts.

Chrissy was an only child. Her parents saw her as shy, but not withdrawn. Mrs. L. reported that she, too, had been shy and had a history of speech dysfluency. Mrs. L. was the primary caretaker and had been home with Chrissy since her birth. The child had never been in the care of babysitters or other caretakers for any period of time. The parents denied knowledge of any stress or trauma in Chrissy's life. They denied any other difficulties with the exception of bed wetting, which occurred practically every night. Because of the wetting, Chrissy wore diapers at night. She did not have daytime accidents. At the time of the assessment, the parents wished to defer any treatment of Chrissy's enuresis.

Assessment

I interviewed Mr. and Mrs. L. and they completed a Child Behavior Checklist (CBCL) (Achenbach and Edelbrock 1983). This standardized child assessment measure yielded a nonclinical profile. In fact, the only items endorsed as "somewhat or sometimes true" were: acts too young for her age; can't concentrate, pay attention for long; can't sit still, restless, or hyperactive; disobedient at home; doesn't eat well; fears certain animals (dogs); refuses to talk; and speech problem (dysfluency). Only one item, wets the bed, was endorsed as "very true or often true." Even with these endorsed items, the profile was flat, suggesting that according to her parents' report, Chrissy did not present with any major psychopathology, despite the serious concerns about her mutism.

During the first three sessions, I observed Chrissy's play and did not introduce specific therapeutic interventions until the fourth session. After her initial hesitation during the first session, Chrissy engaged readily with the materials in the office. She appeared enthusiastic and interested in drawing and toys. I did not try to interview or formally test her, in an effort to communicate to Chrissy that she did not have to talk. I used this assessment period to understand Chrissy better through her play, as well as to communicate to her what the nature of the therapy experience would be like.

THEORETICAL CONCEPTUALIZATION

Background

Children with elective mutism refuse to talk in one or more major social situations, despite an ability to comprehend and speak (APA 1987).

Excessive shyness, social isolation, school refusal, and noncompliance may be present. It is a relatively rare disorder, with fewer than 1% of clinic-referred school-age children diagnosed as elective mute. Etiological factors include traumatic events and/or a family environment that suppresses speech. There is also a noted incidence of maternal overprotection, although the overprotection may be either the cause of the mutism or a response to the child's condition. Most elective mute children fall into one of two categories: those described as immature, withdrawn, shy, and manipulative, and those described as tense and anxious.

Although elective mute children may give the impression of having a language disorder, they often speak normally with someone, often the mother. Only about 20% of cases of elective mutism have specific speech and language delays (Wright 1968). Many of these children have only minor speech articulation difficulties. A higher incidence of other behavioral problems, including enuresis and encopresis, have also been noted in elective mute children (Kolvin and Fundudis 1981).

Assessment and Treatment of the Elective Mute Child

Assessment typically begins with parents or caretakers, so that the therapist can obtain history and information regarding the child. In addition to an overall developmental history, the therapist should gather detailed information about the child's language development. The history should include clear, detailed information regarding the situations in which the child speaks, and those in which the child is silent. The clinician should explore any patterns of speaking and silence. For example, the child may speak only at home or only to female adults. The parent may also be able to provide information regarding how the child perceives his or her silence. For example, elective mute children who speak to their parents may talk about why they do not talk to others. In describing such conversations, the parents may provide the therapist with information that the child might not directly convey to the therapist. This information may become an integral part of the treatment process.

Direct assessment of the elective mute child obviously presents some unique challenges. The young elective mute child who does not speak to the therapist may nonetheless respond through pictures, play, and visual cues (e.g., smiling, eye contact). Therefore, the clinician may base much of the direct evaluation on the child's nonverbal behavior, including interaction with play materials, as well as assessment of the interaction with parents and the therapist.

There is consensus within the treatment literature from a variety of theoretical orientations that direct attempts to force elective mute children to speak will be ineffective (Labbe and Williamson 1984). By definition, the child presenting with elective mutism has chosen not to speak despite the ability to do so. If leaving these children alone were effective, this route might be appropriate. However, there is little evidence that elective mutism gets better without treatment. Therefore, treatment approaches must involve the child in a way that encourages the individual's own wish to speak. A gradual and supportive progression from nonverbal to verbal play characterizes most treatments (Labbe and Williamson 1984).

Early approaches to treating elective mutism were largely concerned with dynamic issues in personality, rather than the removal of the symptom of mutism (Kolvin and Fundudis 1981). The psychoanalytic literature often emphasizes the meaning of the silence and the ways in which the symptom synthesizes conflicts from different developmental levels. Treatment was primarily concerned with modification of personality dynamics, the measurement of treatment success involved a great deal more than whether or not the child spoke.

Since the mid-1960s, behavioral approaches to the problem have focused on efforts to help the elective mute individual talk (Labbe and Williamson 1984). Much of the behavioral literature on elective mutism focuses on directly attempting to increase the individual's speech production. Behavioral approaches often combine a number of different interventions. Several studies document the successful use of contingency management utilizing positive reinforcement of verbal behavior and extinction of nonverbal behavior (e.g., Williamson et al. 1977). Similarly, stimulus fading to gradually change the stimuli controlling speech can be effective for the child who will speak in certain environments or with certain individuals (e.g., Richards and Hansen 1978). With stimulus fading, as new situations become discriminative stimuli for speaking, the child learns to speak in response to new and different situations or stimuli. Another common behavioral approach to initiate speech is through shaping, where the therapist reinforces behaviors that come closer and closer to resembling talking.

Normally children gain satisfaction and a sense of mastery from communicating. However, in some situations, speaking is not reinforcing. In fact for some children, silence becomes more rewarding than talking. Thus, these children may gain control of their environments by remaining silent. Active participation in treatment is important in a disorder in which the main symptom, speech refusal, is entirely under the child's control. Elective mute children have control over their silence. Therefore to change, they must take control over their speaking. Cognitive-behavioral play therapy for elective mute children may be particularly appropriate because it provides the opportunity to be part of the change, to feel a sense of mastery and control over talking, and to learn more adaptive responses to situations that may elicit silence.

Conceptualization of Chrissy L.

Based on history and observation, Chrissy did not seem to be excessively tense or anxious. Instead, Chrissy appeared to fall into the group of elective mute children described as immature, withdrawn, shy, and manipulative. Characterizing her as manipulative came in part from the history that suggested Chrissy was well aware of the consequences of her silence and used it to her advantage.

By history, Chrissy had experienced no major traumas and had consistent parenting from one primary caretaker (her mother). There was no evidence that Chrissy's mutism was the result of any significant traumatic experience. However, she did apparently have a speech dysfluency, which was noted by her parents. The dysfluency could not be adequately assessed by a professional, however, because Chrissy would not talk to adults. She had experienced excessive pressure to "speak correctly" from a preschool teacher. Additionally, she had been the target of excessive teasing regarding her speech difficulties from other children.

These two situations seemed to be precipitating events in the development of Chrissy's mutism. Although neither could be considered extreme or catastrophic stressors, based on her parents' report, they appeared to be quite devastating for Chrissy. Her response was to become silent in many situations. Subsequently, her silence seemed to be very reinforcing. That is, as her silence became her "trademark," she received increasing attention for being quiet. Her parents and many others talked about her silence, tried to get her to talk, and attended to her silence in many ways. My hypothesis was that this focus of attention on Chrissy's silence had become reinforcing. This attention for silence was compounded by Mr. and Mrs. L.'s tendency to infantalize Chrissy, which she also found reinforcing. Mr. and Mrs. L. treated Chrissy like a much younger child and attended to her silence, giving her little reason to want to talk. Mrs. L.'s history of shyness and speech difficulties may have been a contributing factor. I could not determine if there was a genetic predisposition to shyness and speech difficulties, or if these were encouraged or maintained by environmental factors.

Further, Mrs. L.'s overly protective nature may have contributed to the child's mutism or may have been a result of it. There was really no way of knowing which of these factors was the cause and which was the effect.

Given the history, my clinical judgment was that Chrissy would need to *want* to talk before she would do so. Any further direct attempts to convince her or coerce her to talk would likely fail. She would need to be an active participant in change, rather than a passive recipient of an intervention designed to make her talk. Further, she needed to believe that if she did talk, things would continue to be all right for her, and she would not lose the attention she had gained from not talking.

The goals of therapy were to assist Chrissy in wanting to change her behavior and be comfortable talking in multiple situations. It is perhaps a subtle distinction, but a goal of therapy *was not* to get Chrissy to talk. I assumed that if she herself chose to talk and was comfortable with that decision, she would eventually talk. Therefore, talking would ultimately result from the goal that Chrissy would want to change her behavior. Another goal was to deal with the factors reinforcing Chrissy's silence. For example, one aspect of this was to help her cope with feelings associated with being teased by other children.

Cognitive-behavioral play therapy provided an intervention that Chrissy might perceive as noncoercive in regard to her talking. By modeling changes on the part of the puppets, Chrissy could observe specific behaviors and skills, without any expectations that she, herself, talk. It provided a warm, nurturing, safe environment, where not talking was acceptable, but where I provided positive reinforcement for other behaviors. I hypothesized that the combination of these factors would create an environment in which Chrissy herself wanted to talk.

THE PROCESS OF PLAY THERAPY

I saw Chrissy for a total of 33 sessions over the course of one year, including the first three assessment sessions. These sessions were weekly for the first five months, bimonthly for the next three months, and then monthly for the last four months. I saw Mr. and Mrs. L. regularly (usually at every second session with the child) to offer support and obtain information about the child. I encouraged the parents not to question Chrissy or engage her in conversation about her refusal to speak. If she brought up the topic of speaking, I asked them to remain neutral and matter-of-fact in response to her comments. They were to encourage her talking by being positive about it, but not overly attentive to her more infantile and silent behaviors. In a conference with the teacher and principal, it was also agreed that school personnel would approach Chrissy's silence by ignoring it. Although they were not entirely comfortable with this approach, they were willing to deal with her in this way for a trial period of time.

I structured the therapy sessions, in part by using several puppets with a variety of problems. One of the puppets (Mouse) wanted to make some new friends. Another puppet (Frog) talked all the time, and a third (Tiger) did not talk. Treatment consisted of both behavioral and cognitive techniques to "help" the puppets with their difficulties. Thus, the puppets modeled interventions. Because the treatment plan was to avoid directly treating the child's mutism, one of the puppets received direct intervention focused on not talking; however, Chrissy did not.

The behavioral and cognitive interventions I used included *contingency management* techniques. For example, the puppets received *positive reinforcement* for appropriate behavior. I gradually *shaped* closer and closer approximations of the desired behaviors of each of the puppets. Mouse (the puppet who wanted to make friends) learned better peer interaction; Frog (the puppet who talked too much) became quieter; and Tiger (the puppet who did not talk) began to speak. Shaping of socially appropriate expression of feelings was gradual as the puppets learned to put their feelings into words rather than acting those feelings out. After Chrissy talked with me, I "encouraged" her to speak to me in front of others through *stimulus fading*. For example, although she spoke to her parents, she would not do so in front of others. By fading myself into situations with her parents, Chrissy could begin to speak with me in front of her parents. Cognitive techniques consisted of *identifying beliefs*, countering irrational beliefs, and learning to make positive self-statements. Again, I used the puppets. I had each puppet "verbalize" beliefs about its "presenting problem." In an effort to *counter* these beliefs, I challenged each puppet's beliefs and modeled *positive self-statements* with them.

Although Chrissy did not speak at first, it was quite evident that she was listening to what was being said. She interacted actively with the animal puppets (e.g., smiling, hugging) and watched intently when I engaged the puppets in play and conversation.

The following section includes descriptions from therapy sessions with Chrissy. I have used transcribed vignettes to illustrate the nature of the therapeutic process. I controlled all "comments" or activities by the puppets, unless indicated otherwise.

Session 4

I overheard Chrissy talking to her parents in the waiting room, but she stopped midsentence as soon as I walked into the room. Chrissy eagerly entered my office. She began the session by drawing ice cream cones. The frog puppet leaned over and tried to eat the ice cream cones and the rest of the animal puppets interacted with each other, making conversation about how good ice cream was. Although the puppets had been available to the child during the first three assessment sessions, I "formally" introduced them to Chrissy at the fourth session.

Dialogue	*Commentary*
SK: This puppet's name is Tiger and she is shy. She doesn't want to talk.	I was introducing the puppets, and also introducing one puppet as being "shy" and not interested in talking.
[Mouse tries to get Tiger to talk, physically opening and closing her mouth.]	This let her know that I knew that some people try to "make" others talk.
SK: She's not ready, she will talk when she is ready.	I was identifying for her that being quiet is okay. Also, I was letting her know that she was in control of her talking, and she could talk when *she* was ready.
C: (Laughs).	

Session 5

The puppets were playing Tic-Tac-Toe and Tiger hid behind a box and whispered to the others. The frog kept singing and talking, and Mouse told him that he "talks too much." Chrissy interacted with the puppets and mouthed words, but did not speak. I gave a sticker to Chrissy for the picture she drew, one to Tiger for talking, and one to Frog for not talking. The puppets played with the toy phone, each taking turns calling their moms, and Chrissy took the phone and made noises, but did not actually speak.

Session 6

Chrissy began the session by immediately going to the puppets, crayons, and paper. Frog kept up a steady stream of comments and at one point asked Chrissy what she was going to draw, and she whispered to the therapist "mom." She seemed to want Frog to stop talking; at one point she tried to close his mouth. She nonverbally expressed anger at Frog, seemingly because of his nonstop talking, by her facial expressions, physical efforts to make him close his mouth, and destruction of a paper belonging to the puppet.

Dialogue	*Commentary*
SK: [Drawing feeling faces: mad, sad, happy.] This is the mad face, this is the sad face, and this is the happy face. I wonder how you felt when Frog was talking soooo much.	I was labeling feeling faces and words for her. By wondering how she felt, I was trying to let her know that she had feelings, it was acceptable to have feelings, and I was interested in her feelings (even if she did not choose to talk to me).
[C points to the mad face.]	
SK: Oh, you seem mad at Frog. It is important for people to know when you are mad at them.	I wanted her to know that expressing feelings is important, but I said it in a way that would not make her feel that she had to verbalize her feelings.
[C makes an angry face at Frog and whispers in his ear. C makes noises and guttural sounds while pretending to talk on the telephone. She indicates by pointing, that the therapist should answer the telephone.]	

SK: [pauses.]

I waited for the noises she was making to become more audible before "recognizing" that the telephone was ringing and answering it. I was trying not to make assumptions about her intent or to second-guess what she wanted. By so doing, I was gradually shaping her behavior to promote more appropriate verbalizations.

At this session, Mr. and Mrs. L. reported that Chrissy's speech appeared more fluent to them and some of the dysfluencies evident in the past seemed to have lessened. I encouraged them to praise her for the fluency of her speech.

Session 7

In response to Frog when he was talking excessively, Chrissy said, "Shhhh."

Session 8

Dialogue

Commentary

Tiger: [On telephone to her mom.] I hope no one will make a fuss when I talk.

I identified the issue that she did not want people to make a fuss when she talked (as told to me by her parents).

[Frog: Non-word noises.]

[C very quietly imitates noises, but noises become increasingly louder.]

Mr. and Mrs. L. noted this week that Chrissy was aware of a school conference they had with her teacher. She asked about it, and according to her mother, seemed afraid of what was said. Later that evening at bedtime, Chrissy said to Mrs. L., "It's hard to be quiet all the time." Her mom asked her about that, and she responded, "Never mind, I was talking to my puppy."

Session 9

Chrissy listened to a musical tape with Frog. The tape broke and Chrissy appeared upset. I verbalized that it upset her that the tape broke.

Dialogue	*Commentary*
SK [Therapist and puppets play kazoos.]	I introduced the kazoo because the player needs to make noise in order for it to work. However, the noise does not need to consist of speech sounds. This way I was shaping the puppet's behavior toward talking.

[C imitates playing kazoo.]

[C, playing with the doll house, makes noises for the alarm clock, snoring, and the dolls getting dressed. She uses intonation, but no real words, when talking on the telephone, clearly indicating the turn-taking of a telephone conversation without any dialogue.]

SK: I am going to visit your school this week. I will meet your teacher, Mrs. Smith. I can't wait to see your school!	I did not want the school visit to be a surprise, so I told her in advance that I would be at the school.

[C grins from ear to ear.]

Mr. and Mrs. L. reported that they did not cooperate when Chrissy asked them to write out her bunny's name on a piece of paper, so that she could bring it to the session. She also said "boo" to an older relative with whom she had never spoken.

Session 10

Chrissy made noises as she walked around the office.

Dialogue	Commentary
SK: I visited your school this week. I met Mrs. Smith. She is really nice.	Again, no surprises. I was following up on last week's conversation, by telling her what happened.

[C smiles.]

| SK: She told me that you have a rabbit in your class. I wonder what the rabbit's name is. | I knew that Chrissy was very attached to the rabbit. I wanted to introduce the rabbit into the conversation because of her positive feeling about it. I phrased it so that she did not have to answer me. |

C: [Whispers] "Bunny."

| [SK writes "Bunny" next to picture child draws of the rabbit.] | I was nonverbally reinforcing the content of her speech, by writing "Bunny" next to her picture. |

[C continues to draw, this time making a picture of herself with a patch on her eye.]

C: [Whispers to bear] Patch.

Throughout the rest of the session, she played the kazoo, used the telephone with some intonation, whispered, without spoken words, and pointed to feeling faces/words.

Session 11

In the waiting room, Mr. and Mrs. L. mentioned that Chrissy might want to tell me where she was going after the session.

Dialogue	Commentary
SK: [As child and therapist enter office] I wonder where you are going.	I was picking up on her parents' question. I did not want to ask it as a direct question that required an answer. Instead, I phrased it as if I was wondering about it, which did not imply that I expected her to answer.
C: Ho Ho.	
SK: [Acts puzzled.] Ho Ho, I wonder where you are going. Ho Ho, hmmm.	I pretended not to understand what "Ho Ho" meant, in an effort to not "guess" her intent, but rather, expected that if she was going to talk, she must communicate clearly. In other words, I was shaping her talking.
[No response.]	
[C picks up a cat/duck two-sided puppet and plays with it.]	
SK: This side is a cat, but I wonder what this side is.	Again, I wondered instead of asking her directly.
C: Quack, quack . . .	
SK: [Continues to appear puzzled] Ho Ho, Ho Ho . . .	
C: [Seems frustrated, states in angry voice] Santa Claus.	
SK: Wow, that will be really fun to go see Santa Claus. I wonder what you want to get from Santa for Christmas.	I positively reinforced the content of her speech, not the fact that she was talking.
C: [In strained voice] Bouncing babies.	

The session continued with Chrissy talking in mostly two-word utterances, for example saying "tie boots" after she demonstrated her proficiency with tying her shoe laces. At the end of the session, she had a conversation, over the telephone with Frog:

Dialogue	Commentary
Frog: [Over telephone] May I speak to Chrissy, please?	I was introducing simple language that she could respond to with simple utterances, if she preferred. I also had the question come from the puppet, so she did not perceive that I expected her to talk.
C: This is Chrissy.	
Frog: Can you come over to play?	I did not want to appear overly surprised that she was talking nor expect too much. I continued with the conversation as she directed it.
C: Yes.	
Frog: Bring a toy with you.	
C: Bring blocks.	
[This conversation was repeated three times.]	

Session 12

This session was approximately one week before Christmas. Chrissy entered the office, turned off the lights—although it was bright in the room because of the sunlight through the windows—and began talking. She talked about Christmas, what presents she wanted, and what she thought about seeing Santa Claus. Her play centered around themes of Christmas as she and the puppets wrapped presents and decorated the tree.

Dialogue	Commentary
SK: What are you are telling me is really interesting. I am happy to hear about how excited you are about Christmas.	I wanted to praise the *content* of her conversation, not the fact that she was talking.
[SK gives child stickers for how interesting the conversation is and for tying her shoelaces.]	I provided positive reinforcement in the form of tangible rewards (stickers) for the content of her conversation and for tying her shoelaces.

At the end of the session, when Chrissy and I walked into the waiting room, Mr. and Mrs. L. were not there. Chrissy was midsentence, when they walked in and she stopped talking, as if she did not want her parents to know that she had spoken to me.

Session 13

Chrissy was talkative during the session, starting off by introducing Frog to a stuffed animal, Puppy, she brought with her. She indicated that the animal wanted a sticker and tried to figure out what the puppy could do to earn a sticker. She decided that the puppy could sing a Christmas song, which Chrissy sang all the way through. She got angry at Frog, taking him from the police, to Santa (seemingly, the ultimate authority). I indicated that Tiger was still not talking and the following conversation ensued:

Dialogue	Commentary
C: Make her talk.	
SK: I can't make her talk. She'll talk when she is ready.	I was clarifying the idea that no one could "make" her talk, she would talk when she was ready to do so.
C: [To Tiger] When are you gonna talk?	I found it interesting, but did not comment on the fact, that she had very little patience for Tiger not talking.

[Tiger moves lips, uses distorted, unrecognizable voice.]

C: [Seems angry]. NO, use your regular voice like mine and yours. [Pointing to therapist.]

SK: Tiger is at school, and the teacher is asking her to say her ABCs and 123s.

C: I talked at school to a b-b-boy. A bad boy. He tells bad jokes . . .

C: Tiger, talk. Say one.

Tiger: One.   I repeated what she said to model that Tiger could do it

C: Two.

Tiger: Two.

C: Three.

Tiger: Three.

[SK gives Chrissy a sticker for helping Tiger to talk; Tiger gets a sticker for talking.]   Again, I reinforced her for helping, not for talking. Because Tiger's problem had been talking, I reinforced Tiger for talking.

Session 14

Chrissy reminded me that Tiger talked the previous week and the therapist reminded Tiger that she will be going back to school next week when her vacation is over. Chrissy again would not talk in front of Mr. and Mrs. L., although she did show them the puppets. I told her that next week we will all play a game together at the end of the session.

Session 15

Chrissy was excited about the game she would be playing with her parents and the therapist, and asked several questions about it. She asked about Tiger, regarding whether or not she went back to school and if she was talking there.

Dialogue	*Commentary*
SK: Chrissy, Tiger has a question for you. She wants to know what would help her talk at school.	By trying to get her to help the puppet, I was trying to help her verbalize what skills *she* used to talk. My hypothesis was that this might also help strengthen her sense of competence about talking.
C: [Very sternly] Look it.	
Tiger: I don't like talking at school, but I know I need to. What should I do?	I was continuing to try to get her to verbalize what she did.
C: [To therapist] I don't know, you tell.	She did not seem to want to pursue this, but asked me to talk with Tiger.
SK: I should tell her? Okay, Tiger, will you listen to me real carefully . . . I know it is really, really hard, and you're really kinda scared to do it, but I tell you what, if you really try, and you just say a little bit, and then the next day you say a little bit more, pretty soon you'll be ready to talk all the time, and I think you'll even like it. And I don't think you have to worry about kids teasing	I identified that it was hard, and scary and could be done gradually. I wanted to establish that it would be done, it could be a positive experience, and the other children would not necessarily be mean. My hypothesis was that this would label for her what she has done, and what the result was.

you, and I don't think you have to worry about anybody making a big fuss. I just think you'll just really like talking there . . .

Dialogue	Commentary
[C laughs as she puts hat on Tiger.]	Knowing that teasing was a problem, I took her laughing to mean that she might think the Tiger looks silly.
Tiger: Chrissy, I look silly in this hat. Should I wear this hat to school?	I was identifying teasing as a problem for the Tiger.
C: Mmmmm.	
Tiger: The kids will laugh at me.	
C: No, they won't.	She seemed to be getting the message that she won't be teased for everything.

Chrissy and I played a card game, and Chrissy quickly learned the rules. At the end of the session, I asked Mr. and Mrs. L. to join us for a game. Chrissy was quite involved in the game, but would not explain the rules to her parents and talked only in a whisper to Mrs. L. I introduced Mr. and Mrs. L. into the end of the therapy session as a means of encouraging Chrissy to talk to me in front of her parents.

Session 16

Dialogue	Commentary
Tiger: I talked at school this week.	I wanted to continue with the theme.
C: I don't care. [Looking at therapist] You talk to her.	She continued not to want to deal with this issue.

In the game at the end of the session with her parents, Chrissy was quiet, again only whispering to Mrs. L.

Session 17

Just prior to this session, Mrs. L. had telephoned to inform me that Chrissy had talked "nonstop" to the teacher at school that day. Chrissy began the session by immediately showing me the two pins she had received at school for talking.

Dialogue	Commentary
C: I talked with my teacher this week.	
SK: About what?	I focused on the content, not the fact that she talked.
C: Everything . . .	
Tiger: I heard you talked at school, tell me how you did it?	I was trying to get her to label what she did.
C: I don't know, I just did it!	
Tiger: Was it scary?	She did not seem to want to, or be able to focus on the skills. Here, I was trying to get her to focus on the feelings associated with talking.
C: No.	
Tiger: Did it feel good?	I was trying to see if she could identify positive feelings associated with talking.
C: Yes. Maybe you can get a sticker if you talk at school.	
[C draws and cuts out glasses for Frog and places them on the puppet.]	

SK: [To Frog] I know you can see better with the glasses and they look very nice on you.

By reinforcing the frog for wearing glasses and telling him how nice he looked, I was hoping the frog would serve as a model for wearing glasses.

Chrissy became upset when she realized that I was going to talk to her parents at the end of the session. When I acknowledged the anger and tried to label it for her, she at first denied it. Later Chrissy admitted that she was angry with me because she wanted me to spend all the time with her.

In meeting with Mr. and Mrs. L., they reported that Chrissy continued to talk at school with her teacher individually, in class, and was now also talking to the speech therapist.

Session 18

Dialogue

Commentary

C: [To Tiger] Did you talk at school this week?

Child followed up with checking on Tiger.

Tiger: Yes. [Tiger shows Chrissy a piece of paper with stickers on it for talking.]

C: Good girl, Tiger.

Child was repeating the positive reinforcement to the puppet!

C: I talked to my teacher and the speech teacher.

Tiger: That's great. . . .

I had the puppet reinforce her for talking.

SK: I think you were mad at me last week when I had to talk to your mom and dad.

C: Yes. I don't want you to. I don't like it.

SK: Sometimes things like that make you mad. I had to talk to your mom and dad and you were mad about that . . .

I repeated it to clarify that I heard and understood her.

C: Some kid at school called a girl "four eyes" because she wears glasses.

SK: Do you think she was sad when they called her four eyes? Think she was kind of sad and mad about that?

I was guessing at her feelings.

C: NO, she was angry and then that little boy apologized.

SK: He apologized? That was a nice thing to do.

I wanted her to know that what the boy did was wrong and that apologizing was a good thing.

Frog: I wouldn't like it if somebody called me four eyes, that would make me mad.

Because of her identification with the puppets, I had Frog "self-disclose" angry feelings.

C: You would talk to the teacher, Frog.

Frog: Yeah, but I always talk to the teacher. Remember sometimes I talk too much? The teacher has to say, "Frog, you gotta give all the kids a chance, you can't talk all the time, remember?"

C: And then there's Tiger.

SK: What happened to Tiger this week? 'Cause once she started talking in school she really likes talking to her

I was identifying the positive aspects of talking and how happy feelings could be associated with talking.

teacher—she was so happy.
She started talking to everybody.

C: [Puts on the frog's glasses.]
No songs for him until he
wears his glasses for awhile.

She continued to understand the
power of positive reinforcement of
the puppets!

SK: Okay. He looks good in his
glasses, but it may make him
mad if someone teases him
because he wears them.

I was reinforcing the glasses wearing, but also identifying that he
got mad when others teased him.

Tiger: I talked to my teacher, and I
talked to my speech teacher,
and I talked to the kids at
school, but can I start talking
to other people too?

C: Yes.

Tiger: Who should I talk to?

C: Lots and lots of people.

Tiger: Lots of people?

C: Yeah.

SK: [To Tiger] I think you should
talk to everybody because
you have nice things to say.

I was labeling a positive reason for
talking.

C: Yeah, yeah. You talk to
somebody, everybody . . .

Tiger: Okay, I tell you what,
Chrissy. You ask me next
week who I talked to, Okay?

I was encouraging her to follow-up
with the Tiger, as one means of
indirectly reinforcing her own talking.

C: Okay.

SK: [To Tiger] Do you want to know who Chrissy's talked to? Well ask her.

Tiger: Who you talked to Chrissy?

C: Guess.

SK: Umm. Mommy and Daddy . . .

I picked "easy" ones to see what she would say.

C: And the speech lady.

SK: . . . and the speech lady, and Mrs. Smith [her teacher], and Bunny . . . and who else? The principal?

C: How'd you know the principal? I talked to her too. I 'member her name. . . .

Tiger: Should I talk to the principal at my school? Is it hard or easy? . . .

Here Tiger was really modeling progress in talking after Chrissy. I was hopeful that this would help her feel positive about her efforts.

C: It's easy.

Tiger: Oh it's easy. I would like to do it.

Session 19

Chrissy brought in several pictures, including a picture of her house and glasses for the frog. Throughout this session, she repeatedly asked questions about me (e.g., whether I had children, where I lived). I explained that I understood why she wondered about these things, but that I could not answer all of her questions. Chrissy at first became aggressive with the puppets, mostly hitting them. I acknowledged that Chrissy was angry and indicated that perhaps the anger was at me because Chrissy did not feel that I was sufficiently answering her questions. At first Chrissy denied it, but later was able to acknowledge that she was angry at me.

Session 20

Chrissy verbalized that she was still angry, but played positively with the puppets. On the way out of the session she called to the tiger, "Keep talking at school."

Session 21

Chrissy praised the frog for wearing his glasses, "Very good, Frog."

Session 22

Chrissy was intently making hearts for the puppets and herself. As I engaged the puppets in conversation about school and speech class, Chrissy appeared to be listening and offered her opinions from across the room. However, she did not join the conversation.

Session 23

Dialogue	*Commentary*
C: Do you have to see my parents today?	
SK: Yes.	
[C makes angry face.]	
SK: I know that you get very mad about that. Can you tell me that you are mad when I need to talk with your parents?	I was labeling anger and reason for anger for her. Also, I was trying to shape her to label the anger herself.
[C is quiet.]	

[SK shows how Frog makes a   I had the puppet model nonverbal
face and says he is mad.]   and verbal expressions of anger.

Her parents reported that Chrissy was talking to "everyone," including other patrons at fast-food restaurants! She was so talkative at
school that at times the teacher needed to encourage her to be quiet.

Session 24

Chrissy's parents and I had been talking, separately,with her about
changing therapy sessions to meet every other week. Chrissy brought
this up at this session and stated that "every other week is a long time."

Session 25

We had decided to move her sessions to every other week. Chrissy said
that she missed me the previous week and asked questions about the
"other girl" that I saw on the weeks that she did not come in. I assured
her that she is special and that I missed her, too. At this point I was
bringing up the issue of termination at every session, telling her that she
was doing very well and did not need to keep coming. I was also clearly
letting her know that I and the puppets would miss her, but that we
would be happy to know that she was doing so well. I set up a scenario
with the lion puppet in which he did not want to talk and Tiger showed
him how, but Chrissy was uninterested in this.

Session 28

Tiger played out anger at a boy who teased her because she has such
long eyelashes. Chrissy had the boy come over to Tiger and apologize.

Session 29

Chrissy discovered a timer in the room and wanted to use time-out with
Frog for not talking and then reward him with presents. She then timed
Tiger to see how long the puppet could talk. Tiger talked about being
sad because she had to leave kindergarten and how hard it was to say
goodbye. Tiger added that first grade would be good. Chrissy listened,
but told Tiger that she was sad about leaving kindergarten. She did not
seem to be able to focus on the positive side of first grade.

Session 30

We had moved Chrissy's sessions to once a month. Chrissy again put Frog in time-out for not talking. She worked on a book of her life, providing current information about herself. When I asked about her life before kindergarten she said, "I don't remember."

Mr. and Mrs. L. reported that Chrissy continued to do very well. She was talking to most people and planning when she would talk to others to whom she has not yet spoken (e.g., "I will talk to her for her birthday").

Session 31

Chrissy talked about missing her kindergarten teacher. I discussed how she and I would miss each other after therapy ends. Chrissy took a copy of my business card and promised to call. She seemed to need reassurance that even though she did not know where I lived, she would still be able to "find" me. We started to make plans for a final "farewell" party to be held at the last session.

Mr. and Mrs. L. reported that she had been most responsive to others and they continued to be amazed by the settings in which she talked freely. For example, she volunteered to do a magic trick at a theme park and told the large audience her name.

Session 32

Chrissy talked about termination, requesting reassurance that she could call or visit. Mr. and Mrs. L. reported that Chrissy appeared to keep a "list" in her head of those with whom she had yet to speak. Remaining on the list were her first grade teacher (three more weeks until the beginning of school) and her dentist, whom she had not seen since beginning to talk with adults.

Given her dramatic success in talking and increasing reluctance to wear diapers at night, Mr. and Mrs. L. were interested in actively treating Chrissy's nocturnal enuresis. They began to use a urine alarm system with Chrissy with excellent results. They reported that it awakened her immediately, she went to the bathroom, and stayed dry throughout the night. Chrissy was thrilled about finally being out of diapers at night.

Session 33

We held a party with the puppets in attendance. Chrissy repeatedly said, "I will miss you" and wrote her last name on a paper so the therapist "will not forget, in case you have another Chris." She drew a picture of the therapist, "So I won't forget you," and stated she is "happy now. I wasn't before when I wouldn't talk."

RESULTS AND FOLLOW-UP

Chrissy did not speak to me or in my presence during the first three assessment sessions. Gradually, she made closer and closer approximations to talking, moving from laughter, noises, whispering, speech sounds, simple utterances, and then at the twelfth session, Chrissy began to talk. Figure 6–1 shows her progression toward talking over the course of treatment.

Although Chrissy began talking in therapy regularly after the twelfth session, at first she did not talk to any other new adults in her environment. Eventually, between the sixteenth and seventeenth treatment sessions, she began to talk to her teacher, and then gradually to other adults at school and elsewhere.

A CBCL, filled out by the parents at the last session, again yielded a nonclinical profile. Compared with the initial CBCL, this profile was also flat, with even fewer items endorsed than had been at the initial assessment CBCL. The items endorsed as "somewhat or sometimes true" were: can't concentrate, can't pay attention for long; can't sit still, restless, or hyperactive; doesn't eat well; fears certain animals; problems with eyes (farsighted); speech problems (dysfluency); and wets the bed. No items were endorsed as "very true or often true."

Follow-up was obtained via Mr. and Mrs. L. 30 months after the termination of treatment. At that time, Chrissy was talking freely to all individuals with whom she had contact and was doing well with her schoolwork. There had been no relapses in talking, although she was still receiving speech therapy one day a week for her articulation difficulties. The parents had continued to use the urine alarm system for approximately one month after termination of treatment with positive outcome. When they discontinued the alarm, Chrissy had remained dry at night for the past 29 months and there had been no relapses of enuresis. They reported no other problems.

ELECTIVE MUTE 6 YEAR OLD

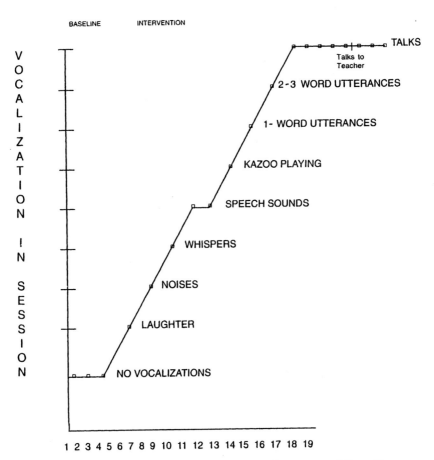

Figure 6-1. Progression toward talking over the course of Cognitive-Behavioral Play Therapy of elective mute 6-year-old

DISCUSSION

I treated Chrissy's mutism indirectly through two major avenues. The first was through the creation of a positive therapeutic environment, in which talking was not the major focus. Instead, I encouraged mastery and accomplishment in other areas. I used positive reinforcement for nonspeech activities (e.g., tying her shoe laces, drawing pictures). I did not assume it was necessary for Chrissy to talk. My comments were often worded as statements conveying interest, but not as questions with the expectation that Chrissy needed to provide an answer. For example, related to her statement "Ho Ho," instead of asking "Where are you going?" I said, "I wonder where you are going. . . ." Also, when Chrissy did speak, I reinforced the *content* of her conversation, not the *fact* that she was talking.

The second therapeutic avenue was via "treating" several puppets for a variety of problems. I gradually shaped talking in one puppet, a shy, nontalkative puppet, and as she "learned" to talk, her efforts provided a model for Chrissy. Thus, although I utilized many of the behavioral and cognitive interventions reported in the literature, I applied them indirectly through modeling, not directly with the child. I based the decision to treat Chrissy's mutism indirectly on the literature as well as clinical judgment that she would not respond positively to another adult who tried to "pressure" her to talk. Chrissy had not responded in the past to other professional efforts to "convince" her to talk or to shape talking and had made clear to her parents that she did not want a big fuss made when she started to talk. It seemed pointless to attempt to coax her into talking.

As much as possible, I tried to avoid responding to Chrissy's nonverbal behavior by making assumptions about what she was communicating. Even when Chrissy began to make closer and closer approximations to speech, I did not make assumptions about what she was intending to convey. For example, when she said "Ho Ho," I did not immediately assume that she meant Santa Claus. Similarly, when Chrissy made low sounds for a ringing phone, I waited until the sounds were more audible before "answering" the phone. This communicated interest, but also conveyed that I would not try to second-guess her intentions or speak for her. At times it was quite difficult not to respond directly when Chrissy did communicate. For example, when Chrissy said, "Ho Ho," it was shortly before Christmas, and I had every reason to believe that she was referring to Santa Claus. Nonetheless, I was able to appear uncertain, because I felt that it was in Chrissy's best interest to do so.

The puppets modeled various adaptive skills for Chrissy and she appeared to respond very positively to their behavior. For example, the puppets modeled appropriate verbal expression as they labeled feelings in response to certain situations. Thus, I *shaped* the puppets *in the socially appropriate expression of feelings*. Before Chrissy started speaking to me, I offered feeling faces so that Chrissy was able to point to the face that expressed her feelings. I also modeled self-statements via the puppets, such as "I don't like talking at school, but I know I need to." As she began to speak, I raised other issues and gradually shaped verbal expression of feelings. Slowly, Chrissy moved from pointing to pictures of feeling faces to making faces to match a particular feeling (e.g., mad, sad), and then eventually to verbal labeling of her feelings.

In providing encouragement and *positive reinforcement*, I also modeled this behavior for Chrissy. She consistently reinforced the puppets for their efforts to meet their goals. For example, Chrissy encouraged Tiger with comments such as, "Keep talking at school." She offered positive reinforcement in the form of praise to Tiger for talking (e.g., "Good talking, Tiger.") and Frog for wearing his glasses (e.g., "Very good, Frog."). This positive reinforcement on her part was unsolicited. I found her efforts to provide such positive feedback to the puppets both interesting and heartening, particularly since it seemed to increase as Chrissy began to feel more positive about herself.

Cognitive techniques were also modeled by the puppets. In order to *identify beliefs*, the puppet reiterated certain statements that Chrissy had made to her parents. For example, I said to Tiger, "Maybe you're afraid when you talk at school that everyone will make a fuss." This was countered by an effort to *change the belief*, when the puppet said, "It would be okay to talk. It would make me happy not to have to be quiet." Finally, the puppet also modeled *positive self-statements* such as, "It's hard to start talking, but it will get easier after I start." My efforts to help Chrissy verbalize her own positive self-statements were never successful. It is my belief that she was able to see herself in a positive way, but could not verbalize these thoughts.

Her ability to see herself in a positive way was clear in many of the statements she made and how proud of herself she seemed to be. However, she was reluctant to deal with any issues related to her previous silence. In fact, she tended to avoid participating in the puppets' conversations related to not talking, except to reinforce Tiger and offer her praise and encouragement. She did deal with the issues of teasing to some extent, although this was largely through comments regarding wearing glasses, something for which she had also apparently been teased. She did not deal with issues related to being teased for her speech difficulties. Working with Chrissy on a book of her life was one effort to deal with these earlier issues. Chrissy's response to her life before kindergarten was, "I don't remember." This was another indication that she preferred not to discuss the time before she talked. My hypothesis about her reluctance to discuss her previous silence relates to the drastic changes in what was reinforcing in her life. Now that talking was pleasant and was being reinforced, she had little use for talking about her previous silence, which was no longer receiving attention from others.

The teacher was apparently frustrated by Chrissy's lack of speech, particularly in view of her knowledge that Chrissy was now talking in therapy. Despite an agreement with the therapist not to directly discuss Chrissy's silence with her, one day between the sixteenth and seventeenth treatment sessions, the teacher merely told Chrissy that she would need to talk in order to go on to first grade in the coming year. The teacher told Chrissy that if she did not begin to speak, she might have to remain in kindergarten. Chrissy spoke to the teacher seemingly in response to the threat that she would need to speak in order to go on to first grade. I believe that this may have been effective because Chrissy was now comfortable talking to me and was gaining some self-confidence about what talking to others would be like. She enjoyed school and learning and found it to be generally rewarding. The teacher's threat about not going on to first grade may have frightened her or given her the impetus she needed in order to talk at school.

Initially, when Chrissy began talking in sessions, she continued to refuse to talk with me in front of Mr. and Mrs. L. She was also still refusing to talk to anyone new outside the therapy sessions. I used a *stimulus fading* paradigm in order to encourage talking in new settings and with new people. I asked Mr. and Mrs. L. to join us and play a game at the end of the session. At first she stopped talking to me when her parents entered the room. Over time, she gradually began to whisper to her mother and then eventually talk with me and both parents in a normal tone of voice. Thus, as I gradually changed the stimuli controlling speech over time, Chrissy began to extend her efforts to talk to include speaking with her parents and myself at the same time. Such a paradigm might have been useful at school had Chrissy not begun to speak there without such an intervention. Had it been indicated, I would have spent some time at school with Chrissy to help her transfer her willingness to talk with me to the teacher and other school personnel.

In addition to the play therapy, a number of other factors may have contributed to the success of this case. By ignoring the mutism, Chrissy's parents and teacher were, in essence, attempting to diminish and eventually extinguish it. This might be considered a form of treatment. Therefore, one explanation of the positive outcome is that efforts to ignore the silence extinguished it. However, this explanation is unlikely for several reasons. First, Chrissy showed a gradual increase in talking that seemed to be related to what was taking place in the CBPT sessions, rather than related to environmental circumstances. Also, the efforts of her parents and teacher to ignore her silence were not always successful, as noted by various occasions where they directly attended to it. Maturation cannot be ruled out as an explanation for the child's success in talking. There is no way to determine if Chrissy would have begun to talk spontaneously without treatment. However, given her dramatic response to specific situations in treatment and lack of responsiveness to previous interventions, it seems unlikely that maturation alone would explain the positive changes.

Assessment of elective mute children presents some unique difficulties because of the lack of direct verbal information provided. Such information must be obtained from parent report, school information, and other sources, as well as from the child's nonverbal behavior. Creative use of feeling faces, drawings, and play materials can provide the therapist with a wealth of information. Currently, most behavioral interventions deal directly with the elective mute child's refusal to speak, either by shaping closer approximations to speech or reinforcing talking when it does occur. These interventions can be problematic, in part because they directly address the child's silence. By dealing with the silence directly, the therapist may convey a message that the child is being "coerced" to speak. Such attempts are typically unsuccessful.

Although many behavioral treatments of elective mutism have been successful without cognitive components, the cognitive-behavioral approach expands the treatment to include cognitive interventions that may directly address the child's perceptions about speaking. Elective mute children may have thoughts about their silence that are not clear to others. In some instances, the parents may have observations about the child that provide a clue to what the child may be thinking. If the therapist has such information available, the child's perceptions can be understood initially through information conveyed to the therapist.

Through CBPT, children can address feelings associated with their silence, as well as learn more adaptive ways of dealing with their feelings. Initially, this may involve nonverbal expression (e.g., facial expressions, drawing feeling faces) and verbal labeling that the therapist models for the child. Later, if the child begins to talk, the therapist might use more direct verbal labeling of feelings.

Elective mutism is clearly a complex disorder. A variety of treatment approaches may be indicated and the choice of a particular approach may be dictated by many factors including the child's age, developmental level, extent of mutism, apparent role of the silence, family dynamics, and previous interventions, as well as parental cooperation and motivation. The applicability of CBPT in the treatment of other elective mute children is at present unknown. Further use of this approach would be helpful in determining which variables would be most amenable to a CBPT approach.

REFERENCES

Achenbach, T. M., and Edelbrock, C. (1983). *Manual for the Child Behavior Checklist and Revised Child Behavior Profile.* Burlington, VT: University Associates in Psychiatry.

American Psychiatric Association. (1987). *Diagnostic and Statistical Manual of the Mental Disorders.* 3rd ed.–rev. Washington, DC: American Psychiatric Association.

Bandura, A. (1977). *Social Learning Theory.* Englewood Cliffs, NJ: Prentice Hall.

Beck, A. T., and Emery, G. (1985). *Anxiety Disorders and Phobias: A Cognitive Perspective.* New York: Basic Books.

Beck, A. T., Rush, A. J., Shaw, B. F., and Emery, G. (1979). *Cognitive Therapy of Depression.* New York: Guilford.

Bierman, K. L. (1983). Cognitive development and clinical interviews with children. In *Advances in Clinical Child Psychology,* vol. 6, ed. B. B. Lahey and A. Kazdin, pp. 217–250. New York: Plenum.

Braswell, L., and Kendall, P. C. (1988). Cognitive-behavioral methods with children. In *Handbook of Cognitive Behavior Therapy,* ed. K. S. Dobson, pp. 167–213. New York: Guilford.

Campbell, S. (1990). *Behavior Problems in Preschool Children.* New York: Guilford.

Knell, S. M. (1993). *Cognitive-Behavioral Play Therapy.* Northvale, NJ: Jason Aronson.

Knell, S. M., and Moore, D. J. (1990). Cognitive-behavioral play therapy in the treatment of encopresis. *Journal of Clinical Child Psychology* 19:55–60.

Kolvin, I., and Fundudis, T. (1981). Elective mute children: psychological development and background factors. *Journal of Child Psychiatry* 22:219–232.

Labbe, E. E., and Williamson, D. A. (1984). Behavioral treatment of elective mutism: a review of the literature. *Clinical Psychology Review* 4:273–292.

Masten, A. S., and Braswell, L. (1991). Developmental psychopathology: an integrative framework. In *Handbook of Behavior Therapy and Psychological Science,* ed. P. R. Martin, pp. 317–336. New York: Pergamon.

Meichenbaum, D. (1985). *Stress Inoculation Training.* New York: Pergamon.

Richards, C. S., and Hansen, M. K. (1978). A further demonstration of the efficacy of stimulus fading treatment of elective mutism. *Journal of Behavior Therapy and Experimental Psychiatry* 9:57–60.

Williamson, D. A., Sewell, W. R., Sanders, S. H., et al. (1977). The treatment of reluctant speech using contingency management procedures. *Journal of Behavior Therapy and Experimental Psychiatry* 8:151–156.

Wright, H. L. (1968). A clinical study of children who refuse to talk. *Journal of the American Academy of Child Psychiatry* 7:603–617.

7

"Born on My Bum": Jungian Play Therapy

John Allan, PH.D., and Susan Levin, PH.D.

In our work in child guidance clinics over the past twenty-five years, we have treated many children with severe behavior disorders. The parents are often at a loss to understand the child and frequently blame themselves for the child's problems. With some of these children, a close examination of their developmental history reveals the presence of clear-cut birth trauma—prolonged and difficult labor, forceps delivery, over- or underuse of oxygen—that in turn has a negative impact on bonding and mastery of some developmental skills (Blackman 1989). Holding, feeding, calming, and attunement are painfully difficult to establish and the child seldom experiences sufficient cycles of distress to relaxation in human contact. This chapter describes a Jungian approach to treating a birth-traumatized child and outlines some of the key theoretical constructs that dictated her treatment process.

INTRODUCTION TO JUNGIAN THEORY

C. G. Jung (1875-1961) was a Swiss psychiatrist who was part of Freud's inner circle until 1912 when he broke away due to strong theoretical differences over the nature of the libido. To Freud, the libido was sexual, whereas to Jung, the main drive in the psyche was that of separation and growth, or to use his term, *individuation*. Though Jung never worked directly with children, his theory and treatment methods are very applicable to children because Jungian theory centers around the

209

role of symbols, dreams, and the creative arts in healing emotional wounds and in facilitating inner development and the reconstruction of an interior life.

Jungian Theory

Jung built his theory on the concepts of conscious and unconscious life and the interplay or dialogue between the two. He saw the ego as the center of consciousness and the self as not only the center of the unconscious but also the whole circumference of the psyche that includes both the conscious and the unconscious. The unconscious, according to Jungian theory, is made up of repressed memories and instinctual drives (personal unconscious) and also archetypal patterns that have evolved over time and play an important part in shaping the human experience (collective unconscious). According to Samuels and colleagues (1986) "the archetype is a psychosomatic concept, linking body and psyche, instinct and image" (p. 26). Archetypes carry strong positive and negative emotional charges, images, and behaviors around "such key basic and universal experiences of life as birth, marriage, motherhood, death and separation" (Samuels et al. 1986, p. 26). The archetype of the self is the central organizing principle in the human psyche that strives toward wholeness and growth.

To Jung, this deep unconscious area of the psyche not only stored knowledge of preverbal wounds, but contained within itself the ability to heal, restore, and regenerate. Healing and regeneration occur when the therapist forms a therapeutic alliance with the client and follows and comments on unconscious processes as they are manifested through dream and other symbolic productions. It is the experience of rapport and therapeutic alliance that activates the self-healing archetype. The skill of the therapist in understanding transference, countertransference, and the language of symbols brings about healing. In this way, core beliefs, internal working models of self, and self in relation to others change and healing occurs. Much of Jungian therapy centers around expression—the act of writing dreams, playing, making, doing, and enacting fantasies in the safety of the therapeutic container. It is only through these acts that the client can express and release negative introjections and experience new and more positive feelings, emotions, images, and behaviors. The client can then use these experiences to build up a new interior psychological life.

Short History

In 1909 at Clark University, Jung (1910) presented a paper called "Psychic Conflicts in a Child." In this paper he described a young girl's dreams and showed how they reflected the psychological conflicts of the parents (and in doing so, he became the first systemic family therapist). Though Jung spent most of his professional life focusing on the psychotherapy of people in mid-life transitions, a number of his followers have done play psychotherapy with children, all of them drawing on various influences of their time and culture. Kalff (1981), who studied under Jung and Lowenfeld, developed the sand-play technique, while Neumann (1973) extended our understanding of archetypal influences on child development. Fordham (1969) integrated Jungian and Kleinian ideas and described how the ego is constructed through processes of deintegration and reintegration. More recently, Sidoli (1989) has instituted seminars on mother/infant observation and written about the advantages of training in both child and adult analysis. Allan (1988) and Allan and Bertoia (1992) have combined the principles of child-centered play therapy and Jungian work, especially in schools and clinics.

Jungian Play Therapy

All certified Jungian play therapists would have had at least four to eight years of their own analysis. This is critically important because Jungians primarily work out of the transference-countertransference paradigm. In order to see and hear clearly and to be sensitive to the nuances of one's own inner processes, one's intrapsychic struggles must be known and understood.

Most Jungians use a traditional fully equipped playroom—doll house, doll figures, art table and materials, two sandboxes (one with wet and the other with dry sand), miniature toys, sink or water table, baby bottle, telephones, puppets, small bed, building blocks, and areas for construction activities and board games. Some analysts use separate boxes for their child clients to store their special toys that they bring in for each session. All analysts evoke the concept of "the container"—that the room is a free and protected space where the child "can play more or less as she or he wishes." This allows for regression, a release from the overburdening demands of consciousness and the possibility of expressing and transforming painful affects and experiences. Limits are typically not set until deemed necessary. The Jungian belief is that children will go to the areas of play that are relevant to their struggles and development. The therapist follows by reflecting or interpreting the emotions, the actions, or the meaning of the struggles. If the child assigns the therapist a role, the therapist asks for clarifications ("What do I do?"–"What do I say?"), plays the role out but always keeps "an analytical attitude" as to the meaning of the play to the child (Allan and Brown in press). Often one sees a pattern in play of chaos, struggle, and resolution that the child repeats until he or she resolves the major issues (Allan and Berry 1987).

The playroom becomes the "temenos," the sanctuary from the demands of the outer world, where regression can occur, and where the child can express, understand, and transform painful affect, giving rise to a new and healthier self. The analyst follows the child's unconscious as it unfolds, believing that the child will go to the problem areas, struggle with the "good versus bad" feelings, and slowly begin to develop appropriate mastery and control.

PRESENTING PROBLEM AND BACKGROUND DATA

We first observed 4-year-old Miko as she darted anxiously around the periphery of the playground of the mental health clinic where we worked. There were dark circles under her eyes, and she looked troubled and unhappy. As she ran about the playground keeping a distance from other children, she appeared frightened, as if she were fleeing imaginary monsters. Indoors, a high degree of hyperactivity characterized her behavior. Outside she could give her energies free rein. Miko looked like a child who was living a waking nightmare.

The personnel at her day care considered Miko a special needs child, even though she appeared normal physically and was strong and energetic, despite a slightly awkward gait. It was her behavior, her emotional and relational responsivity, that was very problematic. Miko exhibited sustained angry and boisterous contact with others in which anxiety and hyperactivity predominated. At home, she was prone to frequent and prolonged tantrums over what appeared to her family to be minor causes. At night her sleeping patterns were highly disturbed. Miko had difficulty falling asleep without one of her parents by her side. She feared monsters, suffered from nightmares, and tended to be enuretic. When traveling to new or even to familiar places, Miko became anxious. She worried whether there would be a bathroom for her use.

Miko displayed some unusual behaviors. At home, she would suddenly urinate on the sofa or on the living room floor. She masturbated frequently. At home or at school Miko liked to disrobe for no apparent reason. Alone with her father and sisters while mother went shopping, Miko had recently pointed at the digital numbers on the television set and screamed inconsolably. This had frightened the entire family.

At school, Miko often engaged in an unusual play sequence. Wearing dress-up clothes and shoes, she veiled her head or waved scarves around in a little veil dance, while singing to herself. Miko's dress-up play was usually solitary and often included solo tea parties. Her peers tended to leave her to these dress-up rituals.

Background Data

Miko was the youngest of three children. She lived with her parents and two older sisters. Her siblings did not suffer from any evident behavioral or emotional difficulties. Her parents, a well-educated and serious professional couple, had immigrated to Canada long before the birth of their first child. The father, Mr. T., and mother, Mrs. T., were devoted to their daughters while they continued to work in their professions, as an engineer and a beautician, respectively.

Miko's difficulties began at birth. Her birth had been a compounded trauma of presenting breech position, a perilous impasse during labor, and the shock of a cesarean delivery. Mrs. T.'s physicians and the hospital personnel had not recognized her breech position before or during the delivery. After many hours, the already difficult labor reached a dangerous and, for the staff, perplexing stage when the baby made no progress through the birth canal for several hours. The specialist who they finally called in quickly identified Miko's life-threatening breech position and ordered an emergency cesarean section. Although this surgical intervention undoubtedly saved Miko's life, as well as that of her mother, the compounded trauma—of many hours of pushing with no success, of exhaustion, and a reduced oxygen supply—took an enormous toll on the psychological well-being of baby Miko and her parents.

Miko did not open her eyes for a week. We believe this unusual postnatal occurrence was in response to her exhausting and traumatic birth experience. A colicky infant, Miko screamed interminably. Exhausted from and disappointed in the delivery for which she felt well-prepared psychologically, Mrs. T. felt frustrated by and distanced from her withdrawn and screaming infant daughter. It was a difficult and disrupted beginning for the attachment bonding between mother and child.

Since infancy, Miko had required frequent medical tests and interventions, including several brief hospitalizations for bone problems. In the pretherapy intake meeting with her parents, when we asked whether Miko suffered from any health problems, her parents detailed at length Miko's many visits to pediatric specialists for continuous colds and flus.

In the summer before we began to treat Miko, Mr. and Mrs. T. had reluctantly agreed to a specialist's prescription of medication for Miko's behavioral difficulties. Miko responded to Ritalin with increased tantrums and intensified antisocial behaviors, such as biting. Her parents immediately discontinued the medication. Later that summer, Miko reacted to a different prescription by another specialist by exhibiting violent physical reactions. She sobbed and screamed in evident pain, vomited, and suffered from severe diarrhea. As Miko's second year at day care began, her parents were emotionally exhausted and near despair. The day care supervision suggested play therapy, which we would be providing at a local mental health clinic, as part of the second author's (S. L.) doctoral internship. Mr. and Mrs. T. eagerly agreed to this treatment for their child, hoping it would help her and feeling that they had nothing to lose.

Attempts at Assessment

Over the years, Miko had been assessed by numerous specialists. Each specialist had identified and focused on a particular problem area: poor adaptive response, poor fine motor coordination, short attention span, immature development, hyperactivity, and so on. Some of the specialists had been perplexed by such traits as head banging in infancy, minimal responsivity to pain, no evident fear of danger, inconsistent eye contact, a tendency for tense and repetitive play, and resistance to holding or cuddling. This array of specialists had advanced an entire spectrum of diagnoses to account for these behaviors: Minimal Brain Dysfunction, Attention Deficit Disorder, social-emotional aspects of a learning disorder, Pervasive Developmental Disorder, and even mild autism. None of these terms had explained to her parents' satisfaction the global nature of Miko's difficulties. Nor had the specialists been able to suggest to Mr. and Mrs. T. ways that they might meaningfully assist their daughter.

When we met with Mr. and Mrs. T. during the pretherapy intake meeting, their feelings were intense. Only hours before our meeting, they had taken Miko to yet another pediatric specialist. They had been stunned to learn that Miko suffered from a degenerative, but potentially correctable, bone condition. Having just returned Miko to school, they were still in shock and terribly upset at the prospect of the required major surgery on her legs. Miko's lifelong difficulties with respiratory infections paled by comparison to this diagnosis. Both parents realized that their already unstable and emotionally at-risk child could suffer a severe emotional trauma with this serious and painful surgery. Their pain and distress over the pending surgery left them distraught, but vulnerable and amenable to our views on their daughter's difficulties.

As we listened to their recounting of Miko's difficulties and her developmental history, we perceived that intermingled with the parents' frustration over the many earlier diagnoses for Miko's problems were their feelings of despair and loss. We also perceived that their discouragement created complications in the parent–child relationship. While earlier diagnoses had left them frustrated, the diagnoses also offered them the security of labels for Miko, labels that, in turn, served to prevent the parents from reassessing and improving their way of relating to their daughter. They were continually in quest of new professional help and opinions.

Although we were aware that head banging and poor responsivity to pain figured in autism, we had observed Miko several times at the mental health center. We knew of her enjoyment of swimming, art, music, and play. Despite the comprehensiveness of her emotional and behavioral difficulties, we considered her a child whose component problems and abilities nevertheless fell well within the normal range. She seemed to be, in fact, quite a bright, verbal, capable, and creative child.

However, as we sat talking with Mr. and Mrs. T., we kept these reflections to ourselves. Above all, we sensed that the parents needed from us a sense of hope and an assessment that offered a framework of understanding within which they could begin to repair their relationship with Miko. We suggested to them that we would explain Miko's apparently bizarre behaviors in terms of anxiety. Their daughter, we explained, had been overwhelmed from an early age by a difficult birth and by frightening, often intrusive, and painful medical procedures. Her contacts with doctors and hospitals had been so frequent and so overwhelmingly fear- and anxiety-provoking that Miko had never had sufficient time or opportunity to recover emotionally before her next health crisis. She had not been able to achieve emotional equilibrium, let alone gain ground. Just as she had appeared on the clinic playground to be running from monsters, Miko indeed must have felt that her own life was a continual attempt to flee the threat of yet another unpredictable, "monstrous" medical procedure.

Both parents eagerly accepted this explanation, which intentionally bypassed any implications about their relationship with their daughter. We offered them several practical suggestions as to how they might reduce her anxiety level preemptively, such as having her draw the monsters she feared at night, and tell a story about them that the parents would write down. Following this, Miko would symbolically destroy them by tearing up the pictures in their presence. Normally, in Jungian work parents and therapists would keep all drawings and stories in a file for the duration of treatment (Allan and Brown, in press). In this situation we thought it was important to empower Miko by letting her "destroy" the monsters. Because the play therapy was part of Susan's internship, Miko would receive a prespecified number of sessions — twenty.

THEORETICAL CONCEPTUALIZATION

We chose play therapy as the primary treatment method because of the age of the child. Play is the language of children — their natural medium and expressive form. Children heal themselves through play. Play enables them to understand and master various developmental tasks and struggles. Miko's developmental history indicated severe birth trauma, which we know can severely impair the bonding process (Prechtl 1963), and the ability of the parents to help their infant experience relaxation while being held (Allan 1976). To help Mr. and Mrs. T. understand and deal with Miko, another therapist in the mental health clinic saw them in couple counseling on a weekly basis. Later they started to talk about their own family of origin issues. This way of working (where the parents are seen by another therapist), is consistent with Jungian theory where some of the issues of the child may reflect the unfinished business (or "shadow" side) of the parents.

Our main therapeutic goal was to be available to the child in more or less any way in which she wanted to use the playroom and the therapist (S. L.). Our goal was simply to follow the lead and the direction of play that the child took. Jungian theory states that in therapy, children innately know how to heal themselves and go to where they need to go in their play activities (Kalff 1981). Based on our prior experiences with these types of children, we expected a lot of regressive play. Because the wounding was at a neonatal and preverbal stage of development, we expected that Miko would want to play baby games and that we would see many ambivalent feelings and behaviors – hate and love, sucking and biting, kissing and hitting, messing and cleaning, regression and progression (Levin 1992). From a Jungian perspective, one of the therapist's tasks is to help the child separate ambivalent feelings and to feel each feeling separately so the child's ego is not overwhelmed by the chaos of mixed emotions (Neumann 1973). To this end, in our clinic, we have divided the playroom into two sections: (a) a dry, warm, carpeted area with the doll's house, soft toys, baby bottles, and a small child's bed; and (b) a vinyl tiled floor area for the sand and water tables, kitchen ware, construction activities, and mess-making.

The therapist's goals are to provide a free and protected space for play and to comment on unconscious processes during play in order to integrate painful unconscious feelings and experiences into consciousness. This process enables the child's ego to grow and to develop and opens up the ego–self axis (Allan and Bertoia 1992, Edinger 1973) enabling the child to live in a healthy and adaptive way with his or her true sense of self. The therapist does this by understanding the child's traumas and developmental struggles, and reflecting the feelings expressed in the play. Later, the therapist focuses on transference and countertransference issues as reflected in the child's relationship to the therapist and by making verbal interpretations to complicated sequences of play. Effective play therapy helps the child's ego mediate between the demands of both the inner and outer worlds without becoming too adaptive or remaining too unsocialized.

Limit Setting

Our own consideration of limits corresponds basically to Axline's (1947) recommendation of a generally permissive atmosphere in which the therapist tolerates behaviors unacceptable elsewhere and which encourages wide-ranging emotional expressiveness. However, the extent and the intensity of Miko's emotional and behavioral problems were so serious that we felt a radical departure from commonly imposed play therapy limits was necessary. The degree to which conventional playroom limits were relaxed in Miko's treatment is, in our experience, unusual. This relaxation of limits generally proved beneficial to Miko, signaling to her that she could express her most outrageous behaviors safely and nonpunitively within the therapeutic playroom. Our experi-

ence has been that allowing this behavior in the playroom decreases its
expression in the "regular" world" (Allan and Lawton-Speert 1993).

As we knew before the start of her therapy, Miko alternated between
an impulsive hyperactivity and a tendency to withdraw from real
emotional contact. Given this tendency to withdraw, we reasoned at the
outset that imposing common playroom limits on this emotionally
fragile child could thwart the expression of her problematic impulses
and therefore block her access to her deeper emotional life. In adapting
and submitting to limits, Miko, we felt, ran the risk of overadapting to
external controls, shutting down, and thereby repressing deeper feelings. Based on these beliefs, the therapeutic risk of imposing conventional playroom limits seemed too great.

We decided to risk emotional chaos and to join her calmly in it. We
tolerated behaviors considered unacceptable not only outside the playroom but within many other therapeutic playrooms as well. We anticipated some of her unusual behaviors, such as disrobing or urinating on
the floor, before therapy even commenced. Miko did not disappoint us.
Susan also relaxed other limits as therapy progressed. In addition, we
reasoned that as the frequency of Miko's unusual behaviors diminished,
we would know with greater certainty that this was due to her own
progress, her increased emotional strength, rather than due to her
acquiescence to imposed limitations.

We acknowledge that such an unorthodox approach to certain limits
would not suit all clients, all therapists, or most settings. Nor would we
employ such a free hand with limits toward all our clients. However,
two factors specific to this case assisted us in our ongoing decision to
maintain a permissive stance. The first concerned Miko's age and size.
We found it more feasible to permit a preschooler free rein than an older
child, as we knew we could, if necessary, gently restrain her physical
outbursts. The second factor concerned the trust that Susan felt in
relation to Miko. Susan believed that, despite the comprehensiveness of
her presenting emotional and difficulties, Miko possessed both the
ability and the strength to find her way through and out of emotional
turmoil.

THE PROCESS OF PLAY THERAPY

Miko's twenty therapy sessions unfolded in three global phases: the
beginning phase, sessions 1 and 2, in which hyperactivity and anxiety
predominated; the middle phase, sessions 3 through 14, in which she
richly elaborated in her play aspects of infant life; and the final phase,

sessions 15 through 20, in which infant play alternated with doctor play, with the figure of a tiny whale serving as both a patient and a friend.

The Beginning Phase: A Polarized Personality

"I don't need toys!" Miko proclaimed, as I (Susan) introduced myself to her and led her down the hall from the clinic waiting room to the play-room. However, Miko lost no time in the first session in playing out the deep and distressing polarization within her personality, between an overadaptive, controlling manner and impulsivity, anxiety, aggression, and anger.

As if already having intuited the purpose of the therapeutic play-room, Miko plunged into engrossed play. Using an accurate but artificial caregiver tone of voice, she enacted the little mother. Standing by the sand tray, she concocted a water, sand, and clay mixture. She told me she was making me (evidently, "the child") "a lovely soup, with all your lovely colors. Now have some dinogetti and bisgetti and eat it all up." As she rushed about her pretend kitchen chores with the anxious hyper-activity that characterized her early sessions, Miko carried out her cooking for me with an almost palpable resentment.

In response to the tense and anxious speed of her speech and move-ments, I intentionally spoke very little. I felt it was important to observe and witness the unfolding of her self. I delivered the few verbal responses I made as "the child" in a low tone of voice, slowly. My verbal responses were emotionally neutral, for example, "Here's my soup" as opposed to "Oh, thank you so much, Mama." I felt that I was encountering a su-perficial outer layer of Miko's personality, and I did not want to engage what I perceived as an aspect of her false self. I was curious as to what lay beneath this resentful maternal behavior. In Jungian terms, this is a "teleological" approach—where is the play and drama going to lead to?

This adaptive aspect of her personality, the insincere caregiver, soon gave way in this first session to aggression. Miko drenched a spongy ball and some baby clothes with water and wrung them out on my head and lap. When her first test of playroom limits did not elicit a negative reaction, Miko undressed completely and urinated on the playroom floor. She then sat on the floor and painted most of her body with water colors. She sank her feet into a small plastic basin that she had filled with water and sand. Near the end of the session, she dumped the basin and its contents all over the floor, commenting that the resulting "storm" was "so confusing." At the end of the session, I felt over-whelmed by the storm of Miko's combined anxiety and aggression. No doubt Miko's ego felt overwhelmed by these same emotions.

An Early Theme: "Mucky Mucky Mess"

Miko devoted the early minutes of the next eight sessions to making messes. On her way to the playroom, she loved to announce happily, "I'm going to make a mucky mucky mess!" Miko's messes were tactile and absolute. On entering the playroom each session, she immediately undressed. Soon after, she urinated on the floor, and spent the duration of each session undressed. She often painted her arms, legs, and torso with water colors. Sometimes she smeared clay on the floor and urinated again on this symbolic fecal target. In the early sessions, she also smeared clay on her body and at times on my hands and clothing. I felt that this direct expression of "messy" anger toward me, by projection the maternal figure, needed to be received without negative reaction. For Miko's sessions, I began to wear old T-shirts over my clothing so that it was possible to accept her behavior without flinching.

Miko often stood and urinated on the playroom floor several times in a session, watching her genital area with interest as she did so. Her interest in messing the playroom with her urine seemed to be compounded with gender confusion and anxiety. This impression was further confirmed when her father later related that at age 3 Miko had watched a younger boy urinate. She had then tried to direct her own urine flow, hoping to "pee like that" using her navel.

Messing seemed to be valuable to Miko as an expression of anger, rebellion, and just plain "letting go" or releasing tension. Often as she was smearing, urinating, painting, or spilling the plastic basin full of water, she said, "I want my mommy to see this!" Based on Miko's expressed wish for her mother to "see this," I inferred that these behaviors held shock value for Miko and that by my responding neutrally to them, her need to engage in this angry acting-out would quickly diminish. Each time I responded to her messes with a neutral matter-of-factness, Miko calmed perceptibly, sometimes almost immediately. Over the course of her therapy, the duration and the intensity of her aggressive, messy play moderated. Although she maintained an interest in spilling water and in occasional urinating, her need to paint herself or smear me with clay diminished and rarely reappeared.

The Middle Phase: The Baby's Birth and Infant Life

By the third session, Miko's hyperactive style of flitting from one activity to the next was showing signs of calming. In this session, Miko initiated the central play theme that was to typify her therapy for the next twelve weeks: the birth of the baby. This theme first appeared as follows. Miko entered the playroom and immediately engaged in what had become an almost ritual session opener for her. She undressed and urinated on the floor. She then played with a few toys in the water basin, painted herself with water colors, and deftly overturned the water basin, flooding the playroom. Shivering from the cold wet floor, she suddenly climbed onto my lap and asked me to wrap her up in a blanket: "I want to be a baby in a cocoon. Baby wants to snuggle because he's [sic] afraid of monsters. You be the mom." I provided her with a colorful flowered sheet. She nestled in my lap, wrapped in the sheet that she came to call affectionately throughout her therapy "my flowered blanket."

In this first appearance of the infant persona, Miko began to determine the identities of herself as infant and of the therapist in the maternal role.

Dialogue	*Commentary*
M: Yes, yes, and I'll be the baby. And she wants to be the . . . That's his mummy. That's his mummy.	That Miko intended therapist to be "mommy" evident in context.
SL: Right.	
M: The baby was so upset about something. So the baby went fast-a-fast asleep.	Remember Miko did not open her eyes for the first week of life.
SL: Okay. The baby was so upset about something that . . .	I was surprised at the intensity of the feelings Miko was expressing: "upset" and "killed." Moments before, she had introduced the notion of "fear." I reflected her statements almost verbatim, wanting to follow her closely through these difficult and frightening feelings that could reflect an experience of being killed during birth trauma.
M: 'Cause something killed him.	

SL: Something killed him. That's why the baby was so scared. He's scared he was gonna get killed. Baby was very scared.

M: He's with his mummy now. He's not scared anymore.

An encouraging sign. Feelings of security and safety are linked with this early infant/mother play. Miko's statements reflect an ability to recover from fear.

SL: Now he's not scared.

M: He's in his little cocoon.

SL: All safe.

M: Like a little bug. Snug in a bug.

SL: Like a little bug. All curled up.

M: [Laughs. Emits faint squeals appropriate to an infant and hums softly.] Do you hear the baby girl?

Miko's laughter is even more encouraging. She has moved quickly from an expression of intense fear to delight. Again in microcosm, I sense her capacity for recovery.

SL: Yes, I think I hear the baby girl making some sounds.

[M emits more squeaks and sounds.]

SL: Ph, I hear something.

[M squeaks.]

SL: What was the baby say telling me? Was the baby telling me something?

M: Pup pup!

SL: [In a whisper.] She's saying something to the mummy.

M: Mummy mummy!

SL: Yes.

M: Mummy.

SL: That's right. I'm your mummy.

I have moved too quickly for Miko. She needs to clarify the lines between fantasy and reality.

M: You're not my real mommy. My mommy is Yama T.

SL: That's right.

M: Yama T.

SL: Um-hm.

M: And you're—the pretend-mommy. You're Susan.

SL: That's right. I'm Susan and we're playing mommy, aren't we. That's right. You have a mommy Yama T. and right now Susan and Miko are playing mommy and baby.

I am attempting to reassure Miko that I understand the complexity of her feelings: that her mother is her primary love object, a role that I do not wish to usurp. By my intimating that this is "just play," her tension is diffused. She calmed noticeably and immediately moved into deeper infant play, with no further need for role clarification.

M: Wah wah wah! There's the baby girl again.

Having clarified for herself and for my benefit the parameters of the therapist's maternal role, Miko turned eagerly to the serious play of being born. Curled in my lap in a fetal position, she completely covered herself with her "flowered blanket." From inside the blanket, she squirmed and made faint squeaks and gentle sounds, an attempt at prenatal communication. She peeked out from beneath the blanket and announced, "It's a baby girl!"

By the next session (4), it was evident that her messing, urinating, painting, and water spilling were attempts to "get out" the bad angry feelings so that she could experience in an uncontaminated way, warm and cozy feelings on my lap. With this in place, she began to reenact what I came to think of as Miko's "birth sequences." In this session, her birth play was particularly intense. Miko repeatedly curled into a fetal position in my lap, hiding herself completely in her flowered blanket. Again she made faint, gentle squeaking sounds, to which I responded, "I hear something very gentle, lovely, and wonderful. It sounds like a beautiful little baby." Slowly, Miko extended a tiny hand, arm, foot, or leg from beneath the blanket, then withdrew back into the flowered womb. Sometimes, she shyly lifted the blanket to gaze quietly at the world, smiling and radiant. In several of these repeated birth sequences, Miko appeared to be enacting the breech position of her own birth. She extended one foot, then both from beneath her blanket, then her legs. As she lifted the blanket off her body and head, she emerged from beneath the blanket and glowingly announced, "She borned on her bum! That be borned!" Miko took great pleasure in her play of infant birth. Her verbal comments about the play revealed a clear understanding of her experience: "I'm in my Mommy's tummy. . . . Baby likes his [sic] mom . . . Crunch crunch crunch. . . . It's crunching out." In contrast to the hyperactive, anxious behavior that had led to her referral, after a birth sequence Miko sat calmly and contentedly in my lap, as peaceful as a newborn, gazing around the room. As the newborn, she often looked radiant, with gleaming eyes, pink cheeks, and a gentle smile.

Once, following a birth sequence in session 5, Miko caught sight of the water, sand, and clay mess she had created on the floor earlier in the session. Cuddled in my lap, she observed proudly, "I made a mucky mucky mess." Perhaps from her state of calm contentment, she could survey her earlier troubled mess with greater clarity. Or perhaps Miko was unconsciously referring to the "mess" of actual birth, and was acknowledging that it was her very own, and good, birth mess. If so, then her earlier messing play would have been a necessary psychological precursor to immersion into the deeper birth experience, and a symbolic dissolution of the constraints of conscious life.

As the therapist, I felt deeply engaged in a process of psychological midwifery. Miko and I were replaying, reconstructing, and remediating the earliest, decisive moments of a traumatic birth and the original, damaged mother–infant bond. I sought to repeatedly acknowledge the presence of "a lovely little baby" or "a beautiful baby girl" with as much warmth as possible. Miko was joyful, open, lucid, and vulnerable in this play.

Progress Outside the Playroom

Emotional and behavioral benefits began to accrue outside the playroom. Mr. and Mrs. T. were pleased with the improvements in Miko's behavior and in her emotional resilience following her first six play therapy sessions. Miko was calmer and happier at home than ever before. She achieved a number of significant behavioral firsts. Miko's parents noted that Miko had a very good weekend with her family, baking, visiting neighbors, and listening to a story at the local library, activities that had been unsuccessful or unpleasant in the past because Miko had deteriorated into hyperactive or destructive behavior. Following this breakthrough, Miko intermittently regressed at home and in her classroom. Despite the positive changes, Miko was still susceptible to being overwhelmed by fear, anxiety, and anger.

Mr. and Mrs. T. still wrestled with the necessity for surgery. Concerned about the psychological impact of surgery, particularly at such a sensitive and vulnerable stage in her therapy, we met with the parents and described to them Miko's birth play. Her birth play mirrored a process of psychological birth. We explained the importance for Miko's psychological recovery of delaying the surgery until Miko was safely delivered in the play. If the specialist felt that a delay would not harm her growth, the continuity of the play sessions could only serve to strengthen Miko significantly for the inevitable surgery. Miko's parents were receptive and understanding of their daughter's psychological needs. They approached the specialist, who permitted an indefinite delay of the surgery, dependent upon the results of periodic checkups. Miko's play therapy continued.

The Therapeutic Playroom as Nursery

Miko gradually created a psychological home for herself within the tiny playroom. The playroom essentially became her nursery, and Miko as the neonate began to play out infant life in increasingly rich detail. She expressed an ever-widening range of infant needs: sleeping, feeding, messing, washing, and baby-at-play.

After a birth sequence, Miko liked to crawl out of her blanket cocoon onto the nearby table. By spreading blankets on the table, and keeping her flowered blanket for her cover, she created a "little bed" for "the little baby" or "the little girl." When she first added sleeping to the infant's repertoire (sessions 3 through 5), she found it difficult to carry out this bed-making calmly or to lie still for more than a few seconds. We surmised that she was unconsciously struggling with the fears that troubled her sleep at home. Over time, her anxiety and tension around this activity diminished, and Miko was able to make her bed quickly and calmly and then lie still for several minutes. Sometimes she asked for the light to be turned off. She was able to tolerate the darkness for anywhere from a few seconds to a minute or two. At times during this play, she asked for reassurance with a statement that sounded more like a question, "There are no monsters in here?" The therapist would reply: "Right. There are no monsters here now, no bad feelings. Life is safe now."

More often, instead of being tired, Miko as the newborn was hungry. "Waaa. Gaga. That means I want food," she explained. In sessions 4 through 10 she created sand, water, and clay mixtures that she spooned into baby bottles. Although she claimed to be hungry, the mixture in the bottle was clearly unappealing. She decided to feed it to me. Piling a tiny spoon high with sand and clay, she told me, "Here is some lovely food for you. This is cherry juice." Deciding to accept her claim at face value, I initially accepted the food, but then spit out the gritty mixture. "No!" said Miko, "You have to eat it!" Expressing what Miko must have experienced both as an infant and more recently around medications, I responded, "Yukky food. You tell me it's going to be good, but it tastes yukky. It's hard for me to know what I'm going to get."

Miko's need to play out scenes with distasteful food was intense. In one instance, the natural flow of this play was thwarted by my intervention. In session 6 Miko had carefully prepared herself a place setting at the table "for lunch." She was ready to enjoy her meal of sand when I became concerned about her ingesting the sand. I decided to provide genuine, good food. I offered her a rice cake from the cupboard, which she enthusiastically accepted. However, once she had crumbled the rice cake with the sand into a baby bottle, she abandoned this play completely for the rest of the session. Her need to experience bad food in fantasy was much more compelling than any realistic need for good food. By offering her a tangible solution to her play scenario, I had disrupted her fantasy play, the realm of the symbolic and imaginary, and so interrupted the therapeutic process.

Spontaneously Miko began to show an interest in ingesting pleasant substances. After repeated birth sequences (sessions 10 through 15), she filled two baby bottles with water and sat contentedly in my lap, drinking from one bottle while holding the other. Her calmness, as she sat in my lap sucking her bottle of water, was so complete and so beneficial to her that by session 15 I decided to make apple juice available for this bottle play. Recalling the play disruption that had resulted from introducing rice cakes, I hesitantly inquired whether the baby, who was searching for her bottles, would like water or juice. Miko answered "water," but later, having thought over the choice, requested juice. The transition from distasteful food (sand), to acceptable substances (water), to tasty substances (juice) occurred gradually. From this session through the end of her therapy, Miko loved to cuddle in my lap and enjoy her bottles of juice, relishing the calm and contentment for sustained periods of up to 15 or 20 minutes.

Within the role of infant, Miko occasionally enjoyed using sand to create a mess. In session 5, after "being born," Miko, still undressed, climbed into the sand tray and asked to be covered with sand. She informed me that the wet sand that she dropped by handfuls onto the floor "looks like poo." She wanted to fling handfuls of sand around the room. I limited this behavior because sand messes were far more difficult to clean up than water messes and because the sand poses a danger to eyes and ears. When I redirected her to flinging the sand into a plastic basin, Miko became extremely agitated and angry. She hurled a preschool epithet at me, "You bonk! You shoe!" When I acknowledged the "angry baby" and repeated that "baby is so angry she called Mommy a bonk and a shoe," Miko relaxed and calmed.

Another favorite activity of Miko as infant was "the baby's bath" which she took in "my special tub" (the plastic water basin). She undressed and jumped into the basin "to take a bath," then climbed into my lap to be wrapped in her flowered blanket for some birth play. She often repeated this sequence in a given session. The themes of messing and cleaning were interwoven, as Miko often enjoyed sitting in her bath and painting her stomach. Still not free from the aggressive impulses that had impelled her earlier messing activities, Miko often climbed out of her "tub" and overturned the water basin. Sometimes, she was able to wait until the end of the session to flood the playroom. Her ability to defer these aggressive impulses and to use the water first to gratify her infant needs was an encouraging sign of her growing ego strength.

Miko found numerous ways to play while still retaining the role of the infant. Some of her infant-at-play activities began while still within the symbolic womb. From under the flowered blanket, Miko uttered faint, playful sounds or engaged me in a game of prenatal peekaboo, by lifting the blanket, peeking at me, and withdrawing.

An enjoyable playful breakthrough occurred in session 9. Baby Miko had just awakened on her table/bed and was feeling very safe and happy. She rocked back and forth, as is typical of a baby in the creeping stage. While she rocked, she made baby sounds, which ranged from shy, faint noises to more aggressive sounds of flatulence. I playfully imitated her sounds in response, just as a mother would with an infant. Miko was delighted with this careful mirroring of her infant speech. She laughed out loud at this boisterous game. It was the first time in her therapy that she had revealed a healthy exuberance.

In later infant play, Miko assumed a toddler persona. She climbed on top of the toy shelves and from this perch proudly showed me how well the "baby" could pound the cobbler's bench "by himself" (session 10). The following excerpt from session 11 shows Miko expanding the infant persona to include delight and pleasure in her first bottle drinking activity. Cuddled in my lap and wrapped in her blanket, Miko was feeling happy and content.

Dialogue	*Commentary*
M: [Singing] Dodododo.	
SL: All covered up.	
M: Ababababababa.	
SL: The baby girl went ababababa- baba.	
M: Shush!	
SL: The baby said shush!	
M: Ah!	
SL: Ah!	I intentionally mimicked or mirrored Miko's sounds. Mirroring by the mother of the infant's sounds, actions, and play is a natural and important part of infant development. I wanted to strengthen Miko's infant persona through the dynamic of mirroring.

M: Ahahahahah!

SL: Ahahahahah!

M: Tsktsktsktsktsk.	Miko's sounds were clearly those of a suckling infant.
SL: Tsktsktsktsktsk. [Whispers] The baby is sucking.	An interpretation of her sounds.

M: I'm a little.

SL: [Whispers] Baby is sucking.

M: I want some milk.

SL: Oh. Okay, baby. I'll give you some oh.

M: Some water!	Miko was not ready for rich, nourishing food, even in fantasy play. She chose a somewhat neutral substance. I followed her wishes.

SL: Okay, I'll give you some water in a . . .

M: Just in a bottle.

SL: Yes, in a bottle.

In the next session (12), Miko sat on my lap after a birth and feeding sequence and initiated her first cooperative play segment within her infant persona. She handed me the "big mommy brush" while she took the "little baby brush." We took turns painting swirls of watercolor on the formica table as the following dialogue unfolded:

Dialogue	*Commentary*
M: Now I have to take the mommy brushes away. Now it's time for baby's turn be-	Miko has set the tone of capably directing this activity. I asked her a question to indicate that I will

cause this is his brush. Now it's your turn, Mommy.

follow her and defer to her direction of the "mommy." I sensed that Miko as infant was entering new developmental territory.

SL: Okay. Do you want Mommy to use the big brushes?

M: Here they are. The nice big Mommy brushes.

SL: Okay. Really big Mommy brushes. Okay. Mommy's gonna paint with the Mommy brushes now. What color should Mommy use? Baby tell Mommy what color to use.

Again, I wanted her to take charge here, to experience the vulnerability of the infant role and at the same time enough safety to direct and order "Mother" about.

M: [Undecipherable.]

SL: Baby can point if baby doesn't know the name. This one?

M: Yup. This one I.

SL: Baby want to do it.

M: You know what to do—is to paint really loud!

By "really loud" Miko meant that the colors should be strong and bold.

SL: Okay.

M: Paint! You do this. Put in your hand and paint!

SL: Okay.

M: I'll do it now. Put in the water.

SL: Okay.

M: You have to paint.

I enjoyed Miko's enthusiastic direction of this activity. In contrast to her first session, when she anxiously ordered me to eat "all the soup," Miko is calm, involved, warmly relating, feeling secure.

SL: Right, oh yeah, it's nice.

M: Now first you need to do this. And you need do it now.

SL: Yeah.

M: And then I made. You do it, Mommy. The baby will help.

An encouraging sign. I made a mental note of the fact that the infant as "helpful" connoted reparation with the mother.

SL: Mommy and baby will do it together.

M: Do it like you do.

SL: Um-hm.

M: You paint the table.

SL: Yes, we're doing a good . . .? A nice job of painting the table.

M: Okay. Now it's my turn, okay?

SL: Okay.

M: This is old, and this is a new one. But this is a new one too. And you put this one inside the other one.

SL: Oh.

M: And paint with two brushes.

Miko was pleased to demonstrate the two-brush technique. Ostensibly still the infant, she was however the 4-year-old self here, happy and secure, proudly demonstrating a new skill.

SL: Two brushes.

M: Now this one has to. These both of these have to go in the water.

SL: Hm.

M: Now I'm gonna put these somewhere else. I have put the Mommy brushes away. They're for baby. This what he would wants to play.

Miko left the painting and turned to the canisters of clay. In this segment, Miko's ability to decide, determine, and direct was evident. Satisfied with the "maternal" contact in the painting activity, she then chose to decrease the contact with the therapist/maternal figure and turned to play with other materials as part of her separation and individuation drive.

A Turning Point

Midway through her treatment, following session 10, Miko's school recessed for two weeks for the Christmas holidays. It was a period that was to prove critical for her. Miko was slated for a series of orthopedic tests and bone analyses before school resumed. Frequent medical examinations had, in the past, at least partially contributed to her being overwhelmed by fear and anxiety. Although she was making progress in her play sessions, at home and at school, Miko was still struggling. Another battery of medical tests threatened to undo her still fragile process. Nevertheless, her intensified limping required that her physicians carry out these tests soon. Mr. and Mrs. T. agonized over whether to stay with her in the hospital for several days as the tests were conducted in series, or to risk a general anesthetic so that all the tests could be carried out painlessly within an hour.

They opted for the general anesthetic. However, the potential benefits of having the tests carried out quickly and painlessly were offset by the risk to her emotional well-being of a trauma of a different sort. A year before, Miko had undergone a procedure under a general anesthetic and had woken up in the recovery room and screamed in terror and rage for nearly an hour.

I consulted with Miko's mother to devise a plan of parental intervention that might reduce the potential for emotional trauma and setback. I recommended that the parents prepare Miko for the pending hospitalization by drawing for her a series of pictures that illustrated, for example, Miko entering the hospital with her teddy bear, Miko sleeping under the care of kind doctors, and Miko waking up to warm hugs from her parents. These drawings would hopefully provide Miko with a cognitive framework for visualizing and integrating potentially traumatic material. In moments of stress, these stored positive images might assist her in managing her fears and anxiety. Mrs. T. responded enthusiastically to these suggestions and said that she would add a picture of recovery in which she gave Miko a popsicle.

I emphasized the importance of both parents' presence with Miko in the hospital, especially when she awoke from the anesthetic. The stated reason was that Miko needed to feel the support of both parents when she was so vulnerable physically. The underlying reason, not expressed, concerned the history of difficulties in the mother–daughter relationship. When awakening, Miko would be particularly vulnerable to any tensions between herself and her mother. Mr. T. needed to be there to counteract this dynamic and to provide support for Miko and for her mother.

Mr. and Mrs. T.'s series of pictures appeared to have had a strong, positive influence on Miko's hospital experience. Instead of tantruming upon awakening, Miko called out, "Where's my popsicle?" Recalling another of her parents' sketches, Miko asked for a "family hug." Both parents were deeply moved as Miko clung to them while they all hugged on her recovery cot.

This brief hospitalization, which could have precipitated a severe emotional setback, instead proved to be an unexpected positive turning point for both Miko and her parents. Their concerted efforts to prevent another medical-related trauma encouraged them to feel that they could, indeed, help their daughter. In addition, Miko's weathering this potential trauma gave them concrete evidence of her progress. Miko did experience minimal regression due to the hospitalization in delayed fashion, as was typical of her. A week or so after the tests, she urinated on the living room floor several days in succession. Urinating on the floor appeared to signal Miko's feeling overwhelmed, with her urine her last weapon and call for help. Miko recovered from this regression within days.

Returning to the Nursery

Following the hospitalization, Miko resumed her play therapy, returning to the infant themes of birth, feeding, sleeping, messing, washing, and playing with increased calm and absorption. In the first session (11) following her hospitalization, Miko, after "being born," crawled into a tiny wooden cradle for the first time and enjoyed her bottle there. Her use of the cradle, rather than the table/bed, represented a deeper immersion into the experience of "being a baby." Although intended for dolls, the cradle easily accommodated her. Her "crib," as she called it, became an important focus in all ensuing sessions. After an initial "baby bath," followed by "being born," Miko loved to curl up in the crib, cover herself with doll blankets and her flowered blanket, and enjoy her bottles of water or juice. Deeply content in this rich interweaving of themes of infant life, Miko sometimes asked for a toy from the shelf. Like any suckling infant, she handled objects as she drank from her bottle. Sometimes, she asked me to read her the only book in the playroom (an infant book of animal pictures) while she enjoyed her bottle.

The Angry Baby

Still within the infant persona, Miko's anger began to surface in sessions 12 and 13. Rather than feeling calmed by her introductory play of bathing in the little basin and climbing in my lap to be cuddled and "born," Miko remained very agitated. She approached the sand tray, dumped sand and water on her own head, and water on me. Still agitated, she lay on her back on my lap, facing me, and began kicking vigorously at my face, shoulders, chest, and stomach. "There's a very angry baby here," I commented. "Baby wants to hurt the Mommy, kick her tummy, her boobies, and her head."

Miko's anger was focused and intense, an emotional breakthrough in terms of trust of me, and an accurate expression of the anger Miko often felt toward her mother. I quickly decided to tolerate the kicking. However, I gently held her ankles so that my hands, rather than my body, safely absorbed the blows.

After 5 minutes of intense kicking, Miko was spent and upset. Beneath her protest and anger, her pain was evident. Almost in tears, a first in her therapy, Miko suddenly nestled into my arms and whimpered sadly, "I want my Mommy." [That she meant Mrs. T. was clear from her tone.] "I want my bottle." "Of course you do," I replied, handing her the bottle. As Miko calmed with her bottle, I sought to offer her an interpretation that could bridge her feelings of rage at her mother toward reparation. This time working within the play metaphor I repeated several times, "Mommy still loves the little baby even when the baby gets mad at Mommy."

Miko was by now not simply playing in the playroom. She was living in the playroom. Her recent successful hospitalization suggested that she was becoming established on the path toward emotional recovery. However, a brief but intense regression occurred. Following session 13, her parents took her on a week-long holiday. The disruption in therapy was unfortunate, given Miko's recent accelerating progress. However, Miko's parents felt it important to indulge Miko, as they were acutely aware that the pending surgery would leave Miko bedridden over a long convalescence. During that vacation, Miko's relationship with her parents warmed and thrived as never before. They were delighted with Miko's accessibility and responsivity. However, after the holiday, Miko fell ill with the mumps and missed an additional week of school. The combination of the holiday and the ordeal of the illness set Miko back.

After a three-week hiatus, Miko appeared for session 14 extremely agitated and anxious. She did not settle into my lap. Soon she was throwing toys off the shelves and attempting to throw handfuls of sand. When I restrained her from flinging sand, she attacked me as in session 13, but this time she quickly stopped herself. "I'm afraid I'll hurt you," she said clearly, and climbed into the sand tray to get away from me. I responded that I was not afraid of her anger and that her anger could not hurt me. "I'm glad to hear that!" she shot back. She then climbed into my lap and resumed an intense physical attack. I again grasped her ankles, so that I could control her kicking. In the fracas, Miko barely touched her head on the sand tray, but the little bump was all the pretense she needed to release her underlying tension and sadness. She collapsed in tears in my lap and asked for her flowered blanket. Calm and centered at last, she peeked out of her blanket and then made herself a little bed on the table. She had begun this session in a tempest of anger, but left markedly calmer.

The Final Phase: The Doctor, Death, and Friendship

Breakthroughs in the therapeutic relationship and in Miko's play themes emerged in session 16, which marked the beginning of the final phase of her therapy. Miko entered the playroom happily and asked me to help undress her. She was sitting on my lap as I undid her shoes, when she suddenly urinated on me. At first Miko looked pleased with herself. On reflection, she assumed a worried look and said, "I'm afraid you'll get angry. My daddy gets angry."

In the previous session, Miko had told me, "I want to pee on you," but she had not carried this out. Forewarned, I had anticipated this behavior and was, in fact, curious as to whether Miko would attempt it. I was also curious as to what the therapeutic ramifications might be of permitting her to carry out her wish. I had decided beforehand to accept this behavior, if only once, to see where this therapeutic risk would lead. I had worn clothes that could withstand this treatment, so I was able to genuinely reassure Miko that I was not angry. I was not totally surprised at the pool of urine in my jeans skirt.

The therapeutic risk proved invaluable. Miko played out her themes of infant life with unprecedentedly intense absorption and trust. For the first time since the infant play began (session 3), Miko bypassed birth sequences and directly entered other aspects of infant life. She climbed into her crib, cherishing her bottles. Perhaps she felt safely delivered.

Having temporarily satisfied her infant needs in this pivotal session, Miko suddenly left the crib and her bottles and began to initiate a new, complex theme that typified this final phase. Miko selected two small animal figures with which she had played occasionally in the past, a plastic fish and a plastic shark. The latter also resembled a whale. Miko perceived the friendly qualities of this somewhat ambiguous play material. She named the whale "Roo" and informed him that she was "the whale doctor." "Would you help [Roo] talk and the whale song is gonna come," she instructed me.

Opening the doctor's kit, she told Roo that he had to have an "owie" (injection) and, reflecting her own difficulty in acknowledging pain, she added, "It will hurt. It won't hurt." She gave Roo repeated injections followed by the application of Band-Aids. In all subsequent sessions, she delightedly offered Roo Band-Aids after his injections "so it won't hurt." Band-Aids for Miko powerfully symbolized comfort and relief. Through this newly established doctor play, Miko began to integrate her numerous experiences with intrusive and painful medical treatments.

In this and in ensuing sessions, Miko ventured even deeper. Pretending to read the little medical chart from the doctor's kit, Miko, still undressed, assumed a professional posture and a serious tone of voice. She read, "Roo is going to die." Over the past few weeks, Miko had frequently lain on the floor at home, telling her family that she was dead. Distressed at this repetitive death play, Mr. and Mrs. T. had asked me to explore this theme with Miko in therapy. However, it was critical to wait until Miko initiated this powerful theme herself.

As Miko "read" from the chart, giving Roo the bad news, she flashed me a quick look as if to ask, "Can you handle this?" Roo, via my voice, expressed surprise and some fear at the news. Too soon, I offered an interpretation through Roo: "When I was a little baby whale, the doctors hurt me all the time. Now I understand that they were trying to help me. But I didn't know that then. I thought they were trying to kill me. That was scary." I should have just acknowledged the death and waited: "Roo is dead."

In sessions 16 and 17, when Miko as the doctor raised the topic of death, I refrained from such premature interpretations. Miko herself ably explored the subject, which was fraught with fear and confusion for her: "You gotta die 'cause you might get hurt." "She doesn't feel when she's dead. That's when you die." "When Roo dies, she'll be sick." Miko gave Roo terrifying news: "Your mommy died" and "Doctors kill you."

Concurrent with references to death were the introduction of positive and hopeful elements and even attempts at solutions to this existential problem: "When you die, I'm gonna help you and give you some Band-Aids to make you better." Involving the small fish in play with the whale, Miko told Roo, "You gotta die, Roo, 'cause you might get hurt. Your friend will help you." When the little fish arrived, Miko remarked, "No more dying, Roo." Band-Aids as well as friendship offered hope to her persistent fears.

Increasingly, references to healing and recovery appeared. The Band-Aids that followed the "owies" were invariably described as a "special treat" or a "surprise." She told Roo, "You're fixed," and she reassured him she was making him "better." At the same time, Miko was not completely certain that he was better. A degree of anxiety about his condition persisted. Many times throughout her medical care of him, she asked him with intermingled hope and fear, "Are you all right?" or "Are you much better now, Roo?"

In these final five sessions, Miko's play alternated between the two well-defined themes of Miko as the infant enacting the gratification of infant needs, and Miko as the whale doctor in representations of pain, fear, death, comfort, and friendship. In any given session, Miko moved comfortably between these two types of play. On entering the playroom during this phase, Miko typically announced, "I'm going to be a baby!" However, as soon as she caught sight of Roo on the shelf, she attended to his "hurts" with Band-Aids. Later, curled in my lap sucking her juice bottle, she incorporated the whale as her transitional object, holding him while she drank. After drinking for a time, she bounded off my lap and proceeded to treat Roo with injections followed by Band-Aids, often repeating this cycle several times within a session.

At the beginning of session 17, I informed Miko that our sessions would be ending after "four more playtimes." Protest over termination did not arise. Rather, Miko plunged with an even greater intensity into her now positively polarized play.

Whale and doctor play did not supplant the previous infant play. Scenarios of infant life continued even into final phase. They did so in a striking and almost rhythmic oscillation with the whale and doctor play. Miko moved back and forth between the roles of the infant and the doctor. In one role, she personified vulnerability and neediness; in the other, control, agency, and authority. She enjoyed regression in the reexperiencing of infant life. With the doctor kit and the whale, she symbolically raised topics pertinent to her current life experience—trips to the doctor, and all the associations of fear, pain, death, and need for comfort that those visits entailed. Miko appeared to be using her retreats into infant life (birth, feeding, and so on) as respites for emotional nurturance from which she drew the psychological strength to deal directly with current concerns.

In the final minutes of her last session, Miko abandoned the doctor play and turned to the creation of a large purple watercolor mural on the playroom wall. She filled the wall with "whales," which had become a symbol of her growing healthy unconscious. As she painted, she retained the role of the infant; however, she appeared a more capable and self-confident, even mature, baby, painting cooperatively with the therapist/maternal figure. The mural concentrated many of the themes and activities that had recurred throughout her therapy: her love of painting and messes, her involvement in the infant role, and the recapitulation of the whale theme. In that respect, the mural seemed a fitting, creative closure to her therapy. However, before leaving the playroom, Miko sought a final foray into infant life. Finishing her mural, she sat on the "baby's chair" and greedily sipped juice from a tiny cup. In taking a final sip of juice, Miko seemed to be conveying that she wanted to take with her one last symbolic gulp of nurturance as she ventured forth from the playroom.

RESULTS AND FOLLOW-UP

Since session 16, there had been accumulating evidence of significant, sustained improvement outside the playroom. At school Miko suddenly discovered her peers. Boys and girls began to seek out her company in play and, likewise, Miko began to talk excitedly about "going to school to play with the girls." At home, Miko related to her parents and sisters with an unprecedented lucid calmness. The family adopted a new communication strategy of slow, careful explanations to Miko of events around her. Their creative efforts calmed and focused Miko. Her anxiety diminished. The simple procedures they used, of drawing events and of slow, careful, verbal descriptions, had the additional benefit of re-building Miko's relationships with family members on the basis of positive verbal communication.

Just before the last session, the parents wrote a long letter to the school, detailing Miko's recent progress at home. Some of Miko's achievements included age-appropriate "firsts," such as dressing herself, brushing her teeth, and using a scissors. Mr. and Mrs. T. were also delighted with a normal family night out to a children's restaurant where Miko ate calmly and played happily with her sisters. The parents reported that they felt as if Miko's brain had began to work with greater clarity and efficiency.

From our perspective, Miko had gradually built islets of calm and strength through her play therapy. Her regression into infant experience and, in particular, her repeated enactments of birth, gradually helped remediate the traumatic circumstances of her own birth and had gratified frustrated infant needs. Through the relationship with the therapist, Miko worked through messy and frightening emotions of anxiety and aggression toward experiences of trust and love. Strengthened through her regressive play, she was ultimately able to begin to depict important current concerns around medical treatment and death, friendship and recovery.

Follow-up is not possible at this stage because treatment has just finished. However, we expect, barring any unforeseen problems, that she will continue to make long-term progress as we have seen in other cases (Allan 1988).

DISCUSSION

The question has to be asked: Why did Miko play in this way? Why did she take her clothes off, urinate on the floor, cover herself with the blanket, and repeatedly play "at being born"? From a Jungian perspective, we would argue that the therapeutic alliance and the transference relationship activated the self-healing archetype in her and she went, in her play, "to where she needed to go to." That is, she went symbolically to the places where she had been traumatized—at her birth and with doctors and hospitals who she had experienced as "hurting her," or even in her own words "trying to kill her." From our experience, it is not unusual for birth-traumatized children to feel that someone or something is trying to kill them because they felt that physical pressure, and lack of oxygen during the difficult labor was life-threatening. In order for these children to heal themselves, we have noticed that they must externalize these "bad, awful feelings"—this means literally "dumping" the feelings into the room and onto the therapist. Frequently they want to hurt or kill the therapist, and want to make messes and mess up the therapist as the child feels messed up by life.

When traumas strike very early in the life cycle, children often want to take their clothes off in play therapy. Likewise when children feel they have been toilet trained too early or disciplined too severely, they will often want to urinate in the playroom and discipline or punish the therapist. To a Jungian play therapist, these activities not only reflect the acting out of aggression, but are also part of the self-generating drive to heal oneself. Miko needed to master or "get on top of" these traumas. She needed to be naked in order to redo the birth experience in her own time. Likewise, she needed to urinate in her own way until she had done enough of it so that she felt she had gained control of her own impulses, her own sense of timing, and her own body. (Here we are referring to activities in the therapy room, not in school or at home where normal limits and controls are needed.)

Jung's psychology is a teleological psychology; he was interested in where the unconscious is going to lead to and how it is going to evolve. To a Jungian play therapist, what happens in one or two of the play sessions is not as important as what the image, fantasy, or behavior is going to transform into or become. Our experiences with profoundly acting-out behavior have shown that indeed these children regress and then emerge out of the regression with much healthier behaviors and new skills. This theory base enables the therapist to trust the child's process, that it will often lead into the pain and that this is necessary and needs to be expressed for true healing to occur. This does not mean that the Jungian therapist allows the child to do anything that he or she wishes. By using the countertransference experiences (i.e., his or her own bodily sensations), the therapist also knows when "enough is enough" and when limits need to be set or acting-out behavior redirected. We noticed that with Miko each regression was matched by progression in the areas of intimacy, trust, and the reworking of various developmental stages from infant to toddler to preschooler. As she expressed, released, and integrated repressed, painful affects around birth into ego consciousness, she established a more flexible relationship between the ego and the self. This resulted in longer sequences of play related to other developmental traumas, for example, repeated visits to doctors and hospitals. Here she verbally disclosed her fear of death, her confusion over hurting, healing, caring, and reparation in doctor–child and mother–child relationships. From a Jungian perspective, it is the archetype of the self that unconsciously orchestrates these developmental narratives and play scenarios that, if fully expressed, result in healing.

A discussion of Miko's therapy would not be complete without setting it in its context in terms of the primal nature of her play therapy. The theorists and therapists who have explored prenatal and perinatal consciousness have focused on the impact of prenatal experiences and birth traumas as causing emotional difficulties in adulthood (Janov 1983, Prechtl 1963, Rank 1929, Verny and Kelly 1981). We are aware of only two accounts in the child psychotherapeutic literature in which the child's traumatic birth experience figured prominently in the assessment and treatment of symptoms (Piontelli 1988, Van Zyl 1977). A review of the play therapy literature revealed no case accounts, including the work by Van Zyl and Piontelli, in which the literal reenactment of birth figured in the child's play treatment.

The South African play therapist Van Zyl (1977) treated a 4½-year-old hyperactive boy who had suffered a violently traumatic birth. Within the play therapy treatment, themes of suffocation and blocking—aspects of his difficult birth—repeatedly recurred within sand-tray play with vehicles.

The Italian analyst Piontelli (1988) carried out the lengthy treatment of a girl who had been born with the umbilical cord wrapped so tightly around her neck that her eyes bulged from the pressure. The child first crawled into the therapy room wearing a heavy chain wrapped around her neck. Surmising from Ms. Piontelli's account, this child made good progress in the verbal, analytically based therapy. However, the therapist was openly pessimistic about the ultimate resolution of the girl's problems, considering her at times "a lost cause and a hopeless enterprise" (Piontelli 1988, p. 79). Further, the therapist reflected that the child "always was and still is so little responsive to my interpretive work" (Piontelli 1988, p. 76).

We suggest that the therapy reached a frustrating impasse because of countertransference issues and because the therapeutic venue relied too heavily upon verbal interaction and verbal interpretation. An emphasis on play treatment, by contrast, might have enabled the child to tap deeper self-curative resources through the play materials and symbolic activities.

One of the reasons that the trauma of birth is so profound is precisely the fact that birth has an impact on the infant long before any verbal and cognitive capacities for processing, for understanding, and for emotional defense are developed. Consequently, therapy for children in which birth trauma has figured must take these factors into account and must treat damage that has occurred deep within the child's psyche. As we have learned from experience with children like Miko, Jungian play therapy has the potential to be effective with children whose difficulties stem from birth trauma. Play provides these children with the symbolic resources with which they can access and, if necessary, even reenact this primal experience.

We acknowledge that it was not the therapist's choice but Miko's deep unconscious or archetypal "choosing" that was responsible for the course her therapy took. Nevertheless, we doubt whether Miko's therapeutic experience would have been so deep had she not been treated in a milieu in which she was free to experience the depth of the regression and to select the materials of her recovery.

Each child we treat has something to teach us, as therapists and as individuals. From Miko we learned, first of all, about the depth at which the play therapy process is capable of working. We saw that, by loosening the behavioral bounds, we could make positive therapeutic gains. Miko clarified for us that this Jungian approach provides birth traumatized children with an appropriately experiential treatment milieu. Should the child choose to use this milieu for this type of regression, play therapy provides a milieu for young children with the force of primal therapy.

As Miko so happily proceeded from birth to bottle, from baby bath to messing, from her crib to infant play, we learned, secondly, that play therapy is much more than "play" in its simplicity, and it is much more than "therapy" in its complexity. Miko was not simply playing at the themes of fears, monsters, baby, infant, death, or killing. She was living them fully. From Miko, then, we learned that play therapy for the young preschool child is a process of living, in all its fullness.

Thirdly, Miko taught us about the intensity of feelings of the 4-year-old child. In the process of living her therapy, Miko held nothing back when it came to experiencing her feelings. From the dubious safety of our adult cognitive defenses, we watched with admiration as little

Miko felt terror, joy, anger, and delight in all their depth and intensity. "Little people, big feelings" was a phrase that frequently ran through our minds as we watched her play. The intensity, the depth, and the dignity of the preschool child should not be underestimated.

Finally, Miko taught us about the interrelationship between trust and courage. She trusted implicitly in and tested the bounds of the therapeutic relationship again and again. Through her most difficult behaviors of undressing and urinating on the floor, Miko dared to express her violent, angry, "bad" feelings, again and again to test us, to fight us, and to call for help with enormous courage.

What we learned about ourselves in this process would fill another chapter. In the treatment of Miko, it was frightening for us at times to risk chaos, and it was difficult to accept the intensity of her anger. We learned that we, like Miko, could take risks. As we relaxed the boundaries for Miko and enabled her to descend into regression and to face the storm of inner emotional chaos, we found that we were loosening the boundaries of our own emotional experience. A strong core carried Miko through the storm. We also endured and were strengthened in her process. Following Miko's example, we discovered that, we, too had the courage to take risks into uncharted emotional waters. We feel stronger as therapists for having experienced how the Jungian play therapy setting can help children to work through birth trauma. We feel richer as individuals for having known such a spirited and courageous child.

REFERENCES

Allan, J. (1976). Identification and treatment of difficult babies. *Canadian Nurse* 72:11–16.

_____ (1988). *Inscapes of the Child's World: Jungian Counseling in Schools and Clinics.* Dallas, TX: Spring Publications.

Allan, J., and Berry, P. (1987). Sandplay. *Elementary School Guidance and Counseling* 21:300–306.

Allan, J., and Bertoia, J. (1992). *Written Paths to Healing: Education and Jungian Child Counseling.* Dallas, TX: Spring Publications.

Allan, J., and Brown, K. (in press). Jungian play therapy in the schools. *Elementary School Guidance Counseling.*

Allan, J., and Lawton-Speert, S. (1993). The play psychotherapy of a profoundly sexually abused incest victim. *International Journal of Play Therapy* 2.

Axline, V. (1947). *Play Therapy.* Boston, MA:Houghton Mifflin.

Blackman, J. A. (1989). The relationship between inadequate oxygenation of the brain at birth and developmental outcome. *Topics in Early Childhood Special Education* 9:1–13.

Edinger, E. (1973). *Ego and Archetype.* Baltimore, MD: Penguin.

Fordham, M. (1969). *Children as Individuals.* London: Hodder & Stoughton.

Janov, A. (1983). *Imprints: The Life Long Effects of the Birth Experience*. New York: Coward-McCann.

Jung, C. G. (1910). Psychic conflicts in a child. *The Collected Works of C. G. Jung*. Vol. 17. *The Development of the Personality*, ed. H. Read, M. Fordham, and A. Adler, pp. 1-37. Princeton, NJ: Princeton University Press.

Kalff, D. (1981). *Sandplay*. Boston, MA: Sigo.

Levin, S. (1992). Thematic transformations in play therapy. Unpublished doctoral dissertation, University of British Columbia, Vancouver, Canada.

Neumann, E. (1973). *The Child: Structure and Dynamics of the Nascent Personality*. New York: A. P. Putnams.

Piontelli, A. (1988). Pre-natal life and birth as reflected in the analysis of a two-year-old psychotic girl. *International Review of Psycho-Analysis* 15:73–81.

Prechtl, H. F. R. (1963). The mother–child interaction in babies with minimal brain damage (a follow-up study). In *Determinants of Infant Behavior*, vol. 2, ed. B. Foss, pp. 53–66, London: Metheun.

Rank, O. (1929). *The Trauma of Birth*. New York: Harcourt, Brace.

Samuels, A., Shorter, B., and Plaut, F. (1986). *A Critical Dictionary of Jungian Analysis*. London: Routledge & Kegan Paul.

Sidoli, M. (1989). *The Unfolding Self: Separation and Individuation*. Boston, MA: Sigo.

Van Zyl, D. (1977). Traumatic birth symbolized in play therapy. *Journal of Primal Therapy* 4: 154–158.

Verny, T., and Kelly, J. (1981). *The Secret Life of the Unborn Child*. New York: Delta.

8

Child, Protector, Confidant: Structured Group Ecosystemic Play Therapy

Kevin O'Connor, PH.D.

INTRODUCTION TO STRUCTURED GROUP ECOSYSTEMIC PLAY THERAPY

The theoretical model upon which the type of group play therapy described in this chapter is based is a subset of the broader theoretical model of ecosystemic play therapy. The ecosystemic therapist views the child as being embedded in a series of nested systems including family, school, peer, culture, legal, medical, and others. Within this model, the play therapist considers the impact and interaction of each of these systems in developing and implementing any psychotherapeutic intervention. Structured group play therapy is simply one way of addressing problems children experience in their peer system. Both the ecosystemic play therapy and the structured group play therapy models have been thoroughly delineated in *The Play Therapy Primer* (O'Connor 1991). Therefore, only a synopsis of the latter, which is the focus of this chapter, will be presented herein.

Structured group play therapy includes components that address the cognitive, behavioral, emotional, physical, and social aspects of the child's difficulties. This multimodal approach promotes rapid change and maximum generalization of the child's progress. The primary function of this type of group is improvement in the quality of the child's peer social interactions. Much of the time, play therapists place children in such groups because they are inappropriately aggressive or because they act out in the context of peer interactions. This chapter, however, focuses on the treatment of a child who was referred because his

245

tendency to interact only with adults in an adult-like manner interfered
with his developing peer friendships.

Components of Structured Group Play Therapy

The Cognitive Component:
Problem-Solving Training and Interpretation

Two elements of structured group play therapy directly address the
cognitive aspects of a child's interactions with peers. Problem-solving
training and social skills training (Camp et al. 1977, Goldfried and
Davison 1976, Meichenbaum 1977, Meichenbaum and Goodman 1971)
were widely advocated in the clinical literature of the 1970s and are still
widely used. The underlying assumption is that both problem solving
and social interactions involve certain basic steps and skills that the
therapist can directly teach to a child. Both types of training are widely
used in public schools and in residential treatment centers. Both types
are represented in packaged programs designed for institutional use.
Think-Aloud (Camp et al. 1977) is an example of a packaged problem-
solving program. *Developing Understanding of Self and Others* (DUSO)
(Dinkmeyer 1973) is an example of a social skills training program.

I have merged the essential features of both problem-solving and
social skills training into a simple, easy to learn, component of structured group play therapy. I use a four-step problem solving strategy
with children from the ages of 4 to 12. I ask children in the group to go
through the following steps whenever they are faced with an interpersonal problem (O'Connor 1991).

> PROBLEM: Identify and operationally define the problem at hand. It is
> important that this phase of the process be done from the child's point of
> view. A child who is hitting another child may not see the hitting as a
> problem, though the victim certainly would. For the child doing the
> hitting, the problem is more likely to be the anger he or she is experiencing
> or the risk of consequences if the behavior continues.

> PLAN: Develop plans that resolve the problem as defined above. All plans
> are acceptable at this stage even those that are impossible in reality or
> socially inappropriate. Ideally, plans developed should solve the current
> problem and decrease the likelihood of the problem recurring in the
> future. The plans should also avoid requesting help from an adult
> wherever and whenever possible. The goal here is to foster creative,
> flexible, and independent thinking.

ACTION: Evaluate the plans made above and determine which one to implement or put into action. At this stage, pragmatics and reality are key aspects of the process. The child should evaluate how the plan chosen will affect the problem as well as the impact it will have on his or her own feelings and the feelings of others involved.

ANSWER: Answer the question: "How did my plan work?" The child is to evaluate the effectiveness of the plan as implemented in the ACTION step according to those same criteria and adjust it as needed.

In the context of structured group play therapy, children primarily address interpersonal problems using this format. Hypothetical situations, events that the children report that occur outside of the session, and any problems that arise during group all provide excellent opportunities to apply the strategy. The goal is to have the children internalize the process to the point that it becomes automatic. This will only occur with near-continuous repetition and rehearsal. The use of situations other than those that occur in the group helps to promote generalization of the skills learned.

In addition to directly teaching the children a problem-solving strategy, it is important to facilitate their overall use of language in interpersonal contexts. One of the best tools for accomplishing this is the therapist's use of interpretation (O'Connor 1991, O'Connor and Lee 1991). First, the therapist models the use of language and may provide the children with additional vocabulary that they can use to convey the subtleties of their experience. Second, the therapist demonstrates the importance of emotions and motives in understanding intra- and interpersonal events. Third, the therapist can help children to understand both the continuity of their behavior over time and the complementarity of behavior between children. Last, the therapist can help the children see connections between their early experience and their current behavior, thereby helping them to break old patterns. The combination of interpretation and the problem-solving strategy can provide children with powerful tools for understanding and subsequently altering their behavior.

The Physical Component: Relaxation Training and Planned Activities

Prior to the onset of formal operations thinking at about age 11, children tend to learn more from experience than from language. They are focused on their bodies and on their interaction with the physical world. For any intervention to be successful with children in this age range, it is imperative that the therapist incorporate a physical component. In structured group play therapy, this can be done in many ways, two of which will be described here. One is to incorporate general relaxation training into group sessions. The other is to plan both fine and gross motor activities consistent with the developmental level of the children. These exercises should expand on the cognitive aspects of the group. Alternatively, the play therapist might use dance, drama, music, martial arts, or exercise programs to accomplish the same ends.

The purpose of the relaxation training is twofold. Primarily, it focuses the children on their bodily states and helps adjust their level of arousal to one where optimal learning can take place. It fosters impulse control. Relaxation training also helps children learn a routine by using a predictable sequence of exercises and repetitive vocabulary.

Virtually any relaxation training program can be effectively employed in a group setting. Progressive deep muscle relaxation (Jacobson 1938) is a standard and the play therapist can employ it with or without the alternate contracting and relaxing of the muscles. Generally, children under the age of 11 seem to do better when using the alternating contraction and relaxation of the muscles. Simply put, the therapist teaches them to repeatedly contract and relax large muscle groups in a consistent order (head to foot or vice versa), while focusing on the experience of muscle relaxation. The play therapist can increase the level of relaxation achieved by helping the children learn to control their breathing rates and through the use of guided imagery.

The structured group play therapist must make the application of the relaxation to social interaction explicit. The play therapist will do this by helping children in the group focus on their bodily experience during both pleasant and unpleasant interactions. The group should include a focus on the bodily experience of different emotions. The children can also be taught to use relaxation to enhance their ability to complete the problem-solving strategy.

Besides using relaxation training, it is important that any group for younger children include activities that facilitate appropriate social interaction and the development of interpersonal skills. High-interest activities that promote sharing, cooperation, turn taking, group problem solving, impulse control, and the like are all very valuable in the conduct of structured group play therapy. A cognitive understanding of the function and implementation of various social skills is imperative if children are to repeat and generalize functional behaviors, but such an understanding is not sufficient to produce behavior change. The play therapist must give children the opportunity to test their understanding and to integrate the information on a physical and/or experiential level.

Each of us has had the experience of trying to follow written instructions for assembling some object and finding that there is often a significant difference in our cognitive understanding of what we have read and the reality of the task at hand. Helping the children in the group translate their cognitive understanding into practical application is an essential element of structured group play therapy.

The Behavioral Component: A Behavior Modification System

All organisms learn best and change the most rapidly in an environment that provides rewards for success and consistent and logical consequences for failure. Children in structured group play therapy are certainly no exception. The type of behavior management implemented by the play therapist may range from one that is extremely detailed and structured in the case of severely disturbed or acting out children to one that is so informal that it remains outside the conscious awareness of the children involved. In either case, it is important that the therapist consider the types of behavior to be reinforced, the types of behavior for which consequences will be imposed, the types of reinforcers and the types of consequences that will be imposed, the reinforcement schedule, and the strategy for fading the reinforcers over time before beginning the group.

The behaviors to be reinforced might include a list of developmentally appropriate social behaviors. The play therapist may or may not choose to explicitly verbalize these target behaviors to the children. The behaviors for which consequences will be imposed generally include, at least, the destruction of property, hurting others (verbally and/or physically), and hurting oneself.

The play therapist will determine the types of reinforcers used and the reinforcement schedule according to the developmental level of the group members. Children in the preoperational stage (ages 2 to 6) often need primary reinforcers administered at very high frequency in order to maintain their behavior. For this age group, the play therapist must impose consequences immediately so that the children are able cognitively to connect the problem behavior and the consequence. Any consequence imposed should also be of very short duration. For example, it is recommended that a "time-out" for a child at this age last no more than 1 to 2 minutes per year of the child's age. Children in the concrete operations stage of development (ages 6 to 11) respond to secondary reinforcers, but usually only if these can be redeemed for concrete reinforcers at some point in the future. These children usually respond well to point systems, but only when those points represent movement toward a specific reward such as a toy or a desired activity. During this stage, children also tolerate more delay between a target behavior and the administration of rewards or consequences. At all ages the liberal use of social rewards is important.

With older and less disturbed children, the play therapist may not need to develop a formal behavioral system so long as social rewards are liberally administered. For all groups, however, it is imperative that the therapist has thought through the consequences that will follow severe acting out that poses a threat to self or others. Is the child to be excluded from group? If so, for how long? Is the child to lose privileges? If so, then the privileges lost must in some way be logically connected to the problem behavior. Is the child to be restrained or physically managed? Each of these questions leads to decisions that have a significant impact on the running of the group and should be made before a crisis occurs. Nothing is more destructive to a group's process than witnessing the severe acting out of one of its members being mishandled. The children may then experience the group as unsafe or punitive or both, resulting in significantly diminished participation or increased acting out.

Finally, it is important for the play therapist to decide how to fade the reinforcement system used over time as the children make developmental progress. For example, a group of severely acting out 10-year-olds may need concrete reinforcers administered at short intervals in order to maintain their behavior at the beginning of the group. However, if the group is successful, then the children should be able to move to secondary reinforcers administered at rather long and intermittent intervals as they progress. Ideally, they would be functioning at a level where social reinforcers were sufficient to maintain their behavior by the time the group ended. Many therapists settle into the use of a particular system and do not change it over time, either because they simply do not think about it or they are afraid the children will regress. Failure to move the children toward developmentally appropriate and socially common reinforcers over the course of the group significantly reduces the chance that behavior learned in the session will generalize to environments where the reinforcers are not present.

The Emotional Component: Guided Discussion and Interpretation

Children's ability to make and sustain peer friendships will benefit from the acquisition of specific social skills and a cognitive understanding of such interactions, but it is not likely to be successful or rewarding if they are unable to integrate their emotional experience into the process. Without emotional integration children will, at best, be going through the motions in their peer interactions. The play therapist accomplishes the goal of integrating emotion into all aspects of the group process by conducting guided discussions and actively interpreting individual children's experience as well as the group process.

Emotion should be a verbal and experiential part of every aspect of the group process. The consideration of one's own and others' emotions is an essential part of effective social problem solving. Emotions should be identified at the PROBLEM, ACTION, and ANSWER stages of the problem-solving process. Relaxation training is most effective when children understand its connection to, and impact upon, their emotional experience. Further, the play therapist can cue children to use a relaxation strategy to manage their behavior in the face of strong negative emotions, particularly anxiety. Lastly, activities that foster the functional expression of emotions facilitate the children developing a sense of control over their feelings and the ability to sublimate those that cannot be fully expressed in reality.

The play therapist may use guided discussions to focus the group on the role of emotion in social interactions. In these discussions the play therapist chooses a topic that is relevant to many of the group members and initiates a discussion that includes problem solving. For example, in a group where many of the children have experienced a parental divorce, the therapist might initiate a discussion about the types of feelings children have in the face of a divorce. One way to do this is by reading the group a story about divorce and then asking the group to compare and contrast their experiences with those portrayed in the story. Once some of the negative consequences of divorce have been owned by the children, the therapist then engages the group in problem solving.

Emotion should be the focus of most of the interpretive work done by the therapist while conducting the group. Children are not prone to processing their emotional experience, in part because doing so requires a certain capacity for abstraction that may go beyond their developmental level. They also tend to try to avoid negative emotions whenever possible. Therefore, it is useful for the therapist to use interpretation to:

1. label emotions: "You seem very angry right now. I think being teased hurt your feelings." "The little boy in the story we just read was jealous of his new baby sister."
2. help the child make the connections between emotions, experiences, and behavior: "Sometimes I think you hit me because you want me

to hold you, but you are afraid to ask." "It seems like you get so excited you just can't hold it in so you start to hop around a lot."
3. help the child incorporate the idea that emotions are a necessary element in guiding their interpersonal interactions: "When you get sad it seems like telling your mom about it works a lot better than going to your room and crying because then she knows you need a hug and kiss." "When you hit someone when you are angry you might feel better, but the other person feels bad and then you get in trouble."

While these examples should serve to get the play therapist started incorporating interpretation in group work, a thorough discussion of the development and delivery of interpretations is beyond the scope of this chapter. For a complete review of this topic see *The Play Therapy Primer* (O'Connor 1991).

The Social Component: Structured Activities

The very nature of structured group play therapy tends to focus children on the social aspects of the experience. After all, they are in a room with other children. It is surprising, however, how often therapists do not make full use of the other children in the group and do not focus the children on one another. Instead, parallel interactions between each of the children and the therapist come to be the norm. The children never come to see the value of their peers in the group setting because they are too focused on the reward potential created by their interactions with the therapist.

Simple strategies for increasing the peer focus of the children include the reinforcement strategies used, interpretation, and structured activities. Directly rewarding developmentally appropriate peer interaction is a powerful tool, but still tends to focus the children on the adult dispensing the rewards rather than the antecedent behavior being reinforced. When the play therapist gives children the means to directly reinforce other group members for engaging in behavior the children experience as pleasurable, the learning is more powerful and more focused. Similarly, peer pressure to conform to a particular standard of behavior is generally more powerful than adult reinforcement. Simply having the entire group wait for one child who is not cooperating to join in can be a very effective form of limit setting if not overused. Also, the use of rewards provided to the group as a whole for a successful collective effort, rather than for individual responses, can increase the positive group focus of the members.

The therapist can use interpretation to focus the children on the reciprocal nature of their behavior and on the impact of their interactions on one another. During the problem-solving process, children can identify ways in which they can get their needs met by approaching peers directly rather than always approaching an adult first. Children can also learn the emotional value that peers have in their daily lives, particularly when focused on the pleasure they receive from positive peer feedback.

Lastly, the therapist can greatly enhance the social aspect of the group through the use of developmentally appropriate activities. As previously discussed, these activities provide the children with the opportunity to engage in safe and pleasurable interactions so as to practice their newfound skills. Such activities also become directly reinforcing, in and of themselves, pushing the children to seek out peer involvement more frequently. Such activities might include cooperative games like Frozen Tag or Red Rover, group art projects, or having the group plan a holiday party.

Basic Assumptions in the Conduct of Structured Group Play Therapy

Children's Developmental Level

Because the focus of structured group play therapy is on the peer socialization of the group members, each child should be at a developmental level where such a goal is appropriate. Children under the developmental age of 2 or 3 are not suitable candidates for this type of group. Their primary focus is on the development of a relationship with a caretaker and nothing should interfere with this. Children between the developmental ages of 3 and 5 are generally not appropriate candidates for this type of group. They continue to be predominantly focused on the development of relationships with adults in general. For this reason, many 3- to 5-year-olds will not have an interest in, or the energy available for, the development of peer relationships. This does not mean that group work is not possible at this age, only that it may be developmentally inappropriate or of low priority.

Once children reach the developmental age of 5, then peer relationships become progressively more important, reaching a peak during adolescence. For children between the ages of 5 and young adulthood, therapeutic group involvement can be a very powerful intervention. The structured group play therapy model presented here seems to be most appropriate for children from the ages of 5 to 12. As children move into formal operations thinking and adolescence, they tend to find the concrete structure somewhat inhibiting. Even some preadolescents do better in a more open-ended, process group.

Children's Pathology

Again, because the focus of structured group play therapy is on the improvement of children's social skills, the group members ought not to be experiencing a level of psychopathology so intense that it precludes any possibility of their effectively interacting with their peers. Three classes of children seem poorly suited to this type of group: (a) children who have significant problems with reality testing or pervasive developmental delays; (b) children who are exhibiting signs of character pathology, such as the ability to hurt others with no evidence of remorse or a preference for social isolation with no evidence of psychosis; and (c) children who have experienced a very recent trauma, as they often require a level of nurturance and support that is difficult for a play therapist to provide within the context of a group. With each of these groups, it is generally best to begin working on the essential features of the children's difficulties through individual play therapy and then to progress to structured group play therapy.

Group Composition

The general rules for the creation of a group are as follows:

1. There should be no more than four to six children in a group run by one adult and no more than six to ten children in a group with two adults.
2. There should be no more than a three-year age spread among the group members, especially among younger children.
3. The socioeconomic status and/or the children's ethnic background should be somewhat similar. This may be one of the least important variables unless the differences between the children are very dramatic, in which case the group may become focused on these issues and unable to address other content or behavioral areas.
4. The children should all be within fifteen IQ points of one another.
5. The ability to mix boys and girls within a group varies with the age of the children, the type of group, and the goals of the intervention. There is no fixed rule, but it is a dimension you should consider (O'Connor 1991, p. 328).

While these general guidelines are helpful, they are by no means required. Any powerful reason for the children being in a group together may alleviate the need to have the children matched on these other dimensions. For example, I chose to include Danny, the child in this case study, in a group that had members of mixed intellectual functioning and socioeconomic status. Their abuse experiences gave them a common ground that precluded the problems these differences might have caused otherwise.

Role of the Play Therapist

The play therapist serves two primary functions in structured group play therapy. The therapist creates and maintains the structure. This includes:

1. all aspects of the creation of the group such as selection of the members, length of the sessions, and duration of the treatment;
2. the selection of a format and activities suited to the particular pathologies and developmental levels of the group members;
3. the development and maintenance of group goals and a treatment plan across group sessions;
4. the maintenance of the structure within each group session; and
5. assuring compliance with the basic rules of not hurting self, others, or property so that the basic safety of the group members is protected.

The play therapist's other function is as the monitor and interpreter of the group's process. The therapist must put words to the children's individual and group experiences so as to facilitate their cognitive understanding of the process. This insight will, in turn, speed the rate of change for the members and increase the likelihood of generalization of those gains.

PRESENTING PROBLEM AND BACKGROUND DATA

Danny Davis was a 10-year-old, European-American, male. He was the only child born to a well-educated, upper middle class couple. His parents were both 32 years old at the time he was born, having waited to complete their education and become financially stable prior to starting a family.

Danny's early history was unremarkable. He experienced no major childhood illnesses. The family moved only twice. They purchased their first home when Danny was about a year old and moved to their current residence when he was 5. Mrs. Davis became aware of the fact that she could not have any more children when Danny was 3 years old. She reports having become moderately depressed at that time, but noted that she came out of it by focusing a great deal of her energy on Danny's upbringing. Mr. Davis worked long hours as an executive in a financial planning firm. Mrs. Davis was a full-time homemaker who did volunteer work for several local groups. Both parents reported that their marriage had been happy until Danny was about 8 or 9 years old.

About one year prior to Danny's referral, Mr. and Mrs. Davis decided to divorce subsequent to a year-long history of escalating marital problems. Unfortunately, the state in which the family lived did not have community property laws. In some such states, a spouse who first vacates a jointly held property risks losing any right to that property. This tends to force divorcing couples to live together until the financial settlement of their divorce becomes final. Additionally, the state in question required that one partner show cause as to why the divorce should be granted if it is contested by either party. This significantly increased the blame-laying between Mr. and Mrs. Davis.

The Davis family owned a very expensive home in a well-to-do suburb. As neither Mr. nor Mrs. Davis wanted to risk losing their right to moneys acquired from the sale of their home, they chose to live there together while pursuing their divorce. They moved into separate bedrooms with an adjoining bathroom.

The intensity of Mr. and Mrs. Davis' animosity for one another only increased as they moved toward divorce. They became preoccupied with the division of assets and the need to place blame for the divorce, each upon the other. Each of them also became preoccupied with gaining sole custody of Danny in order to punish the other parent and get his or her own narcissistic needs met. Since both were aware that there was little reason for the courts not to grant joint custody, each chose to increase the likelihood of getting sole custody by doing two things. Each parent reported the other for spousal abuse. Indeed, the level of domestic violence increased steadily over the course of the year preceding Danny's referral. Each parent also worked to win Danny over to his or her "side," while turning him against the other parent—he was the rope in their tug-of-war.

Danny was referred by Child Protective Services. This was somewhat unusual as Danny had not been either physically or sexually abused. Instead, the referral was based on a determination that he was being emotionally abused through exposure to the violence between his parents. At this point, the couple had engaged in actual physical violence. Although the mother claimed to be the primary victim, it was later discovered that she was often the aggressor. The mother had begun requiring Danny to sleep on the floor at the foot of her bed in order to protect her from her husband.

The parents also tended to use Danny as a messenger between them so that they could avoid contact with each other. Initially, this was simply a strain for Danny who was literally "in the middle." Later, however, both of the parents tended to become abusive toward Danny when they did not like the content of the messages he delivered. Danny soon learned to change the content of the message so as to mollify both parents and earn their approval and gratitude. In other words he convinced both of his parents that he was really on their side.

The primary referral problem was Danny's generally "out-of-control" behavior. He was not directly aggressive in the manner of many out of control children. Instead he was manipulative, controlling, defiant, and verbally aggressive. He had previously been an excellent student and was now getting mostly Cs in school. His mother also reported that he had no peer friendships.

Pretreatment Assessment

The first portion of the intake was separate interviews conducted with the parents during which they relayed the above history and description of the presenting problem. It should be noted that Mr. Davis felt that Danny's difficulties were relatively minor and a result of Mrs. Davis dragging Danny into the marital conflict. Mrs. Davis, on the other hand, saw Danny as a deeply troubled young man with significant internal conflicts arising out of his lack of a significant relationship with his father.

During the intake interview, I also assisted the parents in completing the Developmental Therapy Objective Rating Form-Revised (DTORF) (Developmental Therapy Institute 1992). The DTORF is a scale made up of a hierarchically arranged list of behaviors in four domains: behavior, communication, socialization, and academics. It is particularly useful for determining the developmental goals toward which a child should be working in group. The results of this administration of the DTORF are discussed in the Developmental section of the case formulation that follows.

The intake interview with Danny prior to his acceptance into treatment was a replication of his usual interactions with adults. His mother was so afraid of his reaction to being brought to therapy that she did not tell him where she was bringing him until they were in the waiting room. He responded by leaving and refusing to reenter the clinic. When I informed the mother that I would not take responsibility for Danny until he was, at least, in the waiting room, she went out and pleaded with him until he returned.

Once in the waiting room, Danny came readily to my office. As he entered the office he informed me, while looking at his watch, that I had better talk fast. He said that he had only agreed to come back in the building when his mother had stipulated that he would not be required to stay for more than 5 minutes. He also informed me that I could say whatever I wanted, but he had no intention of talking. At this point I let him know that whatever agreements he had made with his mother were null and void in terms of his interactions with me. He was under his mother's control outside the clinic, but under my control once in my office. I would decide what we talked about and for how long.

At this point Danny picked up a chair and moved to throw it through the huge window in my office. With no hesitation I took hold of the leg of the chair and forced it back to the floor. I moved in very close to Danny and, while making direct eye contact, said "Sit down. Don't talk. And don't move until I tell you it is okay." Danny sat down saying, "Oh, . . . okay." After a brief review of the purpose of the visit and some reflection of his feelings of anger at having been deceived, Danny settled into a very productive intake interview.

Danny was incredibly insightful with respect to his current role in his parents' marital conflict. While I tried to point out the strain the role created, he pointed out the benefits. He said that if he could read his parents correctly and tell them exactly what they wanted to hear from, or about, the other parent then he got rewarded. He said he knew he could make them feel good or guilty as needed. He further noted that in a good week he could woo or cajole thirty to fifty dollars' worth of gifts, cash, or local trips out of each parent. His reality included the fact that his parents' marital conflict was a big money-maker for him.

With respect to his presenting problem, Danny generally responded with denial or blaming. He said he was not really a problem at school, but readily observed that most of his teachers were really stupid. If there was conflict between him and them, he noted, it was generally because he was right and they were wrong about something. Then, because adults hate it when a child is right, they would get him in trouble. He claimed to have many friends, but had difficulty naming any.

THEORETICAL CONCEPTUALIZATION

The style on which the case formulation that follows is based is fully described in the *Play Therapy Primer* (O'Connor 1991). The formulation and treatment planning process is divided into four steps. First, the play therapist delineates the child's present pattern of functioning. From this description the play therapist derives developmentally appropriate treatment goals. Second, he or she develops hypotheses as to the factors that contributed to the child's present functional strengths and weaknesses. From these hypotheses the play therapist derives reparative goals. Third, the play therapist develops hypotheses as to the factors maintaining the child's present functioning. He or she develops treatment goals from these hypotheses to facilitate the generalization of the progress the child makes in treatment. Last, the play therapist synthesizes these goals and develops a treatment plan. Because of the focus of this chapter, I will discuss the individual therapy and broader systems goals developed during this process only very briefly.

Danny's Present Pattern of Functioning

Developmental Level

In observing Danny and conducting the intake assessment, it became apparent that, in spite of his intellectual capacity, he was functioning in many ways like a 2-to 3-year-old. His primary emotional bond was still with his mother. He was obsessed with exerting and maintaining his power in relationships and the world at large. When he could not exert control verbally he would become physically aggressive and demanding. Further, he showed little or no interest in peer relationships. While his social and emotional functioning appeared quite low, it was clear that in other areas he was functioning at or above a level that would be considered developmentally appropriate.

Using the DTORF, the Davises rated Danny as functioning in stage 4 (ages 9 to 12) in the Behavioral domain, suggesting that his behavior and impulse control were within normal limits. Danny was at the end of stage 3 (ages 6 to 9) in the Communication domain, due primarily to limitations in his ability to recognize others' feelings and function as part of a group. He was in stage 2 (ages 2 to 6) in the Socialization domain, primarily because of his extreme difficulty initiating and maintaining interactions with peers. The Academic domain was not rated. At 10 years of age Danny should have been functioning at stage 4 in all domains.

Goals: Danny's developmental level needed to be equalized across areas of functioning; therefore, addressing his deficits in social/emotional functioning was a priority. Danny would be able to (a) respond appropriately to choices for leadership in the group (B-20); (b) indicate beginning awareness of his own behavioral progress (B-21); (c) use words to show pride in group achievements (C-21); (d) channel feelings or experiences through creative, nonverbal media such as art, music, dance, or drama (C-22); (e) participate in interactive play with another child (S-17); and (f) participate in cooperative activities or projects with another child during organized activities (S-18). [These goals are from the DTORF. The code letters stand for the domain (B for Behavioral; C for Communication; and S for Socialization) and the numbers correspond to the DTORF items.]

Cognitions

Danny had been assessed through his school for potential placement in a program for intellectually gifted children. On the *Wechsler Intelligence Scale for Children–III*, he achieved a Verbal IQ of 125, a Performance IQ of 115, and a Full Scale IQ of 123. These scores suggest that Danny was able to function well above average in all intellectual areas. It was apparent in conversations with Danny and from reports made by his teachers that he impressed most adults as being very bright. This impression was created largely by his verbal fluency and language complexity.

Danny maintained several dysfunctional beliefs that derived directly from the role he was playing in his family. First, he believed that he was directly responsible for his parents' well-being. It was his duty to make sure they were happy. Second, he believed that his parents would only respond to his needs if he first met their needs, especially their need for emotional support. Third, he believed he had the power to control the outcome of their marital conflict. Fourth, he believed that any interpersonal interaction that he could not control would turn out badly, resulting in his not getting his needs met. Last, he appeared to believe that peers were not a reasonable source of emotional or material supplies.

Goals: Danny would be able to (a) use his verbal skills in a nonthreatening way in interactions with peers, (b) state the limitations of his power with respect to his parents' marriage, (c) ask directly for emotional and material supplies from either or both of his parents, (d) show pleasure in an interpersonal situation that he was not controlling, and (e) approach his peers for emotional supplies and support.

Emotions

Danny's emotional repertoire was relatively appropriate. He experienced and was able to manifest a broad range of emotions, although he often had difficulty expressing these feelings verbally. He tended to be anxious most of the time secondary to his belief that if he were not controlling every situation it would become problematic. He also tended to become intensely angry when he was not allowed to control a situation, fearing that he would not get his needs met.

Goals: Danny would (a) be able to verbally describe his current emotions, (b) report less anxiety in situations he is not controlling, and (c) demonstrate fewer rage episodes.

Response Repertoire

In this area I considered whether Danny tended to adopt one of two overall styles: autoplastic or alloplastic. An autoplastic style is one in which individuals attempt to correct problems they encounter by changing their own behavior. An alloplastic style is one in which individuals attempt to correct problems by expecting/demanding that others or the environment make the necessary changes. Consistent with his belief that he could and should control most of his interpersonal interactions, Danny tended toward a predominantly autoplastic response style. For example, when faced with the dilemma of his enmeshment in his parents' divorce, he figured out a way to play it to his advantage rather than expecting them to alter their behavior. Only when severely stressed by a situational loss of control would Danny resort to alloplastic responses and expect others to change. This was evidenced by his violent acting upon being tricked into coming to my office.

Goals: Danny would (a) more realistically perceive the level of control he could or should have in various interpersonal situations, (b) be able to ask others (parents and peers) directly to meet his needs, and (c) manifest fewer rage episodes in situations he cannot control.

Origins of Danny's Present Pattern of Functioning

In this stage of the treatment planning, my goal is to develop hypotheses about the factors that contributed to the child's present pattern of functioning and appropriate reparative goals.

Child Specific Factors

Clearly, Danny's intellectual and verbal skills made it possible for him to adopt a primarily internalized, autoplastic mode of responding to his environment. He was capable of interacting with adults on their level and of controlling them in many situations. The subsequent reinforcement he received made this pattern of behavior both predominant and stable. The successful use of this pattern of response, in turn, reinforced Danny's dysfunctional beliefs about his role in the family and his control skills/needs.

With respect to Danny's early history, it seemed likely that his mother's depression when he was 3 years old solidified certain aspects of the family's interactional style. It seemed likely that Danny reacted to his mother's depression and withdrawal as a partial abandonment. This would motivate him to work to reestablish contact with her and would interfere with his pursuing the normal developmental task of this age, namely, the generalization of his primary attachment to his mother to include his father. The father's general unavailability during this period would have exacerbated this problem. Because Danny never generalized attachment behavior beyond his relationship to his mother to include even his father, there would be little chance of his then generalizing that attachment to peers in subsequent developmental phases.

Goals: Danny would (a) use his intellectual skills to become more proficient at interpersonal problem solving; and (b) be able to verbally describe the ways in which his attachment to his mother interfered with his attachment to his father and with his peer interactions.

Ecological Factors

Family As I have noted, Danny's role as the only child in his family significantly contributed to the pattern of strengths and weaknesses he was displaying at the time of intake. He had been expected to meet his parents' narcissistic needs for some time and had become quite skilled at doing so. As the stress of the divorce increased his parents' need for emotional support, Danny attempted to provide for each of them accordingly. Clearly, his resources had become stressed by these demands to the point that he had begun to act out aggressively.

Goals: Danny would (a) be able to verbally recognize the inappropriateness of his current role in his family and redefine himself as a child; (b) ask his parents directly for emotional support; and (c) demonstrate fewer rage episodes.

Peers Since Danny had virtually no peer relationships prior to his entry into therapy, these did not significantly contribute to his present functioning.

Goal: Danny would demonstrate the beginnings of one or more stable peer friendships.

Broader Systems The primary system that seemed to have had an impact on Danny's functioning besides his family was his school. Certainly he had received a great deal of positive reinforcement for his academic success until the year prior to his referral. Teachers may also have contributed to Danny's isolation from peers by using his academic achievements to set him apart. This happens when teachers say things like, "Now children I am very disappointed with the way you did on this last spelling test. I know you can all do better. Danny seems to be the only one who studied because he got a 100 on the test." While such comments are not made with malicious intent, they isolate the child and place him or her in the role of scapegoat.

Goal: Danny's teachers would focus on reinforcing his interactions with peers over academics, at least temporarily.

Factors Maintaining Danny's Pattern of Functioning

Child-Specific Factors

Not only did Danny's intellectual skills contribute to his present pattern of functioning, they allowed for his maintenance of such an autoplastic approach. He engaged adults in long verbal debates about his behavior, thereby avoiding compliance. He was able to manipulate his parents into feeling guilty so as to gain specific rewards. And, he was able to control his peers by speaking to them as an adult would.

The dysfunctional beliefs that Danny had developed about his familial interactions over time now served to maintain his pattern of responding. For example, since he believed his parents would only meet his needs if he first met theirs, he was loath to stop meeting their needs for fear that to do so would result in the loss of their love and support. He may have even believed that either or both of them would choose to "divorce" him.

With respect to Danny's early history, it seemed that his mother's use of her relationship to him as a way of pulling herself out of her depression continued to set the standard for their interactions. At the time of his referral, Danny was not only her child, he was her protector and confidant as well.

Goals: Danny would be able to (a) verbalize the inappropriateness of his mother's dependence on him, (b) recognize his own emotional needs as separate from those of his mother, (c) verbalize some of his dysfunctional beliefs and recognize the degree to which they interfered with his getting his needs met, and (d) use his intellectual skills to engage in interpersonal problem solving relative to his peer interactions.

Ecological Factors

Family The parents' inability to maintain appropriate role boundaries while under the stress of their divorce allowed them to draw Danny into their increasing marital conflicts. Each parent was attempting to pull Danny into the role of spousal confidant and protector. Each parent wanted him to take sides against the other. Each parent also wanted Danny to meet his or her needs for emotional support. All of these combined to force Danny into continuing his pattern of functioning. He perceived himself to be in serious jeopardy of losing what little nurturance he did receive from his parents if he did not comply with their demands.

Goals: Danny would be able to (a) verbalize the inappropriateness of the current demands being placed upon him by his parents, (b) ask his parents directly for emotional support, and (c) reduce his dependence on parental support by identifying other adults and/or peers in the environment who might provide him with emotional supplies.

Peers By the time children enter the third or fourth grade, they tend to have a substantial network of stable friendships if they have continued to live in the same area since beginning school. These networks are frequently rather rigid and new children may have difficulty entering the system. Danny had managed to complete fourth grade without being included in these peer networks. He had the added disadvantage of not being a new child, but rather one already identified by his peers as a loner or outsider. Because of these two factors, it was likely that Danny would have significant difficulty making initial friendships with his school peers.

Goal: Danny would use the members of the group as a transitional peer support network. This would involve his first developing and honing the skills necessary to gain their support and then using the group as a base from which to generalize to relationships with peers in his neighborhood and at school.

Broader Systems School continued to support Danny's dysfunctional patterns of responding by focusing on his steadily declining academic performance and ignoring his peer relationships. His teachers ignored the possibility that school failure might be reinforced by Danny's peers because it reduced the pressure on them to perform.

Child Protective Services made a significant impact on Danny's pattern of functioning simply by referring him to treatment in a child abuse clinic. This referral facilitated Danny's seeing himself, not as the person in control of his family situation with all of the consequent rewards, but as the victim of his parents' conflict. This was the first input Danny received that suggested his parents' expectations were inappropriate. Additionally, he understood that the role of that system was to protect him from his parents rather than promoting his role in protecting his parents from one another.

Family Court appointed an advocate to protect Danny's rights in the divorce process. At one point early in his treatment, Danny requested an Order of Protection against both of his parents. Typically, these orders stipulate that the named parties may not come within a certain physical distance of the petitioner so as to inhibit violence. A violation of such an order can result in the offender serving jail time. At the time of his request, Danny's parents had orders against each other specifying that they must remain at least 100 yards away from each other. If either one violated the boundary, the other party could call the police. Danny wanted a similar order aimed at keeping his parents away from him. This represented overwhelming progress as it reflected Danny's view that he no longer wanted to be a part of such an enmeshed relationship. It was also one of the first times he sought support from another adult.

If the order had been granted, Danny would have felt that someone wished to protect him. On the other hand, such an order would also reinforce Danny's sense that he should be responsible for managing his parents' behavior and his view that they were incapable of responding to his needs directly. In consultation with me, the advocate determined that such an order would not be issued. Instead, the original orders were rescinded. The message to each of the family members was that the court expected them to behave appropriately without the threat of incarceration. The advocate also made it clear to Danny, in front of his parents, that she expected them to protect him with or without a court order simply because it was in his best interest. The parents were strongly chastised for creating a situation where their child felt the need to seek outside protection and informed that failure to alter their behavior could result in both of them losing custody. The advocate did not convey the possibility of both his parents losing custody to Danny as it would have significantly heightened his fear of losing his parents altogether. They responded quite appropriately to this and greatly reduced the fighting they did in front of Danny.

Goals: (a) Danny's teachers would reinforce all positive approaches Danny makes toward peers while minimizing their criticism of his academic performance; (b) Danny would continue to use his court appointed advocate as a source of support; and (c) Danny's advocate would maintain pressure on the parents to meet Danny's needs if either of them was to have any custodial responsibility.

Goal Synthesis

By reviewing the many goals developed in the course of writing the case formulation, the play therapist develops an overall set of goals and then sorts these goals based on their priority. He or she will use two criteria to determine priority. Any goals addressing behaviors that are a danger to self or others become a very high priority. The other high-priority goals are those that reflect the child's developmentally lowest areas of functioning. Second, the play therapist must determine which goals can be addressed through psychotherapy and which must be addressed through some other intervention. Third, the play therapist determines the type of intervention or treatment modality that will best address each of the psychotherapy goals. Last, the play therapist determines the specific techniques or activities to be used with the overall intervention model to address client specific goals or content.

In Danny's case, his aggressive behavior was relatively mild and there was very little threat to the well being of himself or others. Therefore I did not consider any of the goals to be of high priority based on danger. Using the developmental criteria, Danny's very significant delays in social and emotional functioning became the top priority. Since his current functioning in this area was at the preoperational level, I determined that these goals would not be well suited to group therapy. Therefore, I began Danny's treatment with an initial course of individual sessions. Specifically, I wanted the individual treatment to address the issues of Danny's enmeshed relationship with his mother, helping him to separate from her while developing a more positive and stable relationship with his father. Individual treatment was also the context in which I could address the origins and impact of Danny's dysfunctional beliefs about his family and social interactions. Two other therapists in the same clinic also provided individual treatment for each of Danny's parents, with the overall plan of completing some family work prior to termination. The goal of the family treatment was the development of more appropriate role definitions and boundaries within each of the new family units (Danny/Mr. Davis and Danny/Mrs. Davis).

I determined that those goals related to Danny's deficits in peer social skills were second in terms of priority. Once Danny had progressed in individual therapy to the point that his social and emotional functioning was more comparable to that of a 4- to 5-year-old, I decided to begin addressing these goals in group therapy. I used Danny's attainment of three developmental criteria in making this decision. First, Danny demonstrated decreased dependency upon his mother (age 2 or older). Second, Danny demonstrated increased use of his father and other significant adults in his life as sources of emotional and material support (age 3 or older). Last, Danny had become less aggressive and showed an emerging interest in peer interactions (age 4 or older).

During the initial phase of group therapy, Danny participated in both individual and group therapy simultaneously. The individual therapy sessions were rapidly faded to termination by increasing the time interval between sessions. This transitional plan weaned Danny from his one-to-one dependent relationship on me and facilitated his coming to use the group as a substitute for the individual sessions. Although my having provided both the individual and group therapy in this case was not optimal, it was necessitated by the staffing of the clinic. The problem of jealousy between group members was not an issue in this case because all of the children in this particular group had been in individual treatment with me at some time.

I determined a third set of treatment goals to be of relatively high priority, but not suited to psychotherapeutic intervention. These goals consisted of items that could be best addressed through education/ consultation with representatives of the other systems that were affecting Danny's functioning. I established two ongoing consultative relationships. One relationship was with Danny's teachers. I appraised them of the role that the school could play in altering Danny's dysfunctional patterns and presented them with some simple strategies for initiating change. These consultations took place by telephone at irregular intervals over the course of Danny's treatment. I also established a consultative relationship with Danny's court appointed advocate. She was instrumental in setting limits on the family's pattern of interactions that supported the therapeutic goals of establishing appropriate role definitions and boundaries. These consultations continued until the court finalized the Davis' divorce settlement. It is this type of consultation that sets ecosystemic play therapy apart from some of the other more traditional forms of both individual and group play therapy.

THE PROCESS OF PLAY THERAPY

Setting Up

Preparation for the group to which Danny was referred was quite limited. I conducted the sessions in a relatively large (18' × 18') room. It was divided roughly into halves, one carpeted, the other with a linoleum floor. The carpeted side of the room was further divided into two areas. One area was defined by a couch, two armchairs, and a coffee table. It very much resembled a traditional living room. The other half contained a table and enough chairs for each of the group members and the group leader.

The purpose of the arrangement was to provide the members with visual and spatial cues for the types of behavior expected in the group. The living room area was reserved for discussions and quiet activities. This was also where snacks were served. When children were in this area, I expected them to make verbal contributions to the group process and to comply with basic "manners." The group used the table exclusively for table games and art projects. In this area, I emphasized sharing, cooperation, and a "product orientation" among the children. The group used the large empty area of the room for gross motor activities and games. When the group was in this area, I emphasized cooperation. The group also went outside frequently to play at a local park, where I expected behavior similar to that required in the open area of the room.

I brought very few materials into the playroom. My goal was to focus the children on their interactions with one another rather than on their interactions with the toys or materials. I provided food, for two reasons. One reason was simply pragmatic: the group met immediately after school and the members tended to be so hungry that they could not focus on anything else until after they ate. The other reason was more symbolic: the food was a way of sharing nurturance among children who had all been the victims of abuse. Snack time was also a good way for me to teach sharing and simple table manners.

At no time were toys or materials freely available to the group. I selected the materials to be used prior to each group session and placed only these on the table. By limiting access to materials, I maintained the structure of the group and maximized members' developmental progression by presenting materials that challenged, but did not frustrate, the children. Initially, I used storytelling cards extensively to provide the stimulus for group discussions. These included pictures that portrayed themes, events, and conflicts relevant to one or more members of the group. I used art materials quite often throughout the course of the group. I provided crayons, markers, small and large pieces of paper, and clay at different times. I did not introduce board games until the majority of the group members had reached a developmental level where they could tolerate such things as taking turns, following rules, and competition (age 8 and above).

The group consisted of six boys, ages 9 to 12. All of the boys in the group had been abused in various ways. The severity of the abuse ranged from the child who had witnessed his parent murder his sibling, as the most severe, to Danny's, which was the least severe. In spite of their common histories, the boys were not aware that this was one of the criteria for placement in the group. The members were told that they were in the group because they had each expressed sadness at not having friends and a desire to develop friendships.

Prior to a boy entering the group, the parents were required to agree that the child would attend a minimum of nine consecutive sessions. The treatment contract specified that I would review the boy's progress with both the parents and the child after the eighth session. If we decided to terminate at that point, we used the ninth session to accomplish this. If we agreed upon continuation, then I asked the parents to sign another nine-session contract. For returning children, I used the ninth session of the original contract to help them say good-bye to departing members and to welcome new children who were added to the group only at this time.

The format of each group session was also predetermined. The first segment of the group consisted of having the group members complete a simple, directed relaxation exercise. Initially, this was used to focus the group and habituate them to following directions. Because none of the group members had much difficulty settling into the group's routine and none seemed particularly distractible, the relaxation was given up in favor of extended discussion periods.

During the second 15-minute segment of each group, the children sat on the sofa and chairs and had their snack. In this rather relaxed atmosphere, we engaged in "talk time." These were focused discussions about topics of concern to the group members. Initially, I prompted these discussions through the use of selected storytelling cards. As the group became more cohesive, they generated their own discussion topics. I guided them to apply problem solving within the context of these discussions whenever possible.

Following "talk time" came "activity time." For the next 20 to 30 minutes, the boys either sat at the table and completed an art activity or played a table game or moved to the empty side of the room to play a gross motor game. I selected and directed the activities engaged in during this time. I retained primary control of both "talk time" and "activity time" and was responsible for maintaining our established routine during both.

When time permitted, the last 15 to 20 minutes of the group was free-play time. During this portion of the group session, the boys could select their own activity. They could play together or separately, continue what was started during "activity time," or change to something else.

Beginning

During the beginning phase of treatment, a group member usually progresses through several subphases in the process of adapting and responding to treatment. The first of these subphases is exploration, during which the children are focused on absorbing information about the new situation. This phase is usually quite brief in children who are not seriously disturbed or the victims of severe neglect. During the tentative acceptance phase, children appear to be involved in the treatment, but are subtly noncompliant. They will be most involved when the group is meeting their needs and quite resistant when the group is not. Negative reaction is the final subphase of the beginning phase of treatment. At this point children will act out in response to the situational demands for behaviors and responses that are outside their usual repertoire. Further, they will now feel safe enough within the group to manifest their noncompliance more overtly. Not only do all members of the group go through these phases, but the group as a whole moves through them as well. The play therapist must be able to plan activities that address both the treatment stage of the majority of the group members and that of the overall group.

The play therapist can use interpretation to facilitate moving the group members through these stages fairly simultaneously. In order to avoid scapegoating any member who is lagging behind, it is often helpful to make interpretations that compare the progress of each member to that of the group as a whole rather than comparing members to each other. Although it is a difficult decision to make and implement, it is important that the play therapist not allow the progress of the group to be lost due to a single member who is unable and/or unwilling to progress. Sometimes a child will use refusal to progress as a way of controlling the group and will be reinforced by the power he or she wields. In such cases, it is probably better to move the child to another group that is just beginning and to allow the original group to move on.

Exploration

Behaviorally, Danny did very little during the exploratory phase. He did not talk to the other children. He tended to be very reserved motorically and he did not participate in group activities. At best, he engaged in parallel play while visually scanning the environment and obviously attending to all conversations. Danny engaged in this type of exploratory behavior for the first one and one half group sessions.

Here is an example of the types of experiential activities used to address Danny's need to explore his new environment. During Danny's initial session, the group played a simple game designed to facilitate interpersonal focus. One child would stand in the middle of the group allowing all of the other children to visually examine him and try to memorize his exact appearance. The target child then left the room and changed something about his appearance, such as moving his shoes to the wrong feet. When he reentered the room, the group was timed to see how long it would take them to discover the change. Although Danny refused to be one of the target children and made every effort to look like he was not interested, he was among the first to begin guessing what was different when the target child reentered the room.

I used interpretation to put words to Danny's behavior and feelings, as well as to make these a part of the group process. I offered reflections that labeled Danny's anxiety and discomfort with not being in control of this new situation. I interpreted his refusing to play as an attempt (autoplastic) to retain what control he could. I also reflected his ambivalence about participation and noted his interest in the activities.

Tentative Acceptance

Probably because of his previous therapy experience, Danny moved into the tentative acceptance subphase of treatment during the second session. At this point Danny began to talk more, but directed everything he said toward me. He never acknowledged the content of another child's verbalizations directly. Instead, he tended to make very egocentric follow-up statements such as, "Oh yeah, that happened to me once. I . . ." Danny began to complete activities in group that required only parallel play with no more than a minimum of sharing. If possible, he would develop variants on other activities that would allow him to maintain this stance.

While Danny was in the tentative acceptance phase, one of the group activities was a project called "pair pictures." Each of the boys picked a partner and I gave each dyad a single large piece of paper and a single box of markers. I instructed them to draw anything they wanted. I encouraged them to work together, but allowed them to work individually on separate areas of the paper so long as they did not tear it in half. Danny immediately drew a line down the middle of the paper without even consulting his partner. He then proceeded to complete a very small drawing on his half. At this point, most of the other dyads had begun to work cooperatively even if they had initially divided their paper. Apparently, this level of parallel activity was too much for Danny because he found a way to be noncompliant. He folded over one corner of his side of the paper and drew a much more elaborate picture there so it would be completely separate from that of his partner.

While Danny was in this phase, I selected activities that would moderately challenge his usual pattern of behavior. Activities like the "pair pictures" described above were common. The focus of the group was on low-level cooperation. This meant that Danny would not be getting reinforced for the types of parallel play he usually engaged in.

During this phase I used interpretation to reflect Danny's growing frustration with his inability to either get control of the group or to be rewarded for independent activity. When he drew on the back of the paper during the "pair pictures" activity, I labeled his desire to break the rules of the task. Simultaneously, I praised the other children for their compliance. I never directly criticized Danny for his behavior nor did I set any limits. Rather, I consistently reinforced the other children for approximating interactive play. My interpretations always made a connection between Danny's behavior and his belief that if he were not in control he would lose out on reinforcers. I made explicit the fact that, in the group, control would cause him to lose rather than gain reinforcements.

Negative Reaction

Danny moved into the negative reaction phase during the end of his first nine-session contract. He began by becoming more verbally aggressive.

His comments were now both egocentric and intrusive. He would talk over other children or label their comments stupid and substitute his own. He refused to participate in any activity other than snack time, verbally labeling everything as stupid. He became very vocal about his past academic achievements and used these as an attack on the rest of the group members who were experiencing academic difficulties.

Danny also moved to take over my role in the group. This was clearly a manifestation of his move into the parental and spousal roles in the home. He thought he could take control by becoming the adult. He would monitor all of the other member's behavior and report any rule violations to me along with suggestions for consequences. When I would not follow his directions, he would storm out of the room, only to return a few minutes later with a new suggestion. The most benign manifestation of his negative reaction was his tendency to help other members of the group. He would give advice on winning strategies during a game or suggestions for improving another child's art activity. These behaviors were problematic on two levels. Danny tended to use adult language when making suggestions and, therefore, alienated the other children because they believed he was being condescending. Danny also reacted with hostility if they did not take his directions, so that the other children knew he was more interested in control than in being helpful. Danny would also use his role of advice-giver to avoid actually playing a game or completing his own portion of a project.

Activities designed to move Danny through the negative reaction phase were, alternately, ones in which I let him have control and ones in which he had to take direction from others. A simple game of Simon Says proved to be an ideal way of making Danny's behavior evident. He was very enthusiastic when he was picked to be Simon. He gave directions with relish and delighted in getting the other boys to make mistakes. When he had to follow the direction of another Simon, however, he would pout, become argumentative, and then leave the game if he made a mistake.

At this point I regularly labeled Danny's battle to save himself from the anxiety of relinquishing situational control versus the frustration of not gaining my approval for exerting too much control. I also noted the motives for each of his behaviors, and the similarity of his behavior in group to that which he displayed at home and school. I identified the difficulty of the battle and made statements reflecting my belief that he would win in the end. It was at this stage that the other boys really began to talk to Danny and most of what they had to say was quite negative. They did not like his attempts to control them and he heard, "You're not the boss of me," a lot. In spite of this, the group was beginning to coalesce and leave Danny out.

As is often the case, Danny completed the negative reaction phase with a "bang." One day he became furious at being left out of a game when he would not follow the rules. He crashed around the room, and then left. I went to retrieve him and he yelled at me, "You have to make them let me play." I refused and told him he must ask the boys directly to reconsider and include him. When I suggested that he apologize for breaking the rules of the game in the first place, he became further enraged. He threatened never to come back to group. He threatened to tell his parents and then to tell his social worker how mean I was. Then he threatened to hurt me. At this point I grabbed his hands, held him securely and suggested that this was probably the final battle of his war against his old way of handling things and that I knew he would win. He fought for a few seconds then stopped and sat down, resigned.

We then engaged in some problem solving. Danny first identified the problem as the other children being mean. With some help, he redefined it as his feeling hurt and angry at being excluded. He noted that he was really not aware of the behaviors he engaged in that angered other children until after an interaction had already turned sour. Among the many plans we developed was one in which I would cue him to the fact that he was beginning to alienate the other boys by simply saying his name. We also rehearsed what he would say when he reentered the room. As we finished he said he was still not ready to go back to the group. I became aware that Danny was probably gaining a considerable sense of power and reward by keeping me away from the group. I left him saying I knew he would be okay and that he could rejoin the group as soon as he was ready.

While he was out of the room, I coached the boys as to how they might respond if Danny asked for another chance. I had them engage in problem solving with respect to the impact of Danny's behavior on them. Their plan was to provide him with more verbal feedback faster, that is, before they became really angry at him.

A few minutes later he came into the room. At first he said nothing and sat on the sidelines. The other boys kept looking to me for cues as to how they should respond and I suggested they continue with what they were doing. Eventually, Danny came over and tried to join in, but the boys would not let him so he went back to the couch and sat down. I went to him and prodded him in the direction of the group. He then went over, quickly apologized and asked to play. As cued, the group allowed him back in. Danny had been able to approach his peers directly to get his needs met and had encountered success. His negative reaction phase was at an end and he was ready to begin the real work of his group therapy experience.

The group's negative reaction phase is evident in the scenario described above. During this subphase they were not just passively ignoring Danny. They were actively excluding him from things, stating that they did not like him or his behavior. Gentle interpretive comments from me did not undermine their resolve to exclude Danny. They made their response to Danny even more aggressive by choosing to accept another new boy at this time. Only when Danny was able to demonstrate a clear change in his behavior did the group move to change their response to him. Even then, they needed considerable support from me to do so.

Growing, Trusting, and Working Through

Once Danny had experienced one positive, needs-meeting interchange with his peers in a way that violated a behavior pattern of which he was now aware, his treatment progressed rather rapidly. At this stage in the progress of the group as a whole, each of the boys worked out a personal goal toward which he would work in sessions. For some of the boys, the goal was to refrain from hitting others. For some, it was to be less verbally aggressive and for still others, it was to approach others in the group cooperatively. We did this goal-setting in the discussion segment of the group so that all of the boys were aware of each other's goals. When it came time for Danny to develop his goal, I had trouble putting the abstract concept of his trying to be less pseudomature into words. Danny finally said, "I know. I should try to stop being the play therapist and remember that I am one of the kids." While this was not exactly the operationally defined type of goal the other boys had set, it reflected Danny's progress in developing an awareness of his problem and an ability to direct his cognitive skills toward its resolution. Danny requested that I continue to remind him when he slipped into an adult role simply by saying his name as I had done previously.

During the growing and trusting phase, the focus of Danny's treatment was his development of mutually beneficial peer friendships. Initially, this required that I constantly refocus him on his peers and away from me as his primary source of emotional support. I continued to verbally cue him every time he attempted to join me in the play therapist role. I also consistently interpreted the similarity between his style of interacting with me in the group and his style of interacting with his parents and other adults in authority positions. The element of this behavior that he seemed most reluctant to give up was the setting of limits on the other children's behavior. He acted as if his identification of the other children's bad behavior would prevent the adult from giving that child nurturance. This, in turn, would make that adult more available to Danny. Further, if he was to join the adult in setting limits the adult would be less tired and even better able to provide for Danny. I interpreted this dynamic to Danny and he accepted it. However, as all therapists acknowledge, insight does not always bring about behavior change. The reinforcement Danny received for this behavior in terms of anxiety reduction was so great that it withstood any amount of redirection from me.

The intervention that produced the eventual change in Danny's pseudomature, adult-oriented pattern was the selection of activities. Consistent with his developmental age, Danny learned much better from experience than he did from language. This is not to discount the importance of the interpretations and the verbal work that I did. It was this language base that allowed me to process changes in Danny's behavior with him, to compare and contrast the costs and benefits of change, producing rapid generalization.

The types of activities that altered Danny's behavior were ones that involved group cooperation, rather than competition. Games like "Snakes in the Grass" (Fleugelman 1976, O'Connor 1991), where the group must work together to change each of the humans to snakes, were ideal. Other noncompetitive group games can be found in *The New Games Book* (Fleugelman 1976), *More New Games* (Fleugelman 1981), and *The Play Therapy Primer* (O'Connor 1991). Also productive were group excursions to local parks where the children could explore and, consequently, be reinforced by their environment. In this context, one boy could climb a tree and be reinforced for his skill. He could then help another boy up into the tree and be reinforced for his assisting a peer. The recipient of the help was reinforced for reaching the same climbing objective and by having received support from a peer. It should be noted that, while I continued to model the provision of social reinforcement, the group members largely took over reinforcing one another.

I further strengthened the group members' tendency to reinforce one another by periodically abandoning the adult/therapist role. This would not have been possible if the group as a whole had not made the transition into the growing and trusting phase of the treatment process because they still would have required my focusing on maintaining the structure and limits to maintain their behavior. At this point, I tended to join in as an active participant in most of the group activities. I played side by side with the children. I continued to interpret the group process heavily, but disguised these as comments about my personal feelings or reactions to events as they unfolded. Rather than making an interpretation like, "Everyone wants to be 'It' in this game so badly that they are willing to prevent the group from playing rather than let anyone else be 'It.' " I would say, "I'm getting frustrated with everyone fighting to be 'It.' I'll let someone else be it first if we can just go ahead and play." This shift in presentation accomplished two things. On the one hand, I was modeling the use of group process information in interpersonal problem solving. On the other, I was fading the "therapeutic" tone of the group, making it appear more like a typical get-together of peers in order to foster generalization of the children's learning to their everyday world.

I began to fade the structure of the sessions as much as possible, again attempting to simulate a typical interaction of 10-year-old boys rather than a structured play therapy group. We had long since stopped doing the relaxation training at the beginning of each meeting. The snack and discussion time merged and tended to be much more variable in duration. I no longer initiated discussion topics. Some days, the boys would be finished in 5 minutes; other days, they would identify a high-interest or emotionally loaded topic and spend most of the hour talking. At this stage, we had also played a wide variety of games and completed many different activities, so that I began to let the boys plan the activity portion of the next group session during the discussion time. Gradually, they introduced their own ideas for games and activities and we incorporated these in our repertoire. Again, this gradual fading of the structure and facilitation of the boys' self-management of the group promoted generalization of their behavior to other settings.

This group made particularly good progress through the growing and trusting phase largely because of the continuity and stability of the group. After the addition of Danny and one other boy, only one child left and one child entered the group over the next five months. The one boy who joined the group was rather quiet and observed the group for a long time before joining in. When he finally became more active, it was apparent that he had been spending his exploration phase learning a great deal about the group's rules and process because he was immediately accepted and integrated into their interactions.

Termination

Danny remained in the group for approximately 6 months or three nine-session contracts. Danny and his parents made the decision to terminate his group therapy with my full support. At the time of termination, a new DTORF indicated that Danny was functioning at age level in all domains. He was no longer demonstrating any rage episodes and his grades had returned to mostly As and Bs. While problems related to his parents' divorce remained partially unresolved, Danny had made significant gains.

We accomplished termination in the ninth session of his third treatment contract. Consistent with Danny's treatment goals, he was heavily involved in determining the type of termination ritual that would best meet his needs. He chose to have a party similar to that he had seen other children have, which included cake and drinks for snack time. He also chose to ask the other boys for their names, addresses, and phone numbers so that he could call them at some point in the future and get together to play. These types of meetings had already occurred between several of the boys and this was Danny's strategy for retaining some control over the rate at which he separated from the boys in the group.

RESULTS AND FOLLOW-UP

Overall, the outcome of Danny's course of psychotherapy was very positive. He met the primary criteria for termination. He had achieved a level of age-appropriate developmental functioning. He had also met his own goal of developing some consistent peer friendships and feeling less anxious and more happy. Mrs. Davis reported that Danny had begun to develop friendships with some of the children in their neighborhood and even showed early signs of having acquired a best friend.

The least successful part of Danny's treatment was the family component. Both of his parents proved to be very resistant to changing their narcissistic styles. They tended to need an incredible amount of emotional support from others and saw Danny as a viable resource for meeting those needs. Neither parent developed any peer friendships of their own as the divorce progressed and so they remained isolated from other, more appropriate resources. At this level, treatment came to be geared more toward helping Danny resist their demands without acting out, rather than significantly altering their behavior. Danny became very good at recognizing when his parents' expectations were inappropriate and either drawing a reasonable boundary to keep them away or insisting that they seek support elsewhere. While this was certainly an improvement, it maintained Danny in a pseudomature role vis-à-vis his parents. He was the one monitoring boundaries and setting limits, rather than being able to trust those of his parents. However, this application of his pseudomaturity did substantially free both his intellect and his emotions, allowing him to pursue getting his needs met through other relationships and to be a child. Further, this stance allowed him to continue to get those supplies that his parents were able to provide in a way that was much healthier in the long run.

DISCUSSION

Ecosystemic play therapy is a model in which the play therapist considers the impact and interaction of the various systems in which child clients are embedded from the point of intake, through the assessment, treatment planning, and treatment implementation to the time of termination. The play therapist develops broad goals that address the systemic aspects of the problem with which the child is presenting and addresses these either in the play therapy itself or through referral, consultation, and/or liaison work. Structured group play therapy is one intervention technique through which the play therapist can address children's problems with peer socialization.

It is important in conceptualizing a structured group play therapy intervention that the play therapist not view it as a treatment that can be effectively implemented in isolation. The play therapist must consider the developmental level of the child and his or her life situation if the treatment is to proceed optimally. This model was particularly well suited to the case presented as it was the combination of individual, family, and group therapy along with consultation to the school and family court that served to alter the referred client's pattern of functioning. In each of these interventions the underlying goal was the reestablishment of developmentally appropriate behavior in the child as well as an increase in his ability to get his needs met in a way that did not violate the basic needs and rights of others.

In reexamining this case, it is my sense that the outcome could have been significantly enhanced by including the parents in the treatment process to a greater degree. At the time, family therapy was not implemented for two reasons. One was the ongoing combat between the parents and my concern that, should this erupt in session, it would overwhelm Danny's gradually improving defenses. So long as his parents did not directly interact, they did not have the opportunity to be physically violent. My other reason for not conducting family sessions was my concern about fueling Danny's fantasies that he could force his parents to reunite. If this had occurred, then family sessions would have reinforced his acting out behavior. In spite of the divorce, Danny and his parents were probably well suited to family therapy. The goals of such an intervention would have been to establish clearer and more appropriate parent–child role boundaries. This would have freed Danny to be a child in his interactions with each parent.

In spite of the minimal involvement of Danny's parents, I believe the outcome was nearly optimal given the pragmatics of this case. Danny learned many new strategies for getting his needs met. Some of these allowed him to maintain better boundaries between himself and each of his parents and to extricate himself from their marital conflict. Other strategies allowed him to function as a child in his interactions with his peers. The latter provided him with a whole range of reinforcers and supplies that were previously unavailable. Although Danny was required, due to his parents' unresolved narcissistic needs, to maintain an overly mature stance relative to his interactions with them, I believe his prognosis is excellent.

REFERENCES

Camp, B., Blom, G., Herbert, F., and Van Doornick, W. (1977). "Think aloud": a program for developing self-control in young aggressive boys. *Journal of Abnormal Child Psychology* 5: 157–169.

Developmental Therapy Institute. (1992). *Developmental Therapy Objective Rating Form-Revised*. Athens, GA: Developmental Therapy Institute.

Dinkmeyer, D. (1973). *Developing Understanding of Self and Others* (DUSO). Circle Pines, MN: American Guidance Services.

Fleugelman, A., ed. (1976). *The New Games Book*. Garden City, NY: Headlands Press.

———— (1981). *More New Games*. Garden City, NY: Headlands Press.

Goldfried, M., and Davison, G. (1976). *Clinical Behavior Therapy*. New York: Holt, Rinehart & Winston.

Jacobson, E. (1938). *Progressive Relaxation: A Physiological and Clinical Investigation of Muscular States and Their Significance in Psychology and Medical Practice*. 2nd ed. Chicago: University of Chicago Press.

Meichenbaum, D. (1977). *Cognitive-behavior Modification: An Integrative Approach*. New York: Plenum.

Meichenbaum, D., and Goodman, J. (1971). Training impulsive children to talk to themselves: a means of developing self-control. *Journal of Abnormal Psychology* 77: 115–126.

O'Connor, K. (1991). *The Play Therapy Primer*. New York: Wiley.

O'Connor, K., and Lee, A. (1991). Advances in psychoanalytic psychotherapy with children. In *The Clinical Psychology Handbook*, ed. M. Hersen, A. Kazdin, and A. Bellack, 2nd ed., pp. 580–595. Elmsford, NY: Pergamon.

9

From Meek to Bold: A Case Study of Gestalt Play Therapy

Violet Oaklander, PH.D.

INTRODUCTION TO GESTALT THERAPY

Gestalt therapy is a humanistic, process-oriented form of therapy that is concerned with all aspects of the person: senses, body, feelings, and intellect. It is a therapy basically developed by Frederick (Fritz) Perls, M.D., and Laura Perls, Ph.D., and has at its roots principles from psychoanalytic theory, Gestalt psychology, humanistic theories, as well as aspects of phenomenology, existentialism, and Reichian body therapy. Out of these roots there has developed a vast body of theoretical concepts and principles that make up the theory and practice of Gestalt therapy as we know it today (Latner 1986, Perls 1969, Perls et al. 1951).

All the concepts and principles presented in the body of Gestalt literature available can be related to healthy child growth and development as well as to child psychopathology. What follows are some concepts that I consider to be of critical importance in my therapeutic work with children.

The I/Thou Relationship

Although given somewhat passing reference in Gestalt therapy writings, this concept has great implication in work with children. This type of relationship, derived from the writings of Martin Buber (1958), involves the meeting of two people who are equal in entitlement. That is, the therapist, regardless of age, education, degrees, is not a better,

281

more important person than his or her client. The therapist brings herself or himself fully to the session, genuinely and congruently. The therapist meets the child, however he or she presents the self, with respect and honor and without judgment or manipulation. At the same time, the therapist is aware of, and honors, his or her own limits and boundaries in the course of the therapeutic encounter, and never loses himself or herself in the face of the client's situation. The therapist may have goals and plans that he or she brings to a session, but there are no expectations. Each session is an existential experience. The therapist never pushes the child beyond his or her capacity or willingness; the therapist create an environment of safety.

The relationship, itself, can be therapeutic—it may be the only time that the child has had an experience of this kind. Without a relationship, further therapeutic intervention is fruitless.

Organismic Self-Regulation

In its everlasting quest for health, the organism seeks homeostasis. We are constantly faced with needs, whether they be physical, emotional, or intellectual. We experience discomfort until we find some way to satisfy each need and achieve equilibrium, at least for the time being.

I use as a model the natural way that an infant develops. Healthy babies arrive into the world as full functioning organisms encompassing their senses, body, emotions, and intellect. Their very survival depends on their senses. They need to suck to live, and to be touched and held to thrive. As they grow, they learn about their world through smells, sounds, tastes, faces, and colors. They energetically make use of touching, tasting, listening, smelling, and seeing.

Soon they become aware of their bodies and develop new levels of control and mastery through touching, reaching, grasping, dropping, and exploring. As they grow they zestfully make use of their bodies through crawling, walking, running, and climbing.

While becoming more mindful of their senses and their bodies, babies' expressions of feelings become more differentiated. They have yet to learn the art of interrupting their emotional expression. We know without a doubt when they are angry, or sad, or happy, or afraid.

Their intellects, too, are developing at a rapid pace. They learn to use language as a tool for clarity, expression, and getting their needs known and met. As they grow, they begin to express their wants, thoughts, ideas, and curiosities.

The healthy, uninterrupted development of a child's organism—

senses, body, emotions, and intellect—is the underlying basis for the child's sense of self. A strong sense of self leads to good contact with his or her environment and the people in it. As each need surfaces and is met without hindrance, not only does the child achieve homeostasis and balance, but he or she also gains new levels of growth and development (Oaklander 1982).

Contact Boundary Disturbances

We make contact with others and our environment from a place beyond ourselves, from the edge of ourselves—the boundary of the self. "The contact boundary is the point at which one experiences the 'me' in relation to that which is not 'me' and through this contact, both are more clearly experienced" (Polster and Polster 1973, pp. 102–103). If the self is fuzzy and weak, we do not have a clear boundary and contact suffers.

Healthy contact involves a feeling of security with oneself, a fearlessness of standing alone. "What distinguishes contact from togetherness or joining is that contact occurs at a boundary where a sense of separateness is maintained so that union does not threaten to overwhelm the person" (Polster and Polster 1973, p. 102).

We use a variety of guises to avoid strong contact in the misguided hope of protecting ourselves. We project our feelings onto others; we deflect—turn away—from that which makes us uncomfortable; we retroflect—pull inward into ourselves—that which we fear to express outwardly; we will avoid, deny, become confused, and so forth. Children become masters of these maneuvers, developing maladaptive behaviors.

There are several developmental factors that cause children to manifest inappropriate behaviors and symptoms. Although the primary task of children is to separate from their parents and develop their own selves, they are fundamentally confluent with them and see themselves through the eyes of their parents. Moreover, they do not have the cognitive or emotional maturity to discriminate what fits from what does not fit for them, and therefore believe everything they hear, or imagine they hear, about themselves. They take in many faulty introjects— swallow whole information about themselves and how to be in the world: "I am stupid," "I am bad," "I must not show my angry feelings," "I must be very quiet all the time." Each child is developmentally egocentric and imagines that he or she is the center of the universe. Children lack the ability to understand separate experience and separate points of view, and therefore take responsibility for whatever happens in their lives and to those close to them. In addition, children are well aware that they cannot meet their own basic needs and that they are completely dependent upon the adults in their lives to survive in the world.

In order to avoid rejection, abandonment, and to gain approval, children may manifest many behavioral manifestations and symptoms that keep them from engaging in healthy contact with other children, teachers, parents, or books. They may project their feelings as a way of denying personal experience. They may deflect from painful feelings by hitting, punching, or kicking. They may retroflect anger and grief by restricting themselves to the point of having headaches, stomachaches, or asthma attacks. They may be hyperactive or "space out" in order to avoid what they are feeling.

These contact/boundary disturbances are evidence to me that aspects of the child's organism need strengthening, that the child's sense of self is tenuous and frail, and that he or she has lost himself or herself. In fact, the sense of self of some children is so fragile that they will engage in what we call confluent behavior as a means of feeling some segment of self. They will be very good or pleasing to the adults in their lives, willing to do whatever is asked of them, sometimes literally hanging on for dear life.

The very behaviors that bring the child into therapy are actually ways that the child is using to get his or her needs met—to cope and survive. The child has a powerful thrust for life and growth and will do anything he or she can to grow up. In the service of this quest the child will, paradoxically, restrict, inhibit, and block aspects of the self. The child will desensitize himself or herself, restrict the body, block emotions, and inhibit the intellect.

> When a child is brought into therapy, I know that many of her behaviors or symptoms are manifestations of a search for health. I need to find some way to help the child remember, regain, renew, and strengthen that which she once had as a tiny baby but which now seems lost. As her senses awaken, as she begins to know her body again, as she recognizes, accepts, and expresses her buried feelings, as she learns to use her intellect to make choices, to verbalize her wants and needs and thoughts and ideas, and to find ways to get her needs met, as she learns who she is and accepts who she is in her differentness from you and me, she will then find herself once again upon her rightful path of growth. [Oaklander 1982, p. 69]

Often in Gestalt therapy literature contact/boundary disturbances are seen as resistant behavior. Certainly resistance is a way that one has to protect the very self. Resistance with children is expected and respected—it is their only ally. (Confluent children need to build resistance!) In working with children, we meet resistance again and again for, as the child approaches material that may be too difficult and weighty to deal with at that time, the child will close down and break contact. I respect and honor this closing for I recognize it as evidence that the child is on the verge of a new way of being, a new discovery. When I respect this show of resistance, the child becomes more amenable to going over and beyond it—sometimes only after a slight pause, and at other times not until a subsequent session.

Awareness and Experience

Helping the client become aware of his or her process is a prime goal of the Gestalt therapist. Experiencing the process—what I do and how I do it—and acceptance of this process in the moment when it occurs, leads to personal choice and change. Experience, in work with children, plays a key role. As children become more aware of themselves in the therapy experience—who they are, what they feel, what they like and do not like, what they need, what they want, what they do, and how they do it—they find that they have choices they can make, choices for expression, getting needs met, and for exploring new behaviors (Oaklander 1982). This awareness happens through the varied experiences and experiments that the therapist provides in the process of play therapy.

Interpretation

Although many of the techniques I use with children encourage projection, I do not use them for the purpose of providing me with material for interpretation. How I might interpret the child's drawing, sand scene, story, dramatic play, and such would actually be my own projection and would perhaps say more about me than it would about the child. Further, there is an element of arrogance to interpretation. I am well aware that it is almost impossible for a therapist to avoid some interpretation, particularly in work with children. I want, then, to use any interpretations I may have as mere tentative translations, guesses, and hunches that I have the child verify. Through this verification, the child feels listened to and understood and thereby gains strength. So I might say, as I did to a young adolescent client, "Your picture looks so barren and bleak to me. Do you feel that way sometimes?" If the child responds, "Oh, yes" and begins to weep, I know that a kind of therapy is occurring that could never happen had I left these "interpretations" hidden as a notation in a chart.

A child may say, "Oh, no" to my hunches, or suddenly want to do something else, or seem puzzled by my statements. I accept these responses easily and with grace. My suggestions may not be true, or the child may simply not be ready to own them.

I find over and over again that even the youngest of children have a wisdom about themselves that is awe-inspiring. My task is to assist the child in sharing his or her wisdom with me. As I very gently open the doors to self-awareness and self-ownership, through such open and contactful sharing the child strengthens his or her own self and gains new self-support.

PRESENTING PROBLEMS AND BACKGROUND DATA

Ten-year-old Susan was brought into therapy by her adoptive parents. She had severe recurring nightmares, suffered from headaches and stomachaches, often refused to go to school, and was excessively timid and fearful in almost every situation.

The background information provided by Susan's adoptive parents was somewhat sketchy. Her birth parents divorced when she was about 3 years old and Susan had no contact with her birth father after that time. A year later, Jane, Susan's birth mother remarried. When Susan was 8 years old, a teacher noticed unusual bruises on her arms and filed a report with Children's Protective Services. Susan was removed from her home and placed in a children's group home upon discovery that Susan had been beaten with sticks and belts by her stepfather since she was 4 years old. Susan later disclosed that she had also been sexually molested on a regular basis by her stepfather. Physical examination indicated tears within her vagina, as well as swelling and redness in the vaginal area. Further, Susan had been threatened and terrorized by her stepfather. Jane denied any knowledge of the abuse and appeared to have been the victim of physical and psychological abuse, herself. During the investigation period, Jane visited the child fairly regularly at the group home, and then, after leaving a remorseful letter for Susan, took her own life. After her mother's death, Susan lived in a foster home for one year, and was then placed with Jed and Nancy S., the couple who subsequently adopted her.

Susan was an attractive, intelligent, healthy child. She did well in school, though she kept to herself and refused to participate in any playground activities. According to her teacher, other children often made attempts to include Susan in their play, but she would smile shyly and decline. Mr. and Mrs. S. reported that Susan had made a good adjustment to their home and seemed content to spend her time with them. In fact, she had great difficulty separating from them and since she had come to live with them, they had never hired a sitter to spend an evening away from her. Susan also suffered from numerous fears and often woke during the night because of bad dreams.

Mr. and Mrs. S. admitted that when they adopted Susan, they had believed that a loving, stable home would provide Susan with everything she needed to lead a normal, happy life. They revealed, too, that they felt so sorry for Susan that they were at a loss as to the appropriateness of limit setting for her. As the presenting problems developed and persisted, they decided to seek help.

It is my policy to see the parents with the child for the first session. I want the child to hear whatever the parents choose to tell me—I want her to know what I know. Susan sat very close to Nancy as both parents told me about her symptoms and something of her history. I wanted Susan to be involved in this session, so I asked her questions about her life, giving Mr. and Mrs. S. the opportunity to add any information they needed to. "Do you have bad dreams?" "Do you take any medication?" "How's your appetite?" "Do you like school?" "Do you have friends?" "What do you like to do when you're at home?" "Do you have your own room?" "Any pets?" I asked questions from an informal intake sheet that I have. Susan smiled shyly as she answered each question with yes, no, good, yes, yes, shoulder shrug, yes. Her longest response, "No—but I wish I did" was to my question about whether she had any pets. Mr. and Mrs. S. occasionally gave their views regarding some of the questions, but basically this was an interaction between Susan and me. I then described to all of them something of my way of working (my philosophy, my approach, the techniques we use, the process of the therapy), and explained that the first four sessions would be basically diagnostic, and that Susan and I would mostly be establishing a relationship with each other. At the end of the four sessions, I would ask the parents to come back with Susan and we would then discuss the plan of treatment.

At this family session, I found Susan to be agreeable and cooperative. Although she showed much anxiety at the beginning of the session, she made her increasing comfort level evident by her moving away from Nancy as we talked. Susan appeared to have a good relationship with both of her parents, and they manifested genuine love and concern. I knew that Mr. and Mrs. S.'s participation in Susan's therapy would be essential, particularly in terms of their "rescue" attitude and their inability to set consistent limits regarding bedtime, homework, home chores, and such. Mr. and Mrs. S. expressed fear of hurting Susan further and so had fuzzy, weak boundaries of their own.

THEORETICAL CONCEPTUALIZATION

Susan's development had been arrested due to the physical and sexual abuse that she suffered at the hand of her stepfather, and subsequently, the abandonment by her mother. Her trauma caused her to inhibit her senses, restrict her body, block her emotions, and shut off her mind; she was unable to experience herself in appropriate, healthy ways. As a result, Susan felt insecure, lacked a strong sense of self, and was unable to make healthy contact with her environment and the people in it.

Susan used many strategies to cope and survive in her world, and protect herself from the "threat" of contact with others and her surroundings. She deflected the attempts by her classmates to establish friendships. Her physical symptoms appeared to be retroflections of the unexpressed fear, hurt, and anger brought about by her stepfather's abuse and her birth mother's suicide. Since she was not yet secure in her relationship with her adoptive parents, she manifested clingy and fearful behavior.

My prime goal with Susan was to help her develop a strong sense of herself so that she could begin to make healthy contact with the world around her. Her sense of self was so fragile, that she was initially unable to approach and make contact with even the materials in my office. The therapeutic setting is highly attractive to children. It is pleasant, casual, and organized. It is equipped with all of the tools necessary to provide children with the experiences needed to enhance all of the aspects of the self that are prerequisite to healthy engagement in their lives. One can find clay, drawing paper, construction paper, crayons, markers, pastels, colored pencils, musical instruments, miniature figures to use with the sand tray, a doctor set, a doll house, numerous puppets, many different kinds of games, a variety of books, and much more.

Technique is an important aspect in working with children. I use a variety of creative, expressive, and projective techniques, such as guided fantasy, graphic art forms, clay, collage, storytelling, puppetry, the sand tray, creative dramatics, music, body movement, sensory awareness exercises, and photography. From among these techniques, I hoped to find some way to give Susan experiences with those aspects of herself that she had restricted, inhibited, or perhaps lost. I wanted to help her express deeply buried emotions and become more aware of her process. I wanted to help her find healthier ways of being in her world, as well as strengthen her self-support and sense of self.

THE PROCESS OF PLAY THERAPY

Relationship

My focus in the first few sessions with Susan was to establish a relationship with her. She was very timid about approaching any of the materials and merely stood in the center of the room smiling shyly. I brought out a few coloring books and invited her to sit on the floor and color with me. Children, boys as well as girls, who are timid and insecure appear to be comforted by the boundaries represented by the lines in the pictures of the coloring book. I offered crayons, markers, colored pencils, and pastels. She chose the crayons (the safest of these materials) and one of the books and we began to color. We talked about the picture we were working on and the colors we should use. At one point, I made up a silly story about the ducks we were coloring and Susan giggled. We began another picture and through dialogue, Susan made up a story. ("Susan, where does this dog live? Do they treat him well?" and so forth.) We did this casually and easily and I repeated each line before going on to the next question about the dog. I believe that this interaction helped Susan feel comfortable with some expression and to be more contactful with me. We were not dealing with heavy material relating to Susan's life, but finding some pleasure in being together.

When our time in the first session was up, Susan cooperatively helped me to clean up and put things away, an important adjunct to my therapy sessions, except sand-tray scenes. However, she appeared reluctant to leave. She ignored me after I told her several times that it was time to meet her mother in the waiting room, looking around at various objects in the room. Finally I put my arm around her shoulders and gently led her out, reminding her that I would see her next week. She repeated this maneuver for several sessions. Susan had difficulty with boundaries and needed gentle limit setting.

Susan appeared to want me to direct activities for the next few sessions. Children with tenuous selves often cannot make commitments for fear of making the wrong one. At the second session, I gave her two choices: "You could make a sand scene or draw a picture." In later sessions I added one or two more choices. Giving children opportunity to make choices is particularly ego strengthening. That second session, I waited patiently, smiled when she looked at me, and finally she chose to do a sand scene. She made a hospital scene and made up a story about the sick people there getting well.

The first few sessions in Gestalt play therapy with a child are evaluative in nature. It is during this time that I begin to assess the therapeutic needs of the child. Susan was able to establish a relationship with me fairly easily and had no difficulty sustaining contact with me and the activities in which we engaged. Relationship and contact are two important prerequisites of further therapy. If there had been a problem with either, my focus would have remained on helping Susan feel safe enough to establish a connection with me and to help her maintain contact with me and whatever we were doing.

Because of Susan's history, it was evident that we would need to address the issues that we connect with child abuse and abandonment. The impact of child abuse on children can create, among other things, blurred boundaries, confusion about power and authority, poor self-image, poor social skills, lack of trust, lack of confidence, hostility, depression, fears and phobias, and suicidal ideation (Sgroi 1982). Further issues involve self-blame, powerlessness, loss, feelings of betrayal, fragmentation of body experience, stigmatization, eroticization, destructiveness, dissociation, multiple personality disorder, and attachment disorder (James 1989). Abandonment, moreover, can bring on in the child anxiety, anger, sadness, depression, denial, despair, and guilt (Bowlby 1980).

Before we could confront the issues that might have plagued Susan, it was necessary to help Susan develop a stronger sense of herself. So my focus then was to provide experience and activities to facilitate this. Often the child, herself, will know what these experiences need to be.

Susan continued to make hospital scenes in the sand tray and reminded me to get my pad so that I could write her stories down. Each scene involved a different person getting well. (Susan herself had never been in the hospital.) Although I usually hesitate to make interpretations, it was almost obvious that the hospital was a metaphor for her own experience and her hope for her new life.

It was only at the last hospital scene Susan made that I ventured to say, "Does this scene fit with anything about you or your life?" Susan asked, "What do you mean?" "Well," I said, "The story about the person being sick and getting well makes me think about your life with your stepfather. For a long time it made you sort of sick, and now you have a new mother and father, and you come here too, and your life is much healthier now." Susan listened with wide eyes, grinned, picked up the figure in the hospital bed and said, "Did you hear that!!? You can get up and walk now!"

Sensory and Body Experiences

During the assessment phase, I had observed that Susan's body was restricted; she walked in a stiff, rigid manner. Her voice was high and childlike, sounding much younger than her 10 years. She rarely made a clear statement about what she wanted, and, in fact, had great difficulty making choices. These were all indications of a fragile self and a disconnection with her body. Further, I made the assumption, difficult to observe at this point, that Susan had also desensitized herself, since this is a common result of molestation and abuse.

In between hospital scenes, I introduced various sensory and body experiences. Susan enjoyed finger painting so much that she requested this activity for quite some time. We played various games with a soft ball to help free up her body. Many of these games were played with her parents at our sessions and at home. We did numerous pantomime activities to help Susan understand the need to exaggerate the motions of her fingers and hands and legs to get the message across. She delighted in these games.

As Susan gained self-confidence, she began to take more control over the sessions and organized activities involving dramatic play. We played school and restaurant and doctor. She directed these scenes with gusto, telling me what to say and do. Her favorite was the doctor scenario, an apparent extension of her hospital sand-tray scenes. This time, however, I was the patient. "Pretend you are sick and need a doctor and you call me on the phone." With great drama, I would exclaim about my aches and pains as I lay on the couch. She would arrive with a flourish and a smile, reassuring me that all would be well. She would spread out the doctor equipment carefully on a table and proceed to gently examine me, poke me, sprinkle water on me, and pretend she was doing surgery of some kind. She would insist that I rest until she returned. Upon her return, I had made a miraculous recovery and I thanked her profusely. We played this game, with some variation each time, for several sessions.

Other sessions involved helping Susan define herself, as well as achieve a sense of mastery. Children who are abused and grow up in dysfunctional situations do not have the experiences that other children have to give them feelings of mastery. Without that sense of mastery, the self is nebulous. Susan loved to play the game "Hangman" and even made up new rules regarding the words we chose. We often played various games that gave her the opportunity to answer questions about what she thought about something. She began to take over the sessions with her parents, directing us to draw a "safe place" (something she had enjoyed doing with me), as well as various other pictures. At one session, she asked each of us to draw everyone in the room and write how we felt about each person. She participated in every activity along with me and Mr. and Mrs. S., and under her picture of me she had written, "I feel protected with Violet."

Aggressive Energy

After three months of games and activities involving sensory, body, and various dramatic experiences, and witnessing her new-found strength and power, I encouraged Susan to express her aggressive energy. This kind of energy, not to be confused with aggression, comes from a sense of power within the self. It is an energy that involves action. When one bites an apple, one makes use of aggressive energy. I believe that children who are acting "aggressive" are not making use of their own inner strength to express what lies blocked within the self. Children who are meek and fearful, as Susan, more obviously suppress the power within. Children need encouragement to express this kind of energy since I believe it is a major prerequisite to the expression of emotions.

Generally, aggressive energy is first expressed within a playful contact, without relating it to content of any kind. Susan enjoyed making various objects with clay and experimenting with the diverse tools that I presented. One day I asked her to throw the clay as hard as she could onto a board on the table. She threw it rather gently. "Let's have a contest and see who can throw their clay the hardest," I said. And so we did. Susan gradually began to throw the clay with great energy and vigor. I made loud noises when I threw my clay, and I encouraged her to do the same. "I need to put the board on the floor," she said. Susan stood up and used her whole body to throw the clay giving out a great roar. "I love doing this," she said.

In another session I asked Susan to pick a puppet. She characteristically picked a cute kitten puppet. I picked the alligator puppet. "Hello, kitten. You're cute—in fact you look good enough to eat." Susan was startled and began to back her kitten away. "Don't eat me. You could be my friend," she said. "Oh yeah? I'm hungry and I'm going to eat you. But you better not hit me with those paws of yours!" I repeated, "You better not hit me!" loudly, several times, as I came closer and closer to the kitten. Tentatively, the kitten's paw reached out and tapped the alligator. "You hit me! You hit me! Oh! Oh! You hit me! I told you not to hit me!" the alligator moaned and yelled in pain and then finally "died." Susan looked at me in amazement and then said, "Do that again!" In this manner, Susan's kitten killed off the wolf, the shark, the devil, the witch, the crocodile, the bear, and any other mean looking puppet I could find. By the end of the play, she was hitting the enemy vigorously. Susan walked straight and tall as she left that session, in contrast to her usual hunched-over posture.

Emotional Expression

At a subsequent session, I asked Susan to make a figure of her stepfather out of clay. "Do I have to?" she said. "Yes," I replied. It is my contention that children will, as much as possible, avoid confronting material that is uncomfortable for them. Certainly I did not expect Susan to come into a session saying, "I think I need to work on my abuse today." As I observed that she was gaining strength, experiencing a stronger sense of herself, I felt it was time to confront the issues involved with her abuse and abandonment.

Susan made a large head of her stepfather, taking quite a bit of time to add eyelashes and other detail, hoping, I believe, to avoid the confrontation. Checking my watch, I told her that I wanted her to finish her piece since our time was running out. I asked her to say whatever she wanted to say to her stepfather. "I can't talk to him," she said. I reassured her that this was only a clay figure, that we were playing, and that he would never know. "I don't know what to say to him," she responded. I asked Susan if it was okay with her if I talked to him. "Sure," she said. I proceeded to yell loudly, "I don't like what you did to my friend, Susan! I'm really mad about that. I'm very, very, mad!" Susan laughed and giggled as I continued. I said to Susan, as I picked up a rubber mallet, "I think he needs a good whack—here, give it to him!" I reassured her again that we were just playing, and he would never know. "You do it," she said. "No," I replied, "this *you* have to do." Susan took the mallet and began to pound the clay head. "Talk to him now," I said. And so Susan began expressing much of her anger as she pounded with more and more energy. Finally she put the mallet down and spoke to the smashed clay, "You'll get more from me later," and turning to me, "Do we have time to play a game of 'Connect 4'?"

In the very next session, Susan made a new hospital scene in the sand tray, spending much time arranging the figures carefully. And at the session after that, she made a scene involving a castle with a princess placed by it and a fairy godmother-type figure in front of it. She said, "There is a treasure in this castle that belongs to the princess who lives there, and the fairy-godmother is guarding it so that bad people can't get it." I asked her to "be" the treasure. "Just say, 'I'm the treasure,'" I said. "I'm the treasure," she complied. "Well, treasure," I said. "Tell me about yourself." "Well, I'm very valuable." "Who owns you?" I asked. "The princess owns me and bad people are trying to get me. But my fairy-godmother won't let them." We proceeded to build a story that involved a previous experience with the treasure taken by bad guys, and the princess feeling very scared, but now that the fairy-godmother was here, the princess felt safe. "Susan, I wonder if there is anything about this story that reminds you of your own life in any way?" "I don't know." "Well, I wonder if you used to feel afraid, like the princess felt afraid, when you were with your stepfather." "That's right! And now that I have my new mother and father, I feel safe!" she shouted. At my request, she painted the fear feelings she used to have. In later sessions, Susan made several sand scenes involving treasure that was buried (using crystals as the treasure) because it was in danger and was finally discovered and saved by Superman or other hero-type figures.

I did a puppet show for her, using animals as various characters, of a girl who was hurt, physically and sexually, by a bad puppet. The little girl in my story was very frightened each time. Finally, the girl puppet began to pummel the bad puppet, yelling, "Get away from me! I don't want you to do that!" and so forth. The bad puppet slinked away "never to be seen again." Susan was delighted with this story and immediately insisted that she do it for me. In the next session, she performed the story with some variation to make it her own for her parents. When she was through, we all sat around to discuss the metaphor as it related to Susan. She said, "I could never tell him to stop, like the puppet did." Her parents and I assured her that it is pretty much impossible for little girls to do that. Feeling our support, Susan began to sob. "When he first started touching me down there, I kind of liked it. Then it got really bad, but I didn't know what to do. And he said he'd kill me and my mother if I said anything. Sometimes he'd hit me with the belt after that." It was important that Susan could allow these feelings to emerge, particularly her fears regarding her own collusion.

At another session, I asked Susan to draw a picture of Jane, her birth mother. Again she said, "Do I have to?" and when I said "Yes," she asked if she could draw a beautiful, colorful rainbow. This is not the first time that I have had children come into a session and draw rainbows. I realized after awhile that these drawings appeared to serve as a means of support for the child. Finally Susan drew her mother. I placed the drawing against a chair and asked her to speak to her. She sat for quite some time focused on the picture. I waited quietly. Finally she declared, as tears spilled out of her eyes, "Why did you leave me?!" She turned to me then, "I don't want to do this anymore right now." I was happy to reinforce her direct statement and we played a game together until the end of the session. Over the next several sessions, Susan was gradually able to express many feelings regarding her lost mother, using drawings, the sand tray, puppets, and clay.

Self-Nurturing

No matter how much support and reassurance an abused child receives from the therapist and his or her parents, deeper feelings of guilt, shame, and blame persist. Developmentally, a child blames himself or herself for whatever happened, particularly trauma, and this was certainly true for Susan. Susan was able to express some of these feelings to me and to Mr. and Mrs. S.—some children just push them down deeper and deeper. These feelings can cause a split within the child as therapy proceeds. On the one hand, part of Susan was feeling stronger—more acquainted with her senses, her body, her intellect, her emotions. She was gaining self-support, expressing her emotions rather than keeping them buried, and learning a new, healthier way of being in life. Another part was sustaining those bad feelings of self, as well as the negative introjects she had taken in about herself, and true integration and healing had not taken place. Only the child, with guidance from the therapist, can deal with these toxins. This is not a simple task. I have found that the child needs to have the resource of that part of herself that grows stronger and healthier every day to deal with that noxious part of self. I guided Susan to use herself as a resource.

As we played with clay, I formed a figure of a little girl. "Who is that?" Susan asked. "This is you when you were a little girl and your stepfather used to hurt you." She looked at the figure for awhile. "Let's imagine that you can go back in a time machine and talk to her. What would you say?" With encouragement, Susan finally said to the little girl, "I like you." I directed Susan to tell her little girl self some things she liked about her. "Well, you're kind of cute. And you're nice." "Could you tell

her that you know how she feels when her stepfather is hurting her?"
Susan proceeded to do this. "Can you tell her it's not her fault?" Susan
said, "It's not your fault." I asked then, "How did it feel to say that? Is
it true or false?" "It's true!" she said, and turning to the figure again said,
"It's not your fault. You're just a little girl." I asked Susan to choose
something at home—one of her stuffed animals—to be the little girl
Susan, and that every night before going to sleep, to hug her and tell her
it wasn't her fault and that she loved her. We practiced this a bit with
one of my animals. Susan agreed to perform this ritual and took great
pleasure in it.

At another session, I asked Susan to draw a picture of a part of herself
she did not like. She drew a cartoon-like figure labeling it "The Part
That's Afraid of Things."

VO: Susan, I want you to BE that part. Imagine it's like a puppet and
you have to give it a voice.

S: I'm this part.

VO: Tell me about yourself.

S: I'm afraid of everything.

VO: Like what?

S: Well, I'm just afraid of everything, like spiders, and bugs, and the
dark, and things like that.

VO: Susan, look at your picture. What do you think of this part?

S: I HATE it! [This energetic remark represented the retroflective energy
that Susan kept within herself that fed and kept alive that fearful part
of herself. I wanted this energy to come out, so I encouraged her to
yell at the drawing and tell it how much she hated it.]

S: [To the drawing] I hate you! I wish you would go away! You make me
sick!

VO: Yeah! Tell it! [I cheer her on in order to facilitate the expression.]

VO: Susan, how long has this part been with you?

S: Ummm. Always.

VO: How about when you were, say 4 years old?

S: Yeah.

VO: Susan, when you were 4 years old you had a lot of things to be
afraid of. Right?

S: Right. Like especially my stepfather. And also I used to get real scared
when I saw him hit my mother and she would cry.

VO: That's right. So I want to tell you that even though you are safe now, that little girl lives inside of you and doesn't know she's safe. And now she also has someone to be with her that she never had before—beside your new mother and father.

S: Who??

VO: YOU!

S: Me?

VO: Yes, she has you to be with her and you know things she never, ever knew. And you can do things she could never do.

S: Like I can read and stuff.

VO: Yes, and lots more things. Anyway so you need to tell her that you are with her, especially when she's afraid.

S: [To drawing] I'm with you when you're afraid.

VO: Tell her that it's okay to be afraid. You know why! And you don't want her to feel that she's a bad girl because she's afraid.

S: Yeah. You're not a bad girl to be afraid. I know why you are. But you don't have to be afraid anymore because I'm with you now.

RESULTS AND FOLLOW-UP

I worked with Susan for approximately one and a half years, with some time off during the summer. We decided to end the therapy because Susan was functioning very well in her life. She was doing well in school. She had made friends. She was involved in numerous extracurricular activities. She was getting along well at home. Mr. and Mrs. S. reported that she no longer showed any of the symptoms that caused so much concern and prompted them to bring her into therapy. Most of all, Susan stood up for herself, expressed her anger appropriately, and was no longer beset with fears.

The other reason I decided to terminate was that the sessions in the office began to lack energy. Susan was cooperative and contactful with me; however, it was obvious to me that she no longer had much interest in anything I suggested, even games she had previously loved to play. When I suggested that we might stop, she was relieved, and began to tell me how busy she was and how hard it was to come. I suggested that maybe she had been afraid to tell me that she did not want to come anymore for fear of hurting my feelings. She shyly admitted that this was so. I assured her of my delight in her new-found strength—that this ending day was what we had been working toward. We decided to make good-bye cards for each other, and Susan's energy reappeared. As we drew our pictures, we chatted about the phenomenon of mixed feelings: we can be happy to end something and we can be sad, too. I mentioned that I was going to give a workshop for other therapists on treatment of child abuse and asked her permission to tell her story. Susan unhesitantly assented and wrote the following for me to read to the group:

Child Abuse

1. They can go to the hospital.
2. It is a terrible thing to do.
3. If anyone found out about it, the person can get put in jail. Hurray!
4. It can make a child handy cap.
5. It can make a child not do there work. interfears.
6. It can really hurt their feelings after that person has done it. Fell like they should not have done it.
7. It can really hurt a child badly.

Susan asked me several times if the people I would talk to would help other children like her and expressed pride and happiness that she would make some contribution with her list.

Mrs. S. called me two years later to make an appointment. The results of our work together were definitely long lasting—Susan had continued to do well and blossom. However, there were some new issues emerging relating to her entry into adolescence that concerned her parents and they felt they needed some guidance. Susan, they reported, had developed into such a strong personality, a veritable leader in her life, that they were having some difficulty knowing the kind of limits they should set without subjugating her new boldness.

It did not surprise me that Susan's parents decided to seek counseling at this stage of Susan's life. My experience with children who have suffered trauma has shown me that they are able to work through issues related to the trauma only as far as their developmental levels will take them. As they approach new stages in their lives, symptoms or behaviors may emerge indicating that they are now ready to deal with issues at a more mature cognitive and emotional level. I make every effort to advise parents of this phenomenon when we are making closure.

DISCUSSION

My work with Susan verified to me the effectiveness of the play therapy process that I have developed based on the concepts and principles of Gestalt therapy (Oaklander 1978, 1992, 1985). I can use Gestalt play therapy with any child, for if a child is stuck in one aspect of the process and is unable to move forward, I will focus my energy on that particular place. With Susan, we established a good relationship quickly, and she was able to sustain fairly good contact with me, both important preludes to future work. I watched her gain strength and self-support through sensory, body, and self-enhancement activities. As she grew stronger, she was able to express much of the anger and grief locked up within her, and she learned to accept and nurture that little child within her that had suffered through so much abuse and abandonment. The effectiveness of Gestalt play therapy was exhibited by Susan's transformation from a meek, fearful, confluent, fragile child into one who met the world with strength, joy, and boldness. An important element to mention in the success of this work involves the discarding of expectations. Although I certainly had plans and goals and ideas for Susan, and I presented many experiences and activities based on my assessment of her needs as we went along, I was careful to disallow any form of expectation on my part at each session. Each session came to be an existential experience: whatever happened, happened.

> Something significant inevitably happens at each session. I maintain focus and intense awareness to catch those moments of significance, which at times are fleeting and difficult to spot. These moments are the heart and substance of each session. They present many avenues: they provide me with a means for communicating with the child's inner being—a bridge to the child's soul; they are a means for strengthening the child's self-support; they can be clues for new places where I may lead the child or follow; they can indicate an experience by the child that I recognize as one of great importance and that I know I must not interfere with or interrupt. [Oaklander 1982, p. 73]

REFERENCES

Bowlby, J. (1980). *Loss.* New York: Basic Books.
Buber, M. (1958). *I And Thou.* New York: Scribner.
James, B. (1989). *Treating Traumatized Children.* Lexington, MA: Lexington Books.
Latner, J. (1986). *The Gestalt Therapy Book.* New York: The Gestalt Journal Press.

Oaklander, V. (1978). *Windows To Our Children: A Gestalt Therapy Approach to Children and Adolescents*. Utah: Real People Press (New York: The Gestalt Journal Press, 1992).

_____ (1982). The relationship of Gestalt Therapy to children. *The Gestalt Journal* 1: 64–74.

_____ (1985). *The Therapy Process*. (Cassette Recording: 1). Seattle, WA: Max Sound.

Perls, F. S. (1969). *Ego, Hunger and Aggression*. New York: Vintage.

Perls, F., Hefferline, R., and Goodman, P. (1951). *Gestalt Therapy*. New York: Julian.

Polster, E., and Polster, M. (1973). *Gestalt Therapy Integrated*. New York: Brunner/Mazel.

Sgroi, S. (1982). *Handbook of Clinical Intervention in Child Sexual Abuse*. Lexington, MA: Lexington Books.

10

Where in the World is . . . My Father? A Time-Limited Play Therapy

Richard Sloves, PSY.D., and Karen Belinger Peterlin, C.S.W.

In this chapter we present an abridged version of a complete twelve-session, time-managed treatment of a 9-year-old boy with the presenting problem of video game addiction. His parents claimed this addiction was the reason that their son was spending increasingly more time out of the house, why his grades were slipping, and why they felt they no longer had control over him. With this case, we hope to show how quickly the therapist can formulate a central theme and how this process serves to guide and to structure the treatment plan in time-limited play therapy.

INTRODUCTION TO TIME-LIMITED PLAY THERAPY

Psychotherapists have witnessed, in the latter part of the twentieth century, a remarkable growth in competing and complimentary models of brief psychotherapy for adults (Davanloo 1980, Malan 1976, Sifneos 1979). However, there are few models tailored specifically to the brief individual treatment of children. Child therapists have had little choice but to expand upon existing crisis intervention techniques, adapt an eclectic, improvisational approach, or try to modify a brief adult treatment model. In keeping with the belief that treatment should be grounded in a coherent conceptual system in order to avoid patchwork technique, we chose to modify an existing adult model of short-term psychotherapy in our work with latency-aged children. We chose James Mann's twelve-session strategy of treatment presented in *Time-Limited Psychotherapy* (1973).

Clinicians who use time-limited play therapy (TLPT) with children generally agree that its distinguishing characteristic is the specific way the therapist uses time as a metaphor that encapsulates the past, present, and future of the child. In the procedure outlined by Sloves and Peterlin (1986), the authors use the passage of time in the treatment to draw attention to and to intensify issues rooted in the child's unresolved separation-individuation conflict, the phase-specific resolution that forms the very raison d'être of this therapy. Time-limited therapy emphasizes the use of a single, overriding central theme or core conflict to guide the therapy throughout its course. The therapist exercises a directive, focused approach to each session, and structures and restructures the play, as he or she helps the child maintain a positive transference in the face of growing frustration and anxiety (Peterlin and Sloves 1985).

Budman and Stone (1983) conceptualize all forms of brief psychotherapy as a discontinuous process of treatment. Rather than try to provide a permanent cure that will inoculate children from all of life's stressors, treatment simply helps children regain their lost footing and return them to a healthy developmental pathway. Time-limited therapy is most effective when it can assist children to overcome pathological attachments to parents, achieve greater acceptance of the self as differentiated, and remove internal or interpersonal blockages that inhibit their normal press toward individuation. It is especially effective when a child feels trapped or thwarted by external circumstances in an effort to function independently. When specific maturational-developmental tasks lose momentum, brief treatment supports both the child and parents as they negotiate this difficult transitional period. Rapid engagement, brief but intense contact, and withdrawal send a message to the family that they are competent to handle any problems in the future.

Children, during the latency period, struggle daily with issues of self-esteem, autonomy, and conflicts about emotional separateness and interdependency. The limitation of time imposed by the therapy increases and intensifies these conflicts. Because children feel frustrated in their search for an omnipotent, unlimited maternal provider to fulfill all their needs, the time-limited play therapist seeks to use the therapeutic relationship to convey the idea that limited givers are available and trustworthy. If children refuse to accept and internalize this reality, the outside world will offer nothing but constant disappointment. Then too, if the time-limited therapist can tell children when to expect the disappointment of termination from the very onset of treatment, then they have less basis in reality for fearing betrayal by sudden abandonment and may be less frightened by fears of engulfment by the therapist. The time-limited play therapist sets up the treatment to provide an inherent structure that permits children to engage in treatment with an intensity that might not be otherwise expected. The fixed termination date reinforces independence and self-directedness, and offers some security against a loss of self-control.

One way to understand the actual process of time-limited play therapy is to think of the entire treatment as a condensed, intensified rendition of the termination phase of long-term therapy, but without the negative transference. A central theme is extracted from the clinical data and shared with the child. When the therapist states the theme or core conflict in a clear and emphatic manner, children take it to mean that the therapist both understands and shares in their pain. Because the central theme sets the tone for the entire treatment, to be effective it must connect children's present symptomatology with the dynamics of the past. It must reflect and address children's negative sense of self and allow them to discover the etiology of these painful feelings, the discovery of which adds to and intensifies a sense of mastery. In keeping with the adaptive tenor of treatment, the therapist always discusses the central issue in derivative, rather than primary affects. For example, we speak of a child's feelings of disappointment or uncertainty, but never of his or her rage or feelings of abandonment. In long-term treatment, the therapist expects some regression and, in some instances, encourages it because there are few limitations placed on the "working through" process. The opposite is true in brief treatment. Here, technique limits the child's dependence and regression. In psychoanalytic terms, the therapist actively thwarts development of a transference neurosis. The therapist consistently and firmly maintains the focus on adaptation and conflict resolution.

Structured Play

In our version of structured play, we combine both the psychodynamic play interview technique of Conn (1948) and Erikson (1950), and the cognitive-behavioral approach explicated by Meichenbaum (1974). In structured play, it is the therapist who designs specific scenarios, selects the materials, controls the major parameters and constructs the introductory narrative to each session. This is necessary because with rationed sessions, both therapist and child have limited time. Rather than letting children discover implicit rules that govern treatment, the therapist does this for them. The therapist tells the children the dynamic formulation, the length of therapy, and the basic mechanics of the process. Each session is preplanned to optimize time. The therapist spends as much time and energy in contemplating the next session as reflecting on the previous one.

In important ways this method goes against the grain of several prevailing models of Axlinian/Rogerian play therapy. The therapist is sympathetic, friendly, and empathic, but rarely permissive in the relationship. While the therapist respects children's ability to solve problems, it seems unfair to let them do it in their own time, especially when the therapist possesses the collective knowledge of other children who, in similar circumstances, have confronted similar problems. The therapist, as ally, does everything to hurry the therapy along without frightening the child into passivity, active resistance, or flight. The therapist guides the child while maintaining the positive transference in the face of a constantly threatening negative transference.

Because the therapist is active and decides on the theme and course of treatment, specific play materials are used while others are avoided. Puppets, dolls, action figures, toy animals, doll houses and furniture, building blocks, and drawing materials are the primary tools of treatment. The therapist selects play materials for their ability to recreate, in reasonably concrete, literal ways, the core conflict. Any material resistant to psychological regression is acceptable. Obviously, this excludes finger paints, clay, and water play from the treatment. At the same time, the therapist is careful to avoid any play activity that takes too much time to set up, offers sanctuary from the therapeutic focus, or takes too long for the theme to play out. The time-limited play therapist does not use board games no matter how therapeutic their intent. They are, by their very nature, dependent on fixed and invariant rules that limit spontaneity, constrain fantasy, and force the players into a competitive relationship.

To get a head start in treatment, the therapist asks children to bring from home those dolls, action figures, or vehicles that they think helpful in resolving the central theme. Children have a shared history with their personal possessions. They imbue each toy with distinctive aspects of their character and experience. These toys come to therapy with an established and preexistent subtext. The children and these fantasy representations have in common private, interpersonal, and sociocultural experiences. Most importantly, these personalized toys enhance generalization from therapy to the natural environment because the children can continue the work of therapy at home during the week.

The time-limited play therapist does not coerce the child to conform to a prescribed script, but the play materials are perforce limiting. The child is quite free to play out any resistances and any defenses, but the therapist channels the means of expression. Because the child and therapist play as equals, each has as much right as the other to criticize and comment on the play. Watching the therapist play, the child becomes at once an interested observer and active participant in the process of problem clarification and conflict resolution. This collaborative and improvisational switching of roles helps the child identify with the therapist's problem-solving orientation, become more objective about his or her own thinking, and accept some degree of responsibility for these thoughts (Hartner 1977). Having both child and therapist at play enhances the therapeutic alliance and positive transference, making it easier for both to endure conflict. Structured play elevates the therapist to the status of coequal, whereas traditional models of play therapy constrain the therapist and broaden, rather than narrow, the gap between the child-patient and adult-therapist. The therapist is free to shift at will from commentator, to observer, then to participant. Engaged in either parallel or communal play, the therapist is free to ask, "What am I supposed to be doing here? How is this story (action) helping you? What is the point of all this?"

"Play-in-progress" describes a subset of structured play and it combines guided fantasy, mutual storytelling, cognitive restructuring, and symbolic work. The therapist sets the stage, arranging the play materials into a scene shortly *before* the child enters the room. Once the session has begun, the therapist will seamlessly work the play into the ongoing conversation in such a way so that it will appear relevant to his or her introductory remarks. The play is not always a literal representation of the child's life circumstances. At times, it can take on a highly symbolic portrayal of the child's inner world. With this in mind, we use materials directly to illustrate conflict-free spheres of ego and cognitive functioning. We are explicit in our efforts to identify and strengthen the observing ego, and articulate all activities related to self-regulation. We use pictographs extensively to provide children with graphic representations of their internal emotional states and cognitive process—dynamics that children intuitively sense, but which lay just beyond their linguistic and conceptual powers. For example, we use x-ray and cut-away drawings of a human body to diagram and illustrate how the psychological processes of denial, splitting, repression, compartmentalization, and memory operate within the child.

PRESENTING PROBLEM AND BACKGROUND DATA

Evaluation as the opening gambit in time-limited psychotherapy must necessarily be somewhat circumscribed and therefore, at most, we conduct two diagnostic interviews. Detailed assessment of psychopathology is not our primary goal, and even more to the point, may not be particularly helpful. The business of the initial contact is for us to obtain an abbreviated psychosocial history, observe the parent–child interaction, and conduct a mental status examination. Prior to the second interview, parents complete an Achenbach Child Behavior Checklist (Achenbach 1981) and the teacher is asked to fill out a Connors' Teacher Rating Scale (Connors 1972). At the second meeting, we score and review the rating scales, and assess the family history and dynamics. If our selection criteria are met, we present the treatment plan and central theme to the family toward the end of this second session.

Presenting Problem

Ms. Sara B. described the problem of her 9-year-old son, Jamal, as follows:

> This is the last thing I'm doing before I go to Family Court and get a Persons In Need of Supervision (PINS) petition. His guidance counselor said that maybe you can help, but to tell you the truth, no disrespect intended, I don't know what to do with this boy! I don't know if he needs to be in a home or someplace, but unless something gets done fast something is going to happen to him. I tried taking him to a therapist, but he went for four months and it didn't do any good. He's gone AWOL and, for the past eight months, he has been totally out of control. Jamal is addicted. That's right, you heard me right. He's addicted to video games and all he does it hang out at video parlors all over the place and if he doesn't have enough money to play he steals it from home. The last time he took thirty dollars.

It was only on rare occasions that Jamal returned directly from school without getting "lost." Often, he did not return home until 7 P.M. and on several occasions he did not come home until his mother called the local precinct and a police officer brought him home in a squad car. She remarked, "I call there so often the precinct practically knows me by my first name." When Jamal first started to come home late, he would stop off for a slice of pizza and would arrive home 10 to 15 minutes later than expected. Soon the interval between leaving school and walking through the front door increased. His mother tried to put an end to this by asking merchants in the neighborhood not to let him into their stores, but this only served to push Jamal to go even farther afield.

Family History

This was a reconstituted family consisting of the birth mother, the stepfather, Robert, the identified patient, Jamal, and his 2-year-old brother, Andrew. They lived in the same apartment building as the mother's 55-year-old maternal great aunt, who raised her from age 8 following her mother's death. Both parents were high school graduates with some junior college credits and each occupied midlevel clerical positions in a large multinational corporation. They began living together when Jamal was 6 years old and they married shortly before Andrew's birth. Initially, Jamal and his stepfather got along well, but when the therapy began they were "strangers in the night," with Robert deferring to the mother on all issues related to Jamal. As for the mother's relationship with Jamal, Ms. B. said, "I thought I had a good relationship with Jamal, but I noticed things kind of slipping after I gave birth to my youngest child and now I'm so angry I can't begin to tell you." Two recent stressors within the past year seemed especially relevant. Robert had become involved with an adult soccer team that he coached every Saturday afternoon, and both parents' hectic schedule precluded their having meals together.

Jamal's mother and birth father met while she was in her senior year of high school and they married against the strenuous objections of her guardian, her great aunt, who characterized him as a "low life." Jamal was born two years later and accomplished all developmental tasks within normal limits. The parental relationship deteriorated as the father graduated from marijuana to crack/cocaine use. "I thought he was great, but he turned out to be a total idiot. First he began to use the household money for drugs and then he started beating up on me." When Jamal was 4 years old, his parents divorced and that, according to his mother, was the last time he saw his birth father.

School Functioning

Jamal attended an accelerated fourth grade class at a neighborhood public school. He had an excellent academic history from kindergarten to the beginning of the current school year. But at the time Jamal was referred for treatment, his school was not only threatening to place him in a less demanding academic setting, but had gone so far as to suggest the possibility of referring him for an evaluation for a special education placement. According to his teacher, Mr. R., who incidentally was Jamal's first male teacher, Jamal put forth little effort, annoyed his classmates with conversation and rarely completed homework assignments. He failed to bring home notes critical of his behavior and, on the one occasion, he forged his mother's signature. Mr. R. further described Jamal, on the one hand, as very sociable, intelligent, and capable and, on the other hand, highly manipulative to the extreme. The Connor's Teacher Rating Scale (Connors 1972) revealed high scores on items assessing fidgetiness, restlessness, fearfulness, excessive demands for attention, and anxiousness to please. To a lesser degree, his teacher saw Jamal as sad and unusually sensitive to criticism.

Mental Status Examination

Jamal was a slim, handsome, 9-year-old boy of African-American heritage who initially related to the therapist in a cautious, but direct manner. He started out, during the parental interview, by drawing highly stylized, articulated superhero characters. Once he was alone with the therapist, he gravitated to the doll house furniture, all the while providing a running commentary on the thoughts and actions of the dolls. He spoke rapidly and candidly about the presenting problem and was neither defensive nor evasive when asked direct questions.

It was clear that Jamal felt abandoned by both his parents, who he described as "always too busy." He was certain in the belief that the therapist was going "to help them put me away." Surprisingly, he harbored little animosity toward his sibling and enjoyed helping his mother in taking care of him. The predominant mood was one of sadness in the absence of any signs of either a dysthymia or major affective disorder. Receptive and expressive language were commensurate with average cognitive functioning. When asked about the last time he had seen his "real" father, Jamal glanced toward the door, lowered his voice to a whisper, extracted a pledge of secrecy, and disclosed that he had seen his birth father walking in the neighborhood one month prior to the symptoms onset. He reported, "He didn't see me, but I saw him." This was a secret because "my mom hates him and she told my aunt she never wants to hear his name again."

Selection Criteria

Many selection criteria relevant to adults in short-term psychotherapy are not directly applicable to the clinical assessment of children. These include a tendency to be introspective, a willingness to make reasonable sacrifices, psychological mindedness, and an ability to recognize symptoms as psychological in origin. However, precursors of these above criteria are present in most children. In our assessment, we came to the conclusion that Jamal would be honest about his emotional difficulties. He displayed a curiosity about the causes of his feelings and behavior and he responded eagerly once we presented a central theme.

In the final analysis, Jamal would have to engage quickly and positively with the therapist and possess a high tolerance for the separation that would be necessary during the termination phase of treatment. We needed to know whether it was safe to engage Jamal in this intensive modality of psychotherapy or was it best to leave well enough alone. Besides being capable of forming a rapid positive alliance with the therapist, the history must reveal that the child had at least one positive relationship in the past, and that there was, at a minimum, one stable period within the child's life. Multiple losses for a child usually preclude the use of time-limited therapy. With Jamal, the family history revealed a sizable period of stability and that he, at one time, related well to both his mother and stepfather. Further, Jamal has had several good friends and had done well in school until the fourth grade.

Another criterion for time-limited treatment is the ability of the child to understand the passage of time. Integrated into the mental status examination were questions about Jamal's age, date of birth, and the current day of the week, month, and season. Aiming at a higher level of conceptualization, I (Dr. Sloves) asked Jamal to estimate how long it would take to accomplish certain tasks and the length of time that had passed between important life events. Time projections, asking Jamal how old he needed to be to drive a car or get married, were equally revealing. For example, I asked Jamal to pretend his family had recently moved to a new neighborhood and to estimate how long it would take him to make new friends.

There are also family criteria that must be met: time-limited therapy in the context of family instability has limited value (Rosenthal and Levine 1970). It was critical that the family be able to accommodate a change in Jamal and they had to be willing to work toward that end. Other family indicators associated with a favorable prognosis included high parental motivation, parental flexibility, and capacity for change in themselves. In assessing Jamal, it was clear that both his family and he were motivated to change. Moreover, I judged Jamal's problems to be a reaction to external circumstances, rather than a manifestation of a deep intrapsychic or structural disorder. Jamal's mother was neither a shifting nor an unstable object in his early life and his great aunt was supportive whenever his mother was otherwise preoccupied. Time-limited play therapy places a premium on active participation, direct interaction between therapist and child, and a balance between expression through play and verbalization. In the diagnostic sessions, Jamal revealed a readiness to trust and to respond to the therapist. Jamal's environment was sufficiently supportive and stable so external pathological forces would not undermine treatment. Several "rule outs" were absent: there were no severe symptoms including destructiveness, suicidal ideation, or social isolation and withdrawal.

Our assessment reached the following conclusions: Jamal was capable of rapidly developing a positive relationship with the therapist. In addition, his defenses were neither too rigid nor too brittle to thwart rapid resolution of the core conflict represented in the central theme. Furthermore, he had acquired sufficient basic trust for the termination to be integrated as a positive growth experience rather than as yet another abandonment. The next major task to be accomplished toward the latter part of the second diagnostic session was to present the central theme, cement the parental alliance, draft and sign the therapeutic contract, and plan for the family sessions.

THEORETICAL CONCEPTUALIZATION

We identified and isolated a focal dynamic issue to further Jamal's healthy emotional development. For us, the element of loss seemed to be the overriding issue driving Jamal. We did not accept at face value the presenting problem of video game addiction, although we took its attendant behaviors seriously as they propelled Jamal away from the family, placed him in poorly supervised surroundings, and increased the possibility of his becoming engaged in a cycle of ever-increasing dysfunctional behavior.

Ms. B. used the word "addict" to describe both Jamal's seeming preoccupation with video games and his birth father's crack/cocaine addiction. Jamal and his birth father had "stolen" money from family members to support their "habits" and both were threatened with expulsion from the family under the auspices of Family Court. We identified several psychosocial stressors that led to an imbalance in the emotional attachments between Jamal and his parents. At 4 years of age, Jamal lost his birth father, with parental separation and divorce occurring almost concurrently with the onset of normal phase specific paternal identification. The potential for a compensatory relationship with his mother was cut short when, in rapid succession, she married Robert and gave birth to Andrew. Because Jamal did not perceive Robert as a suitable replacement for his birth father, this marriage engendered a sense of estrangement and resentment. From Jamal's point of view, his mother was the source of his unhappiness, while his birth father, preserved and encapsulated in memory, became an idealized object of desire as well as a fellow traveler in crime.

Jamal's initial expressions of hurt and defiance aroused parental anger that only served to intensify, rather than supplant, his identification with the absent/lost father. These vibrant dynamics remained a coercive yet latent force until triggered by his startling encounter with his birth father in the neighborhood. Jamal started to distance himself from the family; first enticed by hunger, then the exhilaration afforded by the arcade game, "Street Fighter II." In this game, Jamal sought compensatory powers that further identified him with his birth father. Also of importance was the fact that Jamal's human figure drawings were replete with muscle-bound superheroes. These commanding, robust figures of fantasy seemed to be an evocation of his longing for sufficient potency to defend against feelings of loss and were emblematic of his need to exercise control. In both the video game and in his drawings, Jamal found a haven from feelings of familial rejection as well as a model for masculine identification. Because of this, Ms. B. impulsively characterized Jamal as "his father's son": he was addicted, irresponsible, and predestined unendingly to roam the streets. It was here that a self-fulfilling prophesy took root and flourished.

In the meantime, Jamal transferred the problematic relationship with his mother to school and replaced it with his teacher. Fortunately for Jamal, his maternal great aunt prevailed as his saving grace. In this unconflicted relationship, the core of his self-esteem was preserved, thereby avoiding more dire psychological consequences. This aunt's indulgence of Jamal, that so infuriated his mother, served to sustain him when he felt most alone. One of the strongest prognostic signs was the fact that Jamal waited for his great aunt whenever she was to pick him up from school. Her strongly voiced disapproval of the birth father never contaminated her relationship with Jamal.

Central Theme

Structured time-limited therapy uses the theoretical formulation in a unique way. The therapist shares the dynamic and historical formulation directly with the family: it is not the sole domain of the therapist, to be shared exclusively with colleagues at a clinical case conferences, chart rounds, or therapeutic postmortem. The therapist does not couch the theme in psychological and psychiatric jargon. The most important test of the theme's veracity is its ability to pass the family's scrutiny with little hesitation and with absolutely no selling on the part of the therapist.

Incorporated into the central theme were three complimentary elements having relevance to Jamal and the family. At the start, I summarized and concretized the developmental and systemic conflict experienced by the family. Second, I explained how the symptom that had aroused the ire, displeasure, and anger of parents, teachers, and neighbors was understandable, that it was a maladaptive, but honest effort on Jamal's part to resolve the family conflict. Finally, I reviewed the history of the problem with Jamal to illustrate both the ineffectiveness of the present solution and the need to find a more appropriate, less conflicted means to achieve adaptation. The central theme gave voice to Jamal's expressed desire to avoid the displeasure of others, while, at the same time, it raised expectations that the future would be a decided improvement on the present.

A properly conceptualized and presented central theme both empowers the parents and advances the child's understanding of the mechanics of psychotherapy beyond vague assertions that it would "make you feel better." In time-limited treatment, the therapist assures the child that therapy will be hard work. I told Jamal pointedly "You are not supposed to like coming to therapy. It is all right if you whine and complain about coming because you can probably think of a lot more fun things to do than to come to therapy. So we are all going to work as hard as we can to get the job done. Then, after twelve sessions, it's finished and you and your family can get on with your lives." However, the therapist buttresses the child's ego by making statements such as "I am certain *we* can work together so that you can get the things you need without getting your parents and teachers angry at you." The twelve-session time limit would assure Jamal that he would not be in treatment forever and that he would get better in a fairly short period of time. When Jamal first entered into the diagnostic process, he thought that all was lost. Now, with the presentation of the central theme, he could understand the problem in concrete terms, and how the process of change would work. The very brevity of therapy was evidence that the solution to his distress was within his grasp.

We organized two interdependent themes and presented the first to the entire family while we reserved the second for Jamal. The family theme was systemic. Rather than regard Jamal's symptoms as the sole manifestation of some deep, intrapsychic psychopathology, we recast his actions as an effort to call attention to the family's precarious stability and tenuous cohesiveness. The simple fact was that, despite their marriage and the birth of their youngest son, the family had not as yet fully coalesced into a supportive and interdependent unit. By absenting himself from the family, Jamal endeavored to draw attention to these deficiencies and, at the same time, to pull his parents away from their entrenched patterns of interaction. Jamal was challenging the family to rise to the occasion and become whole. Perhaps Jamal hoped family members would reach out to one another, but, at the present time, he remained unconvinced that they cared enough to reclaim him as their son. Unfortunately, the parents did not decipher the message quickly enough and they did themselves little benefit and inadvertently confirmed Jamal's worst fears when they threatened him with placement. We asked his parents about the role of men in each of their respective families of origin and they spoke of their own childhood experiences in female-headed households. We asked the parents to consider a question that was to be the focus of the first family session scheduled for the midpoint in the therapy: Were they ready to make a commitment to each other? If the answer was in the affirmative, they would need to communicate this to Jamal in an unambiguous and unequivocal manner in order for treatment to have any real chance of success.

The second theme was weighted more heavily toward the psychodynamic and spoke to Jamal's primarily unconscious and symbolic search for his birth father, his desire to reconstitute the family, reinstate his birth father, and make restitution for whatever he had done that precipitated his birth father's departure. I presented Jamal's theme using play figures while his parents were in the waiting room.

RS: Let me tell you a story about this kid. He's a . . .

J: A boy?

RS: Yes, a boy and he's, let's see, he could be how many years old?

J: Eight?

RS: That's just about right. How did you know?

J: Don't know, he just looks about eight.

RS: Let's see, where was I?

J: [Pointing to the play figures] He lives with them.

RS: He used to, a long, long time ago. When he was 2 and 3 and 4 years old they all lived together and it was great and wonderful and everything was wonderful and he was happy to have a whole complete family. You know, a mother and a father. But then one day, something horrible happened.

J: This is a story?

RS: Sort of, but are you thinking what I'm thinking? Do you think this is a real story?

J: Yeah. Something happened?

RS: Yes. You see, everybody was happy and the boy felt that everybody loved him and then one day something horrible happened to the family.

J: I know! There was an earthquake.

RS: Sort of, but it was even worse than an earthquake because one day the boy came home from school and he knew there was something wrong in the family. Someone was missing.

J: His father. I know this story cause it was on TV or something.

RS: Suddenly the family was broken up and the mother was lonely and cried all the time and the boy kept asking "Where did my father go?"

J: He was kidnapped by crooks.

RS: You think someone took him away against his will, but in this story he was told to leave and he did leave and never, ever came back.

J: It's all wrong here. [Jamal constructs a floor plan of his apartment with blocks and furniture.] There, that's better.

RS: You put the man and the women in bed together. That is interesting. That's how it was. That's how the boy wanted it to be. And you know what? He was sad and mad. Mad at his mother because his father wasn't treating her right, but he treated the boy okay. He asked his mother, "When is he coming back?" and she said . . .

J: He just went out to buy some cigarettes.

RS: Not in this story. He didn't come back, but the boy waited and waited and waited all the way up to the third grade. Then he said to himself, "I better do something about this. Mom has a new boyfriend and a new baby and dad doesn't know about it." The boy thought two things.

J: He thought his father's dead.

RS: He thought his father was dead. First, he went looking for him, every day after school. And then, he thought about living with his father because his mother had a new husband and a new baby. Mom didn't need him around to keep her company.

J: I know this story and I know how it ends. He looked and looked for him, didn't he?

RS: He thought his mother would be proud of him or not even miss him cause he was acting so grown-up.

J: You're wrong. She got not happy. She got . . . [makes sound effect of an explosion].

RS: Absolutely right. She got very angry at him and told all the neighbors, and store people and video people and pizza people and teachers. She told them to stop looking for his . . .

J: . . . father. But he didn't. He was smart and brave.

RS: He didn't stop and kept on looking. All he wanted to do is put his family back together again.

J: Like Humpty Dumpty.

RS: But all the king's horses and all the king's men couldn't . . .

J: . . . put Humpty Dumpty back together again.

RS: Everyone got angry at the boy and all he was trying to do was make everything right.

J: They'll put him in a home for bad boys. He'll become a foster kid.

RS: He feels there is no room for him and his mother, and stepfather and brother don't need him anymore. Then one day, you know what happened?

J: Yes! Yes! He saw him. He saw his father. He saw him but he . . . but he . . . Our time's up?

RS: There is enough time to get the job done. It is a sad story and you need a rest. Hang in there because we're almost finished. But I need you to help figure out the end.

[J begins to draw a picture of a muscle-bound man.]

RS: Who's this? I don't believe we've been introduced.

J: He's an athlete.

RS: And a very strong one at that.

J: He takes steroids.

RS: He needs all the strength and power he can get.

J: No one can beat him up . . .

RS: . . . and no one can take anything away from him.

J: Or he'll punch their lights out.

RS: But you know, not even he can help the kid. The kid wishes he had a special friend just like this guy to help him.

J: He got one?

RS: Yes. You and I will find a way for this kid to have a place in his family so he can get all the love he needs.

J: And his father comes back?

RS: I'm sorry, but no. The boy can get all he needs from the mommy and the stepfather.

Parental Alliance

In order for Jamal's parents to feel invested and empowered by the treatment process, I enlisted their assistance in countering Jamal's inevitable resistance. I could manage Jamal's contentiousness in treatment so long as both of his parents supported the treatment. But, if they had colluded with Jamal in the development of a negative transference against the therapist, the brevity of treatment makes it all but impossible for the therapist to neutralize the negative transference. Several consecutively failed appointments would significantly attenuate the pressure of time and this, in turn, would have a devastating impact on the outcome. Therefore, we discussed in all manner and form how resistances make themselves known at each phase of treatment. We emphasized that Jamal would do his best work on those days when he seemed most determined to avoid therapy. We told them to expect some reduction in the presenting symptomatology within the first two or three sessions and we warned them that it was not all that uncommon for the problem or an entirely new one to reemerge toward the end of treatment.

Therapeutic Contract

The therapist can significantly reduce the number of failed and/or canceled appointments when he or she incorporates a written and signed contract into the treatment plan (Sloves 1988). Clarification and concretization of the passage of time is helpful in mitigating the sense of loss, disappointment, and rejection that the child experiences toward the end of treatment. Jamal's conceptualization of time was variable and in a state of flux, so he would need a therapeutic contract to help make the passage of time in the treatment concrete and tangible. It was important not to have Jamal experience the therapeutic relationship as interminable.

The contract contained Jamal's name, a concise statement of the central theme, the total number of sessions, and the exact date of termination. In the contract were the specific dates for each of the twelve sessions, so Jamal would need to check off each date as it occurred. I took special care to schedule the termination so that it would not coincide with any other planned separations in Jamal's life, such as a school vacation and/or a family holiday. Doing so avoided any dilution or contamination of the termination phase. For example, if the final session were to fall within a week or two of the beginning of summer vacation, Jamal might conclude that the treatment had not actually ended but was being postponed temporarily until the resumption of school in September. I gave copies to both Jamal and his family after all participants, including myself, had signed the contract.

Because cognitive and dynamic factors collude in permitting the child to deny or distort the reality of loss engendered by the termination, it is particularly useful to supplement the contract with graphic or pictorial materials that emphasize time's passage. Given Jamal's chronological and psychological age, I photocopied a calendar and Jamal and I highlighted each session. It is important to note that some children start counting from their first contact with the therapist and they include the two diagnostic meetings as part of the twelve-session contract. This is not a problem during the opening and working through phases of treatment, but, as the termination date approaches, the child may seem unduly anxious because he or she is operating under the mistaken belief that treatment is about to end. In order to avoid this misunderstanding, I told Jamal, "Next week we will begin our *first* session. We will begin working together next week. Last week and today we talked about what was the matter, but next week you and I will begin to fix things up."

Family Sessions

I scheduled two family meetings, one at the halfway point (session 6) and one at the end (session 12). I anticipated Jamal's inevitable question about whether or not he would lose a session to his family, telling him that family meetings were in addition to his twelve individual sessions. I told Jamal that he would be included in the family meetings to safeguard the confidentiality of his individual sessions.

THE PROCESS OF PLAY THERAPY

Briefly stated, the process of time-limited therapy flows through three more or less overlapping and progressive stages. In the opening phase, the therapist systematically nurtures the therapeutic alliance, offering the child a kind of empathic umbrella from the interpersonal and intrapsychic conflicts that cause suffering, which, when externalized in behavior, bring the child to treatment. At this stage, the therapist does not interpret the transference because to do so might suppress the child's magical wish for union. However, during the working-through phase, the therapist begins to resist, gently but steadfastly, any collusion with the very magical fantasies that were encouraged during the opening gambit in order to encourage individuation. At this point, the therapist usually interprets the transference in the light of past relationships with significant others as the therapist functions as a stand-in for ambivalently held objects. Finally, in the termination phase, the therapist helps the child to chose between the ambivalent past and the imperfect future, between magical wishes for restitution and tangible, but flawed, sources of gratification. Here, the relationship between child and therapist is the primary basis of all transference interpretations.

Opening Phase

In the opening phase of treatment, the child, like an infant, reexperiences the "golden glow" of narcissistic identification and feels a sense of omnipotence rooted in the archaic feeling of infinite time. In giving voice to Jamal's conscious and preconscious thoughts and emotions, we anticipated that he would discover me as an all-knowing special friend. Symptoms frequently diminish or disappear altogether because their presence is redundant given the therapist's perceived benevolence. In this atmosphere of empathic linkage, as the therapist sympathetically explores the central issue with the child, intense emotions are released. This abreaction intensifies the positive transference and makes possible the accelerated development of the therapeutic alliance. The therapist unconditionally accepts the child's wish for a perfect bond and with his or her empathic support, they begin to explore the core conflict.

The primary goal at this stage is to magnify the therapeutic alliance by making a direct appeal to that part in Jamal that craved security without dependency and support without regression. I assumed the mantle of the lost and idealized object and gradually created the basis for internalization. By these actions, the therapist engaged Jamal around the unrealistic, albeit understandable, fantasy of union with an all-loving, sustaining figure.

Session 1

The key task during this phase was to foster an alliance against Jamal's feelings of helplessness. To this end, Jamal and I would examine the irrational and unrealistic wish for his birth father's return, and the pain of isolation now that he must compete with his younger, more dependent sibling. If Jamal faltered, my enthusiasm and fearlessness might convey optimism about the future and thereby support the exploration of the central theme. One lesson to be learned from the following vignette is that the therapist must be ready for the unexpected and then "go with the flow." An elaborate play construction, set up to represent his family of origin and reconstituted family, was abandoned the minute Jamal walked through the door. Even though he proclaimed himself "sick," it was clear that he had no intention of assuming any responsibility for his pain nor was he interested in the work of psychotherapy. Treatment began when Jamal offered this unique perspective on the curative process of treatment, and who would do what to whom.

J: I don't feel so good. I have a headache.

RS: Your mom and your teacher seem to feel you have lots of worries inside your head. Maybe the worries don't want to come out today. They're putting up a tough fight.

J: Sometimes I think so hard my head hurts.

RS: Soon it won't hurt so much. You'll feel better once we figure things out.

J: I know. Mom told me all about it in the car. It's your job, right? You're a psychologist and that's what psychologists do.

RS: And what is that?

J: I know all about psychologists 'cause we learned about them in science. They look at dinosaur bones and stuff. We learned about how things began in history times.

RS: You're interested in how things got the way they are and where things come from. By the way, what makes your head hurt?

J: I don't know. Maybe I'm getting a cold.

RS: You know that's not it.

J: I need a rest.

RS: That you do. You've been trying to take care of yourself all this time, not believing your mom and stepfather want you around. I would be tired if I had no one to help me out.

J: Are you kidding! I'm no baby. My brother is a baby, but I can take care of myself. I just can't figure out how to. Can I use the typewriter?

RS: It would be nice to have enough time to play with it, but we have a lot of work to do today. A typewriter won't help you feel like you belong in the family and it won't make your dad come back. Why don't you give your worries to your mom?

J: She'll have a nightmare that will wake up all Manhattan.

RS: Then you must have gigantic worries and want to protect Mom from being scared. We have eleven more times together, eleven more sessions to figure out a way of getting them to realize how lonely you sometimes feel. Of course you can keep your kid worries for yourself.

J: Can't give them to her. I'll give them to you.

RS: How does that work?

J: It's like now. I talk and you listen and then I go home. I'll leave them here with you because you're a psychologist and you'll know what to do with them.

RS: And what will I do with these incredibly gigantic worries and problems?

J: Bury them in the ground and then a zillion years later a psychologist like you will dig them up and study them and then they'll be not gigantic anymore. They'll be all dried up like old bones.

Here, I tried to formulate Jamal's acknowledged and ever-present psychological distress as "worries," a word that Jamal could at once understand and accept without fear of being perceived as a younger child. Worries are legitimate, things that a 9-year-old can deal with successfully, not like frightening feelings. But he initially shied away from the emotional connotation of worries, objectified the conflict, and then decided to give it a decidedly cognitive valence when he intellectualized my role. Avoiding a confrontation, while relentlessly pursuing the cause of his pain, I tried again, and Jamal once again rebuffed me. I supported Jamal, offered a prediction of a positive outcome, and reiterated the central theme, the principal work of doctor and child. Finally, Jamal rescued both himself and his mother from responsibility, suggested that it was the therapist's job to do all the work and accurately foretold the publication of this dialogue.

Session 2

Once again, I was ready with a prepared play scenario, and a rather good one at that. But Jamal had done his homework and came in with a much better idea of how to advance the central theme. He entered the room, cast not a glance at my work and removed two toy helicopters from his backpack.

RS: What have you got there?

J: Helicopters. I can play with them?

RS: Absolutely. You've been thinking about our work together and brought something to help us. I see one is bigger than the other. One's a grown-up helicopter and one is . . .

J: . . . smaller. [They are held at arm's length and circle each other.]

RS: They're not too far away and they're not too close.

J: They can't talk . . . the radio thing is broken.

RS: They can see each other, but can't say what they want to each other.

J: [They land on the tabletop.] See, the helicopter has things, wings on top and they go round and round.

RS: They've landed, but how come they're not talking? What's the matter?

J: It's dangerous. If you get by a helicopter, the wings [rotors] can chop you in little pieces.

RS: Get too close and it's dangerous?

J: It'll cut you up like Freddie Krueger.

RS: They have to stay a safe distance away from each other; a safe space. But they can't get close that way.

J: Get too close and . . . bam!

RS: Getting close is a problem. What do they want to say to each other?

J: This is the baby, I mean little helicopter, and this is the . . . big one.

RS: One is grown up and one is a kid helicopter.

J: That's stupid, helicopters don't grow up.

RS: We're having the same problem as the helicopters. So, they can't understand each other?

J: There's something wrong with the grown . . . Now you got me talking like you . . . I mean with the big one and this one wants to help.

RS: But you said it was dangerous.

J: If he goes real far away, they can't talk. The thing is broke. The tall thing on the roof.

RS: Yeah, the antenna is broken. You were saying that if they get too far apart they can't talk and if they get too close they get hurt.

J: The little one gets hurt.

RS: So what's the solution?

J: They have to find the right, you know. What did you call it? The right space. They do what deaf people do.

RS: When people don't listen, there is a special way to get their attention.

J: Like with their hands. They talk with their hands.

RS: We need to find a better way for the kid, I mean, the little helicopter to get close enough so they can use sign language. Not too close and not too far, just the right spot. We don't want the little helicopter to get hurt anymore.

J: 'Cause helicopters can crash.

RS: That's what will happen if we don't find the right spot. Let's see, what can we do? The little helicopter needs gas, but he can't get it from the big helicopter who has a lot of gas.

J: You got a ruler?

RS: Here you go.

J: [Measures off distance.] Here . . . right here is the spot.

RS: Where he can get gas and not lose anything.

J: It could explode.

RS: Not if he's careful about the distance. What if he goes too far away from . . .

J: He'll crash.

RS: Like people. People sort of need gas too.

J: You mean food.

RS: You know what I mean.

J: Stuff to keep you going.

RS: Exactly. Just like someone you and I both know.

J: [Smiles] There are no helicopters in my family.

RS: Sometimes we need love and affection, but can't find the right spot.

Travel too far away and we get lost: parents get angry. Get too close and people will think you're a baby.

Session 3

Despite Jamal's rejection of structured play in the first two sessions, I tried again. This time I constructed an intricate facsimile of a school classroom with wooden blocks, playhouse furniture, and dolls.

The therapeutic work was placed within an academic context because school represented for Jamal an area of relatively high competence. And, the relatively mild conflicts at school seemed an excellent way to link together problems with his male teacher, stepfather, and birth father.

RS: Hello. I was just working on my school.

J: The police came, to school, and talked about drugs because they're bad for you.

RS: You're wondering about Dad and how's he doing?

J: You can die.

RS: You want to do something about it. Want to protect him like Mom and Robert want to protect and take care of you.

J: I can. Friday I have a birthday party in class. Do you think Superman will come?

RS: Superman?

J: I want Superman to come to the party or maybe Spiderman.

RS: Perhaps he can help?

J: He can come down from the sky and swoosh. [He takes a superhero figure from his backpack and flies it around the table.] He can come down from the sky like He Man and then he will find him.

RS: You wish Superman, Spiderman, and He Man could help you with this serious problem. It interesting that *you* won't let your mother or Robert rescue you, but you'll let these guys do it.

J: I keep telling you I'm not a baby.

RS: No, you're not a baby. You know you have your own Superman and Superwoman to help you.

J: You mean Wonder Woman.

RS: Sorry.

J: She can't fly.

RS: Neither can you.

Session 4

To get at relationships among family members, I arranged dollhouse furniture and blocks to resemble the floor plan of Jamal's apartment.

RS: So how's it going?

J: I'm much better this week. I only had a small problem last week.

RS: Why do you think things have changed? Why are things better for you?

J: Did I tell you my grandmother lives upstairs?

RS: I thought it was your great aunt who lives upstairs?

J: [Jamal tries and fails to explain his relationship with the grandmother/ aunt. Finally exasperated, he says:] I can't figure it out.

RS: Let's see if we can figure it out together. [I draw a genogram representing Jamal, his mother, and great aunt.] Have I got it right?

J: Right. My grandmother died years ago like in the '60s and her sister took care of my mom growing up. I call her Auntie and sometimes Grandma. The family never goes apart.

RS: Never?

J: Mean my dad?

RS: Right again. Let's draw your new family. [I graph a genogram.] So, before when things weren't going so well your mom and Robert and your baby brother were connected together. [I connected them with lines.]

J: Wait a minute, give me the marker. Before it was like this. [He writes "EMPTY" below his name and "FULL" below his brother's name.] Now it's like this. [He writes "HALF" below his name and the same below the name of his brother.]

RS: Well, that is truly remarkable. I'll go back to my original question and the real reason we met together each week. Why do you think things have changed?

J: My father [stepfather] treats me with [he writes "more respect" over his name].

RS: I don't know. Do you think someone else has done something very special to make things better?

J: Maybe my ma.

RS: You're leaving out the most important person.

J: You mean me?

RS: Right again. Here, let me show you something. [I draw a boy standing in front of a video arcade machine.] Now here's his "I'm feeling okay and everybody loves me" gauge on his wrist. When this boy was sad or lonely or felt left out he would . . .

J: I know! He plugged himself in like this. [He draws a hose or umbilical cord from the video game to the boy's wrist.] It's just like a gas station.

Working-Through Phase

In the working-through phase, the child experiences the ambivalence that ensues once the limits of time are realized, and he or she confronts the finite, imperfect nature of all interpersonal relationships. At this critical juncture in the treatment, the child becomes aware of the grief and anxiety surrounding disengagement and termination. With the emergence of separation anxiety, resistances emerge, and the child acts out both ambivalence and discouragement. Confronted with the inevitable, that time is running out, and that much in life is unattainable, both therapist and child gradually acknowledge that they are helpless to ward off its arrival. As time, and its cohort, reality, begin to encroach on the fantasy of an unending affiliation, of interminable symbiosis, the child first confronts the imperfections of the therapist and then gradually of the self. Reality begins to impinge on deeply held fantasies. At this turbulent midpoint, the therapist, ever so slowly, begins to trade on those emotional credits that accrued during the opening phase. The therapist's primary role during the working-through phase is to absorb, deflect, and reframe anger, all the while single-mindedly pursuing the core conflict.

Disenchantment can turn to hostility and it is here that the alliance is most threatened. With the therapeutic alliance on the wane, the child tries to resist the therapist's choice of play materials. With this in mind, the therapist quickly assesses the significance of any shift in the therapeutic alliance in order to avoid becoming embroiled in an unproductive struggle for control. Given the importance of collaboration within the context of the positive transference, the therapist needs to determine whether opposition is a reenactment of the central issue (transference), avoidance of the core conflict (defense), or a valid criticism of the play's irrelevance (self-assertiveness). From the child's perspective, disagreements over power almost always lead to a perception of therapist as impotent or lacking in competence. This can give the child a false sense of power over the therapist that is at once intoxicating and frightening. The child may believe that he or she has enough clout to engage the therapist in a power struggle that replicates those with other significant people in his or her other environment, such as teachers, parents, and other authority figures. What is needed is a therapist who can derail, defuse, and reframe the emerging conflict without becoming embroiled in it.

In the past, when Jamal experienced his dependency feelings as being denied, he recast this experience into pseudoautonomy. Instead of asking for more in the way of emotional support, Jamal acted as though he required very little from others. It was he, alone, who decided when to follow rules or come home from school. Within the treatment, however, I constantly challenged Jamal's effort to conjure up magical solutions to remedy his sense of isolation. I interpreted Jamal's mounting ambivalence toward me as a throwback to infantile feelings of dependency. In Jamal's case, he expressed this ambivalence as anger, but anger that had not destroyed his trust in me. This was demonstrated in session 5, when Jamal burst into my office and said, "Well, you're wrong. Last week you said my mom changed. But you're not so smart 'cause she hasn't changed at all." He then picked up the contract lying on my desk, briefly glanced at it and said, "I'll tell you what she did."

The therapeutic contract and calendar, relatively unimportant and ignored during the previous phase, began to take on meaning that was both metaphoric and tangible. Time began to force its way into the relationship. Jamal, who no more than a few weeks ago gazed at treatment across the wide expanse of time, started to contemplate separation: separation not only from this newly developed relationship, but from the remnants of infantile symbiosis. The session number, mentioned at the beginning and end of each session, became an annoyance and a target of his disdain.

Session 5

Jamal began this session in a somewhat sullen and defiant mood, and went from criticizing me and the therapy, to describing an incident at school in which his teacher chastised him for not paying attention and "daydreaming."

RS: So I guess he's another grown-up who doesn't understand you.

J: Huh?

RS: I mean he didn't understand that you were thinking or trying to figure something out. I'm surprised because after all he was a 9-year-old boy a long time ago.

J: He's a moron.

RS: I've never been to your school. Could you draw me a picture of your classroom?

J: That's what it looks like, but sometimes I have different teachers.

RS: Suppose I make a list of all your subjects.

J: There's reading, math, science, art, gym, and world studies.

RS: Now, where is the best place to worry? Where's the safest place to think about you know what?

J: I think art is the best place, but it's my favorite subject. What are you making?

RS: I'm making a brain out of blocks and I'm going to pretend that it's real. Now, there is a place in our brain where we put our worries so they don't run all over the place and make a mess. Where should we make the worry room?

J: Over here, but it's not big enough. [Jamal enlarges and improves on my construction.]

RS: You made it much better. All we have to do is make a list of your worries. You tell them to me and I'll write each one down on a separate piece of paper.

J: [Jamal reels off a list.] Let me add something to it. I'll draw a picture on them to show what the worry looks like.

RS: You decorated each worry with some artwork. We're almost done. Put each worry in a different place in the worry room.

J: They can come out?

RS: Only if you tell them to. Let's see if it works. Do you want to take one out at a time? But, not all of them at once because that would make a mess and I'd get nervous.

J: Not now. Just leave it there. We can take them out next time?

Session 6

In this session, Jamal made a direct statement about the therapist's possessions, so I went looking for the transference.

J: I'm tired of these stupid, stupid things. I want to play a game.

RS: You want things to change.

J: You don't have any good things here to do. All your stuff is for babies and I'm not a baby, don't you know?

RS: You want me to see that you're all grown up.

J: Yeah, so I don't want to play your games anymore. Your stuff is stupid.

RS: My stuff is stupid and what do you think of me?

J: You're stupid, too!

RS: Why is that? [Jamal is silent.] Because I give you baby games to play when you want me to see you are all grown up?

J: You got it. [Smiles] Maybe you're not so stupid at all.

RS: If you play baby games are you worried that you might be stupid too?

J: [Looks away and is silent for a moment.] Do other kids my age play these games?

When Jamal was either unwilling or unable to answer the question why I was "stupid," he was not allowed to remain in the silence too long. Instead, I quickly reframed the negative transference into a speculative question. Jamal was redirected and protected from an unproductive display of defiance that could only disrupt the alliance and the treatment.

Family Meeting

This conference, held with the child present, provides one of many opportunities to deal with any possible destabilizing effects on the family system as the child begins to change or respond to significant others in new ways. Without parental accommodation, support, and positive reinforcement, progress can be inhibited or undermined. This is especially true should the child feel trapped between the competing and, at times, conflicting requirements of the alliance of therapy and the family. Additionally, it is here that the realignment of parent and child takes place. In the opening phase, the family perceives the therapist as the healer and the mediator, and as being omnicognizant. For treatment to succeed, and for it to continue beyond the twelve-session time limit, the parents must see themselves as empowered. In the family session, this transference of power takes place.

Jamal's parents were pleased with the fact that the presenting symptom, which went into remission by the end of the second session, was "no longer a problem." I was careful to disavow any responsibility for these positive changes. The rule of thumb here is for the therapist to take absolutely no credit for any changes cited by parent or child. I emphasized that the family was choosing to act, to do the work that was leading to significant change.

Session 7

The emergence of resistance in session 6 served as a warning to me that more resistance was in store. For this reason, I was ready to help divert Jamal from unproductive conflict and keep him focused on the central theme. Several options were available. I could have reframed Jamal's provocations as evidence of independent thought or self assertion, interpreted them as a means of resistance, and/or labeled them as unresolved and unreconcilable disagreement between friends. At different times during the working through stage, I used each of these interventions. Whatever the intervention, I later asked Jamal how significant people in his life responded when he tried to assert himself in ways that were misunderstood as acts of defiance.

At some point in this session, Jamal slowly swept the play materials off the table with his forearm as he looked to me for a response.

RS: You are showing me that you want to be grown up. You want to decide for yourself what to do. But, it says here in your therapy contract you are supposed to get what you want without making people angry at you or not like you.

J: [Smiling] I can rip that stupid thing up.

RS: But you can't make sad feelings and worries go away that easily. So, are you finished?

J: I won't do it. Rip it up, I mean.

RS: So how do you feel right now?

J: You're mad at me?

RS: Maybe you're confusing me with someone else who gets angry at you when you try to make your own decisions. I'm not your mommy or daddy. Let's see what we can do about these feelings. But first, what do we do with this mess? [Indicating the blocks that Jamal swept onto the floor.]

J: I can do it by myself.

RS: Yes, you can and we need a safe place to put these feelings. Some place where you can control them so they won't make such a mess.

J: You can't make me. You can't make me.

RS: Absolutely right. I know! I'll just take some of these blocks and stuff and make a castle.

J: [Jamal takes a figure of a medieval knight and smashes into the therapist's production.] But your castle can't stop the enemy and they attack and then . . . [The castle is destroyed.]

RS: I see. You're showing me that I didn't make it strong enough that time. I'll try again.

J: [Jamal hands therapist a large block.] You can use this over here. No, you're doing it all wrong. Let me.

RS: Oh, that's a much better idea than mine. Now, that is a strong castle. It's a place you can put all your messy feelings. They can't escape.

J: Never?

RS: Only you have the key to open the door and let them out. They can't come out without permission.

J: Like you need a pass to go to the bathroom.

RS: There you go. [Holds up a large key.] This is the pretend key to the castle. Only this key and your special powers can open the gate. Only you can decide when it's safe to let them out.

J: I can keep the key?

RS: You already have it in your brain.

J: [Jamal strengthened the walls and placed several knights along the ramparts.] They can defend the castle. When it's dangerous outside, they stay inside.

RS: How will he, I mean how will they know it's the right time to defend the castle against attack?

J: [Places a single figure on the watchtower.] They need a lookout to warn them. He's a spy.

RS: Great idea, but all these knights need a leader. They just can't do whatever they want to whenever they want. Sometimes they need advice or help or they'll get into trouble.

J: The king and queen. He's the boss and he'll listen and decide and punish them if they don't listen.

Session 8

As a follow-up to the previous session, I built a fort from wooden blocks. Once Jamal entered and was seated at the play table, I slowly bumped into it so it would be reduced into rubble. After I built the third fort and demolished it, Jamal expressed annoyance.

J: Why do you keep doing that? Just leave it alone already.

RS: This is not a very safe fort. Let's rebuild it together and make it safer.

J: I don't like it when it crashes.

RS: Every time it falls down I get worried, too. It feels kind of unsafe to me. What do you think we can do to make it stronger?

J: Make the walls thicker.

RS: We tried that and it still falls down. We don't have enough know-how to make it strong and safe for all those mad and sad feelings. Who can help us?

J: You're the doctor. You're supposed to figure it out.

RS: Yeah, you and I are pretty smart, but we don't know everything. Like I don't know much about how to make a strong fort.

J: Get a "Fort Doctor."

RS: You mean like a carpenter. Do you know anyone who works with his hands?

J: Nope.

RS: Think real hard.

J: You mean my father . . . I mean my stepfather because he made the kitchen table?

RS: Great, now I know who we can ask for help.

Again, I reframed the emerging negative transference expressed by Jamal by joining him. I made allusions to his vulnerability, acknowledged his imperfections yet offered a solution that depended on the help of a person external to treatment. Jamal, threatened by my relinquishment of magic, tried to invoke the name of an imaginary doctor, but I redirected him toward a real person.

Termination

The termination phase is the most difficult to manage because it is far more intense than the stages that preceded it. A sense of loss is so palpable that it permeates every aspect of the treatment. However, it is the alliance that is most endangered and the therapist begins each session with the understanding that some unforeseen event might cause the bond between child and therapist to snap, thus ending treatment prematurely. Despite this risk, the therapist has but one path: the aggressive management of the termination. If the child cannot be held to the core conflict and helped to internalize the therapist as a temporary substitute for the earlier ambivalent object, then the time-limited modality has, for all intents and purposes, failed.

The therapist wants the experience of loss and separation, the very act of leaving, to be a genuine maturational event. Every child has his or her own way of saying good-bye, so no strict formula or script can be applied. However, the therapist strives to structure the termination so that the child can leave the therapist in a manner that is at least marginally better than the way a significant person left him or her in the past. In this new context, the internalization will be more positive, corrective, and less anger- and guilt-laden. The guiding principle is that a successful experience with separation engenders feelings of closeness despite feelings of disappointment.

Therapy places children in a kind of Catch-22. They can leave treatment in a way that replicates earlier separations, but this serves only to preserve and perhaps strengthen the conflicted past. On the other hand, they can leave the therapist in a way they would have liked significant others to have left them. However, this means relinquishing any prospect that the lost object will return in the future. The child is quite naturally angered by this state of affairs.

Often, at this phase, symptoms reemerge as the child makes a last ditch effort to prolong the therapy, resist the reality of separation, and the transformation of old dependencies. Every time resistance or its derivatives emerge, the therapist interprets them in light of the child's difficulty with separation from the therapist. Termination makes inordinate demands on the therapist, but the strength of countertransference, which emerges here with a vengeance, is the most difficult to manage. Because all therapists, on some level, are dealing with their own past separations, they must keep this very much in mind, lest they contaminate the endgame. When Jamal expressed discouragement, especially when remnants of the symptom reappeared, I remained confident, and was neither detracted nor detoured by their manifestation. Instead, the treatment remained on track with the central theme kept in focus.

A therapist's uncertainty and doubt will augment analogous feelings and cognitions in the child and then it will be impossible to sort out who owns what feelings. It is only with the family's and therapist's help that the child is able to persist in the face of this calculated loss. If powerful countertransferential issues weaken the therapist's resolve, if the therapist feels conflicted around similar issues of separation, the treatment is effectively sabotaged because he or she will not be able to focus exclusively on the child's struggle toward individuation embodied in the fixed termination. The therapist who dodges this issue, who cannot preserve the therapeutic focus, will be unable to maintain the optimal level of frustration and allow separation and individuation to go forth. Should the therapist pull away from the brink of separation, disillusionment with the therapist's omnipotence cannot occur and the entire treatment process has been for naught.

With Jamal, we devised a plan to evoke both affects engendered by the loss of the idealized father and the emotionally preoccupied mother. To modulate these strong emotions, I directed his attention away from the past and toward present and future time. Over and over again, I showed Jamal that all would not be lost when treatment ended because viable substitutes for the lost object(s) were available for the asking.

Session 9

Because time-limited play therapy is a calculated exercise in the application of optimal frustration, Jamal began to act out the core conflict in session, enabling me to label it as such. I sympathized with Jamal as he fought to express his frustration in a useful way and controlled the intensity of expression by not allowing it to escalate to a point where Jamal would feel guilty or fearful. There was no sense in letting strong affect blur his judgment to the point where he was unable to differentiate between those feelings related to significant objects and those inspired by the alliance. As expected, Jamal tried to ignore or deny the fact that we would soon separate.

In the following incident, in the midst of dramatic play with superhero figures Jamal had brought from home, the interaction between a smaller man and larger woman character suddenly turned violent. The characters pummeled one another, but a satisfactory resolution of the conflict seemed beyond Jamal's grasp. The play increased in intensity, and he was almost on the verge of losing the capacity to verbalize; the observing ego was in retreat. After several failed attempts to connect the play to a recent stressor, such as a fight at school, the central theme, or termination, I intervened.

RS: Time! Time! They're out of control and making me feel scared. They don't even remember what started the fight and they can't seem to agree on how to end this. They lost their memories.

[J intensifies the action.]

RS: This looks like professional wrestling.

J: It's the show "American Gladiators."

RS: [Takes a "father" doll who, in turn, addresses both participants.] But there are no rules here. Everyone is doing whatever they want and there is no fair play. They're out of control. Let me help.

J: What's that?

RS: My stopwatch. I'm the timekeeper, the voice of reason, but most people know me as "Mr. Cooperation."

[J continues banging each figure into the other.]

RS: [In announcer's voice] Both of you will lose points if you continue after the gong. You, little boy, just lost 5 points for that, so now you have 35 points and you're sinking fast.

J: I stopped.

RS: Now, for your next event, you will play by the rules. It's going to be fair and square because I'm "Mr. Cooperation." The winner of the next competition is the person who can stack these Tinkertoy things the highest in 15 seconds. Ready? Go.

J: He won.

RS: Yes, he did.

J: Give me that. I'll be the announcer and you do it.

RS: But there is one more competition before the next show. In this next extremely dangerous and very challenging event, the boy and the lady will work together as a team against the mean and nasty witch and her ugly son, Igor. Whoever can put the most sticks in these holes will win. Ready? Go.

Whenever children bargain for more time, or attempt to mask their fear of loss with anger, the therapist gives them assurances that they have enough time to complete their work. The following intervention, which occurred at the end of session 9, illustrates this emphasis on adaptive competence.

RS: Well, I see our time is gone for today. Session number 9 is history and that leaves three more to go. I'll see you next Friday for session number 10.

J: How about on Wednesday?

RS: Sorry, but that is the only day your mom can bring you.

J: Oh man! I'm going to miss gym for the rest of the year.

RS: It's five months until the end of school, but there are only three sessions to go. What's going on?

J: [In a whiny voice] That's too long.

RS: You are absolutely right. It is too long for things to get better. But you are the kind of kid who can do it faster than that.

J: How long?

RS: It hurts when you even think about it. You try and say it.

J: I know. I know. Three more times.

RS: See you next week.

Session 10

In session 10, I continued the process of challenging the myth of unlimited time and eternal parenting. I urged Jamal to take more and more responsibility for himself, underscoring and supporting both his own capabilities and the resources within his family. I eschewed Jamal's testing and went directly to the heart of the matter: realignment of the family. Negative comments about me, the baby brother, or the mother were either ignored or reframed.

J: [Fiddling with a can of modeling clay.] I can't get this thing open. It's stuck. [Slides the can over to the therapist.] Here, you do it.

RS: [Sliding it back.] Seems to me you can do it yourself. You think it's my job to get everything unstuck?

J: Yeah, but now you're tricking me and stuck it on real good. [He struggles with it some more and is successful.] You tried to trick me, but I tricked you!

RS: You are quite smart and, we see, quite strong and only need help with really big things.

J: Like getting along with my bratty brother.

RS: Your brother?

J: He's always crying and keeping me up all night and I can't even do my homework because he's always annoying me and getting into my stuff.

RS: What have you been doing about it?

J: I tell my mom, but she doesn't do anything. She says he's a baby and what do I expect.

RS: You don't like that answer. So what do you expect and what do you do next?

J: Just get mad. What can I do?

RS: You can't do much by yourself, I guess.

J: [Pointing to a drawing of a family on the wall.] Who's that?

RS: What are you really asking me?

J: Did you ever have a stepfather?

RS: It's tough trying to figure out how to deal with them.

J: Mine is no good at anything except taking my brother's side in everything.

RS: So he's good in taking care of your brother. He's a good-for-something kind of guy.

J: Well maybe . . . Is that what I said?

RS: So you know what that means, don't you?

J: He can take care of me?

RS: How about starting with helping you deal with the baby, since we both agree that he's an expert at that?

J: Or my mom.

RS: What do you mean?

J: Maybe my mom can help me with the brat.

RS: Now that is a second great idea!

Session 11

The pressure imposed by limited time was played out in the therapeutic relationship. At this stage, I remained attuned to and focused on all derivatives concerning time. For example, when Jamal arrived for the eleventh session, he seemed confused about which date to check off on the contract. This led him to question the accuracy of my bookkeeping as well as the number of sessions until termination. "I wasn't here last week and someone put a mark here. I don't make x's, I make checks." While Jamal made no effort to destroy the contract, I kept several copies in reserve for just this sort of occasion. But the contract is not the only symbol of time subject to the child's conscious and/or unconscious anger. One child "accidentally" unplugged my clock, and announced, "There, now we have to go on forever." Another took my keys, locked the door from the inside and remarked triumphantly, "Now you can't leave and I can't go. I guess we'll have to stay here all weekend."

Whenever the therapist discusses time and its derivatives, he or she must clearly label feelings of separation and loss as an expression of the child's thoughts and feelings about termination. At the same time, the prevailing atmosphere of loss that permeates the latter part of time-limited treatment is lightened whenever the therapist can point to existing relationships that are far more permanent and potentially more satisfying than that which is being lost.

During this session, Jamal mentioned that a neighbor's car was recently stolen and wondered aloud if "my mom's car is next to go." He followed this by taking several precious minutes to rummage through his backpack for a misplaced drawing that he thought was "lost." Later, Jamal announced with a touch of defensiveness that he had to "leave early," but couldn't for the life of him come up with a compelling reason to do so.

J: [Picking up a mechanical lead pencil.] This is neat. Can I take it home? I'll bring it back next week.

RS: I have something you want. What else do you want?

J: I don't have this.

RS: And who is not giving you what you need?

J: You mean, them?

RS: Who is supposed to give you these kinds of things?

J: Robert.

RS: Your dad.

J: He's not my father.

RS: There is the word father and then there is the person who acts like a father.

J: I don't want to call him that.

RS: I understand that you're holding that name for father number one. You don't want to use it up in case he returns. It's like leaving a space for him.

J: I know he's not coming back.

RS: How do you fill up this space? Or, do you just leave it empty like a parking spot? Or, do you go looking for it by being an expert video game player?

Five minutes later the issue of time once again emerged as Jamal struggled to reconcile his need for a father, his wish for an all-knowing special friend (the idealized father), and the remote possibility that his stepfather could be a "just good enough" substitute.

J: Will I miss being a child after I'm grown up?

RS: What do you think?

J: Yes.

RS: So what do you think you'll be missing?

J: Playing with Ninja Turtles . . . being a kid.

RS: You'll lose something if you grow up.

J: Do I have to?

RS: Yes and no. What would it be like if you could turn back the clock; rewind the tape?

J: Could I still wind it ahead?

RS: It's up to you.

J:Oh, okay . . . then I would go back to the time before Andrew was born.

RS: How would that change things?

J: I would be born last.

RS: So you'd be the baby and Andrew would be the oldest son. You would reverse things.

J: Then I would get special treatment and I'd be alone with my mother and father. I mean my real father.

RS: So you want to get younger, want to make time go backward, want to keep trying this because it's the only way you know how to get love.

J: It's impossible! I hate them.

RS: You're angry and disappointed. They don't know how hard you're working to try to put everything back together again.

J: It makes me even madder. Like I had a bad day at camp and I tried to tell my mother about it. The swimming teacher, he's like a monster and he embarrassed me in front of everyone and I tried to tell Mom, but she said I was "setting myself up."

RS: What does that mean?

J: I don't want to talk about it.

RS: Because I don't understand like Mom?

J: Just forget it, man! Just forget it.

RS: You feel hurt when people don't understand how hard you're trying. Who are you upset with, me or Mom?

J: Both, you and her, but her more.

RS: Is this what happens at home, at school and at camp? Grown-ups don't listen or understand and you feel they don't love you?

J: They're always too busy, anyway.

RS: What about me? With only two sessions to go, am I too busy?

J: I know what you want me to do. You want me to do something about it, but I can't. I'm only a kid and it's three against one.

RS: You were telling me that Mom said "you're setting yourself up." She was sort of saying it was you who were responsible for the way the swimming teacher spoke to you.

J: I heard them [parents] talking about it. Don't tell them this part, okay?

RS: No problem.

J: My dad said I was having a difficult time with camp, but it was only my first day.

RS: So he was defending you? Did he ever go to camp?

J: I'll go ask him right now. I'll be right back.

RS: Hold it a minute. Actually 10 minutes. We have 10 minutes to go today and we have only one more session left before we stop. You have plenty of time to talk to him and find out if he knows what it's like to be a 9-year-old-boy.

Session 12

This is the last session, at the end of which the therapist meets with both the child and the parents for a 20-minute wrap-up discussion. Both segments are extremely important; the therapist brings together as many aspects of the treatment and supports both parents and child to continue after treatment whatever has been achieved in the twelve weeks. Often, the family cancels the last session or does not come, in a bid for eternal time or because it is too distressing to face the pain and trauma of separation and, subsequently, the realities of one's own finiteness. When this happens, the therapist immediately reschedules the appointment, within the same week, if possible. The therapist brings much pressure to bear on the parents to insure that the family keeps this last appointment.

J: [As Jamal and I leave the waiting room, he runs ahead.] Don't say it, I know. It's our last time today. Good old number twelve. And we have noooooooo more times left, so let's get going.

RS: You are in a big rush to start our session today.

J: Well, I know that you're going to see my parents today and so I want to get our stuff done before.

RS: Stuff?

J: [Pulls a computer floppy disk from his coat pocket.] My dad gave this to me on the way here and I want to play it. Let's do it. It's called "Where in the World Is Carmen SanDiego?" It asks you questions, and if you answer them right, you find her. She's hiding someplace. I thought you had a computer in here someplace. Are you hiding it on me?

RS: Let me see if I have this right: you think the computer is hidden and your job is to find it. You think this Carmen SanDiego person is hidden and it's your job to find her, and if my memory serves me right, your dad, number-one, is hidden and . . .

J: Your job is to find him. No, just kidding. I think he's gone. Maybe he doesn't want to be found. Maybe he doesn't exist anymore.

RS: Doesn't exist anymore?

J: Like he's dead. Could be. Could have been an earthquake or something, or AIDS. Found him once, but haven't seen him in a long time. All kinds of stuff could have happened to him, but maybe he is just hiding.

RS: And your job is to keep looking for him, like Carmen SanDiego? Or do you think it is my job? I'm confused.

J: No. It was my job, but not anymore. Doesn't matter. Even when I did find him, it doesn't matter.

RS: Doesn't matter?

J: He doesn't want to come home anyway, even if he's not dead.

RS: So, now I understand what you mean by not existing anymore. He doesn't really exist for you, is what you're saying.

J: [Fiddles with the computer disk, still in his hands.] Is it time to see my parents yet?

RS: You think time has run out?

J: Not yet. Almost. Let's play with this first. Did someone take your computer?

RS: You look around and feel that something is lost.

J: My dad got this for me, but I know what he's trying to do. Get me to stop going to video parlors.

RS: Or get you to be home with your family.

J: Probably. You never had a computer in here?

RS: Do I disappoint you?

J: You're okay.

RS: And you?

J: You know what I want? Three zillion video games.

RS: Three zillion? Quite a lot.

J: Yeah. But you know what I really want? To be able to come back here three zillion more times.

RS: I will miss you too, but our work is almost done and you've done such a great job that you don't need therapy anymore. You have figured out how to get the people who are around you and care for you to show you that they do love you and want to take care of you. You have learned that you have 9-year-old jobs like making friends, going to school, being part of your new family, and that your parents have their jobs, too, and that, finally, you can't be expected to take on their jobs as well as yours.

J: I can't make my real dad come home either. He can't even make himself do it, so how can I?

RS: You are really clear about that now and know that your family is there for you to help you sort things out when you are not so clear. Together you are . . .

J: Don't say it! Don't say it! The Brady Bunch.

RS: What's the Brady Bunch have to do with this?

J: Number One Son [gesturing proudly to himself], Number Two Son [making a face], Number Two Dad [rolling his eyes], and Number One Mom.

RS: Sounds to me like you figured it out just fine.

I met with Jamal and his parents immediately following this last individual session. A quick overview of the treatment began the session, looking at what brought Jamal into treatment, the kinds of frustrations the family was experiencing, and the behaviors exhibited by Jamal. I helped the family understand that they had come down a very difficult road together, and that any positive changes in behavior or functioning were the result of their own efforts. My aim was to empower the family. Once this was underscored, the family was supported to continue using their own resources for any difficulties that may arise. I went so far as to predict that Jamal would have some kind of relapse in the not too distant future or, failing this, then at some especially stressful moment in the life of the family such as during adolescence when phase-specific frictions between parent and child usually intensify. I assured Jamal and his parents that since they had resolved the present difficulties, they had it within their repertoire to handle any and all problems that might crop up again.

The play therapist formally ends the treatment process with a six-month follow-up when he or she contacts the family and asks them to come in for this purpose. Essentially, this follow-up session is a facsimile of the last family meeting in week 12 of the treatment proper. It serves to reinforce those new lines of communication, and family alignments fostered and nurtured by the therapy. As a psychological tune-up, it serves to revitalize the family's confidence that they have sufficient skills, insights, and abilities to continue without the therapy. Although events and circumstances may conspire against such a face-to-face meeting, the therapist makes every effort to effect it. If a family can be reached by phone, but they are unable to schedule an appointment, the therapist does the follow-up by phone. With this case, events conspired against a follow-up session, but we learned by phone that Jamal continued to make good progress and his parents felt no need to return for additional treatment.

DISCUSSION

Time-limited play therapy is an extremely effective model of treatment when careful attention is paid to appropriate patient selection, the choice of a central theme, and the goodness-of-fit between therapists and the treatment modality. Essentially, therapists engaging in this modality of treatment must be comfortable with an active, directive therapeutic stance and must possess a high tolerance for the pressures this unique model presents. These pressures include enduring many beginnings, intense engagement, and constant separations, as well as confronting their own individual issues of loss and control again and again. Furthermore, time-limited therapists must have high tolerance for brief, yet satisfying relationships. And they must be prepared to say more good-byes than most of us would care to do in a lifetime. Therapists must be prepared to terminate before they have plumbed the depths of the child or the family's psyche. Many mental health workers go into this profession because they enjoy the very satisfactions time-limited therapy will deny them; the enjoyment of intimate and long-lasting relationships that develop between child and therapist over time. There is something deeply fulfilling in the nurturing relationship that is a hallmark of psychotherapy. But, in time-limited therapy, therapists must be willing to redirect or restart the child's stalled psychic engine and then be gone. In most cases, they will never see the complete fruit of their labors, because the family and child do most of the work after the treatment has ended.

Another characteristic of time-limited therapists is that they must remain actively alert to all the derivatives of the central theme, as they screen out the irrelevant and nonessential. They need to be sensitive to the focus, the stage of treatment, the alignment between themselves and the child, searching for negative transference, their own countertransference, as well as for references to time, and resistances in order that they may quickly be deferred. Unflaggingly, they must bear in mind: "What is the plan? Where are we going? How does this particular session, what the patient is saying and doing, fit in with this plan?" In concordance with this, therapists must continually assess when to be supportive of the child and when to be directive.

Time-limited treatment not only requires qualitatively different approaches to treatment than the longer-term models, but an entirely different approach to patient and family assessment, to pinpointing and prioritizing these assessment findings, to the preplanning of each session, to the termination process and to the expectation that the therapeutic gains will continue beyond the treatment. While this is a highly effective treatment, like all modalities, it has limitations; it is only for some children, for some therapists, and for some presenting problems.

By equal turns, this case has as much to commend it as to condemn it. It would be all too easy to dismiss this treatment of Jamal as unrepresentative of the majority of cases presenting themselves for time-limited treatment. For example, one might argue that Jamal was unusually articulate, insightful, and sophisticated, and that virtually any psychotherapeutic modality would have worked given this child's unusual array of strengths. In fact, Jamal was in many ways a very average child. What distinguished him from other children his age, was an astute social-intuitive intelligence and a family that, besides having the usual array of strengths and weaknesses, also possessed a commitment to finding better solutions to their difficulties. So what is so wrong with presenting this emblematic case? First of all, it has the ability both to inspire and to squelch interest in time-limited therapy in that it can give a false impression that this is an easy method to master. Nothing could be further from the truth. This is therapy in a "hothouse" environment where each session is characterized by an almost hurly-burly atmosphere. This affects both training and supervision, in that it requires a decided shift in orientation from "What happened last session?" to "What do you plan to do with the next 50 minutes?" Trainees frequently report that they leave each session emotionally, and, in some instances, physically drained, for it is neither an entirely meditative nor a reflective experience.

A psychotherapist cannot have a full load of time-limited cases, as he or she would almost certainly experience an emotional meltdown within a short period of time. Furthermore, the repetitive pattern of intimacy and loss can be too much to bear over a long period of time. In our treatment of Jamal, we encountered an exceptional child who was insightful enough to articulate the inner workings of our time-limited approach and we were grateful for his trust and friendship. However, it was precisely these characteristics that made it emotionally difficult for me to say good-bye to Jamal. Psychotherapists seasoned in brief treatment are not immune to these transferential issues, especially when a child's comments and actions confirm long-held beliefs about the process of short-term therapy. The authors, who have worked in the time-limited mode for almost ten years, were prepared for the inevitable feelings of sadness that beckoned for the continuation of therapy at the very moment when Jamal was preparing to terminate. The same cannot be said for psychotherapists-in-training and therapists primarily experienced in long-term treatment. They are less prepared for the ordeal and, unless closely supervised, will find a host of ways to prolong the treatment beyond its fixed date of termination, all in an effort to defend themselves against the experience of loss.

Failures in time-limited therapy happen for two major reasons: either the therapist imposes the method on children without any reasoned consideration of the selection criteria or the therapist is ill-suited to the technique. If therapists do not take well to the constraints of time or deadlines and/or take their primary pleasures from the gradual evolution of a parent-like relationship with children, then little will be gained in the way of personal or professional satisfaction in practicing time-limited play therapy.

Brief and time-limited psychotherapy fits the authors' style of inter-action as it satisfies the therapeutic needs of the children whom we serve. Originally trained in the Freudian-Axlinian mode of psychoana-lytic play therapy, as were many of our generation, we were never completely comfortable with this paradigm because by temperament we are neither passive nor capable of keeping quiet for prolonged periods of time. Nonetheless, we did our best to adhere to the prevailing ortho-doxy of therapeutic neutrality and tried to contain an impulse to become more instructive and interactive. The long-term approach ceased to serve us well when we began work in the child psychiatric emergency room of the largest municipal hospital in New York City where a crisis mentality and interventionist attitude were required to meet the needs of our constituents. Around the same time, we were disheartened when long-term psychotherapeutic strategies failed to address many of the problems of an outpatient population. A majority of these families simply "voted with their feet" and withdrew from treatment shortly after it began. This state of affairs eventually led to the approach presented in this chapter.

In conclusion, if you don't like working "at the edge" and if taking risks is not your forte, then this method is best left to those who do. Nonetheless, given the best therapeutic fit, this is an energizing, effective, and practical mode of psychotherapy. It is a venue of great emotion and creativity and it is something that therapists and children can share to the benefit of both.

REFERENCES

Achenbach, T. M. (1981). *The Child Behavior Profile*. Burlington, VT: University of Vermont.

Budman, S. H., and Stone, J. (1983). Advances in brief psychotherapy: a review of recent literature. *Hospital and Community Psychiatry* 34:939–946.

Conn, J. H. (1948). The play-interview as an investigative and therapeutic procedure. *The Nervous Child* 7:257–286.

Connors, C. (1972). Pharmacotherapy of psychopathology in children. In *Psychopatholog-ical Disorders of Children*, ed. H. Quay and J. Werry, pp. 287–299. New York: Wiley.

Davanloo, H. (1980). *Short-Term Dynamic Psychotherapy*. New York: Jason Aronson.

Erikson, E. (1950). *Childhood and Society*. New York: W. W. Norton.

Hartner, S. (1977). A cognitive-developmental approach to children's expression of conflicting feelings and a technique to facilitate such expression in play therapy. *Journal of Consulting and Clinical Psychology* 45:417–432.

Malan, D. H. (1976). *The Frontier of Brief Psychotherapy*. New York: Plenum.

Mann, J. (1973). *Time-Limited Psychotherapy*. Cambridge, MA: Harvard University Press.

Meichenbaum, D. (1974). *Cognitive-Behavior Modification*. New York: Plenum.

Peterlin, K., and Sloves, R. (1985). Time-limited psychotherapy with children: central theme and time as major tools. *Journal of the American Academy of Child Psychiatry* 24:788–792.

Rosenthal, A. J., and Levine, S. V. (1970). Brief psychotherapy with children: a preliminary report. *American Journal of Psychiatry* 127:646–651.

Sifneos, P. E. (1979). *Short-Term Dynamic Psychotherapy*. New York: Plenum.

Sloves, R. (1988). The impact of therapeutic contracts on patient attendance and treatment outcome. *Quality Assurance Report*, OPD, Child and Adolescent Psychiatry, Kings County Hospital Center, Brooklyn, New York.

Sloves, R., and Peterlin, K. (1986). The process of time-limited psychotherapy with latency-aged children. *The Journal of the American Academy of Child Psychiatry* 25:847–851.

11

Internal and External Wars: Psychodynamic Play Therapy

Donna M. Cangelosi, PSY. D.

INTRODUCTION TO PSYCHOANALYTIC DEVELOPMENTAL PSYCHOLOGY

Psychoanalytic developmental psychology is interchangeably called ego psychology. I will use the latter, more concise name in discussing the theory to enhance the "readability" of this chapter.

Several factors led me to embrace this orientation. As the reader will find, the tenets of ego psychology address aspects of functioning and adaptation. The theory is built upon the idea that within all human beings lies a greater or lesser ability to meet the internal conflicts and external challenges that confront them. In practice, then, ego psychology focuses on strengthening existing ego functions and setting up conditions for the development of those that are lacking. I find the theory to be positive and extremely hopeful.

As suggested by the term "psychoanalytic developmental psychology," the tenets of this school of thought derive from observations and investigations of the developmental processes of children. The theory provides a rich clinical framework regarding normality and pathology along what Anna Freud (1965) called "developmental lines." Working from an ego psychology perspective allows the clinician an understanding of ego processes that are working effectively, as well as those that are undeveloped or lacking. I find this understanding of gradations

---

Note: Special thanks to Merle Rosenfelt, ACSW, for her helpful insights and suggestions.

of psychopathology particularly helpful when working with children in clinical settings who, as Anna Freud (1965) noted, often present with weaknesses and immaturities of ego structure.

Historical Description

Ego psychology evolved from Sigmund Freud's structural theory (1923) in which he delineated three mental structures: the id, the ego, and the superego. Within this theory, Freud hypothesized that the ego carries out a defensive function and is responsible for repression. Freud identified the primary goal of psychoanalysis as "removing resistances which the ego displays against concerning itself with the repressed" (1923, p. 7). Stated simply, the goal of psychoanalysis, as Freud saw it, is to make the unconscious conscious.

While Anna Freud (1966) incorporated her father's mental structures and libidinal/psychosexual phases (oral, anal, phallic, latency, genital) into work with children, she focused less on the id and more on the functions of the ego. She was less interested in undoing repressions and much more attentive to the mechanisms that the ego uses to deal with conflicts stemming from id impulses and demands of the superego. Anna Freud's attention was particularly focused on defense mechanisms and the ego's attempts at mastery (A. Freud 1966).

Heinz Hartmann (1958), who is often called the father of ego psychology, focused specifically on the adaptive functions of the ego and was the first to propose that a "conflict-free sphere" exists within the ego. Functions such as perception, reality testing, memory, and concentration are but a few of these. Hartmann (1958) suggested that adaptation depends upon the interaction between the child's innate endowment and the characteristics of the postnatal environment. Here, a reciprocal relationship exists that, in favorable situations, allows the child to develop the ego capacities that promote adaptation to both internal (intrapsychic) and external demands.

More recent developments in the evolution of ego psychology have come from direct observations of infants and mothers. Mahler and colleagues (1975) developed a theory that outlines a series of phases that lead to the child's "psychological birth" or capacity for independent functioning. This process begins with a phase of absolute dependence upon mother or symbiosis. Under optimal conditions, this phase is followed by a gradual separation. The child's growing ability to function separately depends on his/her experience of a mothering person who acts as a "reference point" for the child's activities and at the same time allows him or her the freedom to explore and independently negotiate the external world.

Resolution of this separation/individuation phase of development requires object constancy that "depends upon the gradual internalization of a constant positively cathected, inner image of the mother" (Mahler et al. 1975, p. 109). This gradual process of taking the mother in and identifying with her enables the child to increasingly take on the roles and functions of mother. The child, therefore, functions separately despite a longing for mother. When the child achieves object constancy the "internal mother" or intrapsychic representation of the mother supplies comfort to him or her when mother is physically absent.

This theory holds that psychopathology results from inadequate negotiation of one or more developmental subphases which, in turn, brings about deficiencies of ego structure. It therefore follows that the therapist can analyze developmental arrests and help the client work them through in the therapeutic relationship. For instance, Blanck and Blanck (1974) propose that empathic relatedness by the therapist is a regulatory function that promotes the patient's psychological growth. Establishing a therapeutic alliance is a very important aspect of ego psychology. The therapeutic relationship requires that the therapist be responsive to the child's need, not only for closeness but also for autonomy.

The Therapeutic Relationship

In conceptualizing the therapeutic relationship within an ego psychology framework, Anna Freud (1968) contrasted the differences between adult patients and child patients. One important consideration is that the child-patient never makes the decision to seek treatment, but instead, the child's parents or guardians make this decision. The therapist is a stranger to the child, and therapy, in general, is a totally new and unfamiliar experience. An even greater difficulty is that, in many cases, the child does not suffer nor is he or she aware of a problem. Frequently, the child's symptoms affect the environment and other people more than they affect the child. Child therapy, therefore, lacks three major components that are crucial in adult treatment: insight regarding the illness, voluntary involvement, and the wish to be cured.

Anna Freud (1968) proposed that, unlike adult psychoanalysis, treatment of children requires a period of preparation. During this period of preparation, the therapist's focus is to help the child become "analyzable" by increasing his or her insight, imparting confidence in the therapist, and turning the decision for treatment from one taken by others to one controlled by the child.

Anna Freud (1968) proposed that an "affectionate attachment" is a prerequisite to analytic work with children. She stressed that the therapist must assist the child in developing a strong attachment to the therapist. The child must come to see the therapist as a person who wants to help. Parents have an important role in this process. They must join the therapist and the part of the child's ego that wishes to be helped by conveying a clear, supportive message regarding the treatment.

Within the ego psychology perspective, theorists and clinicians disagree regarding whether or not a transference can develop in the treatment of children and the extent to which it does. I am in agreement with Glen (1978), who notes that the therapeutic alliance is based on both the child's belief in the therapist as a helpful ally and on positive transferences and displacements. Glen defines transferences as "displacements to the analyst of emotions and defenses that appeared toward the parents in earlier periods of life" (p. 176). In addition, he notes, that young children frequently experience feelings and use defenses in the therapeutic situation that may be related to the child's current home situation.

Therapeutic Techniques

Within the ego psychological perspective, therapists use play as a means of getting acquainted with the child, gaining the child's confidence, engaging the child in a positive therapeutic relationship, and as a psychoanalytic tool and means of communication. During the initial phase of treatment, the therapist begins to piece together the history of the child's difficulties from information provided by parents and clinical observations of the child. The child's play provides valuable information regarding conflicts, impulses, interpersonal skills, defenses, fantasy life, and levels of functioning of the id, ego, and superego.

The therapist allows the child's play activity to unfold naturally with as little interruption as possible. By following the child's lead and encouraging him or her to tell the therapist what to do or say or be through dramatic play, the dialogue will depict the child's concerns and needs.

The therapist uses four interventions. Initially, the therapist points out behaviors, play themes, or any important observable phenomenon through "confrontation." The play therapist attempts to make the issue at hand explicit to the child in an attempt to enhance the capacity of his or her observing ego. "Clarification" is used to further this process. Here, the therapist asks detailed questions to clarify the behavior, to paint a picture of what is occurring, to increase the child's awareness, and to explore related affect. The therapist generally points out defenses before content or drives.

Both confrontation and clarification deal with conscious behaviors and are precursors to interpretation. The psychodynamically oriented therapist's "interpretation" is an explanation that he or she uses to help the child understand the source, history, and meaning of defenses, content, and drives. This insight allows for the child to "work through" his or her issues.

In treatment, the child's conflicts and fantasies become more apparent, resulting in increased malleability in his or her defensive structure and the use of more adaptive defenses. Through this process, the child achieves greater drive satisfaction in a more adaptive manner. When treatment is successful, the child proceeds to more advanced libidinal stages. As greater ego maturity develops, the child comes to replace primary process thinking with secondary process thinking (Glen 1978). With regard to technique, focus is on strengthening the ego by supporting all areas of healthy, adaptive functioning and by assisting the child in replacing nonadaptive defenses, symptoms, thoughts, and behaviors with more functional mechanisms. With young children, the therapist commonly takes on educative functions in the working-through phase of treatment to facilitate this process.

Theory of Play

The interest of psychoanalysts in play evolved from the early observations of Sigmund Freud (1920). He believed that the child at play creates a world of his or her own by rearranging things in a new, more pleasing way.

Freud (1920) was concerned with the child's need to transpose his or her role from passivity to activity. He observed that things are done to children over which they have no control. From this experience stems a desire to be grown up and to gain control. This theory explains why, in children's play, they convert passive experiences into active ones and why much play is imitative of adult roles.

Freud (1920) saw play as a critical process for the development of ego strength in the normal child. He believed that play is an act, partially separated from reality, that allows the child's ego to bend with the demands of the id and the superego. The child can try out new mechanisms through play, thus exercising the ego to work out id and superego conflicts. Play, according to this theory, involves the acquisition of control by the ego and the healing of the effects of the child's loss of control.

This tenet of the psychoanalytic approach stems from Freud's (1920) formulation of the repetition compulsion—the organism's need to repeat an experience that had formerly been overwhelming. Freud observed this process in his 18-month-old grandson who repeatedly threw away and retrieved a bobbin of string. Freud understood this act as the child's attempt to master his separation from his mother.

Waelder (1933) explains that repetition of an unpleasant experience is a process by which excessive experiences are divided into small quantities, reattempted, and assimilated in play. This gradual mechanism of assimilation serves the same purpose as the processes of mourning, fantasy, and nightmares: to diminish the residual impact of overwhelming experiences, thus allowing the child to come to terms with them.

In outlining psychoanalytic theories regarding play, Greenacre (1959) describes six psychic functions of play. These are wish fulfillment, instinct of mastery, assimilation of overpowering experiences according to the mechanisms of the repetition compulsion, transformation from passivity to activity, leave of absence from reality and from superego, and fantasies about real objects. In addition to this list, play also serves a cathartic function. It enables the child to purge unvented feelings, through which the child gains increased self-awareness and has an opportunity to develop improved ego functions.

PRESENTING PROBLEM AND BACKGROUND DATA

Eric was $6\frac{1}{2}$ years old at the time of the initial referral. His father contacted me by phone to request play therapy. He stated that Eric had "discipline problems" both at home and at school and that he had been developing a hostile attitude toward his mother. Eric also "refused to do his homework without a fight" and frequently resisted going to school. These problems had begun to surface six months earlier and the school psychologist was providing bimonthly counseling for Eric. At the time of the initial phone contact, Mr. K. noted that although they were still living together, he and his wife were having serious marital problems and were pursuing a divorce. Eric was aware of their plan to divorce.

Mr. K. felt that Eric would need assistance preparing for the impending divorce.

I told Mr. K. that I would like to meet with him and Mrs. K. to obtain more information regarding Eric's current home and school environments, relationships, and developmental history. I asked if he and Mrs. K. were on amiable terms or if he would prefer separate meetings with me. Mr. K. noted that both he and Mrs. K. would prefer to meet together with me to ensure that I understand both perspectives. He candidly noted that they did not trust one another.

I was in my first year of private practice at the time of this call. I had just completed my dissertation, which was a study of the effects on children of parental divorce. Given the fact that this subject was so fresh in my mind, I had many concerns about what Eric might be experiencing. The fact that his parents were telling him that they were divorcing, yet they were still living together could be an extremely confusing message to a 6-year-old child. I had many questions regarding how this was being addressed at home with Eric and what the climate of his home environment was like. What was Eric's perception of his parents' relationship? What was the nature of his own relationship with each parent? What kinds of verbal and nonverbal messages were being conveyed to Eric regarding his parents' differences? The answers to these questions would shed light not only on the symptoms and presenting problems, but also on the most appropriate interventions for Eric and his family.

During the initial parent meeting, Mr. and Mrs. K. sat on opposite sides of the couch. While they spoke with one another, there was a cool distance in their exchanges and a very apparent lack of cooperation between them. They agreed about one thing and one thing only—that Eric's problems were stemming from long-standing marital difficulties. They described Eric as an aggressive and often violent child. Mr. K. clarified that Eric's violence was first evidenced with peers one and a half years earlier, at which time he was transferred to a different school in the same town. More recently, Eric's violence was directed toward his mother.

While Eric had a tendency to be "nasty" and uncooperative with his father, Eric had never demonstrated physically violent behaviors toward him. In contrast, Eric frequently punched, kicked, and threw things at his mother. These behaviors usually followed Mrs. K.'s attempts at disciplining Eric, setting limits, or instructing him to finish homework, to get ready for school, or to carry out other responsibilities. Mrs. K.'s way of dealing with Eric's violence was to hit him back. The latter caused long and often uncontrollable fights.

Mr. K. stated that in the past he took it upon himself to break up the fights between Eric and his mother. More recently, he had decided to stay out of it so that Eric would not see him as "the bad guy." Furthermore, he felt that Eric's anger toward Mrs. K. was warranted because she was frequently unavailable to Eric. Mr. K. accused his wife of working too much and of leading a chaotic life-style. He believed that Eric's aggressive behaviors were Eric's attempts to get much-needed attention from his mother.

At the time of this intake, Mrs. K. was working two part-time jobs and was very involved with a volunteer organization. She agreed that she was extremely busy, but accused her husband of being the one who had been unavailable to her due to his own busy schedule. At the time Mr. K. was working and completing college.

The couple shared that they had been involved in marital counseling five years earlier. While their involvement in counseling lasted for a full year, they were never able to reconcile their differences or their lack of trust toward one another. They had both given up on the marriage, but maintained that they had to continue living together due to financial issues that would be resolved at the time of the divorce. They managed to cope with this arrangement by having as little physical and verbal contact with one another as possible. Each parent spent time with Eric separately. While they were not yet residing in separate homes, they managed to live separately within the same home with Eric as the only bridge between them. Mr. and Mrs. K. no longer argued. Instead, they ignored one another in a kind of "silent war."

Mr. and Mrs. K. presented as two very different people with extremely distinct philosophies and views of child rearing and opposing perspectives regarding Eric and his needs. Mr. K. was very focused on providing structure for Eric. He attempted to schedule playtime after school, followed by dinner, television, and a set bedtime. He criticized Mrs. K. for not having any schedule for either herself or Eric and went on to describe her as "chaotic, unorganized, inconsistent, and messy." Mr. K. believed that Eric needed guidance, structure, consistency, and discipline, while Mrs. K. was very focused on his need for autonomy and experiences outside of the home. She was very invested in involving Eric in extracurricular activities to help him expend his aggressive energies (i.e., karate) and intellectual talents (i.e., enrichment programs).

I set up a second appointment with Mr. and Mrs. K. for several reasons: (a) to complete the developmental history; (b) to further assess their levels of functioning, parenting skills, and openness for intervention; (c) to elicit their support of and involvement in Eric's treatment;

and (d) to work with them regarding how to prepare Eric for his initial session.

Both parents were very involved in describing Eric's developmental milestones. Being their only child, they recalled many details about his development and spoke about him in a proud manner. Minor complications occurred in Eric's delivery that required the use of forceps. He weighed eight pounds at birth. Both parents were "thrilled" about his arrival, despite their many marital problems at the time. Eric "refused to breast-feed" and was therefore bottle-fed. Mrs. K. was unable to expand on this experience.

Eric was hospitalized for acute respiratory problems and was subsequently diagnosed with asthma at 2½ months old. His physician had prescribed Ventolin. Developmental milestones were all within the norm and Eric was consistently described by both parents as bright and advanced.

Eric began a full-day nursery school program at the age of 2. His father was opposed to this, because he wanted his wife to stay home to care for Eric. However, she preferred to work outside of the home and felt that involvement with other children would be positive for Eric because he was an only child.

Eric began kindergarten early due to a late birthday (i.e., at 4 years 10 months old). Mrs. K. reported that she had many regrets about making the decision to enroll him at such a young age. She attributed his aggressiveness toward classmates to his sense of feeling inferior to them. Mrs. K. perceived Eric's aggressiveness as his way of "proving himself" to his older classmates.

Academically, Eric was achieving good grades. However, his resistance to doing homework and reported difficulty with "self -control" by his second grade teacher caused his parents concern. Additional areas of concern, as outlined by Mr. K., were Eric's tendency to be overweight ("like his mother"), resistance to sleeping in his own bed, complaints of stomachaches when going to school, temper tantrums, limited ability to enjoy himself and pervasive tenseness. While Eric's parents described him as a child who makes friends easily, he seemed to have some difficulties maintaining relationships due to fights.

By the close of the second session, I had the feeling that, despite their differences and the animosity between them, Mr. and Mrs. K. were not only very concerned about their son, but also willing to work with me on his behalf. I explained that I would like to meet with Eric individually for several sessions to further assess his difficulties. I informed them that I would be meeting with them again to provide feedback and specific recommendations after these initial sessions with Eric.

Mr. and Mrs. K. came together to bring Eric for his first session. He presented as a very appealing child who was large in stature for his chronological age. Eric seemed eager to meet with me. He separated from his parents without hesitation and presented me with his favorite stuffed animal. His mother informed me that Eric had had this stuffed animal since he was an infant. Throughout this session, Eric spoke timidly in a whisper-like, baby voice. Initially, he shared that his stuffed animal was torn and how he wanted his mother to sew it up. He later shared his understanding that I was a "feeling doctor." We discussed the fact that I had toys in the office and that I would help him to deal with sad, worried, and angry feelings.

Only Mrs. K. brought Eric for his second session. In contrast to the previous session, Eric arrived in an angry mood and resisted entering the office. Eric and Mrs. K. were in the midst of a battle. Eric had thrown a rock at her prior to leaving home for the session. After standing in the doorway for some time, Eric eventually entered the office. He proceeded to explore play materials. Eric took toys out of containers and put them back in repeatedly. When he came upon soldiers, he set up "a war between the United States and Russia." At the end of the session, he asked if he could show his mother the way he set up the scene. I simply highlighted that he wanted to show his mom what a good job he did.

THEORETICAL CONCEPTUALIZATION

The first two sessions with Eric, together with the information shared by his parents, reveal several patterns regarding the challenges confronting this child. Mrs. K. consistently spoke about Eric as if he was a significantly older child. Consequently, she pushed him toward self-sufficiency by enrolling him in nursery school, kindergarten, and extracurricular activities prematurely. She was not attuned to her son's needs for nurturance and closeness. Instead, she involved him in autonomous experiences outside of the home, which caused him to feel alone, disconnected, vulnerable, and needy. While it was difficult to piece together the beginnings of this dynamic, it appeared that this process may have been operative when Eric was an infant and "refused to breast-feed."

I felt that Eric was likely to have experienced being in nursery school on a full-time basis at the early age of 2 as overwhelming if his needs for nurturance were not adequately met. Mahler and colleagues (1975) noted that toddlers become aware of their separateness from mother during the second year of life. At this time, separation anxiety becomes apparent, as well as a fear of object loss. The child experiences a wish to explore and be free, yet simultaneously and in a very real (physical) sense, needs his or her mother to be close, supportive, and emotionally available. It appeared to me that Eric was emotionally on his own during this very sensitive period of development. He did not have the opportunity to separate gradually and at his own pace. My impression was that as soon as Eric could walk he was on his own. Eric's more recent resistance to doing homework and going to school seemed to be his ways of "putting the brakes on." These symptoms suggested that Eric was not ready for the demands being put on him. He wanted his parents to recognize this, but Mr. K.'s anxiety about Eric being out of control (like his mother) and Mrs. K.'s lack of attunement and/or anxiety about Eric's dependency needs were in the way of this insight. The preoccupation of both parents with the impending divorce was further complicating this dynamic.

In Eric's initial contact with me, he talked like a shy, timid baby and through a torn stuffed animal, conveyed his need to be recognized as a little boy. He expressed his feeling of being damaged and needing to be filled and cared for. In this contact, he expressed a wish for his mother to sew the toy. I heard this as a symbolic statement representing his vulnerability and wish to be close, nurtured, and "fixed" by her. Eric's rock-throwing prior to the second session seemed to be a reaction to feelings of vulnerability, as well as an expression of anger at his mom.

Eric's aggression toward his mother typically surfaced when she set limits or instructed Eric to do something. It was at those times when she attempted to exert control that he seemed to feel most vulnerable and out of control.

Mahler and colleagues (1975) pointed out that arrests in the separation–individuation process can result in anal conflicts that provoke intense anger for a child's mother and a simultaneous defensive attachment to her. The first two sessions with Eric clearly demonstrated the presence of this "rapprochement conflict." Eric's separation anxiety (suggested in his stomachaches before school, difficulties sleeping alone, and resistance to going to school) was yet another indication of an arrest in separation-individuation.

It was apparent to me that this delay in Eric's development, together with the climate of his home life, caused problems in his ability to resolve oedipal issues. Divorce research suggests that discord between parents during the male child's oedipal complex is particularly frightening because the boy perceives that his wish to win mother from the rivalrous father has come true (Wallerstein 1983, Wallerstein and Kelly

1972). In Eric's family, this very dynamic had occurred; his mother disliked and ignored his father and made Eric her primary focus. The child's perception of being so powerful is a frightening experience that carries with it a vulnerability and fear that retaliation will be forthcoming from the father.

It appeared that Eric had found a "safe" way to cope with this vulnerability. His overt aggression toward his mother was a way of concealing oedipal wishes toward her, and at the same time overtly showed his father that he was an ally and not an enemy. Unfortunately, this compromised Eric's need for closeness with his mother as well as his need to form a positive identification with his father. This dynamic explained Eric's rage, emptiness, neediness, and anxiety.

In addition to being in the middle of an unresolved unconscious oedipal conflict, Eric was in the middle of the silent war between his parents. Divorce research suggests that a child cannot begin to master the challenges of parental divorce until an actual separation occurs to make the experience "real" (Wallerstein 1983). In Eric's family, both parents seemed unempathic to Eric's experience of living with two parents who did not speak to one another or work together on his behalf. At the onset of treatment, there was absolutely no sense of co-parenting, much less family.

In addition to these issues, I was concerned about Mrs. K.'s approach of keeping Eric on the move whenever they had spare time and wondered what effect this had on him. Likewise, Mr. K.'s anxiety about Eric being "out of control like his mother" raised another red flag. I wondered how the parents dealt with this issue at home, what messages Eric was receiving, and the overall role that his father's focus on control, scheduling, and structure was having on his development.

In assessing Eric and his parents, I was aware that this was a very troubled family with multiple problems. Ideally, it would be helpful for both parents to be in individual treatments of their own. However, Mr. and Mrs. K. made it clear to me when I broached this subject that neither of them was open to this recommendation. I felt that play therapy would be helpful to Eric only if his parents were also willing to be involved in supplemental parent counseling and to make some changes at home. Early on, I was not sure if parent counseling sessions with Mr. and Mrs. K. together would work well. However, I felt it was important to attempt this type of treatment to promote the idea that they must co-parent Eric regardless of their marital status. I was well aware that it would be important not to join the family, but instead to join Eric. Eric's ego was working extremely hard to negotiate the many stressors and conflicts in his world. Given this objective, I saw Eric for weekly play therapy sessions and I saw his parents one to two times per month for supplemental parent counseling.

The parent counseling sessions served to facilitate Eric's treatment. I used them to obtain information regarding Eric's life outside of the treatment, to educate Mr. and Mrs. K. regarding Eric's internal experiences and how to address his psychological needs, and to obtain feedback about Eric's progress.

THE PROCESS OF PLAY THERAPY

During the initial phase of treatment, my goal was to establish a therapeutic relationship with Eric and to help him become acclimated to the atmosphere and process of play therapy. I attempted to create a climate of freedom and acceptance by giving Eric the opportunity to explore toys, as well as a new way of relating to an adult, wherein he could take the lead and set the pace.

I had very warm feelings for Eric and was repeatedly struck by the unusual degree of autonomy in this young child's life. Given his large stature and advanced verbal skills, it was no mystery why many adults treated him as if he were an older child. Nonetheless, Eric's mannerisms and behaviors were clear indications that he was not emotionally ready for so much independent functioning. My countertransferential reaction was that of sadness for this child who appeared to be "emotionally on his own." Consistent with this, I felt empathy and warm feelings toward Eric that were apparent in our exchanges, regardless of Eric's mood or demeanor.

During the first two months of treatment, Eric's presentation from week to week varied significantly. One week he was a baby, the next, he was a soldier (literally dressed in army fatigues), the next, he was a "tough guy" bragging how he "beat up a little kid." Despite this variability, he consistently enjoyed playing. Eric created elaborate scenes with soldiers. He also constructed "mechanical machine guns" out of plastic fiddlesticks and elaborated on the "power" of his creations. Play themes were consistently very aggressive. There were constant explosions, wars, and killings. Eric was unable to neutralize his aggressive impulses, and he frequently became overwhelmed by them, causing him to regress to the vulnerable baby. During this phase, I observed his dynamic and made subtle reflective comments such as, "It feels like you have to be strong and tough."

Throughout this initial phase of treatment, Eric engaged in parallel play. He was well aware of my presence, but he played in a solitary and at times very absorbed manner. I sat on the floor across from him, following his lead and periodically made descriptive comments about his play in order to join him. I hoped to convey the sense that I was attentive and interested in Eric, while at the same time, respectful of his need for autonomy.

Approximately two months into the treatment, Eric became very proficient at asking me for help with his constructions and frequently instructed me where to move "army guys," what to say, and so on. I followed his lead by whispering into his ear, asking instructions on what he wanted the toys to do and say. This transition was an important one for Eric and the manner in which he began to relate to me was very different than it had been. Initially, there was a feeling that Eric had a bubble around himself while playing that isolated him from me and ensured that he was on his own. Now, he was letting me into his world in two important ways. Emotionally, he was sharing his play experience with me by eliciting my help or involvement. At the same time, Eric was symbolically expressing his concerns with the dialogue that he created for the soldiers and other play materials.

During this phase of the treatment, Eric frequently called my answering machine on weekends (when I was not in the office) to inform me that he and his mother were fighting. At times, he talked about his extreme anger at his mother and at other times he regressed, talking "baby talk." Eric was not able to discuss these calls during our sessions. However, Mrs. K. informed me that Eric seemed to calm down after making the calls. While she saw them as a form of "time out," I conceptualized Eric's calls as indications that he wanted my help with his aggression (and his mother's) and that he found solace and a source of hope in his relationship with me. Eric was letting me know the extent of his problems through these phone calls and seemed to be soothed by my voice—a reminder, perhaps, that he was not alone.

During the fourth month of treatment, Eric's parents alerted me that he was scheduled for a tonsillectomy. During the session preceding his surgery (session 15), Eric chose to play with a game for the first time. I was fascinated to see that he chose "Operation." He pretended to be Dr. Eric who was performing surgery on a man with a broken heart. Eric shared with me that the condition was caused by cigarettes and went on to explain that "the man smokes to escape problems." I felt that Eric was attempting to shift his passive patient role to that of the active doctor through this play. This was his attempt at mastery and demonstrated that his ego was, in fact, working hard to negotiate the anxieties that were being stirred by the upcoming surgery. I supported Eric's ego by broaching the subject of his surgery and by providing some information about it. This was the first time I introduced a topic in the session and Eric seemed surprised by my interest and proceeded to talk about his doctor.

Eric missed one session due to his tonsillectomy. In the session that followed, he asked to play a game that involved cooperation and taking turns. Eric's play was significantly more interactive than it had been in the previous sessions. In addition, he was calm and did not speak with either a baby voice or a tough-guy voice. This continued for several weeks. Simultaneously, Eric's parents reported that Eric was significantly less aggressive at home toward his mother.

In the fifth month of treatment, Eric once again became very interested in army soldiers. During session 17, he assembled soldiers in a line and built a bridge so that the soldiers could get to the other side. Eric became very animated and put a great deal of energy into building this bridge. It became the focal point of the session and distracted him from the soldier's war. He was very interactive—describing his plan for designing the bridge and simultaneously asking me to hand him the fiddlesticks he was using to build it. I joined him in his play—he led and I followed.

The bridge seemed to be such a hopeful symbol for Eric—a literal sign of his psychological expansion. His play conveyed what I had been seeing in the previous weeks, that Eric was less cut off and on his own. He was attempting to find a way to have free access to others and to the different sides of himself such as the "vulnerable Eric" and the "aggressive Eric." The bridge seemed to be a metaphor for Eric's ego, which was in the process of being built. Eric's improved ability to neutralize his aggressive impulses was evidence of this enhanced functioning of his ego.

During the next session, Eric became very involved in building a vehicle that he called a "nurse mobile." It was initially designed to "protect the nurses so they could help wounded soldiers." However, over a period of many sessions (sessions 18 to 28), Eric added additional features and functions to this creation. In addition to being a safe and a war tank, it became a street cleaner, a weapon, a hiding place, a house, and eventually a mountain breaker.

The sequence in which these "functions" emerged closely paralleled the treatment and Eric's improved ego functioning. Eric began to construct his nurse mobile three weeks after his tonsillectomy. Its original purpose was nurturant in nature—to "protect nurses" so they could "help wounded soldiers." I saw it as having transferential meaning, that Eric saw me as a nurse or healer for whom he wanted to ensure safety so that I could help him. In this regard he was the "wounded soldier," who had previously been doing battle alone both internally and externally. Eric was no longer alone and wanted to preserve that state by preserving me. As he was building the nurse mobile, he was very animated. I reflected his animation and described the functions of the nurse mobile in a way that paralleled the growth I was seeing in him.

This play theme was overdetermined in that the nurses were also a part of Eric. The "safety" of the therapeutic relationship was transporting him to a place where healing could take place. Eric described the nurse mobile as a "safe," which I interpreted literally as a statement about his experience within the therapeutic relationship. In the midst of the soldiers' war, he had created a safe place. During these play sessions, I reflected how very important it was to have a safe place!

During the weeks in which Eric added to his nurse mobile, he simultaneously became very attached to me. When Eric arrived early for his sessions he became very angry and possessive when I was with another patient. He also resisted leaving sessions more and more each week. The nurse mobile seemed to serve as a transitional object during this point in the treatment. It represented the bond between us and allowed Eric an opportunity to separate in a new way. I was aware that I had to avoid rejecting him; at the same time I had to set clear structure for him. I also shared my own feelings of eagerness about spending time with him. I suggested that his father avoid bringing him a half hour before the session began.

Each week Eric entrusted me to keep this prized creation in a safe "hiding place" (i.e., my closet shelf) where no one else could see or touch it. Between sessions he frequently thought of new ideas for improving it. This process allowed Eric to internalize the therapist and therapeutic situation and thereby promoted object constancy, which began to facilitate Eric's mastery of his separation difficulties.

I took on an active role to help Eric with this process. I confronted his feelings each time he resisted leaving. In doing this, I was careful to avoid "you" statements so as to not threaten the part of Eric that was so overwhelmed by feelings of vulnerability. At the same time, I attempted to convey empathy and to help Eric acknowledge his emotional experience (e.g., "It's really hard to leave when we're having so much fun.") I found it helpful to prepare Eric for the end of each session so that he could achieve some closure and psychologically prepare for the separation from me. Whenever possible, I also attempted to pull together themes that connected the previous session with the present one to promote a sense of continuity in our relationship and our work together.

Several weeks after creating his nurse mobile, Eric added to it the function of a street cleaner. He was very invested in treatment and, like the street-cleaning nurse mobile, was in the process of clearing a path for himself. Interestingly, the very attachment that cleaned streets was later also capable of converting into a machine gun. Eric became very involved in developing the nurse mobile's capacity for warding off enemy soldiers with elaborate weaponry. The multipurpose nurse mobile empowered Eric, enabling him to master his feelings of vulnerability.

While I did not interpret oedipal themes, they appeared to be manifest in this play as well. The parallels between Eric's play themes and the changes in his family dynamics were striking. Eric's aggression toward his mother virtually disappeared and, while control battles persisted, they were now with both parents. Somehow Eric was finding relief from the burden of having to hate his mother in order to be close with his father.

In mid-July, approximately seven months into the treatment, Mr. K. informed me that Eric would be away on vacation for the month of August. In addition to this being the longest break in Eric's treatment, it was also to be the first time that Eric would be separated from his mother for more than a few days.

During the two sessions preceding his vacation, Eric expanded the nurse mobile to make a house for the nurses. I had the feeling that his providing a permanent place for them was an attempt to master his concern about whether or not he would still have a place with me and his mother when he returned from vacation. Considering the short notice that I was given about his vacation and given this child's long history of premature and abrupt separations, I felt it was important to provide reassurance in this regard. I brought up the topic and we discussed the fact that people sometimes miss one another and have feelings about separation when they are apart. During the last session, I attempted to concretize Eric's "place" by specifying the date and time of our next appointment.

Upon Eric's return from his summer vacation, he was eager to show me all the things he had thought about adding to his nurse mobile. Instead of taking the plastic tubes from the bin in which they were, Eric asked me for assistance in organizing the tubes by size and color. Eric made separate piles for each color and commented that he was "organized" like his father. He quickly added, "Don't tell my mother I said that, she'll get hurt." At this point, Eric proceeded to crash the nurse mobile into the couch. He appeared upset and while banging it announced that it was a "mountain breaker out to destroy!" As he was banging it into the couch, I highlighted that the nurse mobile was trying to destroy the mountain, but was being hurt itself. Eric became increasingly agitated and repeatedly banged the nurse mobile, despite the fact that pieces were falling off. Eric proceeded to destroy most of the nurse mobile during the session—leaving just a piece behind. His rage was reminiscent of the anger that he had previously expressed toward his mother—a sign that he was feeling alone and an indication to me that a rift had occurred in the treatment. Although Eric was the one who had left for vacation, I believe that he felt abandoned by me. His rage about this caused him to break the nurse mobile that was symbolic of everything we had built together.

The following week (session 30), Eric arrived speaking in the baby voice that he had not used for months. This seemed to be a direct reaction to the rage and aggression he had experienced in the previous session in his destruction (an "undoing") of the nurse mobile. Eric worked quietly and very diligently to restore what was left of his nurse mobile, repeatedly stating that he wanted to make it "big." This session seemed reparative for Eric. He attempted to restore and rebuild the nurse mobile and, as I saw it, to patch up the therapeutic alliance. Following his lead, I assisted Eric by handing him the various colored fiddlesticks that he needed and by supporting his efforts. Just as in the early sessions, I followed his lead and tried to be supportive of him. While we worked together to fix the nurse mobile, I simultaneously used the creation and our mutual effort to restore an empathic connection and to reestablish my role as a helpful ally.

Although Eric asked me to hide the nurse mobile after this session, he did not add to or play with it again for several months, and at no point in the treatment did he become as cathected to the creation as he had been. It seemed that we had approached a new phase of treatment.

During the months following Eric's return from vacation, his play took on a nurturant quality. Soldiers helped one another, GI Joe protected Smurfland and Eric "cured" patients while playing "Operation." Eric also showed interest in a baby doll and on several occasions, held it and/or changed its diaper. At about this time, Eric had convinced his mother to buy him a baby hamster.

During the session that followed the purchase of his new pet, Eric was happier than I had ever seen him. He discussed how little the animal was (hence its name, Peanut), as well as the many responsibilities involved in caring for it. Eric asked if it would be all right to bring Peanut to the following session, stating that he wanted us to meet each other. I joined Eric in his enthusiasm and welcomed the opportunity to meet Peanut. As planned, Eric brought Peanut to the following session and demonstrated the proper way to handle a hamster, get it out of its cage, and pet it.

I was seeing in Eric a strong identification with me. He was beginning to internalize the nurturant and soothing functions that he had experienced in our relationship. Practicing these new skills with his "little" pet allowed for mastery of his own vulnerability. Eric was no longer passive and "little," but instead active, competent, and capable of "taking care" of vulnerability. I pointed this out to him during our sessions. His role as caretaker to Peanut enabled Eric to further internalize self-soothing abilities. In one session, Eric informed me that he found comfort in petting Peanut (and Peanut's new mate, Jessie) when he was angry or upset at his mother. This indicated that Eric was not only soothing the animals, but was simultaneously comforting himself.

His increased self-soothing capacity was demonstrated more dramatically when in one session Eric accidentally hit his hand on the side of the couch. He exclaimed "ouch," proceeded to kiss his hand and said "that's what mommies do." I responded to this by highlighting that Eric was able to make himself feel better when something hurt.

With Eric's improved ego functions came a shift in the therapeutic relationship. He frequently chose games that involved cooperation, working together, and/or sharing. Eric divided Colorform pieces or blocks equally and asked that we take turns adding to the formation of a picture or building. He asked to read books aloud together, instructing me to take turns reading alternate pages while he read the others. He took an interest in drawing and frequently asked me to draw one part of a picture while he drew another part of the same picture. There was a clear sense that we were working together for a mutual purpose, and Eric related to me as helper, a protector, and, increasingly, a partner.

Eric had extreme difficulty sharing me and continued to become very angry when he arrived early to find me with another patient. As our relationship developed, he became intolerant of any communication between his parents and me at either the beginning or end of our sessions. I made a point to educate his parents about the fact that this possessiveness was a natural part of the therapy process. While his concerns clearly had a possessive, oedipal quality, they were also cast with a fear of losing me. This became more apparent when approximately twelve months into the treatment I announced that I would be moving to a different office.

I provided six weeks notice of this change to Eric and his parents to allow Eric enough time to prepare. During five of the six weeks Eric asked to take turns in reading his two favorite books. When I asked what he liked about the books, he said "I know what's gonna happen."

This statement provided a saga to the subject of my upcoming move. I made up a game that allowed Eric to ask anything he wanted about the new office. The theme of Eric's questions had to do with what I was bringing with me (i.e., "Are you bringing the couch? Are you bringing the toys?"). I answered each of his questions using special wording to dispel his concern about being left behind (e.g., "When you see it you'll see what I mean."). I also pointed out that I would be putting the nurse mobile in a box to ensure its safety during the move.

Upon Eric's arrival to the new office, he threw himself on the couch, put his hands behind his neck and said "I like this place . . . it's a lot bigger!" He proceeded to explore the new toy shelf, commenting that it, too, was bigger and had room for more toys. Eric spent most of the session exploring the office, identifying familiar toys and objects and, as I saw it, "making himself at home." There was a confidence about him that (combined with his comments) suggested that he felt the bigger office space would provide room for his growth.

In the weeks that followed, Eric consistently arrived in good spirits. One week he informed me that his hamsters had three babies. Eric took pride and credit for the expansion and well-being of Peanut's family. Simultaneously, he, himself, was experiencing a psychological rebirth of sorts. He was happy, engaging, and "lighter." Eric frequently asked to play Concentration during this phase of the treatment. We each took turns finding matching pairs of Old Maid cards by recalling their locations. Eric laughed, giggled, and became very excited each time he was able to successfully recall the locations of pairs of cards. He demonstrated an excellent memory. This, combined with Eric's increased "lightness," suggested that his ego had been freed up. Eric was demonstrating clearer thinking, increased energy, and a vivaciousness that I had not noted previously.

During our games of Concentration, Eric consistently demonstrated more competence in recalling the location of cards than I. (This was not artificially staged, but a reality!) While he took pleasure in his ability, he seemed sympathetic that I was not as capable at this task. Eric took on a nurturant, supportive stance toward me and tried to help me by providing hints. Eric was taking this opportunity to nurture and give to me. I responded to Eric's wish to "take turns" helping one another, but I silently questioned unresolved oedipal themes and whether Eric was conveying that he was uncomfortable being "a winner" for fear of hurting someone else and/or making them a loser.

We were into our seventeenth month of treatment when Eric left a message on my answering machine informing me that Peanut had died. The message was very brief and was conveyed in Eric's baby voice that

I had not heard for many months! When I called Eric back, his mother answered and told me that Eric was out with his father. She reported that Eric was quite upset and that he had been very aggressive. She had talked with Eric about Peanut's death, but felt that this talk had not been helpful. I detected a sense of helplessness in Mrs. K. during this conversation. In an attempt to assist her and Eric, I recommended a children's book by Judith Viorst entitled *The Tenth Best Thing About Barney*. I advised Mrs. K. to read the book aloud with Eric. We also scheduled a time for me to meet with Eric the following afternoon. I asked Mrs. K. to let Eric know that I had returned his call and that we would be meeting the following day. I wanted Eric to know that I had heard his cries for help.

The following day, Eric arrived for his session carrying the book that I had recommended. He asked to take turns reading it aloud, with him reading one page and then me reading the next. While doing this, we discussed a list of the ten best things about Peanut that he and his mom had come up with. After reading the book, Eric began to build a "new tank" out of fiddlesticks. While doing so, he asked for my assistance and repeatedly stressed that the tank had to have "plenty of ammunition to fight against the enemy." During this session, Eric spontaneously revealed that when he was scared his "mean side comes out." He told me that he had felt "mean" since Peanut died.

Eric brought two new toys to the next session. He demonstrated that his "Transformers looked like a truck and a car," but in reality, were "weapons that can pop out whenever needed and very quickly." I made statements about how the Transformers (and Eric) appeared one way, but actually felt a different way inside. In the weeks that followed, Eric's play themes frequently reflected sudden drastic shifts from calm to chaos and from peace to war. Things would be going smoothly in Smurfland and suddenly, GI Joe soldiers would attack. Totally unprepared, the Smurfs would find themselves in the midst of a war! Simultaneously, Eric's parents reported that he was beginning to get into physical fights at school.

There were clearly several levels and meanings to Eric's play. However, I was most struck by Eric's attempt to convey the extent to which he was caught off guard—not only by Peanut's death, but also by the awareness that he, himself, was still capable of feeling extremely vulnerable and helpless on the one hand and extremely angry, aggressive, and enraged on the other. His play seemed to be an attempt to integrate the two sides and to come to terms with the idea that, unlike a Transformer, which is one or the other, Eric could have more than one emotion, function, and role simultaneously.

Eric's repetitive play with Smurfs and GI Joe soldier reflected his anxiety about sudden, unforeseen changes. This, combined with loss issues elicited by Peanut's death, and the reality of his parents' upcoming divorce, enabled Eric to address impending changes in his life. As we approached the twentieth month of treatment, Eric's parents were officially divorced. They advised me that they had negotiated a joint custody arrangement. Eric would be living with his father, but spending one night per week and alternate weekends with his mother. Mrs. K. planned to look for an apartment in the same neighborhood so that she could see Eric frequently. She was planning to leave the house in a month or two.

Eric became very focused on his parents' divorce during this phase of the treatment. He talked very openly about it and became very intrigued with a wood sculpture that I kept on a bookshelf. The sculpture consisted of four interlocking family members (a mother, father, and two children) who fit together as a unit, but who could also stand on their own or in separate dyads. The artist who had designed the work attempted to portray that in a functional family, children can come and go freely and at the same time, will always have a place to return.

Eric addressed his uncertainty regarding his "place" after his parents' physical separation through this sculpture. While he never spent more than a few minutes playing with it, Eric touched the sculpture and/or experimented with separating and reassembling family members every week. Whenever possible, I made repeated comments reflecting that the children "fit" with both parents whether they were together or separate and that the same would be true for him. On one occasion, several weeks after his intrigue with the sculpture had started, Eric asked to show it to his mother. I watched as he explained how "there was always a place for the kids."

Two weeks after his parents' divorce was finalized, Eric's mother was diagnosed with mononucleosis. She was unable to work and had to postpone her move. Mr. K. arrived alone for the parent session we had scheduled several weeks earlier and alerted me that he could not pay his bill for the previous month due to lawyer fees and the fact that he now had to carry all financial responsibilities until Mrs. K.'s recovery. He advised me that he would not be returning due to his financial problems. Mr. K. stated that Eric's problems were adequately resolved as well. He saw no need to continue the treatment now that things were settled with the divorce. I made a point to highlight that termination is an important part of the treatment and a process that would take several weeks. Unfortunately, Mr. K. had planned a vacation in three weeks and insisted that the treatment stop at that point. His anxiety about running up a bill prevented Mr. K. from seeing that the timing of this decision was questionable considering that Eric's mother would be moving shortly. Because of this, I had just three weeks to attempt a termination process with Eric.

Eric brought a big coloring book to the next session. He showed me a picture that he had colored with his mother, another that he had colored with his father, and requested that we color one together. Eric was letting me in on this family coloring book! While we colored together, I broached the subject of the upcoming termination. Eric reported that his parents had told him about the plan to stop and said, "I think I'm all right now!" Sadly, there was a sense of bravado in Eric's voice. He returned with his coloring book the following week and again asked to color a picture together. I had a strong sense that Eric was collecting souvenirs of our time together in an attempt to prepare for the separation.

Eric was very animated during our last session. He told me that he and his mother had gone to look at apartments. Eric whispered that his father (who was in the waiting room) did not know about this. Eric enthusiastically described the apartment and highlighted that it was so close that he could ride his bike back and forth and see his mom every day. He played with the wood statue before leaving and told me that he would be going to Florida the following week. These themes of separating, returning, and leaving seemed to be Eric's way of letting me (and himself) know that he was going to be all right.

RESULTS AND FOLLOW-UP

Nearly a year after Eric discontinued treatment, I came upon the remainder of the nurse mobile while cleaning my office. It was hidden on the back of a shelf. Clearly, I had not achieved a sense of closure due to our abrupt ending. While I have heard from Eric several times in the two and a half years that have passed, we have not continued our work together in any formal way. Seven months ago, Eric wrote me a letter asking if we could write to one another. I wrote back saying that I would like to exchange letters with him, but did not hear from him again until a month ago.

One day when I entered my waiting room to greet a patient, I found Eric waiting to see me. I did not recognize him until he said "Hi Dr. Donna . . .remember me . . . Eric?" We had very little time to talk as I had another patient scheduled, but I was surprised, delighted, and very touched by Eric's visit. I thanked Eric for visiting and he responded "I'll see you again . . . maybe I'll drive here someday!" I was struck by this statement and Eric's ability to maintain his connection to me. He no longer needed the nurse mobile to do so . . . just a memory!

DISCUSSION

The memory of Eric's treatment is quite powerful for me as well. A year after Eric left treatment, I wrote a children's book addressing the issue of parental divorce. The book, entitled *They Say There Is Always a Place For Me*, was clearly inspired by Eric!

REFERENCES

Blanck, G., and Blanck, R. (1974). *Ego Psychology*. New York: Columbia University Press.
Freud, A. (1965). *Normality and Pathology in Childhood: Assessment of Development*. Madison, CT: International Universities Press.
——— (1966). *The Ego and the Mechanisms of Defense*. Madison, CT: International Universities Press.
——— (1968). *The Writings of Anna Freud: Vol. 4. 1945–1956. Indications for Child Analysis and Other Papers*. New York: International Universities Press.
Freud, S. (1920) *Beyond the Pleasure Principle*. Ed. and trans. J. Strachey. New York: W.W. Norton, 1961.
——— (1923). *The Ego and the Id*. Ed. and trans. J. Strachey New York: W. W. Norton, 1960.
Glen, L. (1978). *Child Analysis and Therapy*. New York: Jason Aronson.
Greenacre, P. (1959). Play in relation to creative imagination. *The Psychoanalytic Study of the Child* 14:61–80. New York: International Universities Press.
Hartmann, H. (1958). *Ego Psychology and the Problem of Adaptation*. New York: International Universities Press.
Mahler, M. S., Pine, F., and Bergman, A. (1975). *The Psychological Birth of the Human Infant*. New York: Basic Books.
Waelder, R. (1933). The psychoanalytic theory of play. *Psychoanalytic Quarterly* 2:208–224.
Wallerstein, J. S. (1983). Children of divorce: the psychological tasks of the child. *American Journal of Orthopsychiatry* 53:230–243.
Wallerstein, J. S., and Kelly, J. B. (1972). The effects of parental divorce: experiences of the preschool child. *American Academy of Child Psychiatry* 14:600–616.

12

Ann: Dynamic Play Therapy with Ritual Abuse

Steve Harvey, PH.D., A.D.T.R., R.D.T., R.P.T.

INTRODUCTION TO DYNAMIC PLAY THERAPY

When an observer watches a family's interactive scenes closely and listens carefully to stories concerning their emotional experiences, the observer will begin to notice strategies of attachment, relationship patterns, attunement, and empathy between parents and children. These patterns and strategies strongly influence the outcomes and emotional quality of typical, common daily occurrences. The shape and style of such important emotional expression are both created by and reflected in the relationship of such nonverbal elements as physical distance and closeness, facial expressions, matched and mismatched body/vocal rhythms involved in emotional expression, pacing of nonverbal and verbal exchanges, and dramatic role behavior. Though this list is not exhaustive, it is apparent that a family's emotional life has an immediate presence in the personal exchanges.

Using this idea, the play therapist can think of typical family interactions as a "dance/drama of everyday life," in which the nonverbal patterns of relational gestures, postures, and facial and vocal expressions characteristic of family members take on strong emotional and metaphorical significance. The family creates its own unique dance, just as a choreographer might offer patterns of movement for an ensemble of dancers to create a particular emotional effect, using rhythm, matching and mismatching, levels of space, varied degrees of complementary body gestural and postural shaping, different styles of tension/flow, and other movement elements. Such family dances produce and reflect

371

certain basic, core experiences, especially when repeated. The family also uses its dramatic strategies involved with emotional expression, just as a theater or movie director uses blocking and patterning of entrances and exists, spatial awareness and pacing of lines, and role relationships between characters. As in dance and dramatic performance, such expression has the metaphoric quality of producing and expressing organization and meaning in the family's experience. In every family's particular set of dances and dramas, each individual family member has a greater or smaller amount of room to improvise along basic themes to influence and alter these family enactments. More functional families are able to improvise in a creative fashion with their movement, drama, and metaphoric expressions to alter and influence their expression patterns to more adequately satisfy their needs. The more dysfunctional the family, the more these family dance/dramas restrict individuals from developing intimacy and security as they interact with each other.

The central theoretical concept of dynamic play therapy (Harvey 1990, 1991) is that family members are constantly creating the quality and style of intimate relationships within a family in an ongoing, effortless fashion through their nonverbal communication. Past influences with trust-related issues, such as attachment and abuse, influence much of this expressive process. As therapy sessions unfold, the dynamic play therapist uses the actual ongoing dynamic interactions as they occur to help understand and influence subjective experience.

The dynamic play therapist presents the family with a series of interactive art, movement, and dramatic episodes. During these activities, the family's expressive process reveals their essential dance/dramas. These occur especially as family members introduce slight interactive deviations, shifts of focus, changes and breaks of play rules, introduction of new dramatic material, repeated themes and images, and strong emotional themes that interfere with and alter initial activities. The dynamic play therapist notes such deviations and integrates them into subsequent interactions, producing changes within second and third level interactive scenes. As initial play transforms through this incorporation of a family's expressive process, interactions become more relevant and related to core family issues. As these interactive scenes become more defined, the therapist then coaches family members to develop and change their interactive patterns with other significant family members. The most powerful change of dynamic play therapy occurs as the therapist helps the family emphasize the actual, concrete creative process of making new interactions to produce new physically felt experience while generating new dance/drama/art metaphors.

Usually at some point in the therapy, the dynamic play therapist confronts the children and parents with their interactive activity. The play therapist brings about this confrontation by suggesting new metaphors or using the potential options reframed from the expressive elements contained in the deviations and breaks from earlier activities. A "new game" is formed. Such confrontation can produce strong feelings. It is at this point that the play therapist coaches the family to actually re-choreograph or re-direct basic dramas. Through this re-choreography, family members actually make an interactive and emotional change through new active choice-making with different movement or dramatic activity in relation to their significant others. This process helps family members begin to tell their stories of alienation, trauma, and disconnection in fanciful imaginative, and playful ways within their new metaphors. Based on this new understanding, the play therapy begins a process in which family members actually create and undo different and more satisfying scenes for themselves. Such family scenes are then introduced into normal, everyday life through imagery, storytelling, family homework, and other more behavioral techniques common to family therapy.

Though dynamic play therapy emphasizes family relationships, the therapist may see specific family members individually to develop their own art pieces, movement expressions, videos, or dramatic reenactments when necessary. For example, children or sibling groups at times either cannot or will not express themselves to their parents. At this point, the therapist may see the children alone to help them develop a video story, drama, or art pieces to show their parents at some later date. The therapist may also ask parents to address their own family of origin, abuse history, or develop an organized family drama without children present. Some version of such play expressions are then reintroduced in family sessions to find the most important resolution and integration of these expressions. The play therapist may accomplish this division and reintegration within a single session or over several sessions as the need arises.

A particularly telling example of this process occurred with an 8-year-old child who had been repeatedly sexually assaulted by her birth father. Though this assault had been reported, visitation stopped, and the young girl assisted in making verbal disclosures to her mother, her behavior remained very distractible, silly, and highly changeable when she was in any kind of interaction with her mother. Initially in treatment, the play therapist guided the girl and her mother through several drawing, movement, and movie-making activities, such as making faces at each other, playing silly games (dramatic enactment of contests to see who could make the silliest face, silliest body, etc.), running silly races, drawing the girl as being safe, and so on. These initial activities grew out of both the mother's and girl's description of their behavior during the week, as well as their initial interactive presentation during the beginning of the session. I saw the mother and daughter individually during the first half of a few sessions to allow them time to separately talk about their behavior in these "games."

However, in most sessions I saw them together. After doing these interactions, I noticed that the mother would introduce deviations (emotional state changes) in these games by becoming more withdrawn, frustrated, and less effective, while the girl continued to escalate her silly behavior. The girl tended to ignore, yet control, her mother as she was continually giggling with high intensity, changing the games by constantly dominating all aspects of the interaction. This particular pattern produced little emotional exchange between mother and daughter other than anger, frustration and control battles. Using the particular dramatic, vocal, and nonverbal styles of escalation, I asked the young girl to develop a dance and dramatic character who could scream for her mother's attention without her voice, using her body and face. Interestingly, the girl chose to do this by wrestling with a large stuffed animal. I initially coached the mother to go help the daughter. While talking to both mother and daughter, I realized that this scene was clearly representative of the emotional abandonment that the young girl felt following episodes of oral sex with her abuser. I then reframed the activity to fit the sexual activity.

The elements of strong, intense reaching gestures produced by the girl while wrestling and the withdrawal and emotional helplessness felt by the mother formed the basis of a new dramatic metaphor. As the scene continued, the mother was able to begin to respond to each of the young girl's nonverbal bodily cries for help as the girl made silent, strong gestures for her. The young girl was able to direct her attention more clearly toward her mother. Finally, they were able to use a stretch band as a rescue rope, where the mother was able to pull the young girl from a scene with a large stuffed animal. Both the daughter and the mother identified the animal as the father. Though the mother and daughter had discussed the incidents of sexual abuse several years earlier, the actual dramatic production of a new rescue scene was extremely helpful in redefining their relationship around issues of protection, safety, and intimacy. During the actual production of the rescue scene, both mother and daughter showed significant changes in emotional states as each created new dramatic gestures within the new metaphoric scene. The development of this expressive scene from the girl's awkward, controlling, "silly" giggling, coupled with her mother's frustrated, helpless reaction, revealed a more core experience between them. In talking afterward, both mother and daughter recognized the silliness as occurring several times daily and described the enactment of the rescue scene as being a far more emotionally fulfilling extension of the girl's attention-seeking behavior.

Use of Expressive Modalities

Dynamic play therapy makes use of all the expressive modalities in creating interactive scenes. Using art, movement, drama, music, and video, the dynamic play therapist assumes that family members will use the basic core-related interactive strategies within each modality. The dynamic play therapist believes that difficult interactive scenes produced in one modality may be highlighted, clarified, and transformed when expressed in another modality. Such switching of modalities is also helpful in encouraging the creative process of new metaphor-making through a different concrete activity. Quite often, the play therapist sets up an interactive game with movement, for example, only to have some interactive deviation or difficulty appear. At this moment, it is usually very helpful to shift and have the family members draw individual versions of that interaction. In this way, not only is the deviation highlighted, but the art piece assists in making a metaphor about the emergent difficulty. Another use of such shifting modalities involves video. In this shift, family members produce dramatic interactions of typical problems, either in a literal or metaphorical way. The play therapist videotapes these and gives the videotape to the family to watch over the week, with the assignment to observe and make changes in their difficult "movies." In homework sessions, the therapist may ask families to find new endings or beginnings for these "movies," for example.

The goal of approaching interactions through different media is to increase family members' motivation toward adding creative choices to interactive scenes. Often, when in the middle of a power struggle, young children refuse to continue any productive interactive activity and become quite stubborn or tantrum-like, using the tantrum to control the parents. An example of a useful dynamic play therapy technique in this situation has been to introduce a game called "Scribble Wars," where the play therapist asks the parents and child to out-scribble each other with art material. When they are done scribbling, the play therapist asks the parents and child to transform their scribbles into new imaginative characters or stories. Using different modalities at this point

STEVE HARVEY, PH.D., A.D.T.R., R.D.T., R.P.T.

is quite powerful because the shift transforms the interaction involving power conflicts into a creative engagement between parents and children where all family members are actively involved in creating the scribble drawing. A major task of the dynamic play therapist is to highlight and encourage small moments of change while family members are in interaction with each other. These small changes help build the family's reservoir of creative strength to deal with their more basic emotional conflicts. They also demonstrate to various family members that it is possible to interact in new and different ways.

The therapist can also add the additional art pieces, videos, and dances to ongoing scenes as new props. This addition continues to reinforce interactive expression as a creative process of metaphor making. For example, the "Scribble Wars" drawing mentioned above might serve as a marker to label where a family movement argument could occur in the therapy room. Likewise, a child might be encouraged to "scribble a secret" if she says that she cannot talk about something. This secret "scribble" might then be hidden under some pillows in a later game of family hide-and-seek. Family movies or art pieces might also be taken home to include the creative process in the home more directly. For example, a family might take a movie enactment of being in a "safe house" home and watch it before a young child who has been having nightmares goes to sleep.

Initial Family Sessions

During the initial sessions of therapy, the dynamic play therapist observes families in both structured and unstructured play, drawing, movement, and dramatic tasks. Observations of such initial art, story, dance, and drama making provide the therapist with a beginning understanding of core interactive processes and potential strengths. The play therapist observes various family groupings, such as siblings, mother and child, family and child, or individual children alone. Certain controlled interactions have proven to help highlight more specific aspects of the dance/dramas. Some specific directed play tasks used at this point in dynamic play therapy include:

1. Follow-the-Leader (everyone gets a chance to be leader). This task is very useful for highlighting power and control issues, as well as ability to co-create imaginatively among family members. The therapist can also use this activity to observe roles and the switching of

such roles, movement interaction related to leadership of different family members, and conflict resolution.

2. Negotiating obstacle courses made of large pillows, while tied together with stretch ropes. The play therapist can observe mutual problem solving and attachment-related cooperative interactive movement behavior.

3. Parent(s) swinging children into a pile of pillows. This task is particularly helpful at illustrating the natural parent–child choreography associated with affect attunement and excitement or physical matching/mismatching. The more easily parents and children can attune to each other's physical expression of feeling, the more easily they can play this game and the more the parents/children will naturally want to continue. However, problems with physical/ expressive attunement lead to uncoordinated swinging, strong bodily tension, and other choreographic difficulties.

4. Parent calming children down. This task is helpful at observing soothing and restorative behavior.

5. Brief parent separations, solo play with children, and reunion sequences. Observations here are particularly useful in helping the play therapist understand how children have internalized parental figures, their abilities to generate independent themes, tolerate anxiety with play, and use parental figures as a secure base. The resultant play themes and metaphors while children are playing together, compared with solo play help give the play therapist a deeper understanding of attachment-related feelings.

6. Useful art activities to initially observe family dynamics and abilities to make and use metaphors include having each member of the family draw a house on a single, large sheet of paper. The whole family is then asked to draw a system of roads to come out of their houses and develop a story while drawing their interactions. The therapist can ask each member to take several turns. Similar, less elaborate drawings can be completed with younger, preschool children. Even simple interactive mark making can be done with very young children.

7. Dramatic play with different-sized stuffed animals can be completed with families to sample dramatic metaphors, episodes, use of character/ roles, and the creation and resolution of conflict. One beginning is to ask the family to make a home and then tell a story about a family of bears.

This list is meant to provide ideas of initial interactive activities to engage a family's expressive style. Further activities and applications to family evaluations are presented in other works (Harvey 1990, 1991, in press-a). Bell (1984), Dulica (1976), Landgarten (1987), and Meekums (1991) have presented additional interactive expressive movement and art activities that can also be used during the first sessions of dynamic play therapy.

In one initial session, I asked a 7-year-old-boy to play Follow the Leader, develop mutual and solo play, and complete an obstacle course tied together with his maternal grandparents. These caretakers had adopted this little boy following extensive physical abuse and periods of neglect at the hands of his birth mother during his first two years. This boy presented with several behaviors typical of children with attachment-related problems, such as firesetting, lying, and strong oppositional behavior. This family's problematic interactions emerged immediately. The boy loudly chose himself to be the first leader. At this time, the boy began to do large gymnastic movements that his grandparents could not follow. The boy introduced a competition with his grandfather especially. The grandfather tried to slow the boy down, but the conflict merely intensified. The boy pulled at his grandparents and again especially at his grandfather in a tug-of-war fashion as they attempted to complete the obstacle course. Strong tugging allowed for no mutual problem-solving discussion or physical activity, as the pulling dominated the activity. The boy then hid under a parachute during his brief solo play when his grandparents left the room and avoided them on their return, and the family had difficulty restarting mutual activity.

Another case in which I used the swinging, calming, drawing houses, and dramatic family story featuring stuffed animals involved a 3½-year-old girl who was being reunited with her birth mother. The girl had been removed from her home for an extended out-of-home placement since her first year, following a nonorganic failure to thrive situation. When the mother first attempted to swing her child into the pillows, the girl immediately stiffened her torso and became passive in her legs and arms. Her mother likewise had difficulty coordinating a swing through her torso and showed little shaping or sculpting of her body while holding her daughter. The girl did not want to continue the swinging game after the first attempt, expressing only a very nervous laughter. The girl refused to approach her mother to be calmed down. When asked to draw a house and tell an interactive story while drawing themselves coming out of their houses, the girl finished a house, but refused to come out. She also walked away from the picture several times while her mother told a confusing story about two figures who were unrelated to each other. The girl showed similar behavior enacting the family story. She kept leaving her stuffed animal, wandering through the playroom as her mother told another confusing story about two "brother dogs" who had the same name.

These interactive activities show clear reflections of the obvious attachment problems. These problems could also have been predicted from earlier history and/or from verbal interviews with the caretakers. However, the initial activities gave the therapist, the family, and importantly, the children actual interactive behavior to describe the feeling of their relationship. Such behavior also clearly pointed out the way change could occur.

I helped the grandparents and grandson to develop a game in which the grandparents would swing their boy into the pillows while he did favorite gymnastic flips, spontaneously telling them how good he felt telling them the truth. The grandfather and the boy were also coached into developing tugs-of-war with the stretch ropes while the rope was labeled the "getting my own way" rope (their term). I coached the girl and her birth mother into developing rocking rituals using large pillows to encourage more softness, relaxation, and shaping, while they told stories related to the rocking and feelings associated with this activity. In this way, the initial games highlighted the problematic family interactions in interactive game behavior. Such games could be developed into new game metaphors that addressed change within play activity. During these initial activities, I introduced the families to the therapy activity and goals in direct ways using concrete behaviors as examples. The game-like approach also contributed to motivation to engage in therapy from the beginning for both parents and children.

Initial Games

Following these initial observations and an introduction to interactive play, the next step in dynamic play therapy involves the therapist using this information and other presenting behavioral problems to set up "initial games." This is a concept that is primary to dynamic play therapy. Such games usually grow out of the initial activities and are designed to highlight more particular interactive difficulties. For example, an initial game designed for the boy with the leadership dominance mentioned above involved making a house of pillows with his grandfather in a cooperative way. This proved difficult for these two, and the pillows kept falling over while they engaged in disagreements. We decided to call the house the "argument house." These games allow the therapist to ask questions of the family interactive systems using play and interactive scenarios with the family members providing interactive play answers.

The dynamic play therapist expects that each family will transform these initial games using their own style of interaction. This style is related to core interactive processes involved with attachment and intimacy. The family makes these transformations through a series of play breaks—physical deviations, dramatic deviations, and emotional breaks. Physical deviations include spontaneous physical gestures, postural shifts, eye glances, facial affect expressions, and small physical accidents, whereby some family members bump into one another while family members' bodies are in interaction with each other. Dramatic deviations include role shifts and inappropriate role activity, introduction of new dramatic characters not originally stated in the initial game, unusual plot shifts, and breaking of the rules or expectations involved in the initial game. Emotional breaks involve significant shifts of emotional states while interactions proceed. These emotional changes occur along the continuum of withdrawal to high-intensity aggression or dependency. Emotional breaks grow out of each family's and family member's unique history with attachment and intimacy. The therapist watches for such breaks as the initial games proceed. These breaks may cause the game to break down, deviate, or produce other unusual results. Every time the family plays an initial game, members transform it in their own particular way, with deviations and play breaks. The therapist then helps the family incorporate these deviations into new versions of the games, so that the interactions become more personally relevant and challenge each client's creativity while in interaction.

"Monster" is an example of an initial game that is frequently used in dynamic play therapy. In this game, the therapist plays a large, approaching monster. For younger children or more traumatized individuals, the therapist uses a large stuffed animal or a scarf as the monster. Before the approach begins, the play therapist instructs the parents and children to stop the approach of the monster using verbal commands, "Stop" and "Go away," in combination with a simple coordinated hand gesture.

Parents and children produce a wide variety of responses to the approaching monster. Young, traumatized children are sometimes unable to verbalize their stop command, but may show incidental movement behaviors such as eye blinks or finger twitches or slight twistings of their body with the monster's approach. In this case, the play therapist would stop the game and suggest that exactly those movements be incorporated as a "new way to stop the monster." For example, the play therapist could reframe a young child's blinking so that each blink produces a significant physical-spatial retreat by the monster. A family member with trust-related attachment or abuse problems might become somewhat passive with the approach of the monster and fail to coordinate his or her movement gesture in any effective or simultaneous way with other family members. The play therapist could use this information to create new instructions that the parent would need to hold hands with the child and move forward to stop the monster as soon as she felt her child's hand move.

In one particularly dramatic example, a mother and child who were both victims of past physical assault fell down as the monster approached. Following this, I changed the rules of the interaction to have the falling down of the mother and child as the planned gesture to stop the monster. I also added a new rule that the monster was unable to reach below the waist. With the addition of these two new rules, both mother and child were able to play with the therapist "monster" quite freely by crawling under my legs, free of being touched. The goal of incorporating these deviations into the initial game is to increase the personal creative interaction of parents and children as they confront the threat of the approaching monster.

For parents and families who have experienced significant physical or sexual assault, these second- and third-level scenes involving an approaching monster can produce quite dramatic enactments of empowerment. Even though the use of such incorporations as deviations appear relatively small and incidental compared to the amount of traumatic material some families have experienced, the active ingredient of dynamic play therapy intervention is to increase family members' physically felt expression of intrinsic imaginative choice-making while they are interacting to form a new metaphor from the past enactment. Therefore, the experience of the young child who can blink his monster away, while seemingly small on one level, produces a significant new experience of empowerment for that child.

Likewise, the experience of the mother and boy who had both experienced extensive beatings by a large man in their past were able to experience some control of their internally felt distress through their new "ideas" as their dramatic activity of falling down was given new meanings. This mother and her young son were able to intrinsically engage in playful imaginative behavior, while in an imaginative creative feeling state. During this state, both mother and son were able to engage in emotional control and the experience of joint creative choice-making. They were able to create a new metaphor to address their past difficulties, while confronting the dramatic image of a monster to whom only moments before they responded to with shock and helplessness.

In dynamic play therapy, these state shifts, though momentary, form the basis of the therapeutic activity in which families can experience their own natural creativity to reconstruct new relationships on the physical, dramatic, and metaphoric levels in the face of attachment breaks and strong trauma. Through this mother and son's actual movement activity, they not only produced a more creative and imaginative problem-solving style, they also experienced a change in their bodily felt emotional experience. This mother and child could develop new movements in order to change their "dance" of victimization as the larger body of the therapist approached quickly.

Also because of the game aspect, this mother and child were able to use their own intrinsic motivation to achieve the change in a natural, spontaneous, and easy way. Further, as the mother and child were able to talk about the game and identify the monster as the past aggressive father, their dances of change could become both physical and symbolic as they developed their new game metaphor. They continued to happily tease me (the "monster") by asking me to go slow, finding safe areas where I could not go, and the like, extending their activity into a metaphorical dance/drama of "taming their monster" or changing their past experience with domestic violence. By using art in drawing the monster of the family or making movies of the taming dance that they could view at home, this mother and son could together extend their experience of co-creating in a more conscious way a new and more helpful aspect of their relationship.

The dynamic play therapist can use initial games as a beginning to more accurately focus, identify, and facilitate family members' unique interactive behaviors through their natural creativity. The play therapist designs initial games to focus on the physical, dramatic, and emotional deviations and to give these deviations a context. In using these contexts, the therapist can help the family members relabel such seemingly unimportant behaviors as eye blinks or falling over and define them as unique ways of organizing behaviors. Families who have secure attachment relationships and few problems in their interactional patterns develop such games in a relatively easy, creative, and imaginative way. The use of initial games helps focus on the interactive behavior of families who have experienced more problems by identifying their deviations in more manageable units. The dynamic play therapist can then coach the clients through these units. Once the therapist can help the family use this creative process of generating new solutions and metaphors in small ways, the same strategy can be extended and generalized to larger family situations.

Harvey (1989) described several other generic initial games. The dynamic play therapist can also design initial games that specifically fit the interactive dynamics encountered in different families. For example, a mother and father may describe the tantrum behavior of a preschool child while that child remains silent and begins squirming on the couch. The dynamic in this situation might involve control issues on the parents' part, with avoidance and fearfulness on the child's part. Given this situation, an initial game might involve having the child choose a stuffed animal to show the squirming part of the behavior, while the parents continue to list several problems as well as positive behaviors. Once the family starts this activity, the dynamic play therapist would look at all possible interpersonal relationships for their deviations, play breaks, and nonverbal aspects. Ideally, the young child would control the stuffed animal to change movement to correspond with the parents' changes in verbal descriptions, while the parents would be able to list positive as well as difficult emotional reactions for their child. However, if the parents and boy were unable to adapt more favorably to each other's needs, the more likely their interaction might contain parental feelings of accusation, control, and frustration, contributing to more avoidant behavior by their child.

If such activity were to increase, the therapist could incorporate these deviations by having the child build a safe house with pillows, leaving the stuffed animal to confront his parents, while the parents would be instructed to perhaps write lists or draw pictures of ideal behavior for the stuffed animal. This intervention might result in a consideration of whether the child was ready to invite a parent into his house, or the parents producing an interesting-enough artistic or movement activity with the stuffed animal to encourage their child to join them. By highlighting this moment, the play therapist offers both parents and child a natural game-like challenge to deal with their relationship more creatively in a metaphorical as well as physical manner, with the therapist coaching both sides with possible solutions. If no positive interactions developed, the therapist could see the parents and child separately so that they could develop individual expressions and discussion. Often, children can make their own videos to show their parents their feelings at this point.

The aspect of engaging family members in a process of emergent choice-making is more important than the end product of the actual choice itself. In this example, many end results could be positive, with the child asking the parents to join him in his house, or the parents swinging and playing with the stuffed animal in such a way that the child would wish to join them in the activity. However, the most important aspect of using the initial game would be for the play therapist to encourage the actual process of changing the physical and dramatic strategy of interaction and metaphor-making to more completely satisfy needs for security, trust, limits, and boundaries within this family.

Free Play with Props

In addition to using initial games, the dynamic play therapist can also use several props scattered throughout the playroom to highlight and facilitate problematic interactive behavior. These props include several large, different-shaped pillows, stretch ropes, parachutes, large gymnastic balls, several families of stuffed animals of differing sizes, and several large, colorful dance scarves. The playroom is also equipped with track lighting so that different areas of the room can be lighted with red, blue, yellow, and green lights in different combinations. Various art materials, including very large sheets of paper, crayons, markers, and colored pencils are within easy reach. Finally, music is available; besides typical children's music, dramatic selections from a classical, opera, jazz, and rock repertoire can help further elaborate or stimulate dramatic interactive activity. These props are helpful, not only to elaborate and further extend initial games, but as a stimulus for interactive free play as well.

Oftentimes, when no interactive activity appears to be working, or after the family has successfully used an initial game, the dynamic play therapist encourages parents and children to move into the play area with no preset play scenario. As family members use these props, interactive activity immediately becomes highlighted and focused, and can develop potential for metaphorical activity. For example, young children often begin climbing on the pillows. The play therapist can describe such activity as "climbing or escaping or leaving their parents." Other children may begin to climb through the pillows, forming rooms or secret caves that serve as separate "homes" or boundaries. A family member can easily use the larger pillows to help contain movement safely. The play therapist may define these pillows as "Safeland," or even "Mom's/Dad's lap" to identify a focus of security. Several large pillows (approximately three to four feet in diameter) are shaped in hearts and the play therapist can label them "Mom/Dad–land" and "Home." If parents are on these pillows and children have the opportunity to play in the rest of the room, the therapist can use the naturally occurring spatial interactions between Mom/Dad–land and the child to encourage active exploration and security-seeking behaviors by having the children control when they return to or stay away from "Home."

The large parachutes serve to further define areas or become more abstract representation of feelings. Often, as a large parachute moves up and down, it can be defined as representing different feeling states, for example, mad parachute or sad parachute. In order for such prop metaphors to work, the prop must be integrated with the parent and child's immediate, observable interactive behavior.

The families of stuffed animals usually include some animals that are as large as parents, some that are as large as preschool to latency-aged children, and some that are very small. This size variation is very helpful because, as children begin to explore these animals, their movement behavior can help identify relationships between mother and father, brother and sister, parents and children. It has been particularly helpful to have families of "bears" and "dogs." It is important to have animals that represent affective dimensions, such as animals that have more threatening aspects (e.g., wolf and snake), and animals that are more secure (e.g., a large mother dog and a large, soft, mother bear).

The play therapist can use props to help focus the more undefined and disorganized movement behavior into interactive scenarios that involve metaphors and meaning. The dynamic play therapist uses the large stretch ropes to help in defining arguments, such as with tugs-of-war. An example would be a young child who simply moves into the room quickly to avoid his parents, burying himself in pillows. The play therapist can define the pillows as the boundaries of a safe house or a hiding place. The play therapist can use this metaphor to reframe this interaction as representing a natural, creative effort at relationship that involves more contact with a secure caregiver.

It is this aspect of both verbally reflecting and actively using interactive nonverbal behavior to develop more productive dynamic interactive metaphors that is the unique aspect of dynamic play therapy. Often this type of behavior in more traditional play therapy or in verbal interventions merely presents problems for family members and therapists. In dynamic play therapy, the play therapist uses such oppositional, fearful, and other interactive behavior to define problematic situations and to provide a springboard for therapeutic reframing.

Once a family has become more comfortable using initial games and/or free play to develop interactive movement/drama scenes and art work to extend, define, or map such interactions, the dynamic play therapist asks families to set up their own games, dances, or artwork to address more difficult issues. During this time, the therapist may have parents and children begin to tell stories from their past and use these stories as part of various therapeutic activities. The goal here is to encourage family narratives that more accurately address their strengths and create their own new metaphoric activity. During this time, such activities usually become more dramatic. With older abused children whose abuser was never charged by the legal system, for example, the family can stage an "emotional courtroom" with the therapist playing the judge. This activity can help the children define their emotional feelings of betrayal and helplessness and ask that a symbolically created figure of the perpetrator be sentenced to an appropriate emotional retribution. A specific example was that of a 12-year-old boy whose father had sexually assaulted him, but had never been formally charged. The boy told the therapist "judge" that he felt ashamed and humiliated by his father's actions and asked that the judge condemn his father's actions and demands for secrecy. The therapist's intervention was to have the boy draw a life-sized picture of his father and then to sentence the picture to always "feel, in silence, the humiliation for life" that his son had felt.

Development of Repetitive Themes, Imagery, and Posttraumatic Play

When playing individually, young child victims produce posttraumatic play. Terr (1983, 1990) describes this expressive play as including compulsive repetition, showing little mastery or catharsis, and being very literal and concrete. The theme and details of such play exhibit unconscious links between the play behavior and the traumatic event. The quality of such expression lacks the metaphorical or symbolic expression and mastery of feelings normally seen in nontraumatized play. The inclusion of concrete details related to the trauma often serve to only retraumatize, remind, and frighten victims of their over-whelming experience in unconscious ways. Children in individual sessions of dynamic play therapy may also show similar repetitive play behavior (Harvey 1990, 1991, in press-b).

One 8-year-old boy who was having difficulties with fighting with peers as well as with soiling himself at school was seen individually over one year. During many sessions in the first half year, this boy would repeat a play pattern that included first striking the large bears, then crawling under them to lay motionless and limp for several minutes. After several repetitions of this pattern, this boy began to soil himself as he was lying still. As we explored the imagery of the fighting and lying down under the bears, this boy described how he had been anally raped by a much older cousin a few years earlier in the crawl space of a shed. He first fought against the advance, only to later lie still to accept his cousin's advance. Clearly, this boy's repetitive movement/dramatic behavior with the bears expressed his traumatic experience before he could begin to verbally present it to me or to himself.

In watching over one hundred young child victims of abusive trauma in interaction with their nonabusive parents, I have observed that such child victims showed a tendency to repeat elements of (a) strong avoidance; (b) strong aggression; (c) passivity; and (d) direct reenactments when engaged in expressive play with their parents. Such play seems to occur during and following episodes of interpersonal closeness and universally interferes with parent–child nonverbal behavior associated with intimacy, closeness, and comfort. In the avoidant characteristic, children tend to distance themselves from their parents while remaining agitated. When looked at in a more microanalytic way, such children's movement phrasing has little or no rest or organization and tends to be dominated by rapid shifts. This movement style tends to increase with physical closeness to an adult caregiver. Children acting out the characteristic of aggression have aggressive outbursts that seem to have no preceding cue and produce no catharsis once expressed. Those children who show the characteristic of passivity tend to become limp, stopping all nonverbal expressive movement, often merely lying on the floor in the middle of a dramatic play episode. Finally, some children tend to show direct reenactments of abuse while playing with their parents by lying on the floor and pulling animals on top of them, producing scenes that look like the physical attacks or sexual activities they later describe. These children tend to show one or more interactive themes, sometimes in various combinations.

Such repetitive individual and interactive behavior suggests that these children have been strongly affected by their experience with trauma, even though they cannot yet verbally report it. In these cases, it could be that the physical, affective, and sensual experiences of the trauma simply are too strong for verbal integration and expression. The interactive behavior also suggests that the experience with trauma has an impact these children's attachment behavior and therefore their basic ability to trust others, even their most intimate and trusted caregiver. This dynamic of the disruption of interactive trust/attachment behavior may be associated with the actual and implied threats made to such children not to verbally disclose their traumatic experiences.

Given these dynamics, therapists can use the expressive and interactive aspects of dynamic play therapy to help individual children extend and elaborate the repeated themes to better express, integrate, and find new creative metaphors with their traumatic play behavior. Also, dynamic play therapy can guide children and parents toward a recre-ating of interactions that generate trust and security within their relationships.

An example of repeated imagery occurred with a 2-year-old boy who had been threatened with death by an adult who placed a gun to his head while the adult told him not to reveal his experience of sexual abuse to his mother. In play sessions over a period of one year, this boy continued to turn prop pieces into guns that he would raise to his head and then shoot himself. He would then fall over as "dead." While it is true that many older boys play with guns to organize and express their feelings of aggression, sexuality, or modeled role behavior, this boy's play was quite different and served only to continue to frighten him. This play seemed to generate no feelings of mastery. During an intervention, I asked him to extend the gun theme into scribble pictures that could represent the guns. I also asked his mother to draw a house where her son could be safe from the guns on the same page. I then helped him to make a map to get away from the guns and enter the "safe house" of the mother. After repeating this activity several times, the young boy was then able to ask his mother to draw a shield around the "safe house." As the activity continued, the boy sat on his mother's lap in a calm and relaxed way while she sang to him. He was unable to generate this kind of intimacy or trusting behavior during any of the earlier sessions. We were then able to generate several stories and songs about coming home to be safe with mother as she gently rocked him. The mother and boy took their picture home and placed it in the boy's room. Later, she incorporated the picture, songs, and stories into the boy's bedtime activity. After this, the boy had fewer nightmares. In similar ways, the dynamic play therapist coaches children who show avoidant, aggressive, passive, and direct reenactments of abuse in their interactions to develop more secure and elaborated expressive out-comes. As described above, such coaching includes the development of new play imagery, as well as new interactive behavior with their caregivers.

PRESENTING PROBLEM AND BACKGROUND DATA

Ann was referred to me when she was 3 years, 10 months, by a Department of Social Service in northern Colorado. Ann's parents were divorced and she was living with her mother (Julie), having extended visits with her father (Todd). Shortly before the referral, Ann had made statements to her mother, another mental health worker, and the protective caseworker that her father had sexually abused her. When the caseworker began investigating, Todd contended that he had never sexually abused Ann, but that he suspected Julie of physically abusing her. The caseworker requested that I evaluate Ann and provide an opinion about whether she had been abused, and if so, by whom. The caseworker needed this information to make decisions about custody and visitation.

My original evaluations consisted of interactive observational play with Ann and her birth father, Ann and her birth mother, and two individual dynamic play sessions that included projective play and drawings. Another psychologist familiar with the dynamics of sexual assault and the psychological testing of adults conducted full psychological evaluations with both of Ann's parents.

During the time period of the evaluations, a case aide observed Todd sexually assaulting another young preschool child. Todd was convicted of sexual abuse. With this evidence and Ann's statements, the court decided to suspend all visits between Ann and her birth father. This development eliminated the need for opinions from the interactive and psychological evaluations concerning whether Ann had been sexually assaulted and for visitation schedules. Consequently, I saw Ann for play therapy and had no need to deal with outstanding legal issues, so therapy could proceed without the constriction that sometimes affects these cases.

During intake interviews, both Julie and Todd described Ann as showing relatively average development following a normal birth. Physical development included rolling over at five months, sitting at six months, crawling at ten-and-a-half months, walking at approximately thirteen months. Single words and sentences occurred somewhat ahead of schedule at sixteen months. At the time of the initial intake, Julie and Ann's maternal grandmother completed a standardized developmental screening questionnaire. The behaviors reported by these two adult caretakers were similar to those observed in the office, namely that Ann was age-advanced in all areas. They reported social, cognitive, and communicative adaptive behavior to be approximately twelve to eighteen months advanced. At the time of the initial observations, this 3-year, 10-month-old child was able to sing complicated songs and tell stories. She was also able to show some reasoning about cause-and-effect in the stories by being able to answer questions about simple cause-and-effect involved in the narrative. Additionally, play behavior also showed that Ann could identify characters and plots and develop simple scenes and scenarios that suggested a narrative understanding of social cause-and-effect. Later, cognitive testing done when Ann was entering school also estimated an above-average to superior IQ level.

According to Julie and the mental health worker who had been involved with Ann previously, this young girl began to show aggressive and sexualized behavior toward adults and Tiffany, her younger sister, following visits with Todd in the latter part of her second and the beginning of her third year. Her mother also described Ann's symptoms as showing terrified behavior, crying for several days following more extended visits. The sexualized behavior was of great concern and consisted of Ann attempting to perform oral sex activities with Tiffany. Additionally, Ann was able to describe both to her mother, protective caseworker, and the first mental health professional specific games involved with tickling in which she and Todd tickled and licked each other's genitals. Following visits with Todd, Ann had difficulty with bed-wetting, despite the fact that she had been toilet trained quite easily just after she was two. Her mother also noted several sleep disturbances. These included nightmares and several episodes of night terrors where Ann would wake screaming from her sleep and show difficulty being calmed down by her mother. Julie, Ann's grandmother, and later George, her stepfather, were able to report that the nightmares and the aggressive and sexualized episodes seemed to occur in spurts and be related to her visitation with Todd.

When Ann was not engaged in this kind of behavior, she was well behaved and easy to parent, and she appeared good natured. However, when she would become involved in the sexualized or aggressive behaviors, she would become very moody and extremely oppositional, despite anything her mother or other adults around her would do. After these oppositional episodes, Julie reported that she could reason quite easily with Ann to help her control her behavior. However, no amount of planning or consequences seemed able to effect Ann's episodes of misbehavior. Additionally, throughout such episodes, Ann would begin to masturbate in front of the family after taking off her clothes. These episodes of undressing and masturbating seemed to be associated with times when Ann would describe how her father would teach her how to suck or "tickle" his penis. This masturbation and verbal disclosure appeared only to escalate Ann's lack of behavioral control. Following this would be the times when Ann would become extremely aggressive to her mother and family pets, as well as trying to sexually assault Tiffany. When she would finally get over these episodes and be calming down, Ann quite often reported that she was afraid of being kidnapped by Todd. Ann showed similar sexualized behavior and made similar verbal disclosures when she was first taken to a mental health worker who provided her with anatomically correct dolls.

Interactive Observations

In interactive behavior with her mother, Ann presented as a calm, preschool child who was able to follow her mother's leads easily. Julie, for her part, was sensitive to her young daughter's needs and ideas and was able to encourage her in drawing and doll play. No play themes were remarkable during the first interaction. However, when I asked Julie to leave, Ann became overwhelmed with anxiety to the point where I felt it necessary to ask Julie back into the room after separations of only a few seconds. In my opinion, the amount of distress was usually high, with Ann crying and screaming very loudly, holding on to her mother at even the first mention of her brief leaving. This distress came after quite a long time of showing very calm, masterful interaction and interactive play with Julie, which suggested more security. Later, Julie said that the intensity level Ann showed in the office was similar to the kind of distress that she showed during the night terror activity following her return from visits with Todd. When Ann was able to return to play with her mother following the brief episodes of strong distress, her play returned to being highly cooperative and noncoercive, and suggested a return to more secure feelings. However, Ann became hypervigilant around cues that suggested possible separation from her mother again. Taken together, these observations suggested that Ann's reactions to separation may have been more related to trauma than is more typically seen in the coercive interactive styles related to insecure attachment (J. Crittenden in press).

Ann was also evaluated with her father prior to his conviction of sexual assault of the other child. When she was seen with Todd, she showed a marked difference in her interactive style that could best be characterized as apparently seeming to share more high-intensity, positive expression with her father. However, when looked at more closely on the videotape, Todd seemed to lead and cue these episodes of positive good feeling rather than being spontaneous expressions of Ann's feelings. During these play activities, Todd clearly dictated the change of activities, with Ann quickly following his lead. This style of interaction fits the criterion for the style of "obsessive obedience," that Patricia Crittenden (1988) observed in young children who had been physically abused. However, Ann's behavior was different from such children in an interesting aspect. Crittenden's observations of toddler and preschool abused children suggested that these children not only followed their parents' leads and ideas quite quickly, but showed a remarkable restriction in the amount of affect shown, as well as a hypervigilance to their parents' cues and ideas. However, in Ann's case, once she was cued by her father to begin a particular expressive episode, both she and her father were able to express high-intensity pleasure, fun, and laughter in a seemingly mutual and simultaneous way.

Another characteristic of Ann's play that I noticed after looking at the tapes was that these episodes, although initially appearing spontaneous, seemed more to consist of several preplanned and prerehearsed games of enjoyment. These interactions were similar to interactive games of late infancy or early toddlerhood, in which the parent may cue the child to play "I'm gonna get you" or "Peekaboo" with a child following in his or her prescribed way. However, usually with more social development, children are able to develop their own versions and elaborations on these games by toddlerhood or by Ann's age. Though such development and elaborations were clearly apparent in Ann's interaction with her mother, such elaboration, development and use of Ann's ideas to further the interaction were not present in the interaction with her father. In general, this interaction with Todd gave the appearance of him putting Ann through her paces or showing her off, because of the lack of age-appropriate spontaneity and give-and-take of play ideas.

Some other odd characteristics of this interaction between Ann and her father became apparent only after reviewing the tapes several years later, following the completion of Ann's therapy. During this play, Ann introduced statements referring to "Oh, you're in God's land now," or "This is the Devil's side." Her father quickly diverted attention to another game, rather than responding to such questions. Also, Todd whispered to his daughter several times throughout their play, breaking their interactive play. Finally, Ann's father appeared to be making very stereotypical hand gestures involving his fingers to his young daughter during some of the interactive episodes. These same gestures were repeated by Ann a year and a half later when she described a series of hand signs that were supposed to keep her from talking. The main characteristic of these hand signs was that they were very stereotypical and did not fit the more naturalistic flow of gestural activity normally seen in the matching of nonverbal gestures. One such gesture stood out especially, in which Todd was making rapid movements of his hand directly in front of his young daughter's eyes. This movement was also repeated with a play prop in this way. This movement was again very idiosyncratic in the movement flow and had no natural preparation or ending nor did it have any relation to the play material being developed.

Whether or not these gestures were, in fact, a method Todd used to signal to Ann to behave in a certain way may never be known. However, these cues, as well as other play initiations, served the interactive function of capturing Ann's attention and directing her activity in ways that did not serve to encourage the development of her ideas or incorporate her nonverbal and slight emotional mood shifts as they normally would occur in a spontaneous gesture-by-gesture non-verbal dance of intimacy. Such behavior produced a very different style of interaction between Ann and her father than that shown between Ann and her mother. Whereas Ann's behavior showed much more initiation of her ideas in a calm fashion similar to other children her age with Julie, her response to Todd was characterized by quick rhythms and seemed to lack recuperation and redirection that would characterize more normal nonverbal exchange. When Ann first entered the room with her father, she did show some apprehension and fearfulness. After going through these series of cued, high-energy exchanges, she seemed far more comfortable with him. Consequently, she appeared to have sacrificed her own contribution to the "dance/drama of intimacy" created between herself and her father.

Initial Individual Play

Following these interactive observations between Ann and her mother and father, I also saw her in nondirective play by herself. During this play, I provided Ann play props as described earlier in this chapter. I did not use anatomically correct dolls. I gave Ann some large, Raggedy Ann–type dolls that had clothes on, and several stuffed animals. Despite earlier difficulties with separation, Ann was able to separate with much more ease during the sessions after a brief time with her mother. During both sessions, Ann repeatedly developed a pattern where she took off the clothes of the Raggedy Ann dolls and showed a father figure touching one of the dolls between her legs. She also showed a girl figure and a father figure kissing and massaging the breast area of another doll. During these disclosures, Ann became very agitated and giggled, saying many provocative things, such as, "I want to lick her titties."

In the second session, as Ann was repeating these themes, she also became preoccupied with nakedness, seeing the whole room as being naked. At one point she saw a tear in a pillow saying that the pillow was naked, as well as identifying all the bears in the room as being naked. During the episodes of sexualized enactment, Ann identified her father by name as being the father doll or father bear. During the end of this play episode, Ann showed signs of increasing distress and stated that she and the daddy doll had done many bad things and had become "Satan." After she said this word, Ann became extremely avoidant and secretive. She then attempted a get me to play a game of "doctor" with her. This game was initiated by her lying down and wanting me to touch her in her stomach to remove something. She gave this invitation to me even though I was on the other end of the room. I politely refused and continued taking notes.

THEORETICAL CONCEPTUALIZATION

Such play and interactions, in combination with the other information, clearly suggest that Ann may have been sexually assaulted by her father. I could have attempted additional structured play episodes if more collaborative interview information had been necessary to provide an opinion for the social service caseworker. However, as stated above, during the time of the evaluation, Todd was convicted of assaulting another preschool child. With this development, no further evaluation was necessary outside of the recommendations for treatment.

Julie chose not to bring Ann to any treatment for approximately another year. When Ann did return for treatment, her mother reported that Ann continued the aggressive and sexualized behavior around the house and was continuing to have nightmares and show fearfulness. Ann also began to show more strange, phobic reactions, such as seeing bugs and spiders that would terrify her, despite the fact that no insects were present. Additionally, she began to report strong kidnapping fears, despite not having seen Todd for quite some time and his having left the state.

Taken together, Ann's verbal reports of sexual assault, posttraumatic behaviors such as nightmares, aggression, and sexualized acting out, odd fears, the interactive behaviors reported earlier suggesting fear at separation from mother, compulsive following of her father's leads, the sexualized play with the dolls, introduction of avoidance, and the doctor theme strongly suggested the initial formulation that this girl had been sexually assaulted and that the abuser(s) may well have included her father. The continuing fearfulness, aggressiveness, and sexual acting out further supported the idea that Ann's experience had, indeed, been quite traumatic and probably had impacted her sense of trust and her attachment behavior with her family. Given this situation, the initial therapy goals included (a) assisting Ann in developing play metaphors that had meaning for her and that could help her gain an understanding, expression, and resolution of her emotional experience of the trauma; and (b) helping Ann, her mother, and her stepfather develop a trusting/secure relationship despite what seemed to have happened to her. The development of such individual and shared family interactive metaphors could then be used to help reduce Ann's problematic behaviors and feelings in their simpler, more basic elements. Rather than address her fear of bugs, sexual behavior, and periods of uncontrollable behavior toward her parents separately, these therapy goals were to help find a general image, theme, and/or drama to assist Ann in expressing her fears directly and have Julie and George later respond with sensitivity and protection to help Ann develop security and trust. Ann could then truly trust her mother and stepfather and herself. Similar to many of the case examples presented earlier, as Ann could find ways to chase away her inner "monsters" or draw maps of feelings she could share with her parents, this family could generate a beginning strategy and image to understand and appreciate the strong affects influencing their behavior. Following these creative developments, Ann and her parents could be in better position to discuss the actual outer "monsters" with more honesty, and establish safe and more secure actual relationship behaviors at home.

To accomplish these goals, I initially saw Ann and Julie together. In recalling the first interactive observation in which Ann was so frightened of leaving her mother, in combination with the reports of current fears, it seemed important to me to have mother and daughter develop play behavior and an initial metaphor that could address the issue of safety and security successfully. With this development of more mother–daughter security, I believed that Julie could begin to deal with other aggressive and fear-related behavior more productively.

To capture the interactive problems and fearful trauma-related feelings within the play context, I followed the strategy outlined earlier in the chapter. During the first session, I asked Ann and Julie to complete an initial drawing activity and used the deviations of their expressive process to form initial games. I introduced these games in a similar way. Again, I used the deviations and breaks to develop the relevant metaphor that could then be extended to home.

Shortly after this phase, when Ann appeared secure enough in her own play, I asked Ann to play individually in relative free play with the props (pillows, stuffed animals, gymnastic ball, colored scarves, parachutes, etc.). This phase of individual play was important to allow Ann to develop her own themes and images free of her mother's influence. I identified repeated themes and images and creatively extended them with other expressive modalities. Sometimes I accomplished this by asking Ann what other movement, art, or dramatic activity was needed. For example, in one of Ann's repeated movement images, she would fall down and say she was dead. At this point, I asked her what happened next, and she added, "Now I'm buried by the pillows." I extended each repeated theme this way, until Ann reached a natural endpoint to her creativity.

I asked Ann's grandmother, Kathleen, to join the play at this point and she was integrated into this movement/drama/art metaphor. Ann asked that Kathleen join because she was too afraid of having her mother in the room initially. Ann reported that threats had been made toward her family should she reveal anything. After approximately four months of play with her grandmother, Ann was able to have her mother and her stepfather join in the play. The strategy remained for Ann and then Ann and her adult caretakers to extend her art/drama/movement metaphors in ways that could both express her fears and include the adults in protective ways. The core of these metaphors incorporated Ann's repeated themes. Only after approximately eight months of Ann's successfully expressing and contributing creativity to her play imagery did she began to verbally disclose what had happened to her.

THE PROCESS OF PLAY THERAPY

Initial Stages of Treatment

After Ann's mother, Julie, had described her daughter's continuing difficulties in the first session, she and Ann and I completed a structured interactive drawing activity in which each one of us drew a house on a large piece of paper. Because Ann still had some difficulties drawing at this point, her house consisted of a circle next to her mother's image.

During the next part of the activity, Julie, Ann, and myself took turns drawing ourselves coming out of our houses and interacting with each other with drawing activity and storytelling. During this time, Ann began to draw a fire that burned up her own house and her mother's house and covered the entire page. Using this cue, I extended this image into more dramatic activity where Ann and Julie were able to make a safe place with the large pillows in the room. I then enacted a fire coming toward their new place with a parachute. Ann cast herself as a fireman and her mother as the fire chief who were able successfully to put out the fire with a mime of firefighting activity. As presented above in one of the initial games called "Monster," I extended this activity by having Ann and her mother develop different ways to put the fire out, through different styles of singing (e.g., soft singing, loud singing, happy singing), by throwing pillows at the parachute fire, by telling the parachute fire to stop or go away or calm down. Ann was particularly excited and drawn to repeat strong direct movements toward the parachute. Using this cue, I had Ann teach Julie ways to throw pillows at a "fire" to best put it out. Julie appeared best at singing, so she was coached to make up a song about putting fires out with pillows.

As they completed each of these different enactments, Ann became quite excited and motivated to join her mother in these activities. This activity became the model for dynamic art and dramatic activity over the next month, as the approaching dangerous force alternated from being a fire to a ghost to different monsters. I gave Ann choices about how she would describe these images and make them out of different play props (e.g., parachute, different colored scarves, and large animals). I video-taped these scenes, and Ann and her mother were able to watch them with her stepfather in between therapy. They also used these videos to develop bedtime stories.

An interesting elaboration occurred during the first several sessions. The structure of the therapy session included a brief time where both Ann and her mother were to be sitting on the couch, "talking-land," while both were to describe the previous week's activities. During the third and fourth week, Julie began describing the positive results of the fire scene and some other games they had developed, such as chasing away imaginary bugs with an aerosol can that they very creatively called "bug spray." As her mother talked, Ann became agitated and ran through the room, despite our best efforts to help her remain calm. When Ann finally was able to calm down through a brief walk and some light holding by her mother, she reported that her thoughts were making her run away. This theme of intrusive thoughts recurred throughout treatment. I suggested that we transform the fire game into the "Running Thoughts" game where Ann was able to choose a prop (a large colored parachute) that she and her mother could use to chase away these thoughts. She and Julie invented ways to "put out" the thoughts by dancing on and covering them with "safe water." While the calmness that this game produced was usually quite brief, lasting only several minutes in a therapy session, it enabled Ann's mother and I to point out to her how a play activity could affect and change her internal feeling state. I used this procedure of concretely pointing out how an interactive game could help Ann control her own feelings throughout the rest of the therapy.

After Ann and Julie used this game of putting out the fire or chasing away the running thoughts successfully, I began to ask Ann's mother to leave the session after a brief report on Ann's week. I made this therapeutic choice to allow Ann to develop her own play, movement, and graphic imagery that she could use to relate to her mother in a more meaningful way. Ann's successful creative involvement in using the "Running Thoughts" game to give herself a sense of safety and protection with her mother gave the indication that she was able to start to express her distress and have her mother respond to her fears in ways that could successfully begin to produce security. Further, Julie reported that nightmares and other bug-phobic behaviors were decreasing during this time.

Ann's Individual Play

During this next period of solo play, which lasted approximately two to three months, Ann began introducing dramatic activity that was repetitive and literal. I believed that this play may have been related to her earlier trauma. Additionally, some of her drawing material introduced imagery that was quite odd and bizarre. Rather than include Julie prematurely, I decided to facilitate the elaboration of such imagery in a way so that Ann could "play" her own story without being influenced in interactive ways. Also, it was important to help Ann develop a therapeutic alliance with me.

Three main dramatic themes were introduced at this time: (a) the doctor game, (b) playing dead, and (c) a fire truck. In the doctor game, Ann kept lying down and asking me to be a doctor and perform surgery on her by placing my hands over her stomach to remove something. I refused each of these requests and attempted to redirect Ann to become the doctor herself, using stuffed animals, or having the stuffed animal be a doctor. Usually at this point, Ann would stop this activity.

This repetitive theme was particularly interesting because Ann had introduced this same dramatic game approximately a year and a half earlier during her initial solo play with me during the assessment sessions. At this point, I based my choice not to enter this game on my suspicion that the game may have had traumatic origins. I believe that if I had included myself in this game, I might have significantly influenced the relationship between Ann and myself. This was especially true because of her strong insistence that I actually physically touch and manipulate her stomach. Though physical contact does occur during some occasions, these requests appeared much too premature for the relationship between Ann and myself. It also seemed important for this young girl to develop this game into a more metaphorical context where she could control dolls, puppets, or animals rather than in a direct enactment between her and myself.

The second main repetitive action included playing dead. In this activity, Ann would simply fall down in the pillows and say she was dead and lie motionless for approximately a minute and then come back to life and continue what she was doing. These episodes usually had nothing to do with her story and could be considered play breaks as no new play, story, or movement behavior was generated after this action. My intervention during this time was to merely wait and ask Ann what happened when she came back to life. While I made some attempts at verbally describing in concrete terms the connections between playing doctor, playing dead, and how they interrupted the other play activities, Ann seemed to have very little interest in such discussions. Also, these discussions had very little impact on the behavior. As mentioned earlier, Ann extended this "dead" theme by asking to be buried with pillows.

During the initial presentations of these themes, Ann also introduced a third play theme in which she would describe herself as being in a fire truck. My intervention here was to suggest that she be the driver to help her establish more control. These episodes usually occurred after the doctor or dead images.

During this period, sessions 6 to 16, I made the therapeutic choice to maintain a relatively nondirective style so that Ann could generate her dramatic and play imagery as she pleased, rather than attempting to force any corrective scenes, interpretations, or other interventions onto the play. This nondirective stance allowed Ann and me to get to know each other through the play and avoided my inadvertently reenacting her earlier trauma in any way or influencing a verbal report through social reinforcement. During each session, as she introduced these repetitive themes, I would suggest minor interpretations as stated before or minor variations of the play to each of these interventions. Ann would continue her activity, giving me the clear cue that further attempts at manipulating her play were probably too early and would only produce negative effects, such as faulty imagery or premature closure.

Disclosure of More Threatening Material Dealing with Sexual Abuse

During the next phase of the therapy, Ann appeared ready to extend the play naturally. In the first sessions of this phase, Ann described all of the stuffed animal bears as being sick and needing doctors. At another point, Ann made a drawing in which she said that there was a baby who was forced to eat a great deal and that a baby would come out of her stomach. Ann later said that she was the baby to come out of the stomach. During this enactment of the baby, Ann said that there was a lot of white stuff in her mouth and her stomach was full of things that hurt her. Approximately three months into this activity, Ann elaborated her death scene and the imagery related to being sick to her stomach.

Following this game, the level of her disclosure during play increased. During these disclosures, Ann repeatedly said that some of the things that happened were very real, but were secret. She refused to have her mother in the room for fear that someone would be killed or murdered if her mother found out the things she was reenacting, drawing, and discussing.

During a therapy session approximately six months after the beginning of treatment, Ann became extremely agitated and began running around the room, following her mother's departure. At this point, she began saying that God got in her mouth and went to her stomach. With this statement, she began to blink her eyes quite quickly, saying that the "bad people" had taught her how to do this. At the same time, she made very specific gestures, pointing to "God," her "stomach" and to "hell," describing each part of her hand gestures. She then said that these gestures had to do with the Devil and that she knew many real people who were "bad." Following this, she enacted all of the bears being very sick and she began dying repeatedly. Each time she would die, she would ask to be buried by pillows. During one of these requests, I placed a pillow over her. Following this episode, she "arose from the dead" and became a monster. Describing this some minutes later, she said she had been given a pill that changed her into this monster character.

In the next several sessions, Ann continued to describe and enact being given a drink that would change her into a monster. Additionally, she enacted being placed and buried alternatingly with a snake or with bugs. She described these snakes and bugs as eating her. Throughout these scenes, Ann kept bringing up the doctor scene again where she asked me to listen to and touch her stomach. Again, I refused and suggested that she play it out with the stuffed animals. She responded to this suggestion by again enacting the dying scene and being buried. This scene would switch to her being born again as a monster. As Ann enacted this monster character, she adopted a clearly different body attitude and facial expression. Her movements were larger, more intense, as was her face. She also began spontaneously to laugh in a loud way. These expressions were significant as they were not in Ann's previous repertoire. This monster was clearly something very different.

At some points in these scenes, Ann would switch back into a more even voice, describe Satan as being present, and ask me to chase him away. In response to these requests, I entered the drama more actively, talking directly to Satan, saying that this was my office, that all children were safe, that it was important that only good things happen between people, and that Satan had no right to enter my office unless he would obey the rules to not hurt children or other people. These speeches to Satan seemed to help Ann calm down. To involve Ann's creative ideas relative to Satan more directly, I asked her to identify different props (stuffed animals, scarves, and the like) as Satan and put them someplace. She chose to take several of them outside the office. As with my speeches, this activity also appeared to help her calm down.

Seven months after therapy started, Ann described an episode that she said happened "for real" in which many bad people who were dressed up in black had hurt animals in a fire and that she had witnessed this. After she mentioned this, she became quite frightened that she was not supposed to tell this secret. She said that if anyone found out she had "told" her dog and family would be stabbed, and kidnappers would come through her window at night and place her in the ground. She then described these kidnappers as being not only real people, but guardian angels who were with her all the time and listened to everything that she said. During this disclosure, she again began to blink her eyes quite specifically and produced the hand movements described earlier and said her guardian angels had taught her how to do this. After this session, Julie reported a return of the aggression and sexualized behavior at home. In addition, the nightmares and bug phobias returned and Ann was quite afraid to sleep in her own bed.

At this point, because of the return of the strong terror-related behaviors in the home, I decided to have Julie join us. During this discussion, Ann's mother stated that no one could hurt her and that no one was going to steal the dog. We made several plans whereby Ann's window would be made more secure and a night light was added to her room. She was able to draw a picture of her strongest protector who would be in her room. This protector was a combination of a cartoon character with some imagined elaborations by Julie. Both Julie and Ann completed this picture. I also asked her to watch the earlier protective tapes that she had made with her mother. During this session, Ann made it very clear that she could tell no more to her mother about the things she had been discussing with me because of the threats mentioned earlier. She did agree, however, to have her grandmother in the room, as I said it was very important for someone in her family to get to know these scary feelings so they could help her. Ann said she could play with Kathleen because no such threats were made against her. During the following week, Ann's mother and stepfather made several efforts to insure her safety at home and the nightmares and fearful behavior dropped off considerably.

During the next several months, Ann and Kathleen participated in play sessions together following Julie's verbal report about Ann's behavior during the week. In this period, I gave additional homework and home behavior suggestions to Ann's mother to help her adjust the security-related play games, images, and stories she began using at bedtime. During these sessions between Ann and Kathleen and myself, Ann continued to make yet more disclosures and produce more dramatic play that included her, Kathleen, and myself in more elaborated versions of doctor and playing dead, and she was able to begin to describe verbally her versions of what happened to her more clearly. Often, I asked her to draw pictures of what she wanted to say related to the bad man, Satan, and various animal mutilations and bondage situations she had experienced. It is important to note that these disclosures occurred just before or just after elaborated versions of the "doctor," "dead," and other themes that she had developed earlier. The inclusion of Ann's grandmother was quite easy, as I coached Kathleen to follow Ann's lead.

More Elaborated Versions of Torture, Animal Mutilation, and Satanic Activity

During these sessions with Ann and her grandmother, Ann agreed to bring her favorite stuffed animal with her to help her in her play and verbal disclosures. Often, when Ann could not describe what happened to herself, she could describe the events as if they were happening to this doll. It was very clear that this disclosure process was very frightening and painful for her. Occasionally, Ann even refused to come into the room. During these times, Ann, her grandmother, and I would take walks with her doll, telling protective stories involving Ann and her doll. From time to time during these sessions, Ann would also refuse to engage in any play by introducing distracting activities, such as singing songs, talking loudly about another subject, or looking out the window. At these points, Ann, Kathleen, and I would also take the walks until Ann said she was ready to come back in and engage in interactive playing. During the first time I used the walk to confront Ann's more avoidant behavior, we spent the entire session on this walk, while Ann got angrier and angrier at me for not allowing her to continue her distractions. Finally, approximately five minutes before we were to end the session, she agreed to come back in the room. At this point, she was quite disappointed at not being allowed to play longer. This walk technique proved to be one of the best ways of confronting this young girl's anxiety and her anxiety-related avoidance and oppositionalism.

This period of more extreme and specific disclosures lasted approximately four months, and although Ann also introduced the behaviors described above, she spent the majority of the time in either drawing, enactment, or verbal descriptions. Often, Ann accomplished her more specific disclosures using drawings, with the verbal disclosures being made as storytelling to the graphic images produced. Ann elaborated the stories in response to my questions about both story and art material. She usually produced these during the beginning of the session with the more dramatic enactments and play occurring following her disclosures.

During the initial part of these disclosures, Ann described and showed how her doll and another young girl were tied together while they were watching as many as fifteen naked adults dancing around them. Ann also had her doll described how she was placed in a cage or jail underground. Ann stated that there were several bad people around her who were dressed in black robes. During these disclosures, Ann also drew pictures of the Devil who lived underground and also had a special bedroom that could be approached via a series of underground tunnels and crawl spaces under houses. At one point, she had her doll described ceremonies in which several bad people would drink blood and watch animals be mutilated and torn apart with knives. While describing these episodes, Ann began singing popular rock songs, substituting words describing sexual acts in the place of the ordinary words. At one point, she also began singing a song as if it were a chant and walking in a very stylized manner, saying that she was a "soldier of Satan." During this time, she began blinking her eyes very quickly as she had demonstrated before.

After these disclosures during play, Ann would usually introduce the theme of being dead again, enacting short scenes where she would both be dead and fall down, and be buried and ask her grandmother and me to rescue her. During the first such death scene, I sat next to Ann with her grandmother. After lying motionless a while, Ann began to slightly move her fingers. I coached Kathleen to begin finger dances with her granddaughter "to feel" if she could bring her back to life. After a brief time, Ann would become more active again. After several minutes, Ann was able to begin to nonverbally signal for a rope to be thrown, or for us to throw pillows off her that had initially buried her. Interestingly, Ann rarely reintroduced the monster during this time. When she did, I coached Kathleen to tell her that she was not afraid of monsters, and she would love to play with her (the monster). Ann's monster character seemed to begin to transform at this point.

In between these disclosures, Ann also reintroduced the theme of doctor. At this point, she cast me and her grandmother as a doctor and nurse who would begin to take something out of her stomach. After enacting this over several occasions, she described having been forced to eat black widow spiders, and that such spiders were also Satan and that she needed to have the spiders and this force cut out of her. After she had introduced this theme on several occasions, Kathleen and I finally enacted the scene in which we performed a pretend operation to remove the forces. During these disclosures, Ann drew a very detailed picture in which she described the ceremonies as happening in a cave underneath a church, in which there were several magical writings on the wall. She described witnessing many animal mutilations as well as witnessing a death and perhaps participating in the death of a younger child. During these ceremonies, Ann stated that she and the other children were placed in a part of the cave that had snakes and black widows. As she described these very specific allegations, Ann stated that she would have her "tongue cut out" if she disclosed this information.

At one point, Ann described hearing voices from the "bad people" and "Satan" inside her head, which told her to misbehave, hurt her sister, refuse to cooperate, and yell in my office. Ann was able to draw these voices as a spiral-shaped tornado in which she was getting lost. Her behavior became quite agitated during the drawing. Her grandmother and I were able to develop an enactment of "dancing the voices quiet" with movement and whispering by moving with the picture between us. Gradually, Ann, her grandmother, and I developed a whispered song telling the voices to become quieter.

At the same time, Julie reported that her daughter became extremely frightened of a man that she had seen at a store and at another location, reporting that this man would kidnap and kill her with either an ax or a knife. Following these disclosures and fearful home behavior, I decided it was very important to again include Ann's mother and stepfather to help her integrate these fearful disclosures and strong emotional responses into her home attachment relationships. During the first parts of these sessions, I gradually included Ann's grandmother and mother and stepfather. Kathleen began to come to fewer and fewer of these sessions, and the final sessions included joint activities with Ann, Julie, and George only. The goal of these sessions included the development of corrective and more positive activities to develop a sense of safety and reattachment with Ann's nonperpetrating parents.

The Corrective and Attachment Metaphors

This next section of treatment developed over approximately six months of time. During the first four months of this phase, I saw Ann approximately once a week with one or both of her parents. I saw her twice during the last month and once during the last month of treatment in the termination process. As described earlier, Kathleen attended three of these sessions to assist with the transition. However, for the first month, I saw Ann with her mother and stepfather alone. The initial goal of these sessions was to help Ann report the disclosures of ritual abuse to her mother and stepfather independent of the influence of her grandmother and for her caretakers to provide a sense of safety and protection. During this disclosure process, Ann used artwork to graphically illustrate her reports as she had done earlier. These reports were remarkably similar to those reported approximately three to four months earlier to her grandmother, and were made spontaneously without any statements by me reminding her of what she had previously reported.

Ann initially refused to enter the room during the first session with her mother and stepfather. She reported that if she talked about any of the things that she had been describing earlier to her grandmother and myself, her mother would be murdered viciously with a knife, and that the "guardian angels" would be watching her to report back to the "bad people." During this session, Ann's parents continued to reassure her that they would not be killed and could keep themselves, their dog, and their children safe. During these disclosures, Ann would begin making the rapid eye movements and showing quick mood shifts and emotional changes in ways similar to the episodes from earlier sessions. During the next few sessions, Ann continued to use art to describe to her parents the episodes of animal mutilation, children in caves, and the activities of the "bad people" and Satan, including the songs and chants that she had repeated earlier.

After these art sessions, my intervention was to have Ann and her parents build a safe house where none of the guardian angels or Satan or the "bad people" could enter. Ann and both parents cooperatively carried large pillows together, and designed and built a house in the middle of the office. This procedure took a while to accomplish as Ann would at first refuse to work together with one or another parent or they would try to build the whole structure themselves. However, I kept insisting that "in the story of the ghosts" the only kind of house that would really be safe was one that parents and children could work on together, talk to each other, and find mutual enjoyment. The goal of this building activity was first to clearly highlight the interactive difficulties within the completion of the task, reframe these difficulties to be part of the metaphor concerning safety, and then allow the act of making a house together to become making the metaphor together as well. During this time, I coached the activity giving different suggestions on how to complete the task, as well as adding to the metaphorical activity of making a "safe house."

I reintroduced games of chasing away fire, ghosts, and monsters that Ann and her mother had played almost a year earlier, while she and her parents were in the "safe house." Because Julie had used games similar to this throughout the last year to help her with sleeping, it was easy to point out to Ann how her mother and stepfather could now keep her safe from the "bad people." The connections between the monster and safe house games further helped in building the metaphorical value. It was also important that not only were Julie and George receptive to hearing and seeing the pictures of the episodes that Ann described to them, but they were very supportive of her fearful affect as well within the house. Therefore, this activity of building was successful on the task as well as symbolic level. This building activity was so successful that Ann and her parents wanted to repeat it several times in later sessions.

Throughout the next several months, Ann and Julie and occasionally her stepfather were able to participate in developing several corrective or healing metaphorical dramatic enactments. These involved elaborations of the death and doctor scene described earlier. As Ann was verbally reporting information, she began to introduce play of being buried. My intervention to this play was to coach her mother to find and rescue her. Gradually, Ann introduced the idea of animals as being murdered and dead in which she could begin to rescue them. At one point, Ann's mother and grandmother were cast in roles of being doctors and nurses who could sew up the animals after Ann had described them as being torn apart by the "bad people." They enacted this scene by having several of the larger stuffed animals be the "bad people" who tore apart smaller animals. At this point, Ann could enter the scene as a rescuer, chasing away the "bad people," and placing the animals in an ambulance to take them to the safe hospital where her mother and grandmother proceeded to "perform surgery" on them, sewing them up and giving them life again, much to Ann's delight and positive feeling. An interesting detail was having these animals given back their hearts, as Ann had described their hearts being torn out in an earlier drawing.

Another important dramatic scene during this portion of therapy included a series of sessions in which Ann said goodbye to Todd and the "bad people" and was adopted by Julie and George. We developed this scene over several sessions and included drawings as well as dramatic enactments. In several drawings, Ann drew Todd and spontaneously suggested that he be buried as a way to say goodbye to him. At another time, we established a courtroom scene during the time when Ann was in the process of being adopted by her stepfather. In the play court, Ann identified a family of "bad people." This family was set up on one side of the room, and her current family was set up on the other. I played the "emotional judge," asking emotionally relevant questions of Ann's mother and stepfather around such subjects as child safety. I asked them if they would ever hurt Ann and if they could keep her safe. I then gave Ann the task of saying goodbye to the old family and moving to her new "loving, safe family" in which children would not be hurt.

This activity was extremely difficult for Ann to enact, as every time she got close to the family she has identified as being the "bad people," she would become quite silly, provocative, oppositional, and agitated. Interestingly, Ann's movement patterns as she approached the "bad people" were similar to those she had demonstrated more than one and a half years earlier when she was in the presence of her father. To make this scene more clear, I asked Ann to sit with her mother and stepfather while I used a stuffed animal she had cast as herself to complete the ritual of saying goodbye to the old family and being welcomed by the new. At this point, I moved the "Ann" stuffed animal, stopping at each point to ask what the animal would be thinking or feeling. Both Julie and George were able to assist Ann to feel assured, and she reported that she felt both scared and sad to say goodbye to the old "bad people."

We completed the play court activity as the animal and Ann both simultaneously joined her mother and stepfather after they had answered several of the "judge's questions" about not hurting children ever and keeping them safe. At this point, Julie, George, and Ann drew pictures of what they imagined the ideal family would be. These pictures included parents and children being safe, playing, and parents promising never to allow children to be hurt. Ann also agreed to be adopted by her stepfather as well as adopting him, as they completed a family drawing together showing positive and playful interactions. They took this drawing home and placed it in an important place within the home.

These activities produced significant emotional relief and catharsis, helped Ann become much closer to her mother and stepfather, and helped her feel more trusting of them. However, she still would introduce difficult distracting and oppositional nonverbal behavior in their interactions. During therapy, such interactions were characterized by very quick emotional shifts, lack of preparation for new physical transitions, and introduction of high-intensity gestures and postures. This nonverbal behavior made it very difficult for Ann and her parents to develop a cooperative style of nonverbal movement responses more typical of secure attachment. Even as her mother and stepfather were interacting with her, building a new safe house in later sessions for example, Ann would continue to change her behavior, move away, and become somewhat oppositional.

My response to this behavior was to introduce the Follow-the-Leader games to help Ann and her family begin to re-choreograph their nonverbal exchange in order to develop the more reciprocal interactive movement style needed for secure attachment behavior. However, during this Follow-the-Leader game, I nominated Ann's mother or stepfather as the "big leader." I established this role so that either parent could define when the leadership could change in such a way that Ann could lead her parents in nonverbal activities until the "big leader" (one of her parents) would decide who the next leader would be. We videotaped and observed these interactions. During this time, I actively coached the parents to choose the best time to change the leadership so that Ann would stay maximally involved with them and include their intrinsically generated nonverbal, interactive ideas in a free play. I also coached the parents to change the leadership when Ann attempted to control, divert, or otherwise break the interactive patterns. Once they had learned the general game, I gave them homework assignments to watch the tape and practice these interactive games at home. Ann and her family were able to quickly adapt to this style of physical exchange. I gave them different tasks, such as having the parents teach her normal childhood songs and games and drawing using the idea of "the big leader."

Over the period of approximately one month, Ann was able to develop a far more integrated style of physical relating. She began to use her own ideas to freely cooperate with her parents, alternating in an appropriate balance of approach and comfort seeking with distance and exploration. Her parents, on their parts, were able to "learn" how to pace their leadership cues in the interaction in a way that offered the minimum amount of direction needed to accomplish any task, leaving Ann free to develop her own ideas within their relationship quite easily.

As these therapeutic dances and dramas between Ann and her parents became easier for them to accomplish, a more normal, give-and-take, free style of interaction developed. I then brought up the subject of terminating therapy. During this session, Ann and both parents were able to draw and talk about the things they remembered most over the year and a half of therapy intervention. Ann's ideas included drawing the spiders that she had described as being inside of her until her grandmother, mother, and I had removed them in a play enactment. She also remembered the fire that she described in the first part of the sessions as burning down her house. Later Ann remembered burning down her house as being a threat from the "bad people" should she verbally disclose the information about her abuse. During one of these drawing, Ann again introduced the idea of a house burning down and people being burned. Her mother quickly remembered all the rescue scenes that Julie, George, and Kathleen had completed with Ann. Reminding her daughter of this, Julie then drew a fire truck coming to rescue the children from inside the burning house.

From all of these images, we all designed a good-bye drama in which Ann and her mother and stepfather were ultimately able to say good-bye to me one at a time. In this metaphor, both Ann's mother and myself were able to reassure her that none of the things that happened were her fault, and like the people in the house, she had no responsibility for starting the fire and needed to be rescued by her mother. During one of the final good-bye visits, Ann was able to say good-bye to the "bad people" and their memories. At this point, she was able to draw again a picture of the memories, including the scary spiders. After drawing this picture, Ann decided to tear it up as a way of getting rid of the past imagery. During the final termination session, Ann was able to again draw a picture of the fire burning down a house and finally enact rescuing a small stuffed animal she had cast as herself, while her mother, stepfather, and I watched from a safe house. Ann ended the session by bringing this animal into the safe house to be with her family. This dramatic image of rescuing herself (the bear) and bringing the bear to her mother to be safe proved to be very powerful for both Ann and Julie, especially remembering the first image in therapy in which Ann's drawing showed that she was being overwhelmed by this fire.

RESULTS AND FOLLOW-UP

After the last session, Julie and I made arrangements for her to make follow-up contacts with me, as Ann may continue to have problems during stressful times in her life. Though Ann, her mother, and her stepfather certainly had come a long way in reestablishing a more trusting, intimate relationship, the overwhelming experience of such pervasive trauma and Ann's internal representation, physical memories, and belief and expectations about herself in the future may be challenged when she encounters the strong interpersonal challenges of growing up. Through the phone contacts so far, Julie reports that Ann continues to do well in her early elementary grades and she reports no return of the more traumatic behaviors, nightmares, aggression, masturbation, or sexualized activity that first led her to treatment. At this point, Ann's birth father has not attempted to contact her in any way, having had his parental rights terminated. According to Ann's mother, Todd apparently has left the state following his sentence for molesting the other child.

DISCUSSION

Secure family attachments are built upon interactions between parents and children in which parents are physically sensitive to children's nonverbal and emotional cues in a way in which both parents and children experience the intrinsic experience of creative choice making in a moment-to-moment fashion. This style of interaction leads to feelings of security in the flow of nonverbal and dramatic expressions. Internally felt security is reflected as the parents and children successfully negotiate matching and mismatching nonverbal conflict resolution as their interactive flow of movement unfolds. Continuing the image from the performing arts introduced in the beginning of the chapter, the family's inner choreographer provides ongoing dances of attachment that produce gestures, rhythms, and shaping movements, no matter how small. Likewise, in the drama of emotional enactment, attached families are able to successfully resolve their conflicts and roles, which are complementary and encourage independent choice-making. Families who experience love and goodwill repeat and elaborate these dances and dramas in creative ways over and over throughout everyday family life. Such expressions create positive images, metaphors, symbols, stories, and, ultimately, positive rituals to symbolize union.

The experience of abuse frightens and terrorizes children during the moments of the trauma. If such abuse continues, children learn to internalize and ultimately split off from this experience to control, regulate, and survive the emotional intensity they experience. However, the cost of these defenses is that the young child victim's ability to form intimate relationships in a spontaneous and open manner is significantly compromised, setting up disrupted attachment relationships for years following the actual traumatic events. This set of circumstances produces children who experience post traumatic syndromes such as delayed terror reactions, nightmares, night terrors, phobic reactions, and difficulty with achieving developmental, social, emotional, and cognitive tasks, in combination with emotional numbing and blocking. The trauma disrupts these children's sense of the future and negatively impacts their beliefs and feeling toward living a happy life. Because the actual traumatic experience of abuse occurs to these children's bodies and in their physical/sensational level of experience, as in Ann's case, their nonverbal interactional behavior, as well as their ability to make sense of their relationships through metaphors, becomes distorted. Other family relationships can be affected in basic and unconscious ways. It is quite tragic for children and other family members to keep reproducing movement patterns and dramatic enactments that leave them terrified, angry, oppositional, insecure, and ultimately alienated, despite the best of intentions and high need for understanding and belonging.

One of the major contributions of dynamic play therapy is to help such families reestablish trusting, secure relationships. Within this context, it is hoped that young children can be helped to re-create positive expectations of themselves and the world, despite having experienced being overwhelmed and helpless at a basic core physical/sensational/emotional level. By helping parents and children rebuild their primary attachments, the main goal of this intervention is to make concrete the basic hope of every parent to take away his or her child's nightmares and fears, and the basic hope of every child to have his or her parent provide comfort in a real and caring way.

Dynamic play therapy is an integrated expressive arts form designed to help family members use various forms of expression to re-create, re-choreograph, and re-direct the social/emotional part of their relationships in very concrete ways. In this form of therapy, attachment difficulties and experiences with trauma that impact trust and security-related feelings clearly influence the expression between parents and children, both as individuals and as a family. These influences are easily seen in the nonverbal, dramatic, and graphic indicators of play breaks, emotional shifts, incomplete images, and dramatic changes in a moment-to-moment fashion as parents and children interact. As the dynamic play therapist identifies these breaks, he or she designs therapeutic interventions to help family members extend and develop these images within a context of security, exploration, and expression. The interventions allow both parents and children to re-create interactions in which they can experience bodily felt choice and metaphor development in an intrinsic and spontaneous way.

The case presented outlines the struggles of a young girl who described herself as experiencing satanic ritual abuse, through her dramatic, movement, and artistic interactive and solo play. Throughout this intervention, the therapeutic choice was to help this girl and those adults close to her address the physical, emotional attachment, and value/belief aspects of this experience. Because of the amount of physical, emotional, and spiritual devastation this young girl described, I believe as a therapist I did not have the luxury to just address the emotional feelings of these family members in a verbal, insightful manner. This young girl presented such pervasive behavioral symptoms, dramatic imagery, and nonverbal difficulty, including hearing voices and being watched by guardian angels she connected to Satan, who told her to do evil things such as sexually assault her younger sister and hurt her animals. She also reported experiencing intrusive thoughts, terrorizing nightmares, and disorganized attachment behavior in her movement. I decided to use dynamic play metaphors to address all of these issues within the intimate family context. It was also important to let this young girl develop her movement and dramatic and graphic play imagery by herself, without undue influence from the adults involved in her life, including myself, and her parents.

I do not believe that my interpretation of the etiology of Ann's problems or Ann's behavior can be attributed to the therapy process or elements of her relationship with her mother and stepfather. I saw Ann in therapy long before I became familiar with this type of abuse. Her parents reported, and she confirmed, that she had not viewed horror television shows, movies, or any other media presentation that would have taught her the images she played out in sessions. While her parents were religious, they did not participate in any religious practices outside the norms of more common Christian beliefs. Additionally, I am confident that the actual use of movement, drama, art, and video therapy did not produce this level of images, as I have applied the same techniques to several families who are not experiencing problems, as well as families who have experienced more typical problems, such as divorce and adoption, and several children who have experienced sexual abuse by a single perpetrator.

One of the main things I learned from this case was how therapeutic family metaphors can be generated in an emergent process that can stimulate natural creative and restorative attachment experiences. Throughout the therapy with Ann and her family, we kept making positive rituals to counteract the abusive ritual experiences she described. These positive rituals brought the warm, ongoing feelings between Ann and her family together with their imaginative and creative abilities to rebuild their relationship as they made new metaphoric activity.

Interestingly, the most powerful therapeutic images for Ann were constructed from the very frightening imagery that she repeatedly presented. By uniting the repeated fragments of movement, dramatic activity, and story, Ann and her family were able to make successful recombinations. For example, we changed Ann's scene of being dead and turning into a monster to being brought to life and rescued by her grandmother through spontaneous finger dances. This activity ultimately led to Ann rescuing "dead" stuffed animals and bringing them to her mother and grandmother to sew back together at a "hospital." Likewise, the dramatic doctor scene in which Ann could finally have some new "doctor" remove the satanic black widows also had a dramatic ritual quality. Additionally, it seemed to me that the family's building a safe house metaphor together generated a very positive and lasting ritual. These positive metaphors appeared to help this family create experiences of meaningful closeness.

Because the legal and social service systems determined that this young girl would not see her father prior to the beginning of the actual intervention in this case, this girl's actual physical safety was assured. Given cases such as this, this development was a relative luxury, as often contested custody situations and determinations of abuse call for the interventions of social service and legal involvement simultaneous with the therapy, and each of these systems have different agendas, levels of proof, and experiences in dealing with ritualistic abuse. Therefore, this chapter did not address the extremely complex issues involved with the protective, visitation, and criminal aspects that often accompany such cases. This topic is addressed elsewhere (Sakheim and Devine 1992—see Selected Readings list) and warrants the full attention of mental health professionals who need to interact with other professionals. The area of ritual abuse is highly controversial, with mental health, legal, social service, and religious professionals taking both sides of an argument as to whether such abuse even exists.

When these events were reported to the Department of Social Services, the workers in one country were very disbelieving, while the workers and police in another city were quite interested. Personally and professionally, this case and others like it have been very challenging, shocking, and frightening. As a result of this and other cases involving similar material, I believe that my mail was tampered with; my phones were tapped occasionally; my family, myself, and a clinician partner received strange threats; and some local mental health professionals refused to send me additional referrals. Other clinicians dealing with these kinds of cases have reported similar experiences. I have also had to confront my own spiritual beliefs, as well as deal with some secondary posttraumatic symptoms myself. Throughout this turmoil, I have found it important to always keep my focus on the discipline of continuing to develop metaphors using the emergent movement, dramatic, and narrative material presented in the expressive activities.

The atmosphere of sharp and diversive reactions to material such as that presented in this case clearly do not serve us as mental health professionals or the families who find themselves in such situations. This case may present a model for play therapists with similar cases. Ann, her mother, and stepfather were able to generate a new sense of closeness in their therapy together. The emphasis in my interaction with this family was to help them develop secure relationships through creative expression, rather than to attempt to prove or disprove the existence of cult activity.

REFERENCES

Bell, J. (1984). Family therapy in motion: observing, assessing, and changing the family dance. In *Theoretical Approaches to Dance-Movement Therapy*, vol. 2, ed. D. Bernstein, pp. 177–256. Dubuque, Iowa: Kendall/Hunt.

Crittenden, P. J. (in press). Quality of attachment in the preschool years. *Development and Psychopathology*.

Crittenden, P. M. (1988). Relationships at risk. In *The Clinical Implications of Attachment*, ed. J. Belsky and T. Nozworski, pp. 136–167. Hillsdale, NJ: Lawrence Erlbaum.

Dulica, D. (1976). *Movement Therapy with Families*. Monograph of the American Psychological Association. Special Education, 1104.

Harvey, S. A. (1989). *Initial Games in Dynamic Play Therapy*. Copyrighted, unpublished manuscript available from the author.

_____ (1990). Dynamic play therapy: an integrated expressive arts approach to the family therapy of young children. *The Arts in Psychotherapy* 17:239–246.

_____ (1991). Creating a family: an integrated expressive arts approach to adoption. *The Arts in Psychotherapy* 18:213–222.

_____ (in press-a). The development of attachment: long-term family intervention with the adoption of a sexually abused child. In *Dance Therapy: A Healing Art*, vol. 2, ed. F. Levy. Reston, VA: The American Alliance for Health, Physical Education, and Dance.

_____ (in press-b). Patterns of movement interaction observed in child sexual abuse victims. *Journal of the American Dance Therapy Association*.

Landgarten, H. B. (1987). *Family Art Psychotherapy: A Clinical Guide and Casebook*. New York: Brunner/Mazel.
Meekums, B. (1991). Dance movement therapy with mothers and young children at risk of abuse. *The Arts in Psychotherapy* 18:223–230.
Terr, L. C. (1983). Play therapy and psychic trauma: a preliminary report. In *Handbook of Play Therapy*, vol. 1, ed. C. Schaefer and K. O'Connor, pp. 308–319. New York: Wiley.
_____ (1990). *Too Scared to Cry: Psychic Trauma in Childhood*. New York: Harper & Row.

SELECTED READINGS FOR PLAY THERAPISTS DEALING WITH SADISTIC, RITUAL ABUSE ISSUES

Bitz, N. (1990). The impact of ritualistic abuse for sexually abused children and their adoptive families. In *Adoption and the Sexually Abused Child*, ed. J. McNamara and B. H. McNamara, pp. 119–130. New York: Family Resources.
Finkelhaur, D., Williams, L. M., Burns, N., and Kalinowski, M. (1988). *Sexual Abuse in Daycare: A National Study. Final Report*. Durham, NH: Family Research Laboratory, University of New Hampshire.
Gannaway, G. (1989). Historical truth versus narrative truth: clarifying the role of exogenous trauma in the etiology of multiple personality and its variants. *Dissociation* 2:205–220.
Gould, C. (1987). Satanic ritual abuse: child victims, adult survivors, system response. *California Psychologist* 22:1.
Hudson, P. S. (1991). *Ritual Child Abuse: Discovery, Diagnosis and Treatment*. Saratoga, CA: R and E.
Kachin, M. H., and Sakheim, D. K. (1992). Satanic beliefs and practices. In *Out of Darkness: Exploring Satanism and Ritual Abuse*, ed. D. K. Sakheim and S. E. Devine, pp. 73–108. New York: Lexington.
Kelly, S. J. (1989). Stress responses of children to sexual abuse and satanic ritual abuse in daycare center. *Journal of Interpersonal Violence* 4:502–513.
Lanning, K. V. (1989). *Satanic, Occult, Ritualistic Crime: A Law Enforcement Perspective*. Quantico, VA: FBI Academy.
Ritual Abuse Task Force. (1989). *Ritual Abuse: Definitions, Glossary, the Use of Mind Control*. Report of the Ritual Abuse Task Force. Los Angeles, CA: Los Angeles County Commission for Women.
Sakheim, D. K., and Devine, S. E. (1992). *Out of Darkness: Exploring Satanism and Ritual Abuse*. New York: Lexington.
Summit, R. (1989). Ritual child abuse: a professional overview. Ukiah, CA: Cavalcade Productions. (Videotape)
Waterman, J., Kelly, R. J., McCord, J., and Oliveri, M. K. (1990). Reported ritualistic and non-ritualistic sexual abuse in pre-schools: effects in mediators. *Executive Summary, Department of Psychology, UCLA, Research and Education Institute*. Los Angeles, CA: Harper UCLA Medical Center.
Young, W. C., Sacks, R. G., Braun, B. G., and Watkins, R. T. (1991). Patients reporting ritual abuse in childhood: a clinical syndrome. *International Journal of Child Abuse and Neglect* 15:181–189.

13

Oh, But a Heart, Courage, and a Brain: An Integrative Approach to Play Therapy

Jan Faust, PH.D.

INTRODUCTION TO INTEGRATIVE PLAY THERAPY

Integrative play therapy is a form of eclectic play therapy for children. For years professionals and researchers alike have debated the composition of eclectic psychotherapy. Many psychologists disagree as to whether eclecticism is a combination of orientations or the lack of application of any orientation. Norcross (1987) contends that eclecticism evolved in response to professionals' dogmatic adherence to unitary orientations that results in an atmosphere of conflict and partisanship within the profession of psychology.

In fact, professionals have often discussed preferred approaches in the treatment of children as if there exists but one specific approach in treating young clients. The selection of one unitary theoretical orientation over another in child psychotherapy is often not justified, and the therapist may simply follow his or her guru of training rather than accounting for the primary needs of the child. Hence, the therapeutic model or frame guides the therapy often to the exclusion of the particular demands and level of personality development of the child. For example, individuals trained in a psychoanalytic approach of play therapy may focus solely on the child to the exclusion of the family, declining to address overt parenting deficits. Therapists conducting cognitive-behavioral therapy in treating a child's response to trauma may also fail to address the emotional impact of the trauma, as well as the child's changed perception of the family environment (e.g., failure of his or her primary caretakers to prevent the trauma).

Norcross (1987), in his review of the literature, presents three subtypes of eclectic theory that predominate among the multitudes of proposed eclectic models: synthetic eclectism, kitchen-sink eclectism, and linear eclectism. Synthetic eclecticism is equivalent to integrative eclectic theory, upon which integrative play therapy is based. This approach focuses on the integration of a variety of theoretical models into an interactive and coordinated therapeutic effort. The idea is to have a well-developed conceptualization from which to integrate different theories and to do so in a systematic methodological manner, not haphazardly during any given therapy moment. Prior to my presentation of integrative play therapy through case demonstration, it might be useful to discuss how integrative play therapy differs from other eclectic child approaches.

Kitchen-Sink Eclecticism

A slipshod eclectic play therapy approach gives rise to the temptation of the "kitchen-sink" technique with the opposite effect: an atheoretical treatment base and a sense of desperation on the therapist's part to find the magic serum for cure (Eysenck 1970, Norcross 1987). Just as there are many dangers in adhering too tightly and rigidly to treating children from one particular orientation, treating a child eclectically can also be antitherapeutic. A therapist, for example, conducts behavioral parent training with the child and the parents in the first half-hour of a session and then proceeds to meet with the child alone for client-centered play therapy in the second half of the session. The ability of the therapist to maintain a client-centered posture enabling the child to openly learn about him- or herself during the second half of the session may be thwarted by the limit setting and goal-directed behavior of the therapist during the first half hour of the session.

A more subtle example is when a therapist attempts to utilize a humanistic approach in treating an extremely withdrawn and electively mute child, and the therapist "reinforces" the child's verbal communications, disguising such reinforcement within a client-centered reflection. For example, a previously quiet and unassertive child requests assistance with a toy. The therapist responds, "You are asking me for help with the toy. Good for you." These therapists can even provide a rationale for such a technique, attributing the praise as a reinforcement of communication in order to increase the amount of verbalization produced. Then the therapist will be able to reflect the content. In essence, the therapist has put a value judgment on the child and created an emotionalized attitude of an adult expectation and desire for conformity (Axline 1947). Consequently, the behavior no longer belongs to the child or is a part of the child; rather it has become the adult's. This violates one of the basic premises of client-centered play therapy that stipulates that child behavior problems are the result of emotionalized attitudes that develop from adults' maladaptive responses to, and treatment of, the child (Axline 1947). In this instance, attempting to integrate these two models negates the theory upon which the model is constructed and in so doing may actually be destructive for the child. The adult literature refers to this type of therapy as atheoretical eclecticism (Norcross 1987). In atheoretical eclecticism, the therapist ignores the theory that underlies the treatment technique. The clinician simply combines different techniques, thereby predisposing him or her to violate the philosophical basis of the theory from which the technique is derived.

Linear Eclecticism

Linear eclecticism is a move from one orientation to the next after the completion of therapy from within the first model. This type of eclecticism also has limitations. For example, if the therapist were to shift from the role of gatekeeper and messenger to and from the unconscious in psychoanalytic play therapy to superego parent figure in behavioral parent training, there could potentially be a dramatic negative impact on the psyche. This linear form of eclecticism fails to address the historical context of the child and the course of therapy. The therapist approaches each conceptualization and treatment with the idea that every therapy experience is vacuum-packed, an entity within itself. In actuality, every experience, whether physical, experiential, or emotional, is intertwined into the child's psychological fabric.

Clinical Orientations:
A Wolf in Sheep's Clothing or All Sheep?

Many professionals attempt to convince themselves that any real differences among therapy models are only an issue of semantics. These clinicians usually adhere either to an eclectic orientation or to a monogamous approach (without a knowledge base of other therapeutic orientations) and proclaim that all therapy approaches are the same except for the vocabulary utilized in describing the technique. For example, such an eclectic individual may explain depression from a cognitive-behavioral frame as a result of automatic irrational beliefs usually comprised of negative self-worth statements (e.g., I'm incompetent, I'm unlovable). He or she may simultaneously explain depression from a psychodynamic perspective as the result of unconscious intrusions related to guilt (e.g., I'm a bad person), derived from the internalization of rage (cf. Josephs 1992, Klein 1979).

At first glance, the concepts in these different orientations appear to be similar, if not the same. However, on closer inspection, they are not the same at all. The psychodynamic model posits that the unconscious intrusion of guilt is a residue of problems in personality organization and psychological functioning on the whole that have had a long developmental history (Klein 1979). Depression, then, is actually symptomatic of other problems in psychological functioning. On the other hand, the cognitive-behavioral approach attributes maladaptive psychological functioning, such as depression, to learned self-statements that the client has heard so often as to have become habit-forming or automatic (Burns 1981). In this approach, the therapist addresses the depression directly and does not view it as symptomatic of problems in global psychological functioning or adjustment. As a result, and not surprisingly, treatment differs dramatically. The psychodynamic approach focuses on uncovering of unconscious material and associated affects via a solid therapeutic alliance, while the cognitive-behavioral approach focuses on altering and practicing self-statements and attributions so that the client replaces habitual irrational thoughts with adaptive cognitions.

It is apparent, then, that not all therapies are the same with simply disparate language bases. Rather, there appear to be inherent differences among therapies that make them unique, both in practice and with respect to their clinical impact. As a result, it would be fallacious to expect all therapies to differ only in their linguistic properties.

Integration as Alternative

Environment as Therapy Context

Another potential problem associated with adhering too tightly to a particular therapeutic base when treating children arises in developmental differences of children and adults as they relate to external reality. In many traditional therapies, the child's external environment, although considered, is excluded from psychological intervention. Many therapists believe in maintaining a sterile clinical posture, similar to their approach with adults. The preservation of the patient–therapist relationship is focal to the exclusion or lack of therapist involvement with a child's parents, school, or other community resources. Children are environmentally connected individuals, much more so than adults. They do not have the resources to control many events in their lives, nor can they communicate their needs as readily. From a purely survival perspective, children rely heavily on the external environment as a source of information that may be necessary for their survival (Harter 1983). Children, who have limited verbal facility, cue much more readily into the physical environment than adults do. The environment is the basis by which children obtain autonomy and separateness. It would seem logical, then, that an integrative play therapist consider interaction with the physical environment in play therapy sessions. The play therapist must loosely define the environment just as it is in reality: school, family, home, outdoors, indoors, and so on.

Space is important in determining boundaries for everyone, but as children negotiate their ever-changing role from dependency to autonomy, from powerlessness to powerful, space becomes an important determinant of identity. One cannot separate the metaphorical term of space (such as that utilized when a mother is too enmeshed with her child) from physical space, since the latter is altered by psychological changes in space. For example, an overly enmeshed mother restricts her child's activities in order to keep the child in closer proximity to her or in an attempt to protect the child from unseen, yet predicted dangers. This maternal behavior restricts the child's access to his or her environment. Physical space/environment is embedded in the fourth dimension, time. Therefore, the integrative play therapist must also consider the passage of time in assessment (diagnosis) and treatment as it relates to physical space and the historical map of children.

Evolving Conceptualizations

Integrative play therapists must consider all facets of the child's developmental history, and inter- and intrapersonal history (including family systems). In addition, as the play therapist chooses the primary conceptualization and alternative, perhaps competing, secondary conceptualizations, he or she must also consider the historical context of the child and the physical life in which that history is embedded.

So how should the play therapist concerned with individually tailoring therapy to the needs of the child proceed? It is advantageous for the integrative play therapist, armed with a sufficient developmental, medical, and social/familial history, to formulate a detailed, working case conceptualization. The conceptualization, anchored in one particular school of thought, should include alternative as well as complementary conceptualizations from differing theoretical bases. The primary conceptualization will be the map for therapy. The availability of alternative conceptualizations will enable the therapist to maintain a fluidity that facilitates using such a map even when charting unknown territory (with the uncovering of additional historical information).

There are several factors to consider when selecting any conceptualization. The most obvious is related to the individual therapist. First, training, ability, and knowledge will dictate the treatment options available. If the therapist has been trained in three different schools of thought, then other schools of therapy are not appropriate for him or her. The second factor that the therapist must consider in choosing treatment composition involves the child's historical and current contexts. Finally, the resources available to the child, such as those caretakers who are willing to participate in the child's therapy in any capacity, will dictate the composition of the integrative therapies. The latter will help to determine commitment to therapy and the probability of attrition. Commitment is especially important since some types of therapy could threaten the parents emotionally (e.g., parent involvement may increase sense of failure and blame), increasing the likelihood of attrition.

After selecting the primary conceptualization, the therapist then develops secondary conceptualizations from the information used to generate the primary case hypothesis. This does not preclude altering or adding conceptualizations later in therapy as new information becomes available. The therapist then needs to determine the compatibility level of the secondary conceptualizations; that is, are they complementary or incompatible with the primary conceptualization and the environmental context? If they are compatible conceptualizations, the therapist must decide whether to use the additional conceptualizations in conjunction with the primary conceptualization or only as alternatives should the primary conceptualization be insufficient in problem resolution. If the therapist decides to integrate these alternative approaches, he or she should always maintain a clear understanding of the distinct roles the primary and secondary conceptualizations have in the process and treatment of the case. Figure 13-1 provides a graphic representation of this integrative approach. The therapist also decides the level and

ENVIRONMENTAL CONTEXT

Physical, Social, Academic, Familial, Other

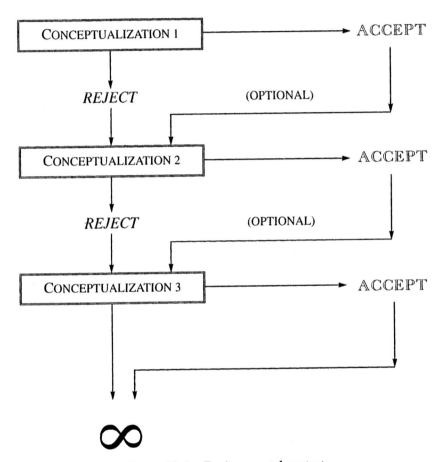

Figure 13-1. Environmental context

process of integration, implementing approaches either sequentially or simultaneously, or a combination of both methods.

If the secondary conceptualizations are incompatible with the primary conceptualization, then the therapist would use only the primary conceptualization, while mentally storing the secondary conceptualizations for future use should the primary fail to contribute to therapeutic effectiveness. For example, a child who had been seen in my training clinic had been labeled as having attention-deficit hyperactivity disorder (ADHD). During the assessment phase, the parents and school officials complained about the manner in which the attention deficit manifested itself via poor peer interactions. Further, behavioral observations also suggested inadequate implementation of social skills in this child's peer interactions. Initially, the student therapist conceptualized this case from a cognitive-behavioral frame, attributing the poor peer interactions of ADHD as the result of misread social cues and faulty learning. We also had evidence from the evaluation period of treatment to question how well the patient's parents had emotionally validated and supported his sense of self as it emerged historically. As a result, we selected, as the primary conceptualization, cognitive-behavioral therapy to increase prosocial behavior in the child through role-playing, as well as instruction and reinforcement of appropriate adaptive social behaviors. As time passed, the child learned more prosocial behaviors, but was unable to generalize the new skills to external environmental settings. As a result, we switched the treatment to encompass the secondary conceptualization, client-centered, and the child's behavior improved dramatically through self-discovery.

Finally, the use of therapy process assessment scales can aid the clinician in determining how well he or she is implementing the targeted treatment in response to the selected conceptualizations. Dr. William J. Burns and I have developed the Nova Assessment of Psychotherapy (NAP) (Faust and Burns 1991) to aid both clinician and researchers in assessing the process and outcome of psychotherapy. The clinical version of the NAP is a shortened version of the research scale and is designed for therapist implementation in a quick and unencumbered fashion at the completion of the therapy session. It helps clinicians track how well they have implemented the therapeutic technique from a variety of theoretical orientations and the impact the selected approach has had on the child.

The Use of Metaphor to Anchor and Convey Integrative Conceptualizations

Metaphor is a powerful form of communication that can transcend the spoken word by conveying a variety of meanings above and beyond its original meaning. A metaphor is a figure of speech designed to compare two entities that are not obviously related to each other (Lankton and Lankton 1983). It produces an amalgam of the two identities that did not previously exist. Hence, the metaphor is a form of communication that either adds information or changes the quality of the original informative message.

The use of metaphor has particular relevance to integrative play therapy. By the very nature of their transcended communicative power, metaphors can help organize various complex theoretical constructs into interactive cybernetic systems that in effect take on a new form or altered form of meaning (Lankton and Lankton 1983). By using metaphor in his or her integrative conceptualization, the play therapist is able to consolidate understanding of the patient through a number of conceptualizations as the metaphor gives form to a multifaceted picture of the patient. This understanding maintains the fluidity of therapeutic process. Metaphorically speaking, integrative play therapy is the equivalent of combining theories via a videotape instead of a series of snapshots. The whole may, in fact, be greater than the sum of the parts.

Therapists practicing individual as well as family systems therapy have used metaphors extensively in order to bring unconscious material forward, to describe metacommunication in a family system, and to help individuals and families view problems from a different perspective. In addition to using a metaphor in understanding the conceptualization of a case, the therapist can also use metaphor to further elucidate knowledge conveyed in educating students. To this end, metaphor can offer students fresh alternatives to problems and their manifestation (Bergman 1992). In response to a metaphor, behavioral and effectual changes can occur among the family members, thereby enabling the system to free itself from a homeostatic feedback loop and hence alter system functioning. The use of metaphor by therapists is designed to effect change in a multitude of ways (e.g., Bergman 1992, Gutheil 1979).

The following case presentation is an attempt to provide the reader with an example of the integrative play therapy approach to treatment. The metaphor of the Wizard of Oz (Baum 1993) was particularly useful in describing this patient and the integrative play therapy process as it pertained to the internal events the child experienced. The metaphor also had relevance to the environment, which played an important role in the understanding and working through of the patient's psychological experiences. The journey of therapy for Paul was a growth experience similar to Dorothy's journey through Oz.

PRESENTING PROBLEM AND BACKGROUND INFORMATION

Paul, a 3-year-old white male, was referred to therapy due to observable aggressive and "out-of-control" behavior his mother noticed after weekend visitations with his father. At the time of treatment, Paul was living alone with his mother. His parents had separated and divorced when he was 2 years old.

It was initially difficult to determine the beginning of the storm for Paul, but the formulation of the funnel cloud, both in his family environment and internally, reached an apex when his parents physically separated. On the morning after Al Johnson moved out of their jointly held house, Paul's mother, Susan, found Paul sleeping by the front door, waiting for his father to return. Dorothy was similarly displaced (at least twice), through the relocation from her parents as caretakers to her aunt and uncle as guardians, and then again when the tornado landed her in Oz (Baum 1993). Through the muddled wreckage of the Johnson's marriage and the havoc the storm waged on Paul's developing personality, it was clear that his road to recovery was not paved with brick, but with mud, mire, and rocks. Paul not only had to endure the pain of loss of his father as a residential caretaker, but also he was caught between the mudslinging of his parents in a bitter divorce.

Prior to his parents' marital separation, Paul's home environment was dysfunctional in that his father had extramarital affairs and would resolve marital conflict with physical violence. Susan's apparent contribution in maintaining the marital conflict included her dedication to the relationship, in hopes that her husband would change, and her exacerbation of the conflict at times in an attempt to change the system. By maternal report, the Johnsons had been married 3½ years before they separated. Susan attributed the dissolution of their marriage to Al's numerous extramarital affairs and his physical and emotional abuse of her. She reported that Al had continually criticized and denigrated her. Later in play therapy, Paul enacted a husband's threat of murder against his wife. This made it clear that Paul's father had threatened to kill Susan when they lived together in the home. Susan confirmed that Al had made numerous threats upon her life. As became so clearly evident in working with Paul, this storm had been building for some time.

After Mr. Johnson physically left the home, he did not contact his son for the eight months it took for the divorce to become final. During my contact with this family, the courts assessed minimal child support, which Al often did not pay. Further, Susan paid all medical and education bills, as Al did not produce his assessed share. Al expressed a renewed interest in visitation approximately four months after the divorce was finalized. He began visiting his son, but only sporadically, and then proceeded to request increased visitation above and beyond the scope of the divorce decree. In order to obtain increased visitation, Mr. Johnson would badger Ms. Johnson at home and at work, effectively intimidating her and wearing her down. Just as Dorothy was hunted and haunted by the Wicked Witch, so too were Paul and his mother tracked and harassed by Mr. Johnson.

Susan and Paul lived in the original residence in which Paul was born until he was about 3½. At that time, Paul and his mother moved in with Ms. Johnson's parents. The maternal grandparents were heavily involved with a conservative church that relied on guilt to control its members and had little tolerance for the expression of negative emotions, particularly anger. Further, Susan appeared to be intimidated by her parents and when Paul had confessed to her that he "said a bad word" in session, Susan told him he could say anything with me. She hurriedly, and with much anxiety, added that it was probably best that he not say these words at home with his grandparents. Paul was expected to alter his behavior and sense of self to avoid confrontation between family members. Similarly, in the film Dorothy had to do the right thing regarding Toto's disobedience, by making amends to her neighbor, Miss Gulch, in Kansas. This reparation resulted in an extremely crucial loss for Dorothy as she had to give away Toto.

Ms. Johnson reported that she was a secretary in a major corporation that enabled her to "climb the corporate ladder." Although very bright and motivated, she had not pursued higher education upon completing her requirements for her high school diploma. Al Johnson had also completed high school and was employed in a family business that had been very lucrative.

Susan reported that her husband was raised in an extremely punitive and rigid home. The use of physical punishment was the primary means of discipline in the household, yet family mores of manhood incorporated looser boundaries than one would expect of such a conservative home. For example, Mr. Johnson's parents tolerated his frequent female overnight visitors commencing at the age of 14. There had also been a historical account of frequent fighting in Mr. Johnson's adolescence, and he had some legal difficulties concerning the use of firearms.

Al Johnson currently worked in his family business and took hunting and camping vacations. Paul had been a frequent guest on these hunting trips, and by the time he was 3 had witnessed the shooting of deer, wild hogs, rabbits, and other animals. During sessions, Paul reported his experiences with hunting as well as sleeping with his father and his father's girlfriend during visitation. His father confirmed these sleeping arrangements, but was unwilling to consider the possible negative consequences of this arrangement for Paul. He did agree to alter this pattern and bought Paul his own bed. Several months after this episode, Paul reported that Lynette, his father's girlfriend, had touched his "pee-pee" and a child protective organization (CPO) investigated. Although the CPO could not confirm this suspected abuse, Paul affirmed it in session and his behavior became increasingly sexualized with specific adult-like sexual verbalizations and actions. Also, CPO informed me that Lynette had unconfirmed reports of child sexual abuse on record with the victims listed as her own children.

During visitation, Paul's father frequently took him to pool bars to "pick up babes." Paul enacted these experiences throughout sessions. He also acted out his exposure to violent and sexualized R-rated movies/videos in his play throughout the course of therapy.

About 6 months after this reported abuse incident, Susan noticed a bruise on Paul's buttocks, which he said originated from a belt buckle used by his father for spanking. Another CPO investigation ensued with an "unconfirmed" report of abuse.

Paul frequently refused visitation with his father. Initially his father would bribe and cajole then threaten and humiliate Paul into complying with the visits. Further, Al would accuse his ex-wife of brainwashing Paul into not wanting to visit, and arguments would often develop in Paul's presence. Although Mr. Johnson's threats of filing legal action to increase visitation never materialized, he did file a suit to prevent Ms. Johnson from leaving the state for her pending interstate job transfer. The Johnsons' original divorce decree stipulated that Susan, primary custodian of Paul, could never move out of state unless Al agreed or if he moved out of state first.

Approximately 2 years after the beginning of treatment, Ms. Johnson's company was closing its branch office in her home town and had transferred her to a city in a neighboring state. It was an opportunity she believed would be difficult to refuse, as she was paid an extremely high salary and benefits for her level of education. She was also reluctant to refuse such an opportunity for advancement. Interestingly, Paul, who traveled often with his parents, wanted to move to this new state. The judge blocked Ms. Johnson's out-of-state transfer and further stipulated that she could not move out of the state or the county. As it turned out, Ms. Johnson's company closed many of its local offices, laying off and transferring hundreds of employees. Her employer, extremely supportive of her domestic situation, was eventually able to relocate her within the company in a different position. Fortunately, she did not lose income, status, or opportunity for advancement.

THEORETICAL CONCEPTUALIZATION

Upon initial consideration, the most prevailing feature of this case is the quantity and quality of developmental traumas or crises Paul had encountered through his early years. Even from the beginning months, he was exposed to an abundance of marital conflict that continued throughout his early childhood. Due to the crises this child encountered at such early, developmentally critical points in his life and the nature of these crises centering around important central figures in his survival and adaptation, I originally chose a psychodynamic theoretical base as the primary conceptualization.

It was difficult to avoid being blind to the intrapersonal dynamics by the whirlwind of the funnel cloud—the divorce and the concomitant emotional turmoil. However, upon closer examination, I decided that the timing of the divorce had a more critical impact than the mere separation of Paul's parents. The divorce and escalating marital conflict coincided with Paul's final crucial negotiation stage of individuation and separation. Paul struggled with a loss of control over his own development as the separation from his father was foisted upon him. Paul's own autonomy and striving toward individuation were confused and thwarted by the father's physical separation from the home, which signaled to Paul the danger of becoming too autonomous. In addition, there is some evidence to suggest that the child begins to negotiate the oedipal striving around this age (Mahler et al. 1975, Rangell 1989).

Paul's understanding of his relationship to both his mother and father became further clouded by the family violence and the marital disruption (his father moving out) as well as the images his father and mother projected. These parental interpersonal interactions during Paul's early years were particularly important in determining his development of a healthy cognitive schema that included both a representation of self and representation of others. According to researchers (Blatt 1993, Diamond et al. 1992), such a schema reflects both an expanding, distinct, yet well-integrated, self-identity and an evolving ability to formulate mature reciprocal and empathic interpersonal relationships. For Paul, the interpersonal and intrapersonal messages he received and incorporated included a lack of consistency with which he could depend upon his needs being met in a nurturing manner. Further, due to the marital violence and conflict between those individuals Paul loved, his environment and sense of self in relation to others was tenuous at best.

In addition to, yet not apart from, the developmental crises, Paul repeatedly received messages to conform to his parents' and grandparents' expectations. His assimilation of the negative emotionalized attitudes from these important figures in his life only served to confirm his sense of badness or wrongness (e.g., Axline 1947). The adults instilled in him their low self-worth and did not validate his separate uniqueness as a worthy and justified birthright. It was evident that Paul had developed emotionalized attitudes in response to the negative and destructive

interactions he had with others and that these interactions had pervaded
his life throughout his childhood. Consequently, a client-centered,
humanistic approach appeared to be a secondary conceptualization that
could enable me to understand and help this child with his pain.

Finally, it was readily apparent that Paul's parents' lack of parenting
skills only served to further aggravate his adjustment. Although it was
evident that Paul was grappling with much more than his parents'
ability to appropriately set and follow through with limits, Mr. and Ms.
Johnson seemed to lack the ability to provide an adequate and healthy
structure for Paul. In general, this secondary (third) conceptualization
could have compromised Paul's response to the other two treatment
approaches. I wanted to help Paul explore his issues, feelings, and
conflicts in a trusting, nonjudgmental atmosphere, without contra-
dicting this approach by setting limits and modeling appropriate parenting skills in session. As a result, I took careful measures to ensure
that I used the third (seemingly incompatible) conceptualization in a
limited manner that did not disrupt treatment. As a result, I conducted
behavioral parent training without Paul being privy to my role in the
instruction, in order to enhance Susan's parenting skills. Mr. Johnson
was resistant to therapy and chose not to participate in this part of Paul's
treatment.

Since, in this case, I could use all three approaches in treating Paul,
I implemented them in careful consideration of the goals of therapy. Both
the psychodynamic and client-centered approaches were complementary in nature. Given Paul's issues, they could be utilized concurrently
without invalidating their theoretical premises and functions. The
behavior therapy had to be integrated differently in that the behavioral
technique (and theory) is in direct contradiction with the other two
conceptualizations. Thus, I implemented the behavioral parent training
without Paul's awareness. Figure 13–2 is a graphic representation of the
integrative play therapy conceptualizations for the case of Paul. This
child was seen in therapy for three years, eight months.

Primary Conceptualization: Psychodynamic

Early Development: Introjected Objects and Projective Identification

Paul initially experienced many threats to his psyche through the
violence present in his family. He experienced both real and subjective
losses and threats to his survival. While simultaneously obtaining some
negative and positive parental object experiences, he was experiencing

"Paul": Case History
ENVIRONMENTAL CONTEXT

<u>Physical</u>	<u>Social</u>	<u>Academic</u>	<u>Familial</u>	<u>Other</u>
Mom's house	School Peers	School	Extended Family	Judicial
Dad's House				
Dad's "Camp"				
Familial Boundaries				

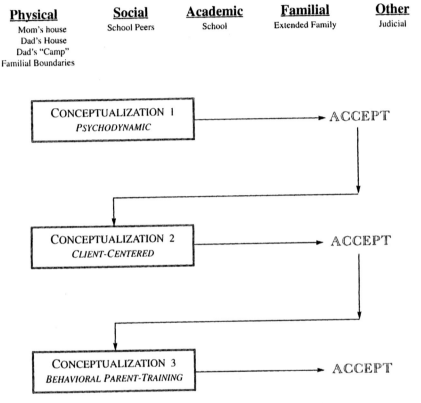

Figure 13-2. "Paul": Case History—environmental context

great difficulty in the integration of these parenting/primary objects. His parents' inconsistency and the unpredictable nature of the volatile marital conflict served to confuse the effectual quality of Paul's object relationships. His attempt at mastery was clear in his splitting off those experienced part objects in his play. The sharks and Mutant Ninja Turtle Shredders represented those punitive, feared parts of his parents. Susan, although she spent much energy hovering over Paul, was ineffectual in helping him battle the very real threatening parts of his father. In his play, Paul would switch playing roles from the shark to the kitten (and sometimes blending such roles as "kitten-shark"), exhibiting his feelings of vulnerability both because of his mother's ineffectiveness at protecting him and as a defensive measure. He played in this manner to distance himself from the seemingly real and scary Shredders, hunters, and sharks in his life. Paul even incorporated the aggressive violent experiences of his father (e.g., Shredder) into his personality. He did this in the course of normal development through assimilation and accommodation, as well as through a defensive maneuver of identification with the aggressor. The identification with the parental aggressor served to ward off anxiety stemming from threats to Paul's survival.

The kitten, in its gentleness and symbolic vulnerability, represented the child part of Paul—where Paul should have been developmentally, had he been on a healthy developmental trajectory. A kitten is a symbol of early childhood and maternal nurturance (e.g., nurturance requirements, both emotional and physical, sleep requirements, and play time—Gutheil 1979). It was difficult for Paul to be a child because of the traumas and crises in his life and because of his parents' parentification of Paul. As a result of their own narcissistic needs, Paul's parents never afforded him the opportunity to be a child, nor did they supply him with the emotional sustenance he needed for healthy growth and identity development. Further, his understanding and integration of healthy, nurturing, primary social relationships were distorted.

Just as Dorothy in *The Wizard of Oz* was orphaned and lived with her rigid nonnurturing aunt and uncle, Paul did not experience a warm and elevating family life. His mother needed Paul to buffer the assaults from her ex-husband and would turn to Paul as an emotional companion during times of loneliness. Mr. Johnson used Paul as a pawn in order to continue a passionate, yet conflictual, relationship with his ex-wife. The conflict between Mr. and Ms. Johnson enabled Al to continue this emotional bond. Just as the Witch, for her own needs, desired to "get to" the magic shoes through Dorothy, so too did Paul's parents want to "get to" each other through Paul. Evidence for Paul's lost childhood was paramount, but one experience that so clearly elucidated this hole in his life was related by his mother. One evening Susan heard a loud thud in Paul's room and subsequent screaming on his part; he had hit his head on the hardwood floor. As she ran to his room, he completely stopped crying before Susan even reached the door. After hearing what happened, Susan, perplexed, questioned Paul about why he stopped crying so suddenly since the injury had sounded painful. The 3-year-old Paul replied: "Only baby sissies cry."

Another example, of Paul's parentification or "childectomy" was evident, when at age 4, Paul's father bought him a pretend rifle for a present. Paul told his father to pretend to be the "hoggie" and then "shot him dead" with the rifle (as he often did to me in therapy session).

Al could not suspend reality and play with Paul, and in this instance, Paul's pretend was a narcissistic insult. In response to this psychological "injury," Al told Paul angrily "That's not nice." In the movie, Dorothy's aunt and uncle, similarly, were so self-absorbed they could not suspend work to attend to their child's urgent fears and needs regarding the conflict between Miss Gulch and Toto.

In addition to Al's ineffectual and frequently destructive interpersonal interactions, Susan exhibited impotence in her ability to protect her son. Rooted in her own developmental history, Susan's poor self-esteem contributed to her selection of a mate who battered both soma and psyche, and also contributed to her hesitant parenting. She often second-guessed her own parenting decisions, allowing Paul too much autonomy in parental limit-setting. As a result, it became evident that when he aggressed toward his mother, she would be ineffective in preventing him from making bodily contact just as she did with Al. Paul did not feel secure with his rage because his omnipotent caretaker could not protect herself from the anger of her own vulnerable small child. The lack of security due to the witnessing of his father's aggression toward his mother and Susan's seeming inability to protect him from his father (e.g., enforced visitation and the abuse that occurred during these visits) only heightened his insecurity and vulnerability. Much as Dorothy and her friends continued along their journey reciting the names of their potential foes (e.g. tigers), hypervigilant to threats that they might encounter, Paul identified in part with his aggressive father to protect himself from subjective anxiety due to threatened and imagined harm. Part of this harm was reality based, in that Mr. Johnson was a visibly punitive and aggressive man and father.

In The Wizard of Oz, the Wizard not only failed to protect Dorothy, he sent her into danger (Baum 1993). The wizards in Paul's life, ironically enough, could be, first of all, the judge, who, cloaked in robes and from behind an altar, dictated supervision and thwarted his escape (with his mother) to the neighboring state. Just as in Oz the good witches worked with the Wizard, Paul's mother was also in collusion with the judge when she complied with the legal visitation order as much as possible (to stay out of jail so that she could retain custody of Paul). Both the judge and the mother, with probably good intentions, set Paul up to confront the "Witch" and all of her symbolic representations. Similarly, the Wizard sacrificed Dorothy to protect himself in several ways, and Paul's mother had offered him up to his father as a way in which she would protect herself (e.g., from Mr. Johnson's wrath or from a legal hassle).

I, too, could easily be cast into the wizard role as the omnipotent caretaker who, endowed with certain therapeutic powers, could lead Paul into health and perhaps save him from the faulty aspects of his parents, especially those many negative attributes of the Wicked Witch, his father. Just as the Wizard was powerless over the Witch (Baum 1993), I, too, could not directly protect Paul from his witch. Paul, like Dorothy, had to rely on his own abilities and resources to conquer fear and threats to his survival.

Further Development: Oedipal Issues

It was also evident that Paul was attempting to negotiate his oedipal urgings. The relationship he had with his parents only served to enhance this developmentally appropriate anxiety. His fear of retaliation from his father in everyday living was enormous. Paul's sense of risked annihilation was further heightened by Al's absence. In addition, Paul's fear of annihilation intensified as mother and son boundaries blurred excessively due to Susan's passive and ineffectual parenting. At the same time, Mr. Johnson continued to tell his son that he and Susan would be getting back together soon. So, in the face of temptation and perhaps the fantasy that obtaining mother was an even greater possibility than it had been previously (with father out of the way and mother's blurred boundaries), as well as his father's promise for a remarriage, Paul's anxiety concerning oedipal feelings were enormous. Paul had evidence of his father's ability to annihilate in observing his physical abuse of women, his slaughter of animals during hunting trips, and his threats of death against Paul's mother. Due to Paul's stage of development, he likely perceived this aggression as both a threat to physical survival and psychological survival, through annihilation and castration.

For Paul, an overidentification with father was in many ways his only hope for survival. Unlike Dorothy, who chanted the names of the threats to her being, Paul's were not animals such as tigers and bears, but characters who had even more unpredictable, yet direct power. His threats were those who would actively search for him such as hunters and the fictional Shredders, and not jungle animals. So instead of hesitantly expressing his fears, chanting carefully and quietly, running in fear, he would take on his monsters in play. He confronted these images, as well as assumed their identities, in order to work through his anxiety and traumas. By actively expecting such beasts and incorporating their caricatures, he could almost become equal with his father and prevent castration and, worse, death.

Secondary Conceptualization: Client-Centered

Paul's identification with his father and incorporation of the maternal and paternal objects included the emotionalized attitudes of many adults in his life. In addition to his parents, both sets of grandparents also conveyed their rigid preconceived ideas of what they expected from children, especially male children. The adults in Paul's life attempted to control and mold Paul's behavior to fit their own expectations and needs. This control or subversion was both covert and overt, and Paul continually heard the message that he was bad and unlovable. Ironically enough, his behavior was the product of the identity given to him by his parents and maintained by their continual response to him through their emotionalized attitudes. His acting-out behavior was the identity that he attempted to preserve and protect, lest he have no identity, as Axline (1947) often observed in children she treated.

Dorothy, in the movie, also had rigid caretakers who had their own difficulties with anger. They relinquished Toto directly to Miss Gulch when she supplied legal papers giving her authority to garnishee the dog. Aunt Em told Dorothy she had to dispense with Toto because that was the law. After Dorothy ran out of the room, Aunt Em told Miss Gulch that for over twenty years she has wanted to tell her the negative feelings she has had for her, but her religious beliefs have prevented her from doing so. And then *she* ran from the room. Anger was taboo for Dorothy (as it was for Paul), lest it get loose and injure. Further evidence of this belief occurred during the beginning of her trip through Oz when she told the scarecrow that he could go with her to visit the wizard but warned him that a wicked witch was angry with her and, as a result, he may be in danger.

Paul needed space, opportunity, and support to experience himself and to understand himself in order to grow and learn. This much-needed emotional and physical environment was not afforded him. Just as Dorothy had to dutifully relinquish Toto to her wicked neighbor Miss Gulch, because of her dog's bad behavior, in order to "correct" some rigidly defined moral faux pas, Paul had to perform to meet his parents' and grandparents' expectations without regard to his feelings and needs. Similarly, Dorothy was told to go away so that she wouldn't be bothersome as she was attempting to communicate with Aunt Em about her problem with Miss Gulch. The people in Paul's family and environment had labeled him directly and indirectly as a "bad boy," and even believed that therapy was a punishment and supposedly a corrective experience (i.e., "to make him good again"). To preserve his identity, he had to continue to be "bad" (e.g., Axline 1947). The spiral (spiraling funnel cloud) persisted as he continued to act out; the adults reaffirmed their judgment that Paul was indeed "bad" and responding accordingly. The amazement on his face when I would respond entirely differently from his parents, grandparents, and teachers in response to his anger and aggression was intense. It was both sad and cute that, in response to his concern over slipping and swearing in session, he did not believe my acceptance of this behavior, and he had to obtain approval from his mother to swear, abruptly leaving the session to do so.

Secondary Conceptualization (Third): Behavioral

While the behavioral conceptualization was not comprehensive enough to account for Paul's psychological adaptation in his short life, it served an ancillary purpose. Based on my understanding of the case history and behavioral observation, I believed that Paul's parents lacked the requisite parenting skills to help nurture Paul's development. He would actively aggress toward his mother, often striking her in my presence. Susan did not know how to prevent him from treating her in this manner, and she felt "out of control." The boundaries were blurred as Susan was unable to set limits and follow through. Paul experienced an increased sense of retaliatory anxiety as he expected his parents to intervene at some point in reaction to his inability to control his rage and aggressive impulses toward them. Additionally, Susan covertly communicated to Paul that she was unable to keep herself safe from a 3-year-old. Paul admitted in session that he questioned his safety in response to his mother's inability at protecting herself from him, a 3-year-old. It was also obvious that Al parented through coercion and aggression. Paul's response to this included fear and rage. Dorothy's Kansas caretakers also had difficulty in parenting her. They were at a loss as to how to nurture her and educate her regarding her inability to take care of Toto. Her adopted support-system family served her well in Oz, rescuing her from the Wicked Witch and asking her to stay with them, expressing their love for her (Baum 1993).

Since behavioral intervention in Paul's presence could damage and undermine the other treatment approaches, I conducted the behavioral parent training through handouts sent to Ms. Johnson and by telephone contact. Further, I recommended that both parents attend formal parenting classes offered through the mental health clinic. Due to Ms. Johnson's intelligence, motivation, and desire to help her child, I believed she could easily manage such intervention with telephone monitoring. She also was receptive to my request to separate my role in teaching her some skills from Paul's therapy. In other words, I asked that she did not associate my name with the skill implementation. For example, she was not to say, "Dr. Faust said you had to sit in time-out for three minutes for hitting me."

THE PROCESS OF INTEGRATIVE PLAY THERAPY

Beginning Treatment Phase – Landing in Oz

It is not surprising that the initial phases of therapy, which lasted four months (twenty sessions), focused on building trust between Paul and myself. Although normal prerequisites of both client-centered and psychodynamic psychotherapy, the development of a trusting relationship was going to be a particularly arduous task given the numerous violations of trust Paul had experienced in his short life. As therapy progressed, it became evident that the violation of trust permeated Paul's life on many more subtle levels than was previously clear to me at the time of intake. For example, Paul's father would tell Paul that Susan did not love him and that soon he would be living with Al. Mr. Johnson's lack of commitment to Paul's therapy was also a subtle rejection of the therapeutic relationship and the therapist, communicating to Paul that I was excluded from the family subsystems and I was not to be trusted. Later in therapy, this was further reinforced. After I had reported both physical abuse and sexual abuse to CPO, directly and indirectly implicating the father as perpetrator, Mr. Johnson told Paul not to disclose anything to me. As both Susan and I are women, Paul was given the message overtly that women are not to be trusted, and, covertly, that men (i.e., dad) cannot be trusted either.

Paul's difficulty with trusting adults was clearly evident in the initial sessions. He would not tolerate a lengthy individualized interaction, leaving the session frequently to check on his mother. In the first session, I structured the play environment so that his mother was sitting directly outside of the therapy room with the door open halfway. Needless to say, I handled the material that evolved sensitively due to the confidentiality break. By the second session, Paul was able to tolerate having his mother sit in the same place, but with the door further closed. He would frequently check for the stability of her presence and use his mother as a safe base. Once refueled emotionally by her, he would return to session. In the third session, Paul told his mother goodbye in the waiting room and went to the therapy session without her. Over the next several sessions, Paul would leave his mother in the waiting room without distress and accompany me back to the playroom alone. However, during these sessions he would leave the room frequently, to check for his mother in the waiting room. He always brought a transitional object, his blanket, to the playroom and would suck his thumb on occasion.

It became evident that space (both physical and emotional space) had a number of meanings for Paul, particularly those revolving around safety and trust. From a client-centered approach, if I failed to accept this and insisted on Paul conforming to my expectations of session attendance, I would again be invalidating his own needs and choices, not allowing him the opportunity to be himself and grow in his own right. Further, from a psychodynamic perspective, by imposing session limits on his ambivalence in session attendance not only would I be destroying the opportunity to develop therapeutic alliance, but he would miss a chance at working through his individuation/separation issues. The latter had already been thwarted by his primary attachment objects.

In the sixth session, due to Paul's lack of trust over his mother's physical stability and my role in his life, I attempted to structure his physical environment within the session for Paul in order to enhance his sense of safety and trust. I placed three stable medium-sized chairs in a vertical row in front of the door. Although Paul could escape, he chose not to and incorporated the pseudobarrier into his play. He could thereby modulate the physical boundary with me and yet escape if need be without having to leave the session. I hoped this would physically discourage him from leaving the session, while simultaneously heightening his sense of safety enough that he could tolerate staying within the playroom. This physical structure initially became his ship, a car, and then a rocket or plane. All structures were modes of transportation within which he could modulate both closeness and distance to me, as well as his issues and conflicts. For example, with respect to the former, Paul would sit within the structure he designated as a ship and assigned me the role of some other character (e.g., shark, kitten) but I was to be swimming in the water (on the ground away from the structure). On several occasions during his play, he was driving toward visitation with his father and then decided to go to my parents' house instead. However, prior to reaching my parents' house, he avoided parent contact whatsoever and would change the actual play itself by driving to McDonald's or some other location. As an example of the use of the physical environment and my approach to Paul's initial trust issues, here is an excerpt from a videotape of one of the early sessions:

P: [In the context of playing kitty, Paul played angry aggressive kitty parents. Angrily:] We're going to my parents. [We both sit in a car made from three chairs; Paul is "at the wheel."]

JF: [I reflect the affect in the tone of my voice.] Oh, no, we're going to your parents.

P: Yeah, we're going to my parents and they will cut you up.

JF: [Again reflecting Paul's fear and anger through the tone of my voice.] They're going to hurt me.

P: [Angrily] We're here at my, my, your parents. We're at your parents, not my parents. Hey I have an idea, let's play bowling.

Paul then shifted his play as the material became too threatening for him, both in terms of threats against his self-concept and personal integrity and with respect to his developmental task. The cutting by the parents represented in its primary form, castration. I chose at this early point in therapy to reflect the content (and its context) in order to heighten Paul's sense of integrity and his trust in me. Had I interpreted the castration and loss issues too soon, Paul could have perceived this as an attack on his self that would have diminished his trust in me. Further, if I had immediately supplied Paul with hypotheses about his conflict, this could have conveyed the message that Paul did not have the resources within to help himself.

After Paul readily began to trust me (around the tenth session), he had difficulty separating from me and therapy. This was not surprising given the tenuousness of his own negotiation of separation-individuation and his incorporation of negative, punitive and abandoning objects. Further, his low self-worth led to feelings of self-defensiveness. Hence, intimate feelings for me engendered a sense of vulnerability and fear that I would disappear or harm him emotionally as had many adults in his life. He would act out his difficulty in separating from therapy by aggressing against his mother in the session. He saw her as responsible for hurting him emotionally by not protecting him and not allowing him to individuate. Termination of the session made him vulnerable and triggered associated rage toward his mother for all the losses and her inability to set boundaries, so his erotic desire for her was fueled and he was unable to separate emotionally. As a result of the above, I sent Susan reading material and guidelines based on Forehand and

McMahon's (1981) parent training program. Further, telephone contact ensued to help Susan effectively implement the behavioral protocol. (I recommended that both the Johnsons attend parenting classes, individual therapy, and couples divorce therapy, but neither one followed through with the recommendations during Paul's treatment.)

Trust was an issue for Dorothy as well, as depicted in the *Oz* movie. First, she could not depend on her aunt and uncle (guardians) to protect her from the witch neighbor who took Dorothy's transitional attachment object (Toto) away from her. Not only did they allow it, but they indirectly supported it by complying with the ordinance the neighbor had obtained. They did not fight for Toto, thereby failing to protect Dorothy. Dorothy again confronted her trust issue as she began to build her pseudofamily, comprised of the Scarecrow, Tin Man, and Lion. Although initially fearful, her fears were soon allayed and Dorothy accepted these characters into her self-selected family. These companions provided Dorothy with the protection and loyalty that she could not procure from her aunt and uncle back home. Through her journey and self-discovery, she grew emotionally and was able to trust her own judgment confronting the Wizard as no one had done before her.

Early Middle Treatment Phase—Following the Yellow Brick Road: Repelling the Sharks, Hunters, and Shredder (Four Months to Six Months, Sessions 20 to 30)

As therapy progressed, Paul began to alter both his self-perception and his perception of others in relationship to himself by better understanding and reintegrating his feelings associated with the primary introjects of the critical objects in his life (his parents). As he explored his relationship to his parents and his feelings of vulnerability and rage in a safe environment, he could more directly confront the sharks, hunters, and monsters in his reality. During therapy, his play unfolded to reveal conflicts with these important objects and hence part of himself. One of the most obvious symbols of his progress in this area was his move up the phylogenetic scale from animals (sharks, reptiles) to roles and characters and then to people. Within the character category, he would gradually move the focus from the animated ones (most disguised from consciousness) to human roles, such as policeman, hunters (least disguised from consciousness), and then to people exactly reminiscent of those in his life.

The following videotape transcript demonstrates Paul's transition from expressing core conflicts and personality integration through more primitive symbols to more advanced constructs such as human roles. In the nineteenth session, Paul played sharks, but further delineated their roles as baby, daddy, and the like. In so doing, his core conflicts emerged closer to consciousness. Due to the strength of our relationship, I implemented the psychodynamic approach, utilizing techniques to launch this latent material into further consciousness. I stopped short, at this time, of tying the material directly into Paul's play.

P: Pretend there's a big daddy shark in here. And you get one of these things [a plastic object, similar to a hammer—he had already donned one]. And we beat the daddy shark up. [He pounded the furniture.] Let's get his eyeballs out.

JF: The daddy shark is mean. [I pounded the chair cushions with Paul.]

P: Oh, he's a . . .he's a baby shark.

JF: We hurt the baby.

P: [Exhibiting the defense of undoing of his aggression against the daddy.] Let's put his eyeballs back in . . .there.

JF: It was too scary, when he was the daddy shark, to take his eyeballs out. So now he is the baby shark.

P: Yes, he is the baby SHARK! [Paul screamed the last word aggressively.]

JF: [Alluding to Paul's legitimate and fantasy trust issues.] He fooled us.

As the sessions progressed, the movement from animals, to characters, and to roles and people became clearly evident. The next tape excerpt is material from the twenty-first session and reflects a progression to humans.

P: [Paul's symbols paralleled more directly (consciously) his family.] There's a baby man with a . . . with a gun. I'm going to beat the baby man up. [Paul banged on the cushion vigorously, then he fell down and pretended to be dead.]

JF: You beat the baby man up and now you fell down dead. It is scary to be mad at the man because it seems like he could make you fall down dead.

Many of Paul's issues can be discerned in this transcript, including his fear of retaliation by his father for his rage and oedipal strivings, his lack of trust in people, his identification with the aggressor and attempts at empowering himself, and individuation/separation issues. Approximately five minutes after the above, Paul's rage and its target became more fully conscious:

P: We can go to camp now and shoot some real wild hoggies. Big black real hoggies. Yeah that's fun. How 'bout you be the hoggie?

JF: Yeah, you're going to shoot me. Oink! Oink! Oink! [Paul shoots and I play dead.] I'm a dead hog. [Paul shoots me again.] Ah, you got me again.

P: [Yells] Get up.

JF: He's really mad at me.

P: [Yells] Crawl.

JF: It feels great to tell grown-up people what to do especially, since adults tell kids what to do all the time.

P: [Shoots me again three times.] Bad hog. You can come to my house and I'll cut you up like your tummy. Come to my house and I'll cut you all up.

JF: I'd bet you'd like to do that to lots of people.

P: Yeah not some, lots. [Even though I had said "lots," he really wanted to ensure that I understood the pervasiveness of his rage.]

During this part of the session, the targets of Paul's rage and conflicts became more conscious as he moved from animals (hog) to human roles (hunter) and the corresponding affect (which was more directly tied into his own life). Further, he used the physical space to help enact boundaries, moving from the "woods" or "camp" to "his house." This not only helped with his sense of safety, but further aided his understanding of his feelings and the concomitant associated people (mother and her home, father and his home, etc.).

After about six months of therapy, Paul would repeatedly request that we play "husband" or "man" with girlfriend and mother, more directly enacting the relationship and conflicts he had with his parents and their significant others. As was happening frequently in his play, Paul would play out these relationship roles, but the baby would often get killed. The oedipal wishes and concomitant fears, as well as the heightened vulnerability he felt with his aggressive, threatening punitive father, exacerbated his vulnerability. This also furthered his exploration of his oedipal issues.

One of our most significant therapy sessions (the twenty-fifth session) was in the bathroom as he used the toilet in a stall, and I waited for him outside the stall, but in the bathroom. Similar to Dorothy's use of her physical environment as a source of tremendous information to aid in problem solving, one of the most important therapeutic transitions in Paul's sessions occurred with the use of physical space. Just as the chairs "boat/car/rocket" had been facilitatory in establishing a trusting therapeutic relationship, the bathroom provided Paul with enough space and an environmental prompt for further exploration of his issues. During this session, Paul enacted father with girlfriend and mother play, switching roles frequently; he exhibited much aggression and rage, "messing" the playroom. More than likely, unconsciously, his play (prior to using the bathroom this session), facilitated exploration of issues that prompted him to use the bathroom. While he used the toilet, Paul wanted to know if I had a penis. In exploring this with him, it became clear that he believed that I did not, as his mother did not. He said this made him sad because then I was not like him. He said that if I had a penis I would be more like him and we could play more and be buddies. I also processed with him his fear that without a penis I could not protect him from his father and others since his mother, without a penis, was unable to do so. We linked these feelings to ones of love and desire of obtaining me and mother as well as fear of retaliation by father. After all, Mr. Johnson seemingly castrated his mother, as observed through his violence and through the anatomical differences between the parents. Therefore, it was likely Paul worried that his father could castrate me and Paul just as easily (or easier since Paul was only a "kitten").

JF: I wonder if sometimes you would like to have me just like you wish you had your mom. [Noticeable pause.] I bet it is scary to feel this way.

P: [Excitedly] Yeah.

JF: You worry if you were to take over your dad's job as husband to your mommy, he might get really mad, . . . and maybe you worry he could hurt you.

P: [Dejected] Yes.

Further, Paul was processing the differences between us in terms of his trust that I could understand his ordeal and be able to help him. We discussed his feelings that perhaps, since I was different from him, that I may not be able to understand and help him. His anxiety began to decrease as we talked about his feelings of disappointment, fear, and anger revolving around the oedipal themes. Dorothy, too, had her own Oedipus/Electra triangle developing, although more subtly than Paul's. Her primary competition was with the witch for the magic shoes, which are representative of power and phallus. The Electra triangle is overt in the witch's statement, "I can still make her my slave, for she does not know how to use her power" (Baum 1993, p. 96), and her numerous aggressive references to Dorothy's physical beauty. In fact, the competition had severe consequences as do the nonnegotiated Oedipus and Electra triangles. The witch tells Dorothy, " . . . See that you mind everything I tell you, for if you do not, I will make an end of you . . ." (Baum 1993, p. 96). Dorothy "won" at the expense of the witch's life. Although she accidentally killed the witch, it was clear to her that her power and rage were beyond her control.

In considering the client-centered secondary conceptualization, it was evident that Paul's aggressive behavior in session also furthered his self-perception about being bad. He needed to destroy the playroom, not only in response to emerging affect associated with core dynamic conflicts, but also in response to how he perceived himself. He would attempt to "set me up" to punish him after acting "bad" (a word I don't believe ever applies to children or adults), baiting me by asking what I was going to do. As I continually reflected his feelings about his behavior and his expectation of having me punish him as his family did, he began to see that I would only support him in his feelings and experiences. He did tell me he expected me to punish him as would his father, with a spanking. When this did not occur, his anxiety dissipated. From a client-centered perspective, the "mess" he left in the playroom mirrored his self-image and the introjection and conditions of worth he received from others. From a dynamic perspective, it represented the remnants of his id in response to the family "mess" (oedipal, poor objects, etc.) and confusion at home and throughout his development.

After this twenty-eighth session, Paul began to spend a lot of time playing and focusing on the roles that were paramount in his life: mother, father, girlfriend (also, husband, wife), baby. He no longer disguised these people in his life as sharks, Shredder/hunter, and kittens, although he could not yet discuss his relationships with and feelings about these people directly. This evolution was a clear demarcation as we moved into the next phase of therapy.

Worthiness issues were also communicated by the adults Dorothy encountered in Oz. Before helping Dorothy, the wizard stated she must show that she deserved his help and nurturance (Baum 1993). The witch told Dorothy that she was not worth all the trouble, she had caused her. During the middle of the movie, Dorothy, the witch's captive, was experiencing much guilt over her angry feelings toward Aunt Em. She cried that Aunt Em treated her well, and she never appreciated it. Because Dorothy ran away, she believed Aunt Em was sick and possibly dying as a result of her behavior.

Middle Treatment Phase–Reaching the Emerald City, Only to Have to Confront the Wicked Witch (Six Months to Two Years, Sessions 30 to 92)

Paul's primary concentration in therapy, during this phase, was playing out the many relationship triangles in his life. His fear and sense of loss and rage associated with the people in his life, both historically and currently, leaked out and flooded his fantasy play. For many months, his characters were seemingly emotionally labile and unpredictable, switching instantly from battering to loving. For example, during one memorable session, Paul had the daddy doll kiss the girlfriend doll and then immediately had him beat her up. In order to facilitate Paul's working through of his issues, beginning in session 31, I confronted him with a less direct emotion than fear or rage and stated that it must be confusing to see people you love or care about treat one another that way. Then my thoughts raced to a 3-year-old's definition of confusion—I knew he needed to understand the word. He admitted he did not know what "camusion" was, so I began to free associate. The definition we settled on was "all mixed up inside." As I left the session that day, I wondered if he understood.

The next session (session 32), Paul repeated the fantasy play, only this time with the mother and father dolls; he stopped amidst the conflictual and contradictory behaviors of the doll play and said: "Say that word again." I asked him for a clarification, and he said "You know that camusion word." I asked him if that was what he was experiencing and if he remembered what the word meant. He answered affirmatively to both parts of the question and added, "All mixed up inside."

During this phase of therapy, Paul enacted out sexual scenes with dolls. He said the dolls were "kissing each others' pee-pees." Further he indicated that his father's girlfriend had been doing this to him. Not surprisingly, he became very aggressive and anxious describing the molestation. This behavior was qualitatively different from when he engaged in fantasy play. In discussing with him my obligation to report this disclosure to CPO and his mother, he told me not to and he said he would "not be my friend." He was visibly angry despite my efforts to process his feelings and explain to him my need to make him safe. Why should he believe me? After all, he did not feel safe during visitation with his father, and neither his mother nor I could protect him during these situations. I sensed he was more fearful of his father's response to the disclosure than anything else.

Interestingly, despite Paul's protests against reporting the abuse, he presented at the next session with an open and forthright attitude, almost as if his trust in me had been heightened. He was able to discuss his feelings about his parents a bit more directly, extending the "confusion" label from characters to people in his life. This pattern of play continued for about 6 months, until his mother reported that Paul returned home from a visit with his father with a bruise on his buttocks that Paul told her was inflicted from a belt buckle his father had used for discipline. After this report (session 57), it became clear that Mr. Johnson had told Paul not to disclose anything to me. During periods of probing and interpreting his play concerning feelings regarding father and girlfriend dolls, he would become enraged and tell me that he was not supposed to tell. It was as if we were in the beginning stages of therapy again, with a resistant, distrustful patient. Only now, I was putting Paul in a bind, without meaning to do so. Many therapists would recommend terminating the therapy due to the lack of commitment (outright sabotage) by both parents to the patient's therapy. This seemed unreasonable to me; if I terminated treatment, this child's prognosis was uncertain, at best.

So, at this juncture in therapy, I decided to switch the main treatment focus from the primary conceptualization to the client-centered approach. The client-centered approach seemed most useful as its primary premise was to help the child grow and mature through self-exploration. I would be the mirror to reflect Paul's self back to him, and he could learn more about himself and his relationship to the significant others in his life. In so doing, perhaps he would have not only a clearer understanding and greater appreciation for who he was, but also a more distinct picture of his parents, apart from himself. I hoped that this would facilitate exploration into his past and the emerging unconscious conflicts in their everyday context.

Toward the end of this phase, Paul had relinquished both thumb sucking and his blanket. He began to verbally acknowledge his fear of and anger toward his father. He also said he was angry that his mother made him visit his father and that he did not feel she could protect him from Mr. Johnson. He said he did not want to visit his father. In *The Wizard of Oz*, there were marked changes in Dorothy as she continued through her growth experience. An overt sign of this intrapsychic transformation was evident when, after reaching the Emerald City the first time, her hair changed from little girl braids to long flowing locks.

Also toward the end of this phase (approximately the ninetieth session), the legal battle ensued wherein Mr. Johnson was attempting to block Ms. Johnson's move to an adjacent state. I was subpoenaed to testify in these proceedings. Although Paul was not directly involved, I briefed him as to my role in the legal proceedings, discussing the general nature of the disclosures and assuring him I would preserve his privacy as much as I could. I did not notice an obvious change in his behavior and effectual state in general or in the transference after disseminating this information to him.

Paul was not deposed and did not attend the hearing. However, it is difficult to say how much exposure he had to this particular conflict. He did tell me that he was excited about a possible move to the new city with his mother. He said he would like to move. Although there was no definitive date for their anticipated departure, pending the judicial decision, we did have to discuss the possibility of the termination of our sessions. However, within just a few weeks, the judge ruled that Ms. Johnson could not move out of state or county. Just as Dorothy reached the Emerald City to meet with the Wizard the first time, so, too, Paul had been given an opportunity to find a different physical life. But for both Dorothy and Paul, this initial trip proved futile.

End Treatment Phase—Confronting the Wicked Witch and Her "Associates/Associations" (Two Years to Three Years, Sessions 93 to 132)

The end phase for Paul was the termination of his therapy journey, but even more importantly this phase of therapy was a culmination of significant interpersonal and intrapsychic development and growth. For it was Paul, himself, who had the capacity to change, just as Dorothy had discovered that all along she had the capacity to go home. But by confronting the Wicked Witch, literally for Dorothy and figuratively for Paul, they were able to learn an abundance more about themselves outright, and in relation to others, which propelled them into a different developmental "plane." The final vehicle for change was a test I accidentally offered: my pregnancy. This event brought Paul's oedipal issues into full consciousness. He discussed his anger at me directly, that I not only was replacing him, but also that I had a "different" husband. He could not accept that someone had such a prominent position in my life, so he "downgraded" my husband's status to "boyfriend." He angrily told me that the baby was his and that he wanted to kill my boyfriend. He became more physically aggressive toward me (and my lower body), wishing to rid himself of perceived competition and a symbol of himself. I had to set limits, not only to protect the baby and myself, but so that Paul would feel safe with his own rage. He was able to examine his behavior and feelings toward me in context of his relationship with his parents. Paul discussed his feelings for his own mother and his fear of retaliation by his father. "If I married mommy, my father would kill me." As Paul worked through these issues, he began requesting, with the adaptive curiosity of a 6-year-old, to meet my baby once he or she was born. We arranged such a meeting after six weeks of maternity leave and two sessions of processing my absence and the birth of my baby. He was very excited and visually pleased to have met my daughter. He frequently stated, "Aww, she's so cute," and the like.

It became clear during this phase of treatment that Paul could ascribe many of the negative ways in which he was treated to those administering the behavior. He had stopped denigrating himself and his verbal aggression had decreased markedly, both in and out of sessions. He was doing well in school with no reports of acting-out behavior. His impulsivity was conspicuously diminished as he negotiated the roles and behaviors of the caretakers in his life. He seemed to be able to put in perspective their behavior toward him and not ascribe these actions as insults against his personal integrity. Furthermore, his own rage became less frightening as he realized that this rage would not engender ultimate retaliation by others (e.g., castration, death, abandonment).

Termination—There's No Place Like Home(s)
(In More Ways Than One)
(Last Eight Months of Treatment, Sessions 133 to 164)

While, earlier in treatment, the probability of unplanned termination existed, this never materialized as an issue due to the judge blocking Ms. Johnson's request to leave the state. We planned the final termination in advance, not only due to the length of time Paul was in treatment, but also due to Paul's original presenting issues surrounding loss, separation-individuation, and identity formulation. We discussed the course of therapy and his readiness to stop the sessions. Although difficult for Paul to understand at first, he handled the discussions about termination without too much anxiety. I drew parallels with respect to my leaving and unavailability and his parents'. We also processed that our cessation of sessions was not due, in fact, to him being replaced by my baby, but due to his growth and negotiation of his relationship to his parents. He exhibited less anxiety and turmoil. His play themes changed markedly as he selected games with rules and expanded on the use of his environment, clearly utilizing space to a marked degree. The anxiety evidenced in the beginning stages of therapy as he earnestly marked off his space was noticeably absent. We would play catch while talking openly about his feelings and problems. When he did suspend reality and engage in fantasy play, his affective state seemed much less confused and his aggression and fear markedly diminished. He played with cars, toy soldiers, and a farm in an age-appropriate manner. Further, he was able to process angry and sad feelings attached to the many events and traumas in his short history; I reflected these and we processed them together. Paul discussed his understanding that, although he loved his father, he realized he had a different view on love and parenting than other people. For example, he told me it bothered him when his father hit his girlfriends and stated this was "not right." He said that visitation was "okay," but that he couldn't wait until he was grown-up because then he would not have to see his father as much. He did admit that he wanted to continue a relationship with his father, but stated that it was often difficult to do this as the father–son dyad boundary was stretched to include his father's girlfriends.

He also discussed how scary it was to know that his mother was unable to protect him completely. And he was able to discuss his love for his kitten and to discuss soft, tender times. He said he wanted to live with his mother until he went to college. Susan reported that Paul's aggressive behavior after visitation and in school had subsided and that he was doing well academically. Further, he had adjusted easily to Ms. Johnson's new boyfriend and seemed to enjoy interacting with him. No reports of jealousy or competition were evident. Similar to Paul's insight about the disappointing qualities of his parents, Dorothy, in the book, also discovered the charlatan quality of the caretaker figure, the Wizard, telling him "I thought Oz was a great head . . . Are you not a great Wizard?" (Baum 1993, p. 123). The Wizard later responded "I'm really a very good man, but I'm a very bad wizard, I must admit" (Baum 1993, p. 123).

During this phase of treatment, Paul presented as more disturbed by his father's current girlfriend than about his former issues with his parenting style. He said, "We always have to bring Carrie with us. We never get to do anything together without Carrie." As Dorothy learned to negotiate several family units (the aunt/uncle unit, pseudofamily from Oz, and the ranch-hand unit from Kansas) and the divergent roles they played in her life, so, too, Paul had to process his feelings, conflicts, and response to the treatment he received by his different families (mom unit, mom and boyfriend unit, Dad and girlfriend unit, grandparents unit).

RESULTS AND FOLLOW-UP

Because of the complexity of children's lives and the influence develop-mental history and environment has on personality development and adjustment, psychological change should be evaluated from a variety of perspectives. Often children do not have the verbal and cognitive capacity to clearly communicate subjective feelings of distress and other psychological states. Further, with respect to Paul's case and the use of integrative play therapy, targeted change often focused on intrapsychic conflicts that traditionally have not been empirically operationalized in the literature. Therefore, the therapist must expand his or her criteria of change in order to have a clear understanding of the impact interven-tions have had on children. Change in this instance must be measured from a variety of domains (e.g., verbal, behavioral, physical) in a number of different environmental contexts (e.g., therapy, school, home).

For Paul, the initial critical issue that had to be addressed was trust. The first observable sign indicative of trust formulation included his ability to tolerate longer separations from his mother in order to attend sessions with me. As insignificant as this may seem (as an indication of change), Paul's ability to trust had a great impact on his ability to utilize therapy. By the sixth session, he was able to leave his mother, without feeling compelled to check on her during the session. For the most part he would stay in session, unless we discussed his rage at and fear of his caretakers, indirectly (through play roles) or directly. For the first two years of therapy, these discussions would occasionally prompt Paul to leave the therapy room and either check in with Ms. Johnson or to change his environment (e.g., go outside, to the bathroom) as an escape from threatening material divulged in session.

Other forms of avoidance Paul utilized initially when confronted with troublesome material included overt acts of aggression against me and other objects in the room and, more mildly, changes of play activity. During the tenth session, for example, Ms. Johnson informed me that Paul had seemed particularly aggressive and angry that day. She believed that his response was the result of a weekend trip with his father. After I asked Paul about his weekend visitation with his father, he shifted his play and began to hammer the toys and shelves aggressively. In linking his aggression to his feelings about his weekend (which he initially refused to discuss), Paul began to aggress toward me. After rechanneling his aggressive behavior away from me and back to inanimate objects, I queried further about his weekend. He refused to disclose the events. In response to my statement, "Sometimes when you talk about something that hurts you inside, it feels better," he replied, "No, it does not." Although he initially avoided his pain through aggression, he was able to verbalize his feelings about disclosure and then was able to tell me about his feelings of fear of his father, without disclosing the actual content of the weekend. Dorothy and her friends of Oz, in the movie summed up the painful process of experience (e.g., psychotherapy) by stating that it seems to get worse before it gets better.

Trust became the foundation for Paul's therapy. Through our relationship, he was eventually able to change his psychological schema of the caretakers in his life and then of himself. Via my unconditional acceptance of him, he was able to learn about himself in a free and accepting atmosphere. This learning facilitated exploration and his ability to tolerate interpretations and clarification of the feelings he had about himself in relationship to his caretakers and about his primary attachment objects. This helped change his self-schema and interpersonal schemas through a reworking of the internalized objects and associated affects, as evidenced in his ability to acknowledge his confusion regarding roles and relationships in his life and his function within these relationships (including his connection between his aggression as a defense). Further, his mother reported a concomitant significant decrease in aggressive behavior at school and a moderate decrease at home, after about 6 months of therapy, also indicating a shift in his perception and affects of internalized objects. Paul's disruptive behavior at home decreased even further after Ms. Johnson was instructed in parent training and implemented the protocol at the end of the first phase of therapy. Overall Paul's aggressive behavior decreased in a linear fashion throughout the course of therapy, although I could readily detect incremental surges in response to continued stresses in his life (abuse incidents, etc.).

After about 1½ years in therapy, Paul relinquished his blanket and thumb sucking, indicating more secure attachment and the negotiation of successful separation and individuation from his primary attachment objects. Since he no longer needed transitional objects to maintain an iconic image of his mother (and father), it seemed likely that Paul had reorganized the introjected objects into a safe stable schema. His identity seemed more secure and his working through of the oedipal conflicts that came out in full force in the transference helped solidify his sense of identity in relation to others. His impulse control continued to increase and his overly sexualized, angry behavior decreased. Toward the beginning of the termination phase of therapy, his sexualized verbalizations decreased markedly. Instead of identifying with the aggressive, sexually acting-out parts of his father, he was able to identify these as father's issues—ones he did not agree with nor hold as part of his behavior any longer. By the end of therapy (approximately the 135th session), his agitation in therapy session decreased, and he no longer exhibited fearful behavior when talking about his father, denying any residual fear. He was better able to objectively evaluate his parents' treatment of him and to connect his behavior with his feelings. He was able to label his feelings without having to act them out destructively.

Termination was held a few months shy of his seventh birthday. At this time, Paul's behavior had improved markedly in all physical contexts. The changes delineated above were maintained at six-month follow-up, the time this chapter was sent to press. Ironically, at follow-up, Mr. Johnson had been fired from his job in his family's company. Mr. Johnson had been unemployed for five months and was anticipating his own move to a neighboring state. Such a move would essentially "break the spell" and enable Ms. Johnson and Paul the freedom to call home any place they choose. However, Ms. Johnson's new position was secure and a move was not pending at the time of follow-up.

For Dorothy, too, her journey facilitated emotional growth as she progressed from a shy, dependent girl ("I am Dorothy, the Small and Meek") (Baum 1993, p. 78) to an assertive differentiated leader. Originally, she ran from her fears, feelings, and anger; then she grew to confront all of her conflicts. At the last visit to the wizard, she yelled at him "you're a very bad man" (Baum 1993, p. 123), and asked him directly how he was going to return her to Kansas. Dorothy also utilized her environment to facilitate her growth, following the yellow brick road, pouring water on the scarecrow and witch.

DISCUSSION

The approach utilized in the treatment of Paul was one that integrated psychodynamic (primary approach), client-centered and behavioral conceptualizations (secondary approaches), and corresponding treatment techniques. I selected the former as the primary conceptualization due to the multitude of developmental traumas and crises Paul had experienced. Paul grappled with separation-individuation issues, oedipal strivings, concomitant trust issues, and associated affects (fear, rage, grief/loss). His self and other schema were pitted with negative introjects that contributed to significant confusion regarding his identity and interpersonal relationships. Further Paul's self-concept, in general, had been poorly defined due to the treatment he received from many of his caretakers. Because of this treatment, his issues with trust and loss, and extratherapy issues (e.g., father's attempt at sabotaging therapy), I used a client-centered conceptualization and treatment as an ancillary approach to the primary psychodynamic one. Finally, I incorporated the behavioral conceptualization to address Paul's adjustment and environment in a specific circumscribed area (i.e., continued poor parenting with a negative impact on Paul's affect and behavior). In addition, I considered the context both inside and outside therapy in treatment, process, and outcome of this integrative approach, as the physical environment is imperative in determining the course of the child's development.

This case also tested the accuracy and durability of the selected conceptualizations, due to not only the patient's history, but also the multitude of intra- and extratherapy issues that were ongoing for Paul. The intratherapy issues included those that Paul brought to therapy through his development and life experiences. The extratherapy issues referred to those directly related to therapy, itself, that originated exogenous to the therapy sessions.

These intratherapy issues were ones that clinicians have found consistently to be critical in negotiating therapeutic process and progress. I was compelled to address a parent's attempt at therapy sabotage, to report both physical and sexual abuse, to testify in legal proceedings, to process my own pregnancy, and to address both planned and unplanned termination of long-term psychotherapy. Further, I had to consider Paul's environmental context during treatment in that physical space and environmental negotiation are imperative in the course of a child's development. The use of the metaphor of the Wizard of Oz in the presentation of the integrative play therapy case study was designed to facilitate communication and understanding of this specific multi-component therapy approach and to give the presentation additional context.

My work with Paul was challenging, albeit rewarding. As with any patient, I learned an abundance, especially about how to maximize the use of a child's environment and the therapeutic context and relationship. The therapist cannot help but learn from each patient, since everyone has a unique life story that impacts significantly on the psychological makeup of that individual. This gives credence to the integrative play therapy approach that tailors each treatment to the individual child. In charting Paul's response to treatment, he responded well to all three theoretical approaches and to the interventions I used in response to his current needs and level of functioning. I believe that the use of integrative play therapy maximized therapeutic effectiveness by addressing the multifaceted complexities of Paul's individual person and environment. The greatest difficulty in utilizing this approach is to maintain a clear understanding of the impact interventions from differing theoretical orientations have on the child in any given moment and context.

Paul was a continual reminder of how much children really understand and incorporate into their personal schema about their environments and interpersonal interactions. It is easy to underestimate the cognitive capabilities of children due to their evolving expressive language abilities, but we must listen closely with our eyes because our ears will not always be privy to all the knowledge that these young patients possess.

It was also a powerful experience to witness the impact my pregnancy had on Paul and to incorporate this phenomenon in a therapeutically advantageous role. My pregnancy was such a reminder for him of his early childhood and his sense of being abandoned, replaced, and nonnurtured. It brought his issues out in full force. Because of his rage, I had to walk a fine line between protecting my future child and allowing Paul to work through his issues without contributing to guilt or persecutory anxiety. At times, this balance contributed to my own feelings of anxiety. The pregnancy also evoked feelings of mothering in me that signaled me to continually cross-check any pull I had toward "rescuing" Paul. This would have only reinforced the sense of enmeshed boundaries he had with his mother and his self-perception of incompetence, thwarting any attempts at separating and individuating. The potential for the mothering countertransference issues were further intensified by the length of the treatment itself. It is odd when one considers Paul's treatment lasted longer than his life-span at the time he began therapy. The beauty in observing a 3-year-old "baby" develop into an almost 7-year-old maturing boy was rewarding, but it was also sad when termination was inevitable.

Finally, I am amazed how much I continue to learn about our judicial system. This system continues to chip away at my liberal, perhaps naive, idealism. In many respects, it was inconceivable to me that our judicial process could actually block a family's move across state lines even though such a move could ensure economic stability for the family, thereby potentially enhancing the physical, educational, and emotional welfare of a child. In light of the fact that women drop three socioeconomic levels when they divorce and men's status remains unchanged (Lahey 1984), thwarting such a move prevents women from becoming emancipated, leaving them subordinate and powerless. However, to deny a child access to a parent and vice versa, may also breach the rights of the parties involved and potentially damage the emotional welfare of these individuals. It is obvious that the goals of mental health practitioners and the legal system are often at odds. During my deposition in the request for out-of-state relocation by Ms. Johnson, Mr. Johnson's attorney, Mr. Adams, in an attempt to discredit my testimony, asked me if I believed "psychology was the truth." I responded, "No, psychological research is the search for truth and the practice of psychology is an application of research." Frustrated, Mr. Adams responded, "You don't like the law or lawyers do you, Dr. Faust?" I passionately stated that "Our legal system is the finest in the world." I followed that statement with an explanation of the fact that it was not my dislike of our legal system that led to my own frustration, but rather that I believed that many times the goals and process of the practice of psychology contradicted those of our judicial system and vice versa—that they were often in conflict. There was a silence of knowing acquiescence by attorneys and health care providers who have shared similar frustrations. And then, Mr. Adams moved on.

"I have always liked you as you were."

Baum 1993, p. 125

REFERENCES

Axline, V. M. (1947). *Play Therapy*. New York: Ballantine.

Baum, L. F. (1993). *The Wizard of Oz*. New York: Tom Doherty Associates Inc.

Bergman, J. (1992). Affect, humor, and metaphor in family therapy. Paper presented at the annual meeting of the American Association of Marital and Family Therapy, Miami Beach, FL, October.

Blatt, S. J. (1993). Object relations perspective on personality development. Paper presented at Continuing Education Conference, Ft. Lauderdale, FL January.

Burns, D. (1981). *Feeling Good: The New Mood Therapy*. New York: Signet.

Diamond, D., Blatt, S. J., Kaslow, N., and Stayner, D. A. (1992). Cohesion, differentiation and relatedness of self and other representations. Unpublished manuscript.

Eysenck, H. J. (1970). A mish mash of theories. *International Journal of Psychiatry* 9:140–146.

Faust, J., and Burns, W. J. (1991). Coding therapist and child interaction: progress and outcome in play therapy. In *Play Diagnosis and Assessment*, ed. C. Schaefer, K. Gitlin, and A. Sandgrund, pp. 663–689. New York: Wiley.

Forehand, R. L., and McMahon, R. J. (1981). *Helping the Noncompliant Child: A Clinician's Guide to Parent Training*. New York: Guilford.

Gutheil, E. A. (1979). *The Handbook of Dream Analysis*. New York: Liveright.

Harter, S. (1983). Cognitive developmental considerations in the conduct of play therapy. In *Handbook of Play Therapy*, ed. C. E. Schaefer and K. J. O'Connor, pp. 95–127. New York: Wiley.

Josephs, L. (1992). *Character Structure and the Organization of the Self*. New York: Columbia University Press.

Klein, M. (1979). The psychoanalytic play technique. In *Therapeutic Use of Child's Play*, ed. C. Schaefer, pp. 125–140. New York: Jason Aronson.

Lahey, B. B. (1984). Child psychopathology. Paper presented at University of Georgia, Athens, Georgia, January.

Lankton, S. R., and Lankton, C. H. (1983). *The Answer Within: A Clinical Framework of Eriksonian Hypnotherapy*. New York: Brunner/Mazel.

Mahler, M. S., Pine, F., and Bergman, A. (1975). *The Psychological Birth of the Human Infant*. New York: Basic Books.

Norcross, J. (1987). *Casebook of Eclectic Psychotherapy*. New York: Brunner/Mazel.

Rangell, L. (1989). Rapprochement and other crises: the specific and nonspecific in analytical reconstruction. *The Psychoanalytic Study of the Child* 44:19–39. New Haven, CT: Yale University Press.

14

As the Child Plays, So Grows the Family Tree: Family Play Therapy

Ruth A. Anderson, PH.D.

The Scotts, a family of four, entered therapy because the 6-year-old twin boys were enuretic. The boys had begun wetting the bed at night about six weeks before the first session. The frustrated mother was tired of airing the mattresses every morning. She had taken the boys to the pediatrician who referred them to family counseling. The first session focused on a history of bed-wetting, what the parents had tried, and what had and had not worked. Nothing worked. During that session, the boys played with Legos, listening to every word that was spoken. It was not until the second session that the mother revealed that her first husband and father of the twins walked out on her before the twins were born. She had not seen or heard from him since.

As the mother revealed this story, the expressions on the boy's faces changed. It was obvious that they had never heard this account of their past, but were closely attuned as the story of their origins unfolded. John, her present husband, had parented the boys since they were 2½. John played professional sports until a year before, when he had knee surgery that prevented him from fulfilling his dream. While recuperating, John had been staying home with the boys. As the mother was narrating this, I was sitting with the twins who were drawing a picture of the family. I noticed that Tim had drawn a very large tree next to John. Mischievously I suggested that John was like a tree for the boys and the family. Both boys said, "Yeah." Then Tim added that they climb on him, just like they do on the tree in their front yard. As the story developed, it became obvious that John, who had just started working as a salesperson, was spending less and less playful time with the boys.

I proposed that John resume some of his sportive activities with the twins. The mother called two weeks later to report that the boys had only one accident since our last meeting.

Tim's picture of this large tree, with the father almost as big as the tree, was an indication to me that there must be some similarity between the tree and John. When I made this connection, the serious expression on the twins' faces shifted to cheerfulness. The affective tone in the room then became much more relaxed and playful. The boys may have been secretly acting out John's mourning over the loss of his dream to be a famous athlete. But he was still big and strong in the eyes of Tim and Tom. Or they may have been anxious over the loss of John as he returned to full-time employment. They still felt entitled to receive parental care from him because of the emotional investments he had made in them. John also admitted that he had grown as a result of the love that he had received from the boys. He enjoyed his full-time father role. For their part, the twins had made to John a loyal commitment of their youthful, boyish activities. The entire family was engaged in trying to make meaning out of the current roles they had been cast into by John's new position as a salesperson. Six months later the family reported that the tree in the front yard was still growing, as were all the family members.

INTRODUCTION TO FAMILY THERAPY

The Essence of Family Therapy

Family therapy is a therapeutic methodology that focuses on the whole family as a dynamic organism or system. Family therapists consider assessment, techniques, treatment plans, and goals as related to the family as a system. The emphasis is on the network of interpersonal relationships, not on intrapsychic phenomena. Although many of the same key elements that are important in play and adult individual therapy are also important in family therapy, the therapeutic thrust in family therapy focuses on the relationship network in the family.

Rooted in general systems theory, the family therapist considers the family to be a powerfully interconnected system that is both stable and changing at the same time. Families are essentially systems open to inputs from and outputs to the environment. Such open systems are characterized by three qualities:

1. Wholeness. Families are not collections of individuals, but rather coherent, irreducible units. A change in one family member will affect every other family member. If the father becomes depressed at the loss of his job, this depression will impact all the other family members.
2. Feedback. All inputs into the family system are modified by the family system. Positive feedback leads to changes in the family system; negative feedback leads to stability in the system. A healthy family needs both types of feedback. In healthy families, for example, rules are adjusted as the children mature; greater freedom is allowed as the children grow up.
3. Equifinality. The same result may be reached from different beginnings. Thus, for family therapists, the family interactions are more relevant than the source or the results of these family patterns. To attain a therapeutic goal (e.g., helping an acting-out child), the family therapist can intervene in the family system wherever he or she believes there is the most likely possibility of change.

Other Key Concepts in Family Therapy

1. The family therapist sees the family as the most influential force in personality development. This is in contrast to the idea that intrapsychic forces are more important, which is the usual basis for individual treatment.
2. Family therapists believe that the disorders of childhood are often manifestations of family problems. Over the past several decades, the child guidance movement moved from a monadic to a dyadic to a triadic model. Behavior is always interactive. In this view, behavior of one family member is related to the behavior of others, especially other family members. This contrasts with the individual view that the children have something solely inside themselves, bothering them.
3. Using circular thinking, the family therapist sees discrete events as part of ongoing, circular loops, for example, child acts out, one parent corrects, second parent withdraws, child responds again. In contrast, the linear thinking of most individual therapists focuses on cause and effect, for example, this emotional hurt causes this symptom.
4. Every system has boundaries that enable it to function. In families where these boundaries are not functional, symptoms often appear among the children. For example, an out-of-control child can possess

power in the family that normally belongs to the parental subsystem. Instead of treating the child as a child, a member of the parental subsystem treats the child as a spouse. This leaves the child in the difficult position of having to choose between being a child or being a spouse. The family therapist seeks to help the family negotiate appropriate roles for each family member and interrupts inappropriate transactional patterns.

5. A two-person emotional system (e.g., husband and wife) tends to form a three-person system (a triangle) when the members of the dyad can no longer manage their interrelational stresses. Children often bear the burden of issues that belong in another part of the family. Husband and wife conflicts may flow over into the parenting area. When parental authority is split, each parent may attack the spouse through the child. The therapist's role is to separate generations and to strengthen the boundary around the husband and wife.

6. Family therapists usually see the symptom-bearer as expressing the dysfunction of the whole family under stress. The identified patient is often the family member strong enough to carry the family stress. In individual approaches, however, the therapist sees the symptom-bearer (e.g., an acting-out child) as the identified patient who needs therapeutic help.

Individual and Family Therapy: A Brief Comparison

For many decades, individual therapy was the only mode of treatment for psychological dysfunctions. This paradigm locates the source of dysfunction as inside the individual. In this model, therapy involves treatment of patients by the therapist in a confidential, supportive, individual relationship. The goal is to change the way patients deal with their own personal world, in order to help them deal more effectively with the environment.

Family therapy is a different way of defining both the problem (as rooted in family interactions, not individual symptoms) and the client (the whole family, not just the child). Family therapists usually consider dysfunctional families to be "stuck," unable to respond to the developing needs of the growing family. Thus, the family therapist tries to bring about change at the level of both the family and of the individual.

Essentially, the process of family therapy requires each family member to step outside the context containing the problem to look at the larger picture. The counseling process involves a redefinition of the family's relationship and changes in the interaction patterns, thus helping the family to become self-healing. The clash of these two different paradigms continues to this day, unfortunately and unnecessarily. Family therapy is simply a different way of conceptualizing clinical issues and conducting therapy. Even if a therapist works with just one person, that can be an aspect of family therapy, since any change the client makes will reverberate through the entire family system.

Focus of the Family Play Therapist

This approach to working with children in the context of family therapy is clearly a different, not necessarily better, way of working with troubled children. Using the systemic paradigm, the family play therapist will normally use a different focus than that used by those who do play therapy with individual children apart from the family environment. The basic principle is that behavior is the expression or acting out of each individual family member's personal experience of the perceived interrelationships within the significant family context. Feelings are the connection between the emotional system of the individual and the relationship system of the family (Bowen 1971). Such a systemic approach will often involve one or more of the following therapeutic thrusts:

1. The family therapist will assist all family members in their definition of the problem. Is the symptom manifested solely in the child? Is there a covert marital conflict expressed in the child's acting out?
2. The family therapist will help to create a positive atmosphere to enable family members to learn new, affirmative ways of relating to each other and of helping all members with their own personal growth issues.
3. The family therapist will attempt to help the family to learn new ways of adjusting to family transitional stages, such as when a child enters school or when a child becomes an adolescent. Often families are "stuck" in such a developmental stage. A classic example is a teenager's acting out when the family system is not adapting to the normal disruptive process of a juvenile family member beginning the individuation process of leaving the family.
4. The family therapist is aware of the heavy emotional investment that most parents have in their children. Thus, the therapist will often attempt to enter the family through connection with the children, especially the child who has the symptom.

5. Finally, the family bond helps to unravel problems because it is the essence of trust and the foundation for change. Believing in this strong interconnectedness in the family system, the family play therapist will attempt to see if the child's play reflects some of the family's core feelings and relationships. At the appropriate time in therapy, the therapist can make that connection in a strong, but caring way.

Children in Family Therapy

The idea of having their children in therapy not only creates anxiety and confusion in most parents, but also taps into parental guilt and shame. Parents begin to ponder, "Is my child just a pronounced terrible two? Is my child just a very difficult adolescent? Is my child normal?"

In family therapy when all the children are present, the therapist has the necessary ingredients for a treatment process that can empower the family while challenging its honesty. This process requires a union of symptom, underlying conflict, and relevant history (Weltner 1982). If the family perceives that there is a problem, there is a problem. The issue, however, may have different dimensions than those of which the family is aware. The family, as the child's original resource system, is the prime source for the establishment of a healthy and growth-filled life for a child. It is within a family that a child is reared, develops, grows, learns, interacts, and matures. Through the family filter system, a child first experiences values, truths, history, people, facts, fantasies, and distortions. It is also within this family context that members learn to proffer their own resource system for the benefit of all.

Family reaches beyond the nuclear family of parents and children to include a multigenerational group of family members who interact in multifaceted ways. These generations influence today's living and self-images (Keith 1986). Involving in therapy as many of these family generations as possible increases the power of the psychotherapy. The generational family context has a strength of history and experiences that can inform, befriend, and encourage the therapist as well as the family. Children in the context of intergenerational family therapy bring a deep sense of hope to the family and to the therapist, as he or she works with the family. By including children in family therapy, their world becomes a better place in the present (Combrinck-Graham 1986).

Play Therapy and Family Therapy

Just as play therapy and individual adult therapy deal with both the conscious and the unconscious, so does family play therapy. Using play therapy methods while working with a family often helps to make the covert *overt*. Adults who will not face their own hurt or loneliness are often deeply touched by their children who spontaneously act out or draw their hurt in a metaphorical way as they play during family therapy. This gift of the child to the parents can often help the adults to go on, to face their own feelings and relationships, and take the risk of being vulnerable and of changing.

Play is children's most natural activity. It is the medium through which children express themselves. Play in the context of family therapy engages the entire family and informs the therapist about family dynamics. It gives the family permission to have fun. Often, play creates energy in the room that provides the impetus for change. Thus, the responsibility for change is not only the parents' or the identified child's but is shared by all the family members. Through play, all members of the family can feel free to experience their own "craziness" (Whitaker 1987, Whitaker and Keith 1981), their own fantasies, and their own frustrations as they shift into the magical world of play and toys. Play helps families understand their maladaptive patterns; it opens up creative avenues, leading to new solutions; and it creates the accessibility for each member to achieve autonomy, while still remaining an intimate part of the family (Carey 1991). Whitaker and Keith (1981) state that a family must learn how to play, since "play is not a leftover for spare time but play must be present to maintain health and facilitate growth" (p. 200). The therapeutic goals of play within the context of the family are to change the family's emotional atmosphere, role expectations, rigid self-image, and structure.

To use play therapy in the context of family therapy, the therapist's playful, creative mode comes into action. Having the mind-set that therapy can be fun frees the therapist to relax and release the creative energies of both family members and therapist. Play helps generate solutions. It also builds an atmosphere of trust facilitating the joining process with the family's pain. Family play therapy enhances positive functioning by creating new realities in communication and interaction.

The Family Interview

Children make a unique and powerful contribution to family therapy. Their mode of communication is often characterized by spontaneous freshness, honest affect, and intriguing candor. Children's excitement at play generates an atmosphere of freedom that can permeate a family therapy session and unleash feelings and covert agendas, and can open future possibilities for the entire family system. New twists and alternatives occur for family members as children exercise their sense of freedom. Through play in the context of family therapy, children lead the family on a journey into forbidden areas behind family rules, roles, masks, and conventions. Children are the windows and doors that let in fresh air to a family.

Some Basic Therapeutic Stances

The first step in working with a family is a process called joining. This involves the therapist entering the family to model a new system. I usually set the tone by saying, "My name is Dr. Anderson. You may call me Ruth." The family members are then free to introduce themselves using the name they prefer. I greet each child, bending down to the child's eye level, asking for a name and age. I make certain not to overlook anyone, even babies. When one family presented itself, the son introduced himself by saying, "My mother calls me J. T. My real name is Joshua Thomas. I want you to call me Josh." Crouching to meet Josh eye to eye, I said, "What are we here for?" Rather than starting with "What brings you here?" I begin by asking each family member what they hope to gain from this session. This provides me with an opportunity to find out what the parents have told the children about coming to therapy. I guide the family to discuss the positives as well as their overt and covert goals. The focus is on the system, not on the "sickness" of an individual family member. By doing this, I take the emphasis off the problem and give the family a sense of hope. The problem will rear its ugly head soon enough.

The therapist begins on the client's level. It is necessary to join with the family in its perception of reality. By so doing, the therapist can develop an affiliation with the family that helps to restructure the family and transform dysfunctional transaction patterns. This leads individuals within the family to see and accept themselves differently in relation to the family.

Both the family as a whole and individual members need to be accepted as they are. The therapist's acceptance of each individual, and his or her verbal, play, and art expressions will encourage further expression and reveal family dynamics. This facilitates the therapist's awareness and assessment of the family's pain and stress.

At the same time that I am joining with the family, which is an ongoing process, I am observing the many expressions of the family, gathering information, and forming hypotheses. One method of learning more about family interactions is to focus questions on circular interactions. To a child, I might say, "Show me how Mom reacts when your brother has a temper tantrum." Or to the family I might ask, "I wonder how the family changes when Mom is gone on one of her business trips."

Establishing clear rules and limits are an important part of working with families and children. In an opening statement about the conduct of children in the therapy session, the therapist makes explicit the expectation that discipline is a joint responsibility shared by the parents. I usually say something like, "In here you may do many of the safe things you would like to do in many different ways. Parents, you are in charge of the children just like you are at home." I want to convey the idea that the family may play as well as talk.

Another important issue when working with families and children is that parents are not to punish the children at home for anything they say or do in therapy. If children misbehave during the session, parents must deal with that behavior in the session. Or if a child announces a family secret, that secret becomes a therapeutic issue for the present session.

Children are entitled to an atmosphere of safety in which to play. One way to achieve this in a family therapy session is by setting limits and establishing rules that are fair for all family members. Trust grows when family members respond favorably to each other for their acts of care, however small. Trust, the foundation of family health, supports this familial concern, fairness, and safety. For example, when a child asks her father to come to school to have lunch with her, she is providing an opportunity to the father to show his love for his daughter. It is also important that the family give the daughter credit for her desire to be close to her father. Thus trust begins to build an atmosphere of safety in which the family can freely play together.

One of the main goals of working with a family with children is to validate the family's primary process of living. Family life can be happy and playful. But the families who come to therapy often have little fun or joy. They go through life looking like they are headed for the dentist's office for a tooth extraction. Thus, play is a powerful tool for changing the hopeless, pain-filled atmosphere and dysfunctional interaction patterns the family has developed over the years. Family members seem quite adept at playing once they have been freed to experience the possibility of change. The challenge to the therapist is to free the family members to trust each other so they can play and enjoy life together.

Without children, the therapist may miss many of the family processes. Children communicate in a metaphorical manner in which they play out a language of symbols that can be universally appreciated. Not having the vocabulary to express feelings and ideas, children use play to communicate. Sometimes, entire families are similar to children; they simply are not at the developmental level where they can openly and honestly express themselves. They are reluctant to be vulnerable because they have to go back home and live with each other. Family play therapy thus provides an atmosphere of safety where the therapist has an opportunity to challenge family members to bring out from within themselves the motivation for change. The family play therapist can encourage the family to express the unspoken and unheard language that is waiting to be verbalized. The therapeutic work becomes an art of uniting the family's inner hopes and dreams with the present reality into a coherent whole.

Suggested Methods

1. Have all the children present at every session because they are a part of the family identity. Every family member contributes to the family homeostasis, a process by which the family balances forces within itself to achieve working and affective relationships. This powerful status quo in a family can block change. Multigenerational dialogue and play, however, give the family a chance for the members of each generation to experience themselves in a new spirit of balance that may lead to change.

   I am always amazed at how wise children are. They know what is going on in the family. Children express the needs and feelings of the family in such simple, sound ways. One family was caught in an endless covert fight over who was the best parent and who was to blame for the son's not eating. Finally, the daughter playing at a small table off to the side said, "They fight all the time. Mom blames Dad; Dad blames Mom. They tell me to grow up and be responsible. Why don't they grow up and be responsible? They can stop all this fighting and get on with living."

2. Have toys available. The toys do not have to be expensive. Here is suggested list: puppets, small cars, dolls, paper and crayons, scissors, a doll house with some furnishings, batakas, a variety of hats, stuffed animals, a toy gun, a telephone, and puzzles. If you do not have toys, ask the children to bring their favorite toys with them to the next session. For latency-aged children, board games and checkers are helpful. Simple play activities, such as making clay objects, help to reduce children's and parent's anxiety as they discuss painful experiences.

   Becky, a demanding 7-year-old, would position herself on the couch between her parents. Then she would withdraw to paint vigorously, but would reappear quickly to show off what she had produced. The mother would acknowledge the drawing and place it on the floor. Both parents appeared disapproving because she was distracting us, but made no comment. I viewed this behavior not as a distraction, but as an opportunity to have the family learn to give and receive care in a way that would leave no one overburdened. Becky's play during the therapy session metaphorically revealed the family dynamics of their struggle for attention and affection.

3. Plan for the specific developmental needs of the children. Plan the length of the counseling session in accordance with the children's ages. Young children have short attention spans. When properly planned, with the right mix of toys and interactive processes, the counseling session can be productive, enjoyable, and beneficial for the entire family.

   Being on the floor or at a small table gives the children their own space and allows them the freedom to be close to each other. I sit on the floor with the children and talk to them using the toys in the room. This makes me more vulnerable and takes me out of the role of being "all wise." Being on the level of the children also helps me be more creatively spontaneous. I hold the smallest infant and join in games with the children. The family interaction patterns in the presence of an infant sometimes give valuable clues to family relationships.

4. Teach misbehavior. Keith and Whitaker (1981) use this idea to disrupt family patterns when a member is trying to solve the family problem by acting out. An adolescent is having a screaming, raging fit; the mother tries to be cool and not raise her voice or lose her composure. Inside, however, she is boiling. The therapist suggests that they both get hot at the same time. Maybe the adolescent could even teach the mother how to raise her temperature, so they could both reach the boiling point. By so doing, the roles change. The teenager is now joined with the therapist in facilitating change in the mother. The basic process becomes teaching the family to have fun. A healing ensues when the entire family makes fun of something they have held ambiguously sacred. The opposite is also true; making serious what seemed foolish can also be restorative.

5. Use positive connotations. When the family play therapist accepts and reframes problem behaviors or situations, this provides the family with new ways of thinking and behaving. It offers the family and each of its members an opportunity to see themselves from a new perspective. The mother has labeled her daughter as, "hot-

headed and stubborn." I accept that and give the behavior a new meaning: "Yes, she has a definite strength of will and determination." This captures the family's attention.

Positive feedback is a natural process that goes along with reinforcing what the family is already doing. For example, a father complains that his son is always doing everything in a hurry. If he only slowed down, he could do a much better job. The son griped that his dad was as slow as a turtle. So I praised both of them by saying, "Sounds like you are a tortoise and a hare; that would make a great team. One is very exact and precise and the other is very swift and expeditious." Thus, I engaged the family in seeing behavior from a new perspective.

6. Make prescriptions for family rituals. The family play therapist designs family rituals to change the rules of the existing family game. Family rituals change the sequence of behaviors. The therapist needs to carefully craft a prescription to fit the family behavior. Families maintain certain behavior patterns because that is what has worked for them. The family requires validation and responsibility for the success of the changes that occur in therapy. The prescription describes the sequence of actions, what is to be done, by whom, and where. Linda, who felt like a single parent mother with her two young children, complained that the children were always fighting with each other. Linda made the statement, "I grew up in a family with five sisters and brothers and we never fought like those two do." After a family discussion about how fighting helps or hurts everyone in the family, how they all felt about the fighting, and the reasons and consequences of the fights, I suggested a family ritual that Blanco (1972) designed. I asked Linda if she had any windows that needed washing. Then I suggested that the two children clean a window, one on each side of the window, facing one another. While washing the window, I encouraged the two children to look really mean and glare at each other just like they do when they are fighting. The first child to smile or break the scowl would receive a sandwich hug from the mother and father. I delivered this prescription at the end of the therapy session without any explanation. The mother and children made a firm commitment to carry out the window washing ritual.

I wanted to connect the family through the strength of working together without fighting. I was also hoping that it would heal some of the tension between the children, between the parents, and between the children and the parents. The hug provided the parents and the children with a sense of security, an affirming, dependable anchor. The ritual worked because it facilitated the destruction of part of the myth surrounding this family, that the only way to get close was through fighting. At the beginning of the next session the children asked, "Do you have another game for us?"

The window washing ritual improved the family functioning; it changed the rules of the existing family game. It was now okay to give and receive hugs. The family structure changed as they built a stronger boundary between the parents and children. The children became secure in their substructure. The sequences of behavior also changed. The children received hugs rather than scoldings. The behavior in the family was directed toward affirming one another. This ritual began to incorporate play and fun into the family life-style.

7. Use storytelling to facilitate understanding and communication. Every family has its own story to tell, just like every individual has a story. The therapist is a master storyteller whose role is to weave a new story from the old worn pattern. The therapist helps the family to create new outcomes with familiar themes. All family members participate in the story's development, opening up new possibilities and scenarios and elaborating on them. Storytelling opens windows and allows the family to think creatively in a fresh and successful way. They can deal meaningfully with feelings and behaviors they are not ready to admit and see unrecognized consequences. Family members can add an individual fantasy in a less threatening manner because the therapy provides an atmosphere of safety.

8. Have family members enact interactional patterns in the session. Enactment is a process that allows the therapist to use the family's own interactional patterns to facilitate change. The family members deal directly with each other in the therapist's presence, thus creating a context from which new possibilities can emerge. Families often come to therapy thinking that they will present their problem to the therapist who, as the expert, will tell them what to do. As the family tells its story, one member will tell something about another that will be a catalyst for an enactment. "Jill never does what she is told. She doesn't come in on time. Doesn't clean up." The therapist can develop an enactment by saying: "She says you're disobedient. I would like you to answer her." Choosing a specific point is more likely to start a dialogue than a vague request, such as "I'd like you to talk these things over." The therapist, through skillful blending of support and challenge, helps Jill experience new relational realities and alternatives during the session.

During an enactment, the therapist can discover family boundaries, rules, and patterns. Are children brought into the communication? Who talks to whom? What are the relationships? Enactments may reveal spontaneously an accurate picture of what goes on in the family at home. They provide the therapist with the opportunity to experience the emotional climate of the family, along with his or her own reactions to the experience itself. They provide a metaphoric blueprint of the emotional processes of recurrent interpersonal interactions and structures.

Enactments also elicit recollections from other family members. If the child feels free to enact her wishes to be autonomous, as depicted by her being messy, then the mother might feel free to recall her struggle to be separate from her family of origin. Mother's acceptance of her daughter's right to be independent allows the child the freedom to proceed.

9. Encourage the entire family to use the puppets and toys to communicate. Like enactments, puppets and toys afford the family an opportunity to act out what they do not have the courage or freedom to say directly. An upset and overwhelmed mother came into my office one day with her four children in tow. The father had walked out on them. The smallest child, age 3½ came into the office, looked around and immediately went after the puppets on the shelf. He then hid himself behind my chair and started talking. The oldest child, a girl, followed him with her puppet. Before long, all four children were behind my chair, each with a chosen puppet acting out their life drama. After listening to the mother's overwhelming story while eavesdropping on the children's play, I asked them if I might join them. I asked the youngest child to choose a puppet for me. Then I proceeded to ask the oldest child what she would like my puppet to say. "You play Daddy and say that you want to come home." Thus the children told the family tale much the same as the mother did. This family exemplifies very clearly the notion that when a problem exists within the family, all family members feel it. It was vital for me to hear how each member perceived what was going on. The puppets became a direct expression and enactment of the family's sense of separation.

PRESENTING PROBLEM AND
BACKGROUND DATA

While I was working at a clinic on a university campus, 6-year-old Adam was referred to me for stealing. The family sought therapy for problems with Adam who was a bright, playful, imaginative child. His parents complained that he was stealing not only from them, but also from grocery stores. Both Betsy and Jerry, Adam's parents, were appalled by his stealing. They seemed to be much more upset about his stealing from several local grocery stores than they were about his thefts of money from the family. While small amounts of change had been disappearing from their house for about a year, they had never investigated or addressed this issue with Adam. However, during the two months prior to their bringing him to the clinic he had been caught stealing candy and small toys from two different grocery stores in their neighborhood. Both parents labeled this behavior as "unforgivable." They feared that people outside the family would find out about this behavior, which would "ruin the family's reputation."

A history-gathering first session with the entire family, including Ana, Adam's paternal grandmother, revealed that Adam and his sister were adopted as infants. Adam, a biracial child, was 2 years old when Carla was brought into the family. Adam was told about Carla's arrival and helped the family prepare for her advent. At the time, he seemed very excited about having a baby sister. Betsy and Jerry, who were Asian, reported their initial enthusiasm when they first received Adam into their family. In passing, Betsy mentioned that "Adam has some black blood." The entire family denied that Adam's biracial heritage was an issue. However, all of the members of the family seemed reluctant to talk within the family about racial issues and what they meant to each member. There seemed to be ambivalence toward Adam's "blackness." Whitaker (1987) stated that human beings have a strong need to see their own faces reflected in their children's faces, but the family denied that this was a problem for them.

The parents described Carla as "loving, bright, and no problem." Adam was described as "a troublemaker, irreverent, disrespectful, and no good . . . He's a bad seed." Jerry felt that Adam's stealing was "wrong" and "bad." He was coming to therapy for one reason, to get Adam "fixed." Adam was not all that Jerry had hoped for and he expressed extreme disappointment in the results of the adoption.

Betsy and Jerry also reported that they had recently had several heated arguments over what to do about Adam. Betsy felt so helpless and overwhelmed that she was ready to turn Adam back to the adoption agency. While Jerry was also disheartened and disappointed over the situation, he was also extremely angry with Adam and angry with the adoption agency. He, however, did not believe it was legally possible to simply return Adam to the agency. Ana joined these disputes even to the point of suggesting that it was Betsy's parenting at fault, rather than Adam's behavior. The conflict between Betsy and Jerry was frightening to both of them because before the recent events, they had experienced very little marital strife.

Ana lived with the family because Jerry was the oldest son in his family. The paternal grandfather had died two years ago and Ana had moved into the family home. I invited Ana to the sessions, not as a parent, but as a grandparent. The purpose of having Ana present was to determine how she could continue to enjoy her relationship with her grandchildren and provide support to her son and daughter-in-law. I wanted to respect the Asian emphasis on generational hierarchy. I complimented Ana on her ability to help her son at this time of need.

Both parents thought Adam would benefit from therapy and agreed to participate in family play therapy. Since Betsy and Jerry did not seem to think their marriage was an issue, I decided to go with the presenting problem. We contracted for five weekly sessions and agreed to evaluate the progress together at the end of that time.

THEORETICAL CONCEPTUALIZATION

Being new to working with families with adopted children, I searched the library for ideas. A book that was helpful to me was *Being Adopted: The Lifelong Search for Self* by Brodzinsky and colleagues (1992). This book gave me the support I needed to develop a persuasive plan for this family.

I theorized that Adam's stealing was an overt expression of his unresolved ambivalence toward both of his adopted parents. It also seemed to be a manifestation of his search to be accepted by his sister, Carla, who shared his adoption experience. It was not an attempt to sabotage Betsy and Jerry's good parenting skills. Another hypothesis was that Adam's behavior was a disclosure of his feelings that he was no longer special. His stealing behavior compromised his parent's attachment to him. Carla seemed to be the fantasy child the parents longed to have and I was guessing that he felt unworthy and unloved compared to her.

It seemed quite obvious that a triangle existed between Ana, the paternal grandmother, Betsy, the mother, and Adam, and another triangle existed between Ana, Betsy, and Jerry. Betsy and Ana did not seem to have clearly defined roles in the family. I had noticed some degree of underlying resentment between them. I viewed Adam as forming an alliance with his grandmother to gain both attention from her and power over his mother. Adam and his grandmother seemed to be in collusion together. The family reaction to Adam's stealing behavior was undermining the closeness between Jerry and his mother and was working to cause conflict in the marital alliance between Jerry and Betsy.

Grandmother was the family switchboard and the family executive. All family socializing and communication passed through her. Before she had come to live with the family, this had not been the case. Because she had been brought up in "the old country," she believed that rigid gender roles needed to be maintained. Jerry, Betsy, and Ana all reported that Ana held Betsy responsible for Adam's behavior. She believed that the man supported the family financially and that the women kept the home and raised the children. Betsy's sense of power and competence seemed to disappear in Ana's presence. I wanted to make sure that Betsy's role as mother was not usurped by Ana. This was very important because Betsy received considerable negative feedback from Ana about her mothering abilities. In order to counteract this negativism, I affirmed Betsy in her strengths as a mother. She truly cared about the children.

To me stealing became Adam's defense against his painful fear of being returned to the agency; in addition, I hypothesized that the stealing symbolized the mother's fear that she might be replaced by the grandmother. She seemed to feel threatened and inadequate as a mother under Ana's watchful eye. Yet Betsy was the primary nurturer in the family; she was the caregiver and the toucher. Jerry, a high-powered professional, was distant in his involvement with the children. He did engage in some play with them primarily on weekends. He described himself as the "breadwinner" and the translator of American rules.

THE PROCESS OF PLAY THERAPY

During the second session I sat on the floor with Adam and Carla. My aim was to help the children feel comfortable and be aware of themselves as individuals, different from one another. Children need to feel that they will be treated as someone special with genuine perceptions and feelings. I wanted to learn more about Adam as he saw himself. Building on Lawson's (1987) storytelling idea, I began, "Adam, this little boy had a dream about a brown and black puppy who had no friends because he was different than the other puppies who were either all black, all brown, or all white. He was sad and would watch the other puppies as they played. He would dream of all the things he would like to do." Then I turned to Adam and asked him to add a few lines. Adam added, "This puppy is very strong. I will call him Tiger." I asked the other family members to help in enlarging the story. I kept the focus on the idea that different is good; it helps one to feel special. The grandmother added, "Tiger was very angry. But as he watched the other puppies having so much fun playing together, he forgot how angry he was and joined them." I concluded the story, "Adam, when the little boy woke from his dream about the puppies, it did not matter that he was different because he knew he was special." Using this story, I began to present Adam with options. He could continue to be a tiger, but he might choose to be a happy puppy.

The family reported that Adam showed reasonable effort in not stealing during that week, mainly because the grandmother had taken away many of his privileges. During the third session I spent most of my time with Adam. I wanted to determine if any of the home stressors were contributing to his stealing. Adam denied that anything was bothering him. Adam was active during the session, moving from one play area to another. Carla started in the sandbox, then Adam joined her. He chose cars, buses, and trucks, having them go through tunnels and over bridges he had built. He was very aggressive in his sand play. The trucks, cars, and buses would crash into each other and knock down the tunnels. Carla made bread and cakes. She was serving them to all of us to eat. Adam entered the nurturing feast by making special cookies for Carla.

RA: You certainly are a responsible big brother by making special cookies for your little sister.

Adam: Yeah. I like to feed Carla.

RA: Oh, it's important to you to care for Carla.

Adam: [Looking at Carla.] Yeah. She knows what it's like. [Adam stopped playing in the sand. He went over to the log that had a bunch of nails in it.] What's this?

Later on during that session, Betsy told me that most of the time Adam stole money from her purse. He used the money to buy "treats" for himself and his sister and he shared the candy and other things he stole from the store with Carla.

As I worked with the adults in the third and fourth sessions, I kept the focus on child-rearing practices that might be useful in helping to eliminate the stealing behavior. My intent was that as both the mother and the father grew stronger in their parenting role, they would provide Adam with the nurturance, safety, and trust that he desperately needed. I affirmed Adam in his efforts to relate with his parents. I encouraged Jerry and Adam to discover activities they could share. This required a new definition of the father role in the family in which Jerry would be engaged in nurturing.

In the fourth session I met with the family, but excluded the grandmother by having her go behind a one-way mirror to watch her son and daughter-in-law parenting the children. The one-way mirror formed a boundary that allowed Ana to feel part of the family, yet required her to relinquish her switchboard role (Minuchin 1974). I also hoped to begin to quench the confusion the children felt with divided loyalties between mother and grandmother.

I asked the children to draw a picture of the family. I was amazed that neither child included Ana.

Dialogue	*Commentary*
Adam: This is my family. You see I am darker than everyone else.	
RA: Oh, so your skin is darker than your mother's, father's, and Carla's.	I deliberately left out grandmother, mirroring what the children had drawn.
Adam: Yeah. I'm different.	
RA: Sometimes it is confusing to be different.	I wanted to let him know that I understood his bewilderment at being different.
Adam: [Looks at his mother.] My mother says I daydream a lot.	
RA: I guess that's one way to try to figure out how you got to be different.	This is a statement trying to normalize his behavior.
Adam: See my Transformer.	Adam pulled a truck out of his pocket. I realized he was squashing any disturbing feelings of being different.
Jerry: Adam, we chose you. We asked for you.	

[Adam looks at his picture and
starts to color everyone darker.]

RA: Oh, so you would like all   Adam did not respond. In his
your family to look like you.   drawing I noticed that he had both
                                  parents standing close to each
                                  other and Carla was near Betsy.
                                  Adam was disconnected.

As a homework assignment I asked the parents to read to Adam and
Carla *The Ugly Duckling*, the fairy tale by H. C. Andersen. By so doing
I hoped to begin to address the cultural and racial issues in the family.

The next session began with Betsy and Jerry talking about some of
their parenting difficulties. They reported that their parenting difficulties had increased after Ana moved in and their communication patterns
became more covert. Parenting is an extremely difficult process. Parents
cannot carry out their executive roles unless they have the power to do
so. These powers seemed to be usurped by the strong matriarchal
system. I worked toward the goal of joining Betsy and Ana together in
a position of mutual support and complementarity. I did this by
challenging the subsystem boundaries between grandmother and Betsy.
I facilitated their efforts to clearly define their roles. Betsy, with a
guarded look of awareness, described how she and grandmother could
work together as a team. Betsy and Jerry were to be responsible for
disciplining. I complimented Betsy and Jerry's efforts and caring. I
affirmed Ana for her strong support of the family.

I tried to convey to Betsy and Jerry that I understood the stress that
Adam and Carla brought to their family and to their marital relationship.
They needed some alone time so they could provide for one another.

During the fifth session we evaluated how the therapy was progressing. The family felt stronger, yet they requested more help. We
contracted for three more sessions. Their goal was still focused on
Adam's behavior. I wanted to see how the family could live with
differences and to reinforce as strongly as possible Adam's worthiness
and ability to be accepted as he was.

I asked for the parents to sign a release of information so that I could
talk with Adam's teacher. Adam's first grade teacher painted this picture
of him. "He is very likeable, active, and constantly visiting others in the
room. Maybe a better word to describe him would be high energy.
Sometimes his constant talking is annoying. He learns quickly, but he
does not always complete his work on time. He is not a bad child; his
school behavior tends to be disruptive and immature. His psychosocial

skills are not quite age-appropriate." Adam's teacher was open to some suggested behavioral modification techniques and concrete, reality-based logical consequences that might facilitate classroom behavior change. I wanted to enhance Adam's academic and social self-confidence. My hypothesis was that once Adam was able to deal with his fear of rejection and his resulting reluctance to commit, he would more likely be able to expend greater energy on learning.

My goal for the sixth session was for Adam to become aware of his abilities and begin to trust himself and others. In this session, Adam drew a monster. It had huge eyes, several horns on its head and sword-like hands and feet.

Dialogue	*Commentary*
RA: You drew that. Tell me about it.	
Adam: It's a monster.	
Betsy: He's always drawing monsters. They all look the same.	I ignored Betsy's comment. Teaching a family rule of communication: family members are to speak for themselves.
RA: Oh, it's a monster. Tell me about these things.	I pointed to the hands.
Adam: Those are its hands and feet. And this is a big hole where lots of sparks fly out.	
RA: Oh, so many sparks come right out of the center of your monster.	
Adam: Yeah. He can keep others away.	
RA: So it's important for your monster to make others keep their distance.	Tracking.

Carla: He's scary. Will he eat other
    monsters?

Adam: Nope. He just shoots
    sparks.

RA: Boy! Really something. And   Using words of competence.
    he does a good job.

Adam: Yeah. Someday the sparks
    will grow smaller.

Carla: [Holds her hands up.] Are
    the sparks this big?

RA: Oh. So in the future the
    sparks will be smaller.

Jerry: He lives in a fantasy world.

RA: Mm-hm.   I wait to see how Jerry and Adam
                                    interact.

Adam: [Ignoring his father.] I
    know exactly when.

Jerry: Tell me, when will they be   I concentrated on positives by ig-
    smaller?   noring Jerry's question.

Adam: When I'm big enough to
    care for myself.

RA: So you know exactly when   Adam has power through his
    those sparks will get smaller.   monster.
    You're just waiting to grow
    up.

For the remainder of the session Betsy, Jerry, Carla, Adam, and I sat
on the floor building towers. It was a chance for the parents and children
to experience a sense of support among themselves.

Adam's drawing of monsters seemed to be a metaphor for how he felt
in the family. I knew I had to challenge the family's conceptualization of

Adam as the problem. I felt that the family's concentration on Adam served to distract them from problems between other family members. I congratulated Adam for the power he had in the family. By creating "sparks" in the family, he was able to keep all family members at a distance. Betsy was distanced from Ana, Jerry from his mother, and Carla and Adam from Betsy and Jerry. I said, "In a funny way, Adam, your stealing seems to keep your family together, yet separate."

As a homework assignment I suggested that the family integrate into one of their family meals some food from black Americans. I also suggested that the family make an effort to meet with a few black families, so that Adam could see others who had similar coloring.

I invited just the parents and Ana to the seventh session. Jerry and Betsy announced that they had a special dinner incorporating some Asian foods and some black foods. Jerry proclaimed, "I have to admit that I'll have to develop a taste for it, but I'm willing to try."

While respecting the family's cultural background and hierarchies, I wanted to challenge the notion that Adam could control the family system. My goal for this session was for the adult members to identify their own part in the family interaction and to accept responsibility for changing themselves. If they did this, my hypothesis was that they could then assist Adam to change. If Betsy and Ana could agree to disagree and Jerry and Betsy could accept their roles in the spousal subsystem, then the existing balance of power would be readjusted. Adam would no longer need to be a scapegoat.

I wanted to create an executive subsystem with Jerry and Betsy in which they are responsible for the child rearing. They needed to have authority to set limits. I wanted to reframe the grandmother's role in this family so that her primary duty was to love and nurture the children. I also wanted to establish a protective boundary where Adam and Carla could learn cooperation, interaction, competition, fighting, and making up.

During this session I worked to redraw the spouse subsystem boundary so Betsy and Jerry could negotiate spouse issues without involving Ana. I was trying to strengthen the boundary around this dyad. I had limited success in this area, because the cultural background played a powerful part in the family's interaction patterns. Jerry's relationship with his mother was vitally important and he was not willing to sacrifice any part of that relationship to begin to build a stronger relationship with Betsy.

Betsy and Jerry discussed their philosophies of parenting and styles of interaction with children. I listened to Jerry's opinion, then turned to Betsy. Betsy tearfully stated, "I feel that both of you blame me for

Adam's problems." Ana acknowledged that she did think Betsy was at fault. She thought Betsy should spend more time with the children. She stated that if this happened, "Adam would not be like this." She said that "Family should always come first." As Ana said this, Jerry nodded in agreement. This alliance between Jerry and his mother created tension and conflict in the family and hurt within Betsy. Betsy seemed reluctant to accept the fact that she would be in a secondary position in relation to Jerry's attachment with his mother. I empathized with Betsy's emotional pain and frustration. I suggested that she work alone with Adam, thus strengthening the boundary around this dyad, which had been weak.

The eighth and final session was a review of what had happened. Betsy and Jerry admitted, "Adam is doing better. He has not stolen any money from the house or anywhere else in over a week." However, even though the problem had ceased, the family interaction style had not significantly changed.

During this session, Adam again drew his monster. This time, I asked Adam to imagine another living creature that could be in his picture with the monster. Adam drew a dog. I then asked Adam if either the monster or the dog had names. There was a long silence. Then he responded, "Yeah. The dog's name is Max." We continued our dialogue with:

Dialogue	*Commentary*
RA: Adam, I would like you to ask the monster if it has a name.	I knew Adam felt safe with the monster. It was a confidant for him.
Adam: [After a long silence.] He says his name is Danger Wolf.	
RA: Ask him if it is okay to pet him.	Trying to enter into his fantasy and create an atmosphere of safety.
Adam: Yeah.	
RA: Ask him if he's your friend.	Making the covert overt.
Adam: Yeah, because I like him and I'm not scared of him. I'll pet him and take care of him.	

RA: As a sign of your friendship   Facilitating Adam's need to trust
     with Danger Wolf, ask him if   his parents.
     you can trust your parents.

Adam: [Looked at his monster. A
       big smile crossed his face.]
       Yeah.

By entering into Adam's fantasy, I tried to facilitate Adam's trust in his own resources. I knew Adam was very resourceful. My aim was to empower him to trust himself and to believe his parents that they would not return him to the adoption agency.

Betsy and Jerry agreed that they loved Adam very much and would not return him to the adoption agency. They both hugged Adam and expressed their love to him. Carla gave him a big hug, too. Adam responded with a gigantic smile.

RESULTS AND FOLLOW-UP

I tried to tap into Adam's profound wishes for understanding, love, and acceptance. The overall goal of treatment was to help the parents and grandmother to behave differently in relation to Adam and his sister and to address all the many domains of the dysfunction (family life, school, and peer interactions) that were involved in Adam's stealing behavior. The focus was on acceptance of the child, warmth, the therapeutic relationship, and inducing change beyond the clinical setting. Specifically, I wanted to see how both parents behaved in relation to their children. In the sessions, the mother would invariably focus on Adam's behavior and how poorly the child was doing. Betsy's confusing feelings about family relationships and her own role in the family all focused on Adam. I would have the parents role-play situations and create enactments right in the sessions, so that they might respond more effectively. I tried to empower Betsy in her role as a parent, as she discovered alternatives in disciplining and relating with her son.

I gave the family homework assignments, such as the parents requesting simple chores from the children (e.g., setting the table, taking out the trash) so that they felt like contributing members of the family. I also encouraged the parents to join a support system for parents with adopted children. This social support system contributed greatly to the success of the therapy. The parents discovered they were not alone. Other families with adopted children had similar issues. In a follow-up session, the mother clearly recognized her fear of being displaced by the grandmother. The parents had gained new perspectives on their struggle with the grandmother's role in the family. Adam was more relaxed as a child in the family.

The concept of mental health was alien to this family. I congratulated the family for going beyond their family boundaries to seek help and for trusting me.

DISCUSSION

Play therapy in the context of family therapy worked with Adam and his family. My goal was to help the family begin to enjoy life, to trust, and to develop friendship and intimacy with each other. Children are natural teachers of this. They help families build bridges by their simplicity and honesty.

For Adam, play proved an important vehicle for expressing his various painful feelings around ethnicity and relationships. It provided a safe context in which Adam could express his fantasy, his fears, and his conflicts. The entire family was able to enter into play. It seemed to help them communicate in a nonverbal, nonthreatening way.

In Adam's family, I felt that the children's behaviors served several functions. The stealing by Adam sustained contact and closeness, but at the same time created an intensity and separateness. For example, Adam's stealing helped to distance him from his mother, distanced the father from the grandmother, and created tension between the parents. However, in some ways the parents were brought closer together as they tried to solve this behavioral dilemma. The children helped to lead the family to greater discussion among one another, to more equitable speaking, and to more spontaneity and fun in their every day life. I helped them reframe the "child's problem" into a larger family and interactional framework.

Treating children with problems is one task; treating their families complicates the undertaking. The integration of family, play, and child treatment paradigms helps to define goals, to organize the change process, and to use imaginative and multiple perspectives in working with families. Play in the context of family therapy is an effective process that creates a dynamic, fluid, and challenging atmosphere that frees the family to love and support each other, to be more open to communication and listening, to foster the development of each individual's unique potential, and to stimulate a sensitivity and capacity for understanding.

REFERENCES

Blanco, R. (1972). *Prescription for Children with Learning and Adjustment Problems*. Springfield, IL: Charles C Thomas.

Bowen, M. (1971). The use of family therapy in clinical practice. In *Changing Families*, ed. J. Haley, pp. 159–192. New York: Grune & Stratton.

Brodzinsky, D., Schechter, M., and Marantz Henig, R. (1992). *Being Adopted: The Lifelong Search for Self*. New York: Doubleday.

Carey, L. (1991). Family sandplay therapy. *The Arts in Psychotherapy* 18:231–239.

Combrinck-Graham, L. (1986). Family treatment for childhood anxiety disorders. In *Treating Young Children in Family Therapy*, pp.22–30. Rockville, MD: Aspen Publications.

Keith, D. V. (1986). Are children necessary in family therapy? In *Treating Young Children in Family Therapy*, ed. L. Combrinck-Graham, pp. 1–30. Rockville, MD: Aspen Publications.

Keith, D. V., and Whitaker, C. A. (1981). Play therapy: paradigm for work with families. *Journal of Marital and Family Therapy* 7:243–254.

Lawson, D. (1987). Using therapeutic stories in the counseling process. *Elementary School Guidance and Counseling* 22: 134–142.

Minuchin, S. (1974). *Families and Family Therapy*. Cambridge, MA: Harvard University Press.

Weltner, J. S. (1982). One to three session therapy with children and families. *Family Process* 21:281–289.

Whitaker, C. (1987). Dynamics of American family as deduced from twenty years of family therapy: the family unconscious. In *The Evolution of Psychotherapy*, ed. J. Zeig, pp. 75–83. New York: Brunner/Mazel.

Whitaker, C., and Keith D. (1981). Symbolic-experiential family therapy. In *Handbook of Family Therapy*, ed. A. Gurman and D. Kniskern, pp. 187–226. New York: Brunner/Mazel.

15

"Please Hurt Me Again": Posttraumatic Play Therapy with an Abused Child

Jamshid A. Marvasti, M.D.

INTRODUCTION TO POSTTRAUMATIC PLAY THERAPY THEORY

Posttraumatic play therapy (PTPT) is not yet considered a school of thought nor a special theory in psychotherapy. However, in general, it may be defined as the treatment of a child who has been victimized and is currently experiencing posttraumatic events and stages. In particular, posttraumatic play (PTP) is a special kind of repetitive play that the survivor of psychic trauma may demonstrate during therapy.

I divide PTP into two distinct types: the positive type and the negative type. In the positive type of PTP, the child reenacts the trauma in a repetitive way and is able, with the help of the therapist, to modify the negative components of the trauma and gradually desensitize himself or herself. Eventually, the child gains ego mastery.

In the negative type of PTP, a kind of repetitive play occurs, described by Terr (1983) as "posttraumatic play." In this repetitive play, the play fails to relieve any anxiety and does not help the child gain ego mastery. Terr (1990) explained that posttraumatic play is monotonous, and at times may be dangerous because with some children it exacerbates their terror.

Johnson (1989) suggested that important goals in posttraumatic treatment are "reexperience, release, and reorganization" (p. 119). In reviewing the literature, I found that several therapists have observed PTP in their cases without identifying or labeling it as PTP. Erikson (1950) gave us the example of a 5-year-old child who witnessed his grandmother's heart attack and the subsequent removal of her body in a coffin, when he was 3 year old. During his play, he "built innumerable variations of oblong boxes, the openings of which he would carefully barricade" (p. 27). Another example is the repetitive play of Bernie following his father's death from a bomb during an air raid (Freud and Burlingham 1942). This 4-year-old boy, who was ill and in bed, had a whole tray full of paper houses on his bed. He would build the houses, cover them with their roofs, then throw them down with small marbles that were his bombs.

Generally, children who have been traumatized react on the basis of their perceptions of the trauma and also their ego structure, pretrauma personality, and posttrauma events. However, each clinician may have a different approach in the treatment of the posttrauma child. In this chapter, I describe the way that I treated a traumatized child. This method is "holistic" and based on the psychodynamic theory of personality development mixed with components of cognitive therapy and education (Marvasti 1989).

I use the psychodynamic principles in both the exploration of deeper conflicts (diagnosis) and in psychotherapy. In this "holistic" approach, I look for and try to deal with transference, countertransference, and resistance. I consider the ego defense mechanisms a protective agent to id impulses (Freud 1936). People use these defense mechanisms to disguise their unacceptable wishes and to avoid the awareness of painful feelings.

Cognitive therapy is a technique that helps to identify and correct maladaptive and distorted attitudes and assumptions. In addition, it gives attention to the dysfunctional beliefs underlying these cognitions. This technique is based on a rationale that a person's emotions and behaviors are largely determined by the way in which he or she construes the world. How an individual thinks determines how he or she feels and reacts (Beck 1976). So, by correcting and modifying the cognitive distortions, one may be able to change the affect and behavior.

The educational component (Marvasti in press) of the therapy is conducted either by the therapist directly talking to the child or the therapist's puppet communicating with the child's puppet (e.g., "This puppet may like father, but can also be angry at him. Let's tell this puppet that it's okay to be angry at grown-ups and still like them.").

The modality of play therapy that I use is a combination of structured play therapy and free play. In this modality, children use projective materials such as dolls, puppets, drawings, and psychodrama to express (in a symbolic way) their internal conflicts and victimization. The therapist observes this expression and tries to identify themes and symbols. Then, with the help of the same play material, the therapist attempts to encourage the children to find better solutions for their conflicts. The therapist may communicate through his or her puppets and limit the discussion to the doll's feelings/behavior and victimization or may connect the doll's feelings/behavior to the child's feelings/ behavior.

Haworth (1990) explains this kind of mixed therapeutic approach and labels it as *ego-dynamic*. Attention at the beginning of therapy is on the present state of the child's reality functioning and ego defenses. As these defenses are neutralized, the feeling and affective state that the child is defending against become the subjects of exploration. In this process, the therapist may become the subject of a child's transference, and reenactments of unresolved conflicts will appear in play and therapeutic interaction (Haworth 1990).

In traumatized children, the concept of repeating the trauma in a symbolic and metaphoric disguise becomes evident. In this way, the child may communicate to the therapist what he or she perceives as a trauma. This may be different from the therapist's preconceived ideas and formulation. The therapist can use clarification, persuasion, suggestion, reflection, interpretation, and "self" as therapeutic tools. The therapist needs to see the world from the child's eyes and then the child is encouraged to see himself or herself from the therapist's eyes. Self-observation and insight are the curative factors in this technique. Other therapeutic goals and elements are identification with the therapist, corrective emotional experience, reworking of the trauma, empowering the victim, resolution of the developmental crisis, and integration of traumatic events (Marvasti 1992).

I call this kind of PTPT the "Persian type" (pending a better term). I have observed how Middle Eastern children (especially Persian children) cope with the simple pain of falling on the ground. For example, when a little boy falls down and hurts his knee, he may start to cry. People who are around him immediately tell him that the ground was responsible for his fall and he needs to get even by kicking and hitting the ground. My observation is that the child immediately stops crying, gets up, and starts to kick and hit the ground at exactly the spot he fell down. This experience gave me some ideas about the treatment of victimized children.

From a psychodynamic point of view, it seems that the child who falls down may blame himself for falling down. However, by reminding him that it is the ground that is responsible for his pain and victimization, he stops the self-blame and possible guilt feelings and accepts the idea that the ground caused his fall and pain. In this example of the Middle

Eastern child falling down, the adult gives the child an explanation and meaning for the victimization. The meaning is that the ground is a bad object, and because it is hard, it inflicts bad things on children when they fall. The second psychodynamic understanding is the issue of getting even or reversing the victimization. Through this role reversal, it is the child who is now the aggressor and the ground is the victim. There are indications that the child who fell is no longer obsessed and preoccupied by his helplessness or pain. In some way he has integrated the trauma and worked it out. This process can also be labeled as the child identifying with the aggressor, which in this case is the ground, and then inflicting the same pain on the ground as it inflicted on him. It is important to remember, however, that in PTPT all these events occur as displacement and in the playroom, rather than the outside world.

A simple example of PTPT would be the case of a child who was bitten by a dog. The process involves a structured play session using a stuffed animal like a dog in which the play therapist informs a child that the dog was responsible for hurting her. The play therapist then asks her to reenact her victimization and gradually reverse the phenomenon by asking the child to get even with the dog. This does not mean that the child needs to bite the toy dog, although this would be acceptable. Using a baseball bat to beat the stuffed animal may do the same job as biting the dog. This kind of therapy may suffice for a child who was attacked by a strange dog, but if this dog is the child's dog, then one also needs to do psychodynamic play therapy in regard to other elements that would emerge as a consequence of trauma by a trusted person or animal. Psychodynamic play therapy could help the child deal with feelings such as betrayal, loss of trust, ambivalent feelings toward the loved object, and possible changes in the child's view of the world.

In the "Persian type" of PTPT the play therapist usually initiates the first stage by asking the child to reenact or revisit the trauma. The child frequently plays out what was done to him or her by using toys and play materials and by using different ego defense mechanisms such as projection, displacement, and symbolization. The second stage consists of the therapist's involvement with the child for the purpose of play modification. As the child repeats the trauma during play, the therapist's task is to gradually change the negative outcome by slowly reversing the helplessness, passivity, and victimization that the child went through. Gradually, the therapist accomplishes the phenomenon of reversal by helping the child reverse the victimization and get even with the offender. The last stage is the neutralization of trauma, or in other words, the integration of the trauma within the child's personality. In this stage, the therapist encourages the child to split the positive part of the offender from the negative part, acknowledge and comprehend the positive part, and finally to get even with the negative part. The child can then integrate the positive and negative parts and acknowledge that both parts belong to one person or object. I call this the de-splitting procedure.

I have interviewed adults who were relatives of murder victims. I consider these relatives as much victims as the dead person. Surprisingly, however, in some of the relatives I did not find the depression or feelings of victimization that I would have expected. What I found was the desire for revenge or getting even. As one relative told me, "That is my life's goal. I will not rest until I have accomplished this goal." It seems that the phenomenon of getting revenge, in both children and adults, creates a tremendous amount of energy and motivation and seems to decrease their depression, helplessness, passivity, and sense of victimization. Although I have never encouraged any victim to get even or get revenge, I must say, having grown up in the Middle East, I have witnessed many families who were able to survive human-induced trauma just with the hope and pleasure of getting even.

Another observation that I have from the Middle East regards techniques used by political prisoners there. Potential prisoners are instructed how to resist mental and physical torture while in captivity. The method used to counteract emotional and physical pressures is for the victims to think about revenge and to increase their anger, rage, and hate toward the torturer. Apparently, experience shows that the victim can resist if he or she is able to do this.

Certain cultures encourage victims of abuse to use specific ego defense mechanisms to cope with the anger, hate, and murderous wishes that they may experience toward their offender. Some of these defense mechanisms are sublimation, reaction formation, denial, and repression. There are also other cultures that encourage the victims of abuse to forego passivity and instead to mobilize their anger in order to get even with the victimizer. I have studied the subject of revenge to see if it has any therapeutic value in psychotherapy with abuse victims. The idea of a "hand for a hand" and an "eye for an eye" traditionally observed in ancient cultures, may be a valuable therapeutic tool when it is used symbolically through displacement on play material in play therapy.

PRESENTING PROBLEM AND
BACKGROUND DATA

Camelot was a 6-year-old child who was brought to my office on the recommendation of the police department. Earlier that day, Camelot had been interviewed by a policewoman because of allegations that her stepfather (Jack) had sexually abused her. I obtained some information from family members before seeing the child. The presenting problem, from the family's point of view, was that the child had been sexually abused by her stepfather and needed therapy.

The family background revealed that Camelot's maternal grandmother (Margaret) was a victim of father-daughter incest. Camelot's mother (Samantha) also was sexually abused by the same man (Margaret's father). Margaret, a very religious Irish Catholic immigrant, was inhibited. She had developed depression and anxiety and had been involved in psychiatric treatment since her mid-thirties. She became my patient several years before I saw Camelot in my office. Margaret was very important in Camelot's life as she was a frequent babysitter and spent time with Camelot when the child's mother was absent. Camelot had a high vocabulary and was very intelligent. I felt that many of the difficult words and expressions she used were the result of the many hours she spent with her grandparents. The grandmother's psychology revealed that she was carrying a tremendous amount of guilt feelings, especially in regard to sexuality. She believed that a child is born crying because it is entering a world that is full of pain and suffering. She viewed death as the end of suffering that would bring happiness. She also believed that people in general are corrupt, and regardless of how much they try not to commit sins they eventually do because people are not in control of the "devil inside." Margaret had little tolerance for happiness or success and had anticipatory anxiety, anticipating that bad things would happen if she had too much success or too much pleasure. She would not buy a lottery ticket, fearing that if she won, people would find out about it and might kidnap her children or sue her for the money.

Camelot's mother, Samantha (Sam), was born and grew up in an intact, but somewhat dysfunctional family. Around the age of 15 or 16, she rebelled against her very rigid and highly moralistic mother and became somewhat promiscuous. She eventually became pregnant and Camelot was the result of that pregnancy. Sam never married Camelot's father, who apparently left her when she told him of the pregnancy. However, Sam had a fantasy that one day he would be sorry and would return to her. She mentioned that she did not know anything about Camelot's biological father; however, she still loved him and believed that one day he would return. She said he was not able to tolerate making a woman pregnant and the minute that he heard she was, he packed his things and moved out of state and she did not know his whereabouts. This same idea was conveyed to Camelot and she fantasized that one day her unknown father would come and rescue her from her misery.

After Camelot's birth, Sam dropped out of school, became involved with marijuana, and totally rebelled against her family's value system. She moved out of the house and lived in an apartment with Camelot. For a couple of years she had multiple boyfriends who stayed in her home. According to Sam, all of them were involved with drugs, alcohol and violence. Sam received alcohol and drugs from them, and at times she was the target of their violent behavior. Sam eventually met a man, Jack, who also had a history of alcohol and drug problems. Jack married Sam and adopted Camelot. Their relationship was mutually enjoyable for a few months; however, before long it started to deteriorate. Sam and Jack frequently fought about money and Sam's diminished interest in Jack. In spite of this, they had a child together, a baby boy, Michael.

The relationship between Camelot and her stepfather became a special one within a short period. They would get together and take care of Michael, or they would make food in the kitchen while Camelot's mother was stoned, intoxicated, or was depressed and sleeping. The marital problems seemed to start because of Jack's need to have some kind of control over Sam and his feeling that Sam was neglecting him. Camelot reported that her relationship with her stepfather eventually became sexual and he sexually molested her many times. In the beginning, he told her that this was a game that any father or stepfather would play with his children. He told her that this was a special secret between the two of them and because of this, Camelot became somewhat distant from her mother. At times Jack asked Camelot to help him spy on Sam. He was somewhat suspicious that his wife might be involved with his best friend who was a very rich drug dealer. This information was given to me by Camelot, Sam, and Camelot's grandmother (Margaret) during the first few weeks of therapy.

Originally, Sam brought Camelot to my office. I interviewed her first, and she appeared to be a woman who was overwhelmed and depressed. She asked me if I would be willing to see her as a patient and I reminded her that she was already in therapy with another clinician and informed her that it would not be appropriate for me to get involved with her daughter and her simultaneously. Later on, she reminded me that I had been her mother's psychiatrist in the past, but I explained that I saw Margaret only in regard to medication and hospitalization and that her "talking therapy" was with another therapist. I told her that I did not see any conflict in prescribing medication for a grandmother and doing play therapy with her grandchild.

In the first session, I felt that Sam was more preoccupied by her own problems than by her child's. She appeared immature and totally overwhelmed. Her life story reminded me of someone with many self-defeating behaviors. She used projection to the highest extent; she blamed everyone else for her problems. She blamed drug and alcohol as the reasons she dropped out of school, had no job, and relied on men to feed her. She also blamed her mother for her problems, although she mentioned that she and her mother loved each other. There was ample indication that there was a love/hate relationship between these two people. Sam had positive feelings toward her father and felt sympathetic toward him, wondering "How has he tolerated my mother for all these years?"

Sam told me about her mother's parenting. Sexuality was something forbidden and she had no sex education. She was not prepared for the onset of menstruation and when she had her first period, the blood "scared me to death." She said she had heard her parents having sex and several times she heard her mother refuse. She frequently fantasized that she was her mother and would satisfy her father sexually. However, she felt that she was not her father's favorite and had a dream that she and her three sisters would get together, throw the mother out, and ask their father to select one of them to take care of him in the kitchen. The father selected Sam's older sister and the older sister transformed the kitchen into a bedroom and took care of the father in this way too. In regards to sex, she overheard her mother tell her older sister the night before her wedding that "Something will happen to you tomorrow night that you will regret for the rest of your life."

Sam had low self-esteem and poor self-image, and she was still involved and stuck in the developmental stage of oedipal rivalry with her mother and siblings. She not only rejected her mother's value system, but she also rebelled against it. There was some indication that Sam was "the other part" of her mother; the part that wanted to rebel against the very religious, subdued, and moralistic part. On several occasions when Sam came home late, Margaret was very suspicious and would accuse her of having sex. She would tell her that boys take advantage of girls and would hurt them. Surprisingly, her mother would go into the details of sex. Sam was also told by her mother that she would become promiscuous, be oversexed, and act out on her sexual feelings and eventually fail her parents. There was some indication that Margaret was projecting the unwanted part of herself onto Sam and Sam eventually acted out this projective identification by Margaret.

Sam explained to me that her childhood was uneventful except for her mother's hospitalizations due to depression. Margaret would withdraw her affection and attention from the children and become some-what seclusive whenever she had one of her depressive episodes. During these periods, Sam's aunt or grandfather would take care of her at home on a part-time basis. There was some indication that, during this time, the maternal grandfather had sexually abused two of the girls in this family. Sam's sister remembered it and admitted to it happening. Although Sam witnessed the sexual victimization of her sister, she had only some vague memories that it "might" have happened to her.

Sam's childhood was full of sibling rivalry with her sisters. She felt that she was the scapegoat of the family and that she was not as attractive as her sisters. She believed that her older sister was her father's favorite and that her brother had become the mother's favorite. She was in competition with her sisters in trying to please her father, but felt that she had failed in all her attempts.

Sam said that she had been open with Camelot and many times they talked to each other "like two friends." She said that many times Camelot had taken care of her, especially when she cried or was depressed. She added that oftentimes her crying was connected to the feelings of loss when her boyfriends left her. In interviewing her, I got the impression that Camelot was a parentified child, with definite indications of role reversal between Sam and her daughter. When I asked Sam what she thought was happening to her child, she com-pletely denied any responsibility for her child's condition, despite her very unstable life situation during the previous several years. She showed anger toward Jack and said she worried that he might have damaged Camelot forever because he sexually abused her. She reported that she had eventually separated from him by using a lot of willpower and with strong encouragement from her family. She felt that she had a choice between staying with her husband or having Camelot. She chose her daughter. Sam said her siblings constantly accused her of distorting reality and went so far as to call her a "pathological liar." This issue of lying became evident later on when I found that it was the husband who filed for separation and divorce, not Sam.

In one session, several months later, Camelot played out the fol-lowing scenario: a mother sacrifices her children for the sake of her husband by kicking her children out and placing them in an orphanage. She then gives him the children's room. In the end, the husband "stabs her in the back" and leaves her. "Stabbing in the back" was a theme that Camelot played out several times. She thought this phrase meant to literally stab someone in the back and that's how she played it. In interviewing the mother and grandmother, I found that these words were often used by the two women during conversation: "I brought this man home, I trusted him, I fed him, and eventually he stabbed me in the back. How could I trust men?"

THEORETICAL CONCEPTUALIZATION

Originally, when I started play diagnosis with Camelot, I did not know if she was in need of PTPT, and it was not evident that she was showing any repetitive play. Camelot's family was very concerned about sexual molestation by the stepfather, but in the beginning she did not show any indication during her play that she had been traumatized by this abuse. However, she did speak about how she felt deceived by him, and how he had hurt her because he had "done things with me that grown-up people do with each other." Her family had explained to her that sexual molestation is bad when "it is done with a child." There was an indication that she blamed herself because at times she participated in sex play with him, and she felt that she was getting a lot of attention and caring from him.

However, after three of four months of therapy, the pattern of repetitive play became evident. The entire play sessions were not exclusively devoted to repetitive play. She could get involved in different kinds of play if I directed her. For example, we did drawings and paintings. However, when she made a story about the drawing, it was always about a man who comes to a home and beats up the woman and then leaves. She started to repeat the type of play that indicates physical and psychological trauma, such as sexual penetration. Originally she started to use the female doll and put clay in the doll's abdomen and genital area. When my puppet asked, "What is going on there?" Camelot answered that the doll "has pain there." Later, in the other play, soldiers with guns would come to a house, shoot the woman and direct their guns toward her genital area. Eventually, the play changed into a repetitive pattern: A man would sit on the genital area of another doll or would pick up a female doll and put it on his genital area. She would say no and he would say yes. The repetitive theme of this play, which later on we called "she said no and he said yes play," continued several times. Eventually, Camelot was able to explain to me that something like that happened to her mother; that once, while he was under the influence of alcohol, Jack had attempted to penetrate her mother while Camelot was in another room.

Sam confirmed that Camelot may have witnessed her being raped, although Sam tried to minimize the issue by saying "I was drunk, I don't know what I said, maybe he forced me, maybe I was screaming and saying no and he was saying yes, and I did not know that she was hearing us from her room." This pattern of a man forcing his penis on a woman was repeated in Camelot's play. It was not possible for me to differentiate if and how much of that was her personal experience and how much was what she witnessed of her mother's experience.

There were several episodes of repetitive play that occurred in the doll house. The male doll physically and sexually abused the female doll and then left her. The female doll cried and called him to come back and begged, "Please hurt me again." In several sessions, this pattern of play was repeated. Again I was not able to distinguish if this was an objective reality and if her mother had really asked, "Please hurt me again," or if it was Camelot's perception of sexual intercourse as a "hurt."

Another pattern of play also became repetitive in a compulsive way. It was that of a man coming home and beating up a woman, taking her money and her food, and leaving her as she cried and asked him to come back. Then a different man would go to the home the next day and do the same thing. Camelot was very absorbed in this play and became very much a part of it. I almost felt that she was inside of the doll house observing everything, as her eyes would show how attentive she was during the play. In the beginning, she denied any similarity between the events occurring in the doll house and those occurring in her house. But eventually she explained to me that there were similarities, such as her mother's boyfriends who were violent, but her mother continued to bring them home.

When these repetitive play patterns continued, I felt that this child had been traumatized and that posttraumatic play was happening. She repeated the pattern of her trauma in a compulsive way, becoming more and more preoccupied with these patterns. She had some difficulty engaging in any other kind of play. Although she tried to please me and responded to me in regard to drawing, painting, or playing with the ball, the minute that she had unstructured play the same repetitive play would emerge. At this time, I decided to use the technique of PTPT, Persian type. I felt that she had difficulty in expressing her anger verbally. I felt that she had been traumatized by her stepfather and by her mother's boyfriends who were coming into her home and terrorizing both her and her mother. Some of the events that she played in the doll house were validated by Sam and some by Margaret. In reality, there were many men who came to the mother's home and, from Camelot's point of view, they were frightening both to her and to her mother. There was no indication that Camelot was ever abused physically or sexually by any of these men. Nevertheless, there was definite indication of emotional abuse, since a couple of the males had hit her mother in front of Camelot. There were times when she, as a parentified child, had attempted to alleviate her mother's pain.

In evaluating Camelot, I felt that she had some strengths and assets: intelligence, physical attractiveness, and talent. I further felt that she may have experienced "good-enough mothering," not from her mother, but most likely from her grandmother. I believed that she had sufficient ego capacity to have withstood many stressful situations without falling apart. Her liabilities were from the pretrauma period. She was born out of wedlock, had feelings of rejection by her biological father, feelings that she was "different" from other children because she did not have a father, had inconsistent mothering, and role reversal with her mother. The parentification of Camelot, as well as the abuse she witnessed at home done by Sam's multiple boyfriends and the abuse by her stepfather, were other negative elements.

In doing therapy with children of divorced parents, many therapists consider the child's lack of an intact parental unit as a narcissistic injury. The child may seek to reestablish the integrity of the parental unit in an attempt to restore an intact sense of self. However, my impression of Camelot was that she had an intact sense of self that was a mixture of her grandmother's ideology and her mother's projection of the image of "a caretaker" on her. I felt that she was a "little adult."

Camelot's lack of a consistent father, especially at the crucial oedipal stage, may have had some impact on her sexual identity and also on her self-esteem and self-image. I felt that at one point, when she became somewhat seductive and started to flirt with me, that this seductive and flirtatious attitude was beneficial behavior for her. She was testing her attractiveness on me and I felt that she considered me safe, nonrejecting, and secure. She seemed to have no fear of abandonment or sexual advances from me. I felt that it was important for her sexual identification and her object relationship that she be able to relate to a man without punishment and abandonment. The identification with parental figures are important factors in the development of the superego, the ego ideal, and sexual identity. However, I felt that Camelot did identify, at least partially, with her grandmother, and partially with her stepfather (two opposite characters.) Part of Camelot's ideology and ego ideal grew from her identification with Margaret's projection of a religion and value system on her, and part grew from Camelot's stepfather's eroticized behavior toward her.

I designed a few therapeutic goals on the basis of Camelot's presentation of the problem. I felt that she looked at women as passive, submissive victims and that she perceived men as abusive and aggressive. I believed that she had developed a parentified role and felt responsible for defending and taking care of her mother and her sibling. I felt that she was also dealing with a betrayal in the same way as her mother: her mother trusted men, brought them home, and eventually they "stabbed her in the back." Camelot had trusted her stepfather and eventually was told that what he was doing to her was criminal and bad. I also believed that Camelot had difficulty in expressing her anger, that many of her grandmother's ideas were present in her, and that she considered anger and hate as forbidden feelings. She especially considered revenge as taboo.

Camelot felt that her role in life was to suffer and be exploited, just like her mother and her grandmother. She had internalized Margaret's ideas and believed that real life is in another world (the afterlife), where there would not be any victimization and suffering. Camelot was preoccupied by two ideas: (a) a man would eventually come and rescue her (which I felt was the lost object: the biological father); and (b) there would be another world where there would not be any suffering. I felt that I needed to "de-identify" her from both her grandmother and her mother and give her the idea that she had a right to experience happiness, justice, and fairness in this world. I felt that Camelot's "world view" was distorted because she was generalizing her experience with a few men to all men. She believed that the way of the world was what was going on in her home, which was full of injustice, unfairness, abuse, and victimization.

One of my therapeutic goals was to reverse and neutralize some of Camelot's painful experiences with her mother, stepfather, and her mother's multiple boyfriends. From the beginning, my first goal was to create a safe "holding environment" as was described by Winnicott (1971). By my creating a safe and nurturing environment, Camelot would be able to reveal to me her confusion, her conception of the trauma, and her preoccupation with her family situation. The second goal was to help Camelot comprehend her trauma and arrive at some kind of meaning in regard to what has happened to her and her family. I considered the reenactment of the trauma in a symbolic and metaphoric way an important element in her therapy. In this safe environment, Camelot could express her feelings through her behavior. She could think about her worries, her fears, her pain, and her wishes. Camelot was a very inhibited child and had internalized some rigid value systems of her grandmother. She had also learned a kind of identity from her mother that involved not showing anger and hate, and, on the contrary, inviting abuse, tolerating it, and possibly enjoying it.

My therapeutic goals with Camelot were very similar to the treatment program for traumatized children, which consists of identifying the psychopathology and focusing on the negative impact of incest. The psychopathology includes self-blame, powerlessness, loss and betrayal, attachment disorder, object relationship problems, erotization of relationship, "damaged goods syndrome" (Sgroi 1982), and a negative world view.

It was very important to find Camelot's perception of traumatic events. I was surprised to find that her mother's neglect and abandonment was more traumatic to her than her stepfather's sexual abuse. However, I found later that the one trauma that she was most obsessed about was witnessing her mother being abused.

THE PROCESS OF PLAY THERAPY

Posttraumatic play therapy has several stages of play. The first stage is play diagnosis. During this stage, I spent most of the time encouraging Camelot to project her internal world onto the dolls and toys in order to identify her preoccupation, trauma, and wishes. In every session Camelot may have expressed a desire or a feeling, but in the first three to four months of therapy I focused my attention primarily on understanding Camelot's perception of her world.

Overlapping with diagnostic sessions, is the relationship stage where transference feelings may start to develop. During this stage, Camelot progressed from suspiciousness of me, to ambivalent feelings and eventually desired that I become her lost oedipal object.

The third stage of therapy consists of the period in which the child's repetitive play becomes evident. During this state, I tried to mobilize Camelot's anger and hate toward "the offender" for the purpose of empowerment. This is the period in which posttraumatic play (positive type) materializes and PTPT becomes the main therapeutic approach.

First Stage

During the first few sessions of therapy, I noted Camelot's desire for her father (oedipal object), as well as her fear of males. Men seemed to be exciting but, at the same time, dangerous to her. This concept was strikingly present during the dollhouse play. For example, whenever the "little doll" was stuck in the chimney or being kidnapped by "Indians," the "father doll" would come to the rescue. The "little doll" and her father would hold hands together and fly over the playhouse, "like Mary Poppins," but there were times that the father doll would drop the little doll from the sky to the ground.

JM's puppet: What is the reason that the little doll fell to the ground?

C: Because she didn't listen to her mother.

JM's puppet: What did her mother tell her?

C: She told her three things. First, never fly when it is raining, "You are not Mary Poppins." Second, never, never go any place with anyone when your mother is sleeping, "You will get hurt." Third, I forgot.

In the first few sessions, I observed anger toward Sam, which I felt originated from two issues. The first was Camelot's feeling that her mother was responsible for getting rid of her biological father. Camelot blamed her deprivation of this oedipal object on Sam. The second issue was connected to her mother's multiple male partners (including Jack), who were abusive and violent toward Sam. I also felt that she had developed role reversal in regard to her mother, thereby adopting a protective attitude toward her, and at times, nurturing her mother as well as her brother. Eventually, these feelings were transferred to me and during the relationship stage she started to take care of me. She worried about my nutrition and wondered if I was getting enough good food. This oral preoccupation became very evident midway through the course of play therapy when she started to be somewhat obsessed with food and nutrition.

Through play and symbolism during the first three to four months of our contact, Camelot expressed her wishes, conflicts, and psychological condition to me. There was evidence of narcissistic injury since the issue of her biological father's abandonment was very important to her. She was thus exposed to several father figures who came into her life and left, just as her father had. In the tenth session we combined "mutual story telling" with doll play. Camelot arranged for a family of dolls in the playhouse. Every doll was in a single room and they could not talk with each other. Camelot and I started, mutually, to make a story about this "lonely" family, and as Camelot mentioned, "People are afraid to get together, because they hurt each other."

JM: How did they hurt each other?

C: I don't know how.

JM: Let's ask Big Bird, he knows everything. Take Big Bird in your hand and pretend that he could magically put the words in your mouth.

C: Okay.

JM: What is Big Bird telling you?

C: Nothing.

JM: Let's ask him to tell us about one of these dolls, the one with the red shirt.

C: That is the red one.

JM: Let's ask Big Bird to tell us what she feels sad about.

C: She is upset, because she has no boyfriend.

JM: Why is that?

C: She is no good.

JM: Because?

C: Because she is ugly.

JM: How did you find out that she is ugly?

C: Because no boyfriends want her, they say "hello" and "bye."

JM: Does she miss any of them?

C: None.

JM: Are you sure? Can we ask her?

C: She may miss one of them. He knows about it and is coming back. [Camelot brought a male doll into the room that the girl doll was in and put them next to each other.]

JM: I have to know what is going on there. What are they telling each other?

C: She is telling him that it is nice to see him.

[Camelot becomes quiet and stares at the doll house, almost motionless.]

JM: And what else?

C: And he is telling her that it is nice to leave her.

JM: What?

C: He left her and she is crying.

JM: How could we help her? Where are her parents?

C: Her parents are dead, she is going to die—No, No, I am here to help her.

Camelot brought Big Bird inside the doll house, put the girl doll on its back, and they both flew over the town. Eventually, the girl doll slept while holding the back of Big Bird and fell down from the sky. "Fortunately," she landed in the roof of her grandparents' house, and they held her in their hands so she did not hit the ground. They yelled at Big Bird, but Camelot told them that it was her fault. If she hadn't fallen asleep she would still be with Big Bird in the sky.

Through her play, Camelot expressed a fear of abandonment and rejection, as well as feelings of object inconsistency, especially in interpersonal relationships.

Camelot's attachment to her grandparents, who were the stable people in her life, was evident as she often quoted Margaret. At times Camelot identified with some of her grandmother's ideas and even her body language and attitudes. For example, Camelot advised me not to drink too much coffee or soda because, "It is not good for you, I tell you, it is not good for you." Her tone of voice and hand movements reminded me of Margaret. I felt that she identified with her grandmother and now, became "a grandmother" to me.

I felt that I needed to play an active role in this play therapy. My hope was that Camelot could eventually identify with some of my ideas or behavior and would modify some of her views of the world. I felt that my role could be defined as a developmental facilitator and at times a kind of auxiliary ego. As other therapists have mentioned (Sgroi 1982), especially in child sexual abuse cases, these children are parentified and "prematurely mature." I felt that I needed to decrease her parentification, help her to understand that adults can take care of themselves and that she did not have to assume the responsibility of protecting or nurturing her mother, me, or anyone else. I wanted Camelot to understand that Sam was responsible for the care of Camelot's brother. These issues were discussed and "practiced" during sessions 8 and 9 that I had with Sam, Camelot, and her grandmother. We all decided to actively object to Camelot's attitude, whenever she became a "little adult" and praise her whenever she behaved like a 7-year-old child. We made the grandmother "responsible" for the care of Sam, and not Camelot. Sam was able to tell Camelot that she was an adult who could take care of herself, and if she needed help, she would get it from her parents. Sam said to Camelot, "I am sorry that I let you worry about me, and the many times you took care of me."

In session 12, Camelot's aunt brought her to my office, but she expected her mother to pick her up and take her home for the weekend. She was very excited and looked forward to spending time with her mother. As it turned out, Sam did not come. Camelot stayed in my waiting room, waiting for her, and at times she would run toward the window to see if her mother's car was coming. After a half hour, when Sam still had not arrived, I tried unsuccessfully to contact her by phone. Camelot started to show some emotion, including worrying about her mother. She expressed fear that "maybe she had a car accident, or was in the hospital." I felt that she was getting very angry at her mother, but showed her anger indirectly by wishing that Sam would get hurt in an accident. She was still able to keep her positive feelings, through the use of denial (to the level of confabulation), that she had a loving, caring mother. Many times I felt that it was not fair or appropriate to confront Camelot's denial because she seemed to have a strong need to believe that she had a caring mother, who was troubled by external events. Whenever she got disappointed in her mother, she shifted to the image of a caring father who would return to her one day.

Dialogue	Commentary
JM's doll: My heart is bleeding for this lonely Bunny. It seems that no one wants this cute little friend.	I demonstrated empathy and sensitivity toward the bunny's pain, which I speculated was due to abandonment/rejection.
C: Don't worry about her.	Camelot was using denial and avoidance.
JM's doll: But I do worry. I see how her mother went out to bring food for her but then saw the wolf on her way back home. She gave the food to Mr. Wolf and decided to go to his house and have some fun. It seems she preferred to be with the wolf rather than with her child. What a lousy mother! Not all mothers are like her. The world is full of good mothers. I know hundreds of them.	I avoided accepting her solution (denial). I interpreted her play, label the mother as "lousy," but then informed her that she should not generalize her concept of the doll's mother to all mothers.
C: She is a good mother. She loves her kids.	She needed to believe that mothers are caring and loving people.

JM's doll: What kind of mother is this? Why doesn't she take care of her kids?

C: Because if she didn't feed Mr. Wolf he would eat her. Then Bunny will have no mother.

JM's doll: She may not have "this mother," but she could find another mother. Bunny is a cute baby, everyone wants to take care of her and be her mother.

I was trying to prepare her for possible placement in her aunt's home. I was trying to decrease "self-blame," and announcing that something was wrong with her mother and not the bunny.

C: But she doesn't want anyone else. She only wants her mother because they love each other.

JM's doll: Okay, but tell me what would happen if little Bunny needed help now? She is hungry and most likely angry because nobody is feeding her. I would also be angry if nobody brought me food.

I was informing her that anger is a normal reaction to deprivation.

C: But you don't know; even Bunny doesn't know. Her mother also doesn't know. I am the only one who knows; that the bunny's father is around, watching her from the top of a mountain. He will come to help her at anytime she needs help. All she has to do is call 911 and he will be there.

She was expressing her wish that there was a father who did not reject her and was caring about her.

JM's doll: Why doesn't she call him now?

C: Because Bunny don't know   This is her self-blame (egocentric
   how to use the phone.   thinking).

During the next two sessions (13 and 14), Camelot's play communicated her involvement with the issue of loss. There was a little girl in the
dollhouse whose parents had died. She buried them in the yard in front
of the dollhouse. My puppet tried to find out if the little girl was angry
at the parents and it was obvious that, although their deaths were
"accidental," the little girl in the dollhouse was very angry at them. In
spite of her anger, she was also crying because of her loss.

JM's puppet: What happened to this little girl's parents Why didn't they
   get help for her?
C: Because they are dead.
JM's puppet: Oh, how did this happen? Were they murdered?
C: It was an accident. They were kissing each other near an open
   window, a storm came and threw them out of the window and they
   died.
JM's puppet: Oh, did they leave any message for their child?
C: Nobody knows.
JM's puppet: Now what will the little girl do?
C: She is burying them in the ground.
JM's puppet: How does she feel now?
C: Not very good, she feels bad.
JM's puppet: What kind of "bad" feeling does she have?
C: It is a very bad feeling.
JM's puppet: I mean is she angry? Is she sad? Is she worried? Is she
   hungry? Does she want to scream? Punch the walls? Yell at God and
   everyone?
C: She is sad because she has no one.
JM's puppet: And she may be angry because . . .
C: No, she is not.
JM's puppet: I wonder if the "storm" was angry at these parents.
   Otherwise, it would not have killed them.
C: It was an accident, not killing.
JM's puppet: Yes, an accident killed the parents. The storm did it. By the
   way, where was their little girl when the storm killed them?

C: They sent this girl to her grandmother's house.

JM's puppet: Why? Didn't they like her?

C: Whenever they want to have fun, they send their child to another home.

JM's puppet: You mean they didn't want the little girl to see them having fun? I wonder why?

C: You don't understand. Kids shouldn't be there.

JM's puppet: Tell me more about it.

C: No, no more. You are making this little girl angry.

JM's puppet: Because I ask too many questions? Because I wonder if the little girl is also angry at her parents, just like the storm?

C: Be quiet! The storm is coming again.

JM's puppet: I wonder if the little girl got angry at me, gave her anger to the storm, and the storm is coming to take care of me.

C: Not at all . . . but, don't stay near the window, go down to the basement because the hurricane is coming.

JM's puppet: I wish that I could talk to the storm. It is okay to be angry. Let's talk about it.

C: [Interrupted my sentence.] Don't talk. The storm is dead and now the hurricane is coming.

JM's puppet: Coming to get me?

C: Don't talk. Go down to the basement.

In the next session (15), Camelot was depressed and had constant crying spells. She refused to play with the dollhouse. She complained that she had a bellyache. I felt that she did not want to go near the dollhouse because in the previous week she had felt responsible for her parents' death and had buried them. If she went near the dollhouse, I might address the issue of murdering her parents or she might have more thoughts about them. In the previous session, my puppet eventually talked about anger, and the focus of the session revolved around anger toward our parents when they disappoint us.

In the next session (16), Camelot was very reluctant to talk so I asked her about her stomachache. She said it was okay, but that she still felt sick. She was in some way giving me a message that she was not ready to talk and was using sickness as an excuse. I invited her to play and she started by bringing a monster to the dollhouse. The monster brought a little elephant to the house to be fed. However, before the monster brought the elephant, the monster talked about how difficult life was for her since she had so many people to care for. The monster also hurt the elephant. The elephant got sick and needed a doctor. During the play, the ambivalent feelings of the little elephant toward the monster was evident. In this session, the little elephant was hostile toward the monster, yet also had a friendly attitude by inviting the monster for lunch and having them together. Play continued and the little elephant eventually became a monster too. I felt that this was Camelot who wanted to decrease her fear of the monster by becoming a monster herself. Then the little elephant monster confronted the original monster, who in my opinion, represented Camelot's mother. After this confrontation, the original monster started to cry and ask for help in order to change, telling the little elephant that it wanted "to see a doctor."

The issue of asking for help in order to change appeared several times in Camelot's play. It seemed that in her mind "change" meant going to a therapist. Also, the court had ordered her stepfather to become involved in some sort of evaluation or counseling. I felt that the little elephant was a victim of the monster, becoming sick because of the monster's abusive attitude. Through my doll, I asked Camelot to help the little elephant by calling the police and other friends to get the original monster and "hurt her the way that the monster had hurt the elephant." In the beginning, Camelot was reluctant and said that the monster was crying and was getting help in order to change. I reminded Camelot that the little elephant might still be very angry at the monster because of what the monster did. Eventually, we brought the little elephant to the "doctor" and the little elephant asked the doctor what to do. The doctor told her it was okay to do to the monster what the monster had done to her. This time the little elephant became very decisive and energetic; it started to fly and jump ("Now it is a flying elephant"), asking everyone to gather around and see what the little elephant was going to do to the monster. Camelot arranged many dolls in a way that almost resembled a court. The little elephant held the monster and hit her in the abdomen; she jumped on her and told her "cry, cry, cry." The monster began to cry and ask for forgiveness. In the end, the elephant was happy and victorious while the monster was subdued and was put in jail to suffer "the rest of her life."

At that time I said, through my puppet, that the little elephant was a good fighter and had done a very good job; however, the little elephant was also good at many other things, including helping people. My puppet instructed the little elephant that she also could make a delicious breakfast for those kids who had no parents to care for them. My puppet brought the little elephant to another dollhouse, an orphanage where my puppet and the little elephant both made a lot of food with clay for these hungry children and animals. They both felt good because they realized that not only could the little elephant do well in fighting and getting even, but could also help needy children.

My plan was to validate Camelot's anger toward her mother. Also, I did not want her to get the message that her only value was being a fighter or that she had to do that to please the therapist. I wanted to remind her of her other qualities, such as her desire to decrease the pain of the needy. Camelot usually felt guilty after showing aggression and would develop self-punishment ideas. By bringing up, after any episode of aggression, some act of charity or sacrifice, I was able to decrease her guilt feelings.

Second Stage

The second stage was for Camelot to develop a relationship with me. This stage overlapped with the first stage, starting in the first few sessions and continuing for five to six months. In the beginning, she was somewhat suspicious of me and she felt that I would hurt her. She believed that all men were abusive. She had heard the story of her great-grandfather who sexually abused her grandmother, as well as her aunt and her mother. She also witnessed several men in her home who emotionally, physically, or sexually abused her mother. What seemed strange to her was her mother's desire to be abused. I wondered if that was a defense or distortion that she used to decrease her fear of men or anger toward them. This was crystallized in the play that was repeated in many sessions, in which the female doll would ask the male doll, "Please hurt me again." It seems that the puzzle for her was why her mother invited these people who hurt her. Eventually she may have felt that there was some pleasure in getting hurt; otherwise why would her mother do that? I also wondered if she had ever seen her mother having intercourse, which a child could perceive as an act of aggression. She may have thought that her mother's desire for sex was a desire "to hurt me again." This issue is still a puzzle for me.

Beginning in session 16, I felt that I became the image of her lost biological father, the father who would one day come to rescue her. There were several episodes of repetitive play in which a man came from the moon and no one knew or heard about him. He came, possessing the power of the six-million-dollar man, and rescued the little elephant, or another doll, whenever they were in trouble. He once took the little girl to the moon and told everyone there that she was the only one that he cared about, that he was happy he had met her after so many years. I felt that this was a projection of her need and desire to meet her biological father after years of hearing about him.

At one point during the fourth month of therapy, she developed the fantasy that I would marry her mother. It was evident that she was getting very close to me, possibly looking at me as a rescuer, one who would not only rescue her but would also rescue her mother from drugs, alcohol, and abusive men. I felt that she gave me this task because many times I had assured her, through play, that she was not responsible for, or capable of, taking care of adults. Although I allowed her to worry about her mother, I did bring up the issue that her mother was an adult with many relatives and friends who could help.

In the eighteenth session, she invited me to her birthday party in her home. I told her that I appreciated her invitation, but was not able to come as I wanted to see her only in my office. She told me that Sam could make very nice food for me; how she could entertain me, especially if she had a little alcohol; and how many people enjoyed her mother's sense of humor, one that could make any man laugh. Her fantasy about my romantic involvement with her mother created countertransference feelings in me. That same week, both Camelot and I had very similar dreams, making me feel that we were somehow connecting with each other in our dreams. Camelot dreamed that she was giving me a piece of cake. I dreamed that it was my birthday and someone sent me a big present that looked like a large cake. When I removed the wrapping paper, a real woman came out and her face was blurred so I could not recognize her identity in my dream manifestation.

I felt that one of the therapeutic elements in Camelot's treatments was her fantasy that one day a man would come and reverse her miserable situation. I felt that she was preoccupied by a lost object and was desperately looking to fill up that empty space inside of her. I actively played the role of rescuer, always bringing a doll and a puppet who gave solutions, hope, optimism, and positive attitudes. Although in reality, I knew that the biological father was not available, and did not care about his child, I actively played the role of believing that eventually a man would come and rescue her. I respected Camelot's wish, as well as her fantasy, in regard to the fact that one day a lost object would be found. I felt that she needed this fantasy (even if it was false) to be able to survive her miserable situation and to decrease her pain. She needed a certain amount of denial in order to endure bitter reality. A certain amount of self-deceptive ideas and behavior was necessary for her to be able to go through her next developmental stages and growing-up process. At that point in her life, reality was too bitter and negative for her. She needed to climb the growth ladder, but this ladder had many missing steps. I was able to help her by creating "fantasy steps." I not only encouraged some of her denial and self-deceptive ideas, I encouraged her to be extremely positive and create fantasy "steps." As a therapist, I became the support system for Camelot in regard to her normal growth process. With each negative revelation, I tried to focus on the positive aspects of her life, such as her intelligence. I tried to balance the negative and positive events in her life. For example, if she lost the grandparents on her father's side, she would still have the grandparents on her mother's side.

During the next two sessions (19 and 20), I felt that Camelot was struggling with her fantasy of having me for a father and staying with her forever. She became curious about the other children who came to my office. She began asking me if I was married or if I had children. She wanted to know if I lived on the second floor of my office. She said that she saw a woman with two children coming out of the back door and she thought they were my children. I answered all of her questions in a matter-of-fact way. For example, I told her that the woman was my sister and the two children were hers. I also told her that I was married, but had no children. She became somewhat curious about my marriage. I explained to her that not all marriages were like her parents' marriage. I explained to her that many marriages are happy ones, although a number of marriages end in divorce. I went on to explain that sometimes divorce is better than having both parents fighting with each other.

During sessions 16 through 24, I felt that Camelot was getting close to me, but was frightened that I might leave or abuse her. There was some indication that she was testing me in regard to my feelings toward her. At one point I felt that she was angry with me. However, she expressed the anger in a distorted way, when she become very concerned about my health. She had seen an accident on my street and she immediately worried that I may have been in a car accident and would not be able to see her on that day. I felt that her anger toward me most likely was connected to my refusal to go to her birthday party. I told her that I would like to make a small birthday for her in my office the next time she came to see me.

C: I saw the car accident near your office when I was coming here. I told my aunt, "Oh God, don't tell me that the doctor had a car accident and can't see me."

JM: So you were worried about me, and of course, if I don't see you, then you may get upset at me.

C: No, I am not upset at you.

JM: It's okay to be upset at me. I encourage you to tell me anything that you feel about me. Here, kids talk to me about how angry and hateful they are toward me, and at times they may tell me I am their best friend. It is okay to feel both anger and closeness toward the same person.

C: I know that.

JM: I wonder if you were upset at me because I didn't come to your birthday party?

C: How did you know that?

JM: I guessed. Because I myself would get upset if I had invited someone to my party and he said no to my invitation.

C: I invited a lot of people. I knew some of them would not come.

JM: So, can you tell me the reason you invited them, if you knew they wouldn't come?

C: I wanted to know what they would say.

JM: And I wouldn't be surprised if you got angry at some of them when they said no to your invitation.

C: Maybe.

JM: Let's get back to the car accident. Do you remember a couple of months ago, when your mother promised she would pick you up at my office and she didn't?

C: Yeah.

JM: And you got angry at her because she disappointed you.

C: Yeah.

JM: And you started to think that maybe she had a car accident, or maybe she got hurt and was in the hospital. Do you remember that?

C: Yeah.

JM: I wonder if there is a connection between the anger and the car accident. That means that when people like your mother and myself disappoint you, you feel upset at them, but you can't tell them about your anger. Do you understand me?

C: Yes.

JM: Instead of telling them how angry you are at them, you start to worry about them, thinking maybe they had a bad accident. Am I right? Please correct me.

C: You are right.

JM: Let's start to practice right here in my office. Whenever you get upset at me, you should immediately tell me about it and I promise you that I will praise you every time you practice this.

C: My grandmother told me people don't stay with you if you get angry at them.

JM: They also can't stay with you if they are in a car accident or in the hospital. Tell Grandma that I promise not to leave you if you get angry at me.

C: Okay.

In session 24, play in the dollhouse changed to a conversation with Camelot. I told her that she had had no luck with the men in her life. I brought up the issue of the biological father whom she perceived had abandoned her. Her great-grandfather was a disappointment when she heard he had been sexually abusive. There were the men who developed relationships with Sam, then exploited her, abused her, and left her. There was her stepfather who was abusive to her. I told her that she had had no luck with men so far, and then I asked her how she felt about me as a man. She answered that she could trust me and she never believed that I would abuse her. However, later on in the same session, she said that "people might do it to their family."

In session 27, we were throwing balls and we both got tired and sat down on the floor. She then lay down next to me and spread her legs invitingly while at the same time her face showed fear. She simply stared at me, quiet and speechless. I offered her a puppet. I also took a puppet and I told her to let these two puppets talk to each other. The two puppets talked, and Camelot's puppet told my puppet "please do it" and "please hurt me again."

Third Stage

The next overlapping stage, which started in the fourth month, consisted of repetitive play. One repetitive theme in play during this month was that grown-up people were victimizing, beating up, and terrorizing a little elephant. In one scene, the policeman even joined the grown-up people and victimized the little elephant. This repetitive play continued in sessions 17 through 23. However, there was some discussion between my doll and Camelot. I brought up the issue of feelings, "How the little elephant felt when he was being beaten by the grown-ups." She sometimes said that the little elephant deserved it. I immediately told little elephant "You are very afraid of these grown-ups, so you believe what they tell you. I wonder if grown-up people told you it is your fault that you are treated so badly. I tell the truth. It is not your fault. It is the fault of the grown-ups." Eventually I actively got involved in this repetitive play.

My goal during this play was to empower the little elephant and be able to stop the abuse and victimization by adults, put them on trial, and then punish them by hurting them, in exactly the same way that they had hurt the little elephant. During one of these play sessions, Snoopy was the one who was being victimized and I brought two dolls, very powerful and strong, who with the help of the little elephant and Snoopy, overcame the "bad grown-up people." We tied them with Scotch tape, we hit them with a baseball bat, and put them in jail. All of this was done very spontaneously and, in the end, all the bad grown-up people were hit in the same way that Snoopy and the little elephant had been hit. Camelot suddenly said, "Oh God, we didn't put them in court." She arranged for a judge who told Snoopy and little elephant that these grown-ups deserve to be punished, but "not as badly as you did, so don't do it anymore."

In the fifth month of therapy, I introduced anatomically correct dolls. This was not for the purpose of sex education or for facilitating communication as is done in evaluating or treating sexually abused children (Marvasti 1989). It was for the purpose of playing out the sexual scene that she witnessed at home. In session 25, there was some indication of posttraumatic stress disorder (PTSD), when she threw the naked dolls on the floor (startle reaction) and became somewhat shaky and frightened. Originally, I felt that this was a "play disruption." However, later on she explained to me that sometimes on nights when she saw pictures of naked people, she had nightmares about her victimization by her stepfather. She talked about how the naked genital area of the male dolls brought her back to when Jack would ask her to touch his penis. To decrease her fear of the naked doll, and also to desensitize her (from PTSD), I covered the dolls and she was able to approach them while they were covered. She added another cover over the male body. The female's naked body did not cause her any symptoms. When the dolls upset her, I offered to put clothes on them and put them in the closet until she was ready to play with them. However, she said that she wanted them now.

In session 26, I began structured play sessions and my puppet planned "to get even" with the male offender who "sat on the girl" even though she said no. I encouraged Camelot to play this scenario with the hope that gradually during play, she would modify and decrease the doll's victimization, the passivity, the submissiveness, and the fear. For example, my puppet would jump in and would put the telephone near the girl and would say "Call the police." Or, "He is lying. That is not a game. He is lying, he is a liar." Or my puppet would jump in and would say "Scream, yell, kick, show anger. He is hurting you, bite him, punch him." In the beginning she completely ignored my intervention. I sometimes said to her "Do you hear my puppet? Listen, listen to her." By session 30, I planned a particular scenario whenever either kind of repetitive play was present: my puppet would call the Bionic Woman to come and stop the victimization. I deliberately brought the Bionic Woman to convey the message that there are women who are strong, powerful, and wise, just like some men.

In sessions 30 to 34, the play, which was repetitive and entirely connected to the doll's being victimized, changed to getting the offender trapped in the home and "By the order of the judge punished." Originally, the punishment was jail and a slap in the face; however, my puppet suggested, "Let's do to him what he did to that woman." This wish was brought up several times by my puppet during the next few sessions and eventually her puppet started to set up the play of "getting even." This stage of therapy, which I will call "reversal," started by punching the male doll in the belly, to eventually putting the male doll on the floor and hurting his genital area with one of the soldier's guns. She took the soldier's gun and brought it near the naked anatomically correct male doll. She moved the gun around, while I took the naked doll screaming "No, no" and I asked the soldiers to yell: "Yes, yes." This direct reversal of play continued for the next few sessions, but she was not initiating this play, and my puppet would ask her puppet to play that scenario. During this period, she was able to get in touch with some of her anger and the concept of revenge and punishing the bad guy in a symbolic way started to work.

Dialogue	*Commentary*
JM's puppet: Oh see how this soldier is hitting the man with his gun.	My plan was to bring the feelings and actions into "words" and verbal expression for the purpose of promoting understanding/communication.
C: Pain all over.	This was a very good imitation of me, as she also put words on feelings.

JM's puppet: Soldier should be very angry at this naked man. He is giving him pain all over his body. I wish someone would tell us what the soldier is angry about.

I speculated about the cause/effect relationship between anger and inflicting pain. Again, I encouraged verbal communication.

C: Watch and see.

JM's puppet: I'll watch and see, but I also like to hear what is going on in the minds of these people.

I was encouraging her to project her feelings and ideas into the "minds" of dolls, so I would be able to identify them.

C: Don't be noisy.

She was trying to stop me from further exploration.

JM's puppet: Oh, please, please, may I be your friend, you brave soldier?

By using the word "brave soldier," I was giving my approval for being angry, and revengeful as a soldier is.

C: [While moving the soldier's face toward the puppet.] Yes, you may.

JM's puppet: Tell me pal, what did this naked man do to you to make you angry at him?

C: [Holding the soldier in her hand near my puppet.] I am angry at him because of what he did to that girl.

JM's puppet: I wonder if the girl is also angry at him?

C: I don't know.

JM's puppet: Let's go inside the dollhouse and ask her.

C: [Moved the soldier into the dollhouse, while my puppet followed her.] Hi, little girl.

JM's puppet: Are you angry at this naked man, little girl?

C: [Holding the little girl in her hand.] NO, no, no.

This was denial of her unacceptable feelings (anger), which was enforced by her grandmother.

JM's puppet: Oh, maybe you gave your anger to the soldier to take care of. Please take your anger back. It's okay to be angry. It's okay to hate someone who hurts you.

C: [Moving the girl doll toward my puppet.] Am I angry? Why should a little girl be angry?

This was a direct imitation from her grandmother.

JM's puppet: Because he may have hurt her, so she got angry, gave her anger to the soldier, and the brave soldier found the naked man and punished him. I wonder if the reason that the soldier gave pain all over to the naked man is because the naked man gave pain all over to the little girl?

I changed the pronoun from "I" to "she." "Am I angry" might be somewhat threatening to her, even if she was quoting from the doll.

C: Yes, yes, yes.

JM's puppet: So, she should be very angry at this naked man.

I was trying to neutralize the displacement of anger (the girl doll was angry, could not accept it, so displaced it on the soldier.) My goal was to bring back the angry feelings to the original owner (girl doll), and eventually from the girl doll to Camelot. (Camelot was angry, cannot accept it, so displaced it on to the girl doll.)

C: [Changing her voice, she talked like a little girl doll.] Yes, yes. She is mad at him, but he should not know.

This was some regression. Now she admitted to anger, but wanted to keep it secret.

JM's puppet: Because . . .?

C: Because . . . he shouldn't know, no one knows.

JM's puppet: But I, a little puppet know how mad the little girl is, the soldier knows, and the naked man's body knows because he has "pain all over" it.

C: Now that everyone knows our secret, let's, let's . . . [Camelot became quiet.]

JM's puppet: [Took the little girl doll and pretended to talk to Camelot.] Let's talk about it, let's tell everyone that the naked man made me angry because he hurt me. I hate him, I wish I was as brave as the soldier and I, myself, could get him and hurt him the same way that he hurt me. By the way [pointing toward Camelot], do you know how he hurt me?

Again, I brought up the concept of "getting even" and revenge.

C: He molested you.

It was easier for her to talk about the "doll's molestation" than hers.

JM's puppet: What is that? Tell me more.

C: He hurt you in your private.

JM's puppet: Oh, that is easier for me to understand.

"Molestation" is an adult word. I gave her the impression that I was interested in her personal experience and feelings and not what adults labeled it.

[At this point I dropped the puppet and directly talked to Camelot.]

JM: There is a similarity between my feelings and this doll's feelings. I am also getting angry at this naked doll, when I heard what he did to this little girl. I wondered if you also got mad like this little doll?

I was neutralizing the displacement and doll's projection and connecting the doll's feelings to my feelings, giving the message that even therapists get angry.

C: I also got mad, he may have hurt many girls.

JM: In their private?

C: And elsewhere.

JM: It is good to talk about our feelings. Camelot, I wonder if you can find any similarity between the naked doll and anyone in your real life?

I was trying to neutralize her defense mechanism (displacement) and bring back the issue to Camelot and her real life.

C: No one. [Became quiet.]

Denial and avoidance.

JM: Are you sure?

C: Sure.

JM: How about your stepfather?

I was challenging her denial and avoidance.

C: Yea, maybe.

The rest of the session was structured by me to acknowledge and talk about Camelot's hatred and anger toward her stepfather. She quoted from her grandmother that "God never wants us angry." But with my encouragement, she started to talk about her negative feelings toward Jack who had hurt her and Sam. I felt that I had accomplished one mission and I was able at least once to defeat Margaret's ideology.

I had become a replacement for Camelot's lost object, her biological father. In some way, I enjoyed having that role. I felt that I partially replaced this lost object, and I felt that Camelot was connecting with me and relating to me as the father who would come and rescue her from her misery. In the beginning, she hoped that I eventually would be a little more than a therapist and possibly marry her mother and become her father. However, later on oedipal rivalry came as she gradually began to talk negatively about Sam, and in some way I felt that she was discouraging me from having any interest in her. It seemed that she wanted me for herself and did not want her mother to have anything to do with me. For example, in the beginning of the second month, she expressed to me that her mother was a good cook; however, midway through therapy (fourth month), she talked about how lousy a cook her mother was as she burned her hot dog. Later during the next month, she played in the dollhouse and demonstrated how the girl doll took over the management of the dollhouse and threw the mother out. The doll then did the cooking and took care of the family, including the father.

There was some indication at one point (fourth month) during play that Camelot was concerned that if she "owned" me, she would lose me as she had lost her biological father and several other men that she tried to develop relationships with. I felt that she blamed her mother for losing her biological father and she needed to create distance between myself and her mother, otherwise Sam would get rid of me, too.

In session 20, Camelot once began calling me "Doc," rather than doctor. During that week she had a dream about ducks. She said she was near a pond with several ducks. Suddenly her mother arrived, scared the ducks, and one after another they disappeared. However, one of them remained, and she was able to play with that duck.

During the same month, Camelot had another dream. This dream had a lot to do with what happened on the day of the dream. Her mother was cooking her a hot dog, but was in a hurry to go out, so the hot dog got "burned." Camelot related to me how bad it tasted. That night she dreamed that she was in a very old building playing with matches and eating candy. After some time, a fireman came and asked if anyone was playing with matches. The fireman said there was a woman in the next room and if there was a fire she may "burn." Then the police came and asked who was in the house and if anyone had stolen candy. Camelot got somewhat embarrassed in the dream; however, she was able to cover up the matches and also lied in regard to the candy. Both men left and she woke up.

The themes of this dream were centered around oral gratification, aggression, and secrecy. When Camelot did free association, I felt that I was in her dream disguised as the fireman and policeman who came to her home. The dream also showed hostility toward Sam because she burned the hot dog and blamed Camelot for talking too much, thus making Sam, who was in a hurry, nervous. There was some indication of secretly defying her stepfather by playing with matches, as Jack was a volunteer fireman in his town.

Gradually in sessions 34 to 42, the doll's victimization decreased. Generally, the repetitive play would start, but soon, with the support of my puppet, "help would arrive." The length of the doll's victimization started to decrease, while, as the victim, her justified anger surfaced and increased. Eventually her puppet suggested "getting even" and reversing the victimization play. The puppets got together and decided to have a trial, "only a two-minute" trial. Her doll wanted to have a short trial and decide on a punishment for the offender. The idea of punishment came from her puppet and there were several sessions in which puppets discussed such subjects as "It's okay to be angry at someone who hurts us, and it's okay to punish the one who hurts us." Eventually, the two-minute trial lasted a little longer and all the puppets said, "He needs to be punished." However, a female doll ran in and tried to rescue him and said that he was innocent (introjection of Sam's ambivalent feelings). But my puppet confronted the woman and Camelot's puppet joined me and yelled at the woman, "You like lazy bums."

Termination and Countertransference

The termination phase was the difficult stage of our therapy. I wonder if it was more difficult for me than for her. In the early part of termination she had a mild regression as, on and off, she became tearful during the session. A few of the initial symptoms returned: her mother reported some abdominal pain, there was a mild increase in her protective attitude, nurturing attitude, and, at times, seductive attitude toward me.

My countertransference was obvious in the sense that Camelot became my special patient. For example, I remember a day that I did not feel well enough to see my patients and I canceled all appointments except hers. I felt very close to Camelot. I felt that she gave me a feeling that I was better than her parents. I believed that I was important and very much satisfied by my rescue fantasy. I felt that I competed with her parents, and with such authorities as judges, lawyers, and protective service and that I had won, that I was better than all of them. I believed that I accomplished my goals of changing a weak victim to an assertive, powerful, and strong person. I had grandiose feelings, and I believed that eventually she would consider me a very important person in her life, the source of nurturing, help, and caring. It reminded me of my feelings toward my psychoanalyst. Camelot brought up my fine memories about my own psychoanalysis. Since I strongly identified with my analyst and picked up many of his ethical and moral issues, I felt that I owed him much of my knowledge and insight about myself and my patients. He was a wise man, my mentor, and I was his disciple, who admired him regardless of whether all or part of these feelings were "transference" feelings.

During the termination phase, I had an interesting dream. In my dream, Winnicott, an English physician, was near me, came toward me and was laughing and telling me that I was a "good enough mother," while he was "holding" me. In reality, I associated this dream with Winnicott's statements in his books in regard to the treatment of children since he mentioned frequently that a therapist's job is to create "a good-enough" mothering or good-enough "holding" environment.

RESULT AND FOLLOW-UP

Camelot learned that I enjoyed being with her without becoming physically involved with her. She felt that I admired her intelligence, her creativity, her caring, and her helpful attitude. She found that she could be powerful without being sexual or abusive. She corrected some of her cognitive distortions and started to believe that men can be strong and powerful, without being abusive or abandoning her. She modified her concept of females as helpless victims. She also changed some of her world view and accepted the idea of happiness in this world. She learned from me that "it is okay to be angry" and "it is okay to show hate and resentment."

In therapy, my most important goal with victims is to prevent the transference of victimization to the next generation. I want to make sure that a victim will not actively victimize his or her siblings, or his or her children, and also (in a passive way) would not allow a victim to witness his or her own victimization.

In the beginning of therapy, I noticed that Camelot was teaching her brother and cousins the rigid, moral, and extreme negative and pessimistic attitude toward the world that she had learned from her grandmother and Sam. I tried to help Camelot de-identify with her grandmother and her mother. I constantly reminded her that she was different from her mother. We discussed in detail how, contrary to Sam, she liked to be with "nice and peaceful people," who were not involved with drugs, alcohol, and violence. I showed her that, although all the men that she had been involved with abused her or her mother, she needed to admit that I had not been abusive to either of them. I felt that I had enough impact on Camelot to stop her from generalizing that all men are abusive and that I was a barrier in her generalization of men as all-negative.

Approximately five years after termination, I saw Camelot in therapy several times. By then she was a teenager and came to me with different problems. One, in particular, was her boyfriend/girlfriend involvement. She said she was "being controlled" by her grandmother with respect to this problem. Margaret did report to me that Camelot was "boy crazy."

In the following year, Camelot left the state to live with her mother. Any information concerning her came to me from her grandmother, who sees me occasionally for medication. Margaret reported to me that Camelot was an honor student, was participating in art and theater at school, and had become very popular; she had also appeared in a beauty contest. In the last few years, contrary to my fantasy and expectation, Camelot was reluctant to talk to me by phone. Sam had suggested that Camelot call me, usually after a conflict between them: "Let's call the doctor and see what he says," but Camelot declined.

I feel that the result of the play therapy intervention was beneficial. It was sustained for several years, since she had developed an awareness of her value other than sexuality. She started to trust boys and changed her cognitive distortion about men. She believed that not all men were abusive. She was able to arrive at some kind of conclusion in regard to her mother's behavior and an understanding of why her mother had invited these abusive men to her home. During her follow-up sessions when she was an adolescent, she also acknowledged that she, herself, some years before, felt that she needed to be abused by men. She also reported that she had believed that I would abuse her some day.

DISCUSSION

My communication with Camelot confirmed that play therapy is a very natural treatment for a child, since play is a natural medium of communication for children. I felt that Camelot was never able to communicate verbally to me what she could show me through play. Her play was a royal road to her unconscious and subconscious material.

In regard to the technique of posttraumatic play therapy, Persian type, I felt it was effective. However, there was no control group or any scientific research that would confirm that this was the most effective way of treating this child. I believe that Camelot could have been treated with any technique. However, my feeling was that if she was able to use her anger and make it an engine inside of herself, she might be able to overcome the victimization, passivity, and helplessness much faster. I have observed how anger, revenge, and "getting even" can shake and shape a victim and change his or her hopelessness, helplessness, passivity, submissiveness, confusion, and state of shock. These negative characteristics can be reversed to powerfulness, hopefulness, and having a direction and goal (to get even or to punish the offender.) I wonder if anger, revenge, and retaliation are the natural and adaptive mechanisms in the postvictimization period. I also wonder if the job of these "normal feelings" in the victim is to maintain the integrity of "self." The rage and revenge reaction may serve to prevent the shattering of "self" during and after traumatization.

What I learned about my theory of PTPT, Persian type, is that it worked. I feel that there are some therapeutic benefits in the concept of getting even and mobilizing the anger and hate toward the offender. Some psychiatric literature may identify it as "identification with the aggressor," but I feel it is a normal human reaction to getting hurt.

In working with Camelot and other children like her, I have learned that they have many angry, hateful, and murderous wishes that they learn to suppress or sublimate. In response to direct victimization, many children are encouraged to sublimate their anger and show it in subtle ways. I feel that this anger and hate can be mobilized and used in a constructive way to overcome feelings of hopelessness, passivity, and powerlessness. Anger can give power and energy to victimized children, and revenge would give them the goal and direction that they desperately need. All these feelings are expressed in a symbolic way during play sessions.

In looking back on the case, another strategy that I might have used, and that might have been effective with this child, was involvement with the family. If I could have changed something, it would have been my limited contact with the family. I was too much of a child advocate, and the stepfather was not able to develop a relationship with me. My lack of neutrality was a very legitimate and normal feeling; I was aware of it and I felt that it would not interfere in my relationship with this family. However, I neglected to develop a relationship with Jack and, therefore, I never realized the possibility of arranging for an "apology session" with him and Camelot.

During therapy with Camelot, I was not aware of my strong identification with my psychoanalyst. Now, years after this therapy, I feel that I really played the role of my analyst and I assigned my role (as an analysand) to Camelot. The same feelings that I had toward my analyst I expected or believed Camelot was having or could have toward me. I become my analyst ("I wouldn't lose him,") and I made Camelot me ("I wouldn't lose her").

As we were going through the termination process, I felt that this was the second significant separation and termination in my adult life; the first one was a few years previously from my psychoanalyst. I feel that the separation from my analyst was an incomplete factor in my life, and I was working through and making it complete through this second separation from my patient. The same feelings of loss that I felt in the termination process from my analyst came back to me. There was a similarity between my feelings toward my analyst and Camelot's feelings toward me. For example, I got angry at my analyst when he planned termination. In the last few termination sessions of my analysis, I remembered thinking that from then on I should check the obituaries; if my analyst died, I would have one last chance to see him in his casket. I was thinking how upset I would be to see him dead. The same feeling occurred in one of Camelot's dreams; she told me she dreamed that a man from the moon was coming to earth who would help her (Camelot), marry her, and have children with her. Then one day he told his wife and children that he might want to go back to the moon, and on that night he slept and never woke up. In the morning they found him dead in his bed. Now, when I look back at these events, I feel I was repeating the "trauma" of separation from my analyst in therapy with Camelot, but it seems this time I was modifying some part of it. I was not the patient, but the therapist, and my passivity and powerlessness were changed to being in control and empowered.

Camelot and I were both repeating our previous traumas (or our leftover issues) with each other and both of us were modifying the outcome as we were repeating it. I still believe that we both re-created our past events for the purpose of ego mastery, and I do not see it as causing any harm toward either of us.

I wonder if, in the process of termination, I used the projective identification mechanism on her; perhaps I projected my leftover issues in separating from my analyst onto Camelot and identified them as hers. She may have felt these and presented them to me as if they were her issues.

One of the things I learned about myself from this therapy was that my separation from my analyst was not worked through completely. I also felt that I had discovered a need to care for a child. My narcissism was still strong to the extent that I expected a child to be thankful to me for the rest of her life. I feel that my parenting needs and fantasies are partially being satisfied by being a child psychiatrist and taking care that I place myself in situations in which I am always the winner: whenever I am compared with the abusive parents of my patients, I am always the winner.

The termination was difficult for both of us, possibly more difficult for me as a dream I had at that time may indicate: I dreamt I was walking in England with a Turkish psychoanalyst and both of us were looking for King Arthur and Merlin the Magician. The dream was interrupted when I woke up. I do not remember any details of this dream, but what comes to mind when I free associate is a book that a psychoanalyst with a Turkish background had written about analyzing his patient who also was a physician (Volkan 1984). In the termination stage, when the analyst was inquiring into his patient's feelings and reactions in regard to termination and not seeing his analyst anymore, his patient expressed sadness in losing his analyst and quoted from King Arthur: "One might yearn forever for Camelot."

And I wonder if I do. . . .

REFERENCES

Beck, A. (1976). *Cognitive Therapy and the Emotional Disorders*. New York: International Universities Press.

Erikson, E. H. (1950). *Childhood and Society*. New York: W. W. Norton.

Freud, A. (1936). *The Ego and the Mechanisms of Defense*. New York: International Universities Press.

Freud, A., and Burlingham, D. (1942). War and children. In *The Writings of Anna Freud*, vol. 3, pp. 143–211. New York: International Universities Press.

Haworth, M. R. (1990). *A Child's Therapy: Hour by Hour*. Madison, CT: International Universities Press.

Johnson, K. (1989). *Trauma in the Lives of Children*. Claremont, CA: Hunter House.

Marvasti, J. A. (1989). Play therapy with sexually abused children. In *Vulnerable Populations: Sexual Abuse Treatment for Children, Adult Survivors, Offenders, and Persons with Mental Retardation*, vol 2., ed. S. Sgroi, pp. 1–41. New York: Lexington Books/ MacMillan Free Press.

——— (1992). Psychotherapy with abused children and adolescents. In *Countertransference in Psychotherapy with Children and Adolescents*, ed. J. R. Brandell, pp. 191–214. Northvale, NJ: Jason Aronson.

——— (In press). Playgroup therapy with sexually abused children. *Handbook of Clinical Intervention in Child Sexual Abuse* (Rev. Ed.), ed. S. Sgroi. New York: Lexington Books/MacMillan Free Press.

Sgroi, S. (1982). *Handbook of Clinical Intervention in Child Sexual Abuse*. Lexington, MA: Lexington Books.

Terr, L. (1983). Play therapy and psychic trauma: a preliminary report. *Handbook of Play Therapy*, vol. 1, ed. C. Schaefer and K. O'Connor, pp. 308–319. New York: Wiley.
_____ (1990). *Too Scared to Cry*. New York: Harper & Row.
Volkan, V. D. (1984). *What Do You Get When You Cross a Dandelion with a Rose?* New York: Jason Aronson.
Winnicott, D. W. (1971). *Playing and Reality*. New York: Basic Books.

16

It's All in the Game: Game Play Therapy

Steven Reid, PH.D.

INTRODUCTION TO GAME PLAY THERAPY

I believe games are used in child psychotherapy much more frequently than one would guess after having perused the major guidebooks on play therapy and child psychotherapy. I suspect, based more on personal experience than anything, that games occupy considerable space on shelves in many child therapists' offices. I have found that traditional play therapy materials and methods often fail to attract or hold the interest of many children referred to me for psychotherapy. Children in the latency period of development often reject play with dolls, puppets, and miniatures as being too babyish. Whereas I have been tempted to interpret this behavior as resistance, I am convinced that the preference for games more closely matches the developmental interests and orientation toward the social world of latency-age children.

To understand the theoretical basis for using games as a therapeutic tool, it is necessary to highlight the similarities and differences between games and play. Play is viewed as a voluntary, intrinsically motivated and pleasurable activity that does not depend on external rewards or other people. It has no particular end point or goal. It often includes fantasy, which allows for the release of unconscious material too difficult for clients to consciously express.

Games typically referred to in the play therapy literature include board games, fine and gross motor games, card games, and street games. Video games, organized sports, math and logic games, and recreational games have not yet found a place in play therapy. Games are similar to free play in that they include a sense of enjoyment as well as pretense. Games are meant to be separate from real life and by definition are supposed to be fun to play.

The primary differences between play and games are the latter's focus on rules and on striving toward the goal of winning the game. Games mimic "real life" more so than play, which is more open-ended, thus allowing for freer expression of impulses and manipulation of reality. Games frequently require more in terms of a player's intellect, emotional control, and social skills. Rules restrict the behavior of the players.

At first glance, then, play appears to be more in line with the goals of therapy, which, depending on one's theoretical orientation, usually include relaxation of defenses and expression of thoughts, emotions, and conflicts. With its open-ended nature and freedom from the restrictions of rules, play often becomes a medium or a substitute for verbalization, fantasy expression, and free association.

Early writings on game playing in therapy, however, pointed out that games also have value for eliciting emotional expression. Loomis's (1957) article on the use of checkers in therapy was the first published work on the therapeutic application of games. Loomis regarded game playing as a medium for expression of resistance and oppositional attitudes. Meeks (1970) and Beiser (1979) argued that game playing is a projection of the relationship between the players involved. Components of the working relationship between the therapist and child, including resistance, transference, and countertransference, are readily observable in the interaction between the players.

But using games as a projective tool is only one of many therapeutic applications developed over the last ten years (Reid 1992). Before exploring in more detail the therapeutic qualities of game play, it will be useful to briefly examine the significance of game playing in normal human development.

Developmental Perspective

Major theories of play are consistent in placing the emergence of game play in normal development between the ages of 5 and 8 years. Interest in games, defined as they are in the play therapy literature as rule-governed, organized social activities, is tied to changes in or acquisition of new cognitive, emotional, and social capacities.

Piaget (1962) links the transition from symbolic play to game play to the development of a higher order of cognitive development characterized by logical thinking and improved perception of reality. The child increasingly prefers more realistic, goal-oriented games typical of those played by adults.

Peller (1954) argues that game playing reflects a reduction of oedipal preoccupations and their accompanying fantasies and magical thinking, and an increase in activities that promote identification with peers of the same sex. It is through identification that the oedipal conflicts are resolved, according to psychoanalytic theory (Peller 1954).

Social theorists such as Mead (1934) have emphasized the growing readiness of children entering the elementary school years to band together as equals, not only for camaraderie but for help in facing the authority of the adult world. Games, with their rule-governing behavior, parallel the laws and codes of conduct that exist in the adult world. Others (e.g., Serok and Blum 1983) describe games as "mini-life" situations in which the basic elements of socialization—control of aggression, rule conformity, and acceptance of group norms—are integral components of the process of play.

Game playing has been linked to identity development in children. Baumeister (1986, 1987) found that the different role structures in children's games reflect the progression of identity development from more stable, passively acquired roles to those that are externally defined, based on competence, and unstable. Preschool children prefer games that have preassigned, passively acquired roles that do not change (e.g., Simon Says, House, Mother May I). These games help affirm the preschooler's growing awareness of stable features of their identity (e.g., gender, ethnicity, place in one's family). Children in early latency (5 to 8) prefer games that involve role switching among a few roles. These children prefer competitive but chance-based games (e.g., Candyland, War, Hide and Seek) that enable them to experiment with new and different roles without requiring them to cope strategically and skillfully with opposition. Preadolescent and adolescent children prefer competitive games based on competence, reflecting the change in identity in which the self becomes increasingly equated with performance (Baumeister and Senders 1988, Erikson 1968).

There is a developmental imperative for playing games that emerges at about the age of 5 or 6 and continues throughout the life span. This is not surprising because games are ubiquitous in society and have been throughout recorded history. Many games have survival value and can be traced to prehistoric times. For example, simple ball toss games served at least two adaptive functions: (1) the practice of throwing improves coordination for the killing of prey by throwing spears or rocks, and (2) the repeated exchanging of one item between people involves practicing the act of sharing of resources, which has survival value.

Freud (see Strachey 1962) viewed games as having a greater role in mastering of anxiety (secondary process) than play, which he saw as being more a product of primary process. Peller (1954) insisted that game playing was different than "pretend play" because it served to promote sublimation, rather than direct expression, of forbidden impulses, especially aggressive ones. Mitchell and Masson (1948) theorized that games contain aggression because fighting is an instinctual response to certain life situations. Fighting releases strong emotions aroused by physiological responses to threatening stimuli. With the development of civilized society came laws and social taboos against uncontrolled aggression. Humans create play and games, therefore, to provide acceptable outlets for anger and hatred, derivatives of the basic fight response.

Games differ widely in their level of competition and, in fact, some games involve cooperation. However, nearly all modern games involve some form of contest, which by itself is a symbolic expression of aggression. The highest level of symbolic aggression is present in games in which one opponent directly attacks another, such as by capturing or neutralizing an opponent's piece (e.g., checkers, chess).

Therapeutic Elements of Game Play

An understanding of the various ways in which playing a game can promote emotional growth of children is essential for the effective use of games in therapy. The therapeutic ingredients of game play include building a therapeutic alliance, pleasure, diagnosis, communication, mastery of anxiety, and socialization.

Therapeutic Alliance

Games are a natural and enjoyable part of children's lives, especially children over the age of 6. Games are even intriguing to resistant children. Games usually involve interaction between two players; therefore, the therapist is a player and not a passive observer. One beneficial effect of this situation is that the adult–child boundary is blurred—from the child's point of view, this might feel like the adult is joining the child's world instead of vice versa.

Pleasure

Game playing even without therapeutic intervention promotes emotional growth, especially for withdrawn or emotionally constricted children. The concept of enjoyment is reciprocal; that is, the child receives pleasure from playing the game, but also is instrumental in giving pleasure to the therapist, who could not enjoy the game without the child's presence. This process results in the child feeling needed and wanted.

Diagnosis

If games are indeed "models of power," as Sutton-Smith and Roberts (1971) contend, then they are particularly useful as projective tools for exploring a child's self-esteem, helplessness, and general ego strength. This is especially true because in the therapy setting the child is playing against someone who is superior in intellect and authority. Additionally, more general diagnostic information about the child's personality can be garnered through game play. For example, an obsessive-compulsive child may insist upon the rigidity of the rules and have trouble accepting defeat. A child's intellectual strengths and weaknesses and coping style will be eventually revealed in his or her responses during game play.

Communication

Although some may view the rules and goal striving of game play as impediments to self-expression, they tend to promote communication between players. A certain level of cooperation, mutuality of purpose, and therefore, social communication is inherent in game play. A high level of affective involvement commonly accompanies game play. An important concept in game play is "points of departure" (Frey 1986, Gardner 1986), in which players "leave" the game to discuss issues brought to light during game playing. Thus, playing games often indirectly leads to self-expression. On the other hand, several new therapeutic board games are specifically designed to promote direct expression of feelings and fantasy material. Rather than attempt to list all of these new games here, the reader would do better to review the Childwork/Childplay catalog, which provides an extensive listing of therapeutic board games.

Mastery of Anxiety

Games invoke ego processes because the competitive nature of games demands concentration, impulse control, and motivation to win. Playing a game frequently arouses anxiety regarding self-esteem, power, and risk taking. Games offer opportunities for children to confront and master these anxieties. Just the process of learning how to play a game, of improving one's performance, and of winning can help improve children's self confidence and sense of mastery.

Socialization

Learning to get along with others is a critical challenge that begins early in childhood and lasts throughout life. Games are particularly useful for socialization because they offer opportunities to experience depersonalized sources of authority in the form of rules, a structure that defines the game, and positive peer pressure for socialized behavior. Norms exist that dictate how winners and losers should behave in relation to one another. Games also require that children compete and assert themselves (by trying to best the other player) within limited boundaries, thus allowing for practice of controlled expression of aggression.

The Process of Game Play Therapy

Game play therapy is not associated with any one theoretical position, nor is it defined by a specific set of procedures or applications. It is best defined as a psychotherapeutic method that utilizes a variety of game forms to help relieve the emotional distress of children. The *therapy* of game play therapy involves much more than merely playing games with the child. The game play therapist is a highly trained clinician who integrates his or her given theoretical orientation with a cluster of therapeutic game materials in order to help the child move systematically toward mental health.

Game play therapy is not separate from traditional play therapy approaches. Game play is theoretically indistinguishable from traditional play therapy. It is not an alternative to traditional play, but an extension and broadening of play therapy to better meet the developmental needs of children in the latency age group.

Regardless of theoretical orientation, there are certain guidelines for choosing games that are more inherently therapeutic than others (see Reid 1992, for a more extensive review of types of games). Complex, intellectually stimulating games like Monopoly or Stratego tend to focus the child's attention on the mechanics of playing rather than on interaction, so they are usually inappropriate for game play therapy. Games that call for more than two players and those that involve solitary play also have limited applicability. The game must be suitable to the space available and should not be too noisy. The game's duration should fit into the therapy hour. Most children in therapy are unable to concentrate for longer games, and playing a game several times within one session promotes learning and provides the opportunity to immediately make up for poor performance in the previous game. The therapist should make available a variety of games, to allow for progression or regression of the child, as needed.

Cheating often becomes an issue in game play therapy. Most therapists would agree that cheating arises out of the child's feelings of inadequacy. However, there is disagreement in the literature about how to manage cheating. Some argue that by allowing cheating the therapist is enabling the child to avoid coping with reality (Cooper and Wanerman 1977, Meeks 1970). Others (e.g., Berlin 1986) contend that the therapist should allow some cheating if he or she acknowledges the child's need to win. My own belief about cheating is that, in general, the therapist should not allow it because this only serves to reinforce and perpetuate the child's feelings that underlie it: I am inadequate and cannot win without playing outside the rules. Nevertheless, the therapist should not view a child's cheating as a problem that needs to be eliminated, but rather as one form of expression of his or her personality and coping style. One way to deal with cheating by a child whose need to cheat is strong is to bring it out in the open and insist that the cheating can be done by both players.

Similarly, there is disagreement about letting children win at games. While on the one hand letting a child win helps his self-esteem and mastery (Berlin 1986), on the other it may communicate the opposite, that the child cannot win on his own (O'Connor 1991). I believe that it is more preferable to handicap yourself as a player to even up the chances for winning, rather than allow the child to win. Allowing a child to win is usually a covert process that sets a tone for secrecy and mistrust. Another technique is to either choose a game of chance or, if possible, modify the chosen game so that chance is a major factor in winning, in order to neutralize the adult's superiority. Attributing losing to chance factors is much less challenging to one's self-esteem.

PRESENTING PROBLEM AND
BACKGROUND INFORMATION

Jason was 6 years old when I began to see him in play therapy. At that time, he recently had been admitted into a large residential treatment facility for emotionally disturbed and conduct disordered boys. Jason was originally removed from his mother's care and placed in a foster home at the age of 2½ years due to allegations of physical abuse and neglect. The courts did not uphold the abuse charge because of lack of proof, but Jason remained in foster placement because the court found his mother, Paula, to be neglectful. It was also suspected that she abused alcohol and drugs, but this also was never proven.

Jason's early history remains sketchy, but it is known that he was raised in and among the homeless. His mother, whose health was poor, never had a stable residence or employment. A variety of Paula's friends and relatives shuffled Jason back and forth. When he first came to the attention of the child welfare authorities, he was undernourished and living in squalor in a crack house in the slums.

The authorities removed Jason from three foster homes before placing him in the residential treatment program. Significant behavioral problems, including hyperactivity, aggressiveness, and self-abusive behavior, precipitated his removal from all three homes. The first placement lasted nearly two years, the second about one year, and the third only one month.

Reports from the foster agency overseeing his placements documented a slow deterioration in the relations between Jason and his first foster family. This was a warm and loving intact family that included two other foster children. A major factor in the decline was the increasingly intrusive presence of Jason's mother in his life. The foster family alleged that Paula turned Jason against them, repeatedly made false promises to him, and left Jason to fend for himself when on weekend visits. The foster parents were described as being deeply hurt and perplexed by Jason's behavior. They stated that Jason was always hyperactive and mildly aggressive, but after he began seeing his mother more frequently, he lost the "sweet" side to his personality, and he became much more hostile and oppositional. Whereas previously the foster parents interpreted his aggressive behavior as a product of immaturity and poor impulse control, they began to see increasing intentionality and provocative aspects in his aggression. The foster family eventually requested Jason be removed from the home.

The second foster family placement reportedly was problematic from the start. By that time, Jason's behavioral problems were more firmly entrenched, and he acquired a set of self-abusive behaviors including biting and scratching himself and hitting himself in the face. The foster parents were a middle-aged couple with three grown children, one of whom lived in the home. These adults had much less tolerance for Jason's misbehavior and were believed to use corporal punishment freely. The authorities removed Jason from this home following a charge against the foster father of hitting him with a belt made of leather intertwined with metal chain. By that time, Jason's behavioral problems had become so severe that it was apparent that he needed a more restrictive placement. His third foster placement was a temporary one pending his admittance into a residential treatment facility.

Jason's developmental history includes a full-term gestation with birth weight of 8 lbs., 1 oz. He was born to a mother who developed a fairly serious heart condition during pregnancy and a father with a history of drug abuse. As an infant, Jason's health was reportedly stable, but his subsequent attainment of developmental milestones was delayed. Most notably, he did not achieve independent toileting until the age of 4.

Formal developmental evaluations done during Jason's preschool years found borderline to low-average intellectual functioning. This was compromised by impaired concentration and attention, as well as mild neurological dysfunction resulting in below average visual analysis and visual-motor integration. He was described as being at significant risk for learning disabilities. His deficient impulse control resulted in poor short-term memory skills and failure to learn from experience. Jason demonstrated average language skills, a fact that suggested average intellectual potential. He was diagnosed with attention-deficit hyperactivity disorder and reactive attachment disorder (*DSM-III-R*).

Jason's problematic behaviors were notably absent during the first few weeks of his placement in the residential treatment facility. Shortly thereafter, however, he began to exhibit the disruptive, destructive, and aggressive behaviors reported by his foster families. His hyperactivity and impulsivity at their worst were very severe. There seemed to be little warning of impending outbursts. Jason often appeared disorganized and motorically restless before lashing out in the form of pushing, hitting, or biting other people without any apparent provocation from them. At other times, however, he would appear calm and even disinterested and then suddenly push or hit another child or an adult. When provoked even mildly, Jason would retaliate with much more force than was warranted.

In his new home, Jason lived in one of many cottages of ten children and two cottage "parents," who were trained child care counselors. The counselors felt that Jason was truly emotionally disturbed as he seemed to be "driven" to provoke and anger them. He responded inconsistently, but generally poorly, to the limits and structured routine of the cottage. Limit setting typically set off a spiral of escalating hyperactivity, defiance, and aggression, and subsequent restrictions and punishments.

Yet Jason presented as a very friendly young child, desirous of affection and affectionate in return. He constantly sought the attention of the counselors and showed little interest in peers. He tried to endear himself to the adults by adopting an exaggerated helper role. The counselors noted that he was extremely independent as he reflexively refused help with tasks or daily self-help activities.

Jason's mother visited him irregularly at the residence, approximately twice per month. Paula seemed to be very harsh, impulsive, and controlling with him, and he tended to be more hyperactive and oppositional in her presence. The caseworker at the residence saw her for parent sessions, and she participated, with irregular attendance, in parent–child therapy groups focusing on nonabusive discipline methods. Paula made some progress in using redirection and ignoring as behavior management tools in dealing with Jason. However, the hostility and impatience that tinged her interactions with Jason never changed. While she voiced a desire to have Jason live with her, she made little progress over a three-year span in securing stable employment or her own apartment. (She was alternately homeless or living with friends.)

Jason was enrolled in a special-education classroom for children classified as emotionally disturbed, in an affiliated school where I was employed as a psychologist. I was familiar with his case, as I also served as a consultant to the residential treatment facility, having worked in the agency several years previously. I participated in the intake evaluation process. Jason took a liking to me and the school and residence personnel decided that he would receive play therapy with me at the school two times per week in 40-minute sessions. I did case planning with the close collaboration of the school and residence.

THEORETICAL CONCEPTUALIZATION

Jason was not unlike most other boys attending the residence and school, a victim of the trauma of abuse and neglect. Jason demonstrated overall impairment in ego functioning in the form of intellectual deficits, poor impulse control, poor self-concept, and hyperaggressivity, all of which are known sequelae of early childhood trauma (Martin 1972, Morse et al. 1970).

Jason's object relations also appeared to be severely disturbed. His highly ambivalent relationships with adults, in which intense emotional hunger and primitive rage were the defining characteristics, originated in attachment failure. I found evidence of a poor attachment not only in the dysfunctional interactions patterns between Jason and his mother, but also in his excessive familiarity with strangers and difficulty maintaining affective ties with caregivers. Although he first impressed me as a friendly, cooperative, and fairly well-related child, it quickly became clear that Jason's relationships with adults remained superficial. He tended to flit from one adult to another without allowing the time for closeness to develop. With repeated exposure to caregivers, he became increasingly anxious, angry, and provocative. Ultimately, to adapt to the stress relationships created for him, Jason distanced himself and never developed a strong relationship with any one adult in his environment.

I knew that failure to establish a secure attachment relationship affects the emotional, cognitive, and social development of the child (Mahler et al. 1975, Sroufe and Waters 1977). Although little factual information was available about the mother–infant relationship between Paula and Jason, their early interactions were played out in an unstable and chaotic environment. This, in itself, would have made it difficult for Paula to provide the consistent emotional availability, attentiveness, and empathy needed for development of a secure attachment (Ainsworth 1979). Children raised in adverse conditions are vulnerable to psychological problems (Farber and Egeland 1987, Guttman 1989).

Jason also was suffering from a sense of loss and grief associated with being separated from his mother. Multiple foster placements had only added to his feelings of rejection and abandonment. His first foster placement appeared to provide Jason with the stability, consistency, and emotional sustenance previously lacking in his life. This kind of substitute parenting can alleviate a child's discomfort from being separated from his mother (A. Freud 1970, Osofsky and Connors 1979).

Finally, Jason exhibited delays and gaps in superego development and male identification. The lack of consistent mothering and the absence of a father figure had left him devoid of a stable sense of self. His self-esteem was poor and his self-image was distorted. Projective drawings revealed his sense of being damaged and unwhole.

Despite this moribund clinical picture, I could see in Jason a warmth and sweetness that must have been nurtured by a parent or caregiver who was emotionally responsive and giving. Thus, it was clear to me that, despite the difficulties in his early life, he had experienced healthy interactions with caregivers at various times, probably for brief periods with his mother, perhaps for a more sustained duration with his first foster family and at certain times with his other foster families. From this information I assumed two things: first, that Jason could establish a working therapeutic relationship, and second, that the positive aspects of his multiple attachments only accentuated the sense of loss he suffered when he left.

Jason was in dire need of play therapy. Initially, I conceptualized this as a long-term case in which traditional play therapy methods and materials would be valuable in helping Jason express painful emotional material, repeat and master anxieties and conflicts, and gain insight into his own motivations and behaviors. A growing body of literature attests to the powerful therapeutic effects of play therapy with children who have experienced abuse and neglect and multiple foster placements (Green 1978, In and McDermott 1976, Masur 1991, Remkus 1991).

I also felt that the relationship Jason and I would develop would be a critical factor in his growth. My thoughts on this subject were influenced by Anna Freud's notion that a lack of fusion between aggressive drives and libidinal drives can lead to unbridled and independent aggressiveness. In her 1949 paper "Aggression in Relation to Emotional Development," Anna Freud postulated that exposure to noncaring environments and frequent changes in object relations deprive the developing ego of a stable love object that binds and neutralizes aggressive urges. The appropriate therapy, Freud insisted, is directed to the neglected, defective side, that is, the emotional libidinal development, as opposed to focusing exclusively on using measures to curtail the aggressive behavior of the child.

In his book, *The Play Therapy Primer*, Kevin O'Connor (1991) presented a developmental context for the practice of play therapy. According to this framework, Jason's age and developmental level placed him in the upper end of the category of the level II child (2 to 6 years old), and at the beginning of the category of the level III child (6 to 11 years old). Children at this developmental level are cognitively and emotionally ready to utilize the type of play forms endemic to traditional play therapy: pretend play, especially with miniature toys; puppet play; dressing up; and art activities, especially three-dimensional art projects. According to most theories of play development, Jason was too young to benefit from a therapeutic program of play with games with rules.

Despite these ostensible indications for the application of traditional play therapy, several factors steered me away from free play and toward the application of game play concepts in my original formulation of a treatment plan. Firstly, psychological and educational assessments consistently noted that Jason showed no interest in pretend play. He refused to play with dolls, puppets, human or action figures, toy cars, trucks, garages, play food, and dollhouses and furniture. He would not engage in dress-up play, and he disliked expressive art forms such as drawing, coloring, or painting. He even refused to play with more primitive sensory materials, such as Play Doh, water, or sand. It was noted several times that he became overwhelmed with affect whenever he attempted symbolic play, which led to increased excitability and acting out. His rejection of this play form represented a healthy avoidance of overwhelming stimuli. Jason preferred more object-specific and goal-oriented play materials, such as pegboards, puzzles, mechanical and constructive toys (blocks, simple models).

In addition to Jason's anticipated resistance to play therapy, his hyperactivity posed a problem in terms of his ability to become engaged in the therapy process. I feared that the freedom of choice, sense of permissiveness, and ambiguity of the play therapy environment would be overstimulating and overwhelming for Jason. Indeed, two play therapists had made previous attempts to engage him in play therapy, one in a mental health clinic and one in his preschool special-education setting. On both occasions, the therapists cited his hyperactivity, oppositional attitudes, and inability to sustain any meaningful play as reasons for premature discharge from therapy.

With this history of failure in mind, I planned to structure the therapy sessions so as to minimize the number of choices for play, reduce visual distractions, and emphasize clear beginnings and endings to tasks, modifications that are consistent with accepted treatment for hyperactive children in the home and school environments (Barkley 1990). I planned to utilize this approach for as long as needed, but with a vigilant eye toward gradually reducing the structure of the sessions, introducing more freedom of choice, and allowing more self-directed behavior.

The structured nature of games, with their strict rules, requirements for cooperation and self-control, and specific objectives, was a suitable match for the modifications I imposed on the therapy program. I planned on using games not only to help engage Jason in an activity he would find enjoyable and nonthreatening, but also to immediately work on reducing his hyperactivity. My choice of games for the first session came from those for which motor activity is a central component. A number of structured motor games have been shown to improve attention and decrease hyperactivity (Bow and Goldberg 1986, Schachter 1986, Swanson 1986). Fine motor games in particular, such as ball toss, penny hockey, soft target games, Perfection, Operation, and ring toss, have a number of advantages that make them useful for hyperactive children. These games involve repeated controlled fine motor movements, thereby providing practice of impulse control. By not being overly engrossing or lengthy, fine motor games allow for immediate feedback without demanding the child's extended attention. Movement by itself is a relaxant and is effective in improving the sensory functioning and perceptual organization among hyperactive children.

My immediate goal of engaging Jason in game play, was, I felt, a necessary step toward establishing a trusting relationship. One could say that mistrust and fear of rejection were central dynamics in Jason's psychic life, in addition to the unconscious determinants of his disordered interpersonal interactions. I anticipated that this early exploratory and relationship-building stage of therapy would be of relatively long duration.

THE PROCESS OF PLAY THERAPY

During the first few sessions, Jason exhibited a consistent pattern. He eagerly came from his classroom to the playroom, began the session by playing in a cooperative and relatively self-controlled manner, then became increasingly active and provocative. While in his "angelic" mode, Jason maintained a distance from me. He would not maintain eye contact, and he focused on the game materials as opposed to social interaction. I felt that Jason was doing his best to ward off anxiety at being rejected in some form by me. Slowly, as if he could no longer contain himself and avoid interacting with me, his behavior became increasingly hyperactive and provocative. For example, he would roughly pull the string to open the window blinds, impulsively grab the phone and press the buttons, curse, and hit or attempt to hit me in the face. Often, quite suddenly, in the middle of all this, he would come to me and hug me warmly, then return to his mischief.

I examined my own reactions to Jason's provocative behaviors and used them as a gauge to measure the overt and covert messages he was communicating. I keenly felt a strong sense of irritation, as it seemed Jason's sole aim in behaving in this manner was to enrage me. It was as if he was seeking to elicit a punishing response from me. At this point in the therapy process, I had several hypotheses as to why he would seek such a response. The most prominent of these theories was that this behavior resulted from a repetition compulsion that drove him to repeatedly evoke and realize painful memories of physical abuse and master the feelings associated with them. I also recognized that his poor self-esteem was partly to blame. Aggressive children often feel it is better to be willfully bad than to risk feeling that people reject them for being inherently unlovable and worthless (Willock 1987). Finally, by provoking adults so effectively, Jason gained a measure of revenge and control over the adult world that had proven so unreliable and hurtful in his young life.

My initial response to Jason's misbehavior was to use reflection (e.g., "You seem like you're very angry right now," "You want to really bash that phone"), but this had to be abandoned as his behavior quickly escalated to the point where I had to use limit setting. I knew that limit setting would be an important therapeutic intervention with Jason. On the one hand, setting limits would help him reestablish his view of himself as a child who is protected by a powerful, but benevolent, adult world. On the other hand, I knew it was critical for me to set limits in a way that did not communicate anger, irritation, or rejection, so that Jason could begin to break the cycle of negative interaction with adults. Controlling my irritation was not always easy as Jason was quite relentless in his attempts to rile me.

Jason showed great interest in the novelty of the game materials. He became engrossed in manipulating the materials of the five or six games I made available and he tended to include me only when he needed help for something. He typically moved from one game to the next, never finishing any game and often playing in a random manner inconsistent with the purpose of the games. For example, he threw the Pic-Up Sticks against the window glass and repeatedly made the buzzer go off on the Operation game just for the effect.

I interpreted Jason's play behavior in two ways: one, as a function of his hyperactivity, for which poor attention and inability to sustain interest with one set of stimuli are characteristic; and two, as a reflection of the manner in which he related to his environment. It was as if Jason was afraid of relaxing and truly involving himself with anybody or anything. This coping style was in reality an isolating and ungratifying compromise. As he became bored with the small set of play materials, the pressure to interact with me increased. Consequently, he "related" to me in the only manner he could, fluctuating between being provocative and aggressive and, less frequently, clingy and affectionate. It seemed to me that the small selection of games actually promoted a transference reaction by preventing Jason from avoiding me by losing himself in play.

By the fourth session, Jason began to show interest in playing some of the games with me, and as I had anticipated, he preferred action games. His favorite was a target game using small light balls covered with Velcro. Over the next few sessions, there came a subtle change in the tenor of Jason's play and the attitudes it reflected. He entered the playroom in a much more subdued fashion, no longer struggling to present himself in a favorable light. He stopped aggressing toward me, and although he continued to provoke limit setting, his provocative behavior lacked the same intensity. I felt I had broken through Jason's very tough outer shell of anger and defensiveness.

Jason totally dominated the game-playing process. He played in typically disorganized, frenetic fashion. He would throw three balls, one after another, at the target hanging on a wall and then move closer and closer to the target to ensure success. Turn-taking was nonexistent, but Jason allowed me to throw a few balls on occasion.

I decided to structure the game in order to strive toward one of the original goals of game play, reducing Jason's hyperactivity in order for him to play games in such a way that I could exploit their therapeutic aspects. I placed a strip of masking tape on the floor that served as an imaginary throwing line and established a rule that we must stand behind the line when throwing the ball at the target. Jason enthusiastically agreed to the new challenge, but had trouble adhering to this simple rule. He impulsively stepped across the line to improve his chances at hitting the target. I then added a new rule, that any time a player stepped across the line, he must give up his turn to the other. I made sure I violated this rule several times in order to help Jason accept this provision.

So it was that I came to teach Jason the basics of playing a game. I realized that he had never learned fundamental game playing skills, such as turn-taking, following rules, and striving toward a goal. I added another component to our play with the target game, a variant of self-instruction, a cognitive-behavioral intervention introduced by Meichenbaum and Goodman (1971). This program involves teaching children a set of self-directed instructions to follow when performing a task. Self-instructions include defining the task, planning a strategy to approach the problem, focusing attention on the task, selecting an answer or solution, and evaluating performance. The rationale for the effectiveness of self-instruction is the diminishing of impulsive responding through increased cognitive awareness and mediation of thoughts associated with actions.

The self-instruction I modeled for Jason was quite informal and presented in a natural way as part of the game. On my turn to throw, I might say something like, "Okay, now it's my turn, let's see, I have to stand behind this line and aim it like this, right at the target, and throw it straight, right?" (turning toward Jason to reinforce his listening). "I think I'll throw on the count of three (then demonstrating making a throwing motion three times), one, two, three, like that, how's that? Nice and slow, that way, I'll be sure to throw it straight. Now watch. All right, I hit the target!"

When it was Jason's turn to throw, I encouraged him to talk about what he was doing along the lines described above. I soon realized this was too abstract for him, so I made a game within a game by ritualizing the steps involved in taking a turn at throwing the balls at the target. Each step included a specific action accompanied by a specific phrase spoken out loud. To illustrate, after a player's turn, that player then put the three balls into a plastic bowl for the next player. The other player then went to the bowl and picked out one ball while saying "Okay, ball number one!" He then went to the throw line and said "Okay, stay behind the line,"and so on.

Jason enjoyed this multilayered game playing and he became less dominating and controlling in his play. He began to take turns spontaneously, to pay attention to me and my game playing, and to interact with me in a less emotional and impulse-ridden manner. Jason was learning to trust me. It seemed to me that the game playing process provided for Jason a less threatening medium for interacting with me. This is not to suggest that his provocative behaviors disappeared. They did not, and I needed to set limits frequently, but his interest in the game enabled me to increasingly use redirection instead of direct prohibitions.

By the tenth play therapy session, Jason and I had sampled most of the fine motor games in the playroom. I approached each of these games in a similar fashion as the ball toss game, structuring and modifying the games to enable Jason to play. His participation and self-control improved as we played each new game. He seemed ready to experiment with new game forms, so I introduced a few simple board games (Candyland, Chutes and Ladders), a deck of cards, a Go Fish card game, and two therapeutic boardgames (Our Game, The Storytelling Card Game). The fine motor games remained available to Jason in the event he would need to return to their familiarity.

I chose the new games because they are relatively simple to learn, with winning based on chance more than skill, and flexible enough to allow for modification or removal of their competitive elements. Jason showed no interest in competing during the ball toss game, a behavior that is consistent with the nascent interest in competition that is characteristic of early latency-age children.

After one and one-half sessions of rifling through the game materials in a manner reminiscent of his first few play sessions, Jason finally settled on Candyland. To my surprise he set up the game correctly, assigning game pieces and placing the cards in a pile, thereby revealing his familiarity with the game. He also revealed his understanding of the competition of the game, and he expressed his desire to be the first to reach "home." It was apparent that winning provided his motivation to play this game.

Candyland emerged as a mainstay of our play during the next several sessions. The process of game play produced a rich body of therapeutic material and interchange. We frequently negotiated new rules, created games within the game, and even developed stories based on the game board. One sequence of particular significance developed after I suggested that we include another game piece at the start of a new game. In keeping with a practice I suggested earlier, Jason assigned names to each of our pieces (often choosing names of nonthreatening fantasy characters such as Big Bird or Batman). This time, his choices were closer to home. The following sequence illustrates how game play can be a projective screen and a catalyst for self-expression.

Session 12

Dialogue

Commentary

J: Okay, I'm Jawan, you're Steve, and she's Paula.

I recognized his mother's name and the name of one of Jason's classmates. I did not ask him if this was his mother. I did not want to risk engaging his defenses at a time when he appeared about to express deeper concerns.

SR: [Pointing to my game piece.] So this is me?

J: Yeah, I'm Jawan, and she's Paula.

SR: Okay.

J: She goes last. [When "her" turn came, Jason picked the

card.] I'll make her go. [He
turned over a card.] Red. She
has to go over here. [He
moved the piece to a red
square near the end of the
long trail.]

SR: You put her there.

J: Yeah, she doesn't have to go
on the road, she can go anywhere she wants.

SR: Anywhere she wants?

J: [Silence.]

SR: She can go anywhere she
wants, huh?

J: Yeah, she's far away from us.

SR: Okay, let's talk. [I moved our
two pieces together, facing
each other, then talked
through my game piece to his
game piece.] Hi, Jawan. How
come Paula gets to move all
the way up there? That's
against the rules.

I had used this technique earlier to
elicit further self-expression, with
some success.

J: Cause she's the mommy, she
can go anywhere she wants.

SR: Does she want to go there?

J: Yeah, she doesn't want to be
with us.

SR: Why not?

J: I don't know, maybe she
wants to be alone.

Jason used the game to project his feeling of being estranged from his mother, as well as his concerns about being abandoned by her. The game continued according to Jason's adaptations of the rules, wherein he and I would move our pieces in the prescribed manner. Jason moved Paula's piece in a pattern that was apparently designed to keep her as far away from his piece on the board. When her piece approached the end of the trail, Jason put her back to the starting point in the game, thus denying her the opportunity to win. Jason and I shifted back and forth from actually playing the game and moving pieces to having characters express feelings by talking to each other—with the notable absence of communication between Jason's and Paula's pieces.

In this session, realistic discussion between Jason and I was minimal. It seemed that he needed the safety of the pretense involved in speaking through the characters in the game. The following sequence reveals more of his feelings about his mother.

Dialogue	Commentary

J: [To his "Paula" piece:] Okay, ha, ha, now you have to go back to the candy cane. [Expressing obvious glee at sending Paula back to near the beginning of the trail.]

SR: Now she's losing. You feel happy about that.

J: Yeah, I hate Paula, she's a motherfucker.

Finally, I thought, Jason was beginning to get in touch with his anger toward his mother. But he was becoming overexcited quickly, so I put myself on alert to intervene if needed to help him control his affect. Jason was embellishing his feelings of being hurt by a more powerful being.

SR: She's bad?

J: Oh yeah, she's been in jail before, she's a killer. She's a really bad bad bad man. She's bad. She shot two people before, with a big rifle. [Jason then used his game piece to kick over Paula's piece.] There, bitch. [Jason then laughed heartily.]

SR: [Speaking through my game piece.] You're mad at her, huh, Jawan?

J: [As Jawan] Yeah, cause I'm her son, and she did it to me!

SR: Did what?

J: She killed me with a gun. But I love her, 'cause she's a very, very, very nice mommy.

I viewed this as reaction formation as well as a sign of an ambivalent attachment pattern.

SR: You love your mommy.

At this point I stopped speaking through my game piece in the hope that Jason would tolerate the subtle shift to more realistic discourse. Fantasies of reunification are central in children who struggle with feelings of abandonment.

J: Of course, don't you love your mommy? Everybody loves his mommy. My mommy's sick now, but when she's better she's gonna take me home so I can go to school on a big school bus.

SR: You want to live with her.

J: Sometimes. I like to live here, too.

SR: You like it here.

J: Yeah, but I don't know where   This revealed Jason's lack of object
     she is. Do you think she's   constancy.
     waiting for me?

SR: Waiting for you?

J: Yeah, waiting for me at home.

SR: Where's home?

J: Where Nicole lives. Also here,   He referred to his foster sibling
     this is my home too. I have a   from his first foster home.
     lot of homes! Okay, let's play.

Through the process of game play with Candyland, Jason continued
to express his ambivalent feelings of love and anger toward his mother,
his lack of object constancy, and his poor sense of being connected to a
family. He did not truly believe his mother was at home waiting for him,
a concept shared by many children living in residential facilities, because
he did not have a stable mental representation of home connected to his
mother. While he did, however, have this connection with his first
foster family, he also sensed, quite correctly, that the ties between
himself and this family were permanently broken.

Game play became a critical medium through which Jason actively
grieved for the loss of his mother—for the broken, incomplete, and lost
relationships he had experienced at so young an age. His insistence on
playing only Candyland, which lasted for about six sessions, attested to
the effectiveness of the game in providing an acceptable outlet for his
pent-up feelings.

The relationship between Jason and me grew stronger, and I knew I
was becoming an important object in Jason's life. While he continued to
test the limits of the playroom and of my resolve not to reject or hurt
him, in general his behavior was much less provocative during the
sessions. Reports from his cottage parents and teacher told of a sharp
decrease in aggression, although his hyperactivity was still severe.
These developments were consistent with Anna Freud's theory that
attributes the cause of aggression to impaired object relations (Freud
1949).

While the focus on grief work continued, there was a gradual shift in
Jason's play away from fantasy expression and magical thinking and

toward realism and rule-governed action. He showed increasing interest in simple competitive games such as checkers, Connect Four, Trouble, War (card game), and Uno. I suspected that Jason needed some time to reestablish his defenses, which had often succumbed to the eruption of unconscious material during our pretend play with the Candyland game. I also felt that Jason had begun to assimilate the painful feelings associated with the different losses he had suffered.

Jason had trouble adhering to the many rules and regulations associated with the competitive games he now chose. Unlike the rules we created for the fine motor games, which were seen as a fun part of a ritualized sequence of movements, Jason seemed to find these new rules to be too restrictive. He had trouble dealing with the symbolic aggression in the games, the relinquishing of control, and the risk of losing. As the following sequence of play with Trouble illustrates, these difficulties were intimately related to his lack of trust and impaired object relations. The session, which I considered to be a turning point in therapy, begins with Jason explaining his idea for a new set of rules for the game.

Session 22

Dialogue	Commentary
J: Okay, you can't send my guy home anymore. If you land on him, you have to go home!	
SR: Okay, that's fine, and the same thing goes if you land on me, right?	
J: No, no, no, no! You have to go back home.	
SR: But that's not fair.	
J: C'mon, let's play.	He was doing his best to ignore reality here.
SR: You want to change the rules so you can win, right?	

J: Yeah, I have to win.

SR: Then you'll be the best.   His desire to be superior is tied to
                                            his foster sibling, who he saw as
                                            better than himself. Perhaps be-
                                            cause she remained with the fam-
                                            ily, Jason is envious of her.

J: I am the best in the whole
     world, nobody can beat me.
     Do you want Nicole to play?

SR: Nicole?

J: She's my sister. She beats me
     all the time.

SR: You never beat her.

J: Naw, she's bigger than me.
     Nicole. . . . hey, maybe she
     can be blue. [Pointing to the
     blue pieces to indicate his de-
     sire to include an invisible
     player as we had done previ-
     ously.]

Throughout this game Jason "reverse" cheated, penalizing himself
whenever possible, quite the opposite effect of his original desire to set
up an advantage for himself. He manipulated the game in order for
Nicole to win. He looked sad and preoccupied during this game.

                 Dialogue   *Commentary*

SR: Wow, you really want to lose
     this game.

J: Sometimes it's better to lose. I
     hate this game. I always lose. I
     stink. You stink! [Yelling at
     one of his game pieces.]

SR: But Nicole won the game.

J: Well, Nicole is a very nice girl, don't you think? She has a mommy and a daddy, and I don't even have a mommy. Except for Manny, he's my daddy. Not my real Daddy.

He ties his self-worth to his lack of a family. Manny is one of his house parents.

SR: Do you have a mommy?

J: Yes, you know her, Paula is her name. But I'm never gonna live with her, cause she's always missing her train. Mommy always has to help a friend.

Referring to her missed appointments at the residence—she took a commuting train to get there.

SR: That's why she didn't come to see you?

J: Yep. When do I come to see you, on Tuesdays?

Jason appears to see me now as a significant object in his life.

SR: Yeah, Tuesdays and Thursdays.

J: Good, let's put this game away for good.

SR: For good?

J: I don't think I want to play with you any more.

SR: You don't want to come to see me anymore.

J: Nope. [Jason said this in a firm voice and looked at me directly in the eye.]

Jason wanted to hurt my feelings.

SR: Well, I feel very sad about
that.

J: [Jason began to angrily smash   He was regressing as seen in his
his fist down on the bubble   attempts to provoke me, some-
dice popper on the game. He   thing he had not done in some
began to throw the pieces   time.
right over my head. He then
grabbed the game board and
smashed it repeatedly over the
door handle, breaking it.] I
hate you and I hate this game
[sobbing].

SR: Jason, are you angry with me?

J: No, I just want to hug you.
[Jason came over to me and
hugged me very tight for a
long time.]

SR: I'm your friend, Jason, I'll always be your friend.

Jason was exhausted and we had to put further exploration on hold.
Several themes emerged in this session. His desire to lose reflected his
devalued sense of self, especially in contrast to his foster sister who
Jason saw as being valued by virtue of her being accepted and loved by
her foster parents. This is why Nicole "deserves" to win. Through this
intervention, Jason revealed his narcissistic injury at being abandoned
and rejected.

Before his memory of Nicole arose, and before his desire to throw this
game, Jason exhibited a strong desire to cheat, as well as sense of
omnipotence. Although not apparent from their brief appearance in the
above sequence, these two themes actually had been quite common in
Jason's play throughout the course of therapy up to this point. I
interpreted these behaviors as signs of grandiosity that Kohut (1971)
explained as a compensatory defense mechanism that serves to deny
low self-esteem. What was different in this session was that Jason did
not cling to his need to be omnipotent, but instead disclosed, in
symbolic form, the underlying sense of worthlessness (e.g., I am not
valued, I cannot win, only Nicole can win, she is lovable). This turn of

events eventually proved to be significant, for Jason's grandiose strivings and related need to cheat gradually abated after this session.

Jason also used this session to consciously discuss his mother. He seemed to be trying to come to grips with the profound sense of loss and disappointment associated with her absence. The experience of actually letting himself feel, even briefly, his sense of aloneness and abandonment led to an expression of his desire to be with me. This, in turn, led to a rejection of me ("I hate you, I don't want to see you anymore"). By rejecting me first, Jason protected himself from the thought of being rejected by me. Over the next few sessions, the relationship between Jason and I took center stage. Jason's flirtations with being nasty and rejecting toward me continued and provided fertile material for discussion. Our discussions revealed the obvious, that Jason had fantasized me as a father figure in his life, although he never consciously admitted this. As gently as I could, I clarified the realities of our relationship, the most potently fearful for Jason being that I would not be a permanent fixture in his life. Jason was able to assimilate this knowledge without responding by acting out his feelings. I viewed this as a positive sign of his emotional growth.

Jason's relationships with adults continued to improve, but his aggressiveness with peers increased. Over the next dozen or so sessions, the themes that emerged centered less on themes of loss and more on Jason's relationships with peers in his current environment. He made fewer and fewer references to his mother and his past. Jason had progressed in making peace with his past, but his fear of rejection and his mistrust were still quite real and at the core of his interpersonal problems. At his young age, Jason's observing ego was largely undeveloped, and he was unable to make much use of insights that linked his particular intrapsychic conflicts (i.e., object constancy and loss) to his behavior. He had achieved the improvements in his behavior for the most part through subtle shifts in his personality structure that occurred largely outside of his conscious awareness.

Game play was particularly useful for helping Jason deal with his problems interacting with other people. He readily projected these problems onto the game situation, which typically entailed interaction on several levels—between Jason and me and between the characters and pieces in the game. Jason took a liking to the Storytelling Card Game (Gardner 1988). The game involves telling stories based on pictures provided in the game kit. According to the game's instructions, players use a spinner to get chips or select from one of several categories of cards, use the dice to determine how many of the fifteen human figurines are to be used on any one turn, and receive chips for telling a self-created story and for then explaining the moral or lesson of the story. The player with the most chips wins the game.

As with most of the games we had previously played, we modified the rules of this game to suit the needs and capabilities of Jason. He wanted me to tell *his* stories, but I compromised by saying we could tell our stories together. He insisted on keeping the game competitive, so we agreed that the better the story, the more chips one would earn. Again, Jason needed to win the game, but I was more concerned with the material he would project in the stories, so I did not argue too much with his decisions about how much each story we told was "worth."

The following excerpt reveals that Jason held a certain belief about the intentions of the peers in his cottage with whom he had the most difficulty interacting. This belief was that these children "were out to get him." Jason expected these boys to be aggressive and hostile toward him. To deal with this anxiety, Jason often behaved in aggressive manner first—in a way, preempting an attack. This distorted perception has been labeled an attributional bias in aggressive children. Studies have shown that aggressive children, compared to their normal peers, believe that other children's intentions are hostile in situations where there is little or no provocation or the provocation is mild at best (Dodge and Frame 1982, Dodge and Newman 1981, Nasby et al. 1979).

Session 31

Dialogue	*Commentary*
J: [Beginning his story.] Okay, now this boy and this girl are playing a game of checkers. They're sitting down. [Laying figurines on their side.]	
SR: Okay, they're playing a game of checkers. So I wonder what happens next?	I always try to be as leading and neutral as possible before actually contributing to a story, which I did only if Jason became truly "stuck."
J: Okay, so they run out of pieces.	
SR: Run out of pieces?	

J: Yeah, she has more pieces than I do! That's not fair.

SR: You mean she wins?

J: No, I mean when she starts she has more pieces than him.

SR: I see, so what happens?

J: Well . . . they both try to find out who stole the missing pieces!

SR: I see.

J: Yeah, they go looking all over the place, then they find the red pieces in Marcus's bed, under his bed.

Marcus is the name of an antagonist of Jason's who lived in the same cottage.

SR: Wow, under his bed. So how did they get there?

J: Well, Marcus knew we wanted to play checkers, so he stole them on purpose just to mess up our game.

SR: Wow, how do you know that?

J: I just know, he's always trying to get one over on me.

SR: So what happens next?

J: So . . . I got it! The next time Marcus plays checkers, I spray him with the hose, all over the place! [Said with glee.]

SR: You mean the hose from outside?

J: Yeah, I get it, bring it inside, and spray him all over with water.

SR: So he gets real wet.

J: Then we have another fight. And I win, I punch his teeth in.

SR: So, let's see, you sprayed him with water because he stole the checker pieces from you?

J: That's right.

SR: Well, maybe, he stole them for another reason. Maybe he wanted to keep something for himself. Like maybe he needed to use them for his own game of hockey.

I was referring to the game of penny hockey that Jason and I had played.

J: Yeah, maybe, could be, I don't really know.

Through the game playing process I was able to challenge Jason's assumptions about the intentions of his peers and offer alternative explanations for the behavior that he attributed to their hostile intentions. I also appealed to Jason's fairness, an idea which he increasingly understood and respected. I argued that it was not fair to retaliate with such a vengeance, especially if he wasn't sure that the child really wanted to harm him. Jason's response to this therapeutic strategy aimed at changing his cognitions was inconsistent. I urged the staff people working with Jason at the residence to employ the same kind of strategies to help him reinterpret the events that led to his aggressive actions directed at peers. Since the intervention was generally simple and concrete it was easy to implement in his home environment.

RESULTS AND FOLLOW-UP

I saw Jason in play therapy for two full years at the rate of twice per week, with interruptions due to normal school holidays and vacations.

I terminated therapy after the second year because I left the school to take another position. Jason remained in the residence for another year. During the third year, he received play therapy with another therapist at the residence. During this year, his mother's rights were officially terminated due to her lack of contact with Jason. She simply dropped out of sight and did not respond to extensive search efforts. Jason's permanency plan was changed to adoption, and he was put on the waiting list for foster home placement. I learned that the first placement in a preadoptive home failed, and he had to be returned to the residence. However, the second placement apparently was a better match and Jason remains with this family.

Jason had difficulty with termination of therapy. Some major regressive episodes occurred. For weeks he refused to leave his classroom, and even getting him into the therapy office became a struggle. Nevertheless, we worked through these difficulties, and Jason left our therapy relationship in a fairly good frame of mind. We completed a scrapbook together that contained pictures of me, the therapy office, his classroom and teachers, and a narrative of the time we had spent together in therapy. This was a significant help for Jason in his adjustment to my leaving, and the scrapbook became a kind of transitional object for him. I also saw the positive side of the termination: Jason would now experience a separation, not unlike others he would face in his life, that resulted not from his "badness," but from impersonal events outside of his control.

I believe the therapy was successful in helping Jason grieve the many losses associated with his poor maternal attachment, separation from significant love objects, and experience of being abused. He began to see himself as someone who is lovable and worthwhile. The timing of the play therapy intervention, although outside of my control, was critical. When therapy began, I believed that Jason was headed for big trouble; conduct disorder and delinquency seemed inevitable. However, Jason was still young. He had not yet generalized his sense of mistrust of parental figures to all authority figures. Therefore, he was more capable of developing a corrective emotional relationship with me.

Jason made significant strides in reducing his aggressive and provocative behaviors. He did show a pattern of regression when faced with new stresses. His hyperactivity continued to cause him problems, but psychotropic medication led to some improvements, especially in the school environment. Overall, I believe that Jason's play therapy helped him move forward in his development and in breaking the cycle of hostility and rejection that his earlier behaviors created.

DISCUSSION

This was one of my more difficult cases, as well as one of my most satisfying cases. When I first met Jason, I had never seen a child who appeared to be as hyperactive and poignantly conflicted. When the therapy ended, I felt it was partially complete. Whereas his improvement was unmistakable, he still exhibited difficulties in his emotional and social functioning. Jason faced many struggles ahead, and he would need a good friend to rely on to make sense of the changes in a way that was self-affirming.

I was pleasantly surprised at the therapeutic effectiveness of the game playing that went on during the therapy sessions. Game playing broke through Jason's resistance to play. It helped lessen his hyperactivity so that he could participate in the therapy process and develop trust in me. Game playing became a blank screen onto which Jason projected aspects of his psychic life. Finally, game playing proved to be an adequate modality by which Jason could confront his fears, his hurts, and his wishes and desires, and subsequently learn new and more adaptive ways of thinking and behaving.

My surprise at the effectiveness of game play was a result of the mitigation of the concerns I had at the beginning of therapy regarding the potential limitations of game play. I was worried that the rules and regulations of the various games offered would hinder Jason's self-expression. Previously, much of game playing I had done in therapy was with older latency-age children (8- to 12-year-old), who generally were much more concerned with following the rules of games. With these children, I had found that emotional expression and discussion of conflictual material typically occurred outside the game.

What Jason taught me was that, if the players are willing, any game can be modified in order to reduce its structure and requirements for rule-bound behavior. The therapist can introduce stories and fantasies into the game rather easily. Game pieces become characters, the goal of reaching "home" becomes a metaphor for separation and reunification, and the interaction of the players in the game becomes an expression of the child's coping skills and interaction style.

On the other hand, the therapist can introduce new rules and codes of behavior into game play to create even more structure than is already explicit in the game's instructions. The flexibility of games made them especially suitable for Jason. Initially, he relied on the structure of games, fortified by a high level of directedness from me, just to become engaged in the process of play. Movement games provided an alternative to unstructured play, which Jason found threatening. Later on in therapy, he required a less-structured approach, and games proved to be useful in promoting expression.

REFERENCES

Ainsworth, M. D. S. (1979). Infant–mother attachment. *American Psychologist* 34: 932–937.

Barkley, R. (1990). *Attention Deficit Hyperactivity Disorder: A Handbook for Diagnosis and Treatment*. New York: Guilford.

Baumeister, R. F. (1986). *Identity: Cultural Change and the Struggle for Self*. New York: Oxford University Press.

—— (1987). How the self became a problem: a psychological review of historical research. *Journal of Personality and Social Psychology* 52:163–176.

Baumeister, R. F., and Senders, P. S. (1988). Identity development and the role structure of children's games. *The Journal of Genetic Psychology* 150:19–37.

Beiser, H. R. (1979). Formal games in diagnosis and therapy. *Journal of Child Psychology* 18:48–490.

Berlin, I. N. (1986). The use of competitive games in play therapy. In *Game Play: Therapeutic Uses of Childhood Games*, ed. C. Schaefer and S. Reid, pp. 197–214. New York: Wiley.

Bow, J. N., and Goldberg, T. E. (1986). Therapeutic uses of games with a fine motor component. In *Game Play: Therapeutic Uses of Childhood Games*, ed. C. Schaefer and S. Reid, pp. 243–256. New York: Wiley.

Cooper, S., and Wanerman, L. (1977). *Children in Treatment: A Primer for Beginning Psychotherapists*. New York: Brunner/Mazel.

Dodge, K. A., and Frame, C. L. (1982). Social cognitive biases and deficits in aggressive boys. *Child Development* 53: 620–635.

Dodge, K. A., and Newman, J. P. (1981). Biased decision making processes in aggressive boys. *Journal of Abnormal Psychology* 90: 375–379.

Erikson, E. (1968). *Identity: Youth and Crisis*. New York: W. W. Norton.

Farber, E. A., and Egeland, B. (1987). Invulnerability among abused and neglected children. In *The Invulnerable Child*, ed. E. J. Anthony and B. J. Cohler, pp. 253–288. New York: Guilford.

Freud, A. (1949). Aggression in relation to emotional development. In *The Writings of Anna Freud, 1967–81*, vol. 3, pp. 118–131. New York: International Universities Press.

—— (1970). The concept of the rejecting mother. In *Parenthood: Its Psychology and Psychopathology*, ed. E. J. Anthony and T. Benedek, pp. 376–386. Boston: Little, Brown.

Frey, D. E. (1986). Communication boardgames with children. In *Game Play: Therapeutic Uses of Childhood Games*, ed. C. Schaefer and S. Reid, pp. 21–40. New York: Wiley.

Gardner, R. A. (1986). The game of checkers in child therapy. In *Game Play: Therapeutic Uses of Childhood Games*, ed. C. Schaefer and S. Reid, pp. 215–232. New York: Wiley.

—— (1988). *The Story Telling Card Game*. Cresskill, NJ: Creative Therapeutics.

Green, A. H. (1978). Psychiatric treatment of abused children. *Journal of the American Academy of Child Psychiatry* 17: 356–371.

Guttman, H. A. (1989). Children in families with emotionally disturbed parents. In *Children in Family Contexts: Perspectives on Treatment*, ed. L. Combrinck-Graham, pp. 252–276. New York: Guilford.

In, P. A., and McDermott, J. F., Jr. (1976). The treatment of child abuse: play therapy with a 4-year-old child. *Journal of the American Academy of Child Psychiatry* 15: 430–440.

Kohut, H. (1971). *The Analysis of the Self: A Systematic Approach to the Psychoanalytic Treatment of Narcissistic Disorders*. New York: International Universities Press.

Loomis, E. A. (1957). The use of checkers in handling certain resistances is child therapy and child analysis. *Journal of the American Psychoanalytic Association* 5:130–135.

Mahler, M., Pine, F., and Bergman, A. (1975). *The Psychological Birth of the Human Infant: Symbiosis and Individuation*. New York: Basic Books.

Martin, H. P. (1972). The child and development. In *Helping the Battered Child and his Family*, ed H. C. Kemp and R. E. Helfer, pp. 94–103. Philadelphia: Lippincott.

Masur, C. (1991). The crisis of early maternal loss: unresolved grief of 6-year-old Chris in foster care. In *Play Therapy for Children in Crisis: A Casebook for Practitioners*, ed. N. B. Webb, pp. 164–176. New York: Guilford.

Mead, G. H. (1934). *Mind, Self, and Society*. Chicago: University of Chicago Press.

Meeks, J. (1970). Children who cheat at games. *Journal of Child Psychiatry* 9:157–174.

Meichenbaum, D., and Goodman, J. (1971). Training impulsive children to talk to themselves: a means of developing self-control. *Journal of Abnormal Psychology* 77:115–126.

Mitchell, E. D., and Masson, B. S. (1948). *The Theory of Play*. New York: Burns.

Morse, C. W., Sahler, O. J., and Friedman, S. B. (1970). A three-year follow-up study of abused and neglected children. *American Journal of Diseases in Children* 120: 439–446.

Nasby, W., Hayden, B., and dePaulo, B. M. (1979). Attributional bias among aggressive boys to interpret unambiguous social stimuli as displays of hostility. *Journal of Abnormal Psychology* 89: 459–468.

O'Connor, K. J. (1991). *The Play Therapy Primer*. New York: Wiley.

Osofsky, J. D., and Connors, K. (1979). Mother–infant interaction: an integrative view of a complex system. In *Handbook of Infant Development*. ed. J. D. Osofsky, pp. 519–548. Lexington, MA: Lexington Books.

Peller, L. E. (1954). Libidinal development as reflected in play. *Psychoanalysis* 3:3–11.

Piaget, J. (1962). *Play, Dreams, and Imitation in Childhood*. New York: W. W. Norton.

Reid, S. E. (1992). Game play. In *Therapeutic Ingredients of Childhood Play*, 2nd ed., ed. C. Schaefer, pp. 323–348. New York: Jason Aronson.

Remkus, J. M. (1991). Repeated foster placement and attachment failure: the case of Joseph, age 3. In *Play Therapy for Children in Crisis: A Casebook for Practitioners*, ed. N. B. Webb, pp. 143–163. New York: Guilford.

Schachter, R. S. (1986). Techniques of kinetic psychotherapy. In *Game Play: Therapeutic Uses of Childhood Games*, ed. C. Schaefer and S. Reid, pp. 95–107. New York: Wiley.

Serok, S., and Blum, A. (1983). Therapeutic uses of games. *Residential Group Care and Treatment* 1:3–14.

Sroufe, L. A., and Waters, E. (1977). Attachment as an organizational construct. *Child Development* 48: 1184–1199.

Strachey, J. (1962). *The Standard Edition of the Psychological Works of Sigmund Freud*. Vol. 1. London: Hogarth.

Sutton-Smith, B., and Roberts, J. M. (1971). The cross-cultural and psychological study of games. *International Review of Sport Sociology* 6: 79–87.

Swanson, A. J. (1986). Using games to improve self-control deficits in children. In *Game Play: Therapeutic Uses of Childhood Games*, ed. C. Schaefer and S. Reid, pp. 233–242. New York: Wiley.

Willock, B. (1987). The devalued self—a second facet of narcissistic vulnerability in the aggressive, conduct-disordered child. *Psychoanalytic Psychology* 4: 219–240.

17

Two By Two: A Filial Therapy Case Study

Louise F. Guerney, PH.D., and Ann D. Welsh, M.S.

INTRODUCTION TO FILIAL THERAPY

It has been nearly thirty years since the concept of parents serving as change agents for their children—with close instruction and supervision from professionals—has been on the scene (Axline 1969, Guerney 1983). In spite of a legion of advocates and much empirical evidence that it is effective, filial therapy (FT), the method that employs this concept, is not as widely used as its success would indicate it could be. We are not sure about the reasons for this, but informal comment suggests that many therapists believe that parents really are too unavailable physically or psychologically to be partners in the play therapy of their children. Or, as some child therapists have told us, they really do not know how to work with parents directly. Instead, they rely on other professionals to see parents. Filial therapy provides a meaningful way for play therapists to expand their role to parent and family work (Guerney 1983, Guerney and Guerney 1985). Play therapists can train and supervise parents in the child-centered play therapy methods of Axline (1969). This powerful method has the means for changing both child and parent behaviors.

We are hoping through this case study that many more practitioners will see that using FT could be very much to their advantage, and, more importantly, helpful to the clients they work with. We would like to interest practitioners in developing the capability to include FT in their therapeutic repertoires. When therapists use FT, they generally achieve good results, frequently much better than anyone can imagine—for example, in working with abusing mothers in an inner-city child welfare agency. Assigning parents a real part in the therapy of their children not only is a recognition of their importance in their children's lives, but also a powerful message to them that they can be a positive rather than a destructive force for their children. This message of hope for parent–child relationships creates an attitude in parents that opens them to new information and professional assistance. Further, the method requires special instruction and observation of parents interacting with their children, so that parents are not sent away simply with vague advice, for example, "Your child is trying to get your attention. You should figure out ways to provide attention more frequently." Generally, except for strict behavioral approaches, the "figuring out" will amount to little more than a few suggestions about trying to be more available and alert to a child. Specific instruction, with feedback, becomes ever so much easier in the context of an observed play session. While some practitioners are concerned that they do not have a place to let parents play, they can usually find a way around this if they are convinced that the method will be helpful. For example, in the inner-city child welfare agency referred to earlier, social workers have parents play in the social workers' offices—far from ideal, but more effective than merely talking to parents about how they might handle home situations differently.

The expectation that parents can serve as the change agents for their children puts a burden upon therapists to be extremely supportive of parents while teaching them. The filial therapist must handle parents' concerns about meeting the responsibilities, objections, and difficulties in carrying out the specific play session behaviors and understanding what their children are trying to communicate, with empathy. Since empathy tends to be a furthering response, parents will frequently at this point discuss their feelings about the process, their family values, their personal conflicts, and other issues that may be interfering with their relationships to their children. The learning of play sessions seems to serve as a catalyst to material that might take months or might never come up in more traditional counseling sessions. Parents receive the same kind of therapeutic understanding and acceptance from the filial therapist that they are learning to give to their children in the play session. In the context of learning play therapy methods, parents' own concerns provide rich material for discussion. However, the filial therapist must never forget that the overarching goal is to teach parents how to relate to their children through the medium of the play session (Glazer-Waldman et al. 1992). Thus, FT has been called a "didactic and dynamic" approach (Andronico et al. 1967).

Another advantage of the FT approach for parents is that they are learning a new and unique method, one that no one expects them to know. Therefore, no expected performance standard exists for them. Their accomplishments and failings in learning *the method* are only that. No one will view their play session performances as global evaluations of them as parents. It is one thing to be told that you are erring when you are being your "parent-self"; it is another to be reminded that the method calls for a different behavior in the play sessions. Of course, when giving feedback, the filial therapist always emphasizes anything parents do in the right direction and limits corrective feedback to only the essential. In fact, for parents (e.g., those who are extremely controlling of their children in real life) really struggling with trying to be more accepting in play sessions, the filial therapist metes out corrective feedback in doses that the parents can handle so that they will always feel that they are making acceptable progress. Of course, while parents are learning to play therapeutically with their children, their children are reaping all of the benefits of play therapy and, furthermore, are learning to perceive their newly accepting parents more positively.

History and Evidence of Effectiveness of Filial Therapy

Having sketched out some of the advantages of FT, it seems appropriate to provide a bit of its history and the rationale for its development, and to cite sources for research that support its efficacy.

In the 1960s, Bernard Guerney developed filial therapy, now sometimes called child relationship enhancement family therapy (CREFT), in recognition of its parent–child (i.e., filial) relationship potential. Guerney undertook the development of the method because of the following beliefs. First, he observed, along with other child therapists, that parents frequently felt alienated from the typical child therapy process and, as a result, removed children from therapy prematurely. Second, he concluded, after years of casework, that parents were not generally malicious or disturbed, but rather lacked the skills to develop positive relationships with, and discipline of, their children. He also recognized that parents have the most meaningful and enduring relationship with their children. Experts temporarily present in their lives, no matter how therapeutic, could not begin to have the impact on children that their parents do. Finally, he postulated that therapists and, more importantly, their clients, would make greater therapeutic gains when parents had a meaningful role in the therapy. This process would reduce resistance and defensiveness and, thus, also reduce therapeutic failures (Guerney 1964).

Of course, this was a radical idea, and Guerney, together with colleagues at Rutgers University, began subjecting FT to empirical study to see if the evidence supported his beliefs. Resistance to the notion that parents, who so frequently contribute to child problems, could serve as primary change agents and achieve positive outcomes has diminished over the years as evidence has increased for the efficacy of FT. Other approaches, such as behavioral therapy, have also successfully employed parents as change agents (Eyberg 1988, Forehand and King 1974). However, the seeming complexity of the FT method appears to remain a concern to many current therapists. This case presentation should be useful to practitioners who believe in the value of the approach, but have not attempted it yet for logistical reasons.

Most early FT studies included only mothers because they usually were the help-seekers. Results of several studies indicated that they could learn the play therapy method and that their doing so resulted in improved behavior in their children in the play sessions (Stover and Guerney 1967). In a large study with fifty-one mothers stretching out over three years, the researchers found that all children reduced major difficulties; most moved to the problem-free category (Guerney and Stover 1971). A follow-up study of the children and their parents two years later indicated that children remained improved, and only one needed any further counseling (Guerney 1975). Studies done more recently at Pennsylvania State University using both mothers and fathers indicated that children's problem behaviors were reduced by more than half. Parents improved significantly on their ability to be accepting of their children (Sywulak 1979). These effects remained three to five years later, across three waves of parents (Sensue 1981). Other research done elsewhere has also supported the efficacy of FT (e.g., Glass 1986, Wall 1979). Even developmental psychologists have generated support for the approach while examining child compliance (Parpal and Maccoby 1985). In observed play sessions, these researchers found that mothers who used methods of empathy, permitted the child to lead, and refrained from negative feedback had children who complied significantly better than a group of mothers who had not learned to follow the above pattern (Parpal and Maccoby 1985).

Results from the major study (Guerney and Stover 1971) showed that noncompliant children improved as well as withdrawn and mixed–behavior pattern children (i.e., both aggressive and withdrawn). Noncompliant children did not improve as significantly as the other child groups, but improved sufficiently enough for the researchers to be able to conclude that the treatment would have value for all types of child problems. The authors' observational experience with noncompliant children in FT is that children improve from the therapy, and parents become much better able to establish limits (as learned for conducting their play sessions) and to make requests in language that facilitates child compliance. This interactional pattern reduces unnecessary power struggles. Thus, we recognize that the FT improvements are a blend of child and parent changes.

Which Clients and What Problems Are Appropriate for FT?

To make a decision to employ FT, practitioners first need to know the population for whom it can be used and how to arrive at a decision to use FT instead of a professional play therapist or a non–play therapy approach.

We believe that any child for whom child-centered play therapy would be the treatment of choice would be a candidate for inclusion in FT with the following provisos. At least one parent would need to get to the treatment site on a fairly regular basis. *Anticipated* regular attendance is basic. If, in the intake procedures, the parents miss appointments for various reasons out of their control (e.g., a car that does not work, repeated personal illness, etc.), FT might not be feasible for them. (Such parents might well miss appointments for their child for any kind of therapy. In such cases, we believe it best not to recommend FT and try, instead, to use an alternative approach that relies less on parent involvement. The problem of the unavailable parent is universal in child therapy and in no way peculiar to requirements of the FT method. Any therapist will attest to that, even those who work with affluent families.

In making decisions regarding FT, the therapist must also assess the question of psychological availability. Our experience is that only serious hindrances in this domain should prevent the FT recommendation. The therapist should not rule out parents with no genuine emotional problems, who simply object to the notion that they will need to be involved instead of an experienced professional serving as the primary change agent. The latter expectation is consistent with the notion of "taking in" a child for help and, in most instances, represents a temporary difficulty in shifting expectations, rather than resistance. Explanations and sincere and prolonged empathy toward their concerns will generally convince such parents to give FT a try. The truly unavailable are those parents too depressed or otherwise mentally or emotionally disturbed to take on additional responsibilities. These parents can make some gains in FT because of the empathic and accepting interpersonal atmosphere, but they may have problems learning the play session skills. They do not have the requisite psychological energy to conduct FT play sessions. Parents who have less serious problems (e.g., anxious, phobic, substance abusers, etc.) generally can handle the task (perhaps via an individually tailored variation) and gain from the nurturance and concern the therapist shows for them.

Therapeutic Procedures

Typically, the filial therapist sees parents and children on a weekly basis at a treatment site. FT proceeds through five stages:

1. The therapist demonstrates therapeutic play to the parents, using their referred children, and also other children in the family, that is, all children in the family who are old enough to play in any way (such as basketball for older children).
2. Parents practice play sessions, supervised by the therapist.
3. Parents play independently with their children; the therapist provides feedback in regular meetings with the parents.
4. The therapist encourages transfer and generalization of playroom skills to real life where appropriate.
5. The therapist and the parents evaluate progress and plan for finishing up.

The latter usually includes a "special times" program to maintain parent–child times together, with the parent in an accepting role, for as long as possible. At stage 4, the filial therapist usually tries to teach the parents any additional parenting skills that they need beyond those transferable from the playroom. The filial therapist uses the book *Parenting: A Skills Training Manual* (Guerney 1988) as a source for the home skills training.

The filial therapist encourages the parents to include all of the children of the family to try to prevent rivalry for parental attention and/or to spare the referral child from feeling singled out as a problem. Also, if pathology is "passed on," as the family therapists would believe, this would serve as a preventive action.

Variations on the Basic Procedures

The method is very robust and can be effective even when major modifications are necessary to accommodate child or parent difficulties in participation. Since FT play sessions are always only one child and one parent, practitioners sometimes become alarmed at the thought of parents needing to conduct individual play sessions for each of their *multiple* children, especially if there is only a single parent involved. With single parent situations abounding, this is an issue indeed. We would like to add, however, that even with two parent families, if only one parent is willing to participate, he or she can use FT. While it is certainly preferable to include both parents, this can be an unrealistic expectation and should not preclude the use of FT. Our studies have shown (e.g., Guerney and Stover 1971) that clinically significant improvements can take place when only mothers are involved, even when there is a father in the wings in one way or another.

What we do to make the burden lighter on the parent(s) is to stagger play sessions so that no parent is doing more than two sessions a week. The target (referral) child always receives a weekly session, while the parents play with the other, presumably less needy siblings, every other week. If both parents play with a single target child and there are no other siblings, that child will receive two sessions per week. If this seems too burdensome to the parents, then they can alternate weeks. The important principle is to keep the task manageable for the parents so that they will not stop playing. We have confidence that FT is robust enough to accept the schedules that will keep parents going. Of course, they cannot miss several sessions in a row. That does not constitute a treatment of any kind. Even when the sessions are done at home, the therapist must keep in touch with and, better yet, see the parents at least every other week, so that the parents will feel accountable for staying with the approach. In extreme cases, where parents give up for real reasons (e.g., their prolonged illness) or for simply a failure to cooperate, a professional therapist can then see the child for a play therapy series.

Home Versus Office Sessions

FT, as originally developed, uses the procedure of parents conducting play sessions at home when they are reasonably proficient in conducting them. However, many practitioners, particularly those in private practice, schedule all of the parent–child sessions in their offices and observe every session with no home sessions. The parent(s)' play session(s), followed by feedback, then some discussion about progress at home, constitute the therapy hour. This is a very effective way to employ FT — especially where parents have no reasonable place or time to play at home. It is certainly preferable to excluding parents from FT, the only other alternative. The authors like to have parents conduct play sessions at home independent of the feedback and progress sessions because, in our opinion, this format enables parents to transfer skills and attitudes learned in play sessions a little more easily to the outside world. We also prefer to work with small groups of parents for FT, because of the benefits of group support. Having some sessions at home makes these group sessions easier to schedule.

However, as in the case described later in this chapter, sometimes parents do not have places to play at home. We then allow them to come in and play at our treatment site, and, unless specially arranged, we do not observe them at that time. Parents' demonstration play sessions during the regular meetings continue and we always observe those. We also request written reports from parents about unobserved sessions.

A typical meeting where the parents are conducting play sessions at home follows this sequence:

1. While the therapist observes, parents conduct play sessions with their child(ren) for 15 minutes per child. (Usually there are two such sessions per meeting.)
2. The therapist and parent(s) discuss the play session(s) feedback, and the filial therapist provides reinforcement.
3. Playing parent(s) discuss real-life child, parent–child, and parent issues.
4. The therapist makes plans for the next meeting and makes any necessary assignments for parent(s)' home practice.

One advantage to the play therapy sessions being held at home, with only short demonstrations observed at the treatment site, is that the filial therapist can hold observation/discussion meetings every two or three weeks if scheduling logistics dictate. Parents continue on their own, with encouragement to call the therapist about any issues. Should problems arise in relation to play sessions, the filial therapist can then schedule meetings more frequently. In geographical areas where travel to treatment sites is difficult, less frequent meetings with regular, scheduled phone parent–therapist conferences in between are a practical alternative.

The major advantage to eliminating parent–child home play sessions is that the filial therapist does not have to observe additional office sessions over and above those conducted in the regular therapy sessions. This does cut down on time required for FT. To our knowledge, no researcher has conducted a study to see if transfer to real life of parent attitudes and skills learned in the play sessions is slower when parents play only at the treatment site and not also at home.

PRESENTING PROBLEM AND BACKGROUND DATA

At our Pennsylvania State University treatment site, The Individual and Family Consultation Center, our question regarding therapy recommendations is only: "Will FT be appropriate for this case or not?" The usual diagnostic question in most other treatment units is: "What kind of therapy, of all those that our therapists are capable of providing, will be the best?" In contrast, we ask what portion or portions of FT and what FT procedures we can employ for the benefit of the child and parent. We are able to limit our services to play therapy and FT, and we want to do this because we believe that FT is the most helpful treatment approach whenever it is feasible. If, as discussed earlier in this chapter, parents are not available to be trainees, we will then recommend play therapy by a professional therapist and/or we will work with parents around parenting skills. If our assessment suggests that other methods, for example, behavioral therapy or psychiatric methods, are more appropriate, we would refer the family to, and help the parents connect with, other suitable services.

When it is clear, as in the case of the Austin family here described, that we can recruit both parents to play and give them adequate supervision, we conclude that the much-preferred route of FT is appropriate. We try to include parents in groups (four to eight parents), but when we do not have a group ready to start, we must further decide whether a wait of two or three months would be detrimental. The wait would follow two intake sessions that parents see as very therapeutic in their own right, and perhaps an additional pretherapy meeting or two to deal with any pressing problems. In some instances, we decide to start treatment immediately, either because (a) of the level of stress being experienced by the child and/or parents, (b) the family is moving soon, or (c) pressure is on from the outside (e.g., a school) to bring about change.

The Austin family fell into the latter category. The preschool staff was complaining about Billy, the son, being too aggressive with other children. No group was close to being formed, so we used the single-family variation for this family. A second variation was that the

family at first, because of cramped space, could not conduct play
sessions at home and had to come into our center to hold their own play
sessions. The third variation was the inclusion of observation and
supervision for some of these sessions that would typically be unsupervised, that is, separate and independent of the weekly meetings with
the therapist. The second author (Ann Welsh), an advanced filial
therapist-in-training, was willing to add this extra component in response to the parents' anxious desire for immediate feedback. Once they
stopped playing at the center, I (A.W.) did not observe play sessions
other than when the family came in for regular sessions. By this time,
the parents felt very confident of their ability to conduct the sessions on
their own.

This case was chosen for this chapter in part because of its variations.
Also, since feedback exchanges were between only the therapist and a
single family rather than a group, reporting the case is clearer for the
reader. We encourage and greatly value the feedback and exchange
among parents in groups. However, the quantity of discussion would
have made reporting of it cumbersome for readers to follow.

We also chose this case because of the obvious problem of the
nonreferred oldest child and the way this was played out in the play
sessions and thus understood by both parents. They were able to
manage their children much more effectively at home at a relatively
early point in the series of 18 regular sessions held with them.

Family Background

The Austin family was seen over a 4½ month period for FT training.
Billy's (age 4 years, 11 months) teacher had referred the family because
of Billy's disruptive classroom behavior of shouting at and jumping on
other children; his unwillingness to do class work; aggression at home;
having no friends; and visual, motor, and language deficits. Mrs. A.
described him as a bright, loving, and even-tempered child, but aggressive and with low self-esteem. She recognized his need for improved
social skills. Billy expressed aggression in the intake play session
consistent with teacher and parent descriptions.

In addition to Billy's problems, it became apparent that his mother
was also very concerned about Beth (age 9 years, 4 months). Mrs. A.
related that she had a "love/hate" relationship with Beth, who was
domineering and overcontrolling. Mrs. A. felt Beth was trying to come
between her and her husband. Beth's controlling behavior was seen in
the intake play session when all three siblings (including Joy, the nearly
3-year-old sister who exhibited no problems) were together.

The Austin's family life was fairly chaotic—they had no routines and irregular schedules. Their income was relatively low and making ends meet was a problem. Mr. A. was a draftsman and Mrs. A. worked part-time as a cook for a day-care centre. They lived in a crowded apartment, but hoped to move to a larger house soon. In the meantime, they had increasing problems in structuring everyday routines, such as bedtime and mealtime or getting ready to leave the house. The children were often not in bed before 10 or 11 o'clock. Beth had particularly severe bedtime problems. She would go to bed when *she* was ready (midnight to 2 A.M.), only if a parent joined her in her bed and stayed until she was asleep. This often meant the parent fell asleep and remained for the night. If they tried to insist that she go to bed alone, Beth had a screaming spell, frequently after midnight, when it was disturbing to Joy, who shared Beth's room. Mrs. A. revealed another factor—she had been physically abused as a child. She worked fervently to prevent abuse in her family, locking herself in the bathroom for as much as a half hour at a time when she was angry and not sure of her control.

THERAPEUTIC CONCEPTUALIZATION

During the first intake interview, Mrs. A. was very aware of Beth and Billy's problems, but was reluctant to do filial therapy. She preferred to have play therapy for the children. At the second intake interview, both parents were present and expressed the need for help with (a) communicating with the children, (b) getting Beth to realize she was a *child*, and (c) improving Billy's social skills. A recurring issue was the parents' concern regarding Beth's control of them and family activities. Mr. and Mrs. A. agreed that Beth "thinks she's a grown-up" and needed to learn that she could not control the family. They talked about the bedtime problems and sibling rivalry. They were frustrated with their inability to control their family life.

Prior to the present intake, Mrs. A. had made two previous contacts with the consultation center. On the first occasion, she attended one of the two scheduled intake sessions and decided she could not go ahead with treatment at that time. On a second occasion, she called and spoke at length and asked to have intake forms mailed, but failed to follow up, explaining upon inquiry that Billy had to have surgery soon on his underdeveloped arm and that they could not undertake anything else. The third contact resulted in a serious involvement. This was about two years after the previous contacts.

I presented FT as the recommended treatment. I explained the FT process to Mr. and Mrs. A., with emphasis on their learning new ways to interact with the children, and with the children having a special place and time where they could be in control. I discussed the possibility that I might need to teach them additional skills, such as specific social skills or structuring family matters, toward the end of the filial therapy program. They were not sure that they could do FT, that it would help Beth's and Billy's personal problems, or that Beth would cooperate and play with the toys. However, they felt they had to try something and agreed, with some hesitancy, to try FT.

PROCESS OF FILIAL THERAPY

Parents

The next four sessions included a demonstration play session with me and one of the children followed by a training/supervision session with the parents and me. The first demonstration play session was with Beth. It was a very moving experience for the parents. They observed Beth behaving as a nice, pleasant *child*, one they did not see at home. During the interview/training session following the play, the parents expressed amazement that Beth actually played. With help from me, they were able to verbalize that she really could act as a child, something they had a hard time seeing because of Beth's behavior at home. They were able to see that Beth did not necessarily feel competent and grown up, even if she was domineering and controlling.

Mrs. A. directly stated that she needed help with limit setting with Beth and with the aggressive behavior of Billy. She tended to look for the hidden meaning of specific behaviors (e.g., during the play demonstration with Billy, she thought Billy must be afraid of policemen when he tied up the police puppet). Through discussion, I helped her to see things from a process perspective (e.g., when Billy tied up the policeman puppet, he was instead enjoying controlling the situation).

Mr. A. focused on learning the technical aspects of FT. Both parents progressed rapidly in their ability to structure play sessions, make empathic responses, and set limits in the training sessions. This was partially attributable to their participation in a parenting skills group I had offered during the previous fall. During that group, they had begun to learn empathic responding, limit setting, and structuring in family situations.

Control continued to be a problem for both parents. Beth voiced resistance to returning after the first session, and two weeks later her parents showed hesitancy and dread in facing up to Beth and telling her it was her week to come. When I said we would still expect Beth to come, Mrs. A. got very quiet and asked to be excused from practice play. As it turned out, Beth was happy to come the following week and did not resist. In spite of this cooperation, Mrs. A. mentioned a television show about parents being afraid of their children. She accepted my reflection that that was "scary" to her and seemed similar to her own feelings regarding Beth at home and about being in the playroom alone with her.

Beth

During the early play sessions with me, Beth was pleasant and polite and seemed to enjoy the play. Several times she degraded her own ability and got frustrated and disgusted with herself. She expressed this through facial expressions and body language, as well as by cessation of the play activity. For instance, she stopped playing a ring toss game because she could not get rings on the post. Then she used masks to have "puppet" people try the ring toss and thought the boy puppet would do better than she. It appeared she was protecting herself from failure by distancing herself through the use of the mask and puppets. She commented she was not very good when drawing with crayons. When Mr. and Mrs. A. used reflective responses at home, she reacted by yelling at them not to talk that way to her. She continued this type of reaction longer with her mother than with her father. She threatened that she would not come back to play sessions, but was willing when the time came.

Billy

Billy's general theme at this stage was mild aggressive play with the rope, guns, bear, and puppets. He particularly enjoyed controlling toys by tying them up. He also did exploration and water play, going from one activity to another. He sometimes asked for help when he could not accomplish a task. The parents' use of reflective responses at home helped him calm down for short periods of time.

Parents Begin Play Sessions with Supervision

After having four weeks of demonstration play and practice with the therapist, the parents agreed to practice with the children. Mr. A. was scheduled to play with Billy. Mrs. A. was to have her first session with Joy so she could first play with the child we expected would be easiest for her to play with. Including Joy had the added advantage of including all the family's children, one of the goals of FT. By this time the parents were beginning to feel more comfortable with giving empathic responses. In fact, Mr. A. had used them at work and had seen good results. He was becoming enthusiastic and looking forward to starting play sessions.

Mrs. A. was nearly euphoric after her first session with Joy, and the next week during supervision she announced she was going to school someday to become a play therapist. From this point on, Mrs. A. was totally "sold" on and identified with the FT method. She made steady progress in improving her reflections and within a month was able to set a limit for Billy and follow through on the time limit with Beth. She still had to think to get at feelings, but often reflected them accurately on the second reflection. Mr. A. felt awkward and unsure of himself at first. However, he made many good reflective responses and seemed to understand what was happening with the children most of the time. He, too, was able to set a limit with Billy and with Beth.

The parents alternated weeks in playing with Beth and Billy. Each week one of them played for a short while with Joy. The following excerpts are from Mr. A.'s first session with Beth and Mrs. A.'s first session with Billy, held during the weekly FT sessions at the consultation center.

First Play Session: *Beth and Mr. A.*	*Mr. A.*	*Supervisory Session*
Beth seemed unsure what to do upon entering and asked Mr. A. what she should do.	Mr. A. answered that in the playroom she could do anything she wanted.	In supervision, Mr. A. was complimented on not giving her a suggestion, but was reminded to reflect her feeling of being unsure. I also reminded him that the limit is "You can do *almost* anything you want to do."

She began her play with her three standby activities of ring toss, jump rope, and drawing.

Mr. A. made such reflections as "I can't see that," or "That surprised you."

It was suggested that he try to get beyond the activity reflections and say such things as, "You don't want me to see that."

A few minutes into the session, Beth started reading long passages from a puzzle book she had with her when she came into the playroom. She asked her father questions to fill in the blanks in the puzzles and thoroughly enjoyed being in charge.

Mr. A. answered questions and once or twice reflected, "You're really enjoying your stories." He seemed somewhat awkward and uncomfortable with the puzzle reading going on for most of the session.

Mr. A. felt it was very difficult to reflect feelings in this situation where she read and he answered questions. He was worried that Beth would continue to want to bring in a book and the play sessions would be difficult for him. I complimented him on reflecting her enjoyment, and we discussed that we could set a limit on bringing in books if it were a recurring problem. [It never came up again.] He seemed to feel her need to control him was related to her need to be successful and in charge of her own activities. This showed growth in his understanding of Beth's control issue.

First Session:
Billy and Mrs. A.

Mrs. A.

Billy headed right for the water and picked up the basin in his first session with Mrs. A.

Mrs. A. reflected, "You're strong!"

In supervision, I said I was glad she was getting at feelings and suggested she look for ways to frame the comment from *his* viewpoint so it would not sound like her judgment. An example would be, "You feel real strong when you can do that." [Billy's left arm movement is impaired.]

Moving around a great deal, he cleaned the blackboard, tried to play with the ring toss, and asked a lot of questions.

Mrs. A. followed him around, staying *very* close. At one point she said, "You're wondering how it goes together and you're working at trying to figure it out."

I noted that Mrs. A. was staying "with" Billy, but told her to give him some more physical space. She was complimented on her handling of questions. We talked about what to do if he asks a question again after she has reflected "You're wondering . . ." I suggested they reflect in a new way working toward finding the feeling behind the question, or telling child that in the playroom he can decide.

"Sometimes I don't like it here." "All a times I like it better at home." [Billy's immature speech in play session is due to his language delay, not regression.]

Mrs. A. responded, "You'd really like to be home," and "You're feeling a little bit sad 'cause your buddies aren't here."

I told her I thought she went ahead of Billy by suggesting he missed his buddies, that maybe he was unsure in the new situation and felt safe and comfortable at home. We discussed staying "with" the children, not going beyond them and interpreting what we think is an issue.

Beth's and Billy's Progress in Play

A week after their first play sessions, the parents reported more positive and fewer negative times at home. Sibling fights and rivalry were lessening. They were thrilled that Beth had read Billy his bedtime story on two different nights. Beth rebelled at reflections once, but generally, all had a good week.

Over the next six weeks, alternating play sessions with mother and father, both Beth and Billy explored more of the toys, became more aggressive with the toys, and, later, were more relaxed and showed more enjoyment of the sessions. Beth started creating roles for her and her parents. Twice she played teacher while her father was a student.

She had a puppet show or telephone conversations with her mother. She was very controlling in her roles, but gradually began to let Mr. and Mrs. A. make a few decisions in the games. She also continued her three routines of jump rope, ring toss, and drawing. In these, she showed less frustration and was increasingly pleased and satisfied with her performance.

Billy played cowboys with guns and rope, shooting dinosaurs, and generally showing strength and power. Gradually he started drawing more and was very proud and pleased when he could demonstrate things he'd learned at school (e.g., writing his name and numbers). He seldom involved parents directly in his games except as an assistant.

Parents Hone Skills in Filial Therapy and Feel More Comfortable with Control

Mother

Mrs. A. learned to maintain an appropriate distance between herself and the children. She became adept at reflecting feelings at least on the second reflection, often giving the activity first and then the feeling. She used such reflections as, "You don't know . . . " "You're worried . . . , " "You're happy . . . , " or "You're so strong you can throw it across the room." She still missed feelings sometimes, but was able to see what she'd done when we discussed it. For example:

Billy and Mrs. A.	Mrs. A.	Supervisory Session
Billy knocked over the kitchen set and things fell all over the floor. He stood back and became very quiet and seemingly unsure.	Mrs. A. said, "You're feeling strong!"	I told the parents I thought that rather than feeling strong, Billy was overwhelmed by his level of aggression, and it might have helped to restructure after acknowledging his feelings. An example would be, when he looked unsure, to say, "If there is anything you shouldn't do, I'll tell you. Thus, he would know he had not actually erred.

Billy asked when he could leave, stayed quiet a little while, and then stayed without complaint until time was up.	Mrs. A. reflected on his wanting to leave.	Parents agreed his concern over aggression was probably what prompted the request to leave—not a real desire to stop the play session.

Mrs. A. was able to set limits with both children, shooting the gun at mirror for Billy, and leaving on time for Beth.

Father

Mr. A. learned to pace his reflections to suit the needs of each child, more frequent responses for Billy than for Beth. He became good at reflecting surface feelings. He made such comments as, "You want it perfect," "You like . . .," "You know all about . . .," and "Makes you feel big when . . ." He was self-critical of his reflections when Beth had long spells of drawing, even though he actually did quite well in this difficult situation. Both parents were able to reflect Beth's enjoyment of being in control and Mr. A. did not feel threatened when she shot him when he said the session was over. It went like this:

Beth and Father	Father	Supervision Session
	Mr. A. announced it was time to leave and headed for the door.	
Beth was holding the gun and deliberately shot Mr. A.		Mrs. A. thought Beth was angry! Mr. A. thought this was a sign she was trying to stay in control and test the limits. I agreed with Mr. A.
	Mr. A. said, "Beth, remember I said there were some things you can't do. In this room, you cannot shoot me with the gun."	Father said it felt good to set the limit, but was hard because Beth wouldn't leave.
Beth put down the gun, giggled a little, and remained in the room.		

Mr. A. left the room.

Beth followed her father.	Mr. A. wasn't sure what he would do if she hadn't followed him.
	When it was all over, it felt good to Mr. A. to be in control. I complimented him on his standing firm on the limit and not arguing or negotiating.

Independent Play Sessions Start for Family: Supervision Continues

One of the high points for the family was when they started family sessions without my presence. By this time they had had eleven training sessions and were ready to begin some unsupervised play. Mr. A. wanted to be sure they would get supervision very soon after the first time alone, hopefully the next day. We arranged to have them play one night alone and with supervision the next night. In the supervision session, they reported that their first sessions went very well, but neither parent wrote up the session as I had requested. The parents were obviously feeling pleased with their ability to conduct play sessions independently. They had a good time and felt that the children were relaxed and had a good time, more than when they knew I was watching them.

In the play session, Mrs. A. and Beth had played with an extended role play on the telephones. Mrs. A. felt herself slipping and had to remind herself it was play therapy, she was having so much fun. I helped her to see she could have stepped out of her role at times to reflect on feelings. She agreed and felt she could have reflected, "Boy, you're really having a lot of fun." She realized that even if it is obvious, it needs to be reflected in play therapy.

Mr. A. had played with Billy and felt he kept the pace of his reflections going. He found it easy to reflect on cowboy play, but difficult when Billy slammed around the kitchen set. I suggested "mad" or "frustrated."

The parents also reported progress in other areas. Both children were accepting empathic responses and even using them occasionally! Billy's teacher reported that his behavior in school was *much* better. He worked hard and no longer grabbed things or hit other children. Beth had not been screaming late at night at bedtime.

The following excerpts are from the supervised play sessions the night after the Austins' first independent sessions.

Beth and Mr. A., 12th Week of Training	Mr. A.	Supervision Session
Beth enters the room before Mr. A. and starts to set things up.		
"Hold it, don't come in yet. Don't come in!"		
	Mr. A. comes to door.	Mrs. A commented, "Beth really does want to be the boss, but she's giving us a little more freedom, giving me more freedom [in my play time with her]."
"I'm still doing something. I'll tell you when you can come in."	"You don't want me to see that."	
"Sit over there."		
	Mr. A. knocks. Beth opens door. (On his way to chair): "You'd asked before, Beth, if anyone was watching, Ann and Mom are watching. They are watching to see if I can do it [the play techniques]."	We had discussed Beth's questions about being watched and decided Mr. A. should bring it up and let her know just who was watching and why.
"You sit over there!" [pointing].	Mr. A. sits.	Mr. A. was very comfortable being ordered around in the role of student.
Beth starts school game and asks a question.	"Do you want me to answer that?"	I had told parents to ask questions if they were not sure what to do when put in a role.

"Who knows something about Pennsylvania?	"I do."	
"Yes, Tom?"	"It's one of the states."	Parents are to play down their role in a game, not take over with their advanced knowledge or ability.
Beth goes on with questions.	"You're thinking really hard to come up with a good one.	Mr. A. was reflecting intent and ability of Beth (complimented for his insight).
"Does anyone know who David Boal is?"	"You make this a hard question."	
"Do you know?"	"No. I think you like it when I don't know the answer to your questions."	Mr. A. was reflecting her feelings of pleasure and satisfaction shown by body language and facial expression. He stepped out of his role to reflect feelings and then returned to his role in game.
("Yes"). "David Boal was . . "	Mr. A. continued to play the student and to step out of role and reflect on her wanting to decide and be in control.	Both children had started agreeing when the parents had a particularly accurate reflection of feelings.
Beth continued an extended game of school. At times she would ask for "Tom's [the name she assigned her father in his student role] choice." If she didn't like it, she would have a vote on his answer with students' heads down on the desk. Then she would count imaginary hands until the vote came out to suit her.		Mr. A. said he was not sure what Beth was feeling except she was the teacher and in control. I agreed that was it and that he reflected accurately on that feeling. I also mentioned that the content of the school lesson was about the town where they were moving.

Ann: " . . . about that
town and school; she's
changing schools."

Mr. A.: "And she's
working it through; I
didn't think of that."

Ann: "You were getting
at Beth wanting to be the
one to decide and be in
control."

Both parents had missed the significance of the school play and were surprised to see it come out in the play session. They were so excited to be getting their own place, they had not thought about the children feeling uneasy about the move. We talked about it in connection with Billy's aggressive play also, and that he could feel in control in the playroom and be as tough as he needed to be. I suggested if they kept notes of sessions, it would be easier for them to realize when an issue came up. They agreed, but did not follow through. It is sometimes the case that parents do not write play session notes regularly.

Billy and Mrs. A., 12th Week of Training	*Mrs. A.*	*Supervisory Session*
Billy did his usual tough-guy play with rope, etc.	Mrs. A. reflected things were going just the way Billy wanted them to, and he was tough.	Mrs. A. is trying to put her reflection in terms of his feeling.
He started to write on paper with a white crayon, "I need help."	"You feel like you need help."	
He moves to write his name on the blackboard. "Me want you help me with the odder one."	"You want to know how to do a 'Y.' "	
"Uh-huh."	"Do you want me to use the chalk?"	She is asking for direction, a recommended response.

"Uh-huh."

"You want to hold the chalk." Mrs. A. helps and he continues with name.

He stands back with hands on hips and looks and smiles.

"Wow! You're happy about that; you did it all by yourself."

She is confirming that he feels competent, but it might have been better to stop after "happy about that," because she *did* help. Accuracy is stressed in feedback.

He maintains his stance.

"You're really pleased; you know how to write your name. So grown up to write your name."

I complimented Mrs. A. on her reflections.

"Me show Daddy this." Shy, pleased body stance and facial expression.

"You'd like to show Daddy; you're proud of it."

By reflecting his feeling, she is accepting his wanting to "show Daddy" without a discussion of whether he'll do it now. There was some hint via his body positioning that he might want to run out to Daddy at *that* moment.

He erases some of the writing and starts making squares with numbers in them, asking for help with some numerals. When he finishes, he stands back, pleased.

"It's time to go yet?"

"You're wondering if it is time to go yet."

Billy gets a strange look on his face.

Mr. A. thought it was a sour face and that Billy didn't like the reflection. I agreed. She should have recognized his desire to leave and said you'd like to leave.

Billy just stands there.	"You're tired."	During supervision I told Mrs. A. I thought this was not an accurate reflection.
Billy gets busy with another activity and drops the idea of leaving.		I thought Billy was wanting time over so he could show Daddy his work. Mr. A. thought so, too.

Independent Family Play Sessions Continue with Intermittent Supervision

We had a supervision/training session, as we had been doing each time I observed the parents play. They were planning to move within a month, so this seemed the logical time to go back and reinforce some of the parenting skills they had learned in the parenting group the previous fall. Therefore, we spent some time talking about structuring routines in their new home. Both parents expressed concern that Beth would start screaming at bedtime again. Bedtime problems had dropped out, but the parents were fearful they would start again when they were in a new house. They agreed, since it was school vacation, that they would buy her an alarm clock and make her responsible for getting up in order to get to her activity in the community. They would enforce the limit of her being in her room at bedtime, but would avoid arguing with her about the unenforceable limit of going to sleep at a certain time. We discussed other structuring skills during subsequent sessions.

We planned for the family to continue independent play sessions once a week in the consultation center. In addition, they would come in every two or three weeks for a supervised play session with one parent and one child. The parents wanted this structure to help them keep from drifting away from the method.

Three and a half weeks later they started holding their independent play sessions in their new home rather than in the center. The family room was arranged so one parent and one child could be there alone. There was water play available, but nothing that imposed unusual limits. Mrs. A. realized the phone needed to be removed during play times and arranged for this. It took a few times before it seemed like "real sessions" at home, but coming back to the center occasionally for a supervised play session seemed to help them focus.

RESULTS AND FOLLOW-UP

Six-Week Follow-Up

Six weeks after the last supervision, I made a follow-up call and talked to Mrs. A. She reported that they were continuing to have play sessions, which were going well. For two weeks they had missed the sessions and everyone could tell. In the course of the skills sessions, Mrs. A. had realized that in order to keep the family running smoothly, she needed schedules. Therefore, the family discussed the necessity of scheduling play sessions. Beth offered to write out a play schedule for the family. The play sessions again became regular and things returned to the same comfortable level experienced as when they were playing regularly.

Mrs. A. found that she wanted to spend more time with her children after she had had play sessions with them. This felt different to her than when she did not have play sessions. In fact, it had made such a difference to her that she recommended FT to a friend. The children were adjusting well to their new schools, liking them, and making friends.

One-Year Follow-Up

A telephone contact to Mrs. A. revealed that things continued to go very well for all the family members. Everyone was doing well in school, both scholastically and socially. Beth was much easier to live with. Mr. and Mrs. A. continued to do "special times" regularly. These were less structured, more informal versions of the play session. The children wanted them. The most interesting comments that Mrs. A. offered were in regard to the way she and Mr. A. reminded each other to empathize with the children and to use parenting skills they had learned. Each supported the other in the joint goal of improved parent–child relationships.

DISCUSSION

Perhaps it is a result of our enthusiasm about the method and the success experienced with it in this case, but we simply cannot imagine the use of any method other than FT for the Austins. They appear to have been tailor-made for FT and vice versa. The Austin family's problems involved the entire family system with the exception of 2½-year-old Joy, who had thus far escaped from the family's negative dynamics. Starting many years earlier, Mr. and Mrs. A. had allowed Beth to exercise control over her parents and siblings. They did not like it, but felt helpless to change it. This made it hard for them to provide Beth with appropriate nurturing and guidance that her tender years required for her optimal development. Essentially, Mr. and Mrs. A. feared Beth, placated her, and reinforced her controlling ways, but felt distanced from her emotionally. A cycle of Beth's needs being unmet, followed by her retaliation through mild tyranny, led to further parent withdrawal and so on. To a lesser extent, the same pattern was in place with Billy. His physical limitations confused the Austins about reasonable expectations for him, and seemed to generate dynamics similar to Beth's.

Teaching the Austins to provide nurturance and understanding and using the affective responses from the play therapy approach addressed the children's emotional needs. At the same time, learning the limits and consequences procedures of the play sessions permitted the parents to practice using limiting and consequences successfully, not only in the play sessions, but outside in real life as well. Thus, the parents began to bring their chaotic home life under control. Moreover, the Austins accepted what to them was a difficult concept—the rationale that parents *should* exercise appropriate controls over their children as well as care about the children's individuality and self-expression.

We were somewhat concerned that Mrs. A. had not explored her personal issues as fully as might be necessary to prevent them from interfering with her new-found parental effectiveness. When Beth reaches adolescence, we believe that the whole family will require additional help, if Mrs. A. has not fully resolved her own control and self-esteem conflicts. Ann discussed these issues with Mr. and Mrs. A. to a certain extent, in relation to FT principles and practices, but we feel sure that there is still more work to do in this area.

In retrospect, we believe that things would not have turned around in so relatively short a time if we had used a more traditional approach, e.g., separate parent counseling and play therapy for the children. FT permitted the parents to see directly how the parent–child dynamics were expressed. And further, they were empowered to initiate changes themselves that, we believe, permitted them to cut through defensiveness and resistance to change. As a matter of fact, we were surprised at how quickly the Austins did progress. It was like a hole suddenly opening up in a defensive (football) line, and the offensive team's quarterback taking off and covering a lot of yardage in a single run. Of course, the natural momentum generated by success helped maintain the new behaviors in place once initiated. We had actually expected that we would have to work at a slower step-by-step pace toward transfer to real life of appropriate attitudes and skills.

Successful as it was and enduring as it seems to have been, the timing of the therapy was unfortunate. The Austin's moving got in the way of regular home session scheduling and resulted in a couple of absences. Moving sapped some of their energy and make FT harder to keep in the desired forefront. At the same time, it was fortunate that the family had the FT sessions to help them through the transition. The Austins could well have experienced a genuine crisis under the strain of it without FT. This was their earlier pattern.

In summary, both authors believe that this case supported our conviction of the value of FT for dealing with adult–child relationship problems. The positive nature of the FT process for family and therapist alike, plus the quickly achieved positive outcome, made the experience rewarding for everyone concerned.

REFERENCES

Andronico, M., Guerney, B., Fidler, J., and Guerney, L. (1967). The combination of didactic and dynamic elements in filial therapy. *International Journal of Group Psychotherapy* 27:10–17.

Axline, V. (1969). *Play Therapy* (Rev. Ed.). New York: Ballantine.

Eyberg, S. (1988). Parent–child interaction therapy: integration of traditional and behavioral concerns. *Child and Family Behavior Therapy* 10:33–45.

Forehand, R., and King, E. (1974). Pre-school children's compliance: effects of short-term behavior therapy. *Journal of Community Psychology* 2:42–44.

Glass, N. (1986). Parents as therapeutic agents: a study of the effect of Filial Therapy. Unpublished doctoral dissertation, University of North Texas, Denton, TX.

Glazer-Waldman, H., Zimmerman, J., Landreth, G., and Norton, D. (1992). Filial Therapy: an intervention for parents of children with chronic illness. *Journal of the Association for Play Therapy* 1:31–42.

Guerney, B. (1964). Filial Therapy: description and rationale. *Journal of Consulting Psychology* 28:303–310.

Guerney, B., and Stover, L. (1971). *Filial Therapy* (Final report on NIMH Grant No. 1826401). University Park, PA: Penn State.

Guerney, L. (1975). Brief report on a follow-up study on Filial Therapy. Paper presented at the Eastern Psychological Association Annual Meeting, New York, N.Y.

_____ (1983). Introduction to Filial Therapy. In *Innovations in Clinical Practice: A Source Book*, vol. 2, ed. P. Keller and L. Ritt, pp. 26–39. Sarasota, FL: Professional Research Exchange.

_____ (1988). *Parenting: A Skills Training Manual*. 3rd ed. State College, PA: I.D.E.A.L.S.

Guerney, L., and Guerney, B. (1985). The relationship enhancement of family therapies.

In *Handbook of Social Skills Training and Research*, ed. L. L'Abate and M. Milan, pp. 506–524. New York: Wiley.

Parpal, M., and Maccoby, E. (1985). Maternal responsiveness and subsequent child compliance. *Child Development* 56:1326–1334.

Sensue, M. (1981). Filial Therapy follow-up study: effects on parental acceptance and child adjustment. *Dissertation Abstracts International* 42:148A.

Stover, L., and Guerney, B. (1967). The efficacy of training procedures for mothers in Filial Therapy. *Psychotherapy: Theory, Research, and Practice* 4:110–115.

Sywulak, A. E. (1979). The effect of Filial Therapy on parental acceptance and child adjustment. *Dissertation Abstracts International* 40:155B.

Wall, L. (1979). Parents as play therapists: a comparison of three interventions into children's play. *Dissertation Abstracts International* 40:155B.

18

I Brought My Own Toys Today! Play Therapy With Adults

Diane Frey, PH.D.

At the beginning of her fourth session, Helen, an adult client of mine, entered my office and exclaimed, "I brought my own toys today!" This client had often seen my child clients coming and going in the waiting room with various toys, games, clay objects, and art work. She had also seen some play materials in my office. Although she had obviously witnessed all this behavior, she had not, up until that point, commented upon it. Quite out of character, she was standing in my waiting room by herself clutching a large white, plastic bag. I had no idea exactly what her toys were. What had she chosen to bring to therapy? What "toys" caused her to exclaim with such delight? I stood there for a few seconds looking at this 66-year-old woman holding a large white bag, beaming with what seemed to be delight. She had piqued my curiosity all right!

Helen rushed into the therapy room and opened the large white bag and proclaimed to me, "See, I told you I brought my own toys!" In the bag was a stuffed teddy bear covered with chenille material. My client held the bear much as a child would and stroked the chenille covering.

When I asked about the history of the bear, Helen reported that she had acquired it after a weekend retreat with a group of women who were part of a hospice support group. During the weekend retreat, which I had encouraged Helen to attend, she had begun to disclose some of her feelings about her mother's death. As she did, she began to cry. Some of the other women had brought teddy bears to the group. One of them reached across the table and handed her bear to Helen with a nod of nonverbal support. Helen really appreciated the quiet understanding and support of another grieving individual. It was the other woman's way of saying, "I know it hurts. I understand. I'm here for you."

This gesture helped Helen to continue to self-disclose. She spoke for quite some time, all the while clutching the teddy bear. After she left the weekend retreat, she thought more and more about that bear. She couldn't believe how much she had opened up in the group. She really liked that bear and the gesture of support. She also liked the chenille covering; it reminded her of old time quilts she remembered from her childhood. The bear and the fabric covering had a comforting effect. They also seemed to give her a sense of security.

In the days after the retreat and before coming to her therapy session, Helen searched for a bear like this for herself. She was gleeful as she told me about finding one that she thought was even more attractive than the one her fellow group member had passed to her—and it was covered with chenille!

Helen passed the bear over to me after having hugged it all the while she told me about it. "Isn't it a great teddy bear? It's cute, isn't it? It feels so great! Doesn't it remind you of old chenille bedspreads? I like the eyes. They look very warm and understanding. I named her 'Rosey.' "

As I held the teddy bear, I had to agree with everything Helen had said. It was a very winsome teddy bear and had the appearance of being very understanding. All the while I was thinking about what all this meant to the therapeutic process, and what Helen was trying to tell me symbolically.

Helen, on the other hand, seemed delighted that I had taken to Rosey so well and was not considering the therapeutic or symbolic implications of her regressive behavior. She simply said, "I knew you would like her too. Maybe you would like one."

As the session progressed it became more and more apparent to me that the teddy bear was extremely valuable to Helen. In fact, I had just reread an article in *Newsweek* about a large stuffed doll that was being used in various therapy settings with adult victims of sexual abuse. It appeared that, as the clients clutched the doll, it helped them to self-disclose, feel more secure, and get in contact with their "child self." It was a form of adult play therapy that was very effective with adults. Helen was utilizing this teddy bear in the same way. It was helping her to feel supported, secure, and safe. It was a nonthreatening way of assisting her to talk about painful issues. She was beginning to return to her childhood identity. Recognizing the positive qualities this teddy bear was eliciting, I returned it to her and encouraged her to tell me more about the pain of her mother's death and the impact it had on her. She actively discussed her feelings. In prior sessions, she had talked about and around her feelings. In this session she was actually "feeling" and expressing the feelings, instead of just telling me about them. This was truly adult play therapy in action.

INTRODUCTION TO ADULT PLAY THERAPY

An early nineteenth century poet, Friedrich Schiller, stated, "Man only plays when he's in the fullest sense of the word a human being; and he is only finally a human being when he plays." These wise words are perhaps even more applicable at the end of the twentieth century. As adults become more and more work oriented and/or serious, they seem to play less. As they play less, they inhibit their own growth.

Adults need play just as much as children do. Play enhances an adult's ability to be creative. Einstein once stated that it was necessary for him to "play with ideas" before he began to think more completely. Play assists adults in their continued physical, social, emotional, and intellectual growth. Play can be very vitalizing for adults. Playing has neurophysiological effects. Play allows for the release of feelings of aggression and disapproval of authority figures. Since customary rules are suspended during play, play can be a diversion from routine societal demands.

Winnicott (1971) stated that "in playing and only in playing . . . the individual . . . is able to be creative and to use the whole personality and it's only in being creative that the individual discovers self" (p. 54). Winnicott (1968) also stated that "psychotherapy is done in the overlap of the two play areas, that of patient and that of therapist. If the therapist cannot play, then he's not suitable for the work. If the patient can't play, then something needs to be done to enable the patient to become able to play, after which psychotherapy may begin" (p. 591).

Types of Play

There are essentially four types of play appropriate for use in play therapy with adults: physical play, manipulative play, symbolic play, and games. In the physical type of play, action is primary. Adult play that is physical includes activities such as football, swimming, golf, and bicycling. In adult play therapy, any activities that are primarily action oriented would be located in this category. When the emphasis in play is controlling or manipulating the environment, the person is engaging in manipulative play. This type of play attempts to answer the questions, "What will someone do?" or "What will happen when I do this?" The use of puppets with adults is an example of this type of play. Helen was using a form of manipulative play by bringing her teddy bear. In addition to its other value, the teddy bear was answering the questions of "What will someone (i.e., therapist) do?" and "What will happen when I do this (use the teddy bear)?" Symbolic play involves the use of fantasy. Sociodrama is an example of symbolic, adult play therapy. Art therapy with adults is also symbolic play. When play includes rules and conversation, it is called a game. Board games, card games, chess, and checkers are all forms of game play for adults.

Adult Clients Who Would Benefit From Play Therapy

While play therapy is appropriate for most adults, certain populations of adults are especially suited for play therapy. Adults who, at an early age, had to parent their own parents have often lost their "child self," and as a result, can benefit from adult play therapy. Adult children of alcoholics (ACOA) and adult children of divorce (ACOD) have frequently lost their childhood through having to deal with serious issues. Play can help them to regain their "child self." Adults who primarily "live in their heads" can benefit from play therapy because it helps them to connect with their affective side. Adults whose work requires them to think extensively and in depth often lose touch with their creative aspects. Play therapy can help them to regain these aspects. Play therapy can also help highly stressed adults become more relaxed. It can provide a catharsis for these clients. Workaholics, with no play in their lives, are also good candidates for play therapy. It can help such clients to avoid and/or manage boredom and depression and teach them to bring fun back into their lives. Developmentally delayed adults are also good candidates for adult play therapy since traditional approaches may be too abstract for them. The elderly are also good clients because they may be threatened by traditional approaches to therapy but will often respond to art or music therapy.

Certain psychodynamics of adults are particularly suitable for play therapy. These clients include resistant clients, clients in denial, psychologically unaware clients, verbally deficient clients, inhibited clients, and non–self-disclosing clients. Helen was an example of the latter. While she was quite often very disclosing and cooperative, the topic of death and dying was a particularly vulnerable and difficult one for her. Adult play therapy was particularly useful in helping her to discuss this topic more thoroughly.

Contraindications

There are contraindications for the use of play therapy with adults. If the client has viewed play as threatening, it is not a suitable modality. Sometimes adults felt seduced by play as a child. A relative may have introduced incest as a "game." Some adults can use play as a defense. Their play becomes calculated or driven and, as such, nontherapeutic. Play can also mask hostility and anger and, as such, direct the interaction from being totally facilitative. Some adults use play as a form of seductiveness in which they try to become disarming. Play therapy is not advised for this type of client. Play can be used to manipulate and control therapy. If an adult is using play to avoid dealing with issues, then it is counterproductive.

It is possible to begin therapy with traditional approaches with some clients and introduce play therapy when the client has a readiness for it. All play therapy with adults requires monitoring the impact of the play on the client to avoid the danger of using play to cover defensiveness, seduction, manipulation, and/or transference. The therapist should also review play therapy with regard to who initiates it—client, therapist, or both. While such monitoring is valuable, it is also important to be spontaneous in play approaches with adults. Play therapists need to be playful themselves.

PRESENTING PROBLEM AND
BACKGROUND DATA

Helen was 58 years old when I initially saw her in therapy, approximately eight years prior to the teddy bear session. The presenting problem at that time was her parenting skills and the effective management of her three children. She was married and her mother was living with the family. Helen expressed some difficulty with mild depression, although she had never been on medication. She was a high school graduate and her husband had earned a bachelor's degree. Helen's married sister lived with her family approximately 200 miles away, but in the same state.

After resolving her parenting concerns, I did not see Helen or her family for about eight years. Helen then referred herself after experiencing the loss of her mother and the death of her sister within a week of each other. Helen had taken care of her mother in her home for about 15 years. As Helen's mother became ill and needed assistance at home, Helen enlisted the aid of Hospice. Much to the surprise of Hospice,

Helen's mother graduated from their care, a rare occurrence. Slightly over three months later, however, Helen's mother died in Helen's arms at home. While Helen had been preparing for her mother's death for several months of Hospice care, she had reversed her thoughts and feelings when her mother improved. Helen now had to deal with another reversal – her mother declining again until she eventually died. It had been an emotional roller coaster ride for Helen.

During this time Helen's sister was relatively uninvolved with the care of their mother. She visited very seldom. One week after the funeral of Helen's mother, Helen's sister died of complications from the recent heart attack that had prevented her from attending their mother's funeral.

Helen's husband was very supportive, as were her children. Nevertheless Helen experienced considerable grief and depression.

While Helen wanted help, she had a somewhat approach–avoidance conflict about therapy. During the first three sessions of traditional therapy, she talked about the problem, but did not seem to be actually feeling much about these life events. I encouraged her to attend a support group sponsored by Hospice. It was there that the woman gave her the teddy bear that inspired her to bring her own bear to her fourth session. It was interesting to me that Helen had named her bear Rosey, a name that certainly did not describe Helen's mood at the moment.

THEORETICAL CONCEPTUALIZATION

Having been a psychologist for twenty-three years, I know that you can learn a great deal from clients about treatment if you listen actively and thoroughly. Helen was a good example of this. She had introduced this stuffed object as a toy she could relate to completely and honestly. Noticing the degree to which she verbalized and the willingness to discuss her grieving while holding the bear, I decided to pursue this type of therapy technique with her. It has always been my approach to do a positive client asset search to ascertain what strengths a client already has. I try to build on these assets to assist the client in dealing with the current problem. My goals for Helen were to help her deal with the grieving and depression she was experiencing and to assist her in rediscovering her identity that was buried in many years of caring for her mother and others. Helen had been a caregiver to others all her life and was now seeking to find her lost self and a new direction in life.

Helen did not seem to fit any of the guidelines about contraindications. She had initiated the teddy bear play, while I spontaneously responded and interacted with her and the bear.

There are many uses of play therapy with adults. It became apparent to me that several of these uses could be appropriate for Helen. First, play therapy could lessen Helen's defenses. Although she intellectually realized that she needed to grieve her mother's death, emotionally she was trying to avoid dealing with it. Being a sincere believer in Thomas Hardy's statement, " . . . if way to the Better there be, it exacts a full look at the Worst," I realized that play therapy could help Helen deal with "the worst." Second, it was obvious from the teddy bear discussion that play therapy could help Helen enhance her verbalization about this issue. She was much more verbal about her feelings while hugging and touching this bear. Third, play therapy could help Helen to uncover unconscious material. I thought of doing this through the use of drawings and play. Helen was experiencing a lot of stress. I wanted to use clay and puppets to help lessen this tension.

At times Helen appeared to be confused about what was happening to her. I decided to use play therapy techniques such as drawings and imagery to help provide insight for her.

Through role playing and/or sociodrama I could also help Helen to do reality testing in play therapy. She needed to learn how to say no to others more often and not overburden herself with too much responsibility. Helen seemed to be a "peace at any price" individual who was willing to internalize emotions rather than express them and cause disharmony.

Other uses of play therapy with adults include diagnostic enhancement of the therapeutic relationship, improvement of communication, lessening of communication barriers, lessening the distance of the client, expanding the range of communication of the client, restructuring the therapeutic relationship, integrating the disoriented self, discovering undeveloped aspects of self, and developing a positive association with the affective domain. I believed that play therapy could help Helen in all of these areas.

While there are many play therapy techniques appropriate for adults, I chose to use (a) play objects, since Helen had already brought one to therapy; (b) music, since Helen was interested in music as a hobby; (c) art, to uncover unconscious material; (d) interactive games, to develop insight and do reality testing; (e) humor, since Helen had reacted to me through this medium before; and (f) drama, to develop insight and enhance verbalization. Other techniques appropriate for adults in play therapy include board games, card games, and role-playing. I did not use these particular techniques in this case, but they are very facilitative in helping adult clients' self-growth and improvement.

THE PROCESS OF PLAY THERAPY

While play therapy with adults can be introduced by the therapist, client, or both at any time, in this case Helen had unknowingly introduced the technique herself. I continued with it. My role was to guide her through the stages of grieving, help her in dealing with depression, and aid in the development of a new identity. I interspersed play therapy with traditional therapy approaches. Each session had some play therapy activity as the center for discussion that day. I usually introduced these strategies, but occasionally Helen introduced them. In session 5, Helen brought another object to the session. This time it was a greeting card with the words, "I just want you to listen" on it. She introduced it by saying that she thought I could put this in a picture frame stand that I had. I told her I wanted to discuss this more as it related to her session. I asked if she was trying to tell me something about our session. Our discussion centered around her ambivalence about wanting to talk and be listened to, but at the same time not being sure that she really wanted to talk about these issues. She was dwelling in the denial state of grieving. While we discussed her ambivalence she held the card tightly, not letting go of it until the end of the session. When she left it on my desk, I told her I wanted to listen very much. I recognized her feelings of pain and frustration in dealing with her ambivalence. I reinforced her idea of bringing the card to the session and perched the card on a small easel on my desk.

Having known Helen from previous work I had done with her, I knew she liked music. She sometimes wrote music and sometimes sang her music and other music for various organizations. Music was a solace for Helen and a vehicle for expressing feelings she sometimes did not express otherwise. Recognizing Helen's positive feelings about music and realizing this was a client asset that could assist me in the therapeutic process, I introduced the song, "Itsy, Bitsy Spider," to Helen in session 6. This well-known children's song has as one of its themes the concept of perseverance. I introduced the song because of its metaphorical message for Helen. After listening to the song, I asked Helen if she knew why I thought of playing it for her that day. She responded by saying that she was beginning to realize that therapy was much like the spider's experience in that you make progress and then sometimes fall down, then you progress again and fall down. Helen went on to state that if she just stayed with it—that is, the process of therapy—"out would come the sun and dry up all the rain."

Using music as a form of play therapy seemed to make it easier for Helen to discuss her feelings, particularly her angry feelings about the losses she had experienced. She realized it was difficult (i.e., raining), but that the sun would appear at the end if she worked through these stages. Her approach–avoidance conflict about therapy seemed to lessen.

As the play therapy continued for Helen and she became more involved in the anger phase of grieving, I introduced art as a play therapy medium. Helen drew her anger with crayons and pounded it out on clay. It was during the clay play that she made a figure of her sister, then spent considerable time destroying it while discussing how angry she was at her sister for not helping her more while their mother was dying. The clay seemed to allow Helen to express her angry feelings in a manner that was acceptable to her. Previous discussions about this anger toward her sister had resulted in Helen's denying the anger because she felt so guilty for being angry at someone who was now deceased. This more traditional approach to therapy—discussion—was not a safe venue for Helen to deal with these feelings. Through the clay and the drawing, she seemed to feel much less threatened.

Helen informed me that in between her sessions she was using Rosey, the teddy bear, to process what had happened in her therapy sessions and the thoughts and feelings that were occurring to Helen during the week. Rosey had become a confidante and source for catharsis and processing what Helen wanted to deal with in subsequent sessions. I applauded her use of Rosey in this way and mentioned that Rosey was welcome to come to therapy anytime. Rosey attended many subsequent sessions.

While considering the effectiveness of art in play with Helen, I decided to continue this medium to assist her in the grieving process. I decided to use Striker's *Anti-Coloring Book for Adults Only* (1983) and the original *Anti-Coloring Book* (1978). On each page is a visual stimulus. The therapist asks the client to finish the drawing. In one session I asked Helen to complete a drawing depicting a telephone with the suggestion that it can be used to "call anyone you want, real or imaginary, dead or alive." Helen drew a picture of her mother as she thought of her now. The drawing and resultant discussion gave me great insight about Helen's belief system about life after death.

We used other drawings from these resources, including one about drawing "your worst nightmare." Helen's nightmare was about her sister being ill and Helen being unable to help her. We discovered many of Helen's "shoulds," "oughts," and "musts" through this technique. She had been feeling guilty for not helping her sister more and for feeling angry toward her when she was most likely ill and Helen did not know it.

Therapy proceeded in this manner, helping Helen to work through the grieving phases until one day she brought another object to her therapy session. This art object was a figurine of an angel with wings outstretched to enfold a lion and a lamb. It was close to Christmas by this time and Helen informed me that she wanted to show this piece to me. She said that she had just purchased it because she believed in world harmony and peace. She liked the way this statue symbolized peace and harmony and wanted to purchase Christmas cards with a lion and lamb scene. As I looked at this beautiful statue, it occurred to me that it symbolized even more than Helen realized.

I process all play therapy interventions using a six-step process (Frey and Carlock 1991). The first step, the introduction, involves discussing with the client the rationale for participating in the play therapy activity to insure that the client understands the techniques being used. I mentioned to Helen that I believed the lion and lamb had additional significance for her at that time and that her enthusiasm for this object seemed to be deeper than one would think at first blush.

I then invited her to proceed to step two in the processing, which is the participation phase. I asked her to think about what else this statue might mean to her. I asked her to imagine that the lion and lamb represented different aspects of herself. If this was true, I continued, I wanted Helen to tell me what words or concepts came to her mind about the lion and the lamb. I asked her to describe each object to me. She described the lion as angry, mean, vicious, unrelenting, and representative of her "shadow" self. She described the lamb as lovable, warm, caring, and a representative of her more ideal self. Helen saw the angel as being representative of a more integrated self that was able to unite the lion and lamb.

Helen had begun to engage in step three—publishing. She was sharing her perceptions and observations about the statue. She was beginning to see the symbolism in the prior steps of this activity.

Step four—processing—involves asking clients to discuss patterns as dynamics they notice while engaging in the technique. Helen continued to hold the statue and stroke each of the figures. She began to explain that she thought she had repressed her lion self much of her life, while in pursuit of her lamb self. In denying her lion self, she had caused herself to become depressed. She mentioned that she was surprised at how she felt that day discussing the lion. She was not denying it anymore. In fact, she felt comfortable petting the lion. She had, in fact, she stated, come to see the beauty of the lion. Helen had indeed worked through many phases of grieving by then and she had processed a great deal about the anger phase.

In step five—cognition—I asked Helen to think about principles of generalizations that she could gather from this technique. She stated that she knew she had denied her anger long before these two deaths and that the deaths had augmented her anger and her denial. She realized that her method of coping before the deaths was the same whenever she experienced losses. She had tried to deny her feelings in order to be liked by others, as the lamb is liked.

In step six—application—Helen revealed that these learnings contained a lot of pleasure for her everyday life. When I asked her how she could apply this to her everyday life, she stated that she needed to recognize her anger more and try to avoid seeing anger as the enemy. Helen said that she really did want to unite her lion and lamb aspects in real life. She believed that when she was able to do this, she would feel more peaceful and more harmonious and complete. She also realized how powerful play techniques are. She was amazed at how much she learned about herself from processing this activity during the therapy session. Helen was glad that she was at a phase where she no longer was denying her anger, and she did indeed want to unite these various aspects of herself.

I reminded myself of how powerful objects were to Helen as a therapeutic modality. In this session, as she continued to hold the statue she disclosed more and more. She stroked the statue as she talked. Objects provided a very therapeutic medium for Helen. They seemed to open the way for her to discuss and process her feelings. While other play therapy approaches were also very helpful to Helen, she kept coming back to the use of objects to facilitate change. I reminded myself to return to this modality again as warranted.

Helen was becoming less and less depressed, and she was in the final stage of the grieving process. I decided to use humor as a play therapy technique with her in the next session. I told Helen about something Woody Allen had once said about death. He said he was not afraid of death. He just didn't want to be there when it happened. We both laughed and she began to discuss her feelings about death and her own mortality. She indicated that before these two deaths she probably would have felt the same way as the humorous quotation. She felt she really understood more about death now, and through dealing with her grieving issues she was able to come to terms more with her own death.

Helen returned the next week with a Ziggy cartoon. Ziggy was on the phone, after having called the time and temperature. Ziggy's comment was, "I don't really care about the time and temperature . . . I just called because I'm lonely!" I realized Helen had turned the corner from the grieving process and depression to wanting to regain her identity and focus more on her needs and not so much on the needs of others. We were ready to begin to use play therapy to help her to regain the self she had lost during all those years.

Since Helen had come to more of an acceptance of her mother's and sister's deaths, we began the journey of self acceptance. I asked her to participate in a type of drama game entitled, "Cutting Loose From Parents" (Frey and Carlock 1989). I asked Helen to close her eyes, relax, and imagine sitting as a child in a very safe room. I continued to ask Helen to imagine one of her parents walking through the door to the room and sitting by her. I asked her to pay close attention to how she was feeling during this. I suggested that she "sit" with her parent for a while and notice how the parent looked and behaved. I asked her to identify her feelings and express them to her parent. I suggested that she express any old business she had with this parent.

Then I asked her to switch to her parent's role and respond to what her "child" said. I asked Helen to tell her "child" how she felt about her. Helen began to gain insight through this activity about the interactional effects of parents on self-concept and self-esteem. We followed this activity with others about the roots of self-concept and self-esteem. Helen was beginning to regain some sense of how her identity evolved.

In a later session, I introduced another play therapy technique to Helen. I gave her a self-esteem fortune cookie. This fortune cookie activity (Frey and Carlock 1991) involves baking various self-esteem quotations into fortune cookies, then asking clients to read the fortune and discuss how the fortune pertains to their lives. In Helen's fortune cookie was the quotation, "By what you say to yourself, you are better in the construction business or the wrecking business of self-esteem" (Frey 1991). Subsequent fortune cookies included quotations such as "Whether you think you can or whether you think you can't, you're right." "Look forward to the butterfly instead of stepping on the caterpillar." After the discussion of the fortune cookie message, I invited Helen to eat the fortune cookie.

Another play therapy activity presented to Helen to enhance self-esteem was a visualization technique called "Rosebud" adopted from Stevens (1991). I asked Helen to relax, close her eyes, and imagine she was a rosebud. I guided her to visualize what type of rosebud she was, where she was growing, what types of roots she had, who took care of her as the seasons changed, what her existence was like as the rosebud and how she felt as the rosebud. When we completed the visualization, I asked Helen to draw what she had seen using pastels and paper I presented to her.

Helen's rosebud was filled with yellow roses in full bloom. She was growing by the corner of her house; she had an elaborate root system, few thorns, and some new buds. As Helen drew the rosebud, she told me of her existence as the rosebud. She indicated that she had been a largely neglected, unseen rosebud growing in this corner space that did not predominate in the landscape of the house. No one had taken care of her as the seasons changed. Even so, she had survived. People around her only began to notice her when other bushes around her withered and she began to blossom profusely. As she began to blossom, more and more little buds developed. She was looking beautiful. She had felt neglected and lonely, but now she was feeling very content and fulfilled. As Helen finished the drawing, she spontaneously added the words, "Hi World, I'm me!" coming from the rosebud's blossom.

The rosebud, of course, represented Helen. The play therapy method of accessing this information about Helen's identity and self-esteem enabled Helen and me to become more aware of her evolving self in ways that traditional therapy could not. This visualization and drawing symbolized more unconscious feelings, mostly unknown to Helen and me before this activity.

Helen and I continued to engage in self-esteem games such as "Self-Esteem Bingo" and a self-esteem scavenger hunt (Frey and Carlock 1991). I asked Helen to search for put-downs she gave herself and positive ways in which others nurture their self-esteem.

It was only a few sessions later that Helen arrived in my office with two different notepads she thought I might like. She had also purchased some for herself. The first one she showed me said, "Choose to be Yourself." The other notepad said, "Listen with Hearts." As I looked at them, I realized this was still another object form of communicating with me and relating to me. Various objects had certainly served as vehicles to enhance communication between the two of us. I was feeling that Helen had come into her own. She was indeed finally brave enough to be herself and trusting her heart. She had shrugged off the previously omnipresent image of herself that she had learned from her mother. At 66 years old she had developed her own identity! We talked about the notepads and a reading Helen shared with me from a small book she had brought with her. The quotation she told me she especially liked was, "Remove the sock from your shoe rather than learn to limp comfortably." Helen indeed had been limping. Since her sock had been removed from her shoe she was walking to the beat of her own drummer. It was a wonderful process to watch.

RESULTS AND FOLLOW-UP

I was very pleased with Helen's progress. I believed we had accomplished our goals of working through the grieving stages of denial, anger, bargaining, depression, and acceptance. Helen had developed a new sense of identity and enhanced self-esteem. Through the use of many and varied play therapy techniques, we had increased Helen's understanding of how she learned and processed information. The process of therapy took approximately thirty sessions occurring over the course of about one year, a very common amount of time to deal with loss issues in therapy. Grieving usually takes one year to eighteen months to complete.

Since Helen lives in the same community where I practice, I sometimes encounter her at the movies or the grocery store. It has been two years since the termination of her therapy. Helen has informed me she has started to collect butterfly objects, much as many people collect stamps or antiques. She still continues to enjoy play objects as a way of self-understanding. Now, though, Helen is more consciously aware of this process.

During my last chance meeting with Helen in a department store during the Christmas holiday, Helen shared that she was volunteering with Hospice, and she continued to meet about once a month with many of the women who had been in her original support group. These women had also moved beyond grieving, but enjoyed each other so much that they agreed to meet as a general support group rotating to different homes or restaurants as meeting places. She was pleased with how well these meetings went, everyone self-disclosing at the same level they had when they were meeting at Hospice. However, when the group met at a local restaurant, Helen noticed the level of self-disclosure diminished and the depth of feelings lessened. She became concerned and pondered about the cause of the change. Not always could they meet in members' homes because of geographic distance for some members and a variety of other reasons. Helen had come across the following poem and decided to take it to the next meeting.

The Elephant in the Room, Hospice of Dayton
by Terry Kettering

There's an elephant in the room
It is large and squatting, so it is
   hard to get around it
Yet we squeeze by with, "How are you?"
   And "I'm fine" . . .

And a thousand other forms of trivial chatter.
We talk about the weather
We talk about work.
We talk about everything else—
except the elephant in the room.
There's an elephant in the room.
We all know it is there.
We are thinking about the elephant
    as we talk together.
It is constantly on our minds.
For, you see, it is a very big elephant
It has hurt us all.
But we do not talk about the elephant
    in the room.
Oh, please, say her name.
Oh, please, say "Barbara" again
Oh, please, let's talk about the elephant
    in the room
For if we talk about her death,
Perhaps we can talk about her life?
Can I say "Barbara" to you and not have
    you look away?
For if I cannot, then you are leaving me
Alone . . .
In a room . . .
With an elephant.

Helen then told me with a gleeful look in her eyes that she thought of a great idea to accompany the poem. She had wanted to get a stuffed elephant or some elephant statue to take to the group. Since she was limited in funds, she thought such a purchase from a store might be too expensive. She decided to look in some thrift shops for a toy elephant. Sure enough, she found a "pink toy elephant" in a thrift shop. At the next meeting of the group she shared the poem. The others really liked it. They were meeting at another restaurant, and Helen suggested that whenever anyone felt that the conversation was becoming too superficial or when anyone felt a need to share something very emotional but did not know how to start, all they had to do was put the toy elephant in the middle of the table and this would serve as a reminder of the poem and of the fact that the person wanted to share something very significant.

I thought to myself of the wonderful cycle that had occurred in Helen's life. Through toy objects in adult play therapy she had been tremendously assisted in her own growth. Now she was passing on the gift of play therapy techniques to others. The women in Helen's group continue to use the pink, toy elephant to facilitate their discussion. I thanked Helen for passing on such a wonderful gift!

DISCUSSION

You can learn a lot from a teddy bear! That was my thought during Helen's therapy, at the termination of her therapy, and, thereafter, when I encountered her in the community. I learned over twenty-five years ago to listen actively to my clients and to flow with their agenda whenever facilitative. In Helen's case, this was most appropriate. Helen had actually introduced the use of play therapy by bringing the teddy bear into the office. By taking her lead and utilizing my knowledge-base of play therapy, I continued to introduce play therapy techniques throughout her therapy. Play objects, the very medium Helen introduced, seemed to be the most effective for Helen, although music, art, games, humor, drama, and visualization approaches were also helpful for her. Although I did not use board games, card games, or role playing with Helen, these media in play therapy might also have been effective. As she opened her experience to play therapy approaches, Helen became more willing to try various approaches to therapy.

What surprised me most was how easily Helen had made the transition from traditional therapeutic approaches with adults to play approaches. It certainly helped, I believe, to have in my office other play materials that I use with children. We made the transition more easily because of this. Helen's watching children come and go in the waiting room with various play objects, paintings, games, and music also helped increase her receptivity to play techniques.

My predictions for Helen are extremely positive. She has already introduced other adults to the play therapy process, and she continues to experience a great deal of personal growth.

My own learning from this client came from my thoughts one day about the play therapy process. I found myself reflecting about how I wished someone had used this modality with me when I was involved in personal growth groups during my doctoral study. I am particularly struck by how effective this approach is with children and adults. While this case was about grieving, play therapy is effective with most concerns adults bring to therapy. It is a very effective use of time in therapy. Play therapy can often reveal much about an adult client that may take many sessions to learn by traditional therapy.

Another thing I learned about myself is how comfortable I am with play and how important that is to the application of this theory into practice. While I was presenting a play therapy conference once, a participant asked me if I played a lot as a child. I was instantly surprised by the insight and then realized how obvious my love of play is to others. As a young child growing up in the Mennonite church, I was forbidden to watch television and movies. Family values and unity were highly prized. As a result, my family played together a lot. We had a great deal of fun. We learned from each other. I saw adults enjoying play. This probably served as an early model for me for choosing play as a child and as an adult.

Since that time, I have learned that many adults are children at heart. During the time I was seeing Helen in therapy, I was also seeing a client named Branden. He was 7 years old. One day as I was discussing some painful issues about his father with Branden, he asked me if we could talk about another boy who was also 7 named Bunden. I agreed. Bunden was actually Branden, but the emotions were so painful to Branden that he could only deal with them through Bunden. For Helen it was the same. Her pain and grieving was so great that she could most readily deal with it through Rosey. Both are symbolic play therapy methods for dealing with real life problems for people age 7 or 58 or 3 or 108.

I recently read an article entitled, "Toys 'r' must for Boomers" (*New York Times* News Service 1992). The theme of the article was that baby boomer adults were not only buying toys for their children, but were also buying toys for themselves as a method for escaping stress and developing effective coping mechanisms. Nearly 45% of 20,000 adults recently surveyed said they had bought a toy or game for themselves or another adult in the past year. Brian Sutton-Smith (1989), professor, University of Pennsylvania, stated, "For decades there has been this assumption that children played and adults didn't." Only now is society realizing that adults play as much, if not more, than children. Perhaps, somewhat intuitively, adults are learning the value of play in their lives. It had been serendipitous for Helen to use play. Through this initial introduction, she began to realize the value of play in her life.

I also used other strategies with Helen. As mentioned earlier, I encouraged her to involved herself with a support group through Hospice. I also used bibliotherapy approaches with her, especially around the issue of grieving. Helen also kept a journal and continues to do so. I used metaphors with her, especially butterfly ones, since Helen liked butterflies even before entering therapy.

The only major change I would have made in this treatment approach for Helen would have been to begin with play therapy approaches earlier because she had a readiness level for this approach earlier. I could have introduced it myself before Helen did. She would have been receptive. Once we began with this modality, however, we devoted part or all of each session to some play therapy method.

The latest interaction I had with Helen was when she sent me a Virginia Satir poster, entitled, "I am Me." She made particular reference to the fact that she especially liked the end: "I own me, and therefore I can engineer me—I am me and I am okay." I felt a keen sense of satisfaction about her growth. Helen had grown a tremendous amount. She had learned and I had welcomed what Friedrich Schiller meant in the nineteenth century when he wrote: "Man only plays when he's in the fullest sense of the word a human being; and he is only a human being when he plays."

REFERENCES

Frey, D. (1991). *100 Inspirational Quotations for Enhancing Self-Esteem*. La Mesa, CA: Educo Learning Systems.

Frey, D., and Carlock, J. (1989). *Enhancing Self-Esteem*. Muncie, IN: Accelerated Development.

———— (1991). *Practical Techniques for Enhancing Self-Esteem*. Muncie, IN: Accelerated Development.

New York Times News Service. (1992). Toys 'r' must for boomers. *Dayton Daily News*, October 27, p. 11A.

Stevens, J. (1991). *Awareness: Exploring, Experimenting, and Experiencing*. Moah, UT: Real People Press.

Stricker, S. (1983). *The Anti-Coloring Book for Adults Only*. New York: Holt, Rinehart, and Winston.

Stricker,S., and Kimmel, E. (1978). *The Anti-Coloring Book*. New York: Holt and Company.

Sutton-Smith, B. (1989). *Practitioners and the modern state of play*. Paper presented at the Association for Play Therapy Conference, State College, PA, October.

Winnicott, D. W. (1968). Playing: its theoretical status in the clinical situation. *International Journal of Psycho-Analysis* 49:591.

———— (1971). *Playing and Reality*. New York: Basic Books.

INDEX

Abuse. *See* Child abuse
Academic achievement
    structured group ecosystemic
        play therapy, 263,
        265–266
    time-limited play therapy,
        307–308
Achenbach, T. M., 177, 306
Achenbach Child Behavior
    Checklist, 306
Adjustment
    Adlerian theory and, 134
    person-centered therapy and,
        10–11
Adler, A., 133–134, 137, 142
Adlerian play therapy, 133–167
    background data and
        presenting problem,
        142–145
    discussion of case, 166
    historical context of, 142
    results and follow-up, 165
    stages in, 138–142
    theoretical concepts, 145–148
    theoretical overview, 133–142
        generally, 133–135
        purposiveness of behavior,
            135–136
        social context, 136–137
        social interest level, 137–138
        unity and holism, 138
    therapy process, 148–165
        insight development, 158–162
        life-style exploration, 155–158
        relationship building,
            148–155
        reorientation/reeducation,
            162–165

Adoption, Gestalt play therapy,
    286–288
Adult children of alcoholics
    (ACOA), adult play therapy
    and, 592
Adult play therapy, 589–606
    background data and
        presenting problem,
        589–591, 593–594
    discussion of case, 604–606
    results and follow-up, 602–604
    theoretical concepts, 594–596
    theoretical overview, 591–594
        contraindications for, 593
        generally, 591
        indications for, 592
        types of play, 591–592
    therapy process, 596–601
Affect. *See* Emotion
Aggression
    game play therapy, 530, 534,
        538
    Gestalt play therapy, 292–293
    posttraumatic play therapy,
        487–488
Alcoholism, adult children of
    alcoholics, adult play therapy
    and, 592
Allan, J., 209–244
Alloplastic style, 261
American Psychiatric Association
    (APA), 177
Andersen, H. C., 476
Anderson, R. A., 457–483
Andronico, M., 562
Animal mutilation, dynamic play
    therapy with ritual abuse,
    402–405

Ansbacher, H., 133, 134, 137, 140
Ansbacher, R., 134, 137, 140
Anxiety
  game play therapy, 532
  Jungian play therapy, 212–216
Archetypes, Jungian theory and,
  210
Arts, Jungian theory and, 210
Assessment
  adult play therapy, 595
  cognitive-behavioral play
    therapy, 177, 178–180
  game play therapy, 531,
    538–539
  Jungian play therapy, 214–216
  structured group ecosystemic
    play therapy, 257–258
Attention-deficit hyperactivity
  disorder (ADHD). See also
  Hyperactivity
  game play therapy, 535
  integrative play therapy, 424
Autoplastic style, 261, 263
Awareness, Gestalt play therapy,
  285
Axline, V., 5, 6, 11, 217, 304, 419,
  435, 436, 561

Bandura, A., 172
Barkley, R., 539
Baum, L. F., 425, 426, 433, 434,
  436, 444, 449, 452, 455
Baumeister, R. F., 529
Beck, A., 486
Beck, A. T., 170, 174
Behavior
  Adlerian theory, 135–137
  behavioral contingencies,
    cognitive-behavioral play
    therapy, 172
  cognitive-behavioral play
    therapy, 171

Gestalt play therapy, 283–285
integrative play therapy,
  436–437
person-centered therapy and,
  8–9
problems in, Adlerian play
  therapy, 142–145
structured group ecosystemic
  play therapy, 249–250
Behavior modification system,
  structured group ecosystemic
  play therapy, 249-250
Beiser, H. R., 528
Bell, J., 378
Bergman, J., 425
Berlin, I. N., 533
Berry, P., 212
Bertoia, J., 211, 217
Bierman, K. L., 174
Birth order, Adlerian play
  therapy and, 140
Birth trauma, Jungian play
  therapy, 242
Bixler, R., 6, 13
Blanck, G., 349
Blanck, R., 349
Blanco, R., 468
Blatt, S. J., 429
Blum, A., 529
Body experiences, Gestalt play
  therapy, 291-292
Booth, P., 50, 52, 53, 55
Borden, B., 140
Boundaries. See Limits and
  boundaries
Bow, J. N., 539
Bowen, M., 461
Bowlby, J., 290
Braswell, L., 170
Brodzinsky, D., 472
Brown, K., 212
Buber, M., 281

Budman, S. H., 302
Burlingham, D., 486
Burns, D., 420
Burns, W. J., 424

Camp, B., 246
Campbell, S., 174
Cangelosi, D. M., 347–370
Carey, L., 463
Carlock, J., 598, 600, 601
Cheating, game play therapy, 533
Child abuse. *See also* Incest; Sexual abuse
    Gestalt play therapy, 290, 298
    posttraumatic play therapy, 485–525. *See also* Posttraumatic play therapy
    ritual abuse, dynamic play therapy with, 371–415. *See also* Dynamic play therapy with ritual abuse
    structured group ecosystemic play therapy, 255–258, 269
Child Behavior Checklist, cognitive-behavioral play therapy and, 177
Child molestation. *See* Sexual abuse
Child relationship enhancement family therapy. *See* Filial therapy
Client-centered concepts, integrative play therapy, 435–436, 437
Client-centered therapy. *See* Person-centered therapy
Clinical orientations, integrative play therapy, 419–420
Cognition
    adult play therapy, 599

structured group ecosystemic play therapy, 246–247, 260–261
Cognitive-behavioral play therapy, 169-208
    background data and presenting problem, 175–177
    discussion of case, 203–207
    results and follow-up, 202–203
    theoretical concepts, 177–181
        assessment and treatment, 178–180
        background, 177–178
        case conceptualization, 180–181
    theoretical overview, 169–175
    therapy process, 181–202
Cognitive change strategies, cognitive-behavioral play therapy, 173–174
Combrinck-Graham, L., 462
Communication
    cognitive-behavioral play therapy, 179–180
    game play therapy, 531
    imagery interaction play therapy, 97–98
    person-centered therapy, 8–9
    toys, person-centered therapy, 14–15
Conn, J. H., 303
Connors, C., 306, 308
Connors, K., 537
Connors' Teacher Rating Scale, 306
Contact boundary disturbances, Gestalt play therapy, 283–285
Cooper, S., 533
Coping strategies, cognitive-behavioral play therapy, 171

Corsini, R., 133, 137
Counterplay, imagery interaction play therapy techniques, 102
Countertransference
  Jungian play therapy, 241–242
  posttraumatic play therapy, 519–520
Crittenden, P. J., 391
Crittenden, P. M., 391
Culture, posttraumatic play therapy, 487-489

Davanloo, H., 301
Davison, G., 246
Developmental factors
  Adlerian theory, 134
  adult play therapy, 592
  filial therapy, 564
  game play therapy, 528–530
  Gestalt play therapy, 283
  integrative play therapy, 428–429, 430–434
  person-centered therapy, 6–9
  psychodynamic play therapy, 347, 348–349
  structured group ecosystemic play therapy, 253–254, 259–260
Developmental Therapy Objective Rating Form-Revised (DTORF), 257, 259–260, 277
Devine, S. E., 413
De Vroom, M.-J., 97–132
Dewey, E., 140
Diagnosis. See Assessment
Diamond, D., 429
Differential reinforcement of other behavior, cognitive-behavioral play therapy, 173
Dinkmeyer, D., 140, 142, 161, 246

Dinkmeyer, D. and Dinkmeyer, D., 134, 135, 136
Divorce, structured group ecosystemic play therapy, 255–258
Dodge, K. A., 554
Dorfman, E., 6
Dreams, Jungian theory and, 210
Dreikurs, R., 134, 135, 138, 142
Dulica, D., 378
Dynamic play therapy with ritual abuse, 371-415
  background data and presenting problem, 388–394
  discussion of case, 410–414
  results and follow-up, 410
  theoretical concepts, 394–396
  theoretical overview, 371–388
    expressive modalities, 375–376
    free play with props, 384–386
    generally, 371–375
    initial family sessions, 376–379
    initial games, 379–384
    themes, imagery, and posttraumatic play, 386–388
  therapeutic process, 396–409
    disclosure of threatening material, 400–402
    elaborated versions, 402–405
    individual play, 398–399
    initial stages, 396–398
    metaphors of correction and attachment, 405–409

Eclecticism, integrative play therapy, 417-456. See also Integrative play therapy

Ecological factors, structured
group ecosystemic play
therapy, 262–263, 264-266
Edelbrock, C., 177
Edinger, E., 217
Egeland, B., 537
Ego psychology, psychodynamic
play therapy, 347, 348
Emery, G., 170
Emotion
behavior and, 8
cognitive-behavioral play
therapy, 171
Gestalt play therapy, 293–295
structured group ecosystemic
play therapy, 250–252, 261
Environment, integrative play
therapy, 420-421, 423, 431
Erikson, E., 303, 485, 529
Experience
Gestalt play therapy, 285,
291–292
person-centered therapy, 7,
9–10, 11
Expressive modalities, dynamic
play therapy with ritual
abuse, 375–376
Extinction, cognitive-behavioral
play therapy, 173
Eyberg, S., 564
Eysenck, H. J., 418

Faber, E. A., 537
Family history. See also
Parent-child relationship
Adlerian play therapy, 140–141,
142–145
cognitive-behavioral play
therapy, 175–177, 180–181
dynamic play therapy with
ritual abuse, 388–394
family play therapy, 470–471

filial therapy, 569–571
game play therapy, 534–536
Gestalt play therapy, 286–288
imagery interaction play
therapy, 104–106
integrative play therapy,
425–428
Jungian play therapy, 212–216
person-centered therapy, 15–16
posttraumatic play therapy,
489–494
psychodynamic play therapy,
352–356
structured group ecosystemic
play therapy, 255–258
Theraplay, 47–48, 49–52
time-limited play therapy, 307
Family play therapy, 457–483
background data and
presenting problem,
470–471
case overview, 457–458
discussion of case, 482
results and follow-up, 481–482
theoretical concepts, 472–473
theoretical overview, 458–470
children and, 462
essential elements, 458–459
family interview, 463–470
individual/family therapy
compared, 460–461
key concepts, 459–460
play/family therapy
compared, 462–463
therapist's focus, 461–462
therapeutic process, 473–481
Family theraplay. See Theraplay
Family therapy. See also Filial
therapy
concepts in, 458–460
individual therapy compared,
460–461

Family therapy (*continued*)
  person-centered therapy and,
    16
  play therapy and, 462–463
  time-limited play therapy, 317
Fantasy, person-centered therapy
    process, 25–30
Faust, J., 417–456
Filial therapy, 561–588
  background data and
      presenting problem,
      569–571
  discussion of case, 585–587
  results and follow-up, 585
  theoretical overview, 561–569
    appropriate uses of, 565–566
    generally, 561–563
    historical perspective and
        effectiveness, 563–565
    home versus office sessions,
        567–569
    therapeutic procedures,
        566–567
  therapeutic concepts, 571–572
  therapeutic process, 572–584
Fleugelman, A., 276
Follow-up. *See* Outcomes
Fordham, M., 211
Forehand, R. L., 439–440, 564
Frame, C. L., 554
Free play, dynamic play therapy
    with ritual abuse, 384–386
Freud, A., 347, 348, 349, 350,
    486, 537, 538, 548
Freud, S., 209, 348, 351, 352, 530
Frey, D., 531, 589–606
Fundudis, T., 178, 179

Galassi, M., 142
Game play therapy, 527–560
  background information and
      presenting problem,
      534–536

discussion of case, 558–559
results and follow-up, 556–557
theoretical concepts, 536–540
theoretical overview, 527–532
  developmental factors,
      528–530
  generally, 527–528
  therapeutic elements,
      530–532
  therapeutic process, 532–533,
      540–556
Games, dynamic play therapy
    with ritual abuse, 371–415.
    See also Dynamic play
    therapy with ritual abuse
Gardner, R. A., 531, 553
Gestalt play therapy, 281–300
  background data and
      presenting problems,
      286–288
  discussion of case, 299
  results and follow-up, 297–298
  theoretical concepts, 288–289
  theoretical overview, 281–286
    awareness and experience,
        285
    contact boundary
        disturbances, 283–285
    interpretation, 285–286
    I/Thou relationship, 281–282
    organismic self-regulation,
        282–283
  therapy process, 289–297
    aggressive energy, 292–293
    emotional expression,
        293–295
    self-nurturing, 295–297
    sensory and body
        experiences, 291–292
    therapeutic relationship,
        289–291
Ginott, H., 6, 13
Glass, N., 564

Glazer-Waldman, H., 562
Glen, L., 350
Goldberg, T. E., 539
Goldfried, M., 246
"Good growing ground" therapy,
    described, 11–15
Goodman, J., 246, 542
Green, A. H., 538
Greenacre, P., 352
Griffith, J., 134, 138
Group composition, structured
    group ecosystemic play
    therapy, 254–255
Guerney, B., 561, 563, 564, 567
Guerney, L. F., 6, 13, 561–588
Gutheil, E. A., 425, 432
Guttman, H. A., 537

Hansen, M. K., 179
Harinck, F. J. H., 104
Hartmann, H., 348
Hartner, S., 305
Haworth, M. R., 487
Head Start program, Theraplay
    and, 46
Hellendoorn, J., 97–132
Holism
    Adlerian theory, 138
    posttraumatic play therapy,
        486
Homeostasis, Gestalt play
    therapy, 282–283
Hyperactivity, Jungian play
    therapy, 212-216. See also
    Attention-deficit
    hyperactivity disorder
    (ADHD); Jungian play
    therapy

Imagery, dynamic play therapy
    with ritual abuse, 386–388
Imagery interaction play therapy,
    97–132

background data and
    presenting problem,
    104–106
discussion of case, 131–132
goals, strategy, and evaluation,
    104
indications for, 103
joint interview in, 115–130
    overview, 115–116
    termination (premature),
        124–126
    termination (second), 130
    working through phase,
        116–121, 127–130
overview of, 97–98
parental counseling in, 102–103
results and follow-up, 130–131
techniques in, 98–102
    counterplay, 102
    limit setting, 101–102
    stimulating, 100–101
    verbalizing and phrasing,
        98–100
theoretical concepts, 106–110
therapy process, 110–115
    parents and, 114–115
    sessions, 110–114
In, P. A., 538
Incest, adult play therapy and,
    593. See also Child abuse;
    Sexual abuse
Incontinence, Jungian play
    therapy, 213, 220
Individual therapy, family
    therapy compared, 460–461
Individuation, Jungian theory
    and, 209
Inferiority, children and, 134
Insight development, Adlerian
    play therapy, 158–162
Intake interview
    Jungian play therapy, 214
    Theraplay and, 47–48

Integrative play therapy, 417–456
    background information and
        presenting problem,
        425–428
    discussion of case, 452–455
    results and follow-up, 450–452
    theoretical concepts, 428–437
        behavioral factors, 436–437
        client-centered concepts,
            435–436
        generally, 428–430
        oedipal issues, 434
        psychodynamic primary
            concepts, 430–434
    theoretical overview, 417–425
        clinical orientations, 419–420
        generally, 417–418
        integration alternative,
            420–424
        "kitchen-sink" eclecticism,
            418–419
        linear eclecticism, 419
        metaphor role in integration,
            424–425
    therapeutic process, 437–450
        end treatment phase, 447–448
        initiation of treatment phase,
            437–440
        middle treatment phase,
            440–447
        termination, 448–450
Intelligence testing, 260–261
Interactive observation, dynamic
        play therapy with ritual
        abuse, 391–393
Interpretation
    Gestalt play therapy, 285–286
    imagery interaction play
        therapy techniques,
        phrasing, 100
Intervention, cognitive-behavioral
        play therapy, 171

Isolation. See Withdrawal
I/Thou relationship, Gestalt play
        therapy, 281–282

Jacobson, E., 248
James, B., 290
Janov, A., 241
Jernberg, A., 45–96
Jernberg, E., 45–96
Johnson, K., 485
Johnson, V., 142
Josephs, L., 420
Jung, C. G., 209, 211
Jungian play therapy, 209–244
    background data and
        presenting problem,
        212–216
    discussion of case, 239–243
    results and follow-up, 239
    theoretical concepts, 216–218
    theoretical overview, 209–212
    therapy process, 218–238
        beginning phase, 219–220
        final phase, 236–238
        generally, 218–219
        middle phase, 220–235

Kalff, D., 211, 216
Keith, D. V., 462, 463, 467
Kelly, J., 241
Kelly, J. B., 357–358
King, E., 564
Klein, M., 211, 420
Knell, S. M., 169–208
Knoff, H., 140, 156
Kohut, H., 552
Kolvin, I., 178, 179
Kottman, T., 1–3, 133–167

Labbe, E. E., 179
Lahey, B. B., 455
Landgarten, H. B., 378

Landreth, G., 6, 12, 13, 14–15, 16
Langeveld, M. J., 97
Language
    mutism, cognitive-behavioral
        play therapy, 175–177,
        178–181
    reality and, 7
Lankton, C. H., 424, 425
Lankton, S. R., 424, 425
Latner, J., 281
Lawson, D., 473
Lawton-Speert, S., 218
Lebo, D., 6
Lee, A., 247
Levin, S., 209–244
Levine, S. V., 309
Libido, 209
Life-style exploration, Adlerian
    play therapy, 155–158
Limits and boundaries
    imagery interaction play
        therapy techniques,
        101–102
    integrative play therapy, 436
    Jungian play therapy and,
        211–212, 217–218
    person-centered therapy,
        13–14, 24–25
Lindaman, S., 52, 53, 55
Linear eclecticism, integrative
    play therapy, 419
Loeven, L., 104
Loomis, E. A., 528
Lowe, R., 135
Lowenfeld, M., 211

Maccoby, E., 564
Mahler, M. S., 348, 349, 356, 357,
    537
Maladjustment
    Adlerian theory, 134
    person-centered therapy, 9–10

Malan, D. H., 301
Manaster, G., 133, 137
Mann, J., 302
Marschak, M., 48
Marschak Interaction Method
    (MIM), 48, 55, 85, 87
Martin, H. P., 537
Marvasti, J. A., 485–525
Masson, B. S., 530
Masten, A. S., 170
Mastery
    cognitive-behavioral play
        therapy, 179–180
    game play therapy, 532
Masturbation, Jungian play
    therapy, 213
Masur, C., 538
McDermott, J. F., Jr., 538
McKay, G., 161
McMahon, R. J., 439–440
Mead, G. H., 529
Meeks, J., 528, 533
Meekums, B., 378
Meichenbaum, D., 174, 246, 303,
    542
Mental status examination,
    time-limited play therapy,
    308
Metaphor
    dynamic play therapy with
        ritual abuse, 405–409
    integrative play therapy,
        424–425
Minuchin, S., 475
Mitchell, E. D., 530
Modeling, cognitive-behavioral
    play therapy, 171–172
Molestation. See Sexual abuse
Mook, B., 97
Moore, D. J., 169
Morse, C. W., 537
Moustakas, C., 6, 11, 13

Mutism, cognitive-behavioral
play therapy, 175–177,
178–181. *See also*
Cognitive-behavioral play
therapy

Nasby, W., 554
Nelson, A., 140
Neumann, E., 211, 217
Newman, J. P., 554
Norcross, J., 417, 418, 419
Nystul, M., 142

Oaklander, V., 281–300
O'Connor, K., 245–280, 533, 538
Oedipal issues
integrative play therapy, 434,
447–448
posttraumatic play therapy, 498
Organismic self-regulation,
Gestalt play therapy, 282–283
Osofsky, J. D., 537
Outcomes
Adlerian play therapy, 165
adult play therapy, 602–604
cognitive-behavioral play
therapy, 202–203
dynamic play therapy with
ritual abuse, 410
family play therapy, 481–482
filial therapy, 563–565, 585
game play therapy, 556–557
Gestalt play therapy, 297–298
imagery interaction play
therapy, 130–131
integrative play therapy,
450–452
Jungian play therapy, 239
person-centered therapy and,
6, 41
posttraumatic play therapy,
520–521

psychodynamic play therapy,
369–370
structured group ecosystemic
play therapy, 278–279
Theraplay, 85–94
time-limited play therapy,
342–345

Painting, person-centered
therapy process, 19–41
Panic attacks, Theraplay and,
49–52. *See also* Theraplay
Parent-child relationship. *See also*
Family history
Adlerian play therapy, 140
adult play therapy, 593
dynamic play therapy with
ritual abuse, 371–372,
376–379
filial therapy, 562. *See also* Filial
therapy
Marschak Interaction Method
(MIM), 55
psychodynamic play therapy,
348–349, 352–356
structured group ecosystemic
play therapy, 264
Theraplay, 46–47
time-limited play therapy, 316
Parents
Adlerian play therapy,
148–155
cognitive-behavioral play
therapy, 178
imagery interaction play
therapy, 114–115, 121–124
imagery interaction play
therapy, counseling of,
102–103
Jungian play therapy, 215
Theraplay process, 81–85
Parpal, M., 564

Peer groups, structured group
ecosystemic play therapy,
263, 264
Peller, L. E., 529, 530
Pepper, F., 140, 156
Perception, person-centered
therapy and, 9, 10
Perls, F., 281
Perls, L., 281
Perry, L., 5-43
Personality development. *See*
Developmental factors
Person-centered therapy, 5-43
adjustment and, 10-11
background data and
presenting problem,
15-16
developmental factors and
behavior, 6-9
discussion of case, 41-42
"good growing ground"
therapy, 11-15
historical perspective on, 5-6
maladjustment and, 9-10
results and follow-up, 41
theoretical concepts, 16-18
therapy process, 18-41
Peterlin, K. B., 301-346
Pharmacology, Jungian play
therapy, 214
Phrasing, imagery interaction
play therapy techniques,
98-100
Physical factors, structured group
ecosystemic play therapy,
247-249
Piaget, J., 528
Piontelli, A., 241
Play, theory of, 351-352
Play disruption, person-centered
therapy process, 33
Pleasure, game play therapy, 531

Polster, E., 283
Polster, M., 283
Positive reinforcement
cognitive-behavioral play
therapy, 173
structured group ecosystemic
play therapy, 249-250, 263
Posttraumatic play, dynamic play
therapy with ritual abuse,
386-388
Posttraumatic play therapy,
485-525
background data and
presenting problem,
489-494
discussion of case, 521-524
result and follow-up, 520-521
theoretical concepts, 494-498
therapeutic overview, 485-489
therapeutic process, 498-520
first stage, 498-507
second stage, 507-511
termination and
countertransference,
519-520
third stage, 511-519
Power, Adlerian theory and,
135-136, 145
Powers, R., 134, 138
Prechtl, H. F. R., 216, 241
Problem-solving training,
structured group ecosystemic
play therapy, 246-247
Prout, H., 140, 156
Psychodynamic play therapy,
347-370
background data and
presenting problem,
352-356
discussion of case, 370
results and follow-up, 369-370
theoretical concepts, 356-359

Psychodynamic play therapy
(*continued*)
  theoretical overview, 347–352
    generally, 347–348
    historical perspective,
      348–349
    play theory, 351–352
    therapeutic relationship,
      349–350
    therapeutic techniques,
      350–351
  therapeutic process, 359–369
Psychopathology, structured
  group ecosystemic play
  therapy, 254
Psychopharmacology, Jungian
  play therapy, 214
Puppets
  cognitive-behavioral play
    therapy, 182
  Gestalt play therapy, 294
  posttraumatic play therapy,
    494, 507–511

Rank, O., 241
Rape, posttraumatic play
  therapy, 494–495
Reactive detachment disorder,
  game play therapy, 535
Reality
  game play therapy, 533
  person-centered therapy, 7
Reid, S., 527–560
Relaxation training, structured
  group ecosystemic play
  therapy, 247–249
Remkus, J. M., 538
Reorientation/reeducation phase,
  Adlerian play therapy,
  162–165
Repetition, posttraumatic play
  therapy, 485, 487, 512

Repetition compulsion, game
  play therapy, 540–541
Repetitive themes, dynamic play
  therapy with ritual abuse,
  386–388
Response repertoire, structured
  group ecosystemic play
  therapy, 261
Results. *See* Outcomes
Richards, C. S., 179
Ritual abuse, dynamic play
  therapy with, 371–415. *See
  also* Dynamic play therapy
  with ritual abuse
Roberts, J. M., 531
Rogers, C., 6, 7, 9, 10, 304
Role-play, cognitive-behavioral
  play therapy, 172
Rosenthal, A. J., 309
Rudolph, L., 135

Sakheim, D. K., 413
Samuels, A., 210
Satanic activity, dynamic play
  therapy with ritual abuse,
  402–405
Schachter, R. S., 539
Schaefer, C., 1
Scheduling, Theraplay and, 54
Schiller, F., 591
Schools, structured group
  ecosystemic play therapy,
  263, 265–266
Self-actualization, person-centered
  therapy and, 16, 41
Self-nurturing, Gestalt play
  therapy, 295–297
Senders, P. S., 529
Sensory experiences, Gestalt play
  therapy, 291–292
Sensue, M., 564

Separation/individuation,
    psychodynamic play therapy,
    348-349
Serok, S., 529
Sexual abuse. *See also* Child
    abuse
    dynamic play therapy with
        ritual abuse, 386, 389-391
    incest, adult play therapy and,
        593
    posttraumatic play therapy,
        485-525. *See also*
        Posttraumatic play therapy
Sgroi, S., 290, 498, 501
Sidoli, M., 211
Sifneos, P. E., 301
Situation, cognitive-behavioral
    play therapy, 171
Sloves, R., 301-346
Social factors
    Adlerian theory and, 136-137
    structured group ecosystemic
        play therapy, 252-253
    withdrawal
        cognitive-behavioral play
            therapy and, 178
        imagery interaction play
            therapy, 104-106. *See also*
            Imagery interaction play
            therapy
Social interest level, Adlerian
    theory and, 137-138
Socialization, game play therapy,
    532
Social learning theory, cognitive-
    behavioral play therapy, 170
Social skills training, structured
    group ecosystemic play
    therapy, 246-247
Soltz, V., 134, 135
Sroufe, L. A., 537
Stevens, J., 600

Stiles, K., 142
Stimulation, imagery interaction
    play therapy techniques,
    100-101
Stimulus fading, cognitive-
    behavioral play therapy, 173
Stone, J., 302
Stover, L., 564, 567
Strachey, J., 530
Striker, S., 597
Structured group ecosystemic
    play therapy, 245-280
    background data and
        presenting problem,
        255-258
    basic assumptions in conduct
        of, 253-255
        developmental level of child,
            253-254
        group composition, 254-255
        psychopathology, 254
        therapist role, 255
    components of, 246-253
        behavioral factors, 249-250
        cognitive factors, 246-247
        emotional factors, 250-252
        physical factors, 247-249
        social factors, 252-253
    discussion of case, 279-280
    overview of, 245-246
    results and follow-up, 278-279
    theoretical concepts, 259-268
        factors maintaining
            functions, 263-266
        goal synthesis, 266-268
        origin of functions, 261-263
        present functions, 259-261
    therapy process, 268-278
        growing, trusting, and
            working through phases,
            275-277
        initiation of therapy, 270-275

Structured group ecosystemic
    play therapy (continued)
  therapy process (continued)
    setting up, 268–270
    termination, 277–278
    toys, 268
Structured play, time-limited play
    therapy, 303–305
Sutton-Smith, B., 531, 605
Swanson, A. J., 539
Sweeney, T., 133
Symbol
  Jungian theory and, 210
  person-centered therapy
    process, 33–34, 37
Sywulak, A. E., 564

Terminal illness of parent,
    person-centered therapy
    and, 15–42. See also
    Person-centered therapy
Termination
  imagery interaction play
    therapy
    premature, 124–126
    second, 130
  integrative play therapy,
    448–450
  person-centered therapy
    process, 38
  posttraumatic play therapy,
    519–520
  structured group ecosystemic
    play therapy, 277–278
  time-limited play therapy,
    331–342
Terr, L., 386, 485
Therapeutic alliance, game play
    therapy, 530
Theraplay, 45–96
  background data and
    presenting problem, 49–52

discussion of case, 94–95
  overview of, 45–49
  results and follow-up, 85–94
  theoretical concepts in, 52–55
  therapy process, 56–85
    parents and, 81–85
    sessions, 56–81
Thompson, C., 135
Time-limited play therapy,
    301–346
  background data and
    presenting problem,
    306–310
  discussion of case, 342–345
  theoretical concepts, 310–317
    central theme, 312–316
    family sessions, 317
    generally, 310–312
    parental alliance, 316
    therapeutic contract, 316–317
  theoretical overview, 301–305
  therapeutic process, 318–342
    generally, 318
    opening phase, 318–325
    termination, 331–342
    working-through phase,
      325–331
Torture, dynamic play therapy
    with ritual abuse, 402–405
Toys
  Jungian play therapy, 211
  person-centered therapy, 14–15
  time-limited play therapy,
    304–305
Trauma
  integrative play therapy,
    417–418, 428–429
  Jungian play therapy, 240. See
    also Jungian play therapy
  posttraumatic play therapy,
    485–525. See also
    Posttraumatic play therapy

Trust, structured group
 ecosystemic play therapy,
 275–277

Unconscious, Jungian theory
 and, 210
Unity, Adlerian theory and, 138

Values, person-centered therapy
 and, 9–10
Van der Kooij, R., 97
Van Zyl, D., 241
Verbalization, imagery interaction
 play therapy techniques,
 98–100
Vermeer, E. A. A., 98
Verny, T., 241
Violence, integrative play
 therapy, 429, 430-431
Viorst, J., 367
Volkan, V. D., 524

Waelder, R., 352
Wall, L., 564
Wallerstein, J. S., 357–358

Wanerman, L., 533
Warlick, J., 133, 139, 142
Waters, E., 537
Wechsler Intelligence Scale for
 Children-III, 260
Welsh, A. D., 561–588
Weltner, J. S., 462
Whitaker, C., 463, 467, 471
Williamson, D. A., 179
Willock, B., 541
Winnicott, D. W., 497, 591
Withdrawal
 cognitive-behavioral play
  therapy and, 178
 imagery interaction play
  therapy, 104–106. *See also*
  Imagery interaction play
  therapy
Working through
 structured group ecosystemic
  play therapy, 275–277
 time-limited play therapy,
  325–331
Wright, H. L., 178

Yura, M., 142